The Revd Philip Nordstrand
June, 1980

WILLIAM JAMES

ALSO BY GAY WILSON ALLEN

THE SOLITARY SINGER

A Critical Biography of Walt Whitman

WILLIAM JAMES
From a sketch in oils by his son William, 1908.

WILLIAM JAMES

A BIOGRAPHY

Gay Wilson Allen

NEW YORK / THE VIKING PRESS

First published in 1967 by The Viking Press, Inc.
625 Madison Avenue, New York, N.Y. 10022

Published simultaneously in Canada by
The Macmillan Company of Canada Limited

Library of Congress catalog card number: 67-10217
Printed in U.S.A. by the Vail-Ballou Press, Inc.

The author is grateful to the following for permission to quote from copyrighted works:

Atlantic–Little, Brown and Company for *The Thought and Character of William James* by Ralph Barton Perry. Copyright 1935 by Henry James.

George Braziller, Inc. for *The Notebooks of Henry James*.

Dodd, Mead & Company for *The Diary of Alice James* edited by Leon Edel. Copyright renewed, Copyright © 1964 by Leon Edel.

E. P. Dutton & Co., Inc. and John Murray (Publishers) Ltd. for *The Story of San Michele* by Axel Munthe.

Holt, Rinehart and Winston, Inc., for *The Philosophy of William James* by Th. Flournoy; authorized translation by Edwin B. Holt and William James, Jr. Copyright 1917, 1945 by Holt, Rinehart and Winston, Inc.

Houghton Mifflin Company for *Charles William Eliot* by Henry James.

The Estate of the late H. G. Wells for *Experiment in Autobiography* by H. G. Wells.

To the memory of
WILLIAM JAMES
1882–1961
(the "Billy" in this biography)

Preface

I

WILLIAM JAMES was America's first world-famous psychologist and first renowned philosopher after Emerson, but most of his students and colleagues at Harvard thought he was greater as a man than as a scholar or teacher. Few teachers have been so loved and valued as a friend as this medium-sized man with blue eyes and iron-gray beard, usually dressed in rumpled tweeds, who in the early years of the present century walked briskly nearly every day from his home on nearby Irving Street to the Harvard Yard.

One of James's students of this period, Rollo Walter Brown, thought he was "an irresistible gust of life coming down the street. Not that he moved along with any noisy kind of strenuousness. Rather he seemed to be a man who had passed through some great fire of suffering and purifying that made him alert to the world about him and responsive to almost every kind of people in it, so that he moved energetically along in a sensitive, universal awareness."

The purifying fire had been hotter than this student could have known, for James had indeed suffered greatly, both physically and spiritually. From youth he had struggled against nervous disorders which more than once had driven him almost to suicide, and by 1900 he was fighting a losing battle against a heart disease which he, as a physician, knew could be alleviated only by the peaceful rest which his own impulsive nature would not permit him to take. Try as he would, he could not ease his inner tensions. Yet almost invariably he impressed others as a man alive to his fingertips—or better, to the roots of his nimble brain and his witty tongue. His charming presence, his informal, conversational lectures, and clear, vigorous writings on psychology and philosophy were unfailingly stimulating to all who saw or heard or read him. And the aim of all his professional lecturing and writing was to promote more abundant health and pleasurable activity in his audience. He never used his Harvard Medical School diploma for the practice of medicine, but he was a healer even in his philosophy.

After graduating from medical school, James became an instructor in anatomy at Harvard College in 1872; but his curiosity about the relationship of his own mind to his body soon led him into the study of nerves, brain cells, conditioned reflexes, and other phenomena of the human psyche. When he published his massive *Principles of Psychology* in 1892, after twelve years of labor on it, James himself predicted that as a contribution to science the book would soon be out of date. He was right; but the *Principles* is still almost universally considered the fullest and best work on the subject published before the twentieth century and has survived as literature though its science has long since become archaic.

A man ambitious for fame would have devoted himself to consolidating his position as the leading American psychologist, but James turned instead to popularizing his discoveries regarding the formation of habit, the influence of ideas and beliefs on conduct and the state of one's nerves—he was a pioneer in somatic medicine —and the psychological need for religious faith of some kind. These interests led him to be sympathetic with the "mind cure" practitioners, notably those of Christian Science, and to defend them against legal reprisals by the medical profession. He also took part in the organization of a Psychical Research Society, with branches in England and the United States, which investigated the claims of mediums, fortune tellers, telepathists, or anyone who claimed to have experienced power transcending the known laws of physiology and physics. Although he never found any clear proof of supernatural powers, he continued to insist that scientists had no right to dismiss any report of a supernatural experience without examining the evidence. Though his own investigations were objective and thorough, he alienated a large part of the contemporary scientific community by even entertaining the possibility of supernaturalism. In fact, he damaged his professional reputation simply by associating with the psychical researchers, forerunners of the recent parapsychologists.

In philosophy, too, James angered the professionals by suggesting, quite early in his career, that philosophy was little more than the biographies of philosophers, and he called one of his early essays "The Sentiment of Rationality." Since Plato, philosophy had claimed to be based on reason, and for James to suggest that emotion—*sentiment*—underlay rationality, or that even a desire to rationalize had an emotional basis, was outright heresy. Then he compounded the felony by arguing in "The Will to Believe" that what a person gives credence to has important psychological consequences in his life, is capable of making him either a "sick-soul" or a "healthy-minded" man, and that therefore everyone has the right to choose those beliefs that will keep him healthy, happy, and at home in the world he must live in. Critics pounced on this doctrine as a license for "wishful thinking" and escaping into a dream world, but James replied that he should have called it "the *right* to believe"; that what he meant was finding ideas or tentative assumptions which would work in specific circumstances. This was the beginning of a still more upsetting theory which he called Pragmatism, the doctrine that a proposition is true only to the extent of its usefulness or reliability in actual life situations.

Finally in his book on Pluralism James said outright:

> A philosophy is the expression of a man's intimate character, and all definitions of the universe are but the deliberately adopted reactions of human characters upon it. . . . If we take the whole history of philosophy, the systems reduce themselves to a few main types which, under all the technical verbiage in which the ingenious intellect of man envelops them, are just so many visions, modes of feeling the whole push, and seeing the whole drift of life, forced on one by one's total character and experience, and on the whole *preferred*—there is no other truthful word—as one's best working attitude.

Thus the great philosophers "willed to believe" when they thought they were being supremely rational.

Whether or not one agrees with Jame's biographical view of philosophy (and it can be said that in anthropology, sociology, and semantics, for example, the notion has grown since his day that a social pattern, a moral value, or the meaning of a word is good or bad only in a specific context), certainly this view makes his own biography of paramount importance in any consideration of his philosophy. In what kind of person and out of what experiences did Pragmatism, Pluralism, and Radical Empiricism take root and grow?

II

It would be difficult to find a philosopher who led a more exciting life than William James, not only in intellectual terms but in those of the senses and emotions. His emotional life fluctuated constantly between crests of happiness and depths of despair, but whether on a crest or in the depths he was always eager for change, new experiences, new scenery, new faces, novelties of almost any kind. What bored him most was repetition, in ideas or places, and this made him an omnivorous reader and a restless traveler. By the time he reached early manhood Europe was "an old story" to him, though he was always hoping for an interesting sequel. He returned there frequently but almost always tired quickly of the familiar scenes and wished he were back in his less predictable native country. Sometimes his satirical comments on the decadence of Venice, the corruption of Rome, or the gloom of London remind one of Mark Twain's "Innocent" abroad.

Of course William James was neither unsophisticated nor provincial. He came from a cultivated and wealthy family. In his adolescence he had acquired from European tutors an easy command of French and German, and later he learned enough Italian for practical purposes. At the height of his career he knew personally every important European psychologist and philosopher and was truly what Ralph Barton Perry has called him, an "ambassador of American thought." He loved Germany, but he had friends in every European country: especially in Switzerland, where he spent one of his happiest years as a student at what later became Geneva University; in France, where his first writings on psychology were published in translation; and in England where he lectured and had honorary degrees conferred upon him.

One of James's characteristically American traits was his mobility. He could live in New York, as he did in childhood, or in Newport and Geneva, as during his youth, and finally in Cambridge, Massachusetts, without becoming emotionally dependent upon the locality—even on Cambridge, though he loved his home there. He could never understand how his brother Henry could be so satisfied in London and so bored with Boston and Cambridge. In the years when he did not go to Europe for the summer or on a sabbatical, or to California or the mountains of western North Carolina, he liked to divide his vacations between the New England seashore and the peaks of the Adirondacks. Even after he had acquired a delightful summer home in New Hampshire, he would slip off by himself for a week at the shore or two weeks in the Adirondacks: he really preferred mountain-climbing to all other diversions.

James's philosophy, too, was mobile. His first effort as a thinker had been to free himself of determinism, both of the scientific and the theological variety, and he went on to formulate a philosophy which recognized no boundaries or limiting traditions, which tested "truth" by personal experience, permitted constant growth and change, and was tolerant of every man's individual experience. From his saintly father, who spent his life writing theological works which few people read, James inherited a religious temperament, but his father's faith in a Deity whose will shaped the destiny of mankind did not satisfy William. Any Deity he accepted must not be responsible for evil; hence He could not be omnipotent and omniscient. More important, God, for William James, needed the help of men as much as they needed Him. But this also meant that man and God could work together in building a better world.

James's melioristic cosmology presumed a world in which men could work effectively together, without the aid or influence of immutable forces, natural or supernatural. By their combined efforts men themselves could eliminate war, pestilence, ugliness—all the evils which human greed and ignorance had permitted to develop. James himself was active in "good causes": he helped to organize a National Committee for Mental Hygiene and joined several peace movements. He opposed the United States occupation of the Philippines after the Spanish-American War, which he had also condemned, and his speech on "The Moral Equivalent of War," first published in 1910, was so widely circulated that eventually several million copies were printed. In it he recognized the appeal of war to human nature and the value of such martial virtues as courage, sacrifice, and endurance but suggested that society must find ways to direct these aggressive impulses and stoic virtues into activities more useful than mass murder. Many of James's other popular essays and lectures are as timely today as when he wrote them.

III

From his eighteenth year until his death at sixty-eight, James's life was a struggle to overcome crippling neuroses. He knew he was neurotic, as were his sister Alice and the two younger brothers—especially the youngest, Bob—but he kept sane by admitting his condition and fighting his symptoms. His scientific training and his honesty with himself enabled him to make contributions of permanent value to the literature of neurology. His unfailing sense of humor also helped him to preserve his sanity, and is not the least enduring of his qualities. But no intellectual insight enabled him to cure himself; the causes lay too deep in his psyche. He was helped at times by "mind cure" therapy, but mainly he had to wrestle with himself. He knew a little about psychoanalysis, though he did not have much faith in what he knew, and no analyst was available for consultation. (He did predict, however, that the future in psychology belonged to Freud.)

What saved James from absolute shipwreck, in his own estimation, was his marrying Alice Howe Gibbens. The story of his meeting with Miss Gibbens, of his troubled courtship, and of her becoming his devoted wife is one of the tenderest and most endearing parts of his biography. William James's oldest son, Henry, had his parents' letters to each other sealed after his mother's death; to shield the sensibilities of persons about whom his parents had made some very sharp and critical remarks, he arranged that the letters not be opened to the public until the year 2023. But he did not forbid their being read by heirs to the estate, and his nephew John S. R. James, the grandson of William James, has read the letters and kindly made their substance available to the present biographer. Fortunately, William's son did not impound his father's private diaries, which are now in the Houghton Library at Harvard. Alice Gibbens James's diaries and letters to her children (among them a few letters to her husband) remained in the possession of her younger son William (the "Billy" to whom this biography is dedicated). Mr. John James, son of Billy, now has these diaries and letters and has generously permitted their use in the preparation of this biography.

James's son Henry was still alive when Ralph Barton Perry wrote his two-volume *Thought and Character of William James* (1935), and he refused to divulge any personal information about his mother, simply because he regarded the publication of such information as an invasion of the family's privacy. Consequently, Perry was not able to write a full account of William James's life, for he was forced to omit almost altogether the important role James's wife played in his biography. Perry's work, though it gives a masterly analysis of James's ideas and of his relationships with other philosophers, was not intended primarily to be a biography. The strictly biographical account is confined to a few chapters in the first volume, preceded and followed by detailed discussions of James's work and his ideas. This plan not only subordinates James's private life to his professional life but obscures the *growth* of his mind and character, depriving the reader of a sense of participation in the experiences being narrated. The present biography is strictly chronological, and attempts to trace the relationship between James's emotional and intellectual life —certainly important for a man who enthroned *feeling* with *thought* in philosophy.

One advantage the novelist or the fictionalizing biographer has over the biographer who limits himself scrupulously to fact is the use of conversation to enliven the narrative. However, a factual biography of William James need not have this handicap, for his letters, so vivid and uninhibited, so pungent, are almost like good conversation. Whether he was being witty and in high spirits or was in one of his complaining moods, his letters show how he thought, felt, and evaluated his own experiences. Of course James loved to exaggerate and to burlesque, and care must be taken to interpret each quotation in its original context.

Alice Gibbens James (she preferred the initials AHJ) did not have the same natural facility with words as her husband, but her simple, unadorned diary entries have the greater pathos for being artless. Whatever emotional effect the last chapter of this biography may be found to have derives largely from the heart-rending diary account of this selfless wife. In this chapter the writer felt, as perhaps the reader will feel, that he was witnessing the final act of a Greek tragedy—but redeemed by what Aristotle called *katharsis*.

Acknowledgments:
My greatest indebtedness is to Mr. John S. R. James, for the reasons indicated above. I am also grateful to his late father, William

(Billy) James, the distinguished painter and art teacher, who gave me permission initially to use the James Papers in the Houghton Library of Harvard University. The staff of the Houghton Library, especially Miss Carolyn Jakeman, has provided generous and courteous assistance. Permission to quote from the James Papers and to reproduce photographs and drawings in the collection has been kindly granted by both Mr. John James and Mr. William H. Bond, Librarian of the Houghton Library.

I also wish to thank my colleague Leon Edel, Henry James's biographer, for having encouraged me to undertake a biography of William James, for much helpful advice, and for having introduced me to the younger William James and his son John. To another colleague, Dan Laurence, I am indebted for information about Henry James Sr. gleaned from the official records of New York City.

Use of the letters of Professor Hugo Münsterberg I owe to the courtesy of the trustees of the Boston Public Library. The Yale University Library kindly gave me access to the voluminous correspondence of the Polish philosopher Wincenty Lutaslawski with William James, from which valuable information was gleaned. For quotations from Henry Adams's letters to William James, grateful acknowledgment is made to the Adams Manuscript Trust and the Massachusetts Historical Society.

My personal indebtedness for advice and criticism is greatest to Malcolm Cowley, who introduced me to the Viking Press and who has been helpful throughout the writing of the book. My friend Miss Anne King gave helpful criticism at one stage in the writing, and the novelist Winifred Halsted has given continuous personal encouragement and unselfishly assisted in reading proof.

I gratefully acknowledge a grant from the American Council of Learned Societies in 1962, and several grants from the Research Fund of the New York University Graduate School of Arts and Science to pay for photographic services.

—G.W.A.

Oradell, New Jersey
August 1966

Contents

Illustrations

Pages 478–479

Except where otherwise indicated, the photographs, sketches, and letters reproduced are in the collection of the James Papers at the Houghton Library, Harvard, and are used by permission.

A Chronology

of the Life of William James

1842	Born January 11, New York City
1843–1844	First trip to Europe
1852–1855	Living in New York City
1855–1858	London, Paris; attend Collège in Boulogne-sur-mer
1858–1859	In school at Newport, Rhode Island
1859–1860	Academy, Geneva; summer in Germany
1860–1861	Painting with William M. Hunt, Newport
1861	Lawrence Scientific School at Harvard
1864	Harvard Medical School
1865–1866	With Agassiz in Brazil
1867–1868	Study and recuperation in Germany
1869	Receives M.D. degree at Harvard
1873–1874	Instructor in Anatomy and Physiology, Harvard College. Trip to Europe (especially Italy) for health
1875	First course in psychology
1876	Assistant Professor of Physiology
1878	Marries Alice Howe Gibbens July 10; signs contract for book on psychology
1879	First course in philosophy
	Birth of son, Henry (Harry)
1882–1883	Travel in Europe: Italy, Germany, England. Death of mother, January 29, 1882; of father, December 18, 1882. Birth of second son, William (Billy), 1882.
1884	Birth of third son, Herman
1885	Professor of Philosophy. (Professor of Psychology 1889–1897). Son Herman dies.
1886	Establishes summer home at Chocorua, New Hampshire
1887	Birth of daughter, Margaret Mary (Peggy)

1889   Builds house at 95 Irving Street, Cambridge
1890   Publication of *Principles of Psychology*
            Birth of son, Alexander Robertson
1892   Sister Alice dies March 6 in England
1892–1893   In Europe with wife and children
1897   Publication of *Will to Believe and Other Essays*
1898   Strains heart in Adirondacks. Lectures in California
1899   Publication of *Talks to Teachers*
1899–1902   Recuperation in Europe
1901–1902   Gifford Lectures at University of Edinburgh
1902   Publication of *Varieties of Religious Experience*
1905   Trip to Greece, Psychological Congress in Rome
1906   Visiting Professor at Stanford University; returns to Cambridge after San Francisco earthquake
1907   Publication of *Pragmatism*. Resigns from Harvard
1908   Hibbert Lectures at Oxford on Pluralism
1909   Publication of *A Pluralistic Universe; The Meaning of Truth*
1910   Europe, March–August. Dies August 26, Chocorua, N.H.

WILLIAM JAMES

CHAPTER I Rebellious Grandchildren

The rupture with my grandfather's tradition was complete; we were

never, in a single case, . . . for two generations, guilty of a stroke of

"business." —HENRY JAMES JR.

"BEFORE I WAS BORN out of my mother generations guided me," declared the poet Walt Whitman. And the same could be said of any man or woman, but the ways and the extent are still subjects for both biological and psychological investigation and controversy. The "guiding" can be either internal, by characteristics transmitted through the genes, or external, through inherited property, traditions, or family relationships.

William James, the American pioneer in psychology and the propagator of the philosophy called Pragmatism, no doubt inherited many of his dominant traits of mind and character from his Scottish-Irish ancestors, but little is known about them except for his grandfather, who was also named William. (Subsequent generations were to have both a William and a Henry, so that they ought to have been numbered like kings, but they were too democratic to adopt such a practice.)

This first American William is of utmost importance in the present biography because the fortune he acquired enabled his son Henry, William's father, to lead a life of leisure, study, travel, and philosophizing during the formative years of the future psychologist-philosopher. And along with his money, the millionaire William also unintentionally bequeathed to his sons and daughters an antagonism to his Calvinist religion and his passion for accumulating wealth which resulted in what his grandson Henry was to call the "rupture with my grandfather's tradition." From the first American William James and his son Henry the William James of this biogra-

[3]

phy inherited or acquired, along with his genius, many psychological problems, and the attempt to solve these in his own life made him a pioneer in the investigation of the human psyche. Moreover, this fact, of which William James himself was well aware and which he freely acknowledged, makes his biography a guide to the understanding of his psychology and philosophy. Thus, to comprehend his life, we begin with his grandfather.

I

In 1789 an attractive dark-haired, blue-eyed boy of eighteen emigrated from Ireland to the United States, with only enough money for his passage and bringing with him, according to family tradition, a Latin grammar, an indication that he was trying to educate himself. His name was William James. His expressed ambition was to visit a battlefield of the American Revolution—strong evidence of sympathy with American history, and perhaps a reason for his one-way trip from Ireland. But he certainly had other ambitions, as his conduct and success almost immediately proved, in which it is doubtful that the Latin grammar was of any use.

Presumably he visited a battlefield, but which one is not known. What is known is that he clerked for a year in a New York store and then traveled up the Hudson to the old Dutch settlement at Albany, which was just beginning a period of expansion and unprecedented prosperity. The energetic Irishman was capable of seizing every opportunity to prosper with the booming city. In a short time he owned a store, then later valuable real estate, stock in the Erie Canal, an express line, salt works at Syracuse, and an interest in numerous other business enterprises. By the early nineteenth century he was a prominent leader in the civic, religious, and educational life of the region. He helped organize a bank and a chamber of commerce, and served as a trustee of the First Presbyterian Church and of Union College at Schenectady. Once when the college was near bankruptcy he lent the president one hundred thousand dollars, taking as security a mortgage on all the grounds and buildings, which he later canceled without having received any payment. By this time he was the wealthiest man in the state of New York except for John Jacob Astor. He owned a fine house on North

Pearl Street in Albany, and was a man of great influence and prestige.

The James household in Albany was a large one. The patriarch of the American line married three times; his first wife died after giving birth to twin sons, the second a year after bearing a daughter. But the third wife, Catharine Barber, from a prominent Scotch-Irish family of Newburgh, New York, produced seven sons and three daughters and survived her husband by more than a quarter of a century. Henry, William James's father, was her fourth son. He always remembered her patience and kindness, which contrasted with his father's rigidity and his maternal grandfather's stoicism. He thought her the "most democratic person by temperament" he had ever known. Though several relatives had fought in the American Revolution, one uncle as aide to General Lafayette, she refused to take special pride in her ancestry. She seemed to enjoy talking to her sewing woman more than to ladies of fashion. This sympathy with ordinary people made a lasting impression on her son.

Another strong influence on this first Henry James in the American line was the "spontaneous" affection of his grandmother Barber. He did not know until he was a grown man that during his childhood she had been greatly troubled by religious skepticism. This knowledge made him feel close to her during his own period of doubt, and he concluded that "this dear old lady had found in the ignorance and innocence of the grandchildren whom she loved to hug to her bosom a truer gospel balm, a far more soothing and satisfactory echo of Divine knowledge, than she had ever caught from the logic of John Calvin."

Henry's own father, William of Albany, had been too occupied with business and civic affairs to pay much attention to his children, except to see that they attended church and gave the appearance of conformity to Presbyterian orthodoxy. "The law of the house, within the limits of religious decency, was freedom itself, and the parental will or wisdom had very seldom to be appealed to to settle our trivial discords." What embittered the sensitive boy was not his father's severity, but the total lack of "a *spontaneous* religious culture" in the home. These are, of course, the words of a mature man analyzing the cause of his childhood unhappiness, but even as a child Henry James had rebelled against the religion forced upon him. "We children of the church had been traditionally taught to contemplate God as a strictly *super*natural being, bigger personally than all the world; and not only therefore out of sympathy with our pigmy infirmities, but exceedingly jealous of the hypocritical homage we paid to his contemptuous forbearance."

This God seemed to hate all the physical joys which largely constituted the emotional life of a child. And of all days of the week, the "paralytic Sunday routine" was the most excruciating. Young Henry was full of animal spirits. "I lived," he recalled, "in every fibre of my body. The dawn always found me on my feet; and I can still vividly recall the divine rapture which filled my blood as I pursued under the magical light of morning the sports of the river, the wood, or the field. And here was a law which frowned—nay, scowled—upon that jocund unconscious existence; which drew a pall over the lovely outlying world of sense, and gave me to feel that I pursued its pleasures only at the imminent risk of immortal loss. Just conceive the horror of leading the tender mind of childhood to believe that the Divine being could under any circumstance grudge it its natural delights; could care, for example, for the holiness of any stupid day of the seven in comparison with the holiness of its innocent mind and body! . . . the fiction of a natural estrangement between me and God . . . turned every hour of unallowed pleasure I enjoyed into an actual boon wrung from [God's] forbearance; made me loath at night to lose myself in sleep, lest his dread hand should clip my thread of life without time for a parting sob of penitence, and grovel at morning dawn with an abject slavish gratitude that the sights and sounds of Nature and of man were still around me."

Then suddenly, as if the God of William James of Albany were punishing the rebellious boy, Henry, in his thirteenth year, suffered a horribly disabling accident. One of his teachers at the Albany Institute had taught the boys how to inflate balloons made of newspapers with the gas given off by burning tow soaked in turpentine. Of course the balloons often ignited, and one day one set fire to a nearby hayloft. The boys rushed to the fire and attempted to stamp out the flames. Henry's clothing caught fire and his right leg was so severely burned that it had to be amputated above the knee. This was before the discovery of anaesthesia, and a stiff drink of whisky did little to lessen the shock and pain of the operation. Moreover it was so crudely performed that infection set in and another amputation had to be performed. During his long recuperation, lasting nearly two years, the boy discovered unsuspected sympathy and tenderness in his father, but not even this could compensate for the loss of outdoor freedom and joy. He did discover new pleasure in reading during the prolonged confinement, and this contributed to his intellectual growth, but it also encouraged him to become more introspective.

After his recovery he entered Union College but soon became bored with the dull instruction and alienated his father by his frivolity and extravagance. He ran away to Boston, and his father felt sure that he would end up in prison. However, he got a job as proofreader in a printing house, studied foreign languages, sampled the preaching of the most famous ministers in the city, and learned a great deal more than he had at college. After a few months there was a reconciliation—or seemed to be—and Henry returned to Union College, from which he graduated in 1830. He then made a conscientious effort to please his father by studying law, which failed to hold his interest, and then bookkeeping, which was no better.

Two years after Henry James graduated from college his father died, leaving an estate of three million dollars tied up in an elaborate and eccentric will. The estate was to be held in trust until the youngest *grandchild* had attained the age of twenty-one, in order, the will stipulated, to prevent "the lamentable consequences which so frequently result to young persons brought up in affluence, from coming at once into the possession of property." Both Henry and his half-brother William were cut off with only a small annuity, but even the income of those who were eventually to share in the estate was subject to the discretion of the trustees, who were to use their judgment "to discourage prodigality and vice, and furnish an incentive to economy and usefulness." Anyone who was judged to be leading a "grossly immoral, idle or dishonorable life" was to receive the same treatment meted out to Henry and William. However, the sons brought suit and broke the will, and Henry shared with the others in a division which gave him an income of ten thousand dollars a year.

The consequences which the Calvinistic father had most feared did result, though not in the way he had thought. Neither Henry nor William became dissipated, but all the children revolted against their father's piety and frugality. As Henry the novelist observed, his grandfather's heirs "were never in a single case . . . for two generations, guilty of a stroke of business; the most that could be said of us was that, though about equally wanting, all round, in any faculty of acquisition, we happened to pay for the amiable weakness less in some connections than in others."

The history of the James family after the death of William of Albany is a dismal record of wasted talent, early deaths, broken homes, orphaned children. F. O. Matthiessen summed it up in this way: "Of the eleven of William James's sons and daughters who reached maturity, seven were dead by forty." These "variously genial, charming, dissipated, or unstable . . . Jameses, and the Temples and Emmets with whom they intermarried," reminded Matthiessen of the "luxuriant tribe" of Henry James's heroine in *The Wings of the Dove:* Milly Theale was "the final flower" of "the immense, extravagant, unregulated cluster, with free-living ancestors, handsome dead cousins, lurid uncles, beautiful vanished aunts, persons all busts and curls. . . ."

II

Freed from the necessity of earning a living, Henry James pondered carefully what he would most like to do with his life. His father had been wrong in suspecting that he and William would sink into riotous living. Both decided to enter the Seminary at Princeton in order to prepare themselves for the Presbyterian ministry. In view of Henry's rebellion against his father's Calvinism, this decision is puzzling, for Princeton College (now University), of which Jonathan Edwards had once been president, was the last stronghold of Calvinist orthodoxy in America. Possibly the two sons who had troubled the conscience of their father harbored pangs of guilt, but this is only conjecture. William completed the course and was ordained, though he never had a church and later resigned from the ministry. For Henry the decision to attend Princeton was certainly unwise, for he had not changed his fundamental attitude toward Calvinism. He decided that both the Princeton students and the faculty knew God only by tradition, not by "natural consciousness."

A trip to England in the summer of 1837 marked a turning point in the life of the theology student. In England he bought a cork leg, which greatly improved his locomotion and made him feel more independent, though he was still not able to ramble the countryside as he had done during the happiest time of his boyhood. He visited his father's birthplace in County Cork, Ireland, and recalled forty years later that he had been "so intoxicated with the roads and lanes and hedges and fields and cottages and castles and inns that I thought I should fairly expire with delight."

But the most important event of the trip was that someone—probably Michael Faraday, the great scientist—introduced Henry James to the doctrines of a Scottish sectarian named Robert Sandeman, a "primitive Christian" mystic, who looked upon Christ as the friend more of sinners than of the righteous. James was already disgusted with Princetonian self-righteousness, and Sandeman, whose letters he edited on his return to the United States, gave him a life-long contempt for pharisaic pride in one's "morality"—the very word became for James a term of contempt. But he did not entirely escape from his Calvinist indoctrination, for he would always believe that man is estranged from God, though not God from man. He believed that man's individual salvation depended upon the salvation of his society: men might "fall from Grace" individually, but they could be saved only collectively. This conviction profoundly affected his attitude toward society, making him spiritually as well as socially democratic. And later it made him a tender, permissive, and almost obsessively loving parent.

At Princeton Henry James had won the intimate friendship of another Scotch-Irish student named Hugh Walsh. Together they reached the decision to leave Princeton. Walsh invited James to visit his home at 19 Washington Square in New York City, where his widowed mother, Mrs. James Walsh, lived with her children. Both her husband and her father had been businessmen like William James of Albany; though not as spectacularly successful as he, both had left substantial estates. The fact that Mrs. Walsh lived on Washington Square was in itself a sure indication of affluence, for in the 1840s this was the most elegant and fashionable residential section of the city. There, in the fine three- and four-story red-brick Georgian houses, with their marble steps, fanlight doorways, and ornamental hitching posts at the curb, lived Commodore Vanderbilt, the De Forests, the Coopers, the Rhinelanders, the De Peysters, and the elite of New York society.

Mrs. Walsh was charmed with her son's effervescent friend, and so were her two daughters near Henry's age, Mary Robertson and Catharine. In the high-ceilinged drawing room, with its Dutch tile fireplace and cut-glass chandelier, the two boys were so eloquent on the delusions of Presbyterian theology that both girls decided to resign from the Murray Presbyterian Church, where they had been christened as babies. This distressed Mrs. Walsh but did not turn her against Henry, nor did she object when two years later her older daughter accepted his proposal of marriage. She even agreed to a civil ceremony, and on July 28, 1840, in the Washington Square house, Mary Robertson Walsh and Henry James were married by the mayor of New York, Isaac Leggett Varian.

In many ways Henry James's marriage was a fortunate one for him. His wife was an Irishwoman with rather plain features, a firm mouth, and unaffected manners. More important, she was the dependable, practical, resolute person she appeared to be, and Henry James needed just such a wife to guard him against the excesses of his own imaginative, introspective, impatient temperament. Mary Walsh James was not unintelligent, but her mind was shrewd rather than brilliant. Her religion contained more ethics than theology. Neither complacent nor smug, she nevertheless accepted the world as she found it and did not lie awake at night contemplating the state of her soul. Her husband, on the other hand, suffered from feelings of guilt and indecision, and brooded on theological matters. He was passionate, vociferous, and restless. But instead of becoming irritated by him, she tactfully calmed and humored him, because she really loved him and sympathized with his ambitions. Lacking his powers of argument, she listened while he expounded his social and religious ideas and accepted them without always fully understanding them. As a consequence, her husband came to depend upon her—a dependence accentuated by his physical handicap—to an extent that sometimes appeared to be parasitic, though on the other hand, her readiness to follow his quixotic schemes on occasion made him seem domineering.

The one thing that Mary James could not do was cure Henry of his compulsive restlessness. During the first months of their marriage they shuttled back and forth between Albany and New York City. For a few months they lived with the elder Mrs. James, Henry's mother, in Albany; then they took rooms at the Astor House in New York, said to be the most luxurious hotel in the country and certainly the most famous at the time. They rented a house on Washington Square near Mrs. Walsh, then returned once more to the Astor House. It was there that their first child, a fine boy whom they named William, was born on January 11, 1842. Looking back, it seems especially appropriate that the future author of *Pragmatism* and *A Pluralistic Universe* should have been born in New York City's busiest, finest, and most commodious hotel.

CHAPTER II Transatlantic Infancy

Willy . . . talks frequently of his transatlantic experiences and ac-

quaintances. —HENRY JAMES SR.

I

WILLIAM JAMES WAS BORN during one of the economic depressions that plagued his country at unexpected intervals. "The year comes in under gloomy auspices and discouraging forebodings," Philip Hone, former mayor of New York and prominent civic leader, wrote in his diary on New Year's Day, 1842. "Real and personal property is diminished greatly in value, and the confidence which promotes success in dealings of men seems to have fled," complained this conservative businessman who had suffered under the inept Harrison-Tyler administration. But Henry James's ten-thousand-dollar income had not been affected, and he was almost completely indifferent to business matters anyway. This ebullient, roly-poly man of thirty with a cork leg and the face of a saint—if one can imagine a saint with a mischievous sense of humor—ignored the "gloomy auspices" and on January 8 bought from his half-brother John for eighteen thousand dollars a splendid three-story brick house on Washington Place, a short street leading from Broadway to the east side of Washington Square. This was the home to which the infant William was brought, after his mother recovered from his birth at the Astor House. Just across Green Street, to the west of the James house, stood the new, imposing, pseudo-Gothic five-story building of New York University.

But the atmosphere of the James home was not in the least academic. Long before he could talk, baby William had become accustomed to the voices of prominent reformers, journalists, and editors. One of these was Horace Greeley, who had just started his

Tribune and opened his columns to the followers of the French socialist, Charles Fourier, who preached that men could return to their original divine nature by breaking up society into small, autonomous communities. William's father and mother had become converts to Fourier's doctrine, and in their home they held animated conversations on his ideas with Albert Brisbane, one of the leading interpreters of Fourier in America, with Parke Godwin, associate editor of the *Evening Post*, and with William Cullen Bryant, the editor of the *Post*. The whole country was seething with schemes for utopias and social reform, from the abolition of slavery to dietary fads, and Henry James shared in the excitement.

Before William was three months old Ralph Waldo Emerson visited the James residence on Washington Place, and the father could scarcely wait to take the tall New Englander with the rich resonant voice upstairs to see his infant son. The unrepressed joy Henry James displayed in exhibiting his cooing, blue-eyed baby must have brought a twinge to the poet-philosopher, who had lost his own idolized son only six weeks before. But William's father, wrapped up in his own happiness, did not notice, or possibly did not even know of Emerson's recent bereavement. At any rate, the "sage of Concord" gave his blessing to the babe, in what might be regarded as a prophetic event for the future philosopher of Pragmatism, and the incident became one of the James family's most cherished anecdotes.

Other New England "transcendentalists" also visited the Jameses at Washington Place. In 1843 both Henry Thoreau and Bronson Alcott called, and Thoreau wrote Emerson that he found Mr. James "the most childlike, unconscious and unblushing egotist it has ever been my fortune to encounter in the ranks of manhood"—interesting testimony from a man who was to become famous for his own use of the first-person pronoun in his writings. But he praised the hospitality he had received. Alcott, a visionary himself, who could match Henry James's pungent exaggeration, resented his host's attempt to translate the "orphic sayings" recently published by Alcott (in the transcendentalist *Dial* magazine) into common sense and called James "a sinner to all eternity" and "damaged goods."

Although Henry James may have appeared to be an "unblushing egotist," inwardly he was seething with uncertainty, especially after the birth of his second son, Henry Jr., on April 15, 1843. On May 11 he wrote Emerson, in response to an invitation to visit: "My wife is grateful for your remembrance, and thinks nothing would so help me as a little intercourse with Concord. Another fine little boy now lying in her lap preaches to me that I must become settled somewhere at home." He had been debating whether to go to France and Germany for a few years, or move to the country. By October he had decided upon Europe, sold his house, and lodged his family at the Astor House between October 10 and 19, when they were to board ship for England.

II

Henry James Sr. booked passage on the *Great Western*, the fastest steamship on the high seas, now making the run regularly from New York to Liverpool in fifteen days. Of course he engaged the best accommodations for his party, which included Mrs. James's sister, Catharine ("Aunt Kate" to the children), and a family servant, Fanny, from Albany. Aunt Kate was going along to help her sister with the two small babies, the younger scarcely five months old.

Arriving in London, the women of the James entourage took turns at baby-sitting and sightseeing while Henry Sr. made the acquaintance of Thomas Carlyle, Lord Tennyson, George Henry Lewes, John Stuart Mill, and other literary figures. On the Isle of Wight he visited John Sterling, a young dramatist "dying in perfect confidence, with no knowledge of the future and no beliefs." James was captivated by Sterling's honesty and courage. But he thought the other men, except for Mill, were cynical: "Their talk was depraved to the last degree. What they had to say was not a tenth part so interesting as the talk you can have in America with the person sitting next you in the horse cars." Underneath the apparent urbanity of Henry James Sr. was a layer of provinciality as tough as that of Fanny, the maid, whose patriotic observation that the British Museum was less impressive than the Museum in Albany became an often-repeated family joke.

By mid-winter, 1844, the James family was tired of England (or at least Henry Sr. was) and they decided to give Paris a try. The weather was rough when they crossed the Channel, and all were dreadfully seasick. As Henry Sr. explained in one of his numerous letters to his mother in Albany, "Willy didn't know what to make of it at all, and screamed incessantly to have 'the hair taken out of his mouth'!" The bad Channel crossing was only a prelude to a miserable three months in Paris. None of them could speak French with any facility, they could not find comfortable quarters, and the damp, cold weather was especially hard on little William. At the end of April they were all glad to return to "tidy old England." This time the crossing was smooth and only Fanny suffered *mal de mer*.

They looked first for suitable lodgings at Clifton, but, failing to find them there, the James party proceeded to Windsor, seat of the castle, where they rented a house called Frogmore Cottage. It seems to have been rather ample for a cottage, and the location was not the least "froggy." Henry Sr. described it in a letter to his mother as "standing between the Great and Little Parks, next to the residence of the Duchess of Kent, and fronting the entrance to the Little Park. The Little Park is called little because it is only four miles around, whereas the Great Park is twenty-three. Either of these will be quite enough for the children's amusement."

The location was ideal for the two little boys. As Henry Sr. explained to his mother, the Great Park "comes 'smack up' . . . to the cottage hedge behind, and Willy and Harry from the nursery windows may hold delightful concourse with the sheep and cattle browsing beneath, the livelong day." On one side of the "cottage" the meadows stretched away for miles, and on the other side the Duchess of Kent's gardens presented a variety of cultivated beauty. At the front, the tree-lined "avenues of the Little Park sweeping over the hill and dale till they reach the Thames, the foresters' lodges, the Queen's private gardens, her aviary . . . ," all these sights, Henry Sr. continued, "combined with many others make Frogmore Cottage a desirable summer residence, even at 4.10 per week."

The widow of the first William James evidently worried about her son's extravagance, and both Henry Sr. and his wife frequently mentioned their economies or justified their expenditures. On taking possession of Frogmore Cottage they were "a little startled by the apparition of a huge watchman's rattle lying in a little room off the hall, and on inquiring its significance were told it was to be used in case of an alarm . . . at night." The master of the house took it to his room, "determined to give it a fair trial on the first symptom of foreign invasion. It will be sure to arouse the Duchess of Kent, whose bed-room is quite near, and who will no doubt 'use her influence' in our behalf." However, thieves could not do much harm, Henry Sr. reflected, because his fortune was in the hands of a trustee of his father's estate. "While *he* endures, the loss of one of my trifling pocketfulls now and then is a mere bagatelle, not worth the naming." Although intended as a joke, this remark gives considerable insight into the psychology of Henry James Sr. Money was the least of his worries, so confident was he of the durability of the trustee. But he hoped his mother would tell his brothers and brothers-in-law how cheaply he was living: "I support my entire family," he said, "upon a sum which they probably throw away every week in superfluities"—thus indicating plainly that he had been criticized for his attitude toward money.

At Windsor Henry James Sr. was also much absorbed in the development of his two small sons, and of course their grandmother was interested in any news he could send about them. "The children are well in the main," he wrote. "Harry's teeth are troublesome at times, but he is as good as the day is long, and the night on top of it. Willy is very good, too, when we are quietly settled. Our wretched Paris excursion broke him up a little, but he is now [May 1] on the mend. He is full of fun—calls me 'Henwy' (he can't pronounce the *r s*) and his mother 'Mawy'—and talks frequently of his transatlantic experiences and acquaintances." It was distinctly not a nineteenth-century custom for children to address their parents by their given names, and this illustrates once again the unconventionality of William's father. Probably, too, Willy's "transatlantic experiences" was merely a humorous exaggeration for his little daily adventures in the parks or toddling around the orchard surrounding Frogmore Cottage. But the sights, sounds, smells, and tastes of the beautiful English countryside were being recorded in his developing memory, and later he would be able to make real transatlantic comparisons.

III

When not strolling with William or driving in either the Little or the Great Park, Henry James Sr. spent most of the day and evening in his study. Before leaving America he had decided that "the book of Genesis was not intended to throw light upon our natural or race history, but was altogether a mystical or symbolical record of the laws of God's *spiritual* creation and providence," and he now planned to write a book on the subject.

At Windsor during verdant May, in a comfortable house surrounded by trees filled with singing birds, Henry James Sr. felt that his thinking and writing had never gone better: "my health was good, my spirits cheerful, and the pleasant scenery . . . furnished us a constant temptation to long walks and drives." Yet under these comfortable circumstances he underwent an almost catastrophic experience (exactly what his son William would many years later, in *Varieties of Religious Experience*, call "mystical") which would influence the remainder of his life, and be re-enacted by William, now only a little over two years old, eighteen years later. This is the way Henry Sr. later described the phenomenon:

> One day . . . towards the close of May, having eaten a comfortable dinner, I remained sitting at the table after the family had dispersed, idly gazing at the embers in the grate, thinking of nothing, and feeling only the exhilaration incident to a good digestion, when suddenly— in a lightning-flash as it were—"fear came upon me, and trembling, which made all my bones to shake." To all appearance it was a perfectly insane and abject terror, without ostensible cause, and only to be accounted for, to my perplexed imagination, by some damnèd shape squatting invisible to me within the precincts of the room, and raying out from his fetid personality influences fatal to life. The thing had not lasted ten seconds before I felt myself a wreck; that is, reduced from a state of firm, vigorous, joyful manhood to one of almost helpless infancy. The only self-control I was capable of exerting was to keep my seat. I felt the greatest desire to run incontinently to the foot of the stairs and shout for help to my wife,—to run to the roadside even, and appeal to the public to protect me; but by an immense effort I controlled these frenzied impulses, and determined not to budge from my chair till I had recovered my lost self-possession. This purpose I held to for a good long hour, as I reckoned time, beat upon meanwhile by an ever-growing tempest of doubt, anxiety, and despair, with absolutely no relief from any truth I had ever encountered save a most pale and distant glimmer of the divine existence, when I resolved to abandon the vain struggle, and communicate without more ado what seemed my sudden burden of inmost, implacable unrest to my wife.

As soon as he could travel, Henry James Sr. went to London and consulted the most eminent physicians, but they took a completely materialistic view of his condition and told him that he had overworked his brain. "They all recommended by way of hygiene a resort to the watercure treatment, a life in the open air, cheerful company, and so forth, and thus quietly and skilfully dismissed me to my own spiritual meditations." Fortunately, at one of the resorts recommended to him, he met a Mrs. Chichester, who told him that he had experienced what the great Swedish mystic, Emanuel Swedenborg, called a "vastation." He rushed back to London to buy Swedenborg's books, and in them he eventually found the relief he sought—or, as William was to put it years hence, when he edited his father's *Literary Remains*, he found his "bundle of truth," which would suffice him for the remainder of his life.

Before leaving New York Henry James Sr. had read an article by a Dr. J. J. Garth Wilkinson of England on Coleridge's marginalia upon Swedenborg, and he now visited Dr. Wilkinson near London. The two men became great friends and James was thoroughly converted to Swedenborgianism, or to his own interpretation of Swedenborg. Actually what he got from the Swedish mystic was not so much definite beliefs or dogmas as clarification and confirmation of ideas which he had already entertained in an intellectual way. In the depth of his "fear and trembling" he longed, like Walt Whitman a few years later, to "turn and live with the animals." In his own words: "The curse of mankind, that which keeps our manhood so little and so depraved, is its sense of selfhood, and the absurd, abominable opinionativeness it engenders. How sweet it would be to find oneself no longer man, but one of those innocent and ignorant sheep pasturing upon that placid hillside, and drinking in eternal dew and freshness from Nature's lavish bosom!"

Despite his earlier revolt, as a theology student at Princeton, against pride in "selfhood," James felt that he had not until now been a sincere "seeker after truth," only desirous "to ventilate my own ability to discover it." His oldest son, who later devoted much time to the study of such experiences as his father had had at Windsor in the spring of 1844, was to conclude that they came after prolonged conflict on the subconscious level. This insight (which anticipates Freud) suggests that Henry James Sr.'s "vastation" had resulted from feelings of guilt he had suppressed as a child when he rebelled against his father and his father's God, perhaps intensified later when, contrary to his father's recorded wishes, he acquired a liberal income from the paternal estate.

It was nearly two years before Henry James Sr. found substantial relief from his neurotic condition, but eventually he derived solace from Swedenborg's doctrine that God is not a personality but "infinite Divine love and wisdom" in union with the soul of man; that Heaven and Hell are states, not places; and that at death the soul is liberated from the body and goes directly into the world of Spirit. Henceforth James's religion was to lose every vestige of anthropomorphism and become completely spiritual.

This period of emotional turmoil in the life of the father naturally affected the close-knit James household. Henry Jr. was perhaps too young to be aware of the tension, but William, who was emotionally precocious, must have felt it. Mrs. James was a dutiful mother, but she managed domestic affairs so that they revolved around her husband: he was always the center of her attention. Under the circumstances William's care was often entrusted to his Aunt Kate, who was even more deliberate and methodical than his mother, and he was not an easy child to discipline.

Already vivid contrasts were emerging in the personalities of the boys: Willy, fretful, impatient, loudly protesting discomforts though "very good" and "full of fun" when the family was "quietly settled"; Henry, patient and stoic even while teething. At two and a half William was talking animatedly, but verbal fluency did not come so quickly or easily to Henry. Yet in his silent absorption of impressions, Henry was equally precocious. Early in 1845 the family revisited Paris, before starting back to America. Three years later, when he was five, Henry startled his parents by describing the streets of Paris as he had seen them at the age of two from a carriage window, seated on Aunt Kate's lap. Questioning convinced them that he did indeed remember details which did not apply to London, New York, or Albany. He could still visualize being conveyed along the Rue St. Honoré, his small feet waggling under a flowing robe. As the carriage crossed the Rue de Castiglione he had taken in for all time the exact appearance of the Place de la Concorde and the Colonne Vendôme.

For William no such precocious feats of memory have been recorded. He was no less impressionable than Henry, but he was too active and impetuous to sit still registering every observable detail on his memory. Even from infancy his mind was restless and dynamic. In America these traits would begin to differentiate the future philosopher from the future novelist.

IV

For two years after returning to America early in 1845 the James family had no permanent residence. William had become accustomed to traveling to and from Albany on the paddle-wheel Hudson River steamboat, which usually docked after what Henry later remembered as "a night of huge strange paddling and pattering and shrieking and creaking." Mrs. James's third child, named Garth Wilkinson for his father's Swedenborgian friend in London, was born in New York on July 21, 1845; her fourth son, named Robertson for her maternal grandfather, on August 29, 1846, in Albany.

In Albany the Jameses lived in the mansion on North Pearl Street with William's grandmother, widow of the first William. All her grandchildren loved her and William no less than the others. She was a soft-spoken old lady with gentle manners, a sweet smile, and a seemingly inexhaustible supply of peppermints, which she dispensed with fingers half-covered by lace mitts. She wore silk dresses which rustled slightly when she walked, which was seldom: she sat a great deal and sighed as if short of breath. Indeed, she had good reason to be tired, for her house was nearly always filled with her numerous sons and daughters and their children. There William could always find some of his twenty-one cousins— Van Burens, Barkers, Temples, numerous Jameses—many of whom lived in Albany.

William especially loved his grandmother's house in summer. The covered piazza at the rear had a swing, and beyond was a garden filled with delightful fruits, green vegetables, and bright flowers. From the house the ground sloped down to the stable, which was surrounded by peach trees. Henry Jr. came to associate his visits to his grandmother with the flavor and odor of peaches; to William, in later years looking back on those carefree days, it always seemed to be afternoon on a warm, drowsy summer day while time stood still.

In 1846 William and his parents and brothers were living in Albany more or less permanently. It was in the autumn of that year that he got his first experience of attending school, a kindergarten or "Dame School," which was conducted by an Albany matron in an old Dutch house just across the cobblestone, tree-lined street from his grandmother's house. Henry Jr. was also sent, and he never forgot being led crying and kicking and protesting to the teacher, while William looked on without the slightest show of surprise, as if he expected such disgraceful conduct from his infant brother. William was almost arrogantly confident and self-possessed. He liked new experiences and he was fond of learning—almost anything. Where Henry found all boys difficult to play with, unless they made the first advances, William had no difficulty in finding playmates of his own age. Henry's slowness in learning to talk increased his timidity and unsociability. William, by contrast, was naturally, effortlessly articulate, unchecked by any emotional disturbance, and this encouraged him to talk recklessly—as he grew older, with witty exaggeration, and often without discretion.

William's father was determined above all to avoid what he regarded as the mistakes of his own father. Of course his reading of Fourier and Swedenborg, as well as his mystical experience in England, influenced his thinking. The most basic tenets in his philosophy of child nurture were freedom, spontaneity, and love. "I desire my child," he declared in 1855 in *The Nature of Evil*, "to become an upright man, in whom goodness shall be induced not by mercenary motives as brute goodness is induced, but by love for it or a sympathetic delight in it. And inasmuch as I know that this character or disposition cannot be forcibly imposed upon him, but must be freely assumed, I surround him as far as possible with an atmosphere of freedom."

Another idea of Henry Sr.'s, derived from Fourier, was that a child's "innocence" must be prolonged and protected as long as possible, for "as you inconsiderately shorten this period of infantile innocence and ignorance [of sin] in the child, you weaken his chances of a future manly character." The fond father did not see that the application of this theory ran counter to his belief in freedom, for to the extent that he preserved his children's "innocence," he insulated them from the actual world of imperfect humanity, thereby limiting the healthy exercise of their free wills. Naturally, despite their father's idealism, the James children could not avoid some knowledge of the world in which they lived, and their more practical mother was not so tender with their sacred "innocence." Nevertheless, William's father did succeed in prolonging his son's childhood to an extent that was to become very unhealthy for him. But it was fortunate that the boy did not con-

tinue to live with his indulgent grandmother, who might possibly
have spoiled him more than his visionary father. In the autumn of
1847 the James family moved back to New York City, and there,
during the next ten years, William was to receive his elementary,
if erratic, education.

V

For several months the James family lived in an apartment at 11
Fifth Avenue, where the Brevoort Hotel later stood. To five-year-old
William the chief attraction of the location was that it was only
two or three blocks from his grandmother Walsh, who still lived
on Washington Square. She fed him cookies and gave him the
attention his little ego craved. But in the spring of 1848 his father
bought a house with a brownstone front at 58 West Fourteenth
Street—not quite so convenient to Washington Square, but still in
easy visiting distance—where the family was to live for seven years,
the longest period William was to spend in one house before he
reached manhood. Here, the last child and only girl, Alice, was
born on August 7, 1848.

Although not as fashionable as Washington Square, Fourteenth
Street was a respectable neighborhood, though a busy and somewhat
noisy one. The James house stood on the south side of the street
near Sixth Avenue, along which a horse-drawn streetcar line made
frequent trips downtown, then still the business center of New
York. Henry Sr., especially, appreciated the "horse cars" because
of his difficulty in walking. He did not keep horses, as many families
in the neighborhood did, but made frequent use of the livery stable
on the corner of University Place and Fourteenth Street, to which
William, and later Henry, as soon as they were old enough to be
trusted out alone, were often sent to order a vehicle for their father.

On the opposite side of Fourteenth Street was a Presbyterian
church, which the Jameses did not attend, and in the same block
nearby a famous dancing school run by Edward Furero, where a
few years later both William and Henry took dancing lessons from
Mr. Furero's sister, Mme. Dubreuil, whose husband sang minor parts
in the Italian operas performed in the Academy of Music, at the
opposite end of Fourteenth Street on the other side of Union Square.
During this and the following decade Italian opera reached its peak

of quality and popularity in New York City, and William's parents sometimes attended performances at the Academy, but William did not find them very interesting.

At quite an early age William began making little excursions by himself, or with other boys of his own age. To an eight-year-old, Henry, only a little over six, seemed like a needless encumbrance. Once when he begged William to take him along, William silenced him by exclaiming: "*I* play with boys who curse and swear!" Poor little Henry had to admit that he did not. But the novelist's later recollection of William's always being around the corner and out of sight before he, Henry, could catch him was not entirely accurate, for there is evidence that on many occasions the brothers did explore the city together.

The boys were allowed a surprising amount of freedom. Of course the region above Washington Square was safer than lower Broadway, or the slums near City Hall Park. Nevertheless, they faced more dangers than their idealistic father or trusting mother realized. Both William and Henry liked to loiter around Union Square, a terminal point for Broadway omnibuses, which had a fountain, a small park, and nondescript policemen whose only uniform was a funny-looking leather hat—hence their nickname "leather-heads." The boys also liked to continue up Broadway to the corner of Eighteenth Street, where there was still a "country place," enclosed by an iron fence, behind which were three cows, numerous chickens, guinea fowl, peacocks, and even fawns.

Around 1850 the boys thought it great fun to go up Fourth Avenue beyond Twenty-third Street to watch the construction of the Hudson River Railroad. Men would wave red flags and shout that a dynamite charge was about to go off. Then there would be a loud explosion, and fragments of rock would be hurled into the air. Sometimes the boys thought they saw the fragments strike down men near the blast, and they felt very brave to be standing so close themselves to such dangerous operations.

After the completion of the railroad in 1851 the Jameses used it instead of the steamboat to travel back and forth between New York and Albany. Now the Albany uncles came to New York more frequently too. At the corner of Fourteenth Street and Broadway Uncle William, just arrived by train from Albany, would pitch his valise from the omnibus window to the feet of one of his brother's servants and yell, "Tell Henry and Mary . . ." The message would be drowned out by the rumble of iron wheels on cobblestones as the omnibus sped down Broadway, but Mary and Henry James Sr. would be informed by the dutiful servant that Uncle William might be expected for dinner that evening.

No matter who the guest was at the James residence, whether an Albany relative or a famous writer, the children were encouraged to take part in the conversation both at dinner and in the parlor. Some of the frequent guests were Charles Dana, the newspaper editor; George Ripley, the Fourier socialist; Bayard Taylor, the famous author-traveler, who told of having his nose frozen in the north; and Parke Godwin, whom the boys thought the homeliest man they had ever seen. In the spring of 1850 Emerson, who had blessed William at the age of three months, was again a house guest, and thereafter the guest room at 58 West Fourteenth Street was designated "Mr. Emerson's room." Two years later Thackeray stayed with the Jameses and made a deep impression on the boys, though perhaps more on Henry than on William, who was not so readily inclined to worship literary lions. But the work of both Thackeray and Dickens became so familiar to both William and Henry that they came to associate areas of London with the settings of these authors' books.

A system of public schools had recently been established in New York, and one was located only two blocks away, but these schools were incompetently conducted and the "better" families did not send their children to them. At various times William had private tutors, who gave him instruction in the James home. But early in the 1850s he and Henry were sent to a private school called the Institute Vergnès, on lower Broadway near Bond Street (a few blocks south of Washington Square). The school specialized in French, taught by Monsieur Vergnès himself, old, irritable, and bristling. Most of the students were little homesick Cubans and Mexicans, sons of wealthy planters and merchants. The whole atmosphere of the school was tense, because M. Vergnès and his assistants seemed perpetually infuriated about something, shouting, gesticulating, even throwing books at dull little foreigners, though never actually whacking them. Needless to say, this attempt by Henry James Sr. to secure for his sons a cosmopolitan education in New York was not very successful.

The Vergnès school was followed by another more satisfactory for William, though apparently not for Henry, who was inclined to find all schools dull. It was conducted by Richard Pulling Jenks on Broadway, near Fourth Street, in two upstairs rooms which were grimy, poorly heated, and ugly. For lack of a playground the pupils roamed Broadway, dodging traffic—there were no stop-lights or traffic policemen in those days—buying sweets and fruits at the shops with their generously provided "pocket money." This was probably one of the times when William seemed "remote" to Henry, for the brothers studied and recited in different rooms.

Mr. Jenks himself taught Latin and Greek, and deplored "the facile text-books of Doctor Anthon of Columbia College, in which there was even more crib than text." Henry was bored by Mr. Jenks, but William thought him an excellent teacher, who deserved a "higher sphere" for his talents. Another teacher named Dolmidge, who wore a formal swallow-tail coat and black satin stock, taught penmanship with fancy scrolls and flourishes. But William's favorite teacher was Mr. Coe, who taught drawing. His specialty was oil painting on little boards or "panels," some of which William brought home after visiting Coe's studio and living quarters in University Building.

William had impressed his drawing teacher by his natural talent for sketching. By this time drawing was his favorite amusement, and Henry later remembered his brother in this period as "drawing and drawing, always drawing, especially under the lamplight of the Fourteenth Street back parlour; and not as with a plodding patience, which I think would less have affected me, but easily, freely and, as who should say, infallibly: always at the stage of finishing off, his head dropped from side to side and his tongue rubbing his lower lip." Henry tried to imitate his facile brother, but no matter how firmly he grasped his crayon it would not perform as William's did.

Henry also began at ten or eleven to write, already feeling that this was what he meant to do in life. In one of his stories, attempting to describe a storm at sea, he wrote that "the thunder sounded and the lightning followed." William found the manuscript and pounced upon the meteorological blunder with such merciless taunting that his mother had to intervene and forbid him to tease Henry about it any more. Thereafter Henry locked himself in his room when he wrote and hid his manuscripts.

William also wrote, but for a very different purpose. The

children of the neighborhood liked to stage comedies, which William wrote and directed, playing the leading roles himself. The children made their own costumes and invited their friends and relatives to see the performances. Henry thought his brother funnier than any of the comic actors they saw in the theatres; in fact, no one was really funny but William—except when he used his comic talents on his younger brother, as he not infrequently did.

The freedom Henry James Sr. permitted his sons extended to the theatre. Many people still had such strong moral prejudice against it that "lecture hall," "lyceum," "music academy," etc., were used to avoid the tainted word *theatre*, but Mr. James had no patience with such hypocrisy. He and his wife went to the theatre often, and the boys either accompanied them or went by themselves or with companions their own age. This was one activity which William and Henry often enjoyed together, as even Henry was to admit in his memoirs.

The brothers had a wide choice of theatrical entertainment in the 1850s, from Shakespeare to contemporary comedy, including broad farce at Burton's Theatre in Chambers Street. They attended the Park in Park Row, the Old Broadway, the Palmo Opera House; the Astor in nearby Astor Place, where rivalry between two British actors caused a notorious riot in 1849; Castle Garden, where Jenny Lind, the "Swedish nightingale," created a sensation in September 1850; Franconi's Hippodrome, up at Twenty-third Street, where chariot races were staged; and Barnum's Great American Museum, way downtown, where freaks and sideshows competed with legitimate theatrical performances. In 1854 William and Henry were delighted with *A Midsummer Night's Dream*, performed with Mendelssohn's music, at the Broadway Theatre. In 1855 they saw *A Comedy of Errors* at Burton's, with William Burton himself playing one of the Dromios. As usual, the play had been read to the boys at home during the day before the family went to see it in the evening. After the final curtain, William made critical comments that made Henry realize for the first time (as he later wrote) that a dramatic performance could be judged as well as enjoyed.

At ten and twelve, however, the James boys did not yet have fastidious theatrical tastes. One of their favorite places of amusement was Niblo's Garden, where they watched acrobats, dancers, pantomimists, tightrope walkers, and similar performers in what

would later be called either vaudeville or the circus. It was to
Niblo's that they took their visiting Albany cousins. But nearly
every Saturday afternoon that they did not have to go to the dentist,
they resorted to Barnum's so-called Museum, where they could view
the bottled mermaids, "bearded ladies," dioramas, and other humbugs,
stuffing themselves with fruits and candies until the "lecture room"
(theatre) opened. There they might see a comedy, a famous dancer,
such as Lola Montez, or a dramatized version of *Uncle Tom's Cabin*.

William and Henry saw so many different versions and performances of *Uncle Tom's Cabin*, at the National, the Chatham, and
other theatres besides Barnum's, that they became experts on the
many ways that Eliza, Cassy, Topsy, little Eva, and faithful Tom
could be played. They were not critical of the many crude illusions
practiced upon them by trick acting or staging; the characters were
as real as life itself to them—as real as the Fagins, Oliver Twists, and
David Copperfields in similar adaptations from the novels of Dickens.

For several years William and Henry attended some sort of theatrical performance nearly every Saturday and on every other holiday
except Sunday. On Sunday the James children could attend church
or not, as they chose. Their parents did not attend, but most of their
playmates did, and they were embarrassed when asked, "What
church do you go to?" When they took this problem to their father,
he was amused by their dilemma and told them to "plead nothing
less than the whole privilege of Christendom," and to say that there
was no communion, including Catholic, Jewish, or Swedenborgian,
from which they need find themselves excluded. Of course this
advice was of little help, but they did visit churches occasionally.
William missed having a church of his own less than Henry, who
even at an early age felt the need for ritual and formality. This
his father did not understand, any more than he understood the
confusion of his children when asked by their playmates about his
occupation or profession. Again he replied banteringly, "Say I'm
a philosopher, say I'm a seeker for truth, say I'm a lover of my kind,
say I'm an author of books if you like; or best of all, just say I'm
a Student." Wilky, who was beginning to worry about such problems, envied a playmate who said his father was a "stevedore." He
didn't know what a stevedore was, but it was definite and sounded
impressive. Why, he asked his brothers, couldn't their father have
been a stevedore?

VI

The chief difficulty with Henry Sr.'s idealistic conceptions of education and child nurture was that they were impossible to realize; hence the frequent changing of tutors, schools, and plans of study. Only he himself could have taught the children as he thought they should be taught, and he either did not have the patience or felt himself incompetent. The last school that he selected for William and Henry in New York was as odd a choice as the others had been. It was something like what would later be called a "business school," though Latin was also taught. It was run by two men named Forest and Quackenboss, the latter teaching Latin and the former, who appropriately looked like Benjamin Franklin, teaching arithmetic and bookkeeping. Several of the boys' uncles had attended this school, and this fact may possibly have influenced their father's choice. Or possibly it may have been because it was nearby, on the west corner of Fourteenth Street and Sixth Avenue. Certainly the father of William and Henry was not trying to make businessmen of them, for he saw no necessity for his sons to master any trade or profession. As Henry Jr. later expressed it, "spiritual decency" was for his father "profession and career enough."

In 1849 Henry James Sr. wrote Emerson that his four stout boys had "no play-room within doors, and import shocking bad manners from the street, with much pity"; adding, "we gravely ponder whether it would not be better to go abroad for a few years with them, allowing them to absorb French and German and get a better sensuous education than they are likely to get here." Europe was the land of aesthetic sensations, and it had a magnetic charm for the imagination of Henry James Sr. New York in 1849 was without doubt untidy, chaotic, unsightly, with commonplace architecture, no fine boulevards, and few public monuments of any kind. It did have some artists, but they had nearly all been trained in Europe, especially in Italy. Moreover, the Albany Jameses had money to travel, and some of them were nearly always in Europe or stopping off in New York on their way to or from Europe.

The Henry James family also found reminders of Europe when they visited relatives, such as the boys' Uncle Robert (the oldest brother of Henry Sr.) at Rhinebeck. Aunt Elizabeth was a great beauty, "mother of the fair and free young waltzing-women in New York," who had named one of her daughters Marie because she had been born in Paris. The Robert Jameses lived like European aristocrats in their large estate called Linwood, overlooking the Hudson River, with gardeners and grooms to attend to their fine horses. In summer the roses were magnificent, and in season so were the grapes, peaches, currants, apples, pears, quinces, and berries of various kinds.

On one trip to Rhinebeck the James boys visited, with their Grandmother James, an orphaned cousin, Augustus (Gus) Barker, at his military school near Sing Sing. Gus took them to visit the prison and they were so impressed by the neatness, order, and quietness of the grounds and buildings that they could not understand its sinister reputation. Later Gus left the military school and went to New York to study languages at the Institute on Tenth Street; but his life was ended in 1863 by a Confederate bullet. A sister was to survive him, but an older brother, Bob, died prematurely after studying sculpture in Europe. Such was the pathetic biography of several cousins, descendants of the heirs to the fortune of William James of Albany: artistic talent, study in Europe, and premature death. And yet they were all attracted by Europe as a moth to a light at night.

In the front parlor of the James home on Fourteenth Street hung a large canvas by the American painter, Thomas Cole, which depicted a scene of Florence from a neighboring hilltop. The back parlor also had a marble bust, supposedly a Bacchante, straight from an American studio in Rome. Over the sofa in the back parlor hung another large painting by a French artist, Lefèvre. It was labeled "View in Tuscany," but a visitor who was familiar with Italy declared that the colors were not soft enough for Tuscany. This observation tarnished the charm of the painting for the James family.

Henry James Sr. seldom missed an opportunity to take the family to exhibitions of paintings, especially of well-advertised new arrivals from Europe. In the 1850s the Düsseldorf school "commanded the market." One evening Mr. James took his wife and older boys to see Leutze's "masterpiece" of Washington crossing the Delaware. They patriotically gaped at every incongruous realistic detail, and did not realize until later that it was "lividly dead." On another evening the Jameses took the Sixth Avenue omnibus downtown to Bryan's Gallery to see an exhibition of Christian art, a "collection of worm-eaten diptychs and triptychs, of angular saints and seraphs, of black Madonnas and obscure Bambinos," which were afterward proved to be fakes. More satisfying were Thorwaldsen's enormous sculptures of Christ and the Disciples at the Crystal Palace exhibition in New York in 1853. This was America's first "world's fair," staged behind the Croton Reservoir, at what is now Bryant Park, behind the Public Library at Fifth Avenue and Forty-second Street, then on the edge of open country.

Most of the art exhibited at the Crystal Palace had been borrowed from Europe. William took the keenest delight in it, but it was Henry who later described his own and William's emotions: "If this was Europe then Europe was beautiful indeed, and we rose to it on the wings of wonder. . . . The Crystal Palace was vast and various and dense, which was what Europe was going to be. . . ." In short, the Jameses were ripe for Europe. But it is possible to exaggerate their homesickness for that ancient continent, for most of our evidence comes from the reminiscences of Henry Jr. set down many years later. William would never find the happiness in Europe that Henry did. At the age of thirteen and a half he was, of course, eager for new experiences, but like his father he would always miss his own country as soon as he was out of it.

By June 1855 plans were made, and on the 26th Henry Sr. wrote his friend and banker, Samuel Gray Ward in Boston, that they had taken passage on the *Atlantic*, which sailed next day. The object of the trip was to "place our dear boys at school in Switzerland." Switzerland had been chosen because some of the wealthy acquaintances of Henry Sr. had sent their sons to Swiss schools. But later Henry Jr. suspected that a book which he and William had been reading in French and translating to their father had something to do with these plans. The book was Rodolphe Toeppfer's *Voyages en Zigzag*, which described in romantic prose, with many engraved illustrations, holiday trips taken by a Swiss schoolmaster and his pupils with knapsack and staff through the Swiss, Italian, and French Alps. "To turn back to Toeppfer's pages to-day is to get the sense of a lost paradise, and the effect for me even yet of having pored over them in my childhood is to steep in sweetness and quaintness some of the pictures. . . . It must have been conceived for us that we would lead in these conditions—always in pursuit of an education—a life not too dissimilar to that of the storied exiles in the forest of Arden. . . ." On this second journey with his parents in search of his father's "lost paradise" William was old enough to make critical comparisons in his transatlantic experiences, and this was to be the next phase in his education.

CHAPTER III Zigzag Voyages

To turn back to Toeppfer's [Voyages en Zigzag] to-day is to get the

same sense of a lost paradise. . . . —HENRY JAMES JR.

America is the lost Paradise restored to boys and girls. . . .

—HENRY JAMES SR.

I

THE BOY WHO HAD MADE his first trip to Europe at the age of two
had not seen that continent for ten years. Never again in his lifetime
would William James stay away so long, and when he sailed on the
S.S. *Atlantic* with his family on June 27, 1855, he was beginning a
more zigzag voyage than any of the Jameses could have imagined.

Their group included—besides the parents and five children rang-
ing in age from William, thirteen, to Alice, seven—Aunt Kate, and
Mlle. Annette Godefroi, a French governess. Aunt Kate, who had
recently left her husband, Captain Charles H. Marshall, had decided
almost at the last minute to accompany her sister and brother-in-law
on their second hegira to delectable Europe. Her brief marriage had
been spoiled by quarrels with her husband over his children by a
former marriage, and she had resumed her maiden name, Catharine
Walsh, though retaining a "Mrs." before it. But if this trip was a
turning point in her life, for William it was to have more turns than
points.

After a miserable twelve-day crossing, the James entourage arrived
in dreary Liverpool on Sunday, July 8, and spent the night in the
Queen's Hotel. Next day they proceeded to London, but were
scarcely installed in the Euston Hotel before Henry Jr. suffered a
severe attack of malaria, which he had probably contracted on a
visit to Staten Island. This illness, from which he did not entirely
recover for several years, made Henry lethargic and accentuated
the difference between his passivity and William's abounding energy.
Because of his patience his parents nicknamed the younger boy

"Angel," and William never tired of playing ironic changes on the name. But Henry did not so much envy William's vitality as despair of competing with it, and he did not try; instead, he read novels, and daydreamed.

Fortunately, Henry's fever was intermittent, and in a few days the whole group was able to start for Paris. Henry Sr. had employed an Italian courier, Jean Nadali, with ferocious black whiskers and gesticulating vivacity, to accompany them the remainder of the journey to Switzerland. They were still accompanied also by the French governess, Mlle. Godefroi, "fresh-coloured, broad-faced and fair-braided, a 'bonne Lorraine.' " This party of ten persons finally arrived in Paris and found rooms in the Hotel Westminster, on the Rue de la Paix.

On one of the days when Henry's fever was in abeyance, William got his first sight of the Louvre, that great treasure-house of old-world masterpieces of painting and sculpture. Jean Nadali, well acquainted with the great museums, acted as guide for the two boys. Neo-classic painting was still in vogue, and William gaped at massive pseudo-historical canvases, at David's helmeted Romans and Géricault's muscular and prancing horses posturing before the broken columns of Greek temples. Henry was awed, and William wondered if he could handle a brush as easily as a crayon. This first glimpse of great art in the Louvre was the beginning of a new era in William's intellectual development.

In 1855 no railroad had yet been built to Geneva, so that from Paris the traveler went by train to Lyon, and then proceeded by carriage or other horse-drawn vehicle across the Jura mountains. After a two-day pause in Lyon at the Hôtel de l'Univers, Henry James Sr. hired two carriages for the rugged journey. Henry Jr. still had his intermittent fever, so that it was necessary to make a couch for him out of a board resting on two seats and covered with a mattress and pillows.

The postillion wore a costume which reminded William and his brother of characters in Italian operas they had seen on Fourteenth Street. Thus the caravan started for Geneva with the operatic Nadali, rosy Annette, faithful Aunt Kate, Mrs. James in new Paris clothes, the semi-invalid on his improvised *wagon-lit*, and numerous trunks and traveling bags tied onto the two carriages. The excited treble of the younger children mingled with the sound of iron wheels and horseshoes striking cobblestones.

The Jameses arrived in Geneva on July 26, and took temporary rooms with New York friends, Mr. and Mrs. Henry A. Stone, at 3 Quai de Mont-Blanc, near the present Hôtel de la Paix, on the shore of Lake Geneva. Gay flowers in numerous pots and hanging baskets brightened the sidewalk in front of the boat landing and majestic swans floated near the shore on the blue water. Gleaming white excursion boats were anchored at the pier, waiting to take passengers to Castle Chillon and other historic places. William was enchanted and could scarcely wait to begin sketching the picturesque scenery so resplendent in the clear, brilliant light, with Mont Blanc twinkling in the distance.

On August 6, after a few days of sightseeing, William, with his younger brothers Wilky and Bobby, was enrolled in a boarding school run by a German political exile named Achilles Heinrich Roediger. Henry Jr. was still recuperating, and was to be instructed at home, with Alice, by a Swiss governess. William's father had chosen Roediger's school because it had fewer American students than the more famous Haccius school, and what he wanted most was for his boys to "learn the languages." Roediger had a polyglot collection of about forty boys from Germany, France, and Russia, with only five Americans besides the three James boys. One lesson a day was conducted in English, and the others in French and German. William had no difficulty with the French, and began almost immediately to make progress in German. Bobby got a bit bumped and thumped in the gymnasium, but the three brothers were well satisfied with the new school, which was conducted in a beautiful old *campagne* on a wooded estate overlooking Geneva and the Rhone River, which joined the Arve to form Lake Geneva.

Henry James was delighted with the arrangements he had made for his three boys and wrote to his mother that she should immediately send over her two wards, Bobby and Willy Temple, to "receive the benefit of Swiss pedagogy." (These small boys were the orphan sons of Henry's sister Catharine Margaret and her husband, Col. Robert Emmet Temple, both of whom had died in 1854.) At Roediger's the playground was nearly as large, Henry Sr. informed his mother, as Washington Square, and every fair day teachers and their students went down to the Rhone to bathe. The teachers also took excursions with their pupils, as in Toeppfer's *Voyages en Zigzag*. Deportment and manners were almost ideal: "I have seen no rowdyism since I left England."

Meanwhile Henry Sr. had rented half a villa (or *campagne*) from
Count and Countess Gerebsow, Russian and Viennese respectively.
It was a lovely old place with balconies and terraces overlooking
Geneva and the junction of the Arve and the Rhone, with Mont
Blanc visible in the distance. But this view and the massive old house
surrounded by shady grounds were enjoyed a great deal more by
Henry Jr. and Alice than by William, who visited only when Herr
Roediger permitted. Moreover, by September 25 William's father
had decided that the Swiss schools were greatly overrated, and he
thought that "home tuition" would be best for the children. The
truth was that he missed his boys dreadfully; he was more emotionally dependent upon them than they upon him. The Stones were
leaving Geneva temporarily and had offered the Jameses their apartment. It was there, consequently, that the vacillating father tried
once more the often abandoned home-tutorial method. But by
October he was ready to abandon Switzerland altogether, and wrote
his friend Dr. Wilkinson for information about the educational
facilities in England. Dr. Wilkinson advised him sarcastically to
stop flitting from "one bit of sunshine after another," and recommended that he settle near London: "Then you shall be like the
Banian [sic] Tree, with sons and daughters in your sylvan shade."
So romantic a thought could not be resisted by Henry James Sr.

II

In an early October dawn the Jameses, Aunt Kate, and Mlle.
Cusin, the Swiss governess, set out for the jolting return journey
by way of Lyon and Paris, this time without Nadali and the two
carriages. In fact, they took the large yellow mail coach, which they
entirely filled. It made only scheduled stops, and the driver relentlessly adhered to his time table. One of the numerous cousins of the
James children, Charlotte King, staying in the country in France,
had been informed of the day and mode of their travel and she
waited along the highway to wave down the coach; *"rien que pour
saluer ces dames,"* she cried to the driver, but he would not pause
even for a salutation to the ladies, and the travelers sat helplessly
watching her wave from the growing distance.

A couple of days later the James family arrived in Paris, to find
the hotels crowded, but one of the ubiquitous Albany uncles finally

came to their rescue and found rooms for them in the Hôtel de la Ville de Paris in the Rue de la Ville-l'Évêque. Such high-sounding names! One reason for the crowded hotels was an Exhibition on the order of the English and American Crystal Palace world fairs at the Palais de l'Industrie. In the British display William saw the works of J. E. Millais for the first time. Painting was becoming one of his main interests.

But the pause in Paris was brief. After another dreadful Channel crossing, the group arrived in London late at night and found lodging at the Gloucester Hotel on the corner of Piccadilly and Berkeley Streets, where, as both William and Henry well remembered, Thackeray's Pendennis had spent his first night when he came to London to study law. Here, fatigued and famished, the family dined on cold roast beef with bread, cheese, and ale. "There's nothing like it after all!" the father exclaimed, and his words seemed to renew the faith of all the family that they had come back to the right place for the next experiment in education.

William's father rented a house for a month at 3 Berkeley Square, called Shiverly Square in Thackeray's *Vanity Fair*. Here all the James children received daily lessons in French from Mlle. Cusin. Henry Sr. considered sending William to various schools, such as the London University Grammar School and a highly recommended school run by a Rev. Mr. Markly in St. John's Wood. But instead he employed a Scottish tutor named Robert Thompson, who later taught Robert Louis Stevenson. Mr. Thompson gave the boys a thorough grounding in English history, pitched ball with them in the garden, and frequently took them to museums and historic buildings such as St. Paul's, the Tower, Westminster Abbey, the National Gallery, and Marlborough House; and of course to places Dickens and Thackeray had used as scenes for their novels.

William and Henry especially liked to stroll on Baker Street; it was not yet famous as the haunt of Sherlock Holmes, but Madame Tussaud's Wax Museum was there. They wore the typical British schoolboy clothes, including "top hats," but British boys would have nothing to do with them, except for the rougher sort, who derided and insulted them, and would no doubt have done worse except for the protection of Mr. Thompson. In fact, they made no friends of their own age, and were only spectators of British life. This galled William, who found this insulated, artificial way of living senseless, without purpose, and a great waste of time. For

Henry it was a chance to absorb new sights, impressions, and sensations; he was not unhappy and could not understand William's irritation and rebellious feelings.

In November Henry James Sr. rented a furnished house in St. John's Wood, the section where Dr. Wilkinson lived. This was a favorite resort for writers, artists, and musicians, with a somewhat Bohemian reputation. One of the most famous residents was Sir Edwin Landseer, the painter. The Jameses looked out upon a spacious garden, beyond which ladies and gentlemen practiced archery on a vast green turf. Regent's Park and the Zoological Gardens, which all the James children enjoyed, were a short walk away. Mr. Thompson took his two older pupils on longer excursions, and frequently to the theatre. The whole family saw Charles Kean in a memorable production of *Henry VIII*.

But best of all for William was the display of B. R. Haydon's paintings at the Pantheon, a combination art gallery and store for artists' supplies. William's assigned studies required so little of his time and energy that he spent many hours in drawing cartoons, sketching people and landscapes, and even dabbling with paint—he had had no instruction in drawing since that brief period in New York with Mr. Coe. He dutifully studied the canvases of Rubens and Titian in the National Gallery, but he found the modern paintings at the Pantheon more interesting. Yet much as he enjoyed this visiting of art galleries and tossing off endless sketches of his own, he felt the need of working at something systematically. He was acquiring some knowledge but in a desultory fashion, and he did not even know which of his several talents he ought to cultivate. Worst of all, he couldn't discuss the subject with his father, who seemed to be afraid that his son might discover a talent or subject of special interest too soon.

William was not disappointed, therefore, when his father began to tire of England. Henry Sr. still occasionally saw Thackeray, but they were not interested in the same ideas. And Dr. Wilkinson seemed "so eaten up with the spirits"—a surprising criticism of one Swedenborgian by another, which makes one wonder how Swedenborgian Henry James Sr. actually was. As for Mrs. Wilkinson, he thought her a conceited, superstitious "dear little goose of a thing," who fancied that Divine Providence was in league with her, giving her prophetic knowledge of the future and remedies for all diseases. But most disappointing of all was Carlyle: "the same old sausage,"

James wrote Emerson, "fizzing and sputtering in his own grease, only infinitely more unreconciled to the blessed Providence which guides human affairs." And William's father found ordinary British men as unapproachable as his sons did the boys—though of course less overtly hostile; merely stonily indifferent. He missed the sociability of the American horsecars. On his daily bus ride into London, he found that if he looked at any of the "stolid visages," an instant film "would surge up from their more vital parts, if such parts there were. . . . They took such extreme pains never to look at one another, that I knew they must be living men, devoutly intent each on disowning the other's life; otherwise I could well have believed them so many sad well-seasoned immortals, revisiting their old London haunts by way of a nudge to their present less carnal satisfaction." He agreed with Dr. Johnson that Englishmen did not "understand the common rights of humanity."

By May 1856 England had become as intolerable to Henry Sr. as it had been for some time to his oldest son; so, with Aunt Kate, he went over to Paris and rented an apartment. Yet he insisted in a letter to his friend Edmund Tweedy that he was not leaving with any bitterness for "brother Bull" and "sister Cow," whom he characterized as "shy, sullen, honest men" and "ill-drest, energetic, longstriding and unaffected women."

III

During June and July the James family lived in Paris on the Champs-Élysées between the Rond-Point and the Rue du Colisée in a luxurious furnished house rented from a wealthy American planter who made frequent trips back to Louisiana. The house, with its highly polished floors, winding stairway, white and gold brocade walls, silk hangings, ormolu vases, and sofas and chairs with gilt frames and red damask upholstery, all reflected in numerous mirrors, was far more elegant than their own in New York. The location, too, gave them a splendid window on the Second Empire in its fourth year.

The Imperial Prince was only three months old when the Jameses came to Paris, and they were witnesses to the excitement and turmoil of his baptism on June 14 at Notre Dame. The occasion was celebrated by all France, and the crowding of Paris was almost incredible. To the James brothers it seemed an interminable hot day, "a day of hanging about and waiting and shuffling in dust, in crowds, in fatigue, amid booths and pedlars and performers and false alarms and expectations and renewed reactions and rushes"; at last all transfigured "by the biggest and brightest illumination up to that time offered even the Parisians, the blinding glare of the new Empire effectually symbolised."

Baron Haussmann had not yet opened up the magnificent radiating boulevards, and the whole region of the Champs-Élysées was half rural, but the Avenue seemed to sparkle with grandeur as the Empress Eugénie rode down it taking the baby Prince to Saint-Cloud for an airing in a splendid coach, protected by the *cent-gardes* in blue and silver uniforms, riding stiffly erect in their saddles with drawn and cocked pistols. This was a scene that Henry Jr. would cherish in memory more than William, but at the time he was as excited and impressed as his younger brothers.

Along the Avenue from the Arc to the Tuileries were many fine old houses, gardens, terraces, hotels, pavilions, cabarets, and cafés of all descriptions. Almost opposite the planter's house where the Jameses lived was the Jardin d'Hiver, lighted at night by many colored oil lamps. William and Henry roamed the neighborhood, from the Arc to the Bois and the river Seine, and having no other friends of their own age, they roamed together. Sometimes they strolled up the Right Bank, looking at books and prints in the stalls on the parapet; at other times they crossed the Seine at the Pont des Invalides and strolled up the Left Bank. Most of all they liked to continue on to the Musée du Luxembourg, which contained a gallery of living French artists.

During the summer the whole family liked to go on excursions to Passy and Auteuil and picnics in the Bois de Boulogne. The Bois seemed to both William and Henry more like virgin forest than anything they had known in America. Actually this two-thousand-acre forest was the most extensive wooded area they had ever seen at close range. They had viewed the New York Catskills only from a boat or a train, and though they had not yet tramped the Alpine forests, they knew the landscapes of Europe far better than those of the United States. And instead of reading Parkman's *Oregon Trail*, published before they had left America, they were reading French classics. But they were not expatriates, like their Pendleton cousins living in the Hôtel Meurice, or Vernon King, another cousin, who was taking his baccalaureate at the Sorbonne.

William had attained complete ease and fluency in French. At the age of fourteen he felt great confidence in his ability to go anywhere in Paris, and his active mind still needed outlets for the energy which his tutorial assignments did not require. In fact, he was getting to be a problem to his tutor and to his family. Neither Mlle. Cusin nor Mr. Thompson had accompanied the Jameses to France, she having contracted a fortunate marriage in London, and William's father apparently having thought it best for William and Henry to replace their Scottish tutor with a French one, a M. Lerambert. This lank, pale, intellectual-looking man, who wore spectacles and a formal black coat, had written a volume of introspective verse which the famous critic, Sainte-Beuve, had praised—one of the few honors the poor man ever received. Henry found him tolerable and translated some of La Fontaine's fables to the tutor's satisfaction. But William disliked him, rebelled against him, and was glad when his father dismissed him after five months.

A Mlle. Danse was employed to instruct the younger children and conduct all of them on sightseeing tours. She had green eyes like Becky Sharp, as both William and Henry were quick to notice, but a more amiable character than Thackeray's selfish heroine. However, William enjoyed acting superior with her, showing off his more exact knowledge, and she frankly thought him *un ours* (a bear), no doubt to his delight. There are indications that he also played practical jokes on her, for he was beginning to experiment with elementary chemistry sets and electrical batteries. At one period every member of the family learned to examine a chair before sitting down to avoid an unpleasant shock.

William's juvenile scientific experiments and pranks were evidence of an approaching dilemma in his life: a conflict between his scientific and artistic talents, for he was also becoming increasingly interested in painting. Everyone who saw his drawings praised them and said he had real talent which ought to be cultivated. One of the leading painters of the time, M. Léon Cogniet, whose "Marius among the Ruins of Carthage" was on exhibit at the Luxembourg, was so impressed that he accepted William as a student—regarded as quite an honor for the fourteen-year-old boy. William also met Couture, a very influential painter, both a heroic classicist and something of a realist, whose recipe was *le morceau bien peint*, "well-painted" meaning to him the multiplying of brilliant (or showy) surfaces. Two of his most famous canvases were "Romans of the Decadence" and "The Falconer." But they were not exactly to William's taste. Nor was he much more impressed by the "costume pieces" of Paul Delaroche, another greatly admired painter who had died recently and whose commemorative exhibition William and Henry visited at the École des Beaux-Arts in 1857. Delaroche had tried to unite the classic and romantic schools in a huge mural on the semicircular wall of the Beaux-Arts school.

The painter who most excited William was Eugène Delacroix. He especially admired a certain exotic use of brilliant colors and mysterious shadows in "Dante and Vergil in Hell," which he copied over and over at home with the aid of lithographs to refresh his memory of this 1822 painting hanging in the Louvre. Delacroix had found his own style by studying and copying the works of Rubens in the Louvre, though his original paintings were not imitative of anyone. Perhaps it was his daring combination of colors that appealed to William. Delacroix was almost a scientist in his knowledge of colors, but he used them to give a general effect of vitality and truth rather than accuracy of minute details, and the results were dramatic. He was in revolt against the pseudo-classicism of David and the superficial imitation of ancient sculpture. Certainly he was a great painter, and William's enthusiasm for him not only indicates the boy's own innate artistic ability but also throws considerable light on his early character. Delacroix's work had a dynamic vitality and conveyed emotion without sentimentality. Even in his teens William had too keen a sense of humor to succumb to sentimentality, but he cared for nothing that did not stir his feelings—all his life he would be interested in *feeling*, later as a psychologist, and finally as a philosopher. Delacroix also gave him a new incentive to spend many hours in the Louvre. Henry Jr. tagged along with him, and at home tried to daub paint too, but he realized that it was William who had the talent.

However, William's discovery of Delacroix did not mean that the winter of 1856–1857 was an entirely happy one for him. Perhaps it might have been if he could have given all his attention to art, but he knew that his father was not ready to assent to such a decision. Henry James Sr. regarded aesthetic experiences as a necessary part of his children's education, but he thought that painters led a shallow spiritual life. It was not that he thought they were immoral; rather, that they were concerned with surfaces, not inner beauty. Besides, he never seemed to think that any of his children would have to earn a living or need to concern himself with a definite vocation.

After dismissing M. Lerambert, William's father made one of the most bizarre decisions in all his impractical educational experiments. During the winter of 1856–1857 he enrolled Willy, Harry, and Wilky in the Institution Fezandié in the Rue Balzac. An idealistic disciple of Fourier (this was what attracted Mr. James), M. Fezandié was a bald, chubby little man with a melancholy, worried look, and a slim young wife. After various failures in life, he had conceived the idea of an institute for the combined edification of young and old of both sexes. The three James boys were *externes* (day students), but most of the English and American pupils were *pensionnats* (boarding students), and most of the older people were tourists looking for a *pension* (boarding house).

However haphazard the instruction, the James brothers had a good opportunity to compare their facility in French with the awkward efforts of the other Americans and English, many of them touring ladies. Men, women, and children of all ages sat around a long table with a green cloth taking dictation from M. Fezandié, or receiving vigorous—or at least dramatic—instruction from his elderly assistant, M. Bonnefons, who was thought to have been an actor. William left no record of this experience, but Henry, with his usual love of reminiscence, did: M. Bonnefons "moved among us in a cloud of legend, the wigged and wrinkled, the impassioned, though I think alas underfed. . . . There were times when he but paced up and down and round the long table—I see him as never seated, but always on the move. . . . I hear him recite to us the combat with the Moors from Le Cid and show us how Talma, describing it, seemed to crouch down on his haunches in order to spring up again terrifically to the height of 'Nous nous levons alors!' which M. Bonnefons rendered as if on the carpet there fifty men at least had leaped to their feet."

M. Bonnefons tolerated the Americans, but he loathed the British, less because of Waterloo than the way they mangled his beautiful language. As usual in learning a foreign language, the children, and especially the James boys, who had had prolonged exposure to

French governesses and tutors, "piped with a greater facility and to a richer meed of recognition." There were also several French boys in the group with whom William, Henry, and Wilky could communicate easily, feeling a bond with them against the awkward babblers.

But to William this whole episode in his life was farcical. He thought he was learning nothing of value to him, and he looked upon most of his associates as zanies. He was astounded at the arrogance of the British, who made fun of the institute—and, in fact, almost everything French—even while they made use of it. Every dish served at *déjeuner* was "rotten." Nothing escaped their supercilious scorn. In his reminiscences Henry claimed he half admired their self-assurance, but it was not in William's nature to do so; nor would he ever become entirely reconciled to the characteristic arrogance of the nineteenth-century Britisher.

At the time that William was getting this overexposure to certain aspects of French and British manners and language, his parents were living almost in social isolation, except for visiting relatives. Despite his great ambition for his children to learn foreign languages, Henry Sr. never learned to speak any language except his own. And his unbookish wife never made any effort to learn more than a few domestic phrases of French. In her opinion the whole country was a vast swindle. She was appalled by the expenses, such as their paying twenty-two hundred dollars a year rent while they rented their New York house for fourteen hundred dollars, outraged by the dishonesty of the shopkeepers, and vexed at the deceptions of her servants, who were, she wrote her mother-in-law, "very inferior to our own." She was disillusioned and homesick. How she longed for just two or three of the peaches "taken in daily at Grandma's" by the basketful. Poor little Alice probably felt the boredom most, without any playmates of her own age; her brothers ignored her except for their habitual teasing, and needlework was almost the only diversion available to her.

When Alice's father became too bored, however, he always came up with a new idea for furthering his children's education—one requiring a change of scene. Thus it happened that a few weeks after having rented an expensive apartment on the Rue Montaigne, he decided that the family should spend the summer of 1857 at the coastal resort of Boulogne-sur-mer.

IV

Boulogne-sur-mer, across the English Channel from Brighton, was a favorite watering place for fashionable British families. As the Jameses already knew from Thackeray's *Newcomes*, it was divided between the *haute ville*, the old town on the heights which the haughty British preferred, and the *basse ville* built around the harbor. Mr. James rented a spacious and well-furnished apartment on the Rue Neuve Chaussée, a street part residential and part commercial, in the *basse ville* not far from the harbor. The landlord, M. Prosper Sauvage, lived with his large family *entre cour et jardin*.

The two main resources of Boulogne were summer vacationers and seafood, the fishing and navigation providing the year-round support of the thirty-five thousand natives. The men went out in the fishing boats and their wives and daughters netted shrimp and crabs from the beaches. Henry Jr. later remembered the women as "so bravely stripped below and so perfectly enveloped above . . . the deep-wading, far-striding, shrimp-netting, crab-gathering matrons or maidens who played, waist-high, with the tides. . . ." To all the Jameses they were far more interesting than the frowsy English ladies in mushroom hats, bestriped scarlet petticoats, tight gauntlets, and "explicit claims to long descent"; or the whiskered, pompous mid-Victorian English gentlemen, who came down from the heights with their "floridly repaired ladies" to bathe in the ocean or patronize the restaurants and the casino. The native women, with their fluted coifs, short dresses, wooden sabots, and long earrings were beguiling subjects for a painter, and the contrast between these sturdy working people and the dowdy British vacationers was good material for a novelist. But William left this field of study for Henry. For the moment his intellectual interest was once more veering toward science.

Boulogne had a Collège Impérial, open to any qualified applicant, for these fisher-folk were instinctively democratic. It was later called a *lycée*, and was actually comparable to an American high school. But *lycée* or *collège*, it gave serious and competent instruction. Henry James Sr. enrolled his three older sons, and for William this proved to be the most stimulating and satisfactory educational experience he had yet known. Here he could indulge his zest for "exact knowledge," with which the Paris governess had been unable to cope, and no longer have the feeling that he was dawdling away valuable time. Before the end of the summer Henry Jr. was suddenly stricken with typhoid fever, then called typhus. For several days he was delirious and his parents feared for his life, and he finally recovered only after eight weeks in bed.

William was the member of the family who enjoyed this summer in Boulogne most. To his mother in Albany Henry Sr. wrote: "Willy is very devoted to scientific pursuits, and I hope will turn out a respectable scholar. He has been attending the Collège Impérial here all summer, and one of his professors told me the other day 'that he was an admirable student, and that all the advantages of a first-rate scientific education which Paris affords ought to be accorded him.' He is, however, much dearer to my heart for his moral worth than for his intellectual. I never knew a child of so much principle, and at the same time of a perfectly generous and conciliatory demeanour towards his younger brothers, always disposed to help them and never to oppress."

Harry, his father had to report, was not fond of study, though a great devourer of libraries, especially of novels and romances. He wanted to be a writer, but his father seemed doubtful of his talent. At this period, William was the son in whom he took most pride. As for the others: "Wilky is more heart than head," his father confessed, "but has a talent for language, and speaks French they say with a perfect accent. They all speak very fluently indeed but Wilky and Bob . . . are particularly forward in it." Alice, too, "speaks very well." Thus at least one ambition of William's father had been accomplished.

V

Henry James Sr. had planned to take his family to Germany for the autumn and winter of 1857–1858, but the illness of Henry Jr. left him, in his parents' estimation, too weak to travel that far. Consequently the James family returned to their expensive apartment in Paris on Rue Montaigne. It was there that Henry Sr. learned that the financial panics in the United States, which his brothers had been writing him about, concerned him personally. A tariff bill, passed by Congress the preceding March, had depressed commerce, and by

August the bankruptcy of a large insurance company had caused banks in New York to stop payment in specie. Yet as late as October 15 the elder James still did not realize that his own income was threatened; however, the failure of several railroads in which his fortune was partly invested and distraught letters from his brothers finally brought the situation home to him.

On October 28 Henry Sr. wrote to his half-brother William that he did not know how long he could keep his family in Paris. "It is something new for us to feel anxious for the future, and I realize now the comfort of remembering the warm hearts at home who will not suffer us to lack anything which their necessities may spare. I wrote to Ma to ask you and Augustus and Howard [brothers in Albany] to aid her to contribute as large a sum as you can, to be put to my credit at Samuel G. Ward's in Boston, in order that we may escape the worst rigors of the crisis. We shall get home as soon as we can command the means, without any undue sacrifice of our present obligations."

Although Henry James Sr. was not his father's youngest child, the tone of his letter to his half-brother sounds rather as if his brothers had treated him in a tenderly protective manner, and there are many other indications that they had helped to shield him from the harsher realities of life. At any rate, the fears to which he had just been subjected confirmed his long-standing Fourieristic convictions: "Was ever anything clearer," he added in his letter to William, "than that these commercial disasters indicate the widest *social* disease in the community. The lack of the sentiment of brotherhood—the prevalence of self-seeking—this is the disease of the common mind as it is of the individual. . . ." This loving father had not the slightest understanding of even the most elementary principles of economics.

But Mary James knew the difference between the eight hundred francs a month they paid for their Paris apartment and the less than half that amount they would pay in Boulogne-sur-mer during the off-tourist season. Consequently, it was decided to return to Boulogne. By December the Paris apartment had been sublet, and the return to Boulogne accomplished. Henry Sr. was able to rent a comfortable house at 29 Grande Rue for two hundred francs a month, or a hundred and fifty if taken for six months. Willy, Wilky, and Rob were again enrolled in the local college, and tutors were employed for Alice and Harry—the latter, in William's words, still "too delicate to go to college." On December 24 Henry Sr. wrote his mother optimistically: "Boulogne is about the most cheerful place in France, prosperous in a business point of view, full of bustle, picturesque in situation and costume. Living is much cheaper than in Paris, schooling quite as good if not better, and I fancy we shall do altogether very well. We keep only two servants, neither of whom ever lived in Paris, and we are not in dread consequently of being cheated out of our eyeteeth." The cook was British and spoke Cockney, but they were "content to miss the French elegance in order to secure English honesty."

Thus the Jameses did not feel themselves too unfortunate at Christmas 1857. But the doting father had a way, quite unintentional, of spoiling Christmas for the younger children—still remembered with bitterness by Alice many years later—by giving them surreptitious peeps at the presents their mother had bought and hidden for Christmas morning. For Alice, and probably for Wilky and Rob, Christmas was always an anticlimax. But on that Christmas in Boulogne Willy at least was tremendously pleased by his father's gift, for it was a microscope. Although it would be several years before he decided on science as a career, his first microscope gave him a strong push in that direction.

William's delight with his microscope was only one new evidence of his scientific bent. He also possessed a Bunsen burner and vials of mysterious liquids which he mixed, heated, and transfused, staining his fingers and clothes, to his mother's annoyance, and sometimes even causing alarming explosions. In Boulogne he had a private aquarium of marine animals—perhaps one reason for his wanting a microscope. And Henry never forgot the cumbersome camera with which William took many pictures, using his younger brother for a model. At that early stage of photography the exposure was long, requiring tiresome rigidity of the subject. Naturally Harry found the posing tedious, and he was even more annoyed by Willy's using the bedroom which they shared as a darkroom.

Before the praise given William by his science teachers at Boulogne, his juvenile "experiments" and shocking people with his galvanic batteries had been regarded by his parents as little more than child's play. Perhaps his mother still so regarded his vials and marine animals and his developing films in the darkroom, but his father was definitely convinced that he had a scientific mind. And truly, no boy's intellectual activities were ever more prophetic of the man. Henry also recalled many years later with considerable distaste his brother's "finely speculative and boldly disinterested absorption of curious drugs" during this period. One can be reasonably sure that Willy's mother knew nothing of his trying drugs on himself just to satisfy his scientific curiosity, and the fact that Harry did not tell her, as apparently he did not, also indicates a surprising loyalty on the part of the younger brother, especially for one who totally lacked such curiosity. Looking back, it is not surprising that William should have grown up to study chemistry, anatomy, physiology, medicine, and finally psychology, all as stepping stones to philosophy.

Except for such excitement as William provided, the James family lived quietly through the winter of 1857–1858 in Boulogne. Henry Sr. had recently published his book, *Christianity the Logic of Creation;* William was absorbed in his studies at the Collège and his "experiments" at home, and Henry recited to an indulgent tutor who demanded so little of him that he had abundant time for reading novels, to the increasing uneasiness of his father. The family remained in Boulogne until the end of the academic year, the longest stretch of uninterrupted schooling any of the children had experienced. Then in June, his financial status no longer in doubt though his income was reduced, Henry James Sr. decided that they should return to America and find a suitable place to spend the summer. This "zag" back to the United States thus brought to a temporary halt the search of the James family for the "lost Paradise" in Europe.

CHAPTER IV

Retraced Steps

I have grown so discouraged about the education of my children

. . . that I have come to the conclusion to retrace my steps. . . .

—HENRY JAMES SR.

I

FOR ONCE, HENRY JAMES SR. had marvelous luck in choosing a place suitable for his family to spend the summer of 1858—much more than the summer, as it turned out. New York City, which can be almost unbearable in July humidity, was definitely not suitable. Besides, after Geneva, London, and Paris, it seemed dirtier, noisier, and uglier than ever to the family fresh from sparkling Boulogne-sur-mer. Their house on Fourteenth Street was still rented; so, with scarcely a pause after landing, they rushed on to Albany, where the widow of the first William was recovering from a stroke suffered during their absence in Europe. Her grandchildren were not prepared to find such a feeble lady in the dear old house on North Pearl Street. But she was still the loving and lovable grandmother, and peaches were once more ripening behind the house.

Toward the end of June William's father and mother left him, Harry, and Wilky with their grandmother while they made a visit to Newport, Rhode Island, taking Rob and Alice with them. Henry James Sr. went with the expectation of finding a house to rent in Newport; two of his best friends, Mr. and Mrs. Edmund Tweedy, after years of wandering in Europe themselves, had settled down happily there and had been urging the Jameses to join them. The Tweedys were not actually relatives, but the fact that they were bringing up four nieces of Henry Sr., the daughters of his dead sister Catharine and Robert Temple, made them seem like relatives. All their numerous uncles and aunts had been willing to provide for the six small children orphaned by the Temples' death in 1854, but the Tweedys took the four girls and raised them as their own. The older boy, Robert, had been sent to school in Scotland while the Jameses were in Europe, but the younger, William, had been attending American schools. Both vacationed in Newport.

Henry James Sr. was immediately charmed by Newport, perhaps in part because it was milder, by contrast with the rest of raw America just before the Civil War, than almost any other place he could have chosen. First settled in 1639 by Puritans who had fled with Roger Williams from Massachusetts, it still retained much of the Colonial and Old World charm. It was not yet the playground of the millionaires who would build their castles on Bellevue Avenue and quaintly call them "cottages," but it was, paradoxically, the favorite summer resort of wealthy Southern planters and merchants and of the New England intelligentsia. The painter William Hunt had recently bought a house in Newport and decided to stay there the year round. And the summer residents included Henry Wadsworth Longfellow; Julia Ward Howe; Thomas Wentworth Higginson; Professor Andrews Norton of Harvard and his son Charles Eliot Norton, who would also become a professor at Harvard and a famous aesthete; Charlotte Cushman, the actress; George Bancroft, still writing his history of the United States; Katherine P. Wormeley, who was translating Balzac; and many others. On Truro Street lived the widow of Admiral Oliver Hazard Perry, hero of the United States naval victory on Lake Erie in 1812. It was not a dull place in summer, whatever it might be during the winter months.

Newport had been one of the major seaports of the Colonies before and during the American Revolution. It had a good natural harbor and the Gulf Stream flowed near enough to prevent its freezing over in winter. But after the War of 1812 its commerce declined, until by mid-century it was rather seedy and run down, with rotting wharves and with clipper ships once famous in the China and India trade lying at anchor, black and moldy. Many of the mansions overlooking the harbor, which wealthy shippers and retired sea captains had built in the eighteenth century, needed paint and repairs.

But approaching this old town by the Jamestown ferry, as the tall church spires and then the straight lines of the other white buildings began to take shape in the hazy sea air, one could not help feeling a pleasurable excitement, which increased as the ferry, its engine idling, sidled among the moored sailboats up to the piles of the landing. Then came the leisurely walk up Thames Street—everyone sauntered in Newport—to the tree-lined streets beyond, while the vegetable carts heading for the next departing ferry rumbled past, and basket wagons driven by pretty girls traveled in both directions.

The square-built old houses had fluted and carved ornamental decorations of eagles, pineapples, acorns, and urns. Newport was a community of culture, tradition, and leisure—not yet of opulent extravagance, though many of the summer residents were wealthy. Kay Street, about midway between Thames at the bottom of the hill along the harbor and Bellevue at the top, had substantial houses of wood or gray stone, with lush gardens in the rear and old elms, a few ginkgo trees, and purple beeches shading the street. On Kay Henry James Sr. found a house for rent, ample for his family and the numerous relatives who would be visiting in the summer.

One of Mr. James's near neighbors was Colonel James MacKaye, a wealthy New York businessman with a town house in Brooklyn Heights and a summer house in Newport. His son James was to become one of the most famous actors of the century. It was Jim Mac-Kaye who became William James's best friend during the summer of 1858. He was about William's age, and the same height, five feet ten inches, though his lithe athletic figure made him appear taller. He had a friendly attractive face, with high forehead, hazel eyes, dark complexion, and dark curly hair. He appeared to be more mature than William and carried himself with a more confident air.

Jim MacKaye had won a local reputation as a boxer, and he gave his new friend lessons. The two boys also spent many hours together that summer on the water, rowing, fishing, or swimming. Henry was still not strong, after his several illnesses, and was not equal to these vigorous activities; Jim regarded Harry as a "sissy." But at times all four James brothers tramped the fields with Jim MacKaye, beyond Bellevue Avenue where it was still open country, or loafed and chatted under the trees.

In Newport all the James children found a greater opportunity for companionship than they had known since they left Fourteenth Street to go abroad. Of course they were already acquainted with their Temple cousins; Katharine (Kitty), the oldest, was the same age as Harry, and Mary (Minny), whose tragic life was to make a deep impression on both William and Henry, was then thirteen. She became especially devoted to William, who could match her vivacious wit.

The James boys made other friends in Newport, too. One of the most important was Thomas Sergeant Perry, grandson of the Admiral. This slender boy with the sensitive face and retiring manner was nearer Henry's age than William's, and his omnivorous reading and more sedentary habits also allied him with Henry rather than William, though all the James brothers liked "Tom." "The first time I saw the James boys," Perry recalled years later, "was at the end of June or early in July in 1858, shortly after their arrival in Newport for a year's stay. . . . Mr. Duncan Pell, who knew Mr. James the father, told his son and me that we ought to call on the boys; and we did, but they were out. A day or two later we called again and found them in. We all went together to the Pells' house and spent the evening in simple joys." Looking back, Perry thought that at first meeting each of the brothers had shown his "characteristic qualities." Wilky hung on his arm and talked as if he had found an old friend. Henry "sat on the window-seat reading Leslie's *Life of Constable* with a certain air of remoteness," and William was "full of merriment."

That summer Jim's great ambition was to be a painter, and he and Willy spent many hours discussing art and artists. At the end of the summer Jim's father agreed to send him to Paris to study painting, and on the afternoon of October 8, the day before Jim was to sail for New York, the two boys sat on a gray stone wall overlooking the harbor and talked furiously, dreading the moment of separation. Of course Jim was excited about going to Paris, a city Willy could talk about endlessly, and Jim's plans and prospects made Willy ponder more seriously than ever whether he too should not apprentice himself to a good painter. For the present, however, he had to think of school; but after Jim's departure he and Harry began to drop into William Hunt's studio on Church Street, where they received a friendly welcome, and occasionally they sketched without supervision.

II

The MacKaye family left Newport soon after their son's departure and rented their house for the winter to Henry James Sr.

Meanwhile, he had enrolled his sons in the Berkeley Institute, in Washington Square. Although named for the English philosopher, Bishop George Berkeley, who had once planned to found a school in Newport, the Institute had little resemblance to the Bishop's dream school. It was called a "classical and commercial school," and resembled the odd institution presided over by Forest and Quackenboss which William and Henry had attended in New York. The principal was the Reverend William C. Leverett, who was also assistant rector of Trinity Church, a cherished old historical and architectural landmark. The Reverend Mr. Leverett had graduated from Harvard with honors in the "Ancient Classics" and had done postgraduate work in Greek and Hebrew, but his students found him dull and an ineffectual teacher. As always, however, study of almost any kind interested William, while Henry was bored and indifferent.

The most valuable reading that William did that winter was of his own choosing, and he spent many hours in the Redwood Library —though not as many as Henry and Tom Perry. Perry later remembered that on one occasion Willy brought home a volume of Schopenhauer "and showed us with delight the ugly mug of the philosopher and read us amusing specimens of his delightful pessimism. It was W.J. too who told us about Renan one cool evening of February when the twilight lingers till after six." At that time William did not have the slightest premonition that he would some day be a philosopher himself, yet he was already interested in the relationship between a philosopher's personal and intellectual life.

It is also quite clear that this period in William James's life was an important one in his own intellectual and emotional growth. When Henry Jr. wrote his reminiscences many years later he completely omitted the year 1858–1859, in order, as he explained to his nephew Henry, to conceal "our poor father's impulsive journeyings to and fro and . . . aimless vacillation"; but he also insisted that "nothing happened in that fifteen months." Indeed, it is probable that very little did—and less for him than for William—except for the forming of some lasting friendships. A very important one for William began early in the summer of 1859. One day he came running up to several of his companions, including Tom Perry, Duncan Pell, and Henry, exclaiming: "There's a new fellow come to Hunt's class. He knows everything. He has read everything. He has seen everything—paints everything. He's a marvel!" Tom asked his age and Willy replied: "Well, he may be sixteen, and he may be seventy."

Actually John La Farge, the exciting "new fellow" who had come to Hunt's studio, was seven years older than William James. He had been born in New York City in 1835 on Beach Street, and had lived in Washington Place within a few years of the Jameses' residence there. And he was indeed a remarkable young man. His father, also named John, had fled France during the turmoil of the French Revolution, then from San Domingo during an uprising of the Negroes against the plantation owners. He had prospered in the United States and been able to send his son abroad to study.

Young La Farge's maternal grandfather had given him expert training in drawing, and during his travels he had studied and painted in the studios of several great artists, including briefly Couture's in Paris. While in Paris he became acquainted with Richard Hunt, who had advised him to go to Newport to study with his brother William. Although he soon found that William Hunt was an apostate from his teacher Couture and was now under the influence of J. F. Millet, who did not interest La Farge, nevertheless John La Farge stayed on in Newport for several years; he married T. S. Perry's sister Margaret in 1860 and established a home in Paradise Valley. Although he had plenty of opinions in 1859 and was not backward in expressing them, it was not until 1860, when William himself was studying under Hunt, that La Farge really had important influence on him.

Had it not been for his father's prejudices, William James would probably have settled down at once to study painting with La Farge in Hunt's studio. But Henry Sr., in addition to distrusting painting as a profession, was now fully convinced that William's abilities were pre-eminently scientific. His own experiences at Union College had made him biased against sending any of his sons to college, but he had nonetheless been considering entering William in the Scientific School at Harvard and had made some efforts to find a suitable house in Cambridge. It was quite characteristic of Mr. James, too, that he would think of moving the whole family to Cambridge instead of merely sending his oldest son to board. However, on July 22, 1859, Henry Sr. wrote his friend Mrs. Francis G. Shaw: "We can't get a house in Cambridge, and are disposed to think it would not be the place for us in all respects if we could." Consequently, once again he was thinking of Europe, "that educational paradise. . . . But we *may* not go, as our minds are still undetermined."

By the end of the summer, however, the decision had been made, as he confided to Samuel Ward on September 18: "I have grown so discouraged about the education of my children here, and dread so those inevitable habits of extravagance and insubordination, which appear to be characteristic of American youth, that I have come to the conclusion to retrace my steps to Europe, and keep them there a few years longer. My wife is completely of the same mind, and though we feel on many accounts that we are making personal sacrifices in this step, the advantages to the children are so clear that we cannot conscientiously hesitate. I am a good patriot, but my patriotism is even livelier on the other side of the water. At all accounts, I am quite sure that my main object in life, which is to do justice to my children, will be so promoted by our return to Europe, as to make all my lesser activities and obligations easily fulfilled."

For both William and Henry leaving Newport friends was an emotional wrench. Jim MacKaye had recently returned from Europe and the group of companions was now more affectionately united than it had been the previous summer. T. S. Perry described the separation from his point of view many years later to Jim MacKaye's son James, who was writing a biography of his father:

October third, 1859, is a date that revives for me the early memory of a poignant sorrow, for on that night Harry and Willie James were going away to Europe, and I was in the depths of a boyish despair. So also was Jim McKaye [later spelled MacKaye], your father, who went down with me to the boat [bound for New York] to bid my comrades good-bye. All of us were intimate friends, school-mates and neighbours. We didn't differentiate our ages; we were all too interested in ideas. Our companionship was a keen natural delight, and our parting was a rather solemn occasion. When Jim and I walked back through the night, up Bull Street, to Kay—where Colonel McKaye's house, with the Gothic roofs and little tower, stood near a rustic lane with stables—I remember tarrying outside with Jim, talking affectionately of our friends, the Jameses, who were to sail from New York to Havre, in the S.S. *Vanderbilt*, on October 8. There we talked on a good while, out of our hearts, til at last Jim turned in the path to his home and I went away through the lane.

III

Stormy weather made the eleven days the James family spent aboard the *Vanderbilt* seem long and tedious. After they finally landed at Le Havre and had rested a couple of days in Paris, they proceeded to Geneva by the now familiar route of Lyon and the Jura mountains. In Geneva Henry Sr. could not find an apartment large enough for his family, which of course included Aunt Kate, but he was able to engage rooms at the Hôtel d'Écu. The school term had already begun, and the boys were enrolled as promptly as possible, William in the Academy, Wilky and Rob in a boarding school outside the city, and Henry in the École Préparatoire aux Éçoles Spéciales. The main purpose of the latter was the preparation of students in mathematics and science for the Polytechnic School in Zurich. It might have been suitable for William, but a less appropriate school could hardly have been found for poor little unscientific Henry. However, he was not qualified to enter either the Academy with William or the Gymnase, and the only alternative was private tutoring, which had never proved satisfactory in the past.

William was more fortunate at the Academy, where he attended stimulating lectures for which his French was entirely adequate, and once again, as at Boulogne, impressed his professors with his ability. He was particularly fascinated by his course in anatomy, perhaps to some extent because of his facility in making accurate sketches of anatomical details, but the scientific information also interested him. In this subject he found his scientific and artistic abilities united. He also enjoyed visiting the Museum in Geneva and drawing the structures of the skeletons.

Because of his interest in anatomy William also attended demonstrations in the dissection of cadavers required of medical students. In the spring Henry dropped out of the École Préparatoire and secured permission to attend certain lectures at the Academy with William. He even accompanied Willy to the dissecting room, but always found the stench unendurable, much to his brother's amusement. This was another period, however, when the two brothers were in close association, and, as Wilky wrote T. S. Perry, got "along very well indeed"—the emphasis implying that they had not always been so congenial.

For William the winter and spring of 1859–1860 was a time of happiness and a sense of achievement. But his father found the cold winds off Lake Geneva unbearable and fled to Paris, and then to London. The letters which his younger children wrote him referred constantly to William's high spirits. In December Wilky reported: "Willie interrupts me here and wants me to go into the parlor with him to hear him deliver a little sonnate on Alice which he has just composed and which he means to perform with much gusto. I will tell you its success when it is finished." Later: "Song went off very well, and excited a good deal of laughter among the audience assembled."

In March Alice in a letter to her "dear old good-for-nothing home-sick papa" also declared that, "Willie is in a very extraordinary state of mind, composing odes to all the family. A warlike one he addressed to Aunt Kate, in which the hero is her husband and dies for her; and he says: 'The idea of anyone dying for her!!' and he wants Mother to take them in to Mrs. Thomas and Mrs. Osbourn [American friends living in the same hotel] to be read and admired by them. We have all come to the conclusion that he is fit to go to the lunatic asylum, so make haste home before such an unhappy event takes place."

On May 28 Wilky wrote Tom Perry about his two author brothers. He was pretty sure that "Harry has become an author . . . , for he keeps his door locked all day long. . . ." But William was not the least bit secretive. "Willie often comes flying in the parlour, in the evening & breaks the family circle, with a poem that he has previously prepared to read. The last one he wrote was an 'Ode to Alice' which he recited in a very flowing manner . . . the only difference there is between Willy & Harrys labours is that the former always shows his productions while the modest little Henry wouldn't let a soul or even a spirit see his."

William did not confine his social exuberance to the family parlor. He entered so fully and successfully into the life of the Academy that he was invited to join the Société de Zofingue, which was a combination of German drinking club and student patriotic society. In the spring the Zofingues held their annual festival, a three-day celebration in a village called Moudon, about twelve miles from Lausanne, to which William was permitted to invite a friend. He invited Henry. Students from all over Switzerland came and the whole village entered into the fun. The chief diversions were drinking beer, smoking big German pipes, and singing. Henry did not find this particularly amusing, but William had a jolly time. On the final night came the ceremony of "Landsvater," adapted from the German universities, which Henry described to Tom Perry as "a kind of oath of allegiance to their country & of brotherhood among themselves accompanied by a great swilling down of beer, of grasping of hands, of clashing of rapiers, and of glorious deep-mouthed German singing. Half the students were roaming in drunken ardour through the town and through the halls of the inns that night seeking whom they might devour. Willie, a German fellow, and I myself did not get scarcely a wink of sleep till near morning because of the constant attacks upon the door of the bed room which we shared together. The weather was fearful a driving storm of alternate hail and rain all the time."

Not long after the Zofingue festival William's glorious year at the Academy came to an end. As so many times in the past, his father seemed unwilling to let him continue in a school in which he was really making progress. Henry Sr. thought he was doing the best thing for all his children by giving them new experiences. By June he had decided that the family should go to Bonn on the Rhine for the summer and to Frankfort on Main for the winter. It was now time to acquire German—that is, for the children to do so. But before leaving Switzerland all the boys must have a chance to enjoy the kind of outing in the Alps which they had read about in those delightful Toeppfer books. The younger boys were taken, Toeppfer-fashion, on trips by their teachers, but Willy and Harry were permitted to travel by themselves except for a guide, who provided a mule to carry the baggage.

Early in July the boys set out for Chamonix, at the foot of Mont Blanc. In a two-hour climb they crossed Montanvert and examined the Mer de Glace, but decided that the Glacier des Battons was more beautiful than the far more renowned "sea of ice." Of course they did not climb the perpetually snow-covered heights (and cable cars had not yet come into use), but they did an incredible amount of walking over mountain passes. In ten hours they crossed the Tête-Noire to Martigny in the canton of Valais. From there they climbed the great Saint Bernard Pass, an ascent that took nine hours, three of them over almost barren rock, as scarcely any vegetation grows at that altitude, and the last hour over the snow.

When they reached the hospice in the Pass they were nearly exhausted and very cold, but a good Father took them in, gave them warm slippers, and set before them hot broth and roast mutton. That night, however, they decided that the mattresses and pillows were filled with wet sand, and they slept very little. Next morning they admired the famous dogs and visited the strange little morgue a short distance from the hospice, where since 1479, when the stone house was built, the monks had kept the corpses of frozen travelers. As Henry explained in a letter to T. S. Perry, they "are stood around the walls in their shrouds and a grim and ghastly sight it is. They fall into all sorts of hideous positions, with such fiendish grins on their faces!"

After their memorable night at the Saint Bernard Hospice, the James brothers found the remainder of their journey an anticlimax. They descended again to Martigny, then went by carriage to Loèche-les-Bains, at the foot of Gemmi. Continuing their tramp, they crossed Gemmi and descended the other side, that evening reaching Interlaken, having spent approximately a week on foot in the Alps. The whole family, with the exception of Robby, who was still in Italy, was waiting for them at Interlaken. After three days of rest and diversion, they all set out for Germany, stopping at Wiesbaden and Frankfurt, and sailing up the Rhine, which seemed a little disappointing after the spectacular beauty of the Alps.

IV

William found it as easy to adapt himself to German life as he had done in Geneva to the life of an Academy student. His father had arranged for him and his two younger brothers to board and study with German families in Bonn, William with a Herr Stromberg and Henry and Wilky with Herr Doktor Humpert, who taught Latin and Greek in the local Gymnasium. Within three weeks William wrote his father, who had retreated to Paris after getting his sons settled, that he was already able to understand and make himself understood in ordinary conversation. He thought learning German was "a mere process of soaking, requiring no mental effort," only time and patience. Wilky had a strong aversion to reading anything in any language, though he quickly acquired enough colloquial German to be ingratiatingly sociable and to keep the conversation on his own uncomplicated level. But Henry abominated the language and almost everything German.

Possibly William was more fortunate in the family to which he had been assigned, though his greater adaptability and fondness for study no doubt made a difference too. At any rate, Henry and Wilky were miserable with the Humperts. The Herr Doktor's wife and sister were supposed, as Henry wrote Tom Perry, "to aid him in the task of conversing ceaselessly with us," but in Henry's opinion they were conversationally handicapped by not possessing, between them, half a dozen teeth. Actually, they knew nothing to talk about except pots and pans, a subject of little interest to the American boys. The Humperts' seventeen-year-old son, Theodore, spent all day at his studies and was seen only at meals. The Herr Doktor himself was a pleasant, genial pedant, more interested in Greek and Sanskrit syntax than the world he lived in. But what Henry most disliked was the food, especially the heavy German pancakes, which gave him an "iron-stomach ache." Dinner, he complained, was likely to be tepid cabbage soup (poured half an hour before Frau Humpert announced the meal), beef boiled to shreds, greasy potatoes, Westphalian smoked ham, black beans, and stewed cherries or tarts for dessert.

William, however, found the Humpert family immensely interesting, though certainly droll, and the food sumptuous, though he may have been intentionally exaggerating when he wrote his father on August 19: "I have just got home from dining at the boys' house. . . . They certainly live on the fat of the land, though they do not seem as sensible of their advantages as they should be. As I had been led to expect nothing of the kind, I was surprised at the sumptuousness of the dinner, rich beef, sausages, pigeons, capital vegetables and soup, all cooked just right, and a most delicious cherry pie, with two bottles of costly Rhine wine in honor of the day. The Doctor was as cordial as usual, and the two old ladies perfect characters for Dickens. They have been so shut out from the world and have been melting together so long by the kitchen fire that the minds of both have become confounded into one, and they seem to constitute a sort of two-bodied individual. I never saw anything more curious than the way in which they sit mumbling together at the end of the table, each using simultaneously the same exclamation if anything said at our end strikes their ear. The boys say they always speak together, using the same words or else one beginning a phrase, the other ending it. It is a singular life." Of course this meal may not have been typical, but, like the wine, "in honor of the day." Besides, William did not have to live with the Humperts. And at this period in his youth everything was grist for his mill.

Continuing in the confident tone of Big Brother, William assured his father that "Henry studies pretty stoutly, but I do not think that you need to be apprehensive about him. There has been no renewal of the stomach aches that I am aware of, and he looks fatter and fresher than when you left. He and Wilky appear to get on very harmoniously together." Sometimes they roughhoused in their bedroom, he continued, and "We are going to put Harry through a slashing big walk daily." William shared his father's opinion that Henry, left to himself, spent too much time reading and did not get enough exercise.

But in spite of the grown-up tone of his report on his younger brothers, William missed his parents more than they did. With a new note of contrition he confessed: "I never value my parents (Father especially) so much as when I am away from them. At home I only see his faults and here he seems all perfection, and every night I wonder why I did not value them more when they were beside me. I beg darling old Mother's forgiveness for the cruel and dastardly way in which I snub her, and Aunt Kate's for the impatience and violence I have always shown towards her. If ever I get back I will be a perfect sherry cobbler to both of them, and to the little Alice, too, for the harsh way in which I have treated her."

In spite of the adolescent sentimentality, which might be found in any teen-age boy's homesick letter, this confession gives us the first direct insight into William James's relations with his parents. He had not shown them the respect and obedience a nineteenth-century son was supposed to show. Of course we must make some allowance for the state of his emotions. We can hardly doubt, however, that Willy's family had found living with him stormy and at times nerve-wracking. But in a family of five children with a permissive father and a harried mother who shared her parental authority with her sister, a bright, nimble, high-strung oldest son would almost inevitably create discord.

Yet at that time William was the center of his father's planning, and he was not unaware of the gratitude he owed him. While the family was all together in Bonn, William had gained his father's consent to return to the United States to study painting under William Hunt in Newport. Henry Sr. wrote his "dear old Tweedius" [Edmund Tweedy] about the change in plans: "We came on here to put the boys in German families for the summer, and take them in winter to Frankfurt or some similar place. But we had hardly reached here before Willy took an opportunity to say to me—what it seems he had been long wanting to say, but found it difficult to come to the scratch—that he felt the vocation of a painter so strongly that he did not think it worth my while to expend any more time or money on his scientific education! I confess I was greatly startled by the annunciation, and not a little grieved, for I had always counted upon a scientific career for Willy, and I hope the day may even yet come when my calculations may be realized in this regard. But as it was I had nothing to do but to submit; and as our motive to stay in Europe was chiefly derived from the imagined needs of his education, so now we are glad enough to turn homewards, and let him begin at once with Mr. Hunt."

In a later letter to Tweedy, Henry James Sr. admitted that his main reason for leaving Newport had been to get William away from the influence of Hunt. But he was now rationalizing his capitulation: the younger children had "been all along perfectly starved on their social side, and not the least bettered on their intellectual . . ."—though he had recently decided that none of them except William was "cut out for intellectual labours." And in reality hotel life in Europe had been lonely for all of them. They doubtless all agreed with him that "we go home profoundly persuaded that no wilder hallucination exists, at least in reference to boys who are destined to grow up into American men," that a better education could be obtained for them in Europe. "America is 'the lost Paradise restored' to boys and girls both, and it is only our own paltry cowardice and absurd ducking to old world conventionalities that hinder their realizing it as such at once. . . ."

William's pleasure in winning his argument with his father was tempered by the realization that the wisdom of his victory was still to be tested. To one of his Geneva friends, Charles Ritter, he confided that he would give up painting if in two or three years his talent proved fragile, for "There is nothing on earth more deplorable than a bad artist." And he also felt that the dialogue with his father was unfinished. As late as August 24 he was still mulling over his father's "reasons why I should not be an 'artist.' " He had asked his father to write out these reasons, but all he got was (in William's paraphrase) "the spiritual danger in which a man is if he allows the bent of his aesthetic nature (supposed strong) to direct his activity." This objection seemed to William without foundation: "I do not see," he wrote to his father, "why a man's spiritual culture should not go on independently of his aesthetic activity, why the power which an artist feels in himself should tempt him to forget what he is, any more than the power felt by a Cuvier or Fourier would tempt them to do the same. . . ."

But it seemed useless to debate this question further by letter when William would be joining his parents in Paris in another week, and like his younger brothers, he was counting the days until their departure. On September 1 the three boys left Bonn by rail. They had as companions in their third-class compartment a French lady's maid, valet, and coachman, whose interminable chatter gave them glimpses of the strange "underworld" of servants and the "great" one which they served. During the prolonged halts at Cologne and Strasbourg Madame la Marquise looked in on them, and smiled in her elegant, condescending manner, as if to remind the American boys that they would soon leave her world of privilege and refinement.

By midnight the three boys were in Paris with their happy parents, their sister Alice, their youngest brother, and Aunt Kate, in the Hôtel des Trois Empereurs, in the Place du Palais Royal. News of the imminent departure for America had been kept from Robby, for fear he would do no studying whatever, until time for the family to reunite in Paris. The older boys enjoyed comfortable beds for the first time since leaving Switzerland, and next morning they were all thrilled to look out upon the new Louvre from their bedroom window.

After a joyous week in Paris the James family sailed September 11 from Le Havre on the *Adriatic*, which docked in New York on Monday morning, September 24. William was eager to join his friends in Newport, but the family had to pause in New York at the Fourteenth Street home of one of the boys' uncles until their father could negotiate for a house. However, La Farge was in New York and he helped to pass the time. Fortunately, Henry Sr. found Colonel MacKaye's house available again, and by the first of October the Jameses were once more settled at 13 Kay Street in Newport. They had retraced their steps from one "hallucination" to another, but they felt that this *was* "the lost paradise restored."

CHAPTER V

The Paternal Grip

I have had a firm grip upon the coat tails of my Willy and Harry

who both vituperate me beyond measure because I won't let them

go. The coats are a very staunch material. . . . —HENRY JAMES SR.

I

THE EIGHTEEN-YEAR-OLD BOY with the short-clipped mustache and serious, brooding eyes who returned to Newport with his family in the autumn of 1860 was outwardly poised and confident. But inwardly William James was already debating whether he had been wise to force his father to bring the family back from Europe so that he might study painting with William Hunt. He was well aware that, though his father had given in, he hoped that William would soon tire of painting and return to the study of science. His victory over his father was not a satisfying one, and this was not a healthy condition for the conscientious boy. Henry James Sr., perhaps unintentionally, restrained his children by indulgence: he appeared to give them complete freedom of choice, but somehow their knowledge of his wishes and opinions did more to curb them than overt opposition. It was difficult to rebel against a father who seemed so untyrannical.

It was entirely accidental but nevertheless a parallel almost symbolic that in 1860 the nation itself concealed an inner turmoil which would soon tear the country apart and almost destroy its political solidarity. Although the Jameses did not feel alienated from their native land, they had nevertheless escaped the rising hysteria over slavery, "free soil," and states' rights during their recent months in Europe. Henry James Sr. had strong convictions on the evils of slavery but trusted to Providence to eliminate them. If asked, William would have been equally emphatic on the inhumanity of slavery, and by nature he was deeply sympathetic to any victim of injustice, but his attention had been focused on his personal problems. In spite of his fashionable clothes and smart mustache he was still a callow youth, disturbed by adolescent dreams and mysterious feelings of guilt. He could be exuberant, witty, and enthusiastic, as he had been in Geneva, Bonn, or Paris, but a close observer would have noticed a growing moodiness, which portended the end of his juvenile self-confidence when he had felt capable of almost anything, and had dazzled his father and brother Harry with his clever dexterity.

Of course, coming back to Newport was like returning home after a few months' absence—to the same house, and many of the same friends; the Temple girls and their kindly foster parents the Tweedys, the Hunts, the Perrys, John La Farge and his recent bride Margaret Perry, and others. In October, with the last of the summer vacationers long since gone, the town seemed spacious and relaxed, sparkling under the bright Indian summer sunlight reflecting from the surrounding blue water and the steep gray roofs of the houses.

To a painter, professional or novice, the most interesting region was the grass-grown Point, terminating in low rocky cliffs, covered with gray lichens, projecting eastward into the Atlantic Ocean. The tonic saline air compensated for the low tone of color in the mingled yellow and gray of mossy rocks, dry grass, and sterile sand. Sparse, stunted, grotesque-shaped trees tried to grow in the rock crevices. But in the evening a purple haze spread over the island, and in October the sun set in a fiery apocryphal luminosity that glorified every object. For scenery this could not compete with Geneva, on the banks of the cool blue lake in the middle of the Alps, or even the tamer picturesqueness of the Rhine, but William's tensions relaxed while he sketched on his tramps with La Farge.

There was no inconvenience for William in starting his new educational regime in Hunt's studio in October, for he and John La Farge were Mr. Hunt's only apprentices, and there was no formal schedule of lessons. But it was late for his younger brothers and twelve-year-old sister to enter school—not that this was a new experience for any of them, for their father had never synchronized his movements with academic calendars. The year before they had arrived in Geneva well after the beginning of the school term. For Henry, in this autumn of 1860, no school at all had been chosen; he was content to read in the Redwood Library and dabble with paint in Hunt's studio, though he did not seriously apply himself to painting as William did. Alice was entered in a private school in Newport.

For the younger boys, Wilkinson, fifteen, and Robertson, fourteen, their father had decided upon what their friends regarded as a very novel and stimulating school.

The family was scarcely resettled on Kay Street before Mr. and Mrs. James took the younger boys to Concord, Massachusetts, to enroll them in a school run by Franklin B. Sanborn, friend of the late John Brown and of runaway slaves whom he had helped on their way to freedom in Canada. This school was considered a daring experiment, not because it had some Negro children enrolled with the white but because it was coeducational. Even Henry James Sr. joked about how the girls would distract his boys from study— as if that were possible, at least for Wilky, who was not likely to study under any circumstances. But the doting father returned to Newport in ecstasy over the autumn colors: "the maple, the oak and the dogwood showered such splendours upon the eye as made the Champs Elysées and the Bois appear parvenus and comical." And he had never tasted such succulent pears as Mr. Emerson served him and Mrs. James. But he felt broken-hearted over leaving his two youngest boys and hoped they "wouldn't die, any of these cold winter days, before the parental breast could get there to warm them back to life or cheer them on to a better."

Though these exaggerated sentiments were uttered in jest, Henry James Sr. was happy only in the midst of his whole noisy family. He was not consciously possessive or demanding, but he liked to hear the voices of his children and know what they were doing and thinking—especially thinking. During the following spring vacation Edward Emerson, son of the poet, visited Wilky and Bob James in Newport and later described the family at mealtime:

'The adipose and affectionate Wilkie,' as his father called him, would say something and be instantly corrected by the little cock-sparrow Bob, the youngest, but good-naturedly defend his statement, and then Henry (Junior) would emerge from his silence in defence of Wilkie. Then Bob would be more impertinently insistent, and Mr. James would advance as Moderator, and William, the eldest, join in. The voice of the Moderator presently would be drowned by the combatants and he soon came down vigorously into the arena, and when, in the excited argument, the dinner knives might not be absent from eagerly gesticulating hands, dear Mrs. James, more conventional, but bright as well as motherly, would look at me, laughingly reassuring, saying, 'Don't be disturbed, Edward; they won't stab each other. This is usual when the boys come home.' And the quiet little sister ate her dinner, smiling, close to the combatants. Mr. James considered this debate, within bounds, excellent for the boys. In their speech, singularly mature and picturesque, as well as vehement, the Gaelic (Irish) element in their descent always showed. Even if they blundered, they saved themselves by wit.

Another visitor to the James home, E. L. Godkin, the journalist and editor, corroborated Edward Emerson:

There could not be a more entertaining treat than a dinner at the James house, when all the young people were at home. They were full of stories of the oddest kind, and discussed questions of morals or taste or literature with a vociferous vigor so great as sometimes to lead the young men to leave their seats and gesticulate on the floor. I remember, in some of these heated discussions, it was not unusual for the sons to invoke humorous curses on their parent, one of which was that "his mashed potatoes might always have lumps in them!"

II

Promptly at ten o'clock every day except Sunday, when William Hunt's studio in an old gray weather-beaten house opposite the Jewish burying ground was opened, William James and John La Farge, and for several months Henry James Jr. also, began working. La Farge had completed several canvases deemed good enough to save during the year that William was in Geneva and Bonn, and he was now less a pupil of Hunt than a guest welcome to paint in his studio. But in the autumn and winter of 1860–1861 William James seriously took lessons from Hunt, paid for by his father. He was already an expert draftsman, for which La Farge warmly praised him, but he had to learn the fundamentals of oil painting—how to mix colors, prepare the canvas, apply the proper stroke, and other technical details.

William and John shared a studio on the top floor, with north windows for proper lighting, while Henry, the hanger-on, copied Hunt's plaster casts on the ground floor. After two or three hours of work Mrs. Hunt would appear with a tea service and provide a light lunch, or continental breakfast, so familiar to all of them. During this interruption there was sociable examination of works in progress. During the working hours Henry usually remained studiously at his downstairs drawing-board, but one day he wandered upstairs and was startled to find his cousin Gus Barker "perched on a pedestal and divested of every garment . . . the gayest as well as the neatest of models." This was Henry's "first personal vision of the 'life', on a pedestal and in a pose, that had half gleamed and half gloomed through the chiaroscuro of our old friend Haydon"—the painter whose works William and he had so much admired in London in 1855. Henry realized instantly and intuitively that he "might niggle for months over plaster casts and not come within miles of any such point of attack. The bravery of my brother's own in especial dazzled me out of every presumption; since nothing less than that meant drawing (they were not using colour) and since our genial kinsman's perfect gymnastic figure meant living truth, I should certainly best testify to the whole mystery by pocketing my pencil." This incident probably took place during Gus's vacation from Harvard, where he, the same age as William, was enrolled. Whenever it was that Henry pocketed his pencil, William continued throughout the winter and spring to draw and paint under Mr. Hunt's professional supervision.

Some forty years later, in writing *Notes of a Son and Brother*, Henry James Jr. felt puzzled at William's coming back to the United States to study painting: ". . . never surely had so odd a motive operated for a break with the spell of Paris." Of course William James knew that in 1860 there were painters in Paris with greater reputations under whom he could study (he had after all taken lessons from Cogniet, a great name in mid-nineteenth-century France, though scarcely remembered today). But his choice of the tall, gaunt New Englander who reminded Henry Jr. of Don Quixote (in appearance only, not in futile idealism) was not at the time a foolish or eccentric choice. William Morris Hunt was a competent painter, and in temperament he was not unlike William James—restless, witty, vivacious, moody at times, always articulate, magnetic in personality. He had been educated in Switzerland, France, and Germany, at places and under cultural influences that William knew and understood. Hunt's return to the United States in 1855 began a new epoch in American art, in which he soon became a dominant influence; his example and rapidly growing reputation stimulated his country to a new art-consciousness. After studying under Couture, he had, before returning to America, come under the influence of Jean-François Millet; in fact he had been the principal purchaser of Millet's canvases, including "The Sower," later to become fatuously renowned. Thus Hunt brought to American art the first strong note of French influence—which happened to be that of the Barbizon School, a group of painters who, like the Romantic poets, interpreted their own souls in terms of nature.

As it turned out, William James's application to painting was to be short-lived, and it would be futile to attempt to trace any lasting influence of William Hunt on his life, though the subjectivity of the Barbizon School would hardly have been uncongenial to the future pioneer in the psychology of consciousness. The influence of John La Farge is another matter, however, and he and William continued to admire each other into old age. La Farge's disappointment over Hunt's having changed his loyalty from Couture to Millet grew into a general disagreement. Hunt's "previous methods," La Farge declared, "which one sees more distinctly in some of his landscapes [rather than his portraits] . . . were nearer what I had been looking for, however less poetic and more commonplace they might be. . . ." In particular, La Farge objected to the "closed light of the studio," which always remained the same. He wanted to paint outdoors, using light and color in such a way that the viewer of his painting could tell the exact time of day—the "certain slant of light" of Emily Dickinson's poem. Throughout his life William James rebelled against confinements and rigidities of all kinds, and he must have preferred La Farge's gambles to Hunt's studio controls. And one definite carryover from his painting experience was his acute consciousness of light, as evidenced in the imagery of his vivid prose in which synesthesia was often to appear. From the seashore, for example, he later wrote Henry that "The broad sky and sea are whanging with the mellow light." And to his sister Alice, after a snowstorm, "the light is shrieking away, outside."

In nineteenth-century America no painter could become fashionably famous without having done portraits of the well-to-do. In Newport William Hunt had already begun to do such portraits, and they were to be the basis of his great reputation and prestige in Boston a few years later. Even in those days Newport was not an inopportune place for an artist to begin, as Hunt may have been shrewdly aware. Another reason for La Farge's finding Hunt uncongenial was his own strong aversion to catering to wealthy Americans who satisfied their vanity with commissions for portraits of themselves or their wives and children. He could paint portraits, but his later and best paintings were mainly of historical, Biblical, or imaginary subjects, many of them allegorical.

To judge from the many sketches and crayon portraits which have survived, William James used his skill at drawing to become a clever caricaturist and, in a serious vein, an intuitive portrayer of character. Portrait work should have come easy for him, and his one surviving canvas, of his cousin Katharine Temple, shows substantial talent. It might even be called brilliant for a young man who had studied painting systematically for only a few months—probably six—though the portrait looks better in a good photograph than in the original, which on close inspection reveals some amateurishness in the brush work. But the fact that this one canvas was carefully preserved indicates that the teacher did not condemn it. Indeed, it is difficult to believe that a novice who could paint so well after only a few months of instruction would not have been encouraged to continue. Yet, soon after completing this portrait William James stopped painting. Why?

William himself never explained why he suddenly decided not to become a painter, and Henry Jr. could only say that he lost interest. The reason may not have been entirely clear to the young man himself. One thing we do know is that by the spring of 1861 he had begun to have trouble with his eyes, which would handicap him for the remainder of his life. Certainly impaired eyesight would have taken much of the pleasure out of painting, and painting or sketching out of doors where the ocean reflected the dazzling sunlight would have been harmful to sensitive eyes. He also had developed a symptom which can only be described as nervous indigestion. Up until his return to Newport his health had been excellent, and these physical debilities clearly indicate psychic disturbances of serious proportions.

Of course a combination of influences and circumstances could have caused both his poor health and loss of interest in painting. Many years later William James told his second son, also named William, who had become a professional painter, that he had asked Hunt at an unfortunate time whether he should continue his apprenticeship, and in a discouraged mood Hunt had replied that America did not value painters and that he could not advise any American to devote his life to a vocation so unrewarding. But such a reply would not have irrevocably discouraged a young man firmly determined to become a painter. Whether cause or effect, his vacillation was closely related to his increasing neurasthenia. It may have been only coincidence that the sudden outbreak of war on April 12, 1861, was so nearly simultaneous with William's decision to give up painting. His impaired health evidently preceded the war news, but the excitement, bewilderment, and indignation felt in the Northern states, and especially in New England, were enough to upset any young man's life plans, and William's were none too firm anyway.

III

The shock of Fort Sumter was followed three days later, on April 15, by President Lincoln's calling the nation to arms. Scarcely anyone could conceive of the four-year war that lay ahead, and preparations were hasty and makeshift. Conscription was not passed by Congress until two years later, and even then a conscript could avoid service by hiring a substitute or simply paying a fee of three hundred dollars. Nevertheless, in April 1861 thousands of young men in the North responded to the President's call. William James's cousins at Harvard, Gus Barker and William Temple, enlisted and became early casualties.

Newport was more divided in its loyalties than most communities in the North, but the Southern families soon departed and patriotic fervor swept Newport too. T. S. Perry recorded in his diary: "April 27: We made bandages all evening." And next day: "April 28: After breakfast we all rolled bullets." Considering the mood of the nation and the friendship between Tom Perry and the James boys, it is safe to assume that both William and Henry Jr. were included in the "we." In a surviving fragment of a letter which Henry Sr. wrote about this time he confided to his correspondent: "I have had a firm grasp upon the coat tails of my Willy and Harry, who both vituperate me beyond measure because I won't let them go [into military service]. The coats are a very staunch material, or the tails must have been off two days ago, the scamps pull so hard."

With cousins approximately their own age enlisting, Willy and Harry might be expected to pull hard on home tethers. But aside from any other considerations, neither was rugged enough for military service. Even if they could have met the lax physical requirements of the enlistment office, they lacked the toughness and endurance needed for long marches, bivouacking in the snow, and the violence of battle. The stories Henry soon began to write and later his reminiscences reveal a strong feeling of guilt at having failed to respond to the President's call, which he later justified by an injury to his back, fused—or confused—in memory with the firing upon Fort Sumter in "the soft spring of '61." His biographer Leon Edel has shown that his "obscure hurt" was actually not suffered until six months later, the following October, while he was helping to extinguish a fire in Newport which began in a stable on the corner of Beach and State Streets and for a time threatened much of the town. William never offered any excuses.

Henry James Sr. was unmistakably torn by conflicting thoughts about the war. At the time he was holding on to the coat tails of Willy and Harry he also confessed: "The way I excuse my paternal interference to them is, to tell them, first, that no existing government, nor indeed any now possible government, is worth an honest human life and a clean one like theirs; especially if that government is likewise in danger of bringing back slavery again under our banner: than which consummation I would rather see chaos itself come again. Secondly, I tell them that no young American should put himself in the way of death, until he has realized something of the good of life: until he has found some charming conjugal Elizabeth or other to whisper his devotion to, and assume the task if need be, of keeping his memory green."

This pacifist attitude was bolstered by mysticism, which, as we have seen before, permitted Henry Sr. at times to ignore the world's ills while he waited for divine forces to overcome them without human intervention. "To the angels, says Swedenborg, death means resurrection to life; by that necessary rule of inversion which keeps them separate from us and us from them, and so prevents our being mutual nuisances. Let us then accept political and all other destruction that chooses to come: because what is disorder and wrath and contention on the surface is sure to be the deepest peace at the centre, working its way thus to a surface that shall *never* be disorderly." This fideism had kept Mr. James hitherto from actively supporting abolition, his neutralism made easier by his having been in foreign countries during much of the decade preceding the Civil War. But he was by no means opposed to abolition, and he admired Frank Sanborn, to whose school he had entrusted his two younger sons.

By July 4, 1861, Henry James Sr. was no longer neutral. In an oration which he gave at Newport at a celebration of Independence Day he declared that "it is Slavery, and Slavery only" that poisons "our body politic"; and he was no longer content to wait for invisible spiritual forces to purge the body politic of this poison; rather, "we must not hesitate for a moment to fight it manfully out to its smiling blissful end, feeling that it is not our battle alone, that we are not fighting for our own country only . . . but . . . for the ineradicable rights of human nature itself." If he thought that

> . . . Mr. Lincoln and Mr. Seward were going at last to palter with the sublime instincts of peace and righteousness that elevated them to power and give them all their personal prestige, by making the least conceivable further concession to the obscene demon of Slavery,— then I could joyfully see Mr. Lincoln and Mr. Seward scourged from the sacred eminence they defile, yes more, could joyfully see our boasted political house itself laid low in the dust forever, because in that case its stainless stars and stripes would have sunk from a banner of freemen into a dishonored badge of the most contemptible people on earth; a people that bartered away the fairest spiritual birthright any people ever yet were born to, for the foulest mess of material pottage ever concocted of shameless lust and triumphant fraud.

Yet despite his aroused militancy, Henry James Sr. did not change his attitude toward the enlistment of his older sons. He may have been wise to shield them, but whether wise or overprotective, he was rewarded by William's turning back to science, thus fulfilling the wish his father had cherished at least since giving him the microscope in Boulogne-sur-mer. Even his decision to enroll in the Lawrence Scientific School at Harvard in the autumn of 1861 was a revival of a plan his father had considered before taking the family back to Switzerland in 1859.

IV

If William's coming back to Newport to study painting at a time when Paris was the art center of the world was as strange as Henry Jr. thought it was forty years later, his going to Harvard the next year to study science was no less odd, for the best scientific schools were in Germany, Switzerland, and France, where most of the few scientists America had in the mid-nineteenth century had been trained. In fact, the Lawrence Scientific School was only fourteen years old and still existed as a loosely attached appendage to Harvard College, which was strong in classical and humanistic studies but scornful of the new sciences. In 1857 Abbott Lawrence, owner of the lucrative textile factories, had donated fifty thousand dollars to start a scientific school at Harvard, with the hope that it would train engineers for his factories. But the trustees of the Harvard Corporation made Louis Agassiz their first appointee to the new school, giving him the title of Professor of Zoology and Geology. Two years later an Engineering Department was started, but by then Agassiz had "stolen the show."

Louis Agassiz, then forty, had come to America only a few months before this appointment, bringing with him an enormous reputation as one of the leading scientists of Europe. A muscular, stocky man, with a massive head like Daniel Webster's, the Swiss-born Agassiz was a human dynamo. He had indeed built a solid reputation on his researches and publications on the origin and action of glaciers, on ichthyology, embryology, anatomy, and pale-ontology. And his genius for discovery and classification was matched by his showmanship. He had not been long in Cambridge before he found subscribers to a Museum of Zoology and Comparative Anatomy, known for many years as Agassiz's Museum, which was to become one of the great institutions of Harvard University.

Actually Harvard already had several scientists who were quietly laboring away at their specialties, with no encouragement and little recognition from the Harvard Corporation, who made no effort to coordinate their activities. One was the unassuming, hard-working Asa Gray, three years younger than Agassiz, whose classification of plants and manuals of botany were already becoming classics in the field. In 1857 Darwin had outlined his theory of evolution to Gray, who became its first champion in the United States, in opposition to Agassiz. At his own expense and on his own property Gray was building a botanical garden, which Harvard was later glad to receive.

In the College Benjamin Peirce was regarded as one of the great mathematicians of his age. And in the Scientific School Jeffries Wyman gave a course in Comparative Anatomy and Embryology "with the facts so cunningly arranged," according to Samuel Eliot Morison, the historian of Harvard, "that the audience could supply the 'missing link.' " Wyman was privately collecting mastodon bones and fossils of American prehistoric vertebrates, exploring Indian graves, and convincing some of his colleagues that he was as learned as Agassiz, though scarcely known beyond Boston.

Despite the presence of genuine scientists at Harvard, William James, with his fluency in French and German, could undoubtedly have obtained a better scientific education in Europe. But that possibility seems never to have been considered because his father could not bear the thought of prolonged separation from his oldest son. When, two years before, he had given up the thought of entering William in the Lawrence Scientific School it was because he could not at the time find a suitable home in Cambridge for the whole family. Whatever school William attended must be within easy visiting distance from Newport. And, everything considered, his father had not made a bad choice, especially as it was further limited by William's irregular academic preparation. Fortunately the Lawrence Scientific School required neither a high school diploma nor an entrance examination. All William needed was a character reference, and some slight evidence that his intentions were serious.

Still another peculiarity of this scientific school was that it had no required curriculum. A student enrolled under one teacher, who received the tuition fee. James wanted to study chemistry, so he was assigned to Charles W. Eliot, who had just been placed in charge of the Chemistry Laboratory. The only chance William had to hear Agassiz or one of the other scientists was at public lectures. To study biology under Wyman, or work in Agassiz's Museum, he would have had to transfer to the Department of Biology or the Museum.

After he was settled, William wrote his mother that he found the chemical analysis bewildering and he would "have to employ most all my time reading up. . . . We are only about twelve in the laboratory, so that we have a very cozy time." He did not yet know Eliot well, though he suspected that he was not "a *very* accomplished chemist, but can't tell yet." Since William was just beginning the study of chemistry (his juvenile experiments could hardly be counted), his suspicion of Eliot's ability was doubtless based on gossip he had heard around Harvard. It was true, however, that Eliot was not actually an accomplished chemist—nor was anyone else at Harvard in 1861. Charles W. Eliot was a truly gifted man, who later, as President of Harvard, made the institution into a distinguished university by modernizing the curriculum, coordinating the various schools and separate departments, and raising to respectability the standards of the professional schools, both for entrance and graduation. But his genius was for organization and administration, not scientific research or scholarship.

Born on Beacon Street in Boston of a distinguished and wealthy family, Eliot had had to overcome the handicap of a liver-colored birthmark that disfigured almost the whole right side of his face. Schoolchildren hooted him off the Boston Common, and he grew up lonely and reserved, but determined. He conquered his painful shyness by will power and stoicism, driving his brilliant mind relentlessly at whatever he undertook. At Harvard he decided to be a teacher of science, and after his graduation he was appointed tutor in mathematics and chemistry. But all the chemistry Eliot knew he had learned from Josiah P. Cooke, who was himself largely self-taught. After six months of study in France Cooke returned to Harvard and was employed to teach chemistry and to set up Harvard's first chemical laboratory, which he constructed in makeshift quarters in a basement, without water or gas. By the time Eliot was placed in charge of it, however, a few weeks before James enrolled, the crude laboratory had been improved and was considered a good one.

After Eliot became President he offered William James his first academic position and took great satisfaction throughout succeeding years in watching his former student rise to world eminence, first in psychology and then in philosophy. He was destined to outlive William, and in a memorandum sent to William's son Henry, when he was preparing a selected edition of his father's letters, Eliot wrote:

I first came in contact with William James in the academic year 1861–62. As I was young and inexperienced, it was fortunate for me that there were but fifteen [twelve in William's letter to his mother] students of chemistry in the Scientific School that year, and that I was therefore able to devote a good deal of attention to the laboratory work of each student. The instruction was given chiefly in the laboratory and was therefore individual. James was a very interesting and agreeable pupil, but was not wholly devoted to the study of Chemistry. During the two years in which he was registered as a student in Chemistry, his work was much interfered with by ill-health, or rather by something which I imagined to be a delicacy of nervous constitution. His excursions into other sciences and realms of thought were not infrequent; his mind was excursive, and he liked experimenting, particularly novel experimenting. . . . I received a distinct impression that he possessed unusual mental powers, remarkable spirituality, and great personal charm. This impression became later useful to Harvard University.

V

Except for a few weeks in Germany in the summer of 1860, William had never been separated from his parents for more than a few days. At nineteen he was emotionally as immature as any Harvard freshman, whose age at that time averaged seventeen. But since William was not enrolled in the College, he was not a direct participator in the social life of the undergraduates, who roomed in the "Yard," as the group of historic old red-brick buildings enclosed by a low fence was called. One advantage was that he was not in danger of being hazed, which could be vicious.

During the Civil War the Commons was closed, and all students ate at nearby private boarding houses. But in the Yard, with its unpaved crisscrossing paths under clusters of elm trees so close together that nearly all were stunted, the noisy life of the undergraduates continued in its traditional ways. From outdoor pumps the boys carried buckets of water to their rooms in the red-brick residential halls, or, if they were wealthy enough, hired porters (known as "Big Mike," "Little Mike," and "Dirty Mike") to supply them with water for their infrequent baths and wood for their open fireplaces. The Yard was a busy place throughout most of the day, and often a noisy one at night when scores of boys returned from Boston, illuminated by gin or wine.

Although enrollment declined during the war, the pattern of college life changed little. A few students formed drill corps and some did volunteer guard duty. Most of the Southern students returned home to serve in the Confederate Army, and at the end of each term a few more Northern students dropped out to enlist in the Union Army, but campus life was affected less than might be expected. Even the son of President Lincoln calmly continued his studies until his graduation in 1864.

William James first rented rooms from Mr. and Mrs. John Pasco on the corner of Linden and Harvard Streets, only a few blocks from the center of Harvard life in the Yard. But he found the rooms uncomfortable and was almost immediately homesick. "The first few days, the first week here," he wrote home, "I really didn't know what to do with myself or how to fill my time," but trips to the post office filled part of it. After receiving letters from his brother Henry and his mother, he wrote the latter almost immediately: "Never before did I know what mystic depths of rapture lay concealed within that familiar word [mother]. Never did the same being look so like two different ones as I going in and out of the P.O. if I bring a letter [out] with me. Gloomily, with despair written on my leaden brow I stalk the street along towards the P.O., women, children and students involuntarily shrinking against the wall as I pass—thus [he drew cartoons of himself in the two moods], as if the curse of Cain were stamped upon my front. But when I come out with a letter an immense concourse of people generally attends me to my lodging, attracted by my excited wild gestures and look."

In this same letter William satirized a suggestion which Henry had passed on in his letter: "I stopped this letter before tea when Wilk, the rosy gilled and Higginson came in. I now resume it after tea by the light of a taper and that of the moon. This room is without gas and I must get some of the jovial Harry's abhorred kerosene tomorrow. Wilk read Harry's letter and amused me metch by his naïve interpretation of mother's most rational request 'that I should keep a memorandum of all moneys I received from Father.' He thought it was that she might know exactly what sums the prodigal philosopher really gave out, and that mistrust of his generosity caused it. The phrase has a little sound that way, as Harry framed it, I confess. . . ."

In another letter he confided, serious for once, "I haven't for one minute had the feeling of being at home here. Something in my quarters precludes the possibility of it, though what this is I don't suppose I can describe to you." Even as he wrote, with "an argand gas-burner with a neat green shade merrily singing" beside him, he still felt unsettled. He said he could hear "the people breathe as they go past in the street, and the roll and jar of the horse-cars is terrific."

William was more fortunate, however, in his choice of a boarding house than in his choice of rooms. After a brief trial of another, he settled upon Miss Upham's on the corner of Oxford and Kirkland

Streets, near the Divinity School. "I like Mrs. [he usually calls her "Miss"] Upham's very much," he wrote home. "Dark, aristocratic dining-room, with royal cheer—'fish, roast-beef, veal-cutlets or pigeons?' says the splendid, tall, noble-looking, white-armed, black-eyed Juno of a handmaid as you sit down. And for dessert, a choice of three, *three* of the most succulent, unctuous (no, not unctuous, unless you imagine a celestial unction without the oil) pie-ey con-fection[s], always two plates full—my eye! She has an admirable chemical, not mechanical, combination of jam and cake and cream, which I recommend to mother if she is ever at a loss; though she has no well-stored pantry like that at good old 13 Kay Street; or if she has, it exists not for miserable me."

But William was not so enthusiastic about Miss Upham's conver-sation. In another letter he reported: "We have very general talk at our table, Miss Upham declaiming against the vulgarity of President Lincoln and complacently telling of her own ignorance as to the way the wind blows or as to the political events going on, and say-ing she thinks it a great waste of time and of 'no practical account' to study natural history." Professor Child's wit kept Miss Upham's abysmal views from being too boring, but there was something about his sallies that made it "impossible to remember what he says." Professor Francis J. Child, who might have been called *the* Harvard English Department, sat across the table from William, "a great joker" and "a little flaxen-headed boy of about 40"—actually thirty-six in 1861. William delighted in drawing caricatures of the dumpy, stooped, lovable, near-sighted little man, whose spectacles seemed too small for his great round face beneath the blond hair. He was to remain a life-long friend. Six years before William met him he had published a monumental five-volume edition of Spenser, and he would later become really famous for his *English and Scottish Ballads*, though it was many years before Harvard gave him a chance to teach anything except "rhetoric" and read the dreary themes of freshmen and sophomores. He needed a sense of humor to keep him sane.

With friends of the James family nearby, such as the Emersons in Concord and the Wards (Samuel Gray Ward was Henry Sr.'s banker) in Boston, William was sure to have social interruptions. Both Edward Emerson and Tom Ward were students at Harvard, and William saw them frequently. Some of his fellow students in the Scientific School also proved congenial, and he formed lasting friendships with several who later became leading scientists, such as Alexander Agassiz, who helped his father found the Museum of Zoology and Comparative Anatomy; Samuel H. Scudder, entomologist; Nathaniel S. Shaler, who became Dean of the Scientific School and a pioneer geologist; F. W. Putnam, later curator of the Peabody Museum; Alpheus Hyatt, for many years the curator of the Museum of Comparative Zoology; and Charles S. Peirce, son of Professor of Mathematics Benjamin Peirce, who was to become a great influence on twentieth-century logic and semantics, though he lived a miserably unsuccessful life, despite the many efforts of William James to help him. In short, at Harvard James knew, either as teachers, lecturers, or students, many of the men who would play major roles in American science.

VI

On a less intellectual plane, William corresponded with his family and friends back in Newport, and occasionally received a visit from one of them. On September 16, while writing a long letter to Wilky, "in he popped," having walked the twelve miles from Concord. "His plump corpusculus looks as always. He says it is pretty lonely at Concord and he misses Bob's lively and sportive wiles very much in the long and lone and dreary evenings. . . ." (Bob had not returned to the Sanborn school in 1861.) William had not yet visited Wilky in Concord because Tom Ward and Edward Emerson had gone, "and I thought he would have too much of a good thing."

Kitty Temple wrote William that Minny had cut her hair, enclosing a picture of the shorn girl, and he wrote his mock condolences: "Do you know, Kitty,—now that it's all over, I don't see why I should not tell you,—I have often had flashes of horrid doubts about that girl. Occasionally I have caught a glance from her furtive eyes, a glance so wild, so weird, so strange, that it has frozen the innermost marrow in my bones. . . . Well, Kitty, after all, it is but an organic lesion of the gray cortical substance which forms the *pia mater* of the brain, which is very consoling to us all. Was she all alone when she did it? Could no one wrest the shears from her vandal hand? I declare I fear to return home,—but of course Dr. Prince has her by this time." (Dr. William H. Prince was the husband of William's cousin Katharine Barber James and superintendent of the State Hospital for the Insane at Northampton, Massachusetts.)

Early in November Henry visited William, and after he had left William wrote his family on a Sunday afternoon: "Wilky & I have just returned from dinner and having completed a concert for the benefit of the inmates of Pasco Hall and the Hall next door turn our-selves I to writing a word home, and he to digesting, in a 'lobbying' position on the Sofa. . . . The radiance of Harry's visit has not faded yet & I come upon gleams of it 3 or 4 times a day in my farings to and fro, but it has never a bit diminished the lustre of far off shining Newport all silver and blue & this heavenly group below [drawing of the family lined up, from left to right, Alice, Aunt Kate, Father, Henry Jr., Mother and 'Robby'] (all being more or less failures [of the artist], especially the two outside ones)." Wil-liam complains that "Harry could in no wise satisfy my cravings to know of the family and friends as he did not seem to have been on speaking terms with any of them. . . ." William says he has never seen anyone so uninterested in "the affairs of those about him. He is a good soul though in his way too, much more so than the light fantastic Wilky who has been doing nothing but disaster since he has been here, breaking down my good resolutions about eating, keeping me from any intellectual exercise, ruining my best hat," wearing it while dressing and washing his face, going to bed with it on, etc. But only one more night before Wilky goes back to Con-cord.

And it will not be long before the whole family can be together for Thanksgiving in Newport. "It is not homesickness I have, if by that term be meant a sickness of heart and loathing of my present surroundings, but a sentiment far transcending this, that makes my hair curl for joy whenever I think of home. . . ." William then launches into an ironical description of the characters in his cartoons: ". . . home comes to me as hope, not as regret, and wh. puts roses long faded thence in my old mother's cheeks, mildness into my fathers voice, flowing graces into my Aunt Kate's movements, bab-bling confidingness into Harry's talk, a straight parting into Robby's hair and a heavenly tone into the lovely babe's temper, the elastic graces of a kitten into Moses' rusty & rheumatic joints." (Moses was Henry Sr.'s horse.) The sarcasms in some of these descriptions are more transparent than in others, as in Henry Jr.'s "babbling confid-ingness," for he neither babbled nor confided in his older brother, but

to us. The radiance of Harry's
visit has not faded yet & I come
upon gleams of it 3 or 4 times a day
in my farings to and fro, but it
has never a bit diminished the
lustre of far off shining Newport
all silver and blue & this heavenly
group below

(all being more or less failures, especially the two outside ones). The more
so as the above mentioned Harry could
in no wise satisfy my cravings to
know of the family and friends as he

A letter from William James to his family, early November 1861.

apparently each one contained a jibe. With William no subject was too serious to bear a little mockery, and his mockery was usually a cover-up for some youthful plan, sentiment, or ambition which he realized to be a survival of adolescence. "As Wilky has submitted to you a resumé of his future history for the next few years so will I hoping it will meet your approval. Thus: 1 year Study Chemistry, then spend one term at home, then 1 year with Wyman, then a Medical education, then 5 or 6 years with Agassiz, then probably death, death, death with inflation and plethora of knowledge. This you had better seriously consider." Actually this was not very far from the plan that he was to follow, and if he had hopes of employment in Agassiz's Museum, even the five or six years with him might have been a serious forecast.

In December, William invited Tom Perry to come to Cambridge as his guest. With much juvenile railing he urged him to arrive on Friday instead of Sunday, "Because on Sunday you can do nothing here, can't even get into Mt. Auburn Cemetery without climbing over the fence." Pretending to talk to a child, he gave Tom explicit instructions on how to reach Cambridge and advised: "You had better read up in order to be able to converse with me . . ." and continued, "I was electrified by Robby's coming down on me today when I did not at all expect him. I should like Harry to come with you. I cou[l]d give you both very comfortable accommodations (comfortable to *me* that is,) I have not time to write him a special note, so please show him this and one of you write to let me know. How quick time flies here! I think you will enjoy your visit and profit by it. The effect Boston has on the rural mind is generally puffeckly indscrib'b'bl. And I expect wonders in your case."

Throughout the autumn term William had been attending public lectures given by Agassiz in Boston on "Method in Natural History," and he had also heard some of Professor Wyman's lectures on comparative anatomy of vertebrates. At first Agassiz dazzled him and it was not until later that he learned to appreciate Wyman. Dr. Wyman, a first-rate scientist teaching in a slipshod, haphazard medical school, was almost the antithesis of Agassiz: cautious, meticulously accurate, and willing to examine new theories or discoveries; but his lectures, William found, were prosy and monotonous.

On Christmas Day William wrote his parents: "The *place*, to me, improves as I go on living here, and if I study with Agassiz four or five years I should like to have you all here, with me, comfortable. I had a long talk with one of his students the other night and saw for the first time how a naturalist could feel about his trade in the same way that an artist does about his. For instance, Agassiz would rather take wholly uninstructed people 'for he has to unteach them all that they have learnt.' He does not let them *look* into a book for a long while, what they learn they must learn for themselves, and be *masters* of it all. The consequence is he makes *naturalists* of them, he does not merely cram them, and this student (he had been there two years) said he felt ready to go anywhere in the world now with nothing but his notebook and study out anything quite alone. He [Agassiz] must be a great teacher."

It may seem surprising that William would still be in Cambridge on Christmas Day, but Puritan New England had been very strongly opposed to making this day a festival and Harvard in 1861 allowed only a single holiday instead of the two weeks' vacation of later years. Apparently Sanborn's school treated the occasion in the same way, for Wilky came over from Concord on Christmas day to take dinner with the Wards in Boston. Of course William had also been invited, but he had intended to decline, after he had "befooled Tom with divers answers." He thought there would be time to set Tom right when he saw him at Miss Upham's the day before Christmas, "But the young viper went home right after breakfast," William wrote his parents on Christmas day, "so I had to go into Boston this morning and explain. Wilky had come up from Concord to dine in said Commonwealth Avenue, and I, as it turned out, found myself in for following the innocent lamb Lily [Barker, visiting the Wards] up and down the town for two hours, to hold bundles and ring bells for her; Wilky and Tom having vanished from the scene."

It was a very cold morning, only five degrees above zero at sunrise, and the streets were covered with a hard glaze of ice. "I had thick smooth shoes and went sliding off like an avalanche every three steps, while she, having india-rubbers and being a Bostonian, went ahead like a Swan." William described in lengthy detail the gyrations and capers he cut, milking the joke to its last drop of mirth. He would never again, he swore, "acknowledge a 'young lady' as a human being." But by the time he got back to his boarding house he had cooled down and behaved "very considerately and paternally" to a young lady who sat next to him. But he was so homesick that he admitted it without his usual protective humor: "Many times and bitterly to-day have I thought of home and lamented that I should have to be away at this merry Christmastide, from my rare family; wondering with Wilky, if they were missing us as we miss them."

VII

Despite the fact that Cambridge improved on acquaintance, William continued to dislike his rooms at the Pascos'; consequently for the second term he engaged rooms with Mr. and Mrs. Samuel Sweetser on Trowbridge Street, near Main (now Massachusetts Avenue). But he soon found these rooms worse than the ones he had vacated, with a smoky stove, "which fills the room with a mephitic and pestilential gas, so that I have to keep the window open." The family he pronounced "worthy of Dickens." It consisted of Mr. Sweetser, his old-maid sister, who "shakes like an aspen whenever she is spoke to," Mr. Sweetser's "three gushing girls, a parrot and a maniac. The maniac is very obstreperous. Her husband left her boarding here 3 months ago and went to Cuba. When she got mad he was written to, but has sent no reply."

These unexpected distractions did not, however, seriously interfere with William's studies. On March 2 he wrote his parents: "I am now studying organic chemistry. It will probably shock Mother to hear that I yesterday destroyed a handkerchief—but it was an old one, and I converted it into some sugar which, though rather brown, is very good." Then he reported that the "hirsute jewel which lent such a manly and martial aspect to my visage is gone, and the place thereof is naked." This was the mustache he had grown in Europe in 1860, apparently to his father's approval, for he adds: "Please don't let Father get excited. I don't think anyone will know the difference, and moreover it is not dead, it only sleeps and some day will rise phoenix like from its ashes with tenfold its former beauty." Then, anticipating a visit from his father, he asks, "When Father comes let him bring *Ganot, if Harry does not want it.*" Certainly Harry would not want Adolphe Ganot's *Traité de physique expérimentale et appliquée* (1853) and the condition was obviously a joke. William's textbook, as Eliot recorded in his notes on the class, was Fowne's *Organic Chemistry*, on which William made an examination grade of 85, according to Eliot, who also recorded that his attendance at laboratory had been irregular.

On February 25 the former President of Harvard, C. C. Felton, died and on March 1 William attended the memorial service in the college chapel "to hear Dr. Peabody's final word on him." Henry James Sr. had always taught his children that death was not something to fear or mourn; rather it was the means by which a human soul returned to the realm of pure spirit whence it had come into the world—a doctrine resembling both the Platonic and the Hindu, though probably derived from Swedenborg. Consequently, William was disgusted with Dr. Peabody's lugubrious tone: "The prayer was a prolonged moan in which the death (not in its consequences but in itself) was treated of as a great calamity, and the eulogy of the sermon was almost ridiculously overcharged. What was most disagreeable throughout the whole was the wailing tone,—not a bit that of simple pagan grief at the *loss* (which would have been honest), but a whine consciously *put on* as if from a sense of duty. . . . The whole style of the performance was so false and unpleasant that I have concluded to have nothing more to do with funerals till they improve."

During the spring John Wilkes Booth (the future assassin of President Lincoln) played in Schiller's *The Robbers* in Boston, and though William called his performance "Rant, rant, rant of the most fearful kind," he went to see and hear him three nights running. On Sunday evening he asked someone to move so that he could get to his seat, and discovered that the person was his cousin Bob Temple, handsome, well-dressed, self-assured as ever. Bob had long been a puzzle and a fascination to the James boys. One reason for his having been sent to Scotland to school was his inability to get along with his older brother, William Temple (now in the Union Army). At Aberdeen University, of all places, Bob had been converted to Roman Catholicism. He had long been cynical; now he was bitterly sarcastic. He defended "Slavery and the wickedness of human society." Bob said he would sail in three days for Europe; no fighting against slavery or for the preservation of the Union for him.

The whole James family, of course, had long ago committed itself emotionally to the Union cause. William's health had not improved, and he no longer debated with himself whether to volunteer for military service, though fellow students were still dropping out of college to go into the army. One of these was Nathaniel Shaler, a tall, intense Kentuckian, who finally joined the Union

Army despite his passionate belief in states' rights. At home Bobby had been begging for permission to join, though he was only sixteen. Since his twelfth year he had brooded over feeling neglected and unappreciated, and had resented his parents' admiration of William's brilliance and Henry's imperturbable serenity. He now threatened to run away and "go to sea."

At the end of the spring term in Sanborn's school, Wilkinson did enlist, with his father's consent; in fact Henry James Sr. accompanied him to the recruiting station. The regiment which Wilky joined was the 44th Massachusetts, being formed in Boston. As Wilky later described the experience:

> A few weeks' stay at the Revere House, until the company was fully enrolled, a drill twice a day upon the Common, a strange youth in a strange land, equipped for battle, and eager for the start of my regiment to the seat of war. My company, it appears, was to be a strange mixture of material. We had a good many graduates and undergraduates of Harvard College, a delegation of some twenty men from the Hanover Street Methodist Church, devout men, who, from their entry into camp until we reached the battlefield, chanted the battle songs of those trained in the army of the Lord.

William was still in Cambridge on June 20, senior class day, and attended the exercises. We may be sure he visited Wilky at Revere House, and probably watched him drill on the Common. Having a brother in the army made the war feel closer to him, but his only immediate plans were to get some rest in Newport, do a great deal of reading, and prepare for his second year of scientific studies.

CHAPTER VI Medical Profession

I embraced the medical profession a couple of months ago. My

impressions are that there is much humbug therein. . . .

—W.J., *February 21, 1864*

I

AFTER A REST IN NEWPORT during the summer, William James returned to Harvard in September 1862, accompanied by Henry Jr., who had become bored with staying at home with his adolescent sister and youngest brother and had decided to enter law school. William found satisfactory rooms for himself with Mrs. H. L. Stewart on Mount Auburn Street, and Henry stayed with him for a few days until he also could locate suitable rooms—as he did, near Winthrop Square. Devoted as the brothers were to each other, they were so different in habits, temperament, and interests that they would not enjoy rooming together, and each was well aware of this fact.

Henry did join William, however, at Miss Upham's boarding house, where he sat beside his brother, opposite Professor Child, whom he had met on his visit the previous year. Of course the major topic of conversation was the war, though Miss Upham did her best to direct attention to more pleasant subjects, innocuous ones which she approved. But the war was on nearly everyone's mind, whether it was discussed or not. Professor Child's cherubic face was a good barometer of the fortunes of the Union soldiers. When the war news was good, he came to the table beaming, full of good humor and jokes. The James family had not yet felt deeply, personally involved in the war, for until October Wilky was still drilling in Boston, but before the end of the month his father came up from Newport to see the 44th Regiment leave for the scenes of battle in North Carolina.

William was continuing his study of chemistry under Professor Eliot, who noted at the time that "James, W." took "quantitative analysis and was tolerably punctual at recitations till Thanksgiving, when he began an investigation of the effects of different bread-raising materials on the urine [his own]. He worked steadily on this until the end of the term, mastering the processes, and studying the effect of yeast on bicarbonate of sodium and bitartrate of potash."

In the memorandum he later wrote for William James's son, Eliot revealed that James worked less steadily than this note indicates:

His tendency to the subject of physiology had appeared clearly during his two years in the Department of Chemistry; so that I enlisted him, in the second year of his study of chemistry, in an inquiry into the effects on the kidneys of eating bread made with Liebig-Horsford baking powder, whose chief constituent was an acid phosphate. But James did not like the bread, and found accurate determination of its effects three times a day tiresome and unpromising; so that after three weeks he requested me to transfer that inquiry to some other person.

It appears, therefore, that he did not complete the experiment, though he had no doubt gone far enough to discover the effects on himself.

Generalizing from his observation of James's performances in the chemical laboratory, Eliot commented further: "The two interesting points about his education are: first, its irregularity—it did not conform to the Boston and Cambridge traditional method; and secondly, it was in large proportion observational, and particularly in the biological sciences. The systematic part of his education did not foretell his subsequent devotion to philosophical studies; but his unsystematic excursions did." Eliot may have been a mediocre chemist himself, but his wise tolerance of the very traits in William James which most teachers would have found intolerable contributed to the making of a great psychologist and philosopher. Chemistry would prove useful in James's later studies, but it was only a mechanical tool for the study of living processes in human beings, and what already interested him was how a man's physiological structure and functions could effect his emotional and intellectual life.

Even his own poor health, which would plague William James for over a decade (and to some extent all his adult life), made him especially observant of the relationships of mind and body. His objection to using his own organs for the baking powder experiment was not mere whim, or academic irresponsibility; his health was already at such a low ebb that to continue eating bread that did not agree with him might force him to withdraw from Harvard. On October 19 he had written his sister that he was much troubled by a boil on his elbow and complained of feeling feverish even with his overcoat on as he sat beside his lamp "writing *à la seule que j'aime* and wishing for nothing so much as an hour or two of her voluble and senseless, though soothing and pleasing, talk." This mixture of compliment and disparagement, incidentally, is typical of his letters to his sister throughout his youth and early manhood, addressing her as he did in the extravagant language of love-making, but treating her as a child who chattered with meaningless volubility. Sometimes it is difficult to tell whether the terms of endearment are intended more to tease and embarrass or to convey affection.

But we have left William sitting with his boil. "Eliot with voice of absolute certainty told me to keep painting it with iodine. . . . It is very painful to apply, and seems only to prolong the boil, and having dropped its use I now curse it aloud." Yet this self-pitying young man who sits in his room cursing his boil—and Eliot for the ineffective remedy—could also be genial, outgoing, and charming, as his brother Henry, who almost never complained and suffered in silence, could not be—or at least not yet. In Miss Upham's dining room William was affable to everyone, no matter how dull or insignificant. It would be difficult to imagine a less snobbish person, although his stylish clothes, his excellent manners, and sophistication gained from travel abroad marked his superiority to most of the other patrons of Miss Upham's. Henry's envious impression was that he had never seen anything "like William's unawareness of exertion after having helped the lame dog of converse over stile after stile."

To Henry most of the diners at Miss Upham's were insufferably dull, and he could not help feeling his utter boredom, which tied his tongue and made him appear aloof. There was Joe May, son of a New York State abolitionist, with fine features, a handsome smile, a "developed moustache and short dark pointed beard." His talk was quite ordinary, but William listened to him patiently. A theology student named C. C. Salter was homely, even sickly in appearance, with stooped shoulders and a sloven appearance, but he had a surprising wit. William assured Henry that he had a superior intelligence, too, but the theological discussions which Henry overheard did not interest him. William seemed capable of talking about anything—or at least listening to anything, which still more encouraged men like Salter and May to talk.

Henry did have a few friends of his own, the closest being T. S. Perry, who had also come to Harvard to enroll in the College. No doubt Henry would have enjoyed knowing Professor James Russell Lowell, with whom later in Europe he did establish a delightful friendship; but Lowell taught in the College and Henry was enrolled in the Law School, though he very soon discovered that he had no interest in law, and continued to attend lectures only because he did not know what else to do. The students at the Law School interested Henry as little as William's fellow students in science. One boarder at Miss Upham's with the glamorous name of John Bancroft, son of the famous historian, had just returned from Europe, having studied in France and painted in Düsseldorf, where he had known George du Maurier, whose illustrations in *Punch*, the *Cornhill*, and *Once a Week* William and Henry had enjoyed and admired for years. But John Bancroft would not let anyone see his paintings, and not even William could draw him into conversation about experiences which both of the James brothers longed to discuss with him.

No one, both brothers agreed, talked as scintillatingly as their father. His coming to Boston in mid-autumn broke the monotony of Henry's law studies, and William took great pleasure in helping him find a printer for his new book, *Substance and Shadow*, which, as usual, he was having to publish at his own expense. William wrote Alice: "I have been with him to the printer's, and think that between us three one of the prettiest books of modern times will be produced —plain, unadorned, but severely handsome." Aside from helping his father, or thinking that he had, William enjoyed visiting a printing office because he sometimes thought he would like to make printing his profession.

William made no reference to the contents of his father's book, and he probably had not read it. Even many years later, while editing Henry Sr.'s *Literary Remains* soon after his death, William confessed that he had never entirely understood his father's extremely individualistic philosophy. And at home, much as Mr. James's sons loved him, they joked and teased him about the unreadable books he wrote. William amused the family by drawing cartoons which he facetiously offered his father as illustrations for his books.

Actually the message of the new book was much the same as that of the others: The insubstantiality of conventional morality and institutionalized religion and the substantiality of real religion. Possibly William might have been better off if he could have shared it—or at least if he could have found for himself a religious faith as sustaining as that of his father. William's poor health was somehow related to his increasing mental and spiritual turmoil. In 1862 his backaches, headaches, eyestrain, and undefinable nervousness increased so much that at the end of the first term of his second year at Harvard he decided to withdraw and spend the spring and summer at home in Newport. This time was not entirely lost, however, because he continued to read extensively in literature, science, and even philosophy.

II

The James family was now beginning to read the newspaper accounts of the war with personal concern. Wilky had taken to army life as if born for it, and before the end of 1862 he had already survived several small skirmishes and wrote home with excited confidence, as on New Year's Day, 1863, from Newberne, North Carolina: "The next fight we have, I expect, will be a pretty big one, but I am confident that under [General] Foster and our gunboats we will rid the State of these miserable wretches. . . ." He wrote jovially of long marches of thirty miles or more a day, of camping in cotton fields with rail-fence fires for warmth at night, and of putting the "Rebs" to flight at Kingston, which gave Sergeant G. W. James the greatest "glee in all his born days."

There is no reason to doubt that Wilkinson James was an excellent and brave soldier, and also Robertson, the "baby" of the family, who had enlisted before his seventeenth birthday in a "nine-months regiment," the 45th Massachusetts, and at the end of his term re-enlisted, being assigned to the 55th as lieutenant. For outstanding bravery at Petersburg, Virginia, he was promoted to captain. Throughout the war the brothers served their separate regiments with similar energy and distinction. The exuberant tone of their letters gives more than a hint that they enjoyed having drawn their parents' attention from William and the less clever though more genial Henry to themselves. Now they had the advantage of complete freedom from their overprotective parents, from which William at least had not liberated himself, though Henry was beginning to. It was not William's nature to be jealous of his younger brothers, but their heroic and vigorous activeness in that time of national crisis could not fail to intensify his mental depression over his own ineffectiveness and uncertain future.

In February the war became more dramatic for Wilky, and more ominous for his family. Governor John A. Andrew, following President Lincoln's Proclamation emancipating the slaves, began organizing a Negro regiment, which became the 54th Massachusetts, under Colonel Robert Gould Shaw—whose statue Professor William James would one day be called upon to dedicate. Colonel Shaw asked the commander of Wilky's regiment, the 44th, to recommend three men for commissions in the new Negro regiment, and Wilky and his friend Cabot Russell were among them. Wilky was offered his choice of captain or adjutant, and chose the latter. On May 28, 1863, after four months of training in camp at Readville, the 54th Regiment marched out of Boston to the accompaniment of both cheers and insults. Some of the Irish Copperheads tried to assault the troops at the dock and caused a near riot.

July 1, 1863, was a long hot day in Newport for William, Henry, Alice, their parents, and several visiting cousins. The local newspaper reported a gigantic and fateful battle in progress at Gettysburg, Pennsylvania, and one of the Jameses or a neighbor frequently visited the newspaper office to see if more telegraphic dispatches had arrived telling of the progress or outcome of the fighting. The James family and their relatives gathered in the garden, unable to do or think of anything except the danger to their young men, while they waited in suspense. It was a situation especially painful for Willy and Harry, who felt ignoble in their safety.

Neither of the younger brothers was at Gettysburg, but on July 18 Wilky was almost mortally wounded in a futile attack on Fort Wagner, which was not taken until September 6. In leading his Negro troops in the first raid on the fort, Wilkinson James was shot both in the side and in his left foot. He saw his commander, Colonel Shaw, killed instantly. He himself was finally picked up and given medical attention, but he lay unconscious for a number of days in a tent of the Sanitary Commission. His family knew nothing of these events until the father of his friend and fellow officer Cabot Russell found him while searching for his missing son. Toward the end of August, after giving up the search for Cabot, Mr. Russell took Wilky back to Newport on a stretcher, still gravely ill. For many days Wilky lay in a semiconscious stupor, and William made a crayon portrait that looked like a death mask. But gradually he recovered, and he always cherished a crude cartoon William drew of him at Fort Wagner holding up his wounded foot with a grim expression on his face. He was still not out of danger when William returned to Harvard at the beginning of September for the new term, though he did recover and return to his regiment. Bob was with the Negro 55th Regiment trying to take Charleston; he had not written for several weeks, and the family waited in suspense for word from or about him.

III

From Cambridge William wrote his sister, whom he addressed as "Chérie charmante de Bal," that he was "nicely established in a cosy little room" at Miss Sophie H. Appleton's, 616 Main Street. Later in the year he moved to Divinity Hall, near the Divinity School on Kirkland, which was intended as a dormitory for theological students but in which other students were permitted to occupy rooms. William still took his meals with Miss Upham, after bargaining with her to let him continue at his old rate of four dollars and fifty cents a week instead of the new rate of five dollars, a maneuver which he felt "redeemed any weaknesses" of past extravagances.

William registered again in the Scientific School, but shifted from chemistry to comparative anatomy, which was regarded as a "premedical" course and was taught by Professor Wyman, whose lectures he had attended the previous year. "I have a filial feeling toward Wyman already," William wrote his sister on September 13 after only two weeks of being his pupil. "I work in a vast museum, at a table all alone, surrounded by skeletons of mastodons, crocodiles, and the like, with the walls hung about with monsters and horrors enough to freeze the blood. But I have no fear, as most of them are tightly bottled up. Occasionally solemn men and women come in to see the museum [i.e., Agassiz's], and sometimes timid little girls (reminding me of thee, beloved, only they are less fashionably dressed) who whisper: 'Is folks allowed here?' It pains me to remark, however, that not all the little girls are of this pleasing type, *most* being bold-faced jigs."

William then asks how Wilky is. "How is he nursed? Who holds his foot for the doctor? [Probably William had.] . . . Everyone here asks about him, and all without exception seem enthusiastic about the darkeys [of Wilky's regiment]." William also sends a photograph of General Sickles "for yours and Wilky's amusement." It is part of "a great anthropomorphological collection" he is making, meaning a file of photographs of famous people, or ones in whom he is interested for one reason or another. Whenever William James read a book or studied the contributions of a scientist or philosopher, he always wanted to know what he looked like, and he continued all his life to add to this collection.

Before he had studied long under his new professor, William James realized that Jeffries Wyman was a greater scientist and teacher than the showy Agassiz. Wyman would always remain his favorite teacher, the one he felt influenced him most. A decade later, in paying tribute to him, James wrote:

> His extraordinary effect on all who knew him is to be accounted for by the one word, character. Never was a man so absolutely without detractors. The quality which every one first thinks of in him is his extraordinary modesty . . . his unfailing geniality and serviceableness, his readiness to confer with and listen to younger men—how often did his unmagisterial manner lead them unawares into taking dogmatic liberties, which soon resulted in ignominious collapse before his quiet wisdom. . . . An accomplished draughtsman, his love and understanding of art were great. . . .

The description foreshadowed William James himself as teacher and scholar.

In praising Wyman for his "incomparable fairness" and (later in the eulogy) "disinterestedness, and single-minded love of the truth," James could not have avoided having in his mind the different attitudes that Wyman and Agassiz took toward Charles Darwin's recent theory of evolution. Before *The Origin of Species* appeared in 1859, Agassiz had already expressed his belief in a "special" Divine creation of all forms of life, each species separate from all others and immutably fixed. Darwin's theory of mutability, whereby variations useful for survival had caused all living creatures to acquire and transmit new characteristics, accounted for the development and separation of species. This "development" theory seemed to Agassiz monstrously wrong, sacrilegious, and even "unscientific." In truth, by the time James knew him Agassiz had closed his mind to all scientific evidence for the Darwinian theory and his own views had hardened into dogma. Wyman, on the other hand, was willing to give a fair hearing to any theory that could be backed up by credible evidence. At first he did not like the implications of Darwin's theory either, but he kept an open mind and studied the evidence with complete impartiality. As a result he won the respect and admiration of his colleagues at Harvard, while Agassiz's reputation with them declined. Wyman was never to become widely known beyond Cambridge and Boston because he did not publish, and James always thought this unfortunate. More ambition "would have greatly increased the sphere of his effectiveness and fame."

After taking the course in comparative anatomy, William James might be expected to enter the Medical School, but in September he was still undecided. To his cousin Mrs. Katharine James Prince he confided: "I am obliged before the 15th of January to make finally and irrevocably 'the choice of a profession.' I suppose your sex, which has, or should have, its bread brought to it, instead of having to go in search of it, has no idea of the awful responsibility of such a choice. I have four alternatives: Natural History, Medicine, Printing, Beggary. Much may be said in favor of each. I have named them in the ascending order of their pecuniary invitingness. After all, the great problem of life seems to be how to keep body and soul together, and I *have* to consider lucre."

Placing "Beggary" at the peak of his "ascending order" was not really a bitter joke, though how to earn a living was beginning to be a real worry for William. "To study natural science, I know I should like, but the prospect of supporting a family on $600 a year is not one of those rosy dreams of the future with which the young are said to be haunted. Medicine would pay, and I should still be dealing with subjects which interest me—but how much drudgery and of what an unpleasant kind is there! Of all departments of Medicine, that to which Dr. Prince devotes himself is, I should think, the most interesting. And I should like to see him and his patients at Northampton [Hospital for the Insane] very much before coming to a decision."

On November 2, William wrote his mother: "I feel very much the importance of making soon a final choice of my business of life. I stand now at the place where the road forks. One branch leads to material comfort, the flesh-pots; but it seems a kind of selling of one's soul. The other to mental dignity and independence; combined, however, with physical penury. If I myself were the only one concerned I should not hesitate an instant in my choice. But it seems hard on Mrs. W.J., 'that not impossible she,' to ask her to share an empty purse and a cold hearth. On one side is *science*, upon the other *business* (the honorable, honored and productive business of printing seems most attractive), with *medicine*, which partakes of [the] advantages of both, between them, but which has drawbacks of its own. I confess I hesitate."

William's father had never urged any of his children to make the decision which his oldest son was now convinced that he must make; in fact, Henry James Sr. had always acted as if none of his children would ever have to earn a living and had actually thrown obstacles in the path of such choices. We do not know the thoughts of Mrs. James, but she evidently was more practical than her husband— someone in the family had to be!—and there are signs and hints that she did not sympathize with William's Hamlet-like indecision. Continuing his letter to his mother: "I fancy there is a fond maternal cowardice which would make you and every other mother contemplate with complacency the worldly fatness of a son, even if obtained by some sacrifice of his 'higher nature'." Certainly his father was not willing to have William make that sacrifice and it becomes very apparent that at this crucial stage of his life the maternal and paternal influences were tugging him in opposite directions; indeed, that this had something to do with his indecision and occasional nervous prostration.

But it is also apparent that William's mother was leaving his decision of a profession up to him. She might apply indirect pressure, but she did not dictate. In the autumn of 1863 she herself was ready for a decision which William had suggested and even urged: moving the family home from Newport to Boston or contiguous Cambridge. In the same November 2 letter William wrote: "To answer the weighty questions which you propound: I am glad to leave Newport because I am tired of the place itself, and because of the reason which you have very well expressed in your letter, the necessity of the whole family being near the arena of the future activity of us young men. I recommend Cambridge on account of its own pleasantness (though I don't wish to be invidious towards Brookline,

Longwood, and other places) and because of its economy if I or Harry continue to study here much longer. . . ."

Neither William nor his mother mentions another motive for the move, and possibly Mrs. James may not have been fully aware of it: her husband had found congenial friends in Boston and the vicinity during his visits of the past two years. He had particularly enjoyed being the guest of the Saturday Club, whose members included, besides Emerson, Hawthorne, and other leading writers of New England, Charles Eliot Norton, who had just become editor of the *North American Review;* Samuel Gray Ward, Mr. James's friend and financial adviser; James T. Fields, editor and publisher of the *Atlantic Monthly;* and a number of other intellectuals who became his life-long friends. In brief, Henry James Sr. was ready for Boston, Boston was ready for him, and his wife was always sensitive and responsive to his needs and pleasures.

As for Henry Jr., he knew even less than William what he wanted to do, though all his impulses were toward writing, and Boston would be a more advantageous place for making experiments, meeting editors, and feeling his way in the literary world than Newport. He had no intention, however, of returning to Harvard, which he had left in the spring of 1863.

Before New Year's William James had made his decision to enter the Medical School. On February 21, 1864, he wrote: "I embraced the medical profession a couple of months ago. My first impressions are that there is much humbug therein, and that, with the exception of surgery, in which something positive is sometimes accomplished, a doctor does more by the moral effect of his presence on the patient and family, than by anything else. He also extracts money from them."

Meanwhile Henry James Sr. had found a house in Boston, on which he took a two-year lease, at 13 Ashburton Place. In May the family moved and of course William rejoined them. Once more he was under the immediate influence of his idealistic father and his practical-minded mother, a situation not likely to help him to attain emotional maturity. However, from the spring of 1864 until April 1865 there is a scarcity of primary evidence for any conclusion about the intimate life of William James. Living at home, he of course wrote no letters to his parents or sister, and his medical studies left him little time to write letters to friends.

IV

The cynicism William James expressed about the medical profession two months after beginning the study of medicine echoed
the views of some of the professors in the Harvard School of Medicine. Dr. Oliver Wendell Holmes, who had been Dean until 1853
and still taught anatomy and physiology, liked to quip that, "If the
whole materia medica (*excepting only opium and ether*), as now
used, could be sunk to the bottom of the sea, it would be all the
better for mankind—and all the worse for the fishes." He also taught
that "a large proportion of diseases get well of themselves, without
any special medication," and that the best the doctor could do was
to calm the patient while nature worked his recovery. And he never
showed any more inclination to practice medicine than William
James did either before or after receiving his M.D.

Both the medical profession and schools preparing for it were, indeed, little respected in the 1860s, and just as little deserving of respect. Harvard nominally required three years of study for the M.D.
degree, but the third year was largely devoted to internship in a
hospital, a perfunctory thesis, and a superficial oral examination. The
degree was the only requirement for a state license; or more accurately, the diploma was the license. The Harvard school was not
one of the worst; in fact it was one of the better, for it at least had
some distinguished scientists who gave either courses or lectures
which medical students could attend.

In 1870, only a year after William James finally presented himself
for the oral examination, Charles W. Eliot, by then President of Harvard, began a campaign to raise the standards of the Medical School,
in which he finally succeeded after a prolonged struggle with the
medical faculty. Dr. Henry J. Bigelow, for example, declared: "We
justly honor the patient and learned worker in the remote and exact
sciences, but should not for that reason encourage the medical
student to while away his time in the labyrinths of Chemistry and
Physiology, when he ought to be learning the difference between
hernia and hydrocele."

At best there was not very much science in the practice of medicine in the United States during the Civil War decade. Before
Pasteur had proved the existence of germs, Holmes had observed

that certain diseases were spread by physical contact, even by doctors themselves. Yet asepsis was unknown in the 1860s, and surgeons took pride in wearing bloody operating clothes, the more soiled the better, like an Oxford student's pride in his tattered gown. It is no wonder that mortality in Civil War hospitals was frightful. Even diagnosis was largely guesswork, and patients were said to have died of a "fever," a "miasma," or something equally vague.

Although in 1863–1864 no one could foresee the discoveries that were soon to make any informed person realize how primitive and even barbaric American medical knowledge was at that time, William James was intelligent enough to have contempt for the Harvard Medical School even while he attended it. One may wonder then, why he did attend it. The explanation is that he was deeply interested in physiology and its relation to the mind and human conduct and, however low the standards of the Medical School were, he did have Wyman, whom everyone admitted to be a first-rate comparative anatomist. For his studies he also had the use of one of the best museums in the country, and the privilege of attending lectures by other scientists who were making history. The practice of medicine never had any attraction for him, either as a student or graduate. What he wanted was, as Eliot had foreseen, the opportunity to study the human body in all its parts and relationships, and the Harvard Medical School got him started in the right direction.

CHAPTER VII

With Agassiz in Brazil

The Professor has just been expatiating over the map of South America and making projects as if he had Sherman's army at his disposal instead of the ten novices he really has.—W.J. to his mother

I

IN THE SPRING OF 1865 the most exciting topic of conversation in Cambridge and Boston, aside from the war, was the collecting expedition to Brazil to be undertaken by Professor Louis Agassiz and his energetic wife, Lizzie. The Agassiz Museum had recently opened in a building especially designed for it, and the ambitious professor was determined to fill it with the most valuable comparative-zoology collection in America. As a young man he had made his reputation with a book on Brazilian fish, but he suspected that the Amazon was inhabited by many species still unknown to science, and now wealthy friends and admirers had made it possible for him to find out. One of the richest men in Boston, Nathaniel Thayer, who had left Harvard without a degree and had become the University's most generous benefactor, would finance the trip, and it was already called Thayer's Expedition. But others were contributing too. Mr. Samuel Gray Ward, who represented the financial interests of the Pacific Steamship Company, arranged for free passage for Agassiz, his wife, and six paid assistants (members of the Museum staff) on one of the Pacific's finest ships, the *Colorado*, bound for San Francisco by way of the Horn.

Then word got out that Agassiz would take several young men as unprofessional assistants if they could pay their own way. Mr. Thayer promptly agreed to pay for his son, Stephen, and Mr. Ward did the same for Tom, one of William James's best friends. Suddenly this trip became William's wildest ambition and he could talk of little else, but he disliked asking his father for the money, and his mother did not encourage him to do so. Fortunately, Aunt Kate, who had ample independent means though she chose to live with her sister and brother-in-law, offered to let William have the money he needed—which his father willingly supplemented.

Though William was already a bit disillusioned about Agassiz, he still regarded him as a great teacher of scientific observation. His own medical studies had wearied him with abstraction and generalization; he thought it would be a relief to deal at first hand with the concrete and particular. What better experience than to be taught by Agassiz to gather and prepare specimens of marine animals for the Museum! Perhaps, too, William had not entirely rejected the possibility of being offered employment in the Museum, as a means of prolonging his scientific studies. But, most of all, he was ready for adventure, and a "scientific expedition to the Amazon" sounded both adventurous and romantic.

William's preparations for the trip were simple, but of course Professor and Mrs. Agassiz's were elaborate and feverish. The United States Government became interested, partly because it saw a chance to counteract the influence in Brazil of European sympathizers with the Confederacy. To Agassiz the war was a nuisance and he did not identify strongly with either side, but the United States Government would be useful to him and he agreed to convey messages. The Secretary of State sent a lengthy one to be delivered to the Emperor of Brazil, Dom Pedro, and the Secretary of the Navy issued orders for all naval officers to render any assistance possible. The expedition was becoming semiofficial, a fact that increased the excitement and sense of importance of the participants.

On Friday, March 30, William wrote his first letter aboard the *Colorado*, which was still in the New York harbor: "We have been detained 48 hours on this steamer in port on account of different accidents. . . . A dense fog is raging which will prevent our going outside as long as it lasts." But William did not have a feeling of inactivity: "The Professor has just been expatiating over the map of South America and making projects as if he had Sherman's army at his disposal instead of the ten novices he really has." These novices included, besides William, Tom Ward, and Stephen Thayer, John Allen, a Harvard senior; Walter Hunnewell, another Harvard senior, son of a wealthy father, who had bought for the trip a newly invented contraption which was supposed to take pictures with less trouble than the daguerreotype camera; and Simon N. Dexter, another rich young man whom William described as "a sunburnt, big-jawed devil . . . from Providence, who is a crack shot, and has hunted all over the U.S." Dexter was also a skilled taxidermist, and Agassiz expected him to be useful in preparing some of the specimens for display in the Museum. Jacques Burckhardt, a European artist who had been making scientific sketches and colored plates for Agassiz for many years, was going along as a paid assistant. Agassiz would employ guides in Brazil, and perhaps, William reported, "some students at Rio to accompany the different parties. . . . I'm sure I hope he will, on account of the language. If each of us has a Portuguese companion, he can do things twice as easily."

Finally about noon on March 31 a tug pulled the *Colorado* out of the harbor and the trip had begun. Hardly had they passed the Narrows before the Professor and his wife announced the instruction they would provide on the way to Brazil. Mrs. Agassiz was to teach the boys Portuguese. She was a remarkable woman, daughter of a wealthy merchant named Cary, younger than her husband, industrious, energetic; she spoke French and Portuguese and was to be the historian of the expedition. As for the Professor, every day at two p.m. he began a lecture on scientific method and aired his favorite theories—some, like his opposition to Darwin, more fanciful than scientific. All the passengers, several officers of the ship, and the captain dutifully attended. William thought the lectures were too long, but his seasickness may have dulled his interest. Mrs. Agassiz worried about her husband's overexerting, but he assured her, according to her own notation, that "it was a rest for him to systematize his own work and arrange it in his own mind."

One of the passengers to San Francisco was Mr. Frederick Billings, a trustee of the new University of California at Berkeley. Another was Alonzo Potter, Episcopal Bishop of Pennsylvania, whom William persisted in calling "Bish" in his letters to his parents. "Bish" had read the "Substance and Shadder" of Henry Sr., admiring the style but rejecting the doctrine. On the first Sunday at sea, April 2, he preached a sermon "and told us we must try to imitate the simple child-like devotion to truth of our great leader. We must give up our pet theories of transmutation, spontaneous generation, etc., and seek in nature what God has put there rather than try to put there some system which our imagination has devised, etc., etc. (*Vide* Agassiz, *passim*.) The good old Prof. was melted to tears, and wepped profusely."

After the sermon the passengers walked the deck on that historic April 2 and were startled to see a strange dark cloud on their right, landward. The captain told them that they were passing Petersburg, Virginia, and that the cloud looked like smoke. "We think," Mrs. Agassiz wrote in her diary, "it may be the smoke of a great, decisive engagement going on, while we sail peacefully along." It was indeed a decisive battle in the Civil War, in which both Richmond and Petersburg were taken by the Union Army. Before surrendering Richmond, desperate Confederate forces set fire to the city, and it was probably the capital on fire rather than cannon smoke that the passengers of the *Colorado* saw. During the following week, as they sailed south, President Lincoln visited the smoking ruins of Richmond, and on April 9 Lee surrendered at Appomattox.

Those on board the *Colorado* knew nothing of these events until weeks later, after they landed at Rio de Janeiro and letters had arrived on other ships. By that time both of William's younger brothers, who had survived the siege of Charleston, had begun planning new lives—plans that would affect the James family for many years. News of peace and his parents' rejoicing William would get in letters from home, but the whole story he was not to know until his own return a year later.

Meanwhile William was finding the voyage anything but the pleasant excursion he had expected. The ship had scarcely passed Petersburg before the trade winds, which Mrs. Agassiz had supposed to be "gentle breezes to float us peacefully southward," began "blowing like fury." The misery the winds caused William James aroused her motherly sympathy. In her diary she described him as "Bright, thoughtful, well-informed; his companionship will always be a pleasure. He has been woefully seasick with that kind of seasickness that makes the head giddy and heavy." It was William's opinion that "No one has a right to write about the 'nature of Evil,' or to have any opinion about evil, who has not been at sea. . . . My seasickness did not take an actively nauseous form after the first night and second morning; but for twelve mortal days I was, body and soul, in a more indescribably hopeless, homeless and friendless state than I ever want to be in again. We had a head wind and tolerably rough sea all that time. The trade winds, which I thought were gentle zephyrs, are hideous moist gales that whiten all the waves with foam. . . ."

II

At ten o'clock Saturday morning, April 22, the *Colorado* sailed into Rio harbor without a pilot. William was agog with excitement and admiration for the magnificent scenery: "The boldest, grandest mountains, far and near," he wrote his parents Sunday evening. "The palms and other trees of such vivid green as I never saw anywhere else. The town 'realizes' my idea of an African town in its architecture and effect. Almost everyone is a negro or a negress, which words I perceive we don't know the meaning of with us; a great many of them are native Africans and tattooed. The men have white linen drawers and short shirts of the same kind over them; the women wear huge turbans, and have a peculiar rolling gait that I have never seen any approach to elsewhere. Their attitudes as they sleep and lie about the streets are picturesque to the last degree." Hunt's former apprentice pulled out his notebook and sketched the exotic types.

At noon William went ashore with eight other members of the expedition. He found the "strange sights, the pleasure of walking on terra firma, the delicious smell of land, compared with the hell of the last three weeks . . . perfectly intoxicating. Our Portuguese went beautifully,—every visage relaxed at the sight of us and grinned from ear to ear. The amount of fraternal love that was expressed by bowing and gesture was tremendous." They had the best dinner William ever ate, costing one hundred forty thousand reis, "Paid for by the rich man of the party." On closer inspection he found the Brazilians "a pale Indian color, without a particle of red and with a very aged expression. They are very polite and obliging. *All* wear black beaver hats and glossy black frock coats, which makes them look like *des épiciers endimanchés*." After returning to the ship at eleven p.m. William lay awake most of the night listening to the "soft notes of the vampire outside of the awning"— maybe not a vampire, but not knowing what it was "we'll call it the vampire." Sunday he and Tom Ward went ashore by themselves and continued to enjoy the new and strange sights. Late April was the beginning of winter in Rio, and the weather reminded William of Newport.

While Professor and Mrs. Agassiz visited the Emperor, William and the other assistants on the expedition explored the city, and in a few days Corcovado, the spectacular peak overlooking the Rio harbor. On the second day of his "shore leave" William suffered an "abdominal tumefaction for having eaten bananas all day." He had gorged himself not because Brazil bananas were more delicious than ripe bananas anywhere, but because they were "*so* filling at the price." On the whole he found his companions "a very uninteresting crew," except for his friend Tom Ward, and Professor Agassiz, who now seemed both "fascinating" and "childlike."

But as usual, separation from his family increased William's appreciation of every one of them, as he confessed in a homesick paragraph: "Dear old Father, Mother, Aunt Kate, Harry and Alice! You little know what thoughts I have had of you since I have been gone. And I have felt more sympathy with Bob and Wilk than ever, from the fact of my isolated circumstances being more like theirs than the life I have led hitherto. Please send them this letter. . . . Thank Aunt Kate once more [for financing the trip]. Kiss Alice to death. I think Father is the *wisest* of all men whom I know."

The actual collecting of zoological specimens began early in May. While the Agassizes made a long visit to the Emperor's summer palace, one group of Americans with native guides set out for the interior, and the following week another began a three-hundred-mile trek to the lower reaches of the Rio Doce and the Rio San Francisco. Agassiz would go several weeks later by coastal steamer up to Pará, at the mouth of the Amazon, where he would rendezous with the two exploring parties. But William James was not assigned to either group, to his great disappointment. Agassiz left him at Rio to set up, with Hunnewell's assistance, an improvised marine laboratory. At low tide he collected and began classifying the jellyfish, though he was tormented by "unlimited itching of the skin, caused by flies and mosquitoes, and worst of all on both cheeks and one side of the neck by a virulent ringworm." Then suddenly the boy was violently ill with a high fever. Hunnewell managed to get him to a hospital, where he stayed eighteen days. The Agassizes, in the country with the Emperor, knew nothing of William's illness until their return to Rio, by which time he was out of the hospital. Hunnewell had nursed him and slept in the room with him without regard to his own danger, even though Brazilian doctors diagnosed the disease

as smallpox. Agassiz, who had taken an M.D. degree before coming
to America, said he thought William had had varioloid, a disease
less severe than smallpox, but William was sure that whatever he
had had, it was not mild. His eyes were so severely affected that for
a while he feared he might lose his sight.

It is not surprising that this experience frightened the young man
and shook his confidence. About the middle of May, after the
danger was over, he wrote his father that it would be foolish for
him to continue the Brazil adventure. He was not strong enough for
the trip up the Amazon, and collecting was not his *forte* anyway.
He had made a serious mistake in coming, and the best thing would
be to swallow his pride, admit his blunder, and return as soon as he
was strong enough to travel. Agassiz was reluctant to "lose a pair
of hands," but he was sympathetic and offered to help William in
any way he could, even to providing money for his passage.

On June 3, four weeks after his illness began, William wrote
again from a hotel where he was staying temporarily: "I sent a
letter home, I think about a fortnight ago, telling you about my
small-pox etc., but as it went by a sailing vessel it is quite likely that
this may reach you first. That was written from the *maison de santé*
where I was lying in the embrace of the loathsome goddess, and
from whose hard straw bed, eternal chicken and rice, and extor-
tionate prices I was released yesterday. The disease is over, and
granting the necessity of having it, I have reason to think myself
most lucky. My face will not be marked at all, although at present
it presents the appearance of an immense ripe raspberry." He then
described how it felt to be able to dress, see friends, go and come, and
feel strength returning. "Now that I know I am no longer an object
of infection, I am perfectly cynical as to my appearance and go into
the dining-room here when it is at its fullest, having been invited
and authorized thereto by the good people of the hotel." He would
remain in the hotel for another week "before returning to my
quarters," despite the expense, because he needed "a soft bed instead
of a hammock, and an arm-chair instead of a trunk to sit upon for
some days yet."

William continued for some time to feel that his coming had
been a mistake, "and a pretty expensive one both for you, dear old
Father, and for the dear generous old Aunt Kate." Instead of
learning natural history he was mechanically packing barrels of

specimens collected by others. And his expenses would be not six hundred to seven hundred dollars as he had been led to expect, but nearer three times that amount. Aside from the expense, he felt that he could not "afford the excursion mentally." He had said to himself before leaving home: "W.J., in this excursion you will learn to know yourself and your resources somewhat more intimately than you do now, and will come back with your character considerably evolved and established." The test had come sooner than he had expected, and the outcome too: "I am now certain that my forte is not to go on exploring expeditions. I have no inward spur goading me forwards on that line, as I have on several speculative lines. I am convinced now, for good, that I am cut out for a speculative rather than an active life,—I speak now only of my *quality;* as for my *quantity*, I became convinced some time ago and reconciled to the notion, that I was one of the very lightest of featherweights."

In some of his self-analysis William James had come near the truth, especially in his conclusion that he was created for "speculative" work, and that monotonous routine was naturally repugnant to him. But he underrated his endurance and "quantity," partly because he had not yet recovered from the debilitating effects of whatever disease he had had, partly because he was trying to justify his giving up and going home—a kind of "rationalizing" which later, as a psychologist, he would understand perfectly. However, getting the money to return home immediately proved a little awkward, and Agassiz really did need him; but—most important of all—with returning health William James recovered his zest for adventure. Actually, he had not yet had any experience of the kind of exploring which all his companions except Hunnewell had been getting while he was lying in the hospital.

On July 28, William was aboard a coastal steamer bound not for Boston but for Belé, do Pará (known today as Belém, but the Agassiz party always called it Pará). An oculist had assured him that the neuralgia-like pains behind his eyeballs would very soon stop, and that his sight would not be impaired. The ship which took him and the Agassizes up the coast was small and dirty, and even Mrs. Agassiz thought very uncomfortable, but it was not sailing against trade winds and the motion did not make William seasick. This was a cause for elation, and gave him confidence in his ability to stand the hardships of a trip up the Amazon.

III

William had left Rio with the Agassizes hoping to find at Pará a ship bound for North America, but he was still with them on August 9 when they boarded the river steamer *Icamiaba*, which was to take them up the Amazon to Santarém, about three hundred fifty miles from the coast. By the time they reached the mouth of the Xingu (then spelled Singu), about two hundred fifty miles from the coast, he had lost all desire to turn back. To his parents he wrote: "Now that the real enjoyment of the expedition is beginning and I am tasting the sweets of these lovely forests here [at the mouth of the Singu], I find it impossible to tear myself away, and this morning I told Prof I would see the Amazon trip through at any rate." The "any rate" referred to the fact that Agassiz hoped to stay on in Brazil after the completion of the Amazon trip, perhaps even extend the expedition to another year.

At last, aboard the *Icamiaba*, William had begun to find that he was learning the zoology and botany he had hoped would be the reward of the trip. The Professor "pitches into me right and left," he wrote home, "and wakes me up to a good many imperfections. This morning he said I was 'totally uneducated.' He has done me much good already, and will evidently do me more before I have got through with him." William's hammock was swung close to the Professor's, and thirty years later he still recalled the moonlit night when his teacher whispered, "James, are you awake? *I* cannot sleep; I am too happy; I keep thinking of these glorious plans." But William was more devoted to Mrs. Agassiz, whom he called "one of the best women I ever met. Her good temper never changes and she is so curious and wide awake and interested in all we see, and so ever busy and spotless, that she is like an angel in the boat."

At Santarém, where the black waters of the Rio Tapajós flow into the yellow Amazon, Agassiz sent William, Dexter, and Talisman (an assistant employed in Brazil) out in a native canoe to collect fish from the Tapajós. William dreaded leaving the comfortable *Icamiaba*, but he dutifully set out with his two companions, a barrel of biscuits, and kegs and cans of alcohol for preserving the fish. The boys would rejoin the Agassizes eight days later three hundred miles up the Amazon at Manáos, at the juncture of the big river with the

Solimões, or Upper Amazon, which would become the temporary headquarters for the expedition.

On September 9 William and his companions arrived "with considerable collections" at Manáos. In her diary Mrs. Agassiz described the place as a small collection of houses, half of which were almost tumbling with decay. Its only importance was as a crossroads of river traffic. To Mrs. Agassiz the boys seemed to have enjoyed their excursion greatly, but William did not feel that he had been on a picnic. To his sister he wrote: "What would the blessed mother say if she saw me now, with nothing on but shirt and trousers, both in a frightfully dilapidated state, with shaven head and fuzzy chin and hacked-up hands and sunburnt feet and cheeks bloated with the remains of my smallpox."

At Manáos William received letters from home, which he answered at intervals between September 12 and 15 on the small steamer which he boarded with the Agassizes for the trip up the Solimões—this river was too shallow for the *Icamiaba*. "It is noon, and the heat is frightful," William wrote his parents. But it was "not the dead, sickening heat of home. It is more like a lively baking, and the nights remain cool. We are just entering on the mosquito country, and I suspect our suffering will be great from them and the flies. While the steamboat is in motion we don't have them, but when she stops you can hardly open your mouth without getting it full of them. Poor Mr. Burkhardt is awfully poisoned and swollen up by bites he got ten days ago on a bayou. At the same time with the mosquitoes, the other living things seem to increase; so it has its good side [for collectors]. The river is much narrower—about two miles wide perhaps or three (I'm no judge)—very darkly muddy and swirling rapidly down past the beautiful woods and islands."

Agassiz's plan at this time was for the group to go as far as Tabatinga. Professor and Mrs. Agassiz would go on into the Peruvian mountains, while the Brazilian guide Bourget and William would "get a canoe and some men and spend a month on the river between Tabatinga and Ega." William expected a "gypsy-like" if very uncomfortable time. "The best of this river," he declared sarcastically, "is that you can't bathe in it on account of the numerous anthropophagous fishes who bite mouthfuls out of you." Tom Ward was still out on his collecting trip, but William hoped he would have reached Manáos "by the time we get back there at the end of

October," adding, "I'd rather see him than any one on this continent. Agassiz is perfectly delighted with him, his intelligence and his energy, thinks him in fact much the best man of the expedition." Doubtless Henry James Sr. passed on this opinion to Tom's father in Boston.

Despite the hardships, which he did not minimize in his letter, William did not regret his decision to stick it out with the expedition. " 'On the contrary,' as Agassiz says, as I begin to use my eyes a little every day, I feel like an entirely new being. Everything revives within and without, and I now feel sure that I shall learn. I have profited a great deal by hearing Agassiz talk, not so much by what he says, for never did a man utter a greater amount of humbug, but by learning the way of feeling of such a vast practical engine as he is. No one sees farther into a generalization than his own knowledge of details extends, and you have a feeling of weight and solidity about the movement of Agassiz's mind, owing to the continual presence of this great background of special facts, than about the mind of any other man I know. He has a great personal tact too, and I see that in all his talks with me he is pitching into my loose and superficial way of thinking." At first William saw only his faults, "but now his wonderful qualities throw them quite in the background." Agassiz had done the work of ten men in Brazil, and William thought he would need a rest when he got back to Cambridge.

But if Agassiz was energetic, the natives were not. By this time William had become exasperated by their laziness and stolidity— making no allowances for the equatorial temperature. "How queer and how exhilarating all those home letters were, with their accounts of what every one was doing, doing, doing. To me, just awakening from my life of forced idleness and from an atmosphere of Brazilian inanity, it seemed as if a little window had been opened and a life-giving blast of one of our October nor'westers had blown into my lungs for half an hour. I had no idea before of the real greatness of American energy."

William also felt proud of his country because of the Union victory. American newspapers did not reach him, but of course all members of the expedition discussed the news they got in letters from home. William hoped "our people will not be such fools as to hang Jeff. Davis for treason. Can any one believe in revenge now?" Lincoln's death had made the deepest impression on him. "I can't tell why, but albeit unused to the melting mood, I can hardly ever think of Abraham Lincoln without feeling on the point of blubbering. Is it that he seems the representative of pure simple human nature against all conventional additions?"

IV

On September 19 the expedition stopped at Tabatinga, a military post near the border of Peru. Agassiz had intended to continue into Peru in search of evidence to refute the scientists who contended that South America had never had an ice age, but war seemed about to break out between Brazil and Peru and he was forced to turn around and start back down the Solimões. Next day at Saõ Paulo he assigned William James and Talisman to explore the two tributary rivers, the Icá and the Jutaí, for three weeks and rejoin him at Tefé.

In spite of discomforts of heat, insects, rain, and one disagreeable companion (unnamed) assigned for the trip, William found his second collecting expedition more exciting than his first. The scenery was spectacular, they dined on fresh fish and turtle every day and slept on the beach at night. The Indians were friendly, and William continued to sketch them in his notebooks. Though he thought them "mentally barren," he called them the "most exclusively practical race in the world." On October 16 William and Talisman arrived at Tefé with a large catch of fish, and were happy to hear from Professor Agassiz that it contained nearly a hundred new species.

After the hardships of his month on the rivers in native boats, Tefé seemed a "beautiful little place," and the house in which the Agassizes were installed wonderfully "picturesque." Both the Professor and his intrepid wife were in good health, but the boys who had been collecting on the rivers were in "an awful condition from a kind of mite called 'muguim' which gets under the skin and makes dreadful sores." Poor Hunnewell's legs were ulcerated badly. Nevertheless, everyone joined in the packing of the specimens in barrels, twenty-nine in all, though "hardly one tight barrel among them." Dexter had become the barrel expert, and he declared that he had the same feeling for a decent barrel that he had for a beautiful woman. The barrels were then loaded onto the *Icamiaba*, which had arrived to take the collections and the Agassizes back to Manáos. Dexter and Tal were to go up the Rio for a month, and William

expected to be sent on another trip too, but first he would go back
to Manáos on the little steamer which he now called "the old
homestead . . . the only haven of rest we have in this country."

Weary from the heat and insects, William once more was fed up
with the expedition. In a previous letter to his parents he had mentioned the possibility of returning to southern Brazil with Agassiz,
but he now found this idea unthinkable and planned to catch any
ship he could from Pará to New York when they arrived at the
mouth of the Amazon some time in December. He had little to do
on the *Icamiaba* except write a lengthy letter to his family, in which
he declared that he was able to rest as long as the steamer was in
motion, but "when we stop at a place, the Prof. is sure to come
around and say how very desirable it would be to get a large number
of fishes from this place, and willy-nilly you must trudge."

Winter would be beginning in Boston, and William "often longed
for a good, black, sour, sleety, sloshy winter's day in Washington
Street. Oh, the bliss of standing on such a day half way between
Roxbury and Boston and having all the horse-cars pass you full! It
will be splendid to get home in mid-winter and revel in the cold."

For the benefit of his sister, William wrote that the expedition
had been far less adventurous than he had expected, but more
picturesque. One night on the beach a "tiger [jaguar?]" did come
within thirty paces of his mosquito net, and then kept "us awake
most of the rest of the night by roaring far and near." It seems that
Alice had worried about his encountering tigers in the jungles. "The
adventure with the wild Indians consisted in our seeing two of
them naked at a distance on the edge of the forest. On shouting to
them in Lingoa Geral they ran away. It gave me a very peculiar
and unexpected thrilling sensation to come suddenly upon these
children of Nature. But I now tell you in confidence, my beloved
white child, what you must not tell any of the rest of the family
(for it would spoil the adventure), that we discovered a few hours
later that these wild Indians were a couple of mulattoes belonging
to another canoe, who had been in bathing." This story, with its
rather forced humor, refers to "wild Indians"; friendly Indians
William had seen in abundance, and even had dealings with them on
his collecting trips, but he was to become much better acquainted
with them on his next trip, which at the time of his writing Alice
he did not know he would make.

William was still in low spirits when the *Icamiaba* arrived back at

Manáos. His own legs were now ulcerated from insect bites, which the heat and oily animal diet aggravated. The only tropical fruits they could get were plantains and pineapples, the latter as big as a beaver hat and sweet and juicy as oranges, but he had had a surfeit of them. And his legs had scarcely healed before the Professor wanted to send him back up the Solimões for another catch of fish. William's reluctance to go was so apparent that Mrs. Agassiz tried to cheer him up with such remarks as, "Well, James, you will have a *very* nice time, won't you[?] I envy you." To his sister William declared her a "silly woman. . . . She seems to fancy we are figures walking about in strange costumes on a stage with appropriate scenery. . . ."

The thought occurred to William that he might be able to get Hunnewell to accompany him, for his friend didn't seem to be doing anything except playing with his photographic equipment. While in Rio Hunnewell had learned not only to use his camera, but also to develop and print his pictures, and in Manáos he had set up a combination studio and dark room. But when William went there he "found Prof engaged in cajoling 3 moas [girls] whom he called pure Indian but who I thought, and as afterward appeared, had white blood. They were very nicely dressed in white muslin and jewelry and flowers in their hair and an excellent smell of pripioca. Apparently refined, at all events not sluttish, they consented to the utmost liberties being taken with them and two, without much trouble, were induced to strip and pose naked. While we were there, Senhor Tavanes Bastos (a Brazilian from Manáos) came in and asked me mockingly, if I were attached to the Bureau of Anthropology." William did not record his reply, but he saw that Hunnewell was too much occupied to go on a collecting trip.

His last evening before departure William spent with Dexter and Hunnewell on the porch of their cottage in homesick talk of what they would do when they got back to New York—"go on a regular bust," and then take the train to Boston because it would make better time than a boat, though William disliked trains. That night he could not sleep. At two a.m. next morning he left with two guides, Senhor Urbano and Senhor "M" (William did not try to spell his name), and four Indians. The oldest Indian, "civilized but still a perfect Indian," took the helm of the canoe, while two "excellent stout fellows and perfect gentlemen paddled," the remaining Indian sleeping on the slatted bottom of the canoe until his turn at paddling.

Before setting out William had found Senhor Urbano, his chief guide, reserved and hard to get acquainted with. He was very dark, seemed about sixty years old, and wore a shiny black alpaca suit. Senhor M., "brown as an Indian but from his features appearing to be a Branca," was also "stiff and queer." But once well under way, "Both my companions seemed to have thrown off their constraint of manner with their shoes and coats and we were soon chatting, laughing and joking like old friends. A weight was taken off my mind." From then on William was on the best of terms with both guides. Senhor Urbano proposed that William go into business with him, importing American goods such as cloth, knives, etc., which they would dispose of at his "plantation," and then the following December (1866) William could go home with a valuable cargo of India rubber. Though this proposition did not appeal to him, William was immensely enjoying the trip by the time dawn revealed the beautiful woods along the river and the "day birds began their singing and crying."

"About sunrise," James wrote in his diary, "we met a large montaria . . . manned entirely by Indian women, seven in all." The head-woman seemed to be a "little old lady" who sat at the mouth of the covered boat, smoking her pipe. She stopped to chat affably in Portuguese with the guides, with an urbanity and politeness that greatly impressed William. He could not quite make out whether the Indian men were in hiding or had already been conscripted into the Brazilian army, but, he wondered, how could such gentle, naturally refined people "care for a war or wish to enter an army? Is it race or is it circumstances that make these people so refined and well bred? No gentleman of Europe has better manners and yet these are peasants."

William did not bother to record in his diary how many fish he caught, but he did catch a considerable quantity, which he promptly dropped into the barrels of alcohol. He did describe the scenery, which he longed to paint. The subjects were not those of any painter of his day—trees overhanging the river, stagnant pools over which flies hovered, driftwood caught on a sandbar: "Nothing could be more simple, plain beach, the red west, the giant trunks with their crooked crowns and roots. . . ."

After he had reached Senhor Urbano's home, William continued to confide in his diary the pleasure he had found on this surprisingly agreeable excursion into the back country: "I now feel perfectly domesticated in this place with these people. Never were there a more decent, worthy set of gentry. Old Urbano, especially, by his native refinement and purity, is fit to be the friend of any man who ever lived, however elevated his birth or gifts. There is not a bit of our damned Anglo-Saxon brutality and vulgarity either in masters or servants. I am always reminded, when the neighbors come in to visit Urbano, of our family and the Tweedy family in Newport. Urbano and his gossips talk with just as much beauty and harmony, or perhaps a good deal more, than Tweedy and Father did, in an easy, slow tone, as if all eternity were before them." This is a new note in William's report of his experiences in Brazil, and indicates that old Urbano taught him more than Professor Agassiz.

The visit to Senhor Urbano's home was the high point of William's adventure in Brazil, but the remainder of his trip was more relaxed and enjoyable than the previous months during which he had frequently been dissatisfied and even miserable. He returned to Manáos with a respectable collection of fish, and in subsequent weeks continued to collect on short trips, sometimes alone.

On December 9 William was at Óbidos, nearly four hundred miles down the Amazon from Manáos, waiting for Hunnewell to arrive on the steamer and join him on a trip up the Trombetas River. By this time Agassiz had decided to return to Rio; he hoped for another full year, but William had definitely resolved to go home as soon as his services could be dispensed with after the whole group reached Pará. Now that he was soon to leave Brazil, however, he had begun to realize that he had spent one of the best portions of his life there, and that he might even at times feel homesick for it. His last fortnight at Óbidos, "this paradisaic spot," was particularly enjoyable. To his mother he boasted that he now spoke Portuguese "like a book," and was "ready to converse for hours on any subject. To be sure," he confessed, "the natives seem to have a slight difficulty in understanding me, but that is their lookout. . . ." Still he hated collecting and longed to get back to books and study after this "elementary existence."

CHAPTER VIII Unsettled Condition

. . . having been in a pretty unsettled condition myself, for which I

hope some positive conclusion might emerge. . . .

—W.J. *to Tom Ward*

I

SOON AFTER CHRISTMAS, 1865, William James and Tom Ward
boarded a ship at Pará bound for New York. This time the vessel
was sailing with the trade winds and the voyage was more comfortable than the trip down to Rio had been the previous spring.
By mid-February both young men were back in Boston with their
families. But within a few days William was "sick unto death of
repeating to people the same sentences about South America," he
wrote to his war-veteran brother Wilkinson, who was in Jackson-
ville, Florida, looking for suitable land for a cotton plantation.
William did not enjoy the role of heroic wanderer, and repetition had always bored him. The Brazil episode was not yet entirely ended for him, however, for every morning he went over
to Cambridge to help Alexander Agassiz unpack the barrels of fish
shipped by his father.

The only change William found in his family was for the better.
To Wilky he wrote, "I think Harry much improved, he is a noble
fellow—so delicate and honorable and true—and Alice has got to be
a very nice girl. But everyone else seems about the same, and even
a white female face can no longer charm me as it did in the first
days." Nevertheless, he was still capable of being charmed. His
cousin Ellen Van Buren and the Temple cousins from Newport
were house guests for several weeks, and William escorted them to
a party in Boston or Cambridge almost every night, falling in love,
he said, with nearly every girl he met. But after a month of parties
and flirtations, he began trying to settle down once more to his
medical studies.

Tom Ward was finding it even more difficult to adjust; he had begun working in the New York branch of his father's great banking firm, Baring Brothers, and he was not at all sure he wanted to be a banker. Through Dexter, William had learned of Tom's unhappiness, and William tried to console him in lengthy letters. On March 27 he wrote Tom that John Allen, the Harvard senior, who had been the first of the assistants to leave Brazil, had just arrived after a ninety-eight-days' passage. "He had a horrible time at sea, being within 160 miles of New York and then blown back as far as St. Thomas." His collections had arrived at Bahia spoiled by the sun. "He was sixteen days crossing a limestone desert on which nothing grew but cacti; so there was no shade at noon, and the thermometer at 98°. . . . Poor Allen! None of us have been sold as badly as he. If I had not been to Brazil, I would go again to do what I have done, knowing beforehand what it would be. Allen says *he* would not, on any account."

William also at this time wrote frequently to his brother Bob, who was in Florida too, considering joining Wilky in the plantation experiment. Unlike Wilky, who never read a book and disliked writing letters, Bob wrote often to his family: "decidedly the letter writer of the family," William called him. But his letters informed his parents only too well of his unhappy, distraught, and unreliable temperament. He had found excitement and satisfying companionship in the army, but not self-control, and civilian life had brought back his old nagging sense of inadequacy, which he tried to deaden with alcohol. But he was not as unfortunate as Cousin Bob Temple, who had been sentenced to a year of hard labor on Bedloe's Island for forging a check in New York. This news William wrote to his brothers while he struggled with his own problems.

By the time William settled down after the excitement of his return home, it was too late to enroll in the current term in the Medical School. Consequently, he applied for an undergraduate summer internship in the Massachusetts General Hospital, the largest and most important in Boston, and was accepted. This work would give him some of the experience he needed, and would also count toward the requirements for his M.D. degree. He hoped, too, that he would have some time for reading in medicine, which actually interested him more than learning how doctors treated their patients and recognized symptoms of diseases.

II

Forming friendships had always been easy for William James, unlike his brother Henry, but in Brazil he had learned to value them more, and during the spring and summer of 1866 several companions near his own age became very important to him. One of these was Oliver Wendell Holmes Jr., the lanky, serious-minded son of the witty poet and professor of the Medical School, whom he had known for several years. After distinguished service in the Union Army Wendell had returned to Harvard to complete his law studies and was taking his second year when William returned from Brazil. To Tom Ward, William declared Wendell to be "a first-rate article, and one which improves by wear. He is perhaps too exclusively intellectual, but sees things so easily and clearly and talks so admirably that it's a treat to be with him." Although only one year older than James, Holmes in 1866 was more mature intellectually and had read even more widely. Sometimes, in fact, William thought he placed too high a price on cold logic, and one evening in the presence of Dr. Holmes he retorted that "feeling counts." Dr. Holmes applauded, but Wendell replied, "To know is not less than to feel." These remarks aptly characterized the two young men at this period: knowing was everything to Wendell, but William, then and always, believed that feeling and thinking could not be separated.

In the spring of 1866 William also met Miss Fanny Dixwell, a comely, round-faced, nimble-minded girl with mischievous gray-green eyes, who lived with her family on Garden Street, a few blocks from Harvard Square. "She is decidedly A-1," he confided to Tom Ward, "and (so far) the best girl I have known." He had already written Wilky that Miss Dixwell was "about as fine as they make 'em. That villain Wendell Holmes has been keeping her all to himself out at Cambridge for the last eight years; but I hope I may enjoy her acquaintance now." However, Wendell Holmes continued to monopolize her affections, though he was so absorbed in his own intellectual development that it would be several years before he could be made to realize that Fanny was in love with him, and that for his own good he ought to marry her—as he eventually did.

William wrote Tom that for the present he would like to narrow his attention and association to Fanny Dixwell, Ellen Hooper, Sara Sedgwick, Holmes, his brother Henry, and the Medical School, "letting no breath of extraneous air enter." Of course he could not limit his social and mental life so drastically, and there were several other friends whom he found as congenial and stimulating. One was Henry Bowditch, a medical student who later, after three years of post-graduate study in Europe, became Professor of Physiology in the Harvard Medical School.

But William found no one to take Wendell's place when the latter left in the middle of May for a summer in England. This came at a time, too, when the James family had given up their home in Boston and rented a house for six months at Swampscott, a seaside resort about twenty-five miles north of Boston. William took a room on Bowdoin Street until July 18, when his own two-month vacation would begin; but he managed to spend most of his weekends at Swampscott anyway. However, this regime was not good for the serenity of mind he was trying so carefully to cultivate.

Gradually William's old restlessness was returning, as he tacitly admitted to Tom Ward while trying to say something that would help Tom combat his own greater emotional instability. "I think," he wrote on June 8, "we ought to be independent of our moods, look on them as external, for they come to us unbidden, and feel if possible neither elated nor depressed, but keep our eyes upon our work and, if we have done the best we could *in that given condition*, be satisfied." In handing out this good advice to Tom he could sound calm and objective, but in his private life William found it impossible to be independent of his moods. However, in his attempt to understand and control them he was gaining psychological insights which would later be of great value to him intellectually if not emotionally. "I myself have felt in the last six months," he wrote, "more and more certain that each man's constitution limits him to a certain amount of emotion and action, and that, if he insists on going on under a higher pressure than normal for three months, for instance, he will pay for it by passing the next three months below par."

Recently William had begun to read the *Meditations* of Marcus Aurelius, and "it seems to me," he said, "that any man who can, like him, grasp the love of a 'life according to nature,' i.e., a life in which your individual will becomes so harmonized to nature's will as cheerfully to acquiesce in whatever she assigns to you, knowing that you serve *some* purpose in her vast machinery which will never be revealed to you—any man who can do this will, I say, be a pleasing spectacle, no matter what his lot in life. I think old Mark's perpetual yearnings for patience and equanimity and kindliness would do your heart good.—I have come to feel lately, more and more (I can't tell though whether it will be permanent) like paying my footing in the world in a very humble way, (driving my physick-ing trade like any other tenth-rate man), and then living my free life in my leisure hours entirely within my own breast as a thing the world has nothing to do with; and living it easily and patiently, without feeling responsible for its future."

How impossible it was for William James ever to acquire the patience Marcus Aurelius extolled in his *Meditations*, his whole sub-sequent life would demonstrate, and especially the crisis of 1866–1867, which his restlessness was already beginning to forecast. This harping on his acceptance (or dreaming of acceptance) of the "hum-ble way" of the "physicking trade" was a sure indication of one of the causes of his half-concealed anxiety. Now that he was making his daily rounds in the hospital, the practice of medicine seemed more unsatisfying than ever. He was by no means indifferent to the suffering of other people, but relieving it with such palliatives and cheerful assurances as the medical profession of the day pro-vided gave him little sense of accomplishment. Aside from the obvious fact that the physician used a great deal less "science" than he encouraged his patients to believe, thus taking advantage of their credulity—something completely alien to the character and inheri-tance of William James—he found that the hospital routine made such slight demands on his intelligence that he quickly became bored and impatient. The work was physically exhausting, so that he left the hospital with his back aching from standing and walking and his mind in a buzz of dissatisfaction. He could read Marcus Aurelius until his nerves calmed, but the *Meditations* were only a temporary sedative—as temporary as the opiates so freely given by the doctors to their patients. What he needed, above all else, was a personal faith such as his father had—faith in himself, in some power outside him-self, and in a goal growing out of such faith; but medicine did not provide it.

III

The summer of 1866 was a time of trial and uncertainty for all the James children. For six weeks, from mid-July to early September, William joined his parents, brother Henry, and sister Alice at Swampscott, but he had settled none of his problems and continued to feel restless. William's father was as bright and witty as ever, and his imperturbable mother was, as always, the chief source of the family's stability. While William was in Brazil Henry had sold his first story to the *Atlantic Monthly*, had begun to write book reviews for the newly founded *Nation,* and seemed well launched on a literary career, but he was too ill during the summer at Swampscott to do any writing.

More serious were the neurasthenic symptoms Alice had begun to display. On August 1, her eighteenth birthday, she looked well, and a stranger visiting the family might have thought her a normal attractive girl. But whenever she became especially interested and animated in conversation, she was likely to fall over suddenly in a dead faint. In her fourteenth year she had begun to suffer violent and unpredictable attacks of hysteria, the symptoms of which had been present since her childhood. It seemed to her that her mind and her will were always engaged in a war over which she had no control. As she recorded later in her journal, "When the fancy took me of a morning at school to *study* my lessons by way of variety instead of shrieking or wiggling thro' the most impossible sensations of upheaval, violent revolt in my head overtook me so that I had to 'abandon' my brain, as it were. So it has always been, anything that sticks of itself is free to do so, but conscious and continuous cerebration is an impossible exercise and from just behind the eyes my head feels like a dense jungle into which no ray of light has ever penetrated."

It is not surprising that Alice James had no "boy friends," and that her girl friends were limited to her cousins or girls from families that knew the Jameses well and could be depended upon not to overstimulate Alice mentally or emotionally. Certainly Mr. and Mrs. James wished all their children to have many friends of both sexes, but Alice's precarious nerves had to be shielded by the family—though they could not have wished more than Alice herself to avoid embarrassing or shocking manifestations of her strange condition. The whole family lavished affection upon her, possibly even too much of it, or in the wrong manner. She was not, however, morbid or introspective in the same way that her brother Robertson was. In fact, she cultivated an objective indifference to her affliction, and laughed away impulses toward self-pity. Years later she recognized in William's essay on "The Hidden Self" a great deal of her own experience; the psychologist had indeed gained much knowledge through sympathetic observation of his neurotic sister.

While the drama of nerves was taking place in Swampscott, William's two younger brothers, Wilkinson and Robertson, were struggling for their physical lives in Florida. During his service as an officer in a regiment of former slaves Wilky had developed great personal attachment to the Negroes under his command. Bob shared his feelings, and after the war they decided to try to operate a plantation in the South with the help of Negro labor, to which they would pay good wages. It is not surprising that such an idealistic plan would appeal to Henry James Sr., who, of course, knew even less about agriculture or the South than his nineteen- and twenty-year-old sons did.

Near Waldo (post office, Gordon), Florida, the James brothers bought a tract of land with fifteen thousand dollars advanced by their father—the experiment would cost him much more before it was abandoned. On March 2, 1866, Wilkinson wrote his father that everything was going well: "It is astonishing what good luck we are having. In everything we do we are helped by the elements and the people. The latter are peaceable and hospitable and treat us with great respect. I can't help feeling great satisfaction in everything we have undertaken." And on April 7 he wrote again full of confidence: "Our seed has all been planted, our corn came up a week ago and our cotton made its appearance yesterday and is doing well."

There was a rumor that the Union troops would soon be withdrawn from the South, and Wilky had some fears for the safety of himself and his men, but he thought that if they traveled in groups they would be safe, and he had known danger before. But weather, insects, and the hostility of the natives began to defeat him before the summer had scarcely begun. Still, he and Bob were not yet ready to give up, and with more money from their devoted and innocent father they prepared for a second year as cotton planters in Florida. Their crisis did not come until two years later when Wilky was threatened and insulted in Gainesville and armed bands of Southern men roamed the countryside at night trying to intimidate both Negroes and their Yankee employers.

IV

The shadow hovering over the lives of both William and Alice grew darker in the winter of 1866–1867. At the beginning of November the James family moved into a commodious old house at 20 Quincy Street, Cambridge, which they rented from a Mr. Louis Thies, recent curator of the Gray Collection of Prints at Harvard. This house, just across the street from the home of the President of Harvard and the shady Yard of the College, was where the Faculty Club stands today. The Cambridge residence which William had recommended to his parents during his first year at Harvard had finally been acquired, and in an ideal location, on a quiet tree-lined street, with excellent neighbors. Half a block away, on the corner of Quincy and Broadway, the Agassizes had built their three-story home. A few blocks beyond Broadway was Shady Hill, the forested estate of Charles Eliot Norton, now editor of the *North American Review*, to which Henry James Sr. and Jr. both contributed, and a good friend of the James family. Of course in a short time they had many other friends in the neighborhood. Here William's parents would live for almost the remainder of their lives, and William himself for the next decade. But during the autumn and winter of his first year on Quincy Street he was in no mood to enjoy it. The exact cause of his brooding despondency is ambiguous, though he had symptoms of both physical and mental illness. A year later he wrote Tom Ward, "All last winter . . . when I was on the continual verge of suicide, it used to amuse me to hear you chaff my animal contentment."

Alice's condition had also grown much worse, and her family had scarcely settled in Cambridge before Aunt Kate took her to New York to be treated by a Dr. Taylor. The treatment did little good, but she continued it until the following spring. William wrote her cheerful letters, carefully avoiding any intimation of his own troubles, and usually alluding to hers, if at all, in a light, bantering manner. On November 14 he wrote "Chérie de Jeune Balle [sic],— I am just in from town [Boston] in the keen, cold and eke beauteous moonlight, which by the above qualities makes me think of thee, to whom, nor to whose aunt, have I (not) yet written. (I don't understand the grammar of the not.)"

Anticipating Alice's first question, " 'Where have I been?' " William reported: " 'To C. S. Peirce's lecture, which I could not understand a word of, but rather enjoyed the sensation of listening to for an hour.' I then turned to O. W. Holmes's and wrangled with him for another hour." William did not say what Charley Peirce's subject was, but maybe even that was not clear to him. This brilliant but prickly son of the famous Professor of Mathematics at Harvard was soon to become a great influence in William James's own intellectual development, giving him some basic ideas and terms, including "pragmatism," which he would develop in his own way. But James, intuitive and introspective, would never fully understand Peirce, who was thoroughly grounded in mathematics and the physical sciences and was a formal, rigorous, coldly impersonal logician. No friends could have been more different in temperament and intellect.

Wendell Holmes also excelled William James in logic and was more advanced in his philosophical studies, despite the fact that his professional field was law; but his was an altogether different mind from Peirce's. He was arrogantly intellectual, scornful of his father's popularity as a humorist, and at this time almost nihilistic in his skepticism. In 1866 he argued for "materialism," though it is doubtful that he had any deep philosophical convictions at the time. But how he could argue! One of William's most stimulating experiences was to visit Wendell at night in his white upstairs room, illuminated by a gas lamp that sputtered and flickered, the whole room reeking with cigar smoke. Wendell found whisky a helpful stimulant for his tongue, and many a night the two young men sipped Wendell's whisky and tried to talk each other down, shouting, gesticulating, and pacing the floor in the bright, smelly room.

Sometimes Wendell visited William in Cambridge and they continued their debates there. After one of these visits William belatedly found words for the thoughts which he could not clearly express in the heat of the argument; accordingly he wrote them out and mailed them the next day. Perhaps the most significant aspect of these written-down afterthoughts was James's psychological approach to materialism as a philosophy: "But as a man's happiness depends on his feelings," he concluded, "I think materialism inconsistent with a

high degree thereof, and in this sense [I] maintained that a material-
ist should not be an optimist, using the latter word to signify one
whose philosophy authenticates, by guaranteeing the objective significance of, his most pleasurable feelings."

In judging philosophical ideas not in terms of ultimate "truth"
but in their bearing on one's *feelings*, James was already anticipating
his mature philosophy. But in the winter of 1866–1867 this attitude
reflected the desperation of his emotional life. As Christmas approached, the house seemed gloomy and depressing without Alice
and Aunt Kate, but Alice had not improved sufficiently to return to
Quincy Street for the holidays. At Christmas William wrote that if
she and Aunt Kate were present: "The quip, the prank, the merry
jibes, the flash of poetry, the tinge of pathos, the gleam of love
would all be . . . where now they are not." When he wished for
Alice "so overflowing with good humor & merriment in the early
morning," he may have been still jesting, though possibly she was
gay in the morning and gloomy later.

In February William's father and mother visited Alice in New
York, and on the eighteenth, after their return, William wrote her
that, "They seem to have had a rather pleasant time and gave a
'graphic' account of you well fitted to tranquilize anxiety & annul
pity but not to kindle enthusiasm or excite envy." William called
this a "good sentence," trying feebly to inject some humor into the
grim situation. "The best thing you can do," he advised, "is to come
home as quickly as you can." He had thought she was coming the
first of March, but his parents said it would not be until the first of
May. If she were not better then, William said, she should quit Dr.
Taylor and "come to me and my pills," which she should have taken
last summer.

Apparently Alice had reproached William for not writing. "Do
not think that because I don't write to you I have no longer any
affection for you. On the contrary. I have, and the house is a weary
& empty place without you. But I have of late contracted such a
distaste for writing letters that my affection ends in procrastination.
(another good sentence) I have also been rather unsociable & have
seen little or nothing of any of your friends lately, except Silvy &
Mary Watson at the Nortons' Sunday night. Silvy is growing as
affected as Adelaide and is quite disagreeable to meet. She asked
about you with great affection." William also commented with
some acidity on several other female acquaintances. But he found

Kitty Temple, who had recently visited the Jameses with some of her sisters, "growing upon me very much." It was Katharine Temple whose portrait William had painted in Newport; she had married Richard Emmett. As if the mention of Kitty's name suggested the idea, William then airily commanded Alice "to find out some handsome, spirited & romantic creature whom I can fall in love with in a desperate fashion. The humdrumness of my life is very tiresome. Find her & bring her on." Beneath the facetiousness was an admission of boredom and a sexual need which William's mind was too "refined" to understand entirely.

As William brought his breathless letter to a close, he remarked that "Herry [sic] is doing finely now, I mean in dorsal, not literary, line." It would seem that pains in his back were not the only inhibiting influence on Henry's muse. At any rate, for the moment Henry was feeling better, William worse. But neither was becoming prematurely gray, while "Mother speaks of certain *curls grey curls*, in a tone which implies—can't be that—but no!—'t were too absurd." Eighteen was an early age for Alice's hair to begin turning gray, but most of her pathological symptoms were extreme.

V

The year William James lost from his medical studies while he was in Brazil prevented his graduating in the spring of 1867. In December 1866, he had written Alice: "The present time is a very exciting one for ambitious young men at the Medical School who are anxious to get into the hospital. Their toadying the physicians, asking them intelligent questions after lectures, offering to run errands for them, etc., this week reaches its climax; they call at their residences and humbly solicit them for their appointment, and do the same at the residence of the ten trustees. So I have sixteen visits to make. I have little fear, with my talent for flattery and fawning, of a failure. The appointments are published in January." But perhaps this was anticipating the time when he would apply, for we hear nothing further about the hospital during succeeding months.

On March 13 William attended the commencement exercises as a cynical spectator, as his letter to his two brothers in Florida reveals: "The Medical School held its commencement today and graduated eighty-two students. It seems a very large number. Agassiz was there and 'made a few neat and appropriate remarks,' as usual, about the transmutation question [Darwinian controversy]. Six of the theses of the graduates were read publicly [The theses must have been surprisingly short, or the commencement astonishingly long],—on what principle they had been selected from the whole lot by the faculty I cannot tell—but the look of mingled wonder, pain and disgust at their flimsy badness on Agassiz's face was very amusing to observe."

In the same letter (March 13) William mentioned attending theatrical performances in Boston and a party at Mrs. Lowell's next door. He was not too ill for recreation and paying visits; nevertheless, he was bothered frequently by pain in his back, which made dissecting in the hospital, or even bending over the bed of a patient, difficult and exhausting. He had heard that mineral baths at one of the spas in Germany were good for such afflictions as his. Besides this attraction, he felt that he ought to get a really good command of the German language, and perhaps after a summer of study and medicinal baths he might be able to attend lectures at one of the famous German universities. When he confided to his parents that he would like to spend a year in Germany, his mother opposed the idea, but his father encouraged it. And Mrs. James, as usual, gave in. Accordingly, William wrote his Uncle Robertson Walsh in New York to engage passage for him on the *Great Eastern*.

CHAPTER IX

Baths in Bohemia

My back will prevent my studying physiology this winter at Leipzig,

which I rather hoped to do. I shall stay here [in Berlin] if I can.

—W.J. *to his father*

I

THE *Great Eastern,* the largest steamship afloat, sailed from New York on April 16, 1867, with William James aboard. It was lightly loaded and rolled constantly, but he was not seasick. He read *Gil Blas, The Cloister and the Hearth,* and other books he had brought with him. On April 27, near the end of the voyage to Liverpool, he tried to write a letter to his sister in the great gilded saloon but was distracted and annoyed by a dozen children "up to their eyelids in the juice of oranges." Why, he lamented, were American children so much ruder and less disciplined than European children?

William's first pause was in Paris, where he wore himself out in five days of sightseeing and attending the theatre. In *Les Idées de Mme. Aubray* by Dumas *fils* Madame Aubray tried "to '*reconstituer l'amour en France*'—but they have so much *esprit*, these Parisians," William wrote his brother Henry, "that they end by having none at all. A young man living as we live in Boston feels the corruption, or rather the inanity, the essential ineptitude in the most hyper-virtuous phrases of this play. . . . Dear Brother, how much I would have given to have you by my side so that we might rejoice together. . . ." And how much Henry would have liked to be there! In fact, he was already resentful that William was having such opportunities while he stayed in dull Cambridge, and William, for his part, had a slight sense of guilt (which would increase) because he was doing and seeing things which Henry would have enjoyed perhaps more than he.

From Paris William went directly to Dresden, a city familiar to traveling Bostonians. The ease with which he found a comfortable *pension* run by a motherly Frau Spangenberg on Christian Strasse indicates that he had been directed there by friends of the James family. This *pension* was evidently a favorite haven for peripatetic New England ladies such as those William mentioned frequently in his letters. The American tourists, however, seemed to him "a poor crowd," while the English were "distinguished by their pure and clean appearance, and by an awkwardness which in a certain way appeals to your sympathies. They have the faculty of *blushing* which is denied to the French and comparatively to the Germans, and in spite of all my prejudices I feel more akin to them than to the others."

William was surprised to find how slight were his "impressions" of this foreign city, which he had long heard praised for its refined culture, but he attributed his mild boredom to the passing of his youth. Of course Germany was not unfamiliar to him, even if Dresden was, and also his physical condition severely restricted his activities. His daily routine consisted of reading all morning, going for a walk and "a lounge in a concert garden in the afternoon," then back to reading German after tea. He was soon reading newspapers and conversing in German with ease—he even felt up to beginning Hegel's *Aesthetik*. But he decided that the language encouraged the German mind to express itself before it knew where it was going, "affixing limitations, lugging in definitions and explanations as fast as they suggest each other, and [you] need never go back to reshape your beginning. While with us you will, as a rule, come to grief if you begin your sentence without a pretty distinct idea of what the whole is going to be." Wilky ought to find German thoroughly congenial: "I am sure that German is the native tongue of all Wilky-isms, and that in Germany [he] would be one of the first authors of the age for style." As for German critical commentary and philosophy, such as Kuno Fischer's essay on Lessing's *Nathan der Weise:* "The way these cusses slip so fluently off into the 'Ideal,' the 'Jenseitige,' the 'Inner,' . . . You never saw such a mania for going deep into the bowels of truth, with such an absolute lack of intuition and perception of the skin thereof."

Among the boarders at Frau Spangenberg's was a "pleasant spinster from Hamburg" who came out "strong in Sanscrit and Greek literature (which she knows of course by translations), and in church history," but she seemed to think that New York and Rio de Janeiro were practically across the river from each other, and she had heard terrible stories about a strange sort of people in America called "Yankees," *das allerschlimmste* (the very worst) in the world. William did his best to set her straight about these fabulous Americans. But he found more entertainment in watching through a telescope a young ladies' boarding school diagonally across the street. The girls were aware of the attention they were getting and waved back or made gestures of kissing their hands. But, sad to confess, "Not one was good-looking." William wrote this account to amuse his sister, who kept him informed of the home news, though it consisted of little more than that the weather had been transcendently beautiful, the air heavy with the sweet scent of lilacs, and Cambridge had never been more resplendent in spite of William's absence. But late in May Alice became ill again while visiting Fanny Morse in Brookline and her mother had to be summoned. It was not a happy spring in the James home on Quincy Street.

As the summer passed William met other Americans either living in Dresden or stopping for a few days or weeks. One of these was the Jameses' landlord, Mr. Thies, who had retired from Harvard and was living in Germany with his wife, daughter, and son. William liked all of them, from the "nice old fellow" who treated him like a second son, to the reserved but friendly mother, and the two genial young people. Miss Thies, William wrote his sister, "seems to enjoy herself and the world, and wears a perpetual open-mouthed smile even at the most serious moments," displaying her white, even teeth. The son impressed William by remarking that Americans were "almost as *gemüthlich* as the Germans, at a fire." This, William declared, "is first class, though it can't be appreciated without an intimate knowledge of the German use of the word *gemüthlich*."

One of the traveling Americans loaned William some copies of the *Boston Weekly Transcript*, which made him squeal with "surprise and satisfaction until deep in the night," when he finally "went to bed tired out with patriotism. The boisterous animal good-humor, familiarity, reckless energy and self-confidence, unprincipled optimism, aesthetic saplessness and intellectual imbecility, made a mixture hard to characterize," but totally different from the German world.

However, William himself was too American to be contemptuous of his country's restless energy, and his mockery was mingled with pride. One afternoon while he was sitting on the terrace, a gentleman and two young ladies came up and sat down beside him. "I knew them to be Americans at a glance and the man amused me very much by his exceedingly American expression [appearance]: red moustache, and tuft on chin, powerful nose, small, light eye, half whimsical, half insolent, and *all* sagacious looking, and a sort of rowdy air of superiority that made me quite proud to claim him as a brother. In a few minutes I recognized him to be Gen. M'Clellan, looking rather different from his photographs, but still no possibility of mistaking him; and I learned afterwards he was here. Whatever his faults may be, that of not being a Yankee is not among them."

Analyzing national character would some day become Henry's specialty, but he had not yet had William's opportunities, and his letters plainly conveyed his impatience to share them. William tried rather unconvincingly to console him. "Tell Harry to keep up his spirits," he wrote. "If I were he I would not put off all German reading till I come here—you can do it just exactly as easily at home." Probably William said this in all sincerity, but reflection would have shown him how much easier he himself had found learning the language in the country where it was used. He did give some pertinent advice, however, when he wrote, "Let Harry read (if he wants to) an essay by [Herman] Grimm on the Venus of Milo, republished by de Vries, and compare it with the St. Victor one [Paul de Saint-Victor, 'La Venus de Mile,' in *Hommes et Dieux*]. Both are imaginative rhapsodies, but how much solider the German!" Yet it was the Saint-Victor essay that was especially pertinent for Henry, to an extent that William could not then have known. Henry did acquire a copy of *Hommes et Dieux* and, according to Leon Edel, kept it in his library, finally writing on the fly-leaf "1867–1915."

Saint-Victor's "Celestial Venus," described by William as without "an atom of flesh in her august marble . . . a virile mind nourished by the Idea and not by the presence of the woman," was the prototype of Henry James's future heroines. But Saint-Victor's conception of the Venus de Milo was not William's idea of Woman. For him *Idea* could never be a substitute for a woman of flesh and blood. But at the moment he was too hypochondriacal to permit himself to think of this deficiency in his life. In fact, his back was giving him more pain than ever, and late in July he consulted a physician in Dresden, who advised him to try the baths at Teplitz (today spelled Teplice) in nearby Austria, in the region once called Bohemia.

William's first visit to Bad-Teplitz, which he would continue to revisit at intervals for the rest of his life, lasted only two weeks. The "cure" consisted of drinking bottles of mineral water and taking thermal baths. Many patients got up at six-thirty to stroll in the Kurgarten, drink mineral water at outdoor tables, and listen to band music. "As for me," William wrote his sister, "I am not such a fool, but gulp the water leisurely down in bed, and at nine o'clock, the bottle finished, I get up, dress myself and go out to get my breakfast." Leaving his hotel, the Fürstenbad, on a square named the Badeplatz, he followed a narrow street between whitewashed houses to the stone gateway of Prince Clary Park, breathing in deeply the crisp freshness and fragrance of the morning air. At a small wooden table under the trees a little maiden who reminded him of his cousin Henrietta Temple served his breakfast, which consisted of a big bowl of curds and whey, a roll, and a glass of yellow frothy milk. "I sit under the trees, and absorb the milk, and the air, and music, and let my eyes feed on all the wonderful details of green light which the woods yield; and then I 'dash away a tear' as I think how impossible it is to enjoy it in company with my little sister, and how happy she would be to be transported here for one brief hour."

After breakfast William would take a three-mile walk, then return to the Fürstenbad to sit on a wooden bench beside the door and watch the "town" go by. In the afternoon he would go riding in the country. The Dresden doctor had advised him not to do any serious reading. This quiet, leisurely, sentimental existence did relax William's nervous tension, which had become very oppressive in Dresden, but he found the thermal baths weakening and both his back and stomach got worse at Teplitz. Toward the end of August he became convinced that he would not be able to do any laboratory work any time soon, but thought he could attend lectures in Berlin and do some reading in German scientific works. With this plan in mind he returned to Dresden and packed his trunk for Berlin.

II

William James arrived in Berlin on the evening of September 4 and engaged a comfortable room near the University at 12 Mittelstrasse. T. S. Perry was spending his second year in France and Germany after finishing his four-year course at Harvard, and William had invited him to be his roommate, but Perry would not come until later in September. The day after his arrival in Berlin, William wrote his father frankly about his true condition, which he had been concealing in his letters: "I think it will be just as well for you not to say anything to any of the others about what I shall tell you of my condition hitherto, as it will only give them useless pain, and poor Harry especially (who evidently from his letters runs much into that utterly useless emotion, sympathy, with me) had better remain ignorant."

Then, beginning with the condition which had caused him to go to Bad-Teplitz, William continued: "My confinement to my room and inability to indulge in any social intercourse drove me necessarily into reading a great deal, which in my half-starved and weak condition was very bad for me, making me irritable and tremulous in a way I have never before experienced. Two evenings which I spent out, one at Gerlach's, the other at Thies's, aggravated my dorsal symptoms very much, and as I still clung to the hope of amelioration from repose, I avoided going out to the houses where it was possible. Although I cannot exactly say that I got low-spirited, yet thoughts of the pistol, the dagger and the bowl began to usurp an unduly large part of my attention, and I began to think that some change, even if a hazardous one, was necessary. It was at that time that Dr. Carus advised Teplitz. . . . I have purposely hitherto written fallacious accounts of my state home, to produce a pleasant impression on you all—but you may rely on the present one as literally certain, and as it makes the others after all only *premature*, I don't see what will be the use of impairing the family confidence in my letters by saying anything about it to them. . . . I have no doubt that you will consider the Teplitz expenditure justified, as I do. My sickness has added some items in the way of medicine and cab hire to the expenses of my life in Dresden, but nothing very considerable."

A week later (September 12) William wrote in the same vein to Tom Ward, comparing his symptoms to Harry's and calling them a "family peculiarity." Leon Edel's suggestion that Henry's back trouble may have been sacroiliac displacement does not apply to William's trembling, weakness, and pain in "the small of the back" rather than at the base of the spine, the location of the sacroiliac. That his pains had other sources is also indicated in a letter to Wendell Holmes on September 17: "I am, as you have probably been made aware, 'a mere wreck,' bodily. . . . A tedious egotism seems to be the only mental plant that flourishes in sickness and solitude; and when the bodily condition is such that muscular and cerebral activity not only remain *unexcited*, but are *solicited*, by an idiotic hope of recovery, to crass indolence, the 'elasticity' of one's spirits can't be expected to be very great. Since I have been here I have admired Harry's pluck more and more. *Pain*, however intense, is light and life compared to a condition where hibernation would be the ideal of conduct, and where your 'conscience,' in the form of an aspiration towards recovery, rebukes every tendency towards motion, excitement or life as a culpable excess. The deadness of spirit thereby produced 'must be felt to be appreciated.' " These sound like neurotic symptoms, as William James himself later decided.

The day before writing to Holmes, William had been discouraged —temporarily—to discover that his German vocabulary was inadequate for a book on electricity, of interest to him because galvanic batteries were being used in German laboratory experiments on animal nerve tissues. He intended, as he wrote Tom Ward, "to try this winter to stick to the study of the nervous system and psychology," on which there was an enormous literature, "from a physical and inductive point of view," in German. Thus William's illness—whatever its cause or exact nature—was propelling him into the very field in which he would some day make his own great contribution. Unable to do the laboratory work which would be required of him in advanced study of physiology, and deeply concerned with his own mental and emotional problems, he turned to the study of psychology through reading and introspection.

In Dresden William had felt that it was always afternoon, and he was reminded of the summer days passed at his grandmother's old house in Albany when he was a small child. But Berlin was "just like home" and the "most American-looking city in Europe," by which he meant both ugly and haphazard, though this did not depress him as it would have depressed Harry's more aesthetic soul. "In the quarter which I inhabit, the streets are all at right angles, very broad, with dusty trees growing in them, houses all new and flat-roofed, covered with stucco, and of every imaginable irregularity in height, bleak, ugly, unsettled-looking—*werdend* [becoming]." Both the people and the place reminded him constantly of America, even to "the very same creative spirit that designs our kerosene-lamp models. . . . Nothing in short that is worth making a pilgrimage to see. To travel in Italy, in Egypt, or in the Tropics, may make creation widen to one's view; but to one of our race all that is *peculiar* in Germany is mental, and *that* Germany can be brought to us."

How much of this disillusioned report was intended as consolation for Henry, who had to remain in Cambridge, it is difficult to judge. But that William's first impressions of Berlin were unexciting all his letters bore witness. He had difficulty in finding a satisfactory restaurant, and the condescension of the waiters made him long for the "honest, florid and ornate ministers that wait on you at the Parker House" in Boston. "These indifferent reptiles here, dressed in cast-off wedding-suits, insolent and disobliging and always trying to cheat you in the change, are the plague of my life."

After his first dinner in a Berlin restaurant William took "quite a long walk under the Linden and round by the Palace and Museum." In a subsequent letter to his sister he explained that "Unter den Linden" did not mean, as he had fondly imagined, "an avenue overshadowed by patriarchal lime trees, whose branches form a long arch. The 'Linden' are two rows of small, scrubby, abortive horsechestnuts, beeches, limes and others, planted like the trees in Commonwealth Avenue" in Boston. But he granted that the numerous statues in Berlin, many of them equestrian, did "light up the place."

While waiting for the lectures to begin in the University and Perry's arrival, William decided to write a review of Herman Grimm's novel, *Unüberwindliche Mächte* [*Invincible Powers*]. Henry had been writing reviews for the *Nation*, and William thought possibly Godkin or some other editor might be willing to pay him for a review. On September 26 he mailed his manuscript to Henry, asking him to "read it, and if, after correcting the style and thoughts, with the aid of Mother, Alice and Father, and rewriting it if possible, you judge it to be capable of interesting in any degree anyone in the world but H. Grimm, himself, to send it to the 'Nation' or the 'Round Table.' I feel that a living is hardly worth being gained at this price. Style is not my forte, and to strike the mean between pomposity and vulgar familiarity is indeed difficult." Still, if "ten beauteous dollars lie down on their green and glossy backs within the family treasury in consequence of my exertions, I shall feel glad that I have made them." William's attitude toward his review was outright contemptuous: "The notice was mere task-work. I could not get up a spark of interest in it, and I should not think it would be *d'actualité* for the 'Nation.' Still, I could think of nothing else to do, and was bound to do something."

The review was not printed in the *Nation* until November 28, but meanwhile Henry had replied that he thought it a success and urged William to try again. Nevertheless, he resented William's condescending attitude and told him so: "I see you scoffing from the top of your arid philosophical dust-heap, and command T.S. P[erry]. to tell you (in his own inimitable way) that you are a damned fool." William's "protesting too much" was obviously an attempt to shield himself against the humiliation of failure in his first attempt to publish, and perhaps Henry was oversensitive in suppos-ing that his brother's characterization of a reviewer's style as neces-sarily falling somewhere "between pomposity and vulgar familiarity" was aimed at him because he had been publishing reviews. But actually what had nettled Henry was his brother's bland assurances that he was as well off in Cambridge as in Europe. "Don't try to make out that America and Germany are identical," he wrote bluntly, "and that it is as good to be here as there. It can't be done. Only let me go to Berlin and I will say as much. Life here in Cam-bridge—or in this house, at least—is about as lively as the inner sepulchre."

Henry also complained that his health had not improved as rapidly as William seemed to assume that it had. He felt that in order to re-cover, he would have to strike a happy medium between reading and social diversion. "The latter is not to be obtained in Cambridge—or only a ghastly simulacrum of it." Boston had no theatre worth at-tending, and he knew few people he cared to call upon. "I say this not in a querulous spirit—for in spite of these things I wouldn't for the present leave Cambridge,—but in order that you may not at distance falsify your reminiscences of this excellent place." In other words, Harry, aware that his father could not afford to support two sons in Europe, was willing for William to have his chance, but he must stop pretending that Henry was not making a sacrifice. Of course part of the friction was caused by the old inability of each to under-stand the other's mind and temperament. In a letter to Wendell Holmes, William expressed exactly the paradox of their relations: "With Harry and my Dad I have a perfect sympathy 'personally,' but Harry's orbit and mine coincide but part way, and Father's and mine hardly at all, except in a general feeling of philanthropy in which we both indulge."

But it was not from lack of effort that William found himself unable to share his father's intellectual orbit. "You live in such mental isolation," he wrote his father, "that I cannot help often feeling bitterly at the thought that you must see in even your own children strangers to what you consider the best part of yourself." He read copies of the *Nation* and the *North American Review* in which Henry James Sr.'s articles appeared, but continued to complain that his father's undefined terms and lack of logic baffled him. For example, Henry Sr. scorned pantheism, yet one of his central doctrines was "the descent of the creator into nature." William wrote his father that he had nowhere explained how this idea differed from pantheism, to which the Swedenborgian mystic replied: "You mean I don't explain it *physically*, for I have done nothing else but explain it *metaphysically*. It doesn't admit of physical explanation. . . ." In spite of his having always encouraged William to study science, he complained that scientists made a superstition of Nature, which they could understand only in physical terms. "I am sure," he declared, "I have something better to tell you than you will be able to learn from all Germany—at least all scientific Germany. So urge me hard to your own profit."

William tried to assure his father that he understood him "now better than before," but the logical difficulties remained. He shared his father's "feeling of philanthropy," but on grounds which he admitted to be almost "atheistic"—actually "existentialist," though he had never heard of Søren Kierkegaard, who had died in Denmark twelve years earlier: ". . . for sympathy is now so much developed in the human breast that misery and undeveloped-ness would all the more powerfully call for correction when coupled with the thought that from nowhere else than from us could correction possibly come,—that we ourselves must be our own providence." He knew that this would "appear most pitiful and bald" to his Swedenborgian father, and he took no joy himself in his conviction; yet in the present "general complexion" of his mind, he could not believe that a Divine Providence was looking after man's welfare.

III

While still waiting for Perry to arrive, William James wrote his brother Henry on September 26: "Today is really a harbinger of winter, and felt like an October day at home, with a northwest wind, cold and crisp with a white light, and the red leaves falling and blowing everywhere. I expect T. S. Perry in a week. We shall have a very good large parlor and bedroom, *together,* in this house, and steer off in fine style right into the bowels of the winter. I expect it to be a stiff one, as everyone speaks of it here with a certain solemnity." However, they had a great porcelain stove which should prove adequate.

Perry arrived at the beginning of October, expecting the University lectures to begin around the middle of the month, but "the lazy professors," William wrote his sister, put them off until the end of the month. At last on October 31 he wrote again to Alice with elation: "I am in great heart and back; took my first lecture at the University today and missed never a word of what the cuss said, at which I was much pleased." His growing confidence in the use of the language had also made him more sociable. Emerson had given him an introduction to Herman Grimm, son of the younger of the famous brother authors of fairy stories, and through the Grimms he met other hospitable Germans. But it was the home of Herman, whose novel William had reviewed for the *Nation,* that he found most congenial.

On October 16 William, "resplendent [in] fresh-biled shirt and collar," though he had neglected to provide himself with a "swallow-tailed coat," strolled through "the pleasant wood called the 'Thiergarten,'" and called at the Herman Grimms' home for his first dinner there. Soon after his arrival other guests made their appearance, including a "Herr Professor" later identified as Wilhelm Dilthey, "overflowing with information with regard to everything knowable and unknowable." This was William's first encounter with a "learned" German professor of philosophy, and he was both impressed and amused: "He talked and laughed incessantly at table, related the whole history of Buddhism to Mrs. Grimm, and I know not what other points of religious history." After dinner he argued tenaciously with Grimm about the identity of Homer.

Next day William had himself measured for a dress coat and thereafter socialized furiously. To his sister he boasted facetiously: "I am beginning to force myself into the hard resisting *society* of Berlin, and through Grimm have come to be on speaking terms with several *countesses!* After the custom of their infatuated nation they prefer speaking to me in English. When they address me in German they call me 'Herr Mister'—and I in English say to them, 'May it please your goodness gracious,' etc." At the Grimms' William also heard some famous musicians perform, among them the violinist Joachim, "a heavy, bilious man, a little like Parke Godwin, with an extraordinary simplicity and goodness. . . ."

Of seven courses and four lectures in physiology and psychology offered at the University of Berlin, William James took five courses and attended three lectures. The course in which he was most interested was given by Emil Du Bois-Reymond in physiology. This professor confirmed William's growing belief that the way to approach psychology was through physiology, but the lectures made him almost despair over his own inadequate and haphazard education. If only he had been "*drilled* further in mathematics, physics, chemistry, logic, and the history of metaphysics" he would not be constantly "going back and picking up loose ends of these elements." Nevertheless, he blocked out an ambitious reading program in physiology and psychology, of course more than he finished because he still found reading German much slower than English. Perhaps the time had come for "psychology to begin to be a science." German scientists had made some measurements "in the region lying between the physical changes in the nerves and the appearance of consciousness-at (in the shape of sense perceptions), and more may come of it. Helmholtz and a man named Wundt at Heidelberg are working at it," William continued to Tom Ward, "and I hope I live through this winter to go to them in the summer."

To Henry Bowditch, who was within a few months of receiving his M.D. degree at Harvard, William wrote on December 12: "The opportunities for study here are superb, it seems to me. Whatever they may be in Paris [which Bowditch was considering], they cannot be better. The physiological laboratory, with its endless array of machinery, frogs, dogs, etc., etc., almost 'bursts my gizzard,' when I go by it, with vexation."

Although William found the short winter days in Berlin, when lamps had to be lighted at 4:15, rather depressing, he was still

illiam James. Pencil sketch by himself, about 1866.

Henry James Sr.
Portrait by Frank Duveneck, about 1880.

Mrs. Henry James Sr., about 1880.

Henry James Jr. at seventeen.

William James at eighteen.

Alice Howe Gibbens at about sixteen.

Garth Wilkinson James
"hard at work (reading),"
sketched by William James about 1863.

Wilky James, recovering from wounds
suffered at Fort Wagner.
Sketch by William James.

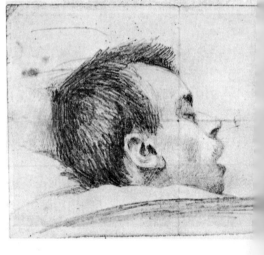

William James about 1865.
From a sketch in his medical-school notebook

Alice James. From a photograph taken by Katharine Loring in 1891.

Robertson James, 1891.

Henry James and William James, about 1902.

The James house at Chocorua, New Hampshire.
From a sketch by D.D.L.McGrew, 1902.

The house at 95 Irving Street, Cambridge.

William James and his daughter Margaret Mary, 1892.

Mrs. William James in the 1900s.

William James at the Putnam Shanty, Keene Valley, in the Adirondacks.

William James in the 1890s.

enjoying his studies and social life when the Christmas season arrived. Now he was invited out to many parties and dinners. One of these was a "surprise" party for Herman Grimm on his fortieth birthday, January 6, instigated by Mrs. Thies and Mrs. George Bancroft, wife of the American Minister to Germany. They planned to drop in on the Grimms unannounced, though they let Mrs. Grimm in on the secret and she ordered crayfish and invited guests. Miss Thies wrote an allegorical poem, which she recited "very prettily," though the theme was vague. William sat behind the American Minister, whom he described to his sister as looking "more like a *villain* than ever. There is no other word for his expression, especially that of the back of his neck and ears. His eyes look like those of a lobster, as if they were on stalks, and T.S.P. says you feel as if he ought to have a pin run through him to be stuck up on the wall like an insect. He speaks German fluently (and audibly) and the Germans speak with ever new admiration of his being minister here, as if they were not able to realize the idea. Mrs. B. is doubtless an excellent lady in private but the impression of an old limp party kid glove which her appearance suggests is but to fill out the form of her conversation."

A Fräulein Bornemann, whom William had met earlier, was also at the birthday party. She had learned that William's family lived in the Thieses' house in Cambridge and had begged William to have his sister send some ivy leaves from the home to present to Miss Thies at Christmas. Alice had dutifully mailed the ivy, and William reported that Miss Thies "sends you the most profuse thanks for them leaves" and Miss Bornemann her "loving thanks." He declared that the latter was so pretty, charming, intelligent, and fluttery with excitement that he "came mighty near falling in love with her."

If he wished, William boasted, he "could see all the best society in Berlin with the openings I now have," but his University work and his ailing back did not permit "a larger visiting circle." The German reserve might be more difficult than the French or English to break through, but, "When you've crossed the sill, I daresay you're as well off [in Berlin] as anywhere else." Well, anywhere except at 20 Quincy Street, for he sadly missed his family, especially "two persons of the moral character of H. James Senr. & H. James Jr." But perhaps he had overextended his strength during the festive holidays, for suddenly he decided that he was wasting his time in Berlin.

IV

On a sunny day, January 18, William James packed his trunk, said good-bye to Perry, and boarded the train for Teplitz. Four days later he wrote his father of his sudden decision and defended his failure to finish the term at the University with the explanation that if he took the course of baths now, he "could have still another turn at it, if necessary, in April,—before the summer semester at Heidelberg began. . . ." He found the Fürstenbad open, with four other "cure-guests" staying there. The staff welcomed him warmly, spring was beginning to "peep out," the theatre was having three performances a week, and with his own books and the circulating library he would be well supplied with reading matter.

Teplitz did not prove beneficial either to William's back or his nerves, but after completing the course of baths he remained in the comfortable Fürstenbad, mainly out of inertia. Then around the first of March he caught influenza, which incapacitated him for travel for a couple of weeks. During these two months at Teplitz in the winter of 1868, William spent many hours writing letters.

His brother Wilkinson had suffered another attack of malaria in Florida, and was now recuperating in Cambridge. "I am sorry Wilky has had a relapse of his fever," William wrote his father, adding, "He and Bob are still the working ones of the family (Harry too, though!), but I hope my day will yet come." Bob had also left the Florida plantation and was now working in Iowa as a timekeeper for the Burlington Railroad. William wrote to him, too, commiserating with him over his bad luck in Florida and praising him for casting his lot "in the West." Bob's mother worried about his finding too many drinking companions among the railroad men, but William felt humble at the thought of his self-supporting younger brothers. "I feel rather ashamed at my age," he wrote Bob, "to stand in the presence of you and Wilky without having earned a cent. But I have not been quite idle notwithstanding, and will, if health only returns, make my living yet."

Actually William had earned twenty dollars for two book reviews. In addition to the one on Grimm's novel, he had written a critique of a novel by Ernest Feydeau, *La Comtesse de Chalis; ou les*

Moeurs de Jour, which the *Nation* printed anonymously on January 23, 1868. Living in Germany had made William quite unsympathetic with French morality, and he condemned this novel for being filled "with all manner of indecent episodes," terminating "in an incident so monstrous that its exact nature is not even hinted to us, and the heroine, in consequence of her share in it, is dispatched by her husband to a mad house."

William's afterthought that "Harry too" was earning money referred to two stories his brother had recently published, "The Story of a Masterpiece" in the *Galaxy* and "The Romance of Certain Old Clothes" in the *Atlantic Monthly*. "I suppose," William wrote to Henry from Teplitz on March 4, "you want to hear in an unvarnished manner what is exactly the impression they make on me." Henry had expressed no such desire, but William gave his opinion anyway: "Both stories show a certain neatness and airy grace of touch which is characteristic of your productions . . . the moral action was very lightly touched, and rather indicated than exhibited." The material "in your stories . . . has been *thin* . . . a want of blood. . . ." By way of apology, "I don't suppose your *literarisches Selbstgefühl* suffers from what I have said, for I really think my taste is rather incompetent in these matters. . . ."

A month later William could not recall exactly what he had written Henry, but feared he had "assumed a rather law-giving tone. I hope it did not hurt you in any way, or mislead you as to the opinion I may have of you as a whole, for I feel as if you were one of the two or three sole intellectual and moral companions I have. If you could have known how I have ached at times to have you by and hear your opinion on different matters, or see how things strike you, you would not think I thought lightly of the evolutions of your mind." Then, a week later, after reading Henry's "latest" in the *Atlantic*, "An Extraordinary Case," William decided that perhaps he had been misunderstanding his brother's purpose in his stories, which now appeared to him to "give an impression like that we often get of people in life. Their orbits come out of space and lay themselves for a short time along of ours, and then off they whirl again into the unknown. . . ." Perhaps Henry had intended nothing more than this fleeting glimpse. "You seem to acknowledge that you can't exhaust any character's feelings or thoughts by an articulate displaying of them. You shrink from the attempt to drag them all reeking and dripping and raw upon the stage, which most writers make and fail in. . . . You wish to suggest a mysterious fulness which you do not lead the reader through."

Henry's reply, if any, to this "discovery" has not survived, but many years later in "The Art of Fiction" he defined a novel as "a personal, a direct impression of life," and observed that "experience is never limited, and it is never complete." William's new view of his brother's fiction was not, therefore, imperceptive, yet all his life he would remain critical of it as too subtle, ambiguous, intellectualized, and "gentlemanly." In fiction, as later in philosophy, William liked to see experience dragged onto the stage reeking and dripping with the rawness of actual life.

By the middle of March William had sufficiently recovered from the influenza to feel the need of a change of scene. Dresden was only forty or fifty miles from Teplitz, not an exhausting trip, and Frau Spangenberg had a room waiting for him. To his sister William wrote a mock-romantic account of his arrival in Dresden on a pleasant Sunday afternoon while the ladies of fashion were promenading in their fine clothes. They were "much struck by the appearance of a young man" wearing a luxuriant beard of two weeks' growth, a handsome soft felt hat ("perhaps a little the worse for wear"), an American overcoat, and a red scarf with gold pin, and carrying an alpaca umbrella. "Who was this noble stranger? Never I ween a maiden, of all those fair ones (faire, aye, and rich, & titled too) whom he met, but tossed sleepless upon her couch that night, & asked herself that question!"

William found Dresden, as he expected, more lively than Teplitz, but quieter than Berlin. Except for a three-weeks repetition of the baths at Teplitz in late April and early May, he remained in Dresden until summer. It was kindly Frau Spangenberg who was the chief attraction. To his sister William declared (May 14), "J'aime la vieille Mme. Spangenberg comme une grand'mère." She had traveled a great deal, spent twelve years in Mexico, and brought back "all sorts of collections, ornithological, botanical, pictorial, and curious," which she cherished "as the apple of her eye." She was so alive and interested in everything that she did not seem like a woman of advanced age; moreover, she was really fond of the hypochondriacal American.

In fact, all German women, from landlady to servant girls, seemed to take a special interest in William because of his poor health, and this led him to generalize about the different attitudes of Americans and Germans toward physical affliction. "I think a person's being sick rather gives him an additional charm in their eyes, instead of making them despise him for a contemptible creature, which the more practical Americans do." Germans were less concerned with outward appearance and more with "the Inward or the Significant. . . . one of these unwholesome, scrofulous, unfashionable musical geniuses for instance, would I am sure in this country receive almost as much admiration from the fair sex as if they were built in a more robust manner."

William was also critical of the gushing sentimentality of the Germans. Once a week a gossipy old maid named Fräulein V. Bose dined with Frau Spangenberg and her young boarder. One day at dinner they had the first strawberries of the season: ". . . I proceeded to eat them in the usual manner—when I was startled by a sudden cry from the Bose: 'Ach! schmecken die Erdbeeren so *wun*derschön!' I looked at her, her eyes were closed, and she seemed to be in a sort of mystic rapture. She had been smashing her strawberries with her spoon so that they made a sort of pulp on her plate with the cream. I replied: 'Ja, wunderschön,' but was rebuked by Mme. Sp. for leaving the berries whole on my plate, for when crushed, 'Sie schmecken *so viel* schöner!' " Such exclamations "implied a sort of religious melting of the whole emotional nature in this one small experience of the sense of taste. The washing out of all boundary lines is implied in the application of the word 'wunderschön.' . . ."

No doubt the Germans "would find us Americans cold, thin, dry, and often prudish and hypocritical," William continued to his sister, but he was becoming surfeited with their gushing sentiment. Even their "sympathy about my health . . . rouses my scorn both for my dorsal infirmity and for the poor deluded beings who see anything touching and 'interesting' in it. How much more pleasing to *this* heart is a good insolent American girl (like yourself), who by her unconcealed repugnance of everything unhealthy about you . . . goads you and spurs you to desperate exertions of manliness. . . ." Alice would later display the same scorn for her own illness, and it is an interesting question whether William transferred his attitude to her or whether it was derived from the whole family's attitude toward physical infirmity, possibly stemming from Henry Sr.'s desire to ignore his missing leg.

During the spring of 1868 William James was tormented by a paradoxical apathy and restlessness which increased his curiosity about the relationships of mind and body. His apathy was physical; his restlessness, mental. The more inactive his body, the more active his mind seemed to become, despite his feeling that this year in Germany was one of the emptiest in his life. He did not lie abed in a torpor, however, but read and wrote incessantly: letters to friends and relatives, meditations in his notebook, even several more reviews which he sent to Henry to submit for publication. He read Shakespeare, Homer, Renan, Cousin, Taine, Kant, Janet, Lessing, Goethe, Schiller, and Darwin, to mention only a few. An American dentist in Dresden loaned him a copy of Mrs. Agassiz's *Journey in Brazil*, recently published, and William was "agreeably disappointed in it," meaning that she spent less time describing sunsets than he had expected, though the book was shallow in content and frothy in style. He was also at the time feeling almost contemptuous of Agassiz because he still refused even to consider Darwin's theory of mutation. To Harry, William wrote: "That scoundrel Agassiz is unworthy either intellectually or morally for [Darwin] to wipe his shoes on, & I find a certain pleasure in yielding to the feeling."

William's intellectual activities were almost as chaotic as his emotions, though underlying motifs could be found in them. He frequently visited the Dresden Museum, which had a fine collection of plaster casts of Greek sculpture. And, like the Germans, he tried to formulate the *Weltanschauung* of those ancient artists. This led him to read Homer and German commentaries on Greek art and literature, and to write out his own thoughts in his notebooks. He wondered if the Greeks' polytheism caused their creations to be *simple*, while our monotheism causes ours to be *simplified*. He wondered, too, why an Italian Madonna could be completely spoiled by an accident to her nose, whereas mutilation of a Greek statue did not destroy all its beauty, which seemed to permeate every part of it rather than the surface, as in Renaissance and later European art. Sitting before casts of metopes and friezes from the Parthenon, he felt that the "moderns should give up the attempt to exhaust thought by expression," for the Greeks did not. To enjoy a painting by Rietschel the spectator must put himself into a sympathetic mood, "Whereas the Greek things never have any point—the eye and the mind slip over and over them, and they only smile within the bounds of their form. They may stand for anything in the scale of human being. . . ."

V

On April 18 William left Dresden for another round of baths at Teplitz, but he took Taine's *Philosophie de l'Art* and Lessing's *Laocoön* with him, and also Schiller's essays on aesthetics, which he summarized and commented upon in his notebooks. His reading, physical sensations, and self-analysis made this April for him a conflict of delight, meditation, and remorse. Long drives in the balmy air of the countryside, when the horse chestnuts were beginning to bloom, gave him sensuous enjoyment almost to the point of ecstasy, but, as he recorded in his diary on April 27: "It seems to me a sin to be doing such things while Harry is moping at home." To Alice he wrote that if she ever felt "any compassion or the like nonsense" for him on account of his back, "let it express itself in renewed and increased attentions and benefits to that 'Angel,' who needs & deserves it infinitely more than I do." This feeling of guilt was all tangled up with his philosophical reading and thinking. Schiller's essay on "Grace and Dignity" seemed to him "very ingeniously thought out but all in the realm of abstractions. He takes for granted the duality of man's being, the sphere of nature or 'Sainlichkeit' being opposed to that of Freedom."

Schiller's doctrine of "grace" touched William's psychological sore spot: "My old trouble and the root of antinomianism in general seems to be a dissatisfaction with anything less than grace." Of course Schiller was thinking of "grace" as an aesthetic effect of supple and coordinated animal movement, but William applied it in the theological sense, that is, unmerited love or favor of God. To William this was not an intellectual abstraction, but a personal, intimate, and urgent problem, all the more urgent because it involved his relations with his adored father. To Tom Ward he confessed during this spring: "I have grown up, partly from education and the example of my Dad, partly, I think, from a natural tendency, in a very non-optimistic view of nature, going so far as to have some years ago a perfectly passionate aversion to all moral praise, etc.,—

an antinomian tendency, in short. I have regarded the affairs of human life to be only a phantasmagoria, which had to be *interpreted* elsewhere in the kosmos into its real significance."

Henry James Sr., as we have seen before, was not indifferent to specific social evils, but his conviction that the source of his own character and actions was God's will, not his own (all wickedness comes from man's assertion of his independent will), gave him peace of mind and an almost saintlike way of life. But his oldest son, lacking both the faith and the physical vigor of his father, could not accept or even understand this antinomian doctrine. In fact, he found it immensely destructive, mentally and physically, his skepticism leading to despair, and despair to sick nerves. In philosophical-psychological terms, the conflict was between uncompromising spiritualism and a naturalism such as William found in Goethe's writings. In a real sense, William felt himself compelled to choose between his father's theism and Goethe's pantheism, and Goethe was to him more congenial and more healthy-minded. Reading Goethe worked no immediate cure, but Goethe did help him to accept evil as an inscrutable fact in nature, not as something ordained by God (as Henry Sr. believed), and therefore capable of being defined and dealt with by practical energy.

On May 1, still in Teplitz, William wrote in his diary: "Have been in a queer state for the last few days, of weak-headedness from bathing, and of a sort of inward serenity, & joy in living derived from reading Goethe & Schiller. Today I finished Goethe's 'Annalen' and feel as if at last I were beginning to feel a little at home in his character. . . . [Goethe's] endless delight in facts & details seems to me no longer the painstaking literalness of a mind which, having no inspiration or intuition of its own, and yet fearing to lose the valuable in anything, gathers the accidental & arbitrary up with the essential in one sheaf; but rather the naif delight of an incessantly active mind & healthy sense in their own operations."

It was with heightened sensibility, therefore, that William returned to Dresden on May 10, where he found Frau Spangenberg's house enlivened by the presence of a number of American women. One of them was a Miss Havens from New York, a small, dainty woman in her late twenties, with a childlike face, and delicate features. Her favorite amusement was improvising (William called it soliloquizing) on the piano. To Tom Ward he wrote that she was "a prey to her nerves and . . . in a sort of hysterical, hypochondriac state, but her mind is perfectly free from sentimentality and disorder of any sort, and she has really genius for music. I never heard a piano speak as she makes it." On May 22 William recorded in his diary that "while listening to Miss H's magic playing & the Dr. and the Italian lady sing my feelings came to a sort of crisis." The intensity and perfection of the music gave him "an unspeakable disgust for the dead drifting of my own life for some time past. . . . It ought to have a practical effect on my own will—a horror of waste life since life can be *such*—and oh God! an end to the idle, idiotic sinking into Vorstellungen disproportionate to the object."

Five days later: "About 'Vorstellungen disproportionate to the object' or in other words ideas disproportionate to any practical application—such for instance are emotions of a loving kind indulged in where one cannot expect to gain exclusive possession of the loved person." These private meditations reveal sexual needs and longings which William only vaguely understood himself because of his extreme idealization of women. The conflict between his longings and his dreamy idealizations certainly aggravated if they were not indeed fundamentally responsible for his own neurotic condition.

On June 23 William wrote his sister that for the past three weeks he had "been smothered in American petticoats," and he did not disguise his pleasure in this situation. "What pleases me most in the female of my dear country is her moral unstainedness—her proud, sensitive & reserved nature—and a total absence of worldly wisdom. . . ." He even admired her "transparency" and naïveté, and declared that "our women are too good for our men," whereas in Europe "they are perhaps often not good enough." William bloomed in the presence of women, and even European women found him charming, but he doted on the unsophisticated New England type, which Henry found "provincial, common, inelegant."

William took great interest in the clothes and jewelry the American women were buying in Dresden, and inquired in his letters about Alice's dresses for the summer. He made a joke of his own sartorial appearance, but his male vanity showed through his mockery. "I have got a neat yellow alpaca coat," he wrote Alice, "white damask vest, blue cravat, and a pair of splendid cinnamon colored pantaloons, *with straps*, very tight & a broad black stripe running adown them." In addition, he had a "magnificent beard," which, if it kept on growing, may rival "that charming tuft which . . . adorned the ambrosial chin of our brother Harry, ere I quit home." He would send samples, but the holes would show, especially in the beard, "which is now even a tighter fit than the trowsers." Miss Thies and numerous other ladies "unconditionally surrendered" when he showed himself in this costume.

But William's conscience reminded him that he had planned to study at Heidelberg during the summer. Finally on June 27 he made the long-planned trip, but six days later he was back in Dresden. He had found the town of Heidelberg shut in by two hills, "the scaling of which constitutes the *only* recreation of the place. As I am inadequate to that, all that remains is to take a turn down a sunny village street and then back to my room. One of the men I went to hear does not lecture, and in the vacation of two months which begins six weeks hence I should find myself absolutely without any source of diversion outside of my own periphery, as the University closes and everyone scatters. I have learned now by experience that, my old resource of walking off tedium and trouble being taken away from me, I require to be somewhere in reach of conversation, music, French and English newspapers, or at least the sight of rushing affairs that a large city gives, to keep of sound mind."

However, William could hardly justify remaining in Dresden for the summer. Besides, he felt better and wanted to travel. Somewhere he had heard that the mineral baths at Divonne, in French Savoy, were especially beneficial; so he decided to go there, after visiting Geneva and Lake Leman. He was surprised to find Geneva so changed during the past decade that he could not find some of the old landmarks that used to guide him to the Academy. In Divonne he was at first disconcerted by the "fire-cracker-like speech" and animated gestures of the French, and felt homesick for the "easy, ugly, substantial ways" of the Germans. But after a few days the French seemed "less heartless and inhuman" and he began to enjoy the neat, facile expressiveness of the French speech and manners. His own facility in French quickly returned. For Alice he drew a fanciful cartoon of himself surrounded by admiring young women, to whom he gave the "cold water cure" [*kalt Wasser Kur*].

The Divonne baths proved as little curative as those of Teplitz, and William finally decided in October that he could not any longer justify the expense of remaining in Europe. Probably his father—or more likely his mother—had ordered him home, for in the third week of October, he wrote from Geneva to his college friend Henry

Bowditch, who was now studying medicine in Paris: "I have been urged by my weeping wife and family to return home without delay, and having sagaciously with finger on nose bethunk me, I believe my wisest course will be to do so. I have a better chance of getting well in the quiet of home, than in tossing about Europe like a drowned pup. . . . I shall turn up at the Hôtel Jean Bart when you least expect me, and have a clean fortnight of talk with you before starting." From Paris, William wrote Tom Ward on October 29: "I am coming home to get well. This vagabond life is not the thing for me. I sail in the *Ville de Paris* from Brest November 7, and if you can manage to be on the wharf when she arrives, you may help me as well as make glad my heart at the sight of you." Tom was still working in the New York bank, and it is to be presumed that he did not disappoint his old friend.

William James looked back upon the months in Europe during 1867–1868 as another wasted period in his life. Certainly he did not find the cure for his back ailment which he had hoped, but he had benefited enormously from the reading he had done in German science, literature, and philosophy. In fact, his reading had been so extensive and useful for his future intellectual development that this year and a half in Europe had been a liberal education—a better one than he could have obtained at Harvard even if he had attended the College and not the Scientific and Medical Schools. And to cap it all, before reaching his decision to return, he had come across a philosophical essay by a Frenchman named Charles Renouvier which would eventually turn out to be of immense value to him. He mentioned this discovery in a letter to his father, though he had not yet read much of the essay and knew only that its author was a nondeterminist empiricist. But we shall hear much more of Renouvier in the near future.

CHAPTER X The End of Youth

. . . For William and myself . . . [Minny Temple's] death made a

mark. . . . We felt it together as the end of our youth.

—HENRY JAMES JR.

I

WHILE IN EUROPE William James, like his father earlier, always
longed for the familiar domesticity of his native land, yet he never
returned home without experiencing a temporary aesthetic and
emotional shock. By temperament he had a typical American contempt for ancient history and the past. And yet after a few months
the hustling disorder, unmannerly haste, and scramble for power of
his countrymen always seemed a bit more uncivilized than he had
remembered. Of course he did not know when he landed in New
York late in November 1868 that the nation was just entering what
Mark Twain would call the "Gilded Age," but he could not help
being aware of an accelerated tempo in the life of the country.
Since May the North American continent had been spanned by rail,
and the frontier was fast giving way to stampeding hordes of
farmers, miners, and land speculators. General Grant had just been
elected President, and the postwar boom was gathering momentum.
In a few years Cambridge and Harvard would have expanded and
changed more than in all their two and a half centuries of existence.

Before long William James, too, would unconsciously respond
to the new rhythm, but in the autumn of 1868 he was weary and
discouraged, though resolved, as he had written Tom Ward, "to
get well." But Cambridge at the beginning of winter did not compare favorably with the health resorts of Europe. The unpaved
streets, little more than country roads, were muddy from autumn
rains. A pedestrian had to be careful to avoid getting splashed by
the hoofs of horses and the wheels of buggies and wagons. Few of

the houses on Quincy Street, most of them wooden structures of nondescript architecture, had shrubs or hedges to shield their dingy exteriors. Behind the red-brick house with the heavy slate roof occupied by the president of Harvard was a row of privies, partially hidden by a scraggy thicket, used by the students because the residence halls did not yet have plumbing. When the students became too noisy in the Yard the president himself, when in residence, would rush out through his back yard to quell the disturbance. Except for these infrequent episodes, Cambridge, suburb of Boston, was a sleepy little rural community. It had changed little since William's first enrollment in the Scientific School seven years earlier—but he was not then just back from a year in European cities.

After the excitement of being welcomed by his parents, Henry, Alice, and Aunt Kate, William's depression returned. Alice's neurotic condition had changed little, and Henry still suffered pains in his back. Undiscouraged by William's failure to find a cure at German or French spas for his back ailment, Henry was eager to seek his own cure in Europe—not at the spas, however, but in a change of scenery, climate, and a more lively social milieu. What he really wanted, whether consciously or not, was to escape the stultifying atmosphere of 20 Quincy Street. Despite the level-headed domesticity of their mother and the vocal histrionics of their patriarchal-looking father, the James home was depressing for all the children. One witness of this period, Lilla Cabot (soon to become the wife of T. S. Perry), has testified to the "poky banality of the James house, ruled by Mrs. James," where her husband limped in and out, "and never really seemed to 'belong' to his wife or Miss Walsh [Aunt Kate], large stupid-looking ladies, or to his clever but coldly self-absorbed daughter." Even as a child Lilla Cabot had perceived that both women were the "very incarnation of *banality*." She thought Henry Sr. genial and delightful, "but he seemed out of place in that stiff stupid house in Cambridge."

Of course Miss Cabot (of the family reputedly spoken to only by the Lowells, the Cabots speaking only to God) may have been a biased observer, and certainly William and Henry did not think their mother "banal," but all evidence does point to the commonplace practicality of Mrs. James and her sister Catharine. And the geniality of her husband was eccentric, or more often satiric than genial. Mrs. James T. Fields, wife of the publisher, tells of attending one of Henry James Sr.'s lectures: "Mr. James looked like an invalid, but was full of spirit and kindness. He not infrequently speaks severely of men and things. Analysis is his second nature. . . . He didn't fail to whip the pusillanimous clergy, and as the room was over-stocked with them, it was odd to watch the effect. Mr. James is perfectly brave, almost inapprehensive, of the storm of opinion he raises." He especially liked to bait the idealistic Bronson Alcott, who once, Mrs. Fields remembered, "talked of the Divine paternity as relating to himself, when Mr. James broke in with 'My dear sir, you have not found your *maternity* yet. You are an egg half hatched.'" William later deduced the reason for his father's verbal combativeness: "He was of such an immense temperament, that when you took him to task for violating the feelings of others in his talk, he would score you black and blue for your distinctions; and all the while he made you feel that the origin of the matter was his divine rage with *himself* at still being so dominated by his natural selfhood which would not be shaken off. I have felt in him at times, away down at bottom of the man, so sheer a humility and self-abasement as to give me an idea of infinity." But a man subject to "divine rages" with himself is not easy to live with, or a soothing influence on a young man trying desperately to avoid a nervous collapse.

It would be a mistake, however, to think of the James home as consistently gloomy, and the unpredictable father as irascible. The house was always open to callers, and William's friends frequently dropped in for an evening of lively argument. One of the most important of these was Wendell Holmes. Wendell had just been admitted to the bar and was working furiously to start a practice. He was writing reviews for the *American Law Review*, of which he would soon be a coeditor, and at the same time reading prodigiously, not only to master his field but also to find a philosophy of law. "This must lead to Chief Justice, U.S. Supreme Court," William predicted.

T. S. Perry had also returned from his studies in Europe and was hoping for an appointment at Harvard. He was still more Henry's companion than William's, but he enjoyed wrangling with them both. There was also the ruddy, convivial Chauncey Wright, twelve years older than William and fond of Henry Sr., with whom he often discussed philosophy. Many thought he had one of the most brilliant philosophical minds of the time, but he had not been successful in his public lectures at Harvard or in his brief period as a teacher and now supported himself by editing the *Nautical Almanack*. Henry Jr. also liked Wright, but philosophical discussion made his head ache.

Another friend who dropped in frequently was Charles Peirce, whom William had known first as a fellow student in chemistry. Peirce was combative as an irate wasp and intellectually arrogant, but William tolerated his unpleasant traits for the sake of his stimulating conversation. Because of his tactlessness he could not secure an academic position. On January 24–25 William wrote Henry Bowditch, still studying in Paris, that a couple of articles Peirce had recently published in *Speculative Philosophy* were "exceedingly bold, subtle and incomprehensible," but "The poor cuss sees no chance of getting a professorship anywhere, and is likely to go into the [Harvard Astronomical] Observatory for good. It seems a great pity that as original a man as he is, who is willing and able to devote the powers of his life to logic and metaphysics, should be starved out of a career, when there are lots of professorships of the sort to be given in the country, to 'safe' orthodox men."

Still impatient for his promised travels in Europe, Henry Jr. sailed for England late in January 1869, and William grimly settled down to reviewing for his Medical School examinations, postponed during his year in Germany. A thesis was required for the M.D. degree, but because of his continued back pains William chose a routine subject, the effects of "cold" on the human body. "I shall not make any experiments for my thesis but just compile what I find in the books under my hand," he reported to Henry Bowditch, still in Europe. To his Geneva Academy schoolmate Charles Ritter he wrote: "At present I can undertake nothing that I am interested in studying because that would lead me to make dangerous excursions in too specialized paths. Nevertheless, I do find time to read a little outside the required grooves."

He pretended not to be apprehensive about the examination, only bored, but of course he worried. Wendell Holmes dropped in once a week to "jaw," and occasionally William went buggy-riding with Fanny Dixwell, not yet engaged to Wendell. But these diversions did not prevent William from "going again through the old medical textbooks," though as he had expressed it to Bowditch, "taking small doses daily, so as not to get *interested* and so fall into *study*—a poor business," meaning injurious to his health. He had made up his mind "to lose at least a year now [after obtaining his degree] in vegetating and doing nothing but survive."

Henry Jr. began writing home from England, and William replied in frequent newsy letters, as on March 22, after John La Farge had visited the James family: "My affections gushed forth to meet him, but were soon coagulated by his invincible pretentiousness, that no one can teach him anything that he does not know already. . . . Father and Mother get on well without you, although Mother and Alice give utterance to maudlin sighs and expressions of affection for you which I endeavor to discountenance." William enjoyed teasing his mother and sister, and the "Angel" himself, about their gushing affection for him. In the same letter William reported that he had written "a notice of a book on spiritualism (*Planchette*) for the *Advertiser* and got $10.00!!!" The review of E. Sargent's *Planchette* in the Boston *Advertiser* (March 11, 1869), which William called a mere "notice," is important only because it shows clearly how early William became aware of psychical research, which later would occupy much of his time.

The James family, like most residents of Cambridge, was keenly interested in the election of a new president for Harvard. The position had been vacant since September 1868, but the Corporation and the Overseers could not agree until the following March even to hold an election, and meanwhile the town seethed with gossip and speculation. Henry Sr. wrote to his son Henry that Arthur Sedgwick, who had become one of the chief contributors to the *Nation* since Henry's departure, was "in the pangs of anxiety . . . that Mr. Eliot should be elected President of Harvard, we [anxious] that someone whom the world thinks better of, should be." The fact that one of the other candidates was Professor Ephraim Gurney, a good friend of the James family, probably had some influence on the senior Henry's opinion, though he was not alone in thinking that Charles W. Eliot was "a man of the grossest lack of tact." But Eliot won the nomination and finally the election. On May 22 William wrote Henry Bowditch: "C. W. Eliot was confirmed President yesterday. His great personal defects, tactlessness, meddlesomeness, and disposition to cherish petty grudges seem pretty universally acknowledged; but his ideas seem good and his economic powers first-rate,—so in the absence of any other possible candidate, he went in. It seems queer that such a place should go begging for candidates."

William had not then the slightest premonition that the election of Eliot would, in a few years, be to his own advantage. On May 21 he turned in his thesis and had his examination set for June 21. "I suppose my star will guide me through it," he sighed to Bowditch, "though I'm ashamed of the fewness of the medical facts I know. I wrote a thesis on cold, nary experiment and nary chance of consulting any books on the subject but those I had, and a few I could send for by name to the library,—so it's of no value. I shall keep quiet till the examination is over, and then go with the family to the country (Pomfret, Conn.) and try whether almost perfect cessation from reading and some degree of exercise out of doors will make a change in my physical condition."

By this time William found it "totally impossible" to study; he could only wait fretfully for June 21. On June 12 he reported to Harry: "My thesis was decent, and I suppose Dr. Holmes [formerly Dean, still a professor of the Medical School] will veto my being plucked no matter how bad my examination may be, but the truth is I feel unprepared. I've no doubt I'll *éprouver* a distinct bodily improvement when it's all over. My feeling of unpreparedness has, so far from exciting me to study, given me a disgust for the subject." But he had made a discovery which gave him some consolation: the actual time he had spent studying medicine was no more than three years and three months. "Three years is the minimum with which one can go up for examination; but as I began away back in '63 I have been considering myself as having studied about five years, and have felt much humiliated by the greater readiness of so many younger men to answer questions and understand cases."

The Medical School examination was oral. Nine professors, in as many separate fields, each examined the candidate orally for ten minutes in a large room. At the end of the ten minutes a bell rang and the candidate proceeded to the next questioner. The examiners graded the candidates by means of cards held up before the Dean. One side of the card was blank and the other had a black spot. If a candidate received no more than four black spots, he had passed, and would be able to practice medicine no matter how ignorant he might be in certain fields. "Buckingham's midwifery gave me some embarrassment," William confided to Henry Bowditch after the examination, "but the rest was trifling enough." And probably his "embarrassment" over midwifery was only his little joke; Dr. Holmes's quizzing was farcical. After asking one question about some obscure part of the anatomy, which William answered correctly, Dr. Holmes said, "If you know *that*, you know everything; now tell me about your family and the news at home." With a vast sense of relief William James could now write himself "M.D., if I choose," as he expressed it to Bowditch. He could also go off on vacation with a clear conscience.

II

William and Alice accompanied their parents on July 1 to Pomfret, where Mr. James had engaged rooms in a farmhouse taking summer boarders. The house, about five miles from Woodstock, Connecticut, stood near the highway, on a hill swept by cooling breezes. "I came here resolved to live the life of an absolute caterpillar," William wrote Henry Bowditch, "and have succeeded very well so far, spending most of my time swinging in a hammock under the pine trees in front of the house. . . . I am far better in every way than when I came, and am beginning to walk about quite actively. Maybe it's the beginning of a final rise of health, but I'm . . . sick of prophesying."

A friendly, pathetic little man named Francis Boott and his artistic daughter, Lizzie, were also vacationing in the farmhouse at Pomfret. Mr. Boott, whom Henry Sr. called "Frank," had fled Boston in 1847 after the death of his wife, taking his eighteen-months-old daughter with him, and had not returned to Boston until the end of the Civil War. William found Lizzie, now twenty-two, "not overpoweringly beautiful," he confided to Bowditch, yet "one of the very best members of her sex I ever met. She spent the first eighteen years of her life in Europe, and has of course Italian, French and German at her fingers' ends, and I never realized before how much a good education (I mean in its common sense of a wide information) added to the charms of a woman. She has a great talent for drawing, and was very busy painting here, which, as she is in just about the same helpless state in which I was when I abandoned the art, made her particularly interesting to me." William advised Bowditch, "You had better come home soon and make her acquaintance—for you know these first-class young spinsters do not *always* keep for ever, although on the whole they tend to, in Boston."

Aunt Kate was now in Europe, having sailed in April with Helen

Robertson, William's "Cousin Helen." Occasionally their path crossed that of the wandering Henry Jr., but most of the time they and he went their separate ways. Henry visited friends of Jane Norton in Oxford (the Nortons had rented Shady Hill and were now living in Europe), then went to Switzerland for midsummer. Once his mother had become alarmed over his expenses, but his vigorous protests caused her to advise him on July 24 to go to Italy for his health, "and do not, I pray you, cramp yourself in any way to hinder your fullest enjoyment of it, you dear reasonable over-conscientious soul!"

Mrs. James was less sympathetic with William, but her reports to Henry Jr. were probably more accurate as a consequence. She wrote that Will spent many hours reading Browning's poems, which he discussed with Lizzie. Henry Sr. talked philosophy and music with Mr. Boott, who had taken singing lessons in Italy and written songs which had a limited reputation among his friends on both sides of the Atlantic. On August 8 Mrs. James wrote Henry, still in Switzerland, that Will had been morbid before coming to Pomfret, but had been greatly benefited by his change of habits. Wendell Holmes had spent a weekend with them, during which he and Will had walked and driven through lush countryside. By September, however, William's health had suffered a slight decline, probably the result of his returning sense of guilt over wasted time. But in spite of the setback, he was planning to visit friends in Newport. Soon after this Henry was in Venice, which reminded him of Newport, where he supposed William to be: "The same atmosphere, the same luminosity."

While William nursed his back and nerves in Pomfret and read Browning in the hammock and Henry reveled in the natural beauties of the Alps or the art treasures of Italy, their younger brothers were having a miserable summer. Wilky had returned to the Florida plantation, where he was futilely trying to raise cotton. Although his ignorance of agriculture had been a handicap, the main reason for his defeat was the hostility of the white natives, who harassed and sabotaged his efforts beyond endurance. Bob expected soon to leave the railroad position he now had in Galveston, Texas, and go to Milwaukee, Wisconsin, to try a new business venture with Wilky. That would require more financial help from their patient father.

Both William and Henry were sympathetic with their younger brothers during these painful months, but their lives were now more than ever completely separated from them. The two older brothers were drawn to each other not only by their closeness in age but also by the similarities of their experience, by their interests—different as their professional ambitions were—and by their intellectual dependence upon each other. Although William had not yet been to Italy, his earlier attempts to paint and the hours he had spent in the museums of England, France, and Germany had given him extensive knowledge of painting and sculpture. It was to William, therefore, that Henry poured out in page after page of enraptured prose his exciting discoveries and observations in the midst of the art treasures of Rome, Florence, and Venice.

William was less dependent on Henry's letters than Henry on his, because he was with his family, and Henry was by himself and often lonely. But the brothers were never again quite as close to each other as in 1869–1870 while Henry was in Europe and William was brooding in Cambridge, a reversal of their roles in '67–'68. From the Hôtel d'Angleterre in Rome Henry wrote on October 30: "Some four days since I despatched to you and Father respectively, from Florence, two very doleful epistles, which you will in course of time receive. No sooner had I posted them, however, than my spirits were revived by the arrival of a most blessed brotherly letter from you. . . . Verily, it is worthwhile pining for letters for 3 weeks to know the exquisite joy of final relief. I took yours with me to the theatre whither I went to see a comedy of Goldoni most delightfully played and read and re-read it between the acts."

Again just after Christmas the receipt of a letter from William moved Henry to reply immediately, though he had mailed a letter only two days earlier. "Your letter fills me with a divine desire to occupy for an hour that old cane-bottomed chair before your bedroom fire." Henry's eagerness for William's letters was by no means due entirely to loneliness, for he frequently met friends of the James family, who were always traveling around Europe. In Rome he ran across Mr. and Mrs. George Ripley, the latter one of his father's Fourier-socialist friends. And there was the ubiquitous Charles Norton, who turned up in London, Rome, and Pisa. In Rome Henry "went about a whole morning with Charles N. and profited vastly by his excellent knowledge of Italian history and art." Later Henry visited the Nortons in Florence, where they were "established in a cold capricious villa not too far from the city gates. . . ."

While in Florence Henry discovered that for a fortnight in Rome he had sat at breakfast with William Lecky, whose *History of Morals* William had been reading and mentioned in a letter, but "we never spoke. He is very young and lanky and blond and soft-looking—but most pleasant of face: with quite the look of a better-class Cambridge [Harvard] divinity student. I have been sorry ever since that I did not address him. . . ." Despite the anticlimax, Henry knew that the anecdote would not fail to interest William, with his great curiosity about the appearance and personality of the authors he read.

After he had left Italy, Henry wrote satirically: "When Aunt Kate gets back make much of her! She's not the common clay you parted with. She has trod the perfumed meadows of Elysium—she has tasted of the magic of the south and listened to the echoes of the past!" What finally forced Henry to leave Italy earlier than he wished was constipation, which in turn caused a revival of the pains in his back. In numerous letters he discussed his symptoms with his M.D. brother and reported the ineffective remedies prescribed by several Italian doctors. He thought he might find a cure in the famous British health resort at Great Malvern, quite fashionable at the time. On February 13, 1870, Henry had been at Great Malvern for a week and was trying to cheer himself up with the "ghastly mockery of a fraternal talk" by letter, his heart reverting "across the awful leagues of wintry ocean to that blessed library in Quincy Street, and to the image of the gathering dusk, the assembled family, the possible guest, the impending—oh! the impending, American *tea!*" Scarcely three weeks later he was so low-spirited that he even berated the English character. The men never uttered a word of appreciation or enjoyment of anything. And the women were so drearily wanting in, "what shall I call it?—Clover Hooper [the future wife of Henry Adams] has it—intellectual grace—Minny Temple has it—moral spontaneity." Presently he took it all back, but it was evidently time for Henry to return to America, where he could at least get fresh vegetables, the lack of which he had finally decided was the cause of his health problem.

But before Henry James returned to Cambridge in May, he learned that William had suffered a nervous collapse—actually as early as January, but Henry never knew when William exaggerated his symptoms and had failed to understand the seriousness of his brother's condition. On January 19 William had written that his eyelids were inflamed "by an overdose of chloral (a new hypnotic remedy which I took for the fun of it as an experiment, but whose effects are already on the wane)." Since those months at Boulogne-sur-mer Henry had been familiar with his brother's "experiments," and had no reason to suspect he had taken the drug for any other purpose than "fun"—though the effects of the chloral on his condition may have been anything but salutary. Nor did Henry have any inkling that for the past several months his cousin Minny Temple, with whom he had compared British women so greatly to their disfavor, had been dying with tuberculosis of the lungs. Minny's death was to have profound psychological consequences for both William and Henry.

III

Ever since the summer of 1858, when the James family had first taken up residence in Newport, Mary Temple—or "Minny," as everyone called her—had been one of William's most admired and admiring friends. All the Jameses were fond of the four orphan girls being reared by the Tweedys, but Minny's vivacity, her wit, and her frankness made her a special favorite of the two older James brothers. In 1858 she was only thirteen, a little too thin, pale, nervous, and perhaps not really beautiful, though her radiant personality made one feel that she was. Henry James Jr. later said that he and all his male friends were in love with her. This statement was somewhat exaggerated, but in memory Henry may have felt it to be true. Minny was almost too fond of dancing, attending the theatre, and social festivities. Because of her infectious high spirits she was frequently invited to visit fun-loving uncles, aunts, and cousins in New York City, Albany, Boston, and Philadelphia, and by her early twenties her life had come to be an almost continuous round of visits, parties, and revelry, though her older sisters thought her "queer," meaning that beneath her apparent frivolity she was thoughtful and introspective—how deeply so no one knew except the young lawyer John Gray, to whom she poured out her mind and heart in long self-revealing letters during the last year of her life.

In 1869–1870 William knew that Minny was not well and may have heard that she was having hemorrhages, but he was not in regular correspondence with her and did not see her frequently. It was pure chance that her physical crisis came to a tragic end just at the time that he was going through a serious psychological crisis himself. And just as William was ignorant of the real inner life of Minny during a crucial phase of his own psychological drama, so was Henry not aware of the depth of William's despair, revealed in his secret diary and in the disguised "case history" which he later published in his *Varieties of Religious Experience.*

On December 21, 1869, William wrote in his diary: "Nature & life have unfitted me for any affectionate relations with other individuals—it is well to know the limits of one's individual faculties, in order not to accept intellectual[ly] the verdict of one's personal feeling & experience as the measure of objective fact—but to brood over them with feeling is 'morbid.'" No matter how one interprets this intellectual statement of the young man's situation, it is obvious that he felt the necessity of controlling (or inhibiting) his emotional longings and normal urges to live a full life of his senses, which would include love and sex (even later, as a psychologist, he had a Victorian squeamishness over this three-letter word) and perhaps marriage. Given the condition of his nervous system, whatever the cause of his back pains and frequent headaches, it is not difficult to understand his conviction that he must and *ought* to deny himself the affectional relations which his nature craved and his conscience rejected.

In the same entry (December 21) William tried to find consolation in the thought that: "I may not study, make, or enjoy—but I can will. I can find some real life in the mere respect for other forms of life as they pass, even if I can never embrace them as a whole or incorporate them with myself." In other words, if he could not actively participate in the life he desired, he could at least be an appreciative observer—the very theme later of some of Henry's stories, such as "The Beast in the Jungle" and "The Jolly Corner," but this was not possible for William, for whom activity was life itself.

On New Year's Day, 1870, William recorded an extremely revealing experience: "For a few days I have had good reason to think that my back is getting into its second stage, one of real improvement; and I have been so weakly excited [i.e., allowed himself to become excited over the hope of recovery] . . . as to have passed several sleepless nights." His New Year's resolution was: "This month I will wait patiently, and if at the end of it things look as they do now I will try the lifting cure. I will try no counter irritation until 3 weeks after *that*. If I do find myself improving instead of steadily running down as hitherto, I must still stifle all eagerness to study. If this year I finish Father's works, Schopenhauer, Maudsley, Boismont, Griesinger, Spencer's Biology, Fechner, & Fichte's Introduction I shall have done well; and must not think of doing more." One would think not! Henry James Sr., the first on the list, had published to date thirteen books, any one of which most readers would have found a formidable task to read.

Except for Schopenhauer, whom James soon came to hate, and Henry James Sr., the books and authors he named * were concerned with the pathology of the brain, or mind-body relationships (*Seelen-frage*), which were at this particular time of marked interest to James. Whether he finished his father's works in 1870 is not known, but the barrier which always prevented his finding satisfaction in Henry Sr.'s theology would have been an even greater one during this year of his mental crisis. The basis of his father's faith was the losing of the individual self in the selfhood of God, but William found it necessary to assert his selfhood to survive. On January 5, after reading Plato, he copied, as if making it his motto: "Ein ganzer Mensch—ein ganzer Wille"—a whole man is a whole will.

On February 1 William recorded at greater length in his diary: "a great dorsal collapse about the 10th or 12th of last month has lasted with a slight interruption till now, carrying with it a moral one. To day, I about touched bottom, and perceive plainly that I must face the choice with open eyes: Shall I *frankly* throw the moral business overboard, as one unsuited to my innate aptitudes, or shall I follow it, and it alone, making everything else merely stuff for it?" The word *moral* must be interpreted here in terms of a philosophical (almost religious) conception of "free will." For most people, no doubt then as now, the doctrine of free will is not a personal, intimate, fateful problem. But for William it was. This is not to say that an unanswered philosophical question made him physically and mentally ill. There were other causes, but his desperate concern to find the answer was a symptom of his sickness. A year before he had written Tom Ward: "I'm swamped in an empirical philosophy. I feel that we are Nature through and through, that we are wholly conditioned, that not a wiggle of our will happens save as the result of physical laws; and yet, notwithstanding, we are *en rapport* with reason." The war between his reason and his sense of helplessness had

* See Notes, p. 531.

been intensified by talks with Chauncey Wright, a formidably logical and relentless determinist, as well as by the reading he was doing of psychologists—Fechner, for example, in his *Elemente der Psychophysik* and *Über die Seelenfrage,* claimed to have measured sensation and reduced it to a mathematical formula. James's later doctrine of "The Will to Believe" and his half-scientific, half-personal interest in faith-healing and psychic research are plainly foreshadowed in the introspection recorded in his diary on a possible relationship between his moral character and his "dorsal collapse."

"Who knows," he continued writing on February 1, "but the moral interest may be developed. Hitherto I have given it no real trial, and have deceived myself about my relation to it, using it in reality only to patch out the gaps which fate left in my other kinds of activity, and confusing everything together. Hitherto I have tried to fire myself with the moral interest, as an aid in the accomplishing of certain utilitarian ends of attaining certain difficult but salutary habits. I tried to associate the feeling of moral degradation with failure, and add to it that of the loss of the wished for sensible good end—and the reverse of success. But in all this I was cultivating the moral . . . only as a means & more or less humbugging myself. Now I must regard these useful ends only as occasions for my moral life to become active. In themselves they are indifferent, symbolic, and may change with health and sickness &c. But while they are what they are today, it is my duty."

These words plainly show the mental and emotional chaos seething in William James's consciousness. He was groping for something to believe in so that he could draw upon his will power and actively pull himself out of his mental depression and physical pain. Then he experienced a great emotional shock: the death of Minny Temple. In his diary he drew three sides of a parallelogram enclosing these cryptic symbols: "March 9/MT/1870/" Minny Temple died at New Rochelle, near New York City, on March 8; March 9, therefore, was the date William James received the news, and he was too stunned to think of anything except the fact of her death. He felt as numb as the crude tombstone he drew in his diary.

Many years later William James's son Henry revealed that a traumatic experience presented in *Varieties of Religious Experience* as that of a Frenchman was actually James's experience, by his own admission to his son, who thought it took place in the spring of 1870. If so, it could well have happened between the news of Minny

Temple's death and the next entry in the diary two weeks later. Certainly it belongs to this period when James was "in a bad nervous condition," like his fictitious Frenchman. Here is the confession which the author of *Varieties* (Lectures VI and VII: The Sick Soul) pretended to "translate freely":

> Whilst in this state of philosophic pessimism and general depression of spirits about my prospects, I went one evening into a dressing-room in the twilight to procure some article that was there; when suddenly there fell upon me without warning, just as if it came out of the darkness, a horrible fear of my own existence. Simultaneously there arose in my mind the image of an epileptic patient whom I had seen in the asylum, a black-haired youth with greenish skin, entirely idiotic, who used to sit all day on one of the benches, or rather shelves against the wall, with his knees drawn up against his chin, and the coarse gray undershirt, which was his only garment, drawn over them inclosing his entire figure. He sat there like a sort of sculptured Egyptian cat or Peruvian mummy, moving nothing but his black eyes and looking absolutely non-human. This image and my fear entered into a species of combination with each other. *That shape am I*, I felt, potentially. Nothing that I possess can defend me against that fate, if the hour for it should strike for me as it struck for him. There was such a horror of him, and such a perception of my own merely momentary discrepancy from him, that it was as if something hitherto solid within my breast gave way entirely, and I became a mass of quivering fear. After this the universe was changed for me altogether. I awoke morning after morning with a horrible dread at the pit of my stomach, and with a sense of the insecurity of life that I never knew before, and that I have never felt since. It was like a revelation; and although the immediate feelings passed away, the experience has made me sympathetic with the morbid feelings of others ever since. It gradually faded, but for months I was unable to go into the dark alone.

So great was the panic that William dreaded even to be left alone in the daytime, and he wondered how other people could live unconscious of "that pit of insecurity beneath the surface of life." His mother, especially, amazed him with her "cheerful unawareness of the danger." She belonged to the type he was to call in his *Varieties of Religious Experiences* the "healthy minded." She had never been a "sick soul" and had neither understanding nor patience with one who was. William says explicitly (still speaking in disguise), ". . . I was careful not to disturb [her] by revelations of my own state of

mind." Of course she did know that he was "morbid," and so char-
acterized him in her letters to Henry Jr. But it was not possible for
William to discuss his almost unbearable melancholy fear with her.
This tells us a great deal about his relations with his mother.

And it also does much to explain his dependence on his father,
whose "vastation" near Windsor Castle when William was a baby
resembled in many ways William's "panic fear" vision. He never
doubted that "this experience of melancholia of mine had a religious
bearing," though he continued all his life to insist that he had never
had a truly religious experience. Elucidating the idea that his experience was "religious," the Frenchman in his book explained: "I
mean that the fear was so invasive and powerful that if I had not
clung to the scripture-texts like 'The eternal God is my refuge,' etc.,
'Come unto me, all ye that labor and are heavy-laden,' etc., 'I am
the resurrection and the life,' etc., I think I should have grown really
insane." This is very curious indeed, for William had very seldom
in his life attended church, and was not in the habit of reading the
Bible. But he had to have a supernatural refuge, an all-understanding,
all-sympathizing parental surrogate. Without becoming a believer,
he surrendered his rational disbelief in order to calm his troubled
mind. And yet in his despair he apparently could not turn to his
saintly father, who would surely have been sympathetic, though
William knew only too well his remedy, which a scientific mind
could not accept. Thus all William could do was to endure his
hellish misery as secretly as possible, not even being able to unburden
himself to Henry, still moping in Great Malvern with his own
problems. And it is very doubtful that Henry, who resembled his
mother (except in his imagination) as much as William resembled
his father, would have fully understood either.

IV

By March 22 William had begun to work out for himself a kind
of crude existentialist philosophy in which he found at least slight
consolation. Under this date he apostrophized the spirit or memory
of his cousin: "By that big part of me that's in the tomb with you,
may I realize and believe in the immediacy of death! May I feel
that every torment suffered here passes and is as a breath of wind—
every pleasure too. Acts & examples stay. Time is long. One human

life is an instant. Is our patience so short-winded, our curiosity so dead or our grit so loose, that that one instant snatched out of the endless age should not be cheerfully sat out[?] Minny, your death makes me feel the nothingness of all our egotistic fury. The inevitable release is sure; wherefore take our turn kindly whatever it contain. Ascend to some sort of partnership with fate, & since tragedy is at the heart of us, go to meet it, work it in to our ends, instead of dodging it all our days, and being run down by it at last. Use your death (or your life, it's all one meaning). . . ."

Although part of his meditation may be regarded as William James's attempt to reconcile himself to the loss of his dear cousin, the stoicism is not a trite echo of Marcus Aurelius. Accept the pain and brevity of life with intensity, and make the most of life while one has it. His thoughts unconsciously echoed Emerson's teaching on "Fate" (in *The Conduct of Life*, 1851), with which he was familiar: " 'Tis the best use of Fate to teach a fatal courage. . . . For if fate is so prevailing, man is a part of it, and can confront fate with fate."

It was now that William took up again the French philosopher Renouvier, whom he had discovered two years earlier, and found what he needed. On April 30 he wrote in his diary: "I think yesterday was a crisis in my life. I finished the first part of Renouvier's 2nd Essay and saw no reason why his definition of free will—'the sustaining of a thought *because I choose to* when I might have other thoughts'—need be the definition of an illusion. At any rate I will assume for the present—until next year—that it is no illusion. My first act of free will shall be to believe in free will. For the remainder of the year, I will abstain from the mere speculation & contemplative Grübelei [musing, meditation] in which my nature takes most delight, and voluntarily cultivate the feeling of moral freedom, by reading books favorable to it, as well as by acting. After the first of January, my callow skin being somewhat fledged, I may perhaps return to metaphysic study & skepticism without danger to my powers of action. For the present, then, remember: Care little for speculation/ Much for the *form* of my action/ [.]"

Another book that gave William James some help at this time was Alexander Bain's *The Senses and the Intellect*, which he had purchased in Paris in 1868. Later he found much in this British psychologist to disagree with, but he would always owe a great debt to Bain's analysis of "habit," both for helping him out of the Slough of Despond in the spring of 1870 and later in the writing of his

Principles of Psychology. In his diary William reminded himself: "Recollect that only when habits of order are formed can we advance to really interesting fields of action—and consequently accumulate grain on grain of wilful choice like a very miser—never forgetting how one link dropped undoes an indefinite number." And again: "Today has furnished the exceptionally passionate initiative which Bain posits as needful for the acquisition of habits." It was not so much a matter of physical acts as controlling his thoughts and imagination: "in accumulated acts of thought lies salvation. . . . Hitherto, when I have felt like taking a free initiative, like daring to act originally, without carefully waiting for contemplation of the external world to determine all for me, suicide seemed the most manly form to put my daring into; now, I will go a step further with my will, not only act with it, but believe as well; believe in my individual reality and creative power. My belief to be sure can't be optimistic—but I will posit life, (the real, the good) in the self governing resistance of the ego to the world. . . ."

By the time Henry Jr. returned to Cambridge in May, William had conquered his temptation to commit suicide, and the resistance of his "ego to the world" was slowly increasing. For both brothers Minny's death made a tide-mark on their spiritual lives, though in different ways. Recalling the event in *Notes of a Son and Brother*, Henry wrote, "there came a moment, almost immediately after [her death], when all illusion failed; which it is not good to think of or linger on. . . ." On hearing of Minny Temple's death, Henry begged his mother to give him more details of her final suffering, the funeral, anything to help him remember her. What Henry always cherished most was *memory*, to recapture and preserve the past in all its linked details. "Try and remember anything she may have said and done. I have been raking up all my recent memories of her and her rare personality seems to shine out with absolute defiant reality. Immortal peace to her memory! I think of her gladly as unchained from suffering and embalmed forever in our hearts and lives. Twenty years hence what a pure eloquent vision she will be." How truly prophetic this letter was anyone knows who has studied the heroines of two of Henry James's greatest novels, *The Portrait of a Lady* and *The Wings of the Dove*.

In his *Notes* Henry concluded that "for William and myself" Minny's death "made a mark. . . . We felt it together as the end of our youth." Perhaps this was true for Henry. It was certainly true for William. But for William it meant not that he had found a "pure eloquent vision" which would become more eloquent with the years, but that he had resolved to accept life as a tragedy to be borne, the darkness to be pushed back as much as possible by accumulated acts of thought, and, if possible, of deed. He had not suddenly found a way to grow strong and robust in a short time, but he would try to conquer his unmanly vacillation. Ironically, near the end of her life Minny had written John Gray: "Willy James sometimes tells me to behave like a man and a gentleman if I wish to outwit fate. What a *real* person he is! He is to me in nearly all respects a head and shoulders above other people." Earlier she had said that "he is one of the very few people in this world that I love. He has the largest heart as well as the largest head, and is thoroughly interesting to me." Whether William was told about these remarks at this time is not known, though it is likely that John Gray had quoted some of them to him; nevertheless, for William Minny Temple was not a memory to cherish, but a person with whose memory he must keep faith.

CHAPTER XI In a Permanent Path

. . . I'm in a permanent path, and it shows me how for our type of

character the thought of the whole dominates the particular moments.

—W.J. *to Henry James Jr.*

I

ALTHOUGH WILLIAM JAMES CONTINUED to have spells of feeling "melancholy as a whippoorwill," as he expressed it on May 7, 1870, in a letter to his brother Henry, not aware that Henry was already on his way home; nevertheless, he had "begun to rise out of the sloughs of the past three months." Even as he recovered from having a tooth pulled, he could not help feeling cheered by the spring sunshine. Quincy Street was shaded by new leaves on the elms and maples, and on "faculty row" the spotty lawns glowed with yellow dandelions.

From the Harvard Yard came the sounds of saws, hammers, and axes, and the clamor of carpenters and masons building Thayer Hall. Under the new president, Charles W. Eliot, William's first chemistry teacher, Harvard had already begun her great era of growth and expansion. One might even see symbolism in the decayed trees' being cut down and removed from the Yard and the remaining ones' being pruned to grace the enlarged quadrangle. Modern plumbing was being installed in all the buildings, and both the unsightly privies and the pine thicket that imperfectly concealed them were being removed. On all sides of Harvard Square one felt the vibration of change and sensed the pulsing vitality.

In May Aunt Kate returned from her European travels, followed soon by Henry Jr., with less exuberance because his poor health and low spirits had forced him home from England. But he too was cheered to find the family in better health than he had expected. To all appearances his parents were unchanged, and to Jane Norton, still in Italy, he wrote on May 20 that "William inspires me with confidence." Alice also was "in strength and activity quite an altered person," meaning for the better. Once more Henry occupied the old green chair in William's bedroom at the back of the house, where the brothers spent hours in talking over their experiences. But after a few weeks each became absorbed again in his own interests and the intimacy decreased—not that any antagonism took its place. Henry turned his attention to writing for the *Atlantic Monthly* and the *Nation*. His friend and editor of the *Atlantic*, William Dean Howells, gave a series of lectures on Venice, which he attended and discussed afterwards nostalgically with him.

William continued to guard his strength and emotions, avoiding philosophical reading and discussion as much as he could and killing time with novels, poetry, biography. But it was impossible to keep his restless mind in a quiescent state. Sometimes his sister Alice would ask if he had read a certain book and he would say, oh, he had glanced at it, and then proceed to mention a detail or give a critical comment which showed that he had gone to the heart of the book. Indeed, he seemed to have a special gift for doing just that; even when he skimmed he took in more than the ordinary reader got from a careful perusal. Thus these months when William felt that he was doing nothing whatever of any importance were not entirely wasted, for he was constantly enlarging his knowledge of literature in English, French, and German. In American literature he read few authors except Hawthorne and Emerson, but these he knew thoroughly; and of course among his contemporaries he read everything his brother Henry and Howells wrote. During the summer, at Mount Desert, in Maine, he read Browning again. On July 10 his mother wrote Henry Sr., who had not accompanied the family to Maine, that Will was discussing Browning's poems with Wendell Holmes. Wendell read beautifully, she reported, and Will sometimes dares to go in bathing. Though not cured, his back was unmistakably better.

During this period when both William and Henry were at home in Cambridge, William was not writing many letters, and therefore documentary evidence for this year in his life is scarce. He was not even keeping up his diary, but this is a good indication that he was successfully avoiding emotional stress, for it was during periods of strain and crisis that he wrote most copiously in the diary. It was not possible, however, for him to protect himself by a shell of indifference. He was trying to toughen his nerves to bear the world he lived in, not to escape from it in some sort of self-induced euphoria. He would always feel much as he had in writing Henry back in May: "It seems to me that all a man has to depend on in this world, is, in the last resort, mere brute power of resistance. I can't bring myself, as so many men seem able to, to blink the evil out of sight, and gloss it over. It's as real as the good, and if it is denied, good must be denied too. It must be accepted and hated, and resisted while there's breath in our bodies."

But good and evil were sometimes so mixed that one scarcely knew one from the other, as in the Franco-Prussian war. Of course that war was not a personal concern for William, but he did keep wondering which side was right—or possibly more in the wrong, for he hardly thought either side was right in going to war. William had heard from Henry Bowditch, still studying and working in German laboratories, just before the outbreak of the war in July. He wondered frequently whether the war was hindering Bowditch's studies, but did not write to him until almost the end of 1870. "You may imagine how excited I was at the beginning of the war," he wrote on December 29. "I had not dared to hope for such a complete triumph of poetic justice as occurred. Now I feel much less interested in the success of the Germans, first because I think it's time that the principle of territorial conquest were abolished. . . . Moreover, if France succeeds in beating off the Germans now, I should think there would be some chance of the peace being kept between them hereafter. . . ."

Returning to his letter to Bowditch two days later (December 31), William confided that he himself was living in a "state of brutal social isolation." He had heard that Professor Jeffries Wyman, the teacher in the Medical School who was his favorite and Henry Bowditch's too, had returned from Florida, where he had gone for the sake of his weak lungs, but William did not feel sufficiently intellectually alive to talk with him. "I fill my belly for about four hours daily with husks,—newspapers, novels and biographies, but thought is tabooed,—and you can imagine that conversation with Wyman should only intensify the sense of my degradation."

In another long letter written on April 7–8, 1871, William reported the Cambridge news as well as his own personal condition. The interesting Cambridge news was that Agassiz was going to make an eight-months' voyage to San Francisco, "accompanied by his faithful and heroic spouse (who is a poor sailor) . . . to make deep sea dredgings. It will rest his mind as nothing else could, and he will at the same time make important scientific discoveries." Agassiz had recently suffered a "collapse," but seemed recovered. "My father was at a dinner club with him t'other day when he told the company that he had within the past six weeks visited 'every whorehouse in Boston'—out of scientific curiosity of course, and because he was unable to study. A-t-il du sang dans les veines! I vow I admire the old fellow. No regular Bostonian of his years and public position would have the courage & animal spirits to amuse himself in that way."

The young man William James did not have such "sang dans les veines," but he was feeling much stronger and had made a good beginning in returning to scientific study. He was taking advantage of a new plan inaugurated by President Eliot to bring some of the best minds of the Cambridge-Boston community to Harvard for lectures on science, philosophy, and literature. "I invested yesterday," he wrote Bowditch, in a ticket "for a course of 'University' lectures on 'Optical Phenomena and the Eye,' by B. Joy Jeffries, to be begun out here tomorrow. It's the first mingling in the business of life which I have done since my return home." It was a wise step, and when in September Henry Bowditch set up a laboratory on Grove Street in Boston, having been duly appointed to the faculty of the Harvard Medical School, William used his laboratory to try some experiments of his own. He still had no definite plans for the future, but Dr. James was nearer the beginning of a career than he realized, and during the past year he had made several of the right decisions.

II

Although Europe had not worked magic cures for either William or Henry Jr., the James family had still not lost faith in a trip to Europe as the best therapy for loss of vigor or jangled nerves. Poor Alice had never had much vigor, though her nerves had been calmer for the past two years. Hearing Aunt Kate's endless chatter about the sights she had seen made Alice wish that she could make a pilgrimage too, and the whole family thought this a splendid idea. Of course she could not go by herself, but Aunt Kate would be delighted to accompany her. Then Henry Jr., who had again become bored with Cambridge, volunteered to go along as guide and protector. Accordingly, toward the end of May 1872, the party of three sailed for Europe. Naturally a vigorous family correspond-ence ensued, in which both William and his parents gave detailed accounts of life in Cambridge.

Before the departure of Alice and her two guardians William had been informally offered a one-year instructorship in Harvard College to teach an elective course in "Comparative Anatomy and Physiology." President Eliot, not only William's former chemistry teacher but also his near neighbor since 1869, was well acquainted with the young man's intellectual progress, as well as his uncertain health. One of Eliot's innovations as president had been to unfreeze the rigid curriculum in the College and introduce some elective courses, the beginning of his controversial "elective system." He was also on the lookout for promising young teachers and had already appointed Henry Adams assistant professor of history, John Fiske instructor in history, and Wendell Holmes instructor in constitu-tional law (in the Law School)—as well as Henry Bowditch to the Medical School faculty. Even at this time William James felt sure that these young men would bring distinction to Harvard, and he fully appreciated Eliot's confidence in him. In August the position of instructor in physiology was formally offered to him, and he accepted it. The course would not actually begin until January and would be shared with an anatomist, Dr. Timothy Dwight. The salary was six hundred dollars.

Writing to his brother Henry on August 24 from Maine, William declared: "The appointment to teach physiology is a perfect godsend to me just now. An external motive to work, which yet does not strain me, a dealing with men instead of my own mind, and a diversion from those introspective studies which had bred a sort of philosophical hypochondria in me of late and which it will certainly do me good to drop for a year." However, William began his career at the age of thirty as a teacher of physiology simply because his first offer to teach happened to be in this field; it was not his first choice. Two months later he confided to Henry Jr.: "If I were well enough, now would be my chance to strike at Harvard College, for Peterson has just resigned his sub-professorship of philosophy [Ellis Peterson was assistant professor of philosophy until 1871–1872], and I know of no very formidable opponent." But William had too little confidence in his health to "strike" for the position.

One immediate advantage of the appointment which William had accepted was that he could now enjoy his vacation. He had already spent part of it at Mount Desert, that scintillating rocky coastal resort with the strange granite formations of mottled yellow and brown, casting blue shadows. At Bar Harbor he had caught a steamboat for Portland, Maine, and then taken a ten-mile trip by carriage to Scarboro, accompanied by Miss Grace Ashburner, a maiden friend of William's parents who lived on Kirkland Street near the Childs and Nortons. "She went on to Boston," William wrote Henry Jr. "I could not resist the temptation of stopping and getting three sea baths. . . . The steady, heavy roaring of the surf comes through the open window, borne by the delicious salt breeze over the great bank of stooping willows, field and fence. The little horse-chestnut trees are no bigger, the cow with the board face still crops the grass. The broad sky and sea are whanging with the mellow light." Though he felt that many "nervous puckers" in his mind had been smoothed out since he had left Cambridge, William confessed that he envied Henry "the world of art" which he was experiencing in Europe, especially in Italy. "Away from it, as we [in America] live, we sink into a flatter, blanker kind of consciousness. . . . I feel more and more as if I ought to try to learn to sketch in water-colors, but am too lazy to begin."

Henry answered William from Paris on September 22. Both he and Aunt Kate thought that Alice had benefited enormously from the Swiss air and scenery and Italian antiquity, and now the two women were shopping in Paris. The Nortons were there too, also Professor James Russell Lowell and wife and Chauncey Wright. "C.W. seems in Paris just as he did in Cambridge—serenely purpurine [probably an allusion to his flushed face, one effect of his excessive drinking]. He lives at the Grand Hotel, and I frequently see him trundling on tip-toes along the boulevard, as he did at home along the Main Street." Henry had visited the Louvre with Charles Norton, and benefited as usual from his expert comments, but could not help feeling that "he takes art altogether too hard. . . . I daily pray *not* to grow in discrimination, and to be suffered to aim at superficial pleasure." Norton had also praised a review of Taine's "On Intelligence," which William had recently published in the *Nation;* Henry said he too had read and admired, though he "but imperfectly understood it."

Henry always professed to admire William's publications, and genuinely wished to encourage him, but as his brother's writings became more philosophical Henry made less attempt to follow their thought. William, however, felt no reluctance in offering literary criticism of Henry's publications, partly, no doubt, because he was "big brother," and partly because he did have a wide knowledge of literature in several languages. While traveling in Europe Henry had been contributing "Trans-Atlantic Sketches" to the *Nation*. William reported that he had enjoyed them, as had "a number of people so large that I confess it rather surprised me; as I thought the style ran a little more to *curliness* than suited the average mind, or in general the newspaper reader. In my opinion what you should *cultivate* is directness of style. Delicacy, sublety and ingenuity will take care of themselves." And again on November 24 William praised a sketch on Chambéry as "a very delightful light bit of work . . . [but I] protest against your constant use of French phrases. There is an order of taste, and certainly a respectable one, to which they are simply maddening." (It is a little amusing that William continued to harp on this mannerism, because since their childhood all the James children had been in the habit of sprinkling their letters to each other with French phrases, to which William added German expressions; but of course French was their second language, which it was not for the general newspaper reader.)

On Henry's stories William offered similar criticisms. He had admired the cleverness of "Guest's Confession," currently being published in the *Atlantic Monthly*, "though not loving it exactly." In addition to the usual French phrases, William believed that many people would find the conversation of the characters "cold, thin-blooded and priggish." He also thought that in his letters to the *Nation* Henry indulged his fondness for literary reminiscence "in the midst of what ought to be pure imagination absorbed in the object." This criticism really characterizes each of the brothers, William wanting a vivid description of the object before him, Henry preferring the rich associations aroused in his memory by the object. Such unlike minds would never be able to meet on neutral ground, and as each developed his own characteristic intelligence the divergence would increase.

Henry had also made a decision which was to be the beginning of his alienation from Cambridge, though it would not weaken his epistolary ties with his family. At the end of September Alice and Aunt Kate returned to America without him. His decision to remain in Paris was not a sudden impulse; now that he was earning from his writings almost enough to live on, he was trying to find the most satisfactory location in which to lead his literary life. First he would try Paris, but he found living there a bit dull. Though he was at ease in the language, he complained that he knew scarcely any French people except waiters and chambermaids, to which William retorted impatiently, "It seems preposterous that a man like you should be condemned to the society of washer-women and café waiters." There were, of course, numerous Boston and Cambridge people in Paris—and other American tourists whom Henry scorned. Once or twice a week he crossed the Seine to dine with Lowell. "Poor little Mr. John Holmes [the idle, eccentric brother of Dr. Holmes], the most unassimilable in Europe, of New Englanders, lives with him and they try to make a little Cambridge together." Henry had a "sense of being in a denser civilization than our own" and yet "outside it." This was also a topic on which he and William would disagree for years to come.

Meanwhile the brother who as a child had been so immensely assimilable, Bob, the youngest, was trying to establish a home in Prairie du Chien, Wisconsin. He had fallen rapturously in love with Mary Holton, a simple, plump, round-faced girl with little education. His mother was extremely apprehensive about his marrying someone with what seemed to her such an inadequate background. But she knew that Bob needed a stabilizing influence and tried to conceal her doubts. In the course of time the James family would come to appreciate the sturdy character of Mary Holton, but in the autumn of 1872 Henry reflected the attitude of the family in this remark in a letter to William: "The picturesque at any rate, has been with you and departed again, I suppose, in the shape of Bob and his plump little spouse." (Robertson James had married in Wisconsin and visited his parents on his honeymoon.) Later, after Henry came to know his sister-in-law, he felt a bond of sympathy with her, especially after Bob proved to be an erratic and undependable husband.

Henry's letters brought back to William the Paris they had known together as boys. In William's memory it seemed "so huge and real in the world," perhaps because it had at one time been his childhood world. "Just about nightfall at this season [November] with drizzle above and mud-paste beneath, and gas-blazing streets and restaurants, is the time that particularly appeals to me with thick-wafted associations." This is one of the few occasions when William was nostalgic for the past. But he was not unhappy in more prosaic Cambridge-Boston. Every morning he went into Boston to hear Bowditch lecture at the Medical School on Grove Street and remained to "paddle round in his laboratory. It is a noble thing for one's spirits to have some responsible work to do. I enjoy my revived physiological reading greatly, and have in a corporeal sense been better for the past four or five weeks than I have been at all since you left."

The letter confirmed the reports Henry had received from Alice and Aunt Kate, as he playfully informed William in his letter dated November 31, 1872: "Aunt Kate and Alice both expatiate gleefully on that threadbare topic, as I believe you consider it, the remarkable salubrity of your appearance and I have ventured to reflect upon it with some complacency. If you are but half as well as they make out that you look I shall be perfectly satisfied." For a fact, William was in better health and spirits than he had known for several years.

III

The most interested observer of William's progress as a teacher was his own father. On January 14, 1873, he wrote his son Henry: "Willy is going on with his teaching. The eleven o'clock bell has just tolled, and he is on the platform expounding the mysteries of physiology." William himself wrote his brother a month later (February 13–14) during a two-weeks' respite, while the boys were taking examinations, that he found the teaching both interesting and stimulating. "It presents two problems, the intellectual one—how best to state your matter to them; and the practical one—how to govern them, stir them up, not bore them, yet make them work, etc. I should think it not unpleasant as a permanent thing. The authority is at first rather flattering to one. So far, I seem to have succeeded in interesting them, for they are admirably attentive, and I hear expressions of satisfaction on their part."

William's father was hardly an objective judge of his success in the classroom, but he was an acute observer of the effects of teaching on his son. To Henry Jr. he wrote again on March 18: "Willy goes on swimmingly with his teaching. The students (fifty-seven) are elated with their luck in having such a professor, and next year he will have no doubt a larger class still, attracted by his fame. He came in here the other afternoon when I was sitting alone, and after walking the floor in an animated way for a moment, exclaimed 'Dear me! What a difference there is between me now and me last spring this time: then so hypochondriacal' (he used that word, though perhaps in substantive form) 'and now feeling my mind so cleared up and restored to sanity. It is the difference between death and life.' He had a great effusion. I was afraid of interfering with it, or possibly checking it, but I ventured to ask what specially in his opinion had promoted the change. He said several things: the reading of Renouvier (specially his vindication of the freedom of the will) and Wordsworth, whom he has been feeding upon now for a good while; but especially his having given up the notion that all mental disorder required to have a physical basis. This had become perfectly untrue to him. He saw that the mind did act irrespectively of material coercion, and could be dealt with therefore at first-hand, and this was health to his bones. It was a splendid confession, and though I knew the change had taken place, from unerring signs, I never was more delighted than to hear it from his own lips so unreservedly. He has been shaking off his respect for men of mere science as such, and is even more universal and impartial in his mental judgments than I have ever known him before."

In the last remark Henry James Sr. was expressing one of his cherished ideas. As early as the Boulogne-sur-mer days, as we have seen, he had believed William's special talents to be scientific, and had encouraged him in various ways to prepare for a career in science and not be diverted, for example, by painting; yet for many years he had also felt that most scientists were blind to the spiritual counterpart of the physical world. They were not satisfied with limiting their knowledge to what they could measure; they seemed to think that whatever could not be measured either didn't exist or was of no importance. Although William would never be able to believe in, or even understand, his father's Swedenborgian spiritual world, he had come to suspect that not all mental life could be accounted for, or mental and nervous aberrations treated, physiologically. As a teacher of physiology he used the methods and nomenclature of science, but he had a growing conviction that the results of the scientific method were more limited than the scientists realized. He had found by experience that what he believed affected his digestion, sleep, and emotions. He did not doubt in the least that his organic functions also affected his mind, but the process could be reversed, as he had found by reading Renouvier, Wordsworth, and Goethe.

Thus William James's "effusion" to his father marked a milestone not only in his gaining a measure of control over his neuroses (complete control would never be possible), but also in his progress toward the essays and books in psychology and philosophy which he would later write. But for a person of his temperament and character the progress could not be orderly and consistent. The journey must be made without a map and might be treacherous. His first problem was to survive, but in the act of surviving from day to day he might be able to form some useful hypotheses.

Fortunately, at the end of three months of teaching William could feel satisfaction in the progress he had made. On April 6, at the beginning of a four-week holiday before the final month of the term, he wrote his brother Henry, "It has turned out a solider job than I anticipated, both in respect of the effort it has taken to put it through, and in respect of the information I have imparted." He felt sure he could do better if he repeated the course, though he doubted that he would continue with it. "Eliot offered me the other day the whole department (i.e., this physiology plus Dwight's anatomy) for next year. But I told him I had resolved to fight it out in the line of mental science [psychology], and with such arrears of lost time behind me and such curtailed power of work now, could not afford to make such an expedition into anatomy. It cost me some perplexity to make the decision, for had I accepted, it might easily grow into a permanent biological appointment, to succeed Wyman, perhaps,—and that study, though less native to my taste, has many things in its favor. But I am satisfied the decision I made was a wise one, and I shall bide my time, they looking for some one man to take the work that Dwight and I have shared between us. I have done enough now to show me that the duty of teaching comes kindly to me, and that I probably should become a good instructor with practice. From what I hear reported the boys have been satisfied so far."

Three days later, however, William had decided that it would be foolish not to accept President Eliot's offer. On April 10 he recorded in his diary the decision and his rationalization of it: "Yesterday I told Eliot I would accept the anatomical instruction [anatomy plus physiology] for next year, if well enough to perform it, and would probably stick to that department. I came to this decision mainly from the feeling that philosophical activity as a *business* is not normal for most men, and not for me." William says nothing about the satisfaction of having at last a permanent position at the age of thirty; though the six hundred dollars a year salary was not munificent, it was not insignificant at that time. But his thinking was on a more idealistic plane: "To be responsible for a complete conception of things is beyond my strength. To make the *form* of all possible thought the prevailing *matter* of one's thought breeds hypochondria. Of course my deepest interest will as ever lie with the most general problems. But . . . my strongest moral and intellectual craving is for some stable reality to lean upon, . . . and the concrete facts in which a biologist's responsibilities lie form a fixed basis from which to aspire as much as he pleases to the mastery of the universal questions when the gallant mood is on him; and a basis, too, upon which he can passively float, and tide over times of weakness and depression, trusting all the while blindly in the beneficence of nature's forces and the return of higher opportunities. A 'philosopher' has publicly renounced the privilege of trusting *blindly*, which every simple man owns as a right—and my sight is not always clear enough for such constant duty. Of course one may say, you could make of psychology proper just such a basis; but not so, you can't divorce psychology from introspection, and immense as is the work demanded by its purely objective physiologic part, yet it is the other part rather for which a professor thereof is expected to make himself publicly responsible."

Before the end of the term, however, William had become discouraged again. On May 25 he wrote Harry: "I have succeeded in doing my college work this half-year without losing ground, so far as I know, in health, but also without gaining an inch. . . . I get utterly collapsed and exhausted with the experimental preparations, and the regular tri-weekly recurrence of the feverish sort of erethism in which the lecture or recitation hour leaves me, cannot be good for [me]. . . . I told Eliot some time ago in accepting the place for the whole of next year, that the acceptance was subject to the right to back out by the middle of August if I feel so inclined. Of course my deep active desire is to go on working uninterruptedly now that, after all this delay, I have begun." Not the least remarkable aspect of this situation was President Eliot's patience with William's vacillation. But on one crucial point he would not yield. The class in physiology had forty-five students [William's father had stretched the number to fifty-seven], and might well increase to one hundred next year. To divide the class into two sections would simply double William's teaching schedule. "The only alternatives are: to back out, and, letting Dwight take them for next year, hope that I shall be *gewachsen* [equal] to the task for the year following; or else to implore that on a plea of the teacher's invalidism my students be forcibly pruned down to a manageable number." President Eliot would agree only to the first alternative, but still did not demand a final decision until August.

The most articulate witness of William's moods and actions during the summer of 1873 was his mother. On July 1 she wrote Henry Jr.: "He has such a morbid sympathy with every form of trouble and privation that he is not strengthening where he most wishes to be. For instance, he broke out last evening on the piazza into a most pathetic lamentation over the servants who had only one arm-chair in the kitchen[.] I promised him at once that I would supply the want, and that there should be three," one for each servant.

Wilky, now employed by a railroad company in Wisconsin, had been urging William to visit him and had offered to get a pass on the railroad. After encouraging Wilky in this plan, William now felt that he was not strong enough for the trip out West. But in a few days, his mother reported to Henry Jr., he would start up the New England coast by steamboat, probably going as far as Mount Desert. "Father's advice to him was to give up the idea of working next winter. . . . I fear unless his resignation is given in at once, and the whole subject dismissed from his mind, that his recreation will yield him neither pleasure nor profit. He is very despondent about himself . . . [but is encouraged by Alice's gains] for he considers her weak, nervous condition very like his own present one. . . ."

While on the trip Willy wrote Harry (July 14–16) that his account of Rome as a place in which he might recuperate without boredom—advice for which William had asked—"was more satisfactory than anything I anticipated. I earnestly hope, however, not to have to verify it next winter, as such a step would be about equivalent to desperation of any continuous professional development, and would leave my future quite adrift again. I shall let July and August shape my decision, and bear whatever comes with as equal mind as I can. What weighs on me perhaps as much as anything now is the ignominy of my parasitic life on the family, in view of the sweating existence of Bob and Wilky and their need of money as married men. Every hundred dollars I take or don't earn is so much less that Father can give them."

In referring to Wilky as a married man William was anticipating, for his brother's marriage was not to take place until November. He was in love with a girl he had met in Wisconsin, Caroline Eames Cary, a friend of Bob's wife, but more reserved, passive, and taciturn. The James family had not yet met her. Probably one reason for Wilky's eagerness for William to visit him was to have him meet her and in that way win a measure of family approval.

Out in Prairie du Chien, in the summer of 1873, Bob and Mary were preparing for their first child. In Cambridge the heat and abnormal drought were dreadful, but Alice and Aunt Kate escaped it by traveling to Niagara Falls and then taking a boat down the Saint Lawrence to Quebec. Because of his difficulty in walking Henry Sr. could not manage the provinces, but found a hotel in Saint John's satisfactory. William, as we have seen, confined his vacationing to the New England coast.

In August William duly notified President Eliot of his final resolve to abstain from teaching for a year. On September 12, now back in Cambridge, his mother wrote Harry that Will was definitely going to Europe, on the S.S. *Spain*, which would dock in Liverpool. He had gained strength but was still "morbid." Some days he felt fine, but after doing "two or three hours study, he says his head gives out and all the strength goes out of his legs. . . . This necessity he is under to measure his strength every day, keeps his mind constantly fixed upon himself which is the worst possible thing for him." Ten days later she added that after Willy decided to go, he felt so well "as to have at times some relentings. But these ought not to be yielded to. He says if he holds on and gets to feeling well, after three months, he will go to Florence or Heidelberg and study." Morbid or not, Willy James was a perennial optimist.

IV

On board the S.S. *Spain*, a big smooth-sailing Cunard liner, William wrote a letter to his family on October 17–18 to be mailed at Queenstown (now Cobh, Ireland) before landing at Liverpool. His cabin-mate was a Bowdoin College graduate who had paid his way through college and saved up enough money for two years of study in Europe "by peddling quack medicines of his own concoction, and cutting corns." William declared him, nevertheless, "an honor to his native land, without prejudices and full of animal spirits"—but "has never tasted spirituous liquor." Harry would have been miserable with him, but Willy called him his "chum." He preferred, however, the companionship of one of the eleven missionaries on board—"She is twenty-four years old and very beautiful"—with whom he "lurched about the deck arm in arm . . . yestereen. I told her that, if I were a missionary, instead of going to the most unhealthy part of Africa, I would choose, say, Paris for a field. She, all unconscious of the subtle humor of my remark, said, 'Oh, yes! there are fearful numbers of heathen there!' "

After a brief stop in London, William stayed in Paris two days and one night at the Hôtel du Louvre, where "the exaggerated neatness and order and reglementation of everything visible . . . all a-kinder turned my plain Yankee stomach, which has not yet recovered from the simpler lessons of joy it learnt at Scarboro and Magnolia last summer." Baron Haussmann's radiating boulevards had transformed Paris into "a terribly monotonous-looking city." William tried to visit the quarters he had known as a boy, but could re-establish no *rapport* with them.

But the "beautifully good-natured easy-going expression on the faces of the [Italian] railroad officials" raised his spirits. They were still undampened on his arrival at Florence on the midnight of October 29 after an eleven-hour ride from Turin, "pouring rain all the way. Ditto yesterday during my twenty-two-hours ride from Paris." Henry had engaged a room for him in his hotel, but William took possession of it without waking his brother, as he explained to Alice: "The Angel sleeps in number 39 hard by, all unwitting that I, the Demon (or perhaps you have already begun in your talks to distinguish me from him as the Archangel), am here at last. I wouldn't for worlds disturb this his last independent slumber."

Although Henry worked steadily every morning on his novel *Roderick Hudson*, he was suffering again from constipation, which gave him headaches, and William did not find him in his happiest frame of mind. Moreover, during the past year each brother had begun to find his own "permanent path" for his intellectual abilities and ambitions and they were not as understanding of each other's problems as they had once been. Henry, in fact, was becoming increasingly alienated from his native soil, while William had become more Americanized even during the past year. On November 16 William wrote Wilky: "At present Harry is my spouse. I have been here with him boarding in a hotel, for two and a half weeks. I was disappointed at finding him not so completely well as I had hoped; but he seems well enough to work hard, and that seems now to be the only thing he lives for." William thought that if he could be persuaded to return to America he might find an editorial position of some kind that would not be as exhausting as his present literary labors, but "his temperament is so exclusively artistic that the vacuous, simple atmosphere of America ends by tiring him to death." Despite his own quick, seemingly more brilliant intelligence, William could never understand the inner impulses which drove Henry to artistic creation. What especially eluded him was Henry's necessity to narrow and limit his life in order to enrich his art. It was a kind of dedication to principle impossible for William, whose natural craving was for ever wider experience and more abundant life.

Surprisingly, William had to get used to Europe again. "For ten days after my arrival I was so disgusted with the swarming and reeking blackness of the streets and the age of everything, that enjoyment all took place under protest, as it were." But now he could enjoy the picturesqueness without a revulsion from the grime. "It is easier in Italy than elsewhere because of the cheerfulness and contented manners of the common people. They don't take life anything like as hard as we do, and suffer privation without being made desperate by it as we are."

William had especially looked forward to seeing the art treasures of Florence which had so thrilled Henry on his first visit in 1869, and he was impressed by the wreath of angels in Botticelli's "Assumption" and Dupré's sculpture for the tomb in Santa Maria Novella, "especially the second female figure, which is however inspired by Michel Angelo." But he could not thoroughly enjoy even these without wondering whether great art were not a thing of the past, and if so why? As a boy he could enjoy a painting for its own sake; now he wanted to relate everything he saw to some law or principle or hypothesis. No doubt this was the penalty of his having turned his back on painting for science, then philosophy, which now attracted him as strongly as writing fiction attracted Henry. To his sister he wrote: "I don't see how, if one lived here, historical problems could help being the most urgent ones for the mind. . . . Even art comes before one here much more as a problem—how to account for its development and decline—than as a refreshment and an edification." And in his diary he recorded: "I am sure that an age will come when our present devotion to history, and scrupulous care for what men have done before us merely as fact, will seem incomprehensible; when acquaintance with books will be no duty, but a pleasure for odd individuals; when Emerson's philosophy will be in our bones, not our dramatic imaginations."

Unlike Charles Norton, and to a certain extent his brother Henry, William could not give himself up to reveling in the past glories of Florence with a feeling of scorn for his own sorry world. It might be sorry, but it was his and it was living. Like Emerson he felt that it was important not that poets had written poems or sculptors carved statues but that poems and statues could be and were being created still. William respected artistic creation as activity but not as artifact. This was not only his disagreement with Norton and Henry (though Henry was less idolatrous of the past than Norton), but it was also his American quarrel with European or traditional culture. To be a tradition was to be dead, and his concern was with the living. Here again we see the emergence of his "Pluralistic" philosophy.

It is not surprising that William would find Rome even more repugnant, when he went there with Henry on November 28. His first reaction to its gaudy decay, its embalmed history, its traditional paganism was a moral revulsion, which he spilled out like hot lava in a letter to his father. After a few days his indignation cooled, but on December 17 he could still write to his sister: "The barbarian mind stretches little by little to take in Rome, but I doubt if I shall ever call it the 'city of my soul,' or 'my country,' " as several Cambridge friends, including the Nortons, had. "Strange to say, my very enjoyment of what here belongs to hoary eld has done more to reconcile me to what belongs to the present hour, business, factories, etc., etc., than anything I ever experienced." In an earlier letter (December 11) he had confessed a "strong sympathy with Ellen Emerson [daughter of the poet], who, I am told, actually grew afraid at last that she might be going to think Rome a greater place than Concord." But there was little danger. William's feelings continued to be more like those of Mark Twain in *Innocents Abroad*, published in 1869, though William may not yet have read it—Mark Twain could not see beauty in anything that was old and dingy.

But William's unfavorable opinions of Rome did not spoil his sense of humor. To his sister he also wrote: "Every day I sally out into the sunshine and plod my way o'er steps of broken thrones and temples until one o'clock, when I repair to a certain café in the Corso, begin to eat and read 'Galignani' and the 'Débats,' until Harry comes in with the flush of successful literary effort fading off his cheek. (It may interest the sympathetic soul of Mother to know that my diet until that hour consists of a roll, which a waiter in wedding costume brings up to my room when I rise, and three sous' worth of big roasted chestnuts, which I buy, on going out, from an old crone a few doors from the hotel. In this respect I am economical. Likewise in my total abstinence from spirituous liquors, to which Harry, I regret to say, has become an utter slave, spending a large part of his earnings in Bass's Ale and wine, and trembling with anger if there is any delay in their being brought to him.) After feeding, the Angel in his old and rather shabby striped overcoat, and I in my usual neat attire, proceed to walk together either to the big Pincian terrace which overhangs the city, and where on certain days every-one resorts, or to different churches and spots of note. I always dine at the table-d'hôte here; Harry sometimes, his indisposition lately (better the past two days) having made him prefer a solitary gorge at the restaurant."

Of course William's parents and Alice knew him well enough to know how much of this was sarcasm or burlesque, with the sly dig at his mother's "sympathetic" (parsimonious) soul, and the de-flation of the Angel's virtuous character. But the allusion to Henry's constipation sounds like sober fact. Henry's account of William also contained some exaggeration, but simply for the sake of reassuring his parents and Alice; he could paint the lily with grace and suavity: "He seems greatly contented with his condition and is sensible of its growing constantly better. He has just been into my room, flushed with health and strength, to see whether I had found any letters at the bankers this morning and to ask where he should go today. See-ing me writing, he says,—'Give them my love and tell them I am doing splendidly.' He does in fact, a great deal, and walks, climbs Roman staircases, and sees sights in a way most satisfactory to behold. It has been a measureless blessing that the weather, ever since our arrival in Rome, has been the finest, on the whole, I ever saw. . . . what I said about Willy . . . doesn't seem to me at all too *couleur de rose*. Certainly, a man couldn't look better—and what he dis-tinctly says of himself quite justifies his looks. . . . Willy, who at first hung fire over Rome, has now quite ignited, and confesses to its sovereign influence. But he enjoys all the melancholy of antiquity under a constant protest, which pleases me as a symptom of growing optimism and elasticity in his own disposition. His talk, as you may imagine, on all things, is most rich and vivacious. My own more sluggish perceptions can hardly keep pace with it."

The only news of significance from Cambridge concerned the visit of Wilky and his new wife on their honeymoon. Henry Sr. wrote the first melancholy account, and they all apparently felt very much as William's mother did in her letter to Henry Jr. on December 8: "Our last letters have all been full of our strange experience of Wilky's visit with Carrie, and our disappointment. There is one great consolation in it, that he seems to have no shadow of a misgiving himself, about his having drawn a prize—and let us hope that it may turn out that we have made the mistake—not he."

The other bit of interesting news was that Bob and Mary had a son, not yet named. On December 11 William wrote Alice: "We got 3 days ago from Father . . . a letter giving an account of Miss [sic] Cary, and announcing to us that we had given birth to a nephew. So the 3rd generation of the J. family is in full swing! We are uncles, grandmothers, aunts, &c, all drawing our subsistence as such from that one worm-like being in Wisconsin. It seems to me the pyramid points the wrong way, and the spreading end ought to be the youngest, instead of the trunk being more numerous than the twiggery. . . . Poor old Bob will no doubt be renovated by the new experience. . . . Harry says: 'for Heaven's sake don't make it another Henry!' He feels sure that if you do it will become a magazinist, and mix up the family articles more than ever. . . . I need not say how sorry we both were to get from Father an account of Wilky's bride so much the reverse of enthusiastic. . . . If Wilky is happy, we ought not to be unhappy, but only to trust that he will keep so." He had written Wilky an affectionate letter of congratulations on his marriage, and later sent Carrie warm greetings. And to his sister he wrote two months later, "What you say of Carrie is too painful to dwell upon, but I feel so capable of being victimized by a hard nonentity myself that I have the most perfect sympathy & esteem for Wilky."

Near the end of December William thought he had caught the notorious Roman (malarial) fever and hastened back to Florence. It was probably not malaria, for in a few days he had sufficiently recovered to enjoy Florence, and then went on to Venice, which put him on his "sight-seeing feet," as he wrote Alice on February 13 —addressing her with the atrocious epithet of "Beautlet." "Three days have I gondoled and picture-gazed, under a cloudless sky, but an eager and nipping air—especially in the Academy, where the poor custodians have a cold time of it. Such glory of painting and such actual decay, I never saw. This afternoon I mounted the Campanile and got a view which explained to me much of Venetian art—i.e., the light as one of the *dramatis personae*. While the gondola . . . makes one understand how figures seen from below against the sky . . . came so natural to them."

Next day William departed for Munich, stopping for a few hours in Verona. In Dresden he visited the Tweedys. At Bremen he boarded ship for home and arrived in Cambridge about the middle of March. Soon after his arrival his mother wrote Henry Jr. that he had not let them know he was coming, but that she had had a premonition "and every night when I heard the high March wind howl, I felt as if I were tossing with him on the stormy main." She was not sure about his physical condition; of course he was still fatigued from the trip. "The trouble with him is that he *must express* every fluctuation of feeling, and especially every unfavorable symptom," without considering the effect upon his auditors.

In the same letter Mrs. James reported that Father had just returned from a lecture at Providence. "All that he has to say seems so good and glorious, and easily understood to him, and it falls so dead upon the dull, so sceptical souls who come to hear him. . . ." This conscientious mother worried about all her children and her husband too. In April she wrote that Willy was better and studying industriously at home. But Wilky was going to resign from the railroad and go into business making iron chains and bolts. "Wilky is so sanguine that one can place no reliance upon his judgment, and little upon his prudence . . . ," she wrote on April 3. In May she was worried about Henry Jr. and wished he would consider marrying. If he must live in Europe, and she knew the advantages for him, she would feel easier about him if he had a wife to look after him. By July Henry had promised to come home in September and try again to write in America. Of course his mother was happy over this news, but she almost despaired of Willy, who said he was no better, though he looked well and worked hard in preparation for his autumn teaching: "his temperament is a morbidly hopeless one, and with this he has to contend all the time, as well as with his physical disability."

However, Mrs. James sometimes worried as needlessly about Wil-

liam as he worried about himself. A letter which he had written
Henry back in April most adequately summed up his actual condition between his return from Europe and the beginning of his permanent association with Harvard College: "Any gossip about Florence you can still communicate will be greedily sucked in by me,
who feel towards it as I do towards the old Albany of our childhood,
with afternoon shadows of trees, etc. Not but that I am happy here,
—more so than I ever was there, because I'm in a permanent path,
and it shows me how for our type of character the thought of the
whole dominates the particular moments. All my moments here are
inferior to those in Italy, but they are parts of a long plan which is
good, so they content me more than the Italian ones which only
existed in themselves."

When summer came, William made his usual tours of the resorts
along the coast of Massachusetts, New Hampshire, and Maine and
found many more moments of contentment. In spite of temporary
setbacks, and unrepressed groans which disturbed his mother, his feet
were indeed in "a permanent path," and the right path for him.

CHAPTER XII

Muscles to Mind

In the College he began his teaching with comparative anatomy,

but soon found bones and muscles of no consequence apart from

functions . . . [and] bodily functions were merely subsidiary to

mental . . . —GEORGE HERBERT PALMER

I

IN THE AUTUMN OF 1874 William James resumed his teaching at Harvard as instructor in full charge of the course called "Natural History 3," which was further described in the college catalogue as "The Comparative Anatomy and Physiology of the Vertebrates." As this title indicates, James was teaching not an elementary course in "physiology," but one (actually two) which cut across a number of what would later be regarded as distinct fields: biology, physiology, and anthropology. Moreover, Jeffries Wyman had died on September 4, after several years of illness, and thus on short notice, even before classes began for the new term, William had also to take charge of the Museum of Comparative Anatomy, which Dr. Wyman had started and maintained.

Dr. Wyman had done extensive research in the history and archaeology of American Indians and had collected valuable artifacts; this explains in part why James's "Natural History" courses covered so much more than the rudiments of anatomy and physiology. Dr. O. W. Holmes, the witty Dean of the Medical School, paid this tribute to Dr. Wyman and his collections:

How many skulls, broken so as to be past praying for, he has made whole; how many Dagons, or other divinities, shattered past praying to, he has restored entire to their pedestals, let the myope who can find the cracks where his cunning hand has joined the fragments tell us. His manipulation of a fractured bone from a barrow or a shell-heap was as wonderful in its way as the dealing of Angelo Mai with the scraps of a tattered palimpsest.

Harvard had at the time several museums with overlapping purposes and holdings. There was the vast collection of bones, glacial rocks, and fishes and animals preserved in alcohol made by Louis Agassiz for his Museum of Comparative Zoology. Then in 1866 the great philanthropist George Peabody had endowed a Museum of American Archaeology and erected a grand building for it between Divinity Avenue and Oxford Street. The collections of Agassiz and Wyman were never assimilated by the Peabody Museum. When James took charge of the Wyman collection, it was in Boylston Hall, but the following year it was moved to the University Museum, where it was still kept separate from the Agassiz collections. Eventually (1914) the University Museum and the Peabody were joined by a connecting wing.

Charles Loring Jackson remembered that when the Museum of Comparative Anatomy was moved in the autumn of 1875, because the Chemistry Department needed its space in Boylston Hall, William James had come back for a few items that had been left behind and paused for conversation with the young chemist:

His call on us must have been at the beginning of [the academic year] '75–6, as he stayed half an hour, and if I had got started on my benzyl work (a month after the beginning) he could not have stayed five minutes. I had just returned from two years in Europe, and, talking of my work, I said that once when I was working with amyl nitrite in Berlin an Englishman who was also in the loggia began singing and laughing as if he were drunk. By the evening I was in the same state. James was immensely interested and asked to try some of it. At first he very properly held the bottle at a distance, and waved the vapor toward himself; but when to his continual questions, 'Is my face flushing?' we answered 'No,' he at last put it against his nose and took a good sniff. Then he felt blindly for the table, put the bottle on it and said, 'O! how queer I feel!' took up two battery-jars full of alcohol (two quarts if I remember) and started across the Yard.

Apparently James was able to make it without mishap to Oxford Street, and we hear of no after-effects of the rash experiment, so similar to those he had made as a boy.

This personal trial of amyl nitrite was another indication that William James's deepest interest was still the relationship of mind and body rather than comparative anatomy, though his knowledge of anatomy and physiology would always provide useful background for his psychological studies. In the autumn of 1875 he began giving a graduate course in "The Relations between Physiology and Psychology." With this course he also introduced laboratory experiments, such as he had been performing himself in Bowditch's laboratory. Though other institutions were to claim priority in establishing psychological laboratories in America (partly an argument over definition), this seems to have been the real beginning. No record has survived of the experiments James's students performed, but it is a safe guess that they were similar to those he had observed briefly in the laboratories of Helmholtz, Hering, and Wundt in Germany, or read about in their publications.

In 1876 James began giving a similar undergraduate course in the relations of physiology and psychology and set up an improvised laboratory in Lawrence Hall, which later developed into a "laboratory for Psychophysics." It was perhaps a year or so later, as G. Stanley Hall, the first student to take a Ph.D. in Psychology-Philosophy at Harvard, recalled, that "in a tiny room under the stairway of the Agassiz Museum he [William James] had a metronome, a device for whirling a frog, a horopter chart and one or two bits of apparatus."

Although James continued to teach anatomy and physiology until 1878, he was steadily making progress toward the fields in which he was to gain fame: first psychology, and then philosophy. In 1876 he was promoted to an assistant professorship, at a salary of twelve hundred dollars a year, with a promise of two thousand the following year. There were then no regulations or formal concepts of "tenure," but he was nevertheless professionally established with this promotion and could look forward to steady progress in his academic world.

Graduate study had just begun in America and was mainly an adaptation of the methods of the German universities. During the first two years of his presidency of Harvard, Eliot had experimented with courses of public lectures given by outstanding scholars or thinkers to provide some advanced training beyond the A.B. degree and the courses of the professional schools. William James, as will be recalled, had attended lectures on "Optical Phenomena of the Eye" after taking his M.D. degree and before he began teaching. But Eliot soon realized that the public lectures were not a success, and he set about organizing a Graduate School, though called a "Department" at its inception in January 1872. For many years any graduate of Harvard College known to be of good character had been able to obtain the Master of Arts degree by paying a fee of five dollars. When Henry Thoreau said, "Let the sheep keep his skin," he was referring to the purchased M.A. diploma, which he himself refused. But each commencement many Harvard graduates did come back to receive this unearned honor. Eliot abolished the custom, and thereafter the Master's degree could not be obtained without at least a year of residence spent taking approved courses and passing a formal examination. The Doctor of Philosophy degree was modeled on the German Ph.D., which required at least three years of study, a thesis judged to be a contribution to knowledge, and the passing of an oral examination which often resembled an initiation.

Though the only degree William James had was his M.D., few men in America were better acquainted with the scholarship in psychology, in German, French, or English, and his medical studies were an extra advantage. Thus he was well qualified to begin graduate instruction in psychology. But the course in the relations between physiology and psychology he had proposed in 1875 was regarded as pertaining to philosophy more than physiology, and the authorities decided that it must be offered in the Department of Philosophy. The chairman of that department was George Herbert Palmer, a man exactly the same age as James, who later won popular acclaim for a biography of his deceased wife, Alice Freeman Palmer, a pioneer crusader for higher education for women. He was methodical, cautious, and conventional, a contrast in almost every way to the nervous, mercurial, and sometimes erratic James. Palmer had become a tutor in Greek in Harvard College in 1870 after his return from two years of study in Germany, and then an instructor in philosophy in 1872. Thus on the academic totem pole he was little higher than James.

In Germany Palmer had become imbued with Hegelianism, a pure form of philosophical idealism, hostile to science; James's scientific training made him antagonistic to this doctrine. Ironically, Karl Marx was to derive his dialectical materialism from Hegel, but Palmer's Hegelianism was more like a rationalization of the Christian dogma his predecessors in philosophy had taught at Harvard. Intellectually and temperamentally he and James were in almost complete contrast, but Palmer was able to appreciate the character and ability of his more impulsive and spontaneous colleague. To the historian of Harvard, Samuel Eliot Morrison, Palmer recalled that soon after James began teaching comparative anatomy he found bones and muscles things of no consequence apart from functions, and so he crossed over to physiology. He had been engaged with this but a short time when he announced to me that bodily functions were merely subsidiary to mental and could be understood only from the point of view of psychology. Accordingly he came over into our Department, gave delightful instruction for several years to large courses of beginners, led a little band of graduates in psychological research, and amused his leisure with building up his monumental book [*Principles of Psychology*].

However, Palmer thought James too tolerant and sympathetic with his students: "His judgment of men was not good; it was corrupted by kindness." Perhaps nearly everyone who knew William James at Harvard, especially during the early part of his career, would have agreed that this statement was partly true, but Palmer's own judgment was certainly faulty when he declared that James's "over-estimation of Charles Peirce, and too ample acknowledgment of his debt to Peirce's thought, I believe to have sprung quite as much from pity as admiration." Today it would seem to be greatly to William James's credit that he recognized Peirce's genius while nearly everyone else thought he was an intolerable bore. Yet, with all his own limitations, Palmer's summing up of James's characteristics as a teacher and colleague tallies fairly well with other evidence and is worth quoting:

Among his colleagues, there was a hearty tolerance of divergent beliefs [probably referring to a later period than the 1870s]. James accepted the principle no less for the workings of his own mind. Consistency was counted negligible, fidelity to facts the sole obligation. While his mind was certainly hospitable to an astonishing variety of ideas which are usually thought to conflict, it was a sane and usually evolutionary variety, where the latter did not forget the earlier. There was far more order and consecutiveness in him than he ever claimed, perhaps more than he himself saw. It is true that so soon as he had seen anything through, his interest flagged. To hold attraction for him a subject must offer opportunity for adventure and exploration.

This last statement is corroborated in a letter of William James dated November 14, 1875, to his brother Henry, who had tried living in America for another year and had gone back to more congenial Europe: "My busyness at the Museum has begun to slacken a little of late owing to my decision not to sweat so hard at making osteological preparations which after all are to go before long to another man's professorship. I have never felt so well and have never on the whole been so busy as since your departure, though I've read absolutely nothing of a 'general' sort." A year later (December 30, 1876), after having begun his undergraduate course in psychology, using Herbert Spencer's *Principles of Psychology* as a text, James wrote his old friend Tom Ward that his Spencer elective was "quite exciting and arduous," but he regretted that he found little time for reading biographies, histories, etc., "for I think a professor, in addition to his *Fach*, should be a *ganzer Mensch*—but I can read nothing"—and then mentions editions of some letters in French he has evidently been reading, which "show the *disease* of love about as completely as anything I ever saw. But I like human nature, and can't breathe without some suggestion of contact with lives of other people—vigorous ones, I mean. All the men here seem so dry and shopboard like. . . . I have some bright boys in my Spencer class,—but I am completely disgusted with the eminent philosopher, who seems to me more and more to be as absolutely worthless in all *fundamental* matters of thought, as he is admirable, clever and ingenious in secondary matters. His mind is a perfect puzzle to me, but the total impression is of an intensely two and sixpenny, paper-collar affair."

One thing that can certainly be said of James as a teacher: he did not let the text interfere with the free play of his own vivacious mind. And he did not set himself up as an authority to which his student must make obeisance. He frankly learned as he taught, and he and his students shared the adventure together. One who took advantage of his tolerance was a bumptious, nearsighted boy named Theodore Roosevelt, who interrupted lectures to argue with his teacher; but Dr. James let him have his say, and then went quietly on with his exposition.

II

Even if William James had written out and preserved his college lectures, they might tell us less about his intellectual development in the early years of his teaching than the essays he published at that time in the *Atlantic Monthly* and the *Nation*. Perhaps it was fortunate that he did his early writing for these literary magazines rather than for scholarly or professional journals, because almost at the beginning of his career he learned to write for the general public in nontechnical language—though his own personality was the main source of his clarity and pungency of style. He wrote for the public much as he talked or expressed himself informally in his personal letters, with directness, vigor, and an enthusiasm that often took the form of exaggeration and metaphor. William James *felt* his thought, and from his own experience he had discovered that even so-called abstract thought is more indebted to the thinker's emotions than he usually realizes.

In a critical essay on George Henry Lewes's *Problems of Life and Mind*, published in the *Atlantic* in 1875, James considered the question of the *usefulness* of philosophical speculation, for "of all forms of earthly worry, the metaphysical worry seems the most gratuitous." If it leads to skepticism, "it is worse than superfluous," as James knew from painful experience. If it ends by "reinstating us in the possession of our old feelings, motives, and duties," is the effort worth the trouble? James thought it was, if for no other reason because the mental effort to understand is the source of great human satisfaction.

> Consciousness is the only measure of utility, and even if no philosophy could ever alter a man's motives in life,—which is untrue,—that it should add to their conscious completeness is enough to make thousands take upon themselves its burden of perplexities. We like the sense of companionship with better and more eager intelligences than our own, and that increment of self-respect which we all experience in passing from an instinctive to a reflective state, and adopting a belief which hitherto we simply underwent.

Lewes was one of the British skeptical philosophers then in the ascendancy, who denied "substantial cause," or at least the human ability to know cause and effect. According to this view, all that men know about their world is their own experience of it. With this empiricism James was sympathetic, but it seemed to him that Lewes's positivism rested on nothing except faith in positivism.

> We wish that Mr. Lewes had emphasized this volitional moment in his Positivism. Although the consistent pyrrhonist is the only theoretically unassailable man, it does not follow that he is the right man. Between us and the universe, there are no "rules of the game." The important thing is that our judgments should be right, not that they should observe a logical etiquette. There is a brute, blind element in

every thought which still has the vital heat within it and has not yet been reflected on. . . . May it not be that in the theoretic life the man whose scruples about flawless accuracy of demonstration keep him forever shivering on the brink of Belief is as great an imbecile as the man at the opposite pole, who simply consults his prophetic soul for the answer to everything? What is this but saying that our opinions about the nature of things belong to our moral life?

Here the influence of Renouvier is very apparent, that French philosopher who had taught him that he could sustain a thought because he chose to do so, when he might have other thoughts. If he could do this, regardless of weak logic or the lack of scientific proof of "free will," why could he not entertain "opinions about the nature of things" which would strengthen his "moral life"? Once again we see James steadily working toward his mature philosophy.

In the same year he demonstrated his talent for satire in a biting review for the *Nation* of a book on *Der Modern Pessimismus,* by a Dr. Edmund Pfleiderer. "In other countries," says James,

aristocratic misanthropes, dyspeptic pleasure-seekers, and unappreciated geniuses have existed, and their utterances never passed beyond the sphere of splenetic or pathetic individuality. . . . It was reserved for Schopenhauer to show his countrymen that the cursing and melting moods could be kept alive permanently, and extended indefinitely . . . and Schopenhauer's disciple Hartmann, whose work, the *Philosophie des Unbewussten* [Philosophy of the Unconscious], has met with one of the greatest literary successes of the time, and carried the new gospel into regions where the torch of metaphysics had never yet begun to glimmer, has made everything so simple and perfect in his system, that all who have a quarrel with destiny, whether peevish or tragic, can be housed there side by side, without altering their mode of life or losing any of their "home comforts" in the process of cure. For it would be unpardonable in these philosophers to preach disgust with life unless the disgust were likely to lead the way to a cure. Existence being of course the original sin of that substance or essence of things which Schopenhauer calls "Will," and to which Von Hartmann gives the name of "the Unconscious," annihilation or *nirvana* is of course the cure. And in both philosophies this may be attained through the thorough and final intellectual persuasion of the vanity of all the goods of life and the consequent extinction of every desire.

But there is a difference, James notes, between the master and his pupil:

Schopenhauer's philosophy, says Hartmann, is one of despair. So far is this from being the worst of all possible worlds, . . . it is the best, for it tends invincibly to the *summum bonum* of extinction. Let no man then desert the ranks, but each labor in the Lord's vineyard, sneering, lamenting, and cursing as he pleases, getting indigestion himself, and begetting young, to inoculate them with a disgust greater than his own, and co-operating so with the grand movement of things which is bound to culminate in deliverance. Above all, let us have no standing aloof and trying prematurely to save one's individual self, like Schopenhauer's ascetics. This delightful unselfish submission to epicurean practice in the midst of pessimistic theory is Hartmann's cleverest stroke.

To James's Anglo-Saxon mind what "seems so outlandish is that crowds of dapper fellows, reveling in animal spirits and conscious strength, should, enroll themselves in cold blood" as Hartmann's apostles.

These Germans can attain their absolute luxury of woe only by speaking of things transcendentally and metaphysically. As far as the outward animal life goes, the existence of a Walt Whitman confounds Schopenhauer quite as thoroughly as the existence of a Leopardi refutes Dr. Pangloss [the optimistic philosopher satirized in Voltaire's *Candide*]; and Hartmann's elaborate indictment of the details of life is precisely on a par in point of logic with the "wisdom and beneficence" philosophy of the most edifying and gelatinous Sunday-school orator.

We then get a glimpse of James's later-elaborated theory that the universe is still in process of formation, and may be eventually either good or bad depending upon the forces at work upon it, among which is the mind of the human race. "The world is thus absolutely good only in a potential or hypothetic sense, and the hypothetic form of the optimistic belief is the very signature of its consistency, and first condition of its probability."

It was also in 1875 that the most consistent and thoroughgoing agnostic James had known died, his old eccentric bachelor friend Chauncey Wright. In the past few years Wright had become lonelier and more unhappy than ever, and on a Saturday night, September 11, when most of his friends, including William James, were out of town, he suffered a stroke at his desk. His housekeeper discovered him next morning, barely alive, and gave the alarm. Henry James Jr., who had not yet departed for Europe, heard the news and ran through the quiet Sunday morning streets to Wright's house, but arrived a few minutes too late.

After William's return to Cambridge he wrote an article about Wright for the *Nation* which was both a public memorial and a personal tribute, and an unconscious revelation of the contrast between his own mind and thought in 1875 and that of this Cambridge "Socrates." Chauncey Wright's death "reminds us most sadly of the law," he began, "that to be an effective great man one needs to have *many* qualities great. If power of analytic intellect pure and simple could suffice, the name of Chauncey Wright would assuredly be as famous as it is now obscure, for he was not merely the great mind of a village—if Cambridge will pardon the expression—but either in London or Berlin he would, with equal ease, have taken the place of master which he held with us."

But Wright failed to be "an effective great man" because his "best work was done in conversation," which affected only the few friends who knew him. He was shy, lacked ambition, and was even indolent. His philosophical defense of Darwin's theory of "natural selection" was so well thought of by Darwin that the great evolutionist had it reprinted in England and distributed at his own expense —Wright's most notable recognition.

In philosophy Wright "was a worker on the path opened by Hume, and a treatise on psychology written by him . . . would probably have been the last and most accomplished utterance of what he liked to call the British school." Although Wright accepted biological evolution, he rejected the "nebular hypothesis" in astronomy, because he could see no way of proving that cosmic change moved from chaos to organization, and he conceived the

happy phrase, "cosmical weather," to describe the irregular dissipation and aggregation of worlds; so, in contemplating the totality of being, he preferred to think of phenomena as the result of a sort of ontologic weather, without inward rationality, an aimless drifting to and fro, from the midst of which relatively stable and so (for us) rational combinations may emerge. The order we observe in things needs *explanation* only on the supposition of a preliminary or potential disorder; and this he pointed out is, as things actually *are* orderly, a gratuitous notion.

Probably James never knew another mind so "disinterested"—so willing to observe dispassionately and accept whatever conclusion impersonal reasoning turned up—as that of this modest, unselfish,

unegotistical man. In later years James's own thinking was often influenced or clarified by certain doctrines or published essays of
Wright, one notable example being the chapter on "Reason" in the
Principles of Psychology, in which James acknowledged indebtedness to Wright's "Evolution of Self-Consciousness," written at Darwin's suggestion. But William James's relationship with Chauncey
Wright was more personal and deep-rooted than this. Wright's
philosophical skepticism had pushed him to the limits of his forensic
and emotional strength, and he never felt satisfied with his answers
to Wright's destructive criticisms. For years after Wright's death
he continued to think of refinements to the answers which he might
have given but could not quite think of on the spot. Not until his
own empiricism had matured did he gain sufficient confidence in his
own thinking to cease worrying about the holes that Chauncey
Wright had torn in his immature logic.

Throughout the first two decades of his professional life, the
philosophical subject which interested James most continued to be
free will *versus* determinism. In a review published in the *Nation*
June 8, 1876, called "Bain and Renouvier," he contrasted Bain's
cautious refusal to entertain any idea which had not yet been scientifically proven with Renouvier's freedom to accept needed or useful
beliefs. He also continued to correspond with Renouvier, to whom
he had addressed his first letter in 1872. On July 29, 1876, he assured
Renouvier that "it is a mere affair of time" before "you will take
your place in the general History of Speculation as the classical and
finished representative of the tendency which was begun by Hume,
and to which writers before you had made only fragmentary contributions, whilst you have fused the whole matter into a solid,
elegant and definitive system, perfectly consistent, and capable, by
reason of its moral vitality, of becoming popular, so far as that is
permitted to philosophic systems."

In an essay published posthumously as "Some Problems of Philosophy" James asserted again: "Renouvier was one of the greatest of
philosophic characters, and but for the decisive impression made on
me in the seventies by his masterly advocacy of pluralism I might
never have got free of the monistic superstition under which I had
grown up." So great was James's admiration for Renouvier—though
he admitted there were some "psychological and moral facts" in
Renouvier's doctrines which he could not yet (1876) wholly accept
—that he became an enthusiastic propagandist of this French philos-

opher and urged both his students and colleagues to read him. Renouvier in turn showed his appreciation by helping his assistant François Pillon translate several of James's essays, which Renouvier published in the *Critique Philosophique;* in this way William James first became known in France.

The encouragement he received from Renouvier stimulated James's ambition to be transferred entirely to the Department of Philosophy, which he expected to develop in the new academic atmosphere at Harvard. In 1876 G. Stanley Hall wrote an open letter to the *Nation* condemning the neglect of philosophy in American colleges:

> Within the last few years I have visited the class-rooms of many of our best institutions, and believe that there are few if any branches which are so inadequately taught as those generally roughly classed as philosophy. Deductive logic, or the syllogism, is the most thoroughly dwelt upon, while induction, aesthetic and psychological and ethical studies, and especially the history of the leading systems of philosophy, ancient and modern, and the marvellous new developments in England and Germany, are almost entirely ignored.

On September 21, 1876, the *Nation* printed an amplification of Hall's charges contributed anonymously by James:

> The philosophical teaching, as a rule in our higher seminaries is in the hands of the president, who is usually a minister of the Gospel, and, as he more often owes his position to general excellence of character and administrative faculty than to any speculative gifts or propensities, it usually follows that "safeness" becomes the main characteristic of his tuition; that his classes are edified rather than awakened, and leave college with the generous youthful impulse, to reflect on the world and our position in it, rather dampened and discouraged than stimulated by the lifeless discussions and flabby formulas they have had to commit to memory.

The fact that James withheld his name from this letter suggests that he had Harvard partly in mind in writing it, though philosophy had not for some years been taught by the president, and Eliot was capable of understanding what a department of philosophy should be. Nevertheless, in addition to Palmer, the courses in philosophy were taught by Francis Bowen ("Fanny" Bowen to the students), who had offered a course in "Psychology" before James began his, to Bowen's annoyance; and by Andrew Preston Peabody, Professor of Christian Morals. Perhaps to cushion the impact of this letter on Harvard sensibilities—for its authorship was sure to become known—James concluded: "Meanwhile, when we find announced that the students in Harvard College next year [1877–1878] may study any or all of the following works under the guidance of different professors,—Locke's 'Essay,' Kant's 'Kritik,' Schopenhauer and Hartmann, Hodgson's 'Theory of Practice,' and Spencer's 'Psychology,'—we need not complain of universal academic stagnation, even today." Although this was a respectable beginning, compared to other American colleges, with Bowen and Peabody teaching the courses James could not have expected very impressive results, except possibly from his own class in Spencer's "Psychology."

III

Absorbed as William James was in his teaching, museum directing, and starting a psychological laboratory, he was able through his correspondence with Henry Jr., now living in Paris at 29 Rue du Luxembourg, to feel that he was not entirely out of touch with the world of literature and art. In Paris Harry had become well acquainted with Turgenev and was on less familiar terms with Flaubert, Maupassant, Renan, and other famous writers and artists. Henry's first novel, *Roderick Hudson*, was published late in 1875, and he was eager to hear news of its American reception. On December 12 William wrote that it "seems to be a very common theme of conversation." He himself had found the story better in the book than he had thought it in its magazine installments, "but I must tell you that I am again struck unfavorably by the tendency of the personages to reflect on themselves and give an acute critical scientific introspective classification of their own natures and states of mind, *à la* G. Sand. Take warning . . . !"

Charles Peirce was another source of interest to the two brothers. He was spending several months in Europe, visiting astronomical observatories and performing experiments in gravity. Early in December Henry wrote, "He is busy swinging pendulums at the Observatory, and thinks himself indifferently treated by the Paris scientists. We meet every two or three days to dine together; but tho' we get on very well, our sympathy is economical rather than intellectual." William replied promptly: "I am amused that you should have fallen

into the arms of C. S. Peirce, whom I imagine you find a rather uncomfortable bedfellow, thorny and spinous, but the way to treat
him is after the fabled 'nettle' receipt: grasp firmly, contradict, push
hard, make fun of him, and he is as pleasant as anyone; but be
overawed by his sententious manner and his paradoxical and obscure
statements—wait upon them, as it were, for light to dawn—and you
will never get a feeling of ease with him any more than I did for
years, until I changed my course and treated him more or less
chaffingly. I confess I like him very much in spite of all his peculiarities, for he is a man of genius, and there's always something in that
to compel one's sympathy." Before Peirce left Paris for Berlin three
months later, Henry saw him infrequently, but confirmed William's
impression of him: "He is a very good fellow, and one must appreciate his mental ability; but he has too little social talent, too little
art of making himself agreeable."

William himself was now leading a more sociable life, but at times
it only made him feel a stronger sympathy for the "spinous" Peirce.
On January 22, 1876, he wrote Harry: "Last night I went of all
places in the world to Mrs. Sargent's aesthetic tea in Chestnut
Street. [Mrs. Sargent was the widow of a prosperous Boston physician, Dr. Howard Sargent.] Certain individuals read poetry, whilst
others sat and longed for them to stop so that they might begin to
talk. The room was full of a decidedly good-looking set of people,
especially women—but New England all over! Give me a human
race with some *guts* to them, no matter if they do belch at you now
and then."

In literature, too, William had been nauseated by the overrefine-
ment displayed in Renan's *Dialogues et Fragments Philosophiques*,
which he reviewed for the *Nation*. The book made him wonder
about the health and sanity of France: "It seems to us no less than
an example of mental ruin—the last expression of a nature in which
the seeds of insincerity and foppishness, which existed alongside of
splendid powers, have grown up like rank weeds and smothered the
better possibilities. The dialogues which form the only new part of
the book are simply priggishness rampant, an indescribable unmanli-
ness of tone compounded of a sort of histrionically sentimental self-
conceit, and a nerveless and boneless fear of what will become of the
universe if 'l'homme vulgaire' is allowed to go on. M. Renan's idea of
God seems to be that of a power to whom one may successfully go
like a tell-tale child and say: 'Please, won't you make "l'homme

vulgaire" stop?' As the latter waxes every day more fat and insolent, the belief in God burns dim, and is replaced by the idea of a kind of cold-blooded destiny whose inscrutable and inhuman purposes we are blindly serving, with at most the relief of making piquant guesses and epigrams as we go, about our Master and ourselves."

Henry had written William about meeting Renan and his wife at a dinner: "Renan is hideous and charming,—more hideous, even, than his photographs and more charming even than his writing. His talk at table was really exquisite for urbanity, fineness and wit,—all quite without show-off. I talked with him for three-quarters of an hour in the corner after dinner, told him that I couldn't measure his writings on the side of erudition, but that they had always been for me (and all my family!!) '*la plus haute perfection de l'expression*,' and he treated me as if I were a distinguished savant."

In June of 1876 Henry commented on Renan's *Dialogues* in a letter to the New York *Tribune*, but after reading William's sterner criticism (first expressed in a personal letter to Henry and then amplified in the review for the *Nation*), Henry wrote his brother on July 4: "Your remarks on Renan were most refreshing, and (strange as it may appear to you after my worthless account of his book in the *Tribune*) quite in accordance with my own sentiments. I suspected what you say, but as it was only a vague feeling (mingled with a great admiration of his artistry) I attempted to make nothing of it (since I could make so little), and chose the tack of rather wholesale and general praise. But I am ready to believe anything bad of him. The longer I live in France the better I like the French personally, but the more convinced I am of their bottomless superficiality."

Almost at the same time that Henry was writing William on the Fourth of July, William was writing Henry with the affectionate defiance he often exhibited when he was feeling well: "Your letters breathe more and more a spirit of domestication in the modern Babylon which is very pleasant to me to receive. I suppose from your gilded and snobbish heights you think of us here with great pity, but for my part I hurl it back at you, being on the whole contented with my outward lot. . . . Your spiritual condition is evidently felicitous, with your Turgenevs, your de Broglies, your Montargis and your Longchamps. Long may you enjoy them, only keep watch and ward lest in your style you become too Parisian and lose your hold on the pulse of the great American public, to which after all you must pander for support. In your last *Tribune* letter . . . there were too many traces of Gallicism in manner. It will be a good thing for you to resolve never to use the word 'supreme,' and to take great care not to use 'delicate' in the French sense of a 'cultured and fastidious' person."

William had just returned the night before (July 4) to Cambridge from a three-day visit to Wendell Holmes and his bride, Fanny Dixwell, at Mattapoisett, near Plymouth: "I fell quite in love with she [the same "she" William had found Wendell "monopolizing" on his return from Brazil]; and he exemplified in the most ridiculous way Michelet's *'mariage de l'homme et de la terre.'* I told him that he looked like Millet's peasant figures as he stooped over his little plants in his flannel shirt and trousers. He is a powerful battery, formed like a planing machine to gouge a deep self-beneficial groove through life; and his virtues and faults were thrown into singular relief by the lonesomeness of the shore, which as it makes every object, rock or shrub, stand out so vividly, seemed also to put him and his wife under a sort of lens for you."

The exuberance of this letter, for all of its high-handed advice to Henry Jr. and sharp analysis of Wendell, gives no indication that William's own sensibilities had been disturbed by a discovery he had recently made in reading the second installment of Henry's *The American* in the June *Atlantic*. "The morbid little clergyman is worthy of Ivan Sergeyevich. I was not a little amused to find some of my own attributes in him,—I think you found my 'moral reaction' excessive when I was abroad."

The Unitarian minister in *The American*, called Mr. Babcock, has recognizable characteristics of William James, though perhaps he should not be called an outright caricature. William was, like Mr. Babcock, "fond of pictures and churches" (though at the time of his sojourn with Henry in Italy he was less fond of these than Henry himself); and he did, as his diary shows, regard "works of art as questions and his relations with them as experiences" which he must analyze. Though Henry had always doted on *remembering* experiences in all their nuances of emotion, reducing experiences to a psychological principle or a philosophical theory always struck him as futile.

But the psychologizing was not the only "Williamish" trait that William himself might have recognized in the moralizing traveling companion of Christopher Newman: "In his secret soul he detested Europe and felt an irritated need to protest against Newman's easy homage to so compromised a charmer, mistress of a cynicism that appeared at times to have made him cynical. . . . He mistrusted the 'European' temperament, he suffered from the 'European' climate, he hated the 'European' dinner hour; 'European' life seemed to him unscrupulous and impure." All of these "distrusts" William had expressed, though sometimes partly in jest, and perhaps sometimes to tease Henry, who also took Europe hard, though not in Mr. Babcock's New England way. Possibly the relations of William and Henry might be seen in Mr. Babcock's remark to Newman, "You think I take all questions too hard, and I think you take them too superficially." But this is a doubtful parallel. A more palpable hit is, "Goethe recommended seeing human nature in the most various forms, and Mr. Babcock thought Goethe perfectly splendid." So did William, who also "got his plans into a tangle and talked one moment of doing one thing and the next of doing another."

It is not necessary, however, to regard this very minor character in *The American* as Henry James's method of paying off a grudge against his brother. William did annoy him at times—sometimes even with malicious amusement. But there was no grudge between the brothers. They loved and respected and depended upon each other too much for that. Furthermore, like most novelists, Henry borrowed hints for his characters wherever he could find them. And William had given him several for Mr. Babcock's moral revulsion against the decadence of Europe. William was entirely correct when he said he found "some of my own attributes in him," and there is no reason to doubt his "amusement" over the discovery.

In spite of their many differences in taste and temperament, already noted, the two older James brothers often agreed in their judgments. The widely publicized American Centennial in Philadelphia was similar to the Crystal Palace Exhibition which the boys had seen together in New York in 1851. At the beginning of his vacation in the summer of '76 William had conscientiously paid his visit, being interested especially in the "pictures," and wished Henry Jr. were home to describe them instead of the official cataloguer, who lacked discrimination and indulged in superlatives. Most of the art exhibit impressed William as simply "trashy." France had nothing good to show, but "an unexpected thing that much pleased me was the high average of the American pieces. It is obvious that we are a people of artistic sensibility. Not that there were there any very great American works, but there was almost nothing vile, such as every foreign school gives you in its degenerate pupils, who without a grain of inward decency or cleverness of their own, manufacture a far-off echo of someone else's *chic* or ability. An immense preponderance of the American work was landscape, and in almost every case the animus was a perfectly sincere effort to reproduce a natural aspect which had affected in some particular way the painter's sensibility. There was little schooling through it all, but genuine native refinement and, speaking in a broad way, intelligence of purpose. The English school was a most curious study, being so good in its best works, but so utterly preposterous and inartistic in some of its worst things of thirty or forty years ago. . . ."

Henry replied: "Your letter, with its superior criticism of so many things, the Philadelphia Exhibition especially, interested me extremely and quickened my frequent desire to converse with you. What you said of the good effect of the American pictures there gave me great pleasure; and I have no doubt you are right about our artistic spontaneity and sensibility. My chief impression of the Salon [from reading the catalogue] was that four-fifths of it was purely mechanical and, *de plus*, vile."

Without any trace of resentment Henry also thanked William for his criticisms of *The American*. "I can't judge it. Your remarks on my French tricks in my letters are doubtless most just, and shall be heeded. But it's an odd thing that such tricks should grow at a time when my last layer of resistance to a long-encroaching weariness and satiety with the French mind and its utterance has fallen from me like a garment. I have done with 'em forever, and am turning English all over."

It was not until late autumn, however, that Henry James Jr. actually did move to England. On January 12, 1877, he wrote William that he had been living in London for five rainy, foggy weeks, but he believed that the inconveniences and drearinesses he would feel less as time went on, and this proved to be true. He soon discovered that he had attained more literary reputation in England than in America, and he was presently extended the privileges of the exclusive Athenaeum Club, "a place it takes sixteen years for a Briton to become a member of!—if things go smoothly." They were going very smoothly indeed for Henry Jr. On February 28, 1877, he wrote William, "What is your 'Herbert Spencer elective'?—to which you have alluded, but without explaining its sudden genesis [—though William had already taught this graduate seminar for a whole semester]. I often take an afternoon nap beside H.S. at the Athenaeum, and feel as if I were robbing *you* of the privilege."

CHAPTER XIII Psychology and Psyche

. . . what is this mythological and poetical talk about psychology and Psyche and keeping back a manuscript composed during a honeymoon?

—W.J. *to Francis J. Child*

I

DURING THE ACADEMIC TERMS for 1875–1876 William James often took walks with G. Stanley Hall, who was that year an instructor in English at Harvard, at the end of which he was to return to Germany to continue his study of psychology before coming back to take his Ph.D. at Harvard. Aside from their intellectual interests, the two men enjoyed talking about their experiences in Germany, which had been as different as their own temperaments and youthful backgrounds. Hall had left a rocky New England farm to attend Williams College; then he had worked in New York to support himself while studying at Union Theological Seminary and trying to convert Bowery streetwalkers. Through the influence of the Reverend Henry Ward Beecher he unexpectedly obtained funds for study in Germany, where he quickly lost his Calvinistic theology and his puritan inhibitions. Though two years younger than James, at thirty-two he was far more sophisticated and self-reliant, and emotionally better adjusted.

It is quite possible that William James might have got rid of his neurotic symptoms if he could have shed his inhibitions in Germany as successfully as Hall had, but he had come back fully as inhibited and neurotic as he had been before leaving home. Hall, like William's father, had grown up observing Sunday as a day of gloom and depression, but in Berlin and Heidelberg he found it to be a time of excursions, games, theatre, concerts, and dancing. "Servants went out and families dined together with friends in public resorts. Soldiers released from their barracks were everywhere; courting and lovemaking were carried on in the open, and young couples seemed not only unabashed but almost fond of having others observe their enjoyment of one another." Good German beer consumed with convivial companions relaxed nervous tensions, banished reticence, and promoted friendships. This William James had discovered too as a member of the student fraternity in Switzerland. But his beer-drinking, unlike Hall's, was with male companions, and did not lead to intimacies with *Fräuleins*. William had been decidedly interested in the *Fräuleins*, but during his year in Germany he was a semi-invalid, and also lived much alone at the spas or in his Dresden boarding house protected by his grandmotherly landlady. Further-more, in spite of his father's Fourieristic free-love doctrines, which were so idealistic that they were apparently not very real even to Henry Sr. himself, William had grown up with exalted ideals of chastity.

Thus, where James had merely observed the nubile German girls or exchanged innocent sentimentalities with them, two *Fräuleins* in succession taught Hall "what love really meant and could do." With neither was there any engagement or plan for the future, or any awkward consequence, and both girls later married and had large families. Hall was convinced that the temporary liaisons harmed neither of them, and as for himself:

> I learned how great an enlightener love is and what a spring of mind Eros can be. . . . Not only did these companions facilitate my use of German but, what was vastly more important, they awoke capacities hitherto unusually dormant and repressed and thus made life seem richer and more meaningful. If passion was aroused, the power to moderate and control it was also gained and I have never had regret but only a sense of enlargement of soul from it all.

William James had returned from Brazil, as we have seen, starved for female companionship, and it is possible that if Fanny Dixwell had not been so firmly attached to Wendell Holmes, he might have fallen in love with her at that time. But until he was thirty-four years old he never had a real love-affair. Ever since his first student days at Harvard he had hoped that he might someday be able to marry and have a family, but until he began teaching at Harvard he had consistently felt that his poor health and consequent inability to support a wife required that he refrain from even think-ing of such a goal. Although he had grown up outside any church, and had no theological beliefs, he had strong religious predilections and even stronger moral convictions. In fact, in almost all his serious thinking and social conduct moral considerations were uppermost in his mind.

This fact is quite apparent in many passages of James's *Principles of Psychology*, which he would soon begin writing. For example, in explaining the functions of the lower and higher centers of the brain we find these remarks about chastity and moral responsibility:

> No one need be told how dependent all human social elevation is upon the prevalence of chastity. Hardly any factor measures more than this the difference between civilization and barbarism. Physiologically interpreted, chastity means nothing more than the fact that present solicitations of sense are overpowered by suggestions of aesthetic and moral fitness which the circumstances awaken in the cerebrum; and that upon the inhibitory or permissive influence of these alone action directly depends.

> Within the psychic life due to the cerebrum itself the same general distinction obtains, between considerations of the more immediate and considerations of the more remote. In all ages the man whose determinations are swayed by reference to the most distant ends has been held to possess the higher intelligence. The tramp who lives from hour to hour; the bohemian whose engagements are from day to day; the bachelor who builds but for a single life; the father who acts for another generation; the patriot who thinks of a whole community and many generations; and finally, the philosopher and saint whose cares are for humanity and for eternity,—these range themselves in an unbroken hierarchy, wherein each successive grade results from an increased manifestation of the special form of action by which the cerebral centres are distinguished from all below them.

However "old-fashioned" and didactic this kind of psychologizing may seem today, it opens a window on the mind and character of William James. Undoubtedly the prevailing American and British prudishness of the mid-nineteenth century had conditioned his attitudes toward sex far more than he could possibly realize. He was naturally emotional and impulsive, always impatient, and often indiscreet in "speaking his mind"; but he had so firmly controlled or repressed his own sexual urges that he could not fully appreciate their power in a less inhibited society than his own genteel one. In his chapter on "Instinct" in his *Principles* he could offer this analysis:

> Of all propensities, the sexual impulses bear on their face the most obvious signs of being instinctive, in the sense of blind, automatic,

and untaught. The teleology they contain is often at variance with the wishes of the individual concerned; and the actions are performed for no assignable reason but because Nature urges just that way. Here, if ever, then, we ought to find those characters of fatality, infallibility, and uniformity, which, we are told, make of actions done from instinct a class so utterly apart. But is this so? The facts are just the reverse: the sexual instinct is particularly liable to be checked and modified by slight differences in the individual stimulus, by the inward condition of the agent himself, by habits once acquired, and by the antagonism of contrary impulses operating on the mind. One of these is the ordinary shyness . . . ; another is what might be called the *anti-sexual* instinct, the instinct of personal isolation, the actual repulsiveness to us of the idea of intimate contact with most of the persons we meet, especially those of our own sex. Thus it comes about that this strongest passion of all, so far from being the most "irresistible," may, on the contrary, be the hardest one to give rein to, and that individuals in whom the inhibiting influences are potent may pass through life and never find an occasion to have it gratified. . . .

Amplifying his notion of the "instinct of personal isolation," James says that it "exists more strongly in men with respect to one another, and more strongly in women with respect to men. In women it is called coyness, and has to be positively overcome by a process of wooing before the sexual instinct inhibits it and takes its place." Such, of course, all "nice" women of the period were taught, so successfully that most of them would have most sincerely agreed with James; and belief most powerfully influences conduct, at least on the conscious level. These deeply imbedded beliefs in instinctive aversion to physical contact, and woman's natural coyness, will help to explain the agonies William James went through in his own wooing, delayed until his thirty-fourth year.

II

Early in 1876 Henry James Sr. returned one night from a meeting of the Radical Club in Boston and announced to William that he had seen his son's future wife. That he would ever have a wife was news to William, and he was eager to hear about her. His father could say only that she was a teacher in Miss Sanger's School for Girls in Boston, and that he had been greatly impressed by her personality and the few words he had exchanged with her. With considerable interest William himself attended the next meeting of the Radical Club and was introduced by an eccentric friend of his, Thomas Davidson, a huge, burly, blue-eyed Scot with whom James often talked philosophy, to Miss Alice Howe Gibbens.

Miss Gibbens was a woman of twenty-seven, short, stocky, with somewhat heavy features, but with soft brown hair and sparkling dark eyes which lighted up her face and gave her wild-rose complexion a surprising luminosity and glowing vitality. And as soon as she spoke, William felt the weight of his father's prophecy. Her voice was so resonant that even commonplace words sounded musical in her pleasantly vibrant enunciation. She was poised, unaffected, but rather startling in the unreserved candor of her remarks, which could either repel or charm a new acquaintance. It delighted and stimulated William and challenged his own spontaneous wit. But however caustic her tongue, her serious eyes seemed to tell him that she was capable of the sympathy and understanding he needed.

The very fact that Miss Gibbens attended the meetings of the Radical Club tells something about her. It was an informal association of Unitarian ministers and liberal laymen, formed to discuss the abolishing of all vestiges of supernaturalism in the Christian religion and finding ways to make the human religious experience more spiritual. That this group would arouse the curiosity of William's father is not surprising; but Miss Gibbens attended the Congregationalist church and was in many ways fairly conventional in her religion. However, she enjoyed the intellectual stimulation of new ideas, and especially of people who held them. But no one had ever interested her as much as this intense, witty young Harvard teacher. She was almost as spontaneously attracted to him as he to her, though of course her well-bred "coyness" prevented her from disillusioning him by unseemly capitulation. To William's father the mutual attraction was almost as if predestined. Knowing William's conscientiousness and his worries about being able to support a wife on an assistant professor's salary, Henry Sr. urged his son to marry Miss Gibbens without delay and depend upon his father for any financial assistance he might need.

Alice Gibbens had only three years previously returned to America after living for five years in Europe with her widowed mother and two younger sisters, whom she was now partly supporting on her teacher's salary. She and William had barely missed being in Heidelberg and in Dresden at the same time in 1868, and in Florence during William's visit there in 1873. But their knowledge of these places gave them a feeling that they were not strangers to each other, and they also soon discovered mutual tastes in literature, French, German, and English, but especially Browning's poems. Their first act of friendship was an exchange of books, which they discussed on leisurely walks under the great elms of Boston Common. Because of her mother's dependence upon her, emotional as well as financial, the thought of marriage had occupied Alice's daydreams less than those of most young women; it was not repugnant, merely seemed remote. Then as this brilliant, emotional, but hypochondriacal teacher of psychology stirred affections which she had never felt before, she began to wonder if she were the right wife for him, and their relationship became troubled and fragile.

Although William undoubtedly idealized Alice Gibbens and in his imagination made her more than human, he was not wrong in thinking her a very remarkable person. She in no way resembled the stock type of the spinster schoolteacher. Though, like William, she had never before been in love, her experience had given her a maturity of character and practicality in judgment which he, in his more protected life at home, had not yet attained. Both her parents were descendants of early New England settlers, a mixture of British and Irish. But her father and mother had been an ill-matched couple—he, Dr. Daniel Lewis Gibbens, a large, hearty, convivial country physician; she, Elizabeth ("Eliza") Putnam Webb, a delicate, genteel woman, whose sensibilities were frequently exacerbated by her husband's tastes and fondness for saloon cronies. As if to accentuate his awkward position in his wife's ultrafeminine world, fate gave Dr. Gibbens three daughters: Alice, born February 5, 1849; Mary Sherwin, two years later; and finally Margaret Merrill, in 1857.

Before the birth of his third daughter Dr. Gibbens moved his family in 1856 to California, where two of Mrs. Gibbens' brothers were living. Alice always remembered the trip with pleasure, although it was long and exhausting, and in crossing the Isthmus of Panama her mother had nearly died of cholera, with the second sea-voyage to San Francisco still to be made. Dr. Gibbens bought a ranch in the Santa Clara Valley, and Alice was delighted with the new flowers, trees, and birds, and learned all their names. They were in one of the gold-rush communities, but Alice's father was interested in ranching instead of mining or speculating—apparently he did not consider trying to practice medicine. The venture might have succeeded if a legal dispute had not arisen over Dr. Gibbens' title to the land because of a previous Spanish claim, which resulted in his losing the property. He attempted to settle on another ranch at Los Altos, but soon had to return to Boston, so "broke" that Mrs. Gibbens was forced to live with her grandmother, Mrs. Christopher Webb, near Weymouth, a small town a few miles south of Boston, while Dr. Gibbens returned to his mother's home in Boston. During this separation of her parents Alice often visited her father and grandmother on Chauncey Street. In Weymouth she attended public school and her mother's Congregational church. She was a devoted student of the Bible, and after her marriage often suggested appropriate quotations for William to use in his speeches and writings. In 1861 Mrs. Webb died, but Mrs. Gibbens and her three daughters continued to live in the old farm house.

At the outbreak of the Civil War no one in Alice's family was of military age, but she felt such great sympathy for the soldiers that she slept on the floor in order to share vicariously some of their hardships. She also helped in a more practical way by shredding lint for bandages. Her father, now in control of his weakness for alcohol, went to New Orleans to fill a civil administrative position during the military occupation of Louisiana by the Union Army. He was successful in his work and became private secretary to the mayor. During his stay in New Orleans Alice corresponded with him regularly and was elated over his plan to return to his wife and daughters and live in the country somewhere near Boston. As Christmas of 1865 approached, she impatiently awaited his homecoming; but the day before he was scheduled to arrive Mrs. Gibbens received a telegram stating that on the following day his body would be at the Boston railroad station. He had left New Orleans as planned, but stopped in Mobile, Alabama, where he was found dead, shot with his own revolver.

The shock of this tragic news prostrated Mrs. Gibbens. She was not even capable of making funeral arrangements. Alice, now sixteen, took charge and did everything that was required, not only for the funeral but also afterward in running the household. She nursed her mother, prepared meals, and took charge of her younger sisters. In actuality she became the head of the Gibbens family, and her mother continued to depend upon her for nearly every practical decision long after her slow recuperation. It is hardly surprising, therefore, that premature domestic responsibility should have made this sturdy girl somber-faced and strong-willed. But she was never cross or bitter. On the contrary, she was unfailingly cheerful, and not without a sense of humor, though she seldom smiled. Naturally a certain stoicism became ingrained in her character, though she permitted herself some pleasures. She thought, for example, that she was too awkward to waltz, but enjoyed "round-dancing."

Dr. Gibbens had managed to save some money and left his widow twenty thousand dollars, but even with the addition of some modest property which she had inherited, Mrs. Gibbens's total income was only about eighteen hundred dollars a year, hardly adequate for the support of four people during the period of inflation in the postwar years. Mrs. Gibbens had been told that one could live more cheaply in Europe, and from an American woman who had lived in Germany she got the address of a pastor in a village near Leihgestern who agreed to board her and the three girls at cheap rates.

Thus it came about that in July 1868 Mrs. Gibbens, her three daughters, and a cousin, Helen Merrill, sailed for Bremen. None of them could speak German, and except for the kindness of strangers they would have been helpless. The captain of the ship took them to his home in Bremen for lunch, then put them on a train headed for Leihgestern bei Giessen. Someone met them and took them to an expensive hotel which they could not afford. Next morning a book dealer acted as interpreter for them and they learned that the pastor with whom Mrs. Gibbens had corresponded was ill and had assigned them to another pastor; but they found his house dirty and depressing, and all these disappointments reduced Mrs. Gibbens to hysterics. Alice, however, guided the family to Heidelberg, found an inexpensive pension in the suburbs, and later more desirable quarters in the city. (Many years later, in May 1900, Alice Gibbens James and her husband stopped at the Hotel Victoria on the Anlage in Heidelberg, and she discovered that this was not far from Frau Förster's, where she had lived with her mother and sisters in 1868. The Heidelberg University students seemed unchanged: the same caps, the same saber-scarred cheeks, even the same bull terrier dogs trotting at the students' heels—but they no longer leered at her!)

Soon the Gibbens family learned to speak German and to enjoy their expatriation. From Heidelberg they moved to Dresden, where William James had also lived for several months in 1867–1868, and later Berlin. They remained in Germany throughout the Franco-

Prussian War. In a village near Baden Baden Alice took voice lessons from Clara Schumann, widow of the composer and a famous pianist herself. She continued taking voice lessons in Florence, where the Gibbenses spent their fifth year in Europe, under Luigi Vanuccine, a singer, composer, and conductor of considerable renown in Italy at that time. But in 1873 the Gibbens family returned to Boston, mainly because Mrs. Gibbens' income had declined; during her absence her property had been mismanaged, and it no longer yielded enough for the support of herself and her daughters. Alice and one of her sisters both secured positions, and she was in her third year of teaching at Miss Sanger's school when she met William James.

III

The only impediments to the marriage of Alice Gibbens and William James were their tormenting consciences. William still believed that he was a physical wreck, or at the very least a neurasthenic, in spite of the respectable amount of work he had managed in the past two years to accomplish in the classroom, in starting a psychological laboratory, and in directing a museum; and he wondered if he had the right to inflict his disabilities on a healthy, normal woman such as Alice Gibbens. After she had adjusted her thinking to marriage, with her mother's encouragement, she was ready to accept William as a husband. But then his agonizing letters made her wonder if she were the right woman for him, and it was now she who had the moral scruples. Finally she decided that for his sake she ought not to marry him, and almost in despair she went to Quebec in the summer of 1877 to remove temptation and reconcile herself to giving him up—a noble-minded renunciation that reminds one of some of Henry James's heroines. But this was exactly the psychology (though not so intended) to bring the psychologist to his senses. He now began to woo in earnest. To be sure of making the right decision, however, she kept him in suspense until the following spring.

William's frustrating courtship cast a shadow over his professional life, though he continued to perform his duties as best he could. Dr. D. C. Gilman, president of the newly founded Johns Hopkins University, modeled after German universities, was interested in obtaining James for his Psychology Department and invited him to give ten lectures in February 1878 in psychology. James accepted and chose for his subject "The Brain and the Mind." Though he had already written out the lectures, he unavoidably carried his personal worries with him to Baltimore, as Professor Francis J. Child, who was also lecturing at Johns Hopkins, reported in a letter to James Russell Lowell, currently the United States Minister to Great Britain: "I had William James with me a fortnight in Baltimore. He gave ten lectures on the brain as the organ of the mind, and made a decided impression. I heard the last, in which he offered reasons for not accepting the theory that we are automatons unreservedly. . . . [He] was sleepless and restless, and, as it turned out, not because the lectures troubled him, but because his fate was in the scales and Miss Alice Gibbens would not say the word he wanted."

Not until May 10, 1878, did Miss Gibbens finally "say the word." On that day, as she often recalled in later years, when the flowering trees and shrubs of the Boston Common perfumed the air, William proposed again and she accepted. Both felt that they might be acting on emotion rather than reason, but they decided to trust their deeper instincts—a decision entirely in harmony with William James's evolving philosophy.

Two days later William wrote his sister-in-law, Mary Holton James: "You may remember my writing to you a couple of years ago that I had seen at a party the evening before, 'the future Mrs. W.J.' I have now the pleasure to announce, not that she is already that, but that she has succeeded in overcoming her natural reluctance to contemplate it as a future possibility, and is in short 'engaged' to me since last Friday. Her name is Miss Alice Gibbens. She teaches at present in a Boston school and is the pink of perfection in all respects, as you may well imagine; reminding me of what you were in that fleeting glimpse I had of you before your marriage, only being a little older. Bob, who has had an inkling of this and of the thorns of my path will be glad to hear that they are all plucked & nothing but the roses remain."

William's letter to Henry Jr. has not survived, but Henry's reply on May 29 has. "Your letter came to me yesterday," he wrote, "giving me great joy, but less surprise than you might think. In fact, I was not surprised at all, for I had been expecting to get some such news as this from you. And yet of Miss Gibbens and your attentions I had heard almost nothing—a slight mention a year ago, in a letter of mother's, which had never been repeated. The wish, perhaps, was father to the thought. I had long wished to see you married; I believe almost as much in matrimony for other people as I believe in it little for myself—which is saying a good deal."

Henry had long been determined to avoid the complications of matrimony in his own life, but he knew William's need for the right kind of wife, and he liked what he had heard about Alice Gibbens— later confirmed by a friendship which was to last beyond his brother's life and until the end of his own. After insisting, with delicate and tactful teasing, that he believed every word of what William wrote him about her—though he would not mind receiving a description from an impartial judge, such as his father, mother, or sister Alice—Henry begged for a photograph, and sent to his future sister-in-law "my cordial—my already fraternal—benediction. I look forward to knowing her as to one of the consolations of the future."

The match was enthusiastically approved by all members of both Alice's and William's families with one apparent exception. No record has survived of Alice James's emotions on first meeting Alice Gibbens, but the second Alice soon developed a violent antipathy for the first, and it is unlikely that this attitude was unprovoked. About the time William's engagement was announced his sister became gravely ill and was nearly insane for several months. Henry Jr. wrote a few weeks later (July 23): "I know it must be a sad summer in Cambridge, and my thoughts are constantly in Quincy Street." It may have been entirely a coincidence that this most serious of Alice James's many attacks of hysteria occurred just at the time when she learned she must share her devoted brother's affections with another woman, but, whatever the cause, the antagonism was unmistakable. This, however, was the only unharmonious note in the rejoicing of the two families over the marriage— and there was never to be any other disharmony. William adored and was adored by Alice's mother, and his own parents were jubilant.

The marriage ceremony was performed on July 10 by the Reverend Rufus Ellis in Alice's grandmother Gibbens' house at 153 Boylston Street, where Alice had lived while teaching in Boston. The wedding was attended only by the relatives and friends of the bride and groom, who immediately set out for Keene Valley in the Adirondack Mountains, where they planned to spend the summer in a farmhouse which William and his friends Henry Bowditch and James Putnam had bought for a few hundred dollars and converted into a vacation camp. On the horizon could be seen the rugged summits of the Giant, Noonmark, Colvin, and the Gothics, and the highest mountain in the Adirondacks, Mount Marcy, was only a day's walk away. Even nearer was Lake Placid, and the Ausable River ran near by. For the reminder of his life this would be William James's favorite vacation retreat, to which he would come back summer after summer, though often alone after Alice had maternal responsibilities.

Henry James Jr. did not receive the news of the exact date of the wedding until after the event had already taken place; then he wrote promptly on July 15: "The abruptness of your union has prevented me from a becoming punctuality in sending Alice a small material emblem of my good wishes; and now I shall wait till next autumn and the beginning of your winter life. I thank her meanwhile extremely for the little note—a charming note—that she sent me in answer to my own—and I feel most agreeably conscious of my intensification of kinship. I envy you your mountains and lakes—your deep free nature. May it do you both—weary workers—all the good you deserve. Ever your fond and faithful brother H.J.,Jr."

A month before his marriage William James had signed a contract with Henry Holt and Company for a book on psychology for Holt's American Science Series. Mr. Holt wanted the manuscript within a year, but James wrote him: "My other engagements and my health both forbid the attempt to execute the work rapidly. Its quality too might then suffer. I don't think I could finish it inside of two years—say the fall of 1880." Little did either prospective author or publisher dream that it would take twelve years. Nevertheless, preliminary work on the book was actually begun on William's honeymoon, to the amusement of his friends. Francis Child reported to James Russell Lowell: "William has already begun a Manual of Psychology—in the honeymoon;—but they are both writing it."

The bride and groom had invited Professor Child to visit them, but he declined to intrude upon their Edenic world and made jokes about their psychological activities, to which William replied on August 16, renewing the invitation but protesting the professor's levity—one of his first letters in his wife's handwriting, for he had dictated it to her: ". . . As for the remaining matter of your somewhat illegible letter, what is this mythological and poetical talk about psychology and Psyche and keeping back a manuscript composed during a honeymoon? The only Psyche now recognized by science is a decapitated frog whose writhings express deeper truths than your weakminded poets ever dreamed. *She* (not Psyche but the bride) loves all these doctrines which are quite novel to her mind, hitherto accustomed to all sorts of mysticism and superstitions. She swears entirely by reflex action now, and believes in universal *Nothwendigkeit* [determinism]. Hope not with your ballad-mongering ever to gain an influence.

"We have spent, however, a ballad-like summer in this delicious cot among the hills. We only needed crooks and a flock of sheep. I need not say that our psychic reaction has been one of content —perhaps as great as ever enjoyed by man.

"So farewell, false friend, till such near time as your ehrwürdig [very worthy] person decorate our hearth at Mrs. Hanks's in Harvard St."

The couple had decided to board in Cambridge until they could acquire a suitable house and furnish it, and the illness of William's sister ruled out their staying with William's parents. At the beginning of the new academic term they were installed in furnished rooms at 387 Harvard Street, where on December 26 William dictated to Alice a letter to their mutual Boston friend, Miss Frances R. Morse, who was traveling in Europe and the Near East and had recently ascended the Nile with the Longfellows: "We are very happily 'boarding' on the corner of Harvard and Ware Street, next door to old Mrs. Cary's, where the Tappans used to live [special friends of William's parents]. We have absolutely no housekeeping trouble; we live surrounded by our wedding presents, and can devote all our energies to studying our lessons, dining with our respective mothers-in-law, receiving and repaying our 'calls,' which average one a day, and anxiously keeping our accounts in a little book so as to see where the trouble is if both ends don't meet." The account book sounds like Alice's practicality—so similar to William's mother's.

IV

When William James indicated his reluctance to leave Harvard, President Gilman offered him a position for three months of the year at Johns Hopkins, evidently hoping that this special arrangement would eventually make James willing to reside permanently in Baltimore. However, this inducement was resisted, mainly, one would suspect, because both Alice and William wished to remain near their parents. William's marriage had made him dissatisfied with his salary and assistant professor's rank, but President Eliot encouraged him to stay at Harvard and trust to promotion. The promotion did not come immediately, but lectures in the autumn of 1878 at the Lowell Institute in Boston supplemented the Harvard salary.

James's professional as well as personal life benefited almost immediately from his marriage, if his great upsurge of creative energy is any indication. In the previous decade he had published about forty-five essays and reviews, many of them brief, and none of outstanding significance. But soon after his marriage he published several major essays, including a critique of Herbert Spencer's *Definition of Mind as Correspondence*, "Brute and Human Intellect," "Quelques considérations sur la méthode subjective," and (in 1879) "The Sentiment of Rationality" and "Are We Automata?"

In the lecture on "The Brain and the Mind," given first at Johns Hopkins and repeated at the Lowell Institute in October and November of 1878, James traced the development of scientific theories on the nature and function of the brain and then analyzed the relations of the brain and the mind. Most of the laboratory psychologists had become increasingly antagonistic to "the subjective method," which James defended in his article in French. They contended that only statistical data based on physiological measurements yielded scientific "truth." But, James pointed out, "the whole theory of different local habitations in the brain for different classes of ideas with fibres connecting the localities together—so that when one locality is excited the excitement may travel along the fibres and waken up the other locality—this whole theory, I say, was originally derived from our introspective knowledge of the way in which our feelings awaken each other."

In spite of all the data the physiologists had accumulated about the nervous system, they had not, James contended, been able to explain consciousness. That still remained in the realm of metaphysics, which these materialists would banish as exploded superstitions and sophistries. "Many persons nowadays seem to think that any conclusion must be very scientific if the arguments in favor of it are all derived from twitching of frogs' legs—especially if the frogs are decapitated—and that, on the other hand, any doctrine chiefly vouched for by the feelings of human beings—with heads on their shoulders—

must be benighted and superstitious." The deep gulf separating these "scientific" physiologists and subjective philosophers was already almost unbridgeable and had become a problem to James in his own classroom. "I have for some years past, in thinking of my duties as teacher in Cambridge, been inclined to deplore the rather wide surface over which my instruction had to be spread. I have been obliged to teach a little anatomy, a little physiology, a little psychology; and I have felt that where one's wisdom tried to cover so much ground it must needs be thin at any given spot."

But now James had come to feel that his misfortune had its advantages. As a teacher of both physiology and psychology, with a keen interest in philosophy, he had read and pondered all the "evidence" and arguments of both sides, and it seemed to him that no theory of the automatic response of nerve cells to physical stimuli could explain a human being's mental life. Thinking-feeling-consciousness was a complex process of *interaction*, not of *automatism*. In fact, not all stimulation of the brain cells came either from physical stimuli outside the body (noise, light, odor, etc.) or from the chemical actions taking place inside the body (digestion, circulation of the blood, absorbing oxygen, etc.).

> The truth is that science and all these other functions of the human mind are alike the results of man's thinking about the phenomena life offers him. . . . I, for one, as a scientific man and a practical man alike, deny utterly that science compels me to believe that my conscience is an *ignis fatuus* or outcast, and I trust that you too, after the evidence of this evening, will go away strengthened in the natural faith that your delights and sorrows, your loves and hates, your aspirations and efforts are real combatants in life's arena, and not impotent, paralytic spectators of the game.

In rejecting the *automatism* in psychology James was consistently following his greatly admired French philosopher, Renouvier. But he had carefully examined the "scientific" arguments for determinism, and he did not reject the conception of the "reflex arc," now firmly established in psychological theory. He insisted, however, that the brain did not act with the consistency and predictability of the spinal cord, and its indeterminacy made choice possible —even necessary. As he expressed it three years later (1881) in "Reflex Action and Theism": "The willing department of our nature . . . dominates both the conceiving department and the feeling department; or, in plainer English, perception and thinking are only there for behavior's sake." Thus James restored *purpose* to the operations of mind and brain, and not only causal explanation, but moral purpose as well. This was to be the psychological foundation of his future philosophical doctrines of freedom and choice; of the influence of a man's emotions on his creative thinking and of volition on his character; of a world which not only affects man, but which he in turn can affect by his own thought and action. James had been working toward these convictions for the past decade, and his marriage in no way changed his thinking, but the stabilizing influence of his wife made it possible for him to give his ideas coherence and expression.

CHAPTER XIV

Fathers and Sons

. . . as my own boys grow up, I shall learn more and more of the

kind of trial you had to overcome in superintending the development

of a creature different from yourself . . . —W.J. *to his father*

I

DURING THE FIRST FOUR YEARS of his marriage, William James twice became a father and lost his own mother and father. It was a period of dramatic change in the lives and fortunes of every member of the James family. Henry Jr. became a literary celebrity and was entertained by lords and ladies, millionaires and statesmen, and the elite of British society; still better, he could now live wholly on the income from his writings and no longer have to draw on his father's letter of credit. Sickly Alice found the friend she needed in Miss Katharine Peabody Loring, a strong, energetic, somewhat masculine young woman of thirty-one (a year younger than Alice), who lived at nearby Beverly, Massachusetts. Under her influence Alice grew strong enough to make a trip with her to New Hampshire, and in the summer of 1881 even a voyage to England. To William's Alice the relationship looked suspiciously Lesbian, but everyone was grateful for Alice's improvement in health.

For the younger James brothers life had turned dark. Bob drank, philandered, quarreled with his wife, and separated from her and his children. Wilky, ill with rheumatism and a diseased heart, ran eighty thousand dollars in debt and had to go into bankruptcy. The debt was too great for his father to pay off, especially after he too had lost money in 1879 by the failure of a western railroad in which he had investments. William's mother continued to keep the household in Quincy Street functioning smoothly, but she was weary from a lifetime of sacrifice for husband and children.

Although William's professional successes were still modest compared to Henry's spectacular triumphs, this was also for him a period of professional growth and establishing a family. His wife was four months pregnant when he took her to Newport for the 1878 Christmas vacation to visit the Tweedys and other friends still living there. In the spring she bore her confinement with some impatience, as might be expected with the first child, but on May 18 she gave birth to a healthy boy, whom William named for his father, so that there were now three Henrys in the family.

William's own views of his fatherhood can only be surmised from the responses of Henry the novelist to the letters of William and his parents, for William's letters of this period were destroyed by Henry Jr. in one of his numerous epistolary immolations. On June 15 he wrote William: "I gather from father's p.s. to mother's letter of last night that your wife is so well on the way to her normal condition again that you have no longer any cause of anxiety. I delight in the image, indistinctly as I yet perceive it, of your infantine Henry. . . . He will be for many a day the flower of Quincy St. and I hope he will bloom with dazzling brilliancy. I can fancy the interest you will take (as a psychologist) in watching his growth, and can trust you to give him a superior education."

Naturally William was proud of his son and took keen interest in his growth, but he was not always the doting father one might expect. His eyes still prevented him from reading or writing at night and this often made him irritable. Alice tried as best she could to protect him from the distractions of the baby's wailing, from which he could not escape in their narrow quarters on Harvard Street. At times both of them became short-tempered. She was not a patient Griselda herself and was no more accustomed to curbing her tongue than he; consequently, when he stormed, she stormed back. The marriage was never in danger of a rupture, and William later felt that it saved him from hopeless neurasthenia, but he found parenthood a distraction from mental concentration and creative thinking.

It was not domestic cares, however, which most worried James at this time but his inability to make any visible progress on the psychology book. He was not willing merely to write a manual summarizing current theories, though apparently Holt would have been satisfied with that. James wanted—in fact, felt he *must*—write the most reliable exposition of the operation of the mind and nervous system that he possibly could. He knew all the books in the field published in Germany, France, and England—there was none of consequence in America—, but the knowledge they contained was incomplete and contradictory. Many gaps still remained to be filled in, and James had no one to discuss them with him. In 1878 Hall had declared that James taught "the only course in the country where students can be made familiar with the methods and results of recent German researches in physiological psychology." But Hall was back in Germany, and no one else in the Department of Philosophy and Psychology at Harvard had any real interest in the subject.

In the summer of 1879 William took his wife and infant son to the Maine coast. From Prout's Neck he wrote Hall on September 3: "The college year ended satisfactorily. Poor Palmer has gone abroad to steep himself I suppose still more deeply in that priggish English Hegelism. Much good may it do him. He is an extraordinarily able man, but associating with him is like being in a dentist's chair the whole while." James was trying to write a chapter on the perception of space (finally published as one of the later chapters in the *Principles*), and had taken books with him to Maine, but most of them seemed "an awful waste of precious time." However, he was enjoying Lotze's *Metaphysik*, and thought him "the most delectable . . . of all German writers. . . . But how I wish you were back,— I fairly pine for psychologic intercourse. . . . You don't know, my dear fellow, what great advantages you are enjoying over the rest of us in being able at your mature age to pump the German founts of wisdom. . . . I feel conscious of any amount of thirst, and of a good deal of digestive and assimilative power, but the supplies of material are to me so small."

Back in Cambridge James wrote to Hall again on October 10: "College has begun. I have three rather lowly graduates in 'Physiological Psychology,' five seniors in Renouvier, about thirty juniors etc., in Spencer's *First Principles*, and a lecture a week on Physiology. Enough to do! My psychology hangs fire awfully, and my ideas are stagnant from want of friction. Palmer is back from Caird [i.e., from studying with Edward Caird, Professor of Moral Philosophy at Glasgow University] in splendid condition and (I fear me) fully *aufgegangen* into the great arcanum of the identity of contradictories. Of all mental turpitudes and rottennesses, that may claim the prize. But the delicious bewilderment it engenders will always attract certain poetic and priggish natures. The worst of it is, it makes an absolute sterility where it comes. If Palmer doesn't recover, good-bye to him. His ability strikes me more and more. For a non-original man, he seems to me the ablest I know. He has three students to my one now, but I'm not afraid of him at all in a fair field. . . ." A few months later: "Palmer is fully enrolled in the white-winged band of seraphim *illuminati*. Caird has done the business for him. . . . Nothing but the thought of you keeps my head straight. Our Club doesn't meet this winter." The Club was a group which called itself the Philosophical (or sometimes Metaphysical) Club, that had meetings about once a month in Boston, but it too had turned Hegelian and James had lost interest in it.

William had written Henry on November 27 complaining of his scientific isolation and his longing to talk with the German experimenters, and on December 16 Henry had replied with sympathy but bewilderment: "I am sorry you 'outgrow' so, and hardly know what remedy to suggest—as I can't, like Joshua, bid science to stand still. But keep up your heart, and sometime you will have your year or so of leisure in Europe—which I will endeavour, in the future, to further." Although this consolation may sound like a hollow fraternal gesture, the phrases are worth a closer look, both because they reveal Henry's incomprehension and his genuine desire to help. In the first place, William's dissatisfaction was not that he had outgrown the courses he was teaching and his knowledge of his subject, but that in Cambridge, cut off from all personal contact with men who were contributing to the growth of psychology, he felt that he himself was not growing in his field. What Henry thought was restlessness or need of "leisure" was intellectual hunger—at times, William thought, near-starvation. It was less for a restful vacation in Europe that he longed than for the opportunity to talk with Hermann von Helmholtz in Berlin, Paul Fleshing and Johannes von Kries in Leipzig, and other physiological psychologists, but especially with Wilhelm Wundt at Heidelberg, where Wundt had established the leading psychological laboratory in the world. Although Henry James the novelist had heard the names of some of these men, their world was more alien to him than his world of literature and art was to William, for William did know some artists and authors.

Probably at the time William did not fully understand or appreciate Henry's vague promise to "further" his year abroad "in the future." Later correspondence shows unmistakably that Henry was now so confident of the earning power of his pen that he expected in another year or two to have enough money to be able to help

William, Bob, Wilky, or any other member of the family in need. Perhaps success was just a little "going to his head," but in his generous dreams he was being true to his own "angelic" nature.

III

As we have many times seen, William had always criticized Henry's fiction without reserve or tact. Usually Henry thanked him for the criticism, and occasionally admitted its justice, but in the first year of William's marriage he began to criticize in a way that Henry thought showed downright incomprehension of what he was doing. William's marriage had nothing to do with the sharpness of this dialogue, but the two men were developing their dissimilar talents in different directions, and the divergence had now reached an acute phase.

In 1878 Henry James published a novel called *The Europeans*, a rather slight story of two European aristocrats' visit to their Boston cousins. It was a study in cultural contrasts, but to New England readers it seemed very close to a satirical attack on their provincialism. As Henry became more cosmopolitan, William seemed to take an almost perverse delight in flaunting his sympathy with the American point of view—though at other times he could be critical of America too. At any rate, he disliked *The Europeans* and attacked it for being thin, empty, and trivial, unworthy of his talented brother. On November 14 Henry replied: "I was much depressed on reading your letter by your painful reflections on *The Europeans;* but now, an hour having elapsed, I am beginning to hold up my head a little; the more so as I think I myself estimate the book very justly and am aware of its extreme slightness. I think you take these things too rigidly and unimaginatively—too much as if an artistic experiment were a piece of conduct, to which one's life were somehow committed. . . ."

It was not, therefore, that Henry disagreed with William's judgment on this particular book, but that William seemed not to understand how a novelist had to work. Henry said he hoped William would continue to write his frank opinions, though he didn't think that they were "always right, by any means. . . . I don't trust your judgment altogether (if you will permit me to say so) about *details;* but I think you are altogether right in returning always to the importance of subject. I hold to this, strongly; and if I don't as yet seem to proceed upon it more, it is because, being 'very artistic,' I have a constant impulse to try experiments of form, in which I wish to not run the risk of wasting or gratuitously using big situations." Henry did not consider that he had yet written a novel in which he had displayed his full power, but he was working on such a novel, which he said in one of his letters would be, compared to his previous efforts, as wine to water, and his family frequently joked about Henry's forthcoming "wine-and-water" novel. That was to be his first masterpiece, *The Portrait of a Lady*.

Meanwhile Henry continued to annoy his older brother by his aspersions upon American cultural sterility. In 1879 he published his *Nathaniel Hawthorne*, a biographical-critical study, in which, taking his cue from Hawthorne himself, he excused the romancer for the slightness of his achievement because of the "crude and simple society in which he lived. . . . It takes so many things, as Hawthorne must have felt later in life, when he made the acquaintance of the denser, richer, warmer European spectacle—it takes such an accumulation of history and custom, such a complexity of manners and types, to form a novelist."

In spite of the fact that Henry James was almost paraphrasing Hawthorne himself, especially in another passage in which he enumerated "the items of high civilization . . . absent from the texture of American life," his interpretation of Hawthorne's handicaps aroused almost universal indignation in America, and William sympathized with the American critics. The more Henry sank into his contentment with London, the more impatient William became with his acquired manners and expatriated mind. And on his side Henry continued to misjudge William's reasons for wanting to revisit Europe. On May 9, 1880, Henry wrote: "I deplore your decision with regard to giving up Europe, for I had hoped that something pleasant (for both of us) would come of your plan. I should have been very happy to do the honours of London for you." As we shall see, it was not "the honours of London" that William wanted, or, in fact, very much of anything that Henry could do for him. Nevertheless, Henry looked forward to the "pleasure postponed—to a time, I trust, when Alice will be able to share it."

William's father had suggested that his lot on Quincy Street was large enough for two houses and invited William to build a house behind his. For several months William drew plans and talked of building. This and other personal considerations had made him decide to postpone a trip to Europe in the summer of 1880, but toward the end of May he changed his mind and postponed the house instead, though it meant leaving Alice and the infant behind.

Mrs. Gibbens had bought a house in Cambridge at 18 Garden Street, a few blocks west of the Harvard Yard, in order to be near the daughter on whom she had depended for so many years. She now suggested that when the Jameses' lease on the Harvard Street rooms expired at the end of May Alice and baby Henry should spend the summer with her while William traveled in Europe. This plan was quickly accepted and relieved William of worry about his wife's comfort and happiness during his absence. His buoyant mood is apparent in a letter which he wrote on May 30 to Bowditch, who was again in Germany: "I'm to sail on Wednesday for Berlin, where I hope Helmholtz's lectures, Munk's vivisections in the veterinary school, *and a year of laboratory work under Hall* will bring peace to my distracted soul." If Bowditch had been misled by the other statements, the underscored "year of laboratory work under Hall" gave the joke away. William was not going for a year but only three months, and he had never, as Bowditch knew, spent a whole year doing laboratory work under anyone's supervision, nor was likely to; he was not a laboratory man. He did look forward to seeing Bowditch, talking psychology with Hall, and meeting a few of the great men in psychology and philosophy. But first he would stop in London and pay his fraternal respects to Harry.

A few days after William's arrival in London, Henry Jr. wrote his father on June 30 that he had his brother "domiciled here in the apartment beneath my own. It is very delightful to see him again, and we have had much interesting talk, which as well as most other things, he seems to enjoy." To Henry he seemed "little changed, looking no older and with the same tendency to descant on his sensations—but with all his vivacity and Williamacy of mind undimmed." Several days later to his mother, whose sympathy Henry could depend on, he expressed his undisguised impatience with William's complaining: ". . . I can't get rid of the feeling that he takes himself, and his nerves, and his physical condition too hard and too consciously. As he takes himself, however, so one must take him, but I wish he had a little more of this quiet British stoutness."

William did find Henry slightly changed, though only more Anglicized and more absorbed in his constant round of engagements.

Henry tried to introduce his brother into the elite of British society, but this was not the society William craved. Surely, Henry thought, William would want to spend an evening with Thomas Huxley, but William was impatient to visit friends on the continent and left abruptly without meeting the great English biologist. From Amsterdam, on July 13, he wrote his father his impressions of Harry: "I think as he grows older that he is better suited by superficial contact with things at a great many points than by a deeper one at a few points. The way he worked at paying visits and going to dinners and parties was surprising to me, especially as he was all the time cursing them for so frustrating his work."

Actually, Henry's social life, with its contacts with a great many people, was exactly what he needed not only for his personal happiness but also for getting impressions and ideas for his fiction. William's life as a scholar and teacher was so different, as was his less gregarious temperament, that he could not understand the kind of "depth" that Henry's life in England had—nor Henry what went into William's work on psychology and philosophy. Even Henry's predilection for bachelorhood seemed to William another aspect of his brother's unwillingness to settle down, strike cultural roots, and attain full manhood. William's parenthood had widened the gulf of misunderstanding between the brothers. After visiting Saint John's Wood, where he had been so unhappy in 1856, William wrote his father (in the same Amsterdam letter) that when he contrasted "the life you led there with that which Henry is now leading in Bolton Street, it made me feel how few things you laid claim to, and how entirely at that time your lives were given up to us. There is a strange inability on the part of children to project themselves out of their egocentric standpoint, so far as their parents are concerned." Perhaps William was at least partly apologizing for his rebelliousness in Saint John's Wood twenty-four years ago when he added that now his own "parental condition" made it possible for him to understand his father's sacrifices.

Henry was hard at work finishing up his "wine-and-water" novel, and this may have caused William's eccentricities to annoy him more than usual. At any rate, he was obviously relieved by his brother's hasty departure. And William was in high spirits when he wrote Bowditch on July 19, berating him for their failure to make contact: *"Schurke, Lump, Unverschämter Mensch, Halb-Physiolog, und so weiter!* [Scoundrel, scamp, impudent man, half-physiologist,

etc.] See what you lost by breaking your promise and running off
in that cowardly way: I reached Cöln Wednesday midnight; found
your letter and cards sent on from London assuring me you would
wait Thursday for me in Heidelberg. I accordingly sacrificed one
day I expected to spend on the Rhine, telegraphed you at nine
o'clock, got to Heidelberg Thursday night only to find your *teu-
flisch höhnisch selbstsüchtig* [diabolical, sneering, selfish], badly-
spelt illegible note saying you couldn't wait and boasting of your
shameless carousals with Kühne [Professor Wilke Kühne of the
University of Heidelberg] (which by the way I will report to your
poor wife). Meanwhile Hall (who arrived also on Thursday night)
and I have been carrying on the highest and most instructive conversation, which we would have let you listen to gratis had you been
here. We talked twelve hours steadily on Friday, thirteen with a
two-hour intermission at Kühne's lecture on Saturday, and thirteen
and a half without an instant's intermission yesterday. He is a
herrlicher Mensch [magnificent man] and singularly solidified since
being here. Speaking seriously, I wish to heaven you had stayed;
three would have been better than two, even though the third were
only an H. P. Bowditch. Hall left this A.M. for Paris via Cöln. He
goes soon to London and almost certainly thence in August home,
where I hope he'll get a place in Baltimore next winter. [Hall did
secure the position at Johns Hopkins which had been offered to
James.] I start in an hour for Strassburg where I'll try to speak to
Goltz [Friedrich Leopold Goltz, Professor of Physiology at the
University of Strassburg], and then to Basel and der Schweiz."

After a vacation in Switzerland William paid a brief visit on
August 15 to Renouvier at Uriage-les-Bains, a health resort near
Grenoble, where Renouvier was enjoying mineral baths and a rest
with François Pillon, his philosophical disciple and collaborator. In
addition to the gratitude which James still felt toward Renouvier for
the help his ideas had provided in the black despair of ten years
earlier, he had recently taught a graduate course in Renouvier's
Essais at Harvard, and had some questions to talk over with the
French philosopher. They had by correspondence exchanged ideas
on the infinity of space and time—Renouvier maintained they were
finite—and James's critique had appeared in translation in *Critique
philosophique*.

James spent only one day with Renouvier and Pillon because he
wanted to stop off in Paris and still have several days with Henry in

London before sailing for home on August 22. But nothing went according to schedule. He spent only twelve hours in Paris and arrived in London on the 19th, only to discover, as he wrote Renouvier on the 21st, "that it was impossible to get a place in tomorrow's steamer and that I must wait till next Wednesday, the 25th." He regretted now that he had not remained longer at Uriage, "For hardly had I left when a number of questions that I might have asked you, but did not, arose in my mind. . . ."

Henry had also planned to return to America late in August, but he did not accompany William because in the end he decided he could not spare the time from his writing. He was considering several projects—one of them a study of Dickens, similar to his *Hawthorne* —which could more easily be carried out in London. Serial publication of *The Portrait of a Lady* had begun, but he was still working on the novel, and was already anticipating his great literary triumph with it. These excuses seem convincing enough for his reluctance to return with William, though there may have been other psychological motives, conscious or unconscious. To his parents Henry wrote, as consolation, "for the present, William will take you plenty of news." And to William himself on August 31: "I enclose you herewith a letter that has just come for you, and which may be of importance. You are at the present moment on the lonely deep, but so near home, I hope that you will begin to take an interest in the post again. The weather, in England, has been so lovely since you left that I pray you may have had something like it on the Atlantic: if so, you must have had the pleasantest of voyages. But of this you will tell me."

William's summer in Europe had been exhilarating, and he was returning to Cambridge to resume his teaching with the new title of Assistant Professor of Philosophy. It was not really a promotion, and did not affect the courses he would teach, but he had desired the official change in his academic title. He still had a long way to go before completing his book on psychology, but he was already looking ahead to a career in philosophy. It would be an exaggeration to say that Dr. James went to Europe in June a psychologist and returned in September a philosopher. But at least his desire for the transition had been stimulated by the men he had met, especially Charles Renouvier.

IV

After being lovingly welcomed home by his wife, at his mother-in-law's home, William was immediately faced with a problem that slightly blunted his happiness in resuming his life as husband and father. It was more than his usual temporary letdown on returning to America from Europe. He had never before returned as the head of a family without a house to live in. Alice did not want to live with his parents, and he preferred not to live with her family, much as he liked them. In short, he had to go house-hunting without delay. Well, not for a house but for rooms, for his salary was not adequate for a house, and he did not want to borrow from his father.

Nothing suitable was found for rent in Cambridge, but rooms they could afford were finally located on Louisburg Square in Boston, a short distance from the Charles River and near the State House. It was not a bad location, and fairly convenient to the horsecars to Harvard Square. But the noise and cooking odors from adjoining rooms annoyed William, and in a letter to his brother Henry written on September 30 he complained of the lingering smell of soup. The "low tone" of this letter caused Henry to delay in answering it, not knowing just how to respond, and unable himself to take an optimistic view of American life. But on November 13 he hoped "the feeling you expressed has melted down a good deal since you have got into your work again and ceased to see Boston and London in immediate juxtaposition. I hope you are physically comfortable and that Louisburg Square stands the test of time." Then, perhaps without intentionally contrasting their situations, "I am afraid that if you found me basely naturalised here when you came out, I am no less so these few months later."

The "melting down" which Henry hoped for William had taken place, and on the 27th of November Henry could write in reply to a more cheerful letter from William (later destroyed), "It gives me great pleasure to hear that your work this year leaves you leisure for reading and study, which must be a great satisfaction." He also thanked William for his praise of *Washington Square*, but regarded that novel as sketchy compared to *The Portrait*, which *Macmillan's* in England and the *Atlantic* in America had just begun to serialize. He thought *The Portrait* would be found to increase "in merit and interest as it goes on, and being told in a more spacious, expansive way than its predecessors, is inevitably more human, more sociable. It was the constant effort at *condensation* (which you used always to drum into my head—àpropos of Mérimée etc—and when I was young you bullied me,) that has deprived my former things of these qualities." But if there was any bitterness in this announcement of his emancipation from William's doctrine of "condensation," Henry quickly countered it by the assurance that he would "read what J. Allen and Fiske reply to you in the *Atlantic,* but shall be sure not to enter into what they say as I did into your article, which I greatly appreciated." The article, published in the October *Atlantic Monthly*, was "Great Men and Their Environment," in which William James had argued vigorously against Herbert Spencer's disciple, Grant (not J.) Allen, who "maintained that individuals have no initiative in determining social change."

During the winter of 1880–1881 William James continued to complain about the limited use of his eyes. He could dictate letters to his wife, but his reading had to be budgeted. In thanking Renouvier (December 27) for his translation of James's long psychological article on "Feeling of Effort" he had to confess that he had not been able to read all of the French version. But his eyes did not prevent his continuing to oppose the spread of Hegelianism. "My principal amusement this winter," he delighted in writing Renouvier, "has been resisting the inroads of Hegelism in our University. My colleague Palmer, a recent convert and a man of much ability, has been making an active propaganda among the more advanced students. It is a strange thing, this resurrection of Hegel in England and here, after his burial in Germany. I think his philosophy will probably have an important influence on the development of our liberal form of Christianity. It gives a quasi-metaphysic backbone which this theology has always been in need of, but it is too fundamentally rotten and charlatanish to last long. As a reaction against materialistic evolutionism it has its use, only this evolutionism is fertile while Hegelism is absolutely sterile."

In the spring of 1881 William began planning to take Alice and his son to Europe for a year. Henry would be back in England (after travels in Italy), and the trip would not be as difficult for Alice in 1882 as for his mother in 1843 when Henry James Sr. had taken his family to Europe before William was two and Henry Jr.

less than five months old. Throughout the spring William continued to bombard his brother with questions about places where they could afford to live, and Henry, still in Italy, gave the best advice he could, though he pointed out that he had had no experience in housekeeping in any country. But he thought Paris would be too expensive, Florence too far away, and he advised London, possibly Bloomsbury, where lodgings were said to be inexpensive and the British Museum, which contained the finest library in the world, was nearby. However, when Alice became pregnant again in the autumn William gave up this dream of taking his little family abroad.

In March Alice and William received a visit from Bob, still separated from his wife and children. During his stay he divided his time between his brother's rooms in Boston and his parents' home in Cambridge, but neither household was made happy by his presence because he was moody, began carrying on an affair with a woman in Boston, and frequently got drunk. In a recent letter Henry Jr. had begged William to explain what his mother had meant by saying that Bob was "a trial" to them and himself.

Though occupied and often worried by his own problems, William continued to sympathize deeply with the experiences of his brothers and sister. He attempted to help Bob, who had almost stopped trying to earn a living, by employing him as a scribe. Wilky was becoming so crippled with rheumatism that he could not work, and all the Jameses were concerned about him. But William's sister Alice continued to grow stronger under the healing influence of Katharine Loring. During the summer of 1881 she and Katharine toured England and Scotland. Henry wrote that he had spent a few days with them, but he felt that he was almost an intruder, and left them most of the summer to their own happy companionship.

William wrote Henry that their parents were becoming frail, and encouraged him to return to America while they were still alive. Henry was very eager to meet his sister-in-law Alice too, and he decided to return, after a six-year absence, solely to see his family, not to gather literary material. On arrival he was distressed by the weakness of his mother, and his father showed his age more than Henry had expected. But the novelist liked William's wife immediately, as he had anticipated he would, and she in turn got along well with the large, stout, bright-eyed man with the neatly trimmed brown beard, who carried himself with such grave dignity. The "little Henri-trois," as his uncle called him, announced he was "Uncle Henry's fascinating little nephew." Now two and a half, he talked with the precocity his father had shown at the same age.

During Christmas William's parents were joined by all their children, for even Wilky, badly crippled as he was, had managed to make the trip from Milwaukee. But before the holidays were over it was quite apparent that Henry Jr. was weary of Quincy Street and homesick for his Bolton Street rooms in London. Early in January he escaped to New York, and then went on to Washington, D.C. Late in January William's mother suffered an acute attack of pneumonia (called at the time "bronchial asthma"), but Bob wrote Henry that Aunt Kate and his sister would be able to nurse her through the illness. Both William and his wife visited her frequently. On Sunday night, January 29, Henry's sister-in-law telegraphed him: "Your mother exceedingly ill. Come at once."

Henry could not get a train until next day, and his mother died that evening before he could leave Washington. By the time he arrived in Cambridge William and Bob had made all arrangements for the funeral to be held on Wednesday, February 1. Aunt Kate was always dependable in such emergencies, and William's Alice had, as usual, risen to the occasion. His sister Alice surprised everyone by her self-control and helpfulness.

On February 4 Robertson James wrote his estranged wife an account of his mother's burial:

"Dear Mother's funeral occurred on Wednesday. We four boys took her coffin to the grave and kissed her quiet face for the last time. Dr. James Freeman Clarke read a simple burial service, at the house—some scriptures and at our request omitted any reference to her personally—a thing no one could have done for us and spoken our thoughts. I sometimes think Father's loneliness must be appalling but he gives no sign of it save in physical weakness. . . . The secret of their union was a religious one. It had its inception during their engagement, when Mother relinquished all the narrow sectarian habit in which she had been bred [Calvinism], to his and her own everlasting peace. There have been no mutations on that score between them.

"We have all been educated by Father to feel that death was the only reality and that life was simply an experimental thing and for this reason . . . we have taken Mother's going as such an orderly transition. None of us would recall her for we feel that we are more near to her now than ever before, simply because she is already at the goal for which we all cheerfully bend our steps. An hour after we laid her out, I do not think that either father, Alice or myself have shed a tear. But the boys coming later were very much shocked, Harry especially who had a passionate childlike devotion to her.

"I feel as if I had not much else in life to live for now but keep very close to father and dissipate as much as possible the loneliness in which he must remain. I sleep beside him in mother's empty bed and we have quiet happy talks at night about mother's nearness and about our pride in her. The last two weeks of my life have been the happiest I have known. . . ."

The effects of his mother's death on William can only be surmised because he did not record his sensations in any detail either in letters that have survived or his private journal, as Henry did. He did not have Bob's mysticism to make him feel nearer to her in spirit than in life. Though tolerant of such feelings, he never experienced them. But the immediate effect of his mother's death on his father was dramatic—one might even say traumatic. She had been the stabilizing force in his emotional life and the guardian of his material well-being for over forty years, and it was almost impossible for him to continue living without her. Her body was scarcely in the vault in the Cambridge cemetery (the casket later to be placed in a grave after the ground thawed) before he began cherishing every preference and whim she had ever had. Without any intentional turning away from William or his other children, Henry Jr. now became his favorite because he had been dearest to his mother.

Henry James Sr. also began to long for an end of his weary, burdensome material life and to look forward eagerly to becoming, like his wife, all spirit. His daughter Alice seemed to gain strength in her desire to help and protect her father. But the Quincy Street house was too large for the two of them, and the incompatibility of the two Alices made it impossible for William's family to share it with them. Furthermore, William had finally given up his plan to build on his father's property and had bought a small house near the Harvard Yard, a few blocks west of the main gate, at 18 Appian Way. So father and daughter moved into a comfortable house in Boston, 131 Mount Vernon Street, near Louisburg Square, where William and Alice had recently lived. The daughter Alice surprised everyone, and not least herself, by her ability to keep house for her father—so well, in fact, that early in May Henry Jr. felt that his father no longer needed him and that he could return to England.

William was ailing at the time of Henry's departure, and his wife was expecting her second child in June. On May 9, a few days after Henry Jr. left Boston, his father wrote him, addressing him as "My darling Henry": "I went out early after breakfast to see William yesterday, and he came down from his bedroom *dancing* to greet me. . . . It was delightful to witness the elasticity of his spirits, and we had a capital talk about Renouvier and Hodgson [Shadworth H. Hodgson, a British psychologist]. Dear Alice looked so burdened to sight by her new maternity, and her anxiety about Willy, and her solicitude in behalf of Harry [her son], that all my compassion was drawn to her, and I expressed it very tenderly, I assure you. Harry was incomparably sweet. I had met him in company with his Aunt Margaret [Gibbens] Sunday afternoon in a Park Square horse-car, and he had been so preoccupied with the people in the car that he scarcely noticed his granddaddy. And I, in reproaching him with this remembrance before the family, got no satisfaction but what lay in these exact words: 'Yes, I thought almost I wouldn't even speak to Grandpa.' This *even* was too expressive. . . ."

This letter leaves no doubt of Henry Sr.'s affection for his oldest son, his wife, and grandson namesake. Perhaps an intensification of affection for one son need not mean any diminution of love for another. But whether this was true or not, Henry Sr. certainly loved "darling Harry" more intensely after Mary James's death. "And now, my darling boy," he continued in his letter, "I must bid you farewell." Presumably "farewell" was a way of saying "bon voyage," but it might well have contained also a premonition that the father would never again see his son in life. ". . . I feel that I have fallen heir to all dear mother's fondness for you, as well as my proper own, and bid you accordingly a distinct widowed farewell."

In William's youth it was he whom his father thought had most talent, and of whom he expected the greater achievements. Although his father had never indicated disappointment in him, and in fact had good reason during the past few years to expect a distinguished academic career for him, up to 1882 it was Henry who had enjoyed the greater professional success. However, Henry James Sr. was not the kind of man to be swayed one iota by such considerations; he felt somehow committed to his wife's partiality—a partiality which she had felt without such tender compunctions as her husband now exhibited in striving to be in "no way unjust" to the other children while preferring Harry.

"That blessed mother, what a link her memory is to us all henceforth!. . . . She was not to me 'a liberal education,' intellectually speaking, as some one has said of his wife, but she really did arouse my heart, early in our married life, from its selfish torpor, and so enabled me to become a man. And this she did altogether unconsciously, without the most cursory thought of doing so, but solely by the presentation of her womanly sweetness and purity, which she herself had no recognition of. The sum of it all is, that I would sooner rejoin her in her modesty, and find my eternal lot in association with her, than have the gift of a noisy delirious world!" The old man's desire for death had not yet become a fixed resolution, but the "good-bye," repeated several times, was clearly prophetic.

V

William James, of course, knew of his father's ineffable sense of loss, but there was nothing that he, or anyone else, could do about it. Furthermore, he was absorbed in his own problems, the coming of his second child and his continued hunger for intellectual contact with the best psychological and philosophical minds in Europe. Since his return to Cambridge in the autumn of 1880 he had felt mentally more isolated than ever, and early in 1882 he had begun planning to spend another year abroad, alone if necessary. It was not because he was callous, or indifferent to the discomfort and dangers of his wife's pregnancy, that her impending confinement worried him less than his own intellectual deficiencies. She had borne one healthy child without difficulty, and his medical observations indicated that this pregnancy was perfectly normal. Also her mother and sister Margaret, now living practically around the corner from Appian Way, were in frequent attendance. There were times, in fact, when he felt that the women could get along better without his presence. Alice was exacting in domestic performances and regarded him as clumsy and inept in household chores.

Thus if William James appears to have been most restless during his wife's pregnancies, she encouraged him to attend to his own affairs while she bore the children and she and her mother and sister took care of them. It was not a bad arrangement if a man only understood it, and had a sense of humor; he certainly had a sense of humor, and he seemed to understand the situation. He was really fond of his mother-in-law, who understood and sympathized with him more than his own mother had. Moreover, he appreciated Alice's desire to protect him from anything that might distract him from his work and thinking, though she was seldom satisfied with her efforts.

In planning to renew friendships in Europe William James also saw a chance to help a young man in California whom he had met first in his father's house in Cambridge one summer day in 1877. He was a chubby, round-faced, red-haired young man thirteen years younger than James named Josiah Royce. Since that first meeting Royce had taken a Ph.D. in philosophy at Johns Hopkins and had returned to the University of California at Berkeley to teach English, because this new university did not have a department of philosophy. But he was unhappy at Berkeley both because he was not teaching his chosen field and because he felt the same intellectual loneliness that James did in Cambridge.

James had already made one unsuccessful effort to get Royce appointed to the Harvard faculty, but when he finally received permission from President Eliot to take a year's leave of absence on half pay, beginning in September 1882, provided he could find someone to teach his courses on the other half, he saw his chance to help Royce and himself at the same time. On April 12 he wrote Royce about the circumstances, explaining that this would be a temporary appointment, and would pay only twelve hundred and fifty dollars, scarcely enough for Royce and his recent bride to live on in Cambridge, let alone paying their transportation from California. It was a big gamble, but James thought that if Royce's teaching was satisfactory, about which he himself had no doubts, there was a strong likelihood that he would be appointed to a vacancy in the department likely to occur at the end of the year. Royce accepted the gamble—which proved to be a lucky one for him.

Thus William James was assured of his leave long before his wife's confinement. On June 17 she gave birth to another fine boy, whom this time they named William. Alice's recovery was satisfactory, and the parents had the whole summer to adjust to their renewed parenthood before William's departure. Meanwhile Professor C. H. Troy rented the Appian Way house for the coming academic year, and this left Alice free to accept her mother's invitation to live with her again at 18 Garden Street during her husband's absence. All arrangements were now complete for William's next intellectual adventure in Europe.

CHAPTER XV

Ambassador of American Thought

James was now able to play that important rôle for which his early

training, as well as his personal traits, so admirably fitted him—ambas-

sador of American thought . . . to the countries of Western Europe.

—RALPH BARTON PERRY

I

ALTHOUGH WILLIAM JAMES was a restless man to whom new experiences were a necessity of life, the tedium of travel annoyed and exhausted him. In a mood of exasperation he descended from the boat train at Euston Station in London in September 1882 to greet his apprehensive brother with: "My!—how cramped and inferior England seems! After all, it's poor old Europe, just as it used to be in our dreary boyhood! America may be raw and shrill, but I could never live with this as you do! I'm going to hurry down to Switzerland . . . and then home again as soon as may be. It was a mistake to come over! I thought it would do me good. Hereafter I'll stay at home. You'll have to come to America if you want to see the family."

These remarks were reconstructed by William James's son Henry many years later from his uncle's account, and show unmistakable signs of caricature, but caricatures are only exaggerations of basic truths. William could complain, and he liked to shock the Anglophile sensibilities of his less volatile brother. William's son also caricatured his uncle's reactions:

Time never accustomed [Henry] to these collisions, even though he learned to expect them. England inferior! A mistake to come abroad! Horror and consternation are weak terms by which to describe his feelings; and nothing but a devotion seldom existing between brothers, and a lively interest in the astonishing phenomenon of such a reaction, ever carried him through the hour.

[246]

In two days William rushed off to the continent, leaving Henry gasping and sputtering in his dignified way over such blasphemous utterances. By September 23 William had reached Vienna, where he visited an International Art Exhibition. Next day he wrote his wife about a French painting of a peasant woman which had greatly impressed him, perhaps because it confirmed the "deepest impression" he had received in Germany, "that made on me by the indefatigable beavers of old wrinkled peasant women, striding like men through the streets, dragging their carts or lugging their baskets, minding their business, seeming to notice nothing, in the stream of luxury and vice, but belonging far away, to something better and purer. . . . They are the venerable ones whom we should reverence. All the mystery of womanhood seems incarnated in their ugly being—the Mothers! the Mothers! . . . Yes, Alice dear, what I love in you is only what these blessed old creatures have; and I'm glad and proud, when I think of my own dear Mother with tears running down my face, to know that she is one with these."

However one looks at these declarations, they are curiously revealing. William James was not usually mawkishly sentimental, and his assurance to Alice that he loved in her "only what these blessed old creatures have" is a little difficult to comprehend. But she knew her husband well enough to understand that he intended no unflattering comparison with those peasant women, though a vainer woman might have been offended. And perhaps the remarks did unconsciously reveal the psychology of the situation: he on his intellectual odyssey while she, the home-keeping Penelope, took care of the two baby boys.

William had intended to begin his year in Europe with a leisurely tramp through the Austrian and Italian Alps, but by the time he reached Salzburg the continuous rains had caused floods in many places and he had to give up his "mountain plans." He had also expected to go to Berlin, perhaps for a couple of months, after his vacation in the mountains, but on September 28 he was still in Vienna. From there he wrote Renouvier, whom he had hoped to visit in Southern France, that for the present he had given up the Berlin visit (Renouvier had recently urged him not to expose his soul to "the philosophical malaria of Germany"), and found himself "obliged to come as far east as Vienna, so as to get to Venice by way of Trieste. It results in my passing my weeks of *flâneries* in large cities instead of spending them in the bosom of nature. Fortunately I can be sure of no further inundation in Venice than that to which she has always been accustomed, and on the whole I have no doubt that my present lot is as useful to me as the plan I originally formed."

Venice, however, was another disappointment. On October 23 James wrote to Renouvier that he was leaving earlier that he had expected to "because I think the air is bad for my sleep. I left home with the hope that my chronic insomnia would improve, but it has been here as bad, or worse, than ever, notwithstanding the fact of my mind being like a stagnant pool and all outward influences somnolescent to the last degree. If you knew my life, you would confess that my little stream of work runs on under great disadvantages." This last statement was not uttered in any exaggerated mood of self-pity. It was literally true. But insomnia had not entirely spoiled James's enjoyment of Venice, which he pronounced "delicious, in spite of gloomy and rainy weather four days out of five." It was not the rain, however, which most depressed him, but the ever-present reminder in Venice "of the inevitable decay of every art, as soon as it reaches the full bloom of maturity." And yet, "Because I think I can see why, it does not make *me* a fatalist."

With his moving on to Germany, James's luck improved, and so did his health. The combination of cooler, brighter weather and stimulating conversation made him feel like a different man. Prague (then under Austrian rule) was a triumph. William went there, as he wrote his wife Alice from Aussig, Bohemia, on November 2, "with much trepidation to do my social-scientific duty. The mighty [Ewald] Hering [physiologist] in especial intimidated me beforehand; but having taken the plunge, the cutaneous glow and 'euphoria' (*vide* dictionary) succeeded, and I have rarely enjoyed a forty-eight hours better, in spite of the fact that the sharp-nosed [Carl] Stumpf (whose book 'Über die Raumvorstellungen' [Space-perception] I verily believe thou art capable of never having noticed the cover of!) insisted on trotting me about, day and night, over the whole length and breadth of Prague, and that [Ernst] Mach (Professor of Physics), genius of all trades, simply took Stumpf's place to do the same." Mach is best known for his formula giving the ratio of the speed of an object to the speed of sound in the same atmosphere, but he was, as James said, a "genius of all trades," and had made important contributions to psychology.

William heard Hering give "a very poor physiology lecture" and

Mach "a beautiful physical one," probably with demonstrations. Both men "received me with open arms. I had an hour and a half's talk with Hering, which cleared up some things for me. He asked me to come to his house that evening, but I gave an evasive reply, being fearful of boring him. Meanwhile Mach came to my hotel and I spent four hours walking and supping with him at his club, an unforgettable conversation. I don't think anyone ever gave me so strong an impression of pure intellectual genius. He apparently has read everything and thought about everything, and has an absolute simplicity of manner and winningness of smile when his face lights up, that are charming."

With Carl Stumpf James began a friendship which was to continue throughout the years. Stumpf had not yet published his monumental *Tonpsychologie* (2 volumes, 1883–1890) but he was far advanced in his investigation of the sensations of sound. James spent five hours with him on Monday (October 30) and in all seven hours on Wednesday—"so I feel rather intimate. A clear-headed and just-minded, though pale and anxious-looking man in poor health." Stumpf was six years younger than James, but had got an earlier start in his profession and was as mature intellectually; perhaps their struggles against poor health also gave the two men sympathetic understanding of each other.

It always surprised William to discover that his command of German was adequate for conversation with distinguished scholars. To Alice he bragged: "My native *Geschwätzigkeit* [loquacity] triumphed over even the difficulties of the German tongue; I careered over the field, taking the pitfalls and breastworks at full run, and was fairly astounded myself at coming in alive. I learned a good many things from them [Hering and Stumpf], both in the way of theory and fact, and shall probably keep up a correspondence with Stumpf. They are not so different from us as we think. Their greater thoroughness is largely the result of circumstances. I found that I had a more *cosmopolitan* knowledge of modern philosophic literature than any of them, and shall on the whole feel much less intimidated by the thought of their like than hitherto."

This gain in self-confidence was one of the major benefits of James's sojourn in Germany. And he was not deceived in his own cosmopolitanism, for the German psychologists and philosophers largely ignored the French and the French the German, whereas James knew both the men and their work in the two languages.

Moreover, he had thoroughly absorbed the work of the British school, and he would soon become personally acquainted with the remaining outstanding English psychologists and philosophers. In fact, he attempted to introduce the men of these three countries to one another but never broke down their national prejudices to any great extent. But since there was no "school" of psychology or philosophy in America, he was accepted freely in all three countries without jealousy. Of course his command of French and German was a potent aid such as no contemporary in his field possessed. He was indeed a cosmopolitan, though not in manners like his brother Henry.

Of all experiences William James had in 1882, the visit to Prague was undoubtedly the most enjoyable and beneficial. "My letters will hereafter," he assured Alice, ". . . have a more jocund tone. Damn Italy! It isn't a good thing to stay with one's inferiors. With the nourishing breath of the German air, and the sort of smoky and leathery German smell, vigor and good spirits have set in. I have walked well and slept well and eaten well and read well, and in short begin to feel as I expected I should when I decided upon this arduous pilgrimage. Prague is a —— city—the adjective is hard to find; not magnificent, but everything is too honest and homely,—we have in fact no English word for the peculiar quality that good German things have, of depth, solidity, picturesqueness, magnitude and homely goodness combined. They have worked out a really great civilization. . . . I say German of Prague, for it seems to me, in spite of the feverish nationalism of the natives, to be outwardly a pure German city."

In Berlin the good talk and intellectual stimulation continued. On November 8 James visited the veterinary school, where H. Munk, "the great brain vivisector," taught and experimented. "He was very cordial," William wrote his wife next day, "and poured out a torrent of talk for one and a half hours, though he could show me no animals." Dr. Munk introduced James to Dr. Baginsky, regarded by ear specialists as an authority on the semicircular canals. "So we opened on the semicircular canals, and Baginsky's torrent of words was even more overwhelming than Munk's. I never felt quite so helpless and small-boyish before, and am to this hour dizzy from the onslaught."

It is quite possible that these two specialists in the veterinary school were showing off to the professor from Harvard, but that evening, at a small dinner party given by a lecturer (Docent) on ethics named Gizycki, James had more of the kind of talk that most delighted him: "Good, square, deep-chested talk again, which I couldn't help contrasting with the whining tones of our students and of some of the members of the Hegel Club—I hate to leave the wholesome, tonic atmosphere, the land where one talks best when he talks manliest—slowest, distinctest, with most deliberate emphasis and strong voice."

From Berlin James went to Leipzig, where one of the largest and most famous universities of the time flourished. After he had been there several days he wrote his wife on November 13: "Yesterday was a splendid day within and without. . . . The old town delightful in its blackness and plainness. I heard several lecturers. Old [Carl Friedrich Wilhelm] Ludwig's lecture [on physiology] in the afternoon was memorable for the extraordinary impression of character he made on me. The traditional German professor in its highest sense. A rusty brown wig and broad-skirted brown coat, a voluminous black neckcloth, an absolute unexcitability of manner, a clean-shaven face so plebeian and at the same time so grandly carved, with its hooked nose and gentle kindly mouth and inexhaustible patience of expression, that I never saw the like. Then to [Wilhelm] Wundt, who has a more refined elocution than any one I've yet heard in Germany. He received me very kindly after the lecture in his laboratory [one James had hoped to work in fourteen years earlier], dimly trying to remember my writings, and I stay over today, against my intention, to go to his *psychologische Gesellschaft* tonight."

However, the "psychology club" meeting was postponed, and Wundt did not suggest an alternative occasion, so that James simply lost time in staying over. Nevertheless, he insisted in his letter to Alice written on the train to Liége that Wundt "made a very pleasant and personal impression on me, with his agreeable voice and ready, tooth-showing smile. His lecture also was very able, and my opinion of him is higher than before seeing him." Previous to meeting him James's admiration for the founder of the first laboratory for experimental psychology had declined as he himself had drifted away from purely physiological psychology to a growing conviction that not all operations of the mind could be measured mathematically.

Although Liége did not prove as exciting as Prague, James found the best hospitality of the trip at the home of the Belgian philosopher and psychologist, Joseph Rémy Léopold Delboeuf, famous for his work in both logic and hypnotism. Though eleven years older, he was like James in temperament, lively, enthusiastic, witty, and generous. On November 20 William wrote Alice: "I am still at Delboeuf's, aching in every joint and muscle, weary in every nerve-cell, but unable to get away till tomorrow noon." He had intended to start for Paris that day, but stayed over to rest.

This pause, however, gave James time to sum up the "total lesson of what I have done in the past month." Briefly, the effect had been "to make me quieter with my home-lot and readier to believe that it is one of the chosen places of the Earth. Certainly the instruction and facilities at our university are on the whole superior to anything I have seen; the rawnesses we mention with such affliction at home belong rather to the century than to us (witness the houses here); we are not a whit more isolated than they are here." When James asked Delboeuf what he taught, the latter replied: "Greek and Latin philology, at the University of Liège" and "Greek grammar at the École Normale des Humanités." Even when James had taught anatomy at Harvard, the subject had some relationship to his other interests.

"In all Belgium," William continued to his wife, "there seem to be but two genuine philosophers; in Berlin they have little to do with each other, and I really believe that in my way I have a wider view of the field than anyone I've seen (I count out, of course, my ignorance of ancient authors). We are a sound country and my opinion of our essential worth has risen and not fallen. We only lack abdominal depth of temperament and the power to sit for an hour over a single pot of beer without being able to tell at the end of it what we've been thinking about. Also to reform our altogether abominable, infamous and infra-human voices and way of talking. . . . The first thing to do is to establish in Cambridge a genuine German plebeian Kneipe [beer-house] club, to which all instructors and picked students shall be admitted. If that succeeds, we shall be perfect, especially if we talk therein with deeper voices."

Two days later William James was in Paris, where he met M. and Mme. Pillon. Renouvier did not feel strong enough to make the trip from Provence, so that James's only philosophical talk was with the Pillons, which, he reported several days later to Renouvier from London, "was of the very pleasantest. I shared their hospitality several times, and we talked of all things under the sun." But this delightful reunion was suddenly terminated by a cablegram from William's wife telling him that his father was very ill. William left immediately for London. There on December 6 he wrote Renouvier: "Arrived in London, I received another despatch saying the peril was not immediate and that I, at least, must not come home. My brother has sailed, and I am waiting in his apartments until he telegraphs me on his arrival what to do."

II

While Henry's ship sped toward America, William apprehensively waited in his brother's gloomy Bolton Street flat. Of course his insomnia returned, and his eyes ached so that he could not read. The short December days were so cloudy and dark that he could not read even in the daytime without lighting the gas lamp, and he found it impossible to read for any length of time by the artificial light. He was more miserable than he had been even in Venice back in October. It took all his will power not to take ship himself immediately. But aboard ship he would be completely out of touch with Cambridge and Boston for the duration of the voyage.

Until he received his wife's first cablegram in Paris, William had not known that for several weeks his father had been deliberately, with sane but firm resolution, starving himself to death—because he was tired of his physical life and wanted to become all spirit. Doubtless Alice had kept this news out of her letters so that the benefits of her husband's visits and talks in Germany might continue. For a person of her stoic honesty, this dissimulation could not have been easy, but she knew she must protect William's nerves and his sabbatical.

Of course William knew that his father's health had been steadily declining since his mother's death, and he was prepared to lose his father at no distant date. Nevertheless, in spite of their different views and religious beliefs, William was emotionally dependent on his father in much the same way that Henry had been upon their mother. Scarcely two days after Henry had left England, on December 14, William wrote his father a letter so remarkable for its revelation of the mind and character of the writer that it deserves quotation in full:

"Darling old Father.—Two letters, one from my Alice last night, and one from Aunt Kate to Harry just now, have somewhat dispelled the mystery in which the telegrams left your condition; and although their news is several days earlier than the telegrams, I am free to suppose that the latter report only an aggravation of the symptoms the letters describe. It is far more agreeable to think of this than of some dreadful unknown and sudden malady.

"We have been so long accustomed to the hypothesis of your being taken away from us, especially during the past ten months, that the thought that this may be your last illness conveys no very sudden shock. You are old enough, you've given your message to the world in many ways and will not be forgotten; you are here left alone, and on the other side, let us hope and pray, dear, dear old Mother is waiting for you to join her. If you go, it will not be an inharmonious thing. Only, if you are still in possession of your normal consciousness, I should like to see you once again before we part. I stayed here only in obedience to the last telegram, and am waiting now for Harry—who knows the exact state of my mind, and who will know yours—to telegraph again what I shall do. Meanwhile, my blessed old Father, I scribble this line (which may reach you though I should come too late), just to tell you how full of the tenderest memories and feelings about you my heart has for the last few days been filled. In that mysterious gulf of the past into which the present soon will fall and go back and back, yours is still for me the central figure. All my intellectual life I derive from you; and though we have often seemed at odds in the expression thereof, I'm sure there's a harmony somewhere, and that our strivings will combine. What my debt to you is goes beyond all my power of estimating,—so early, so penetrating and so constant has been the influence. You need be in no anxiety about your literary remains. I will see them well taken care of, and that your words shall not suffer for being concealed. At Paris I heard that Milsand, whose name you may remember in the 'Revue des Deux Mondes' and elsewhere, was an admirer of the 'Secret of Swedenborg', and Hodgson told me your last book had deeply impressed him. So will it be; especially, I think, if a collection of *extracts* from your various writings were published, after the manner of the extracts from Carlyle, Ruskin, & Co. I have long thought that such a volume would be the best monument to you.—As for us; we shall live on each in his way,—feeling somewhat unprotected, old as we are, for the absence of the parental bosoms as a refuge, but holding fast together in that common sacred memory. We will stand by each other and by Alice, try to transmit the torch in our offspring as you did in us, and when the time comes for being gathered in, I pray we may, if not all, some at least, be as ripe as you. As for myself, I know what trouble I've given you at various times through my peculiarities; and as my own boys grow up, I shall learn more and more of the kind of trial you had to overcome in superintending the development of a creature different from yourself, for whom you felt responsible. I say this merely to show how my *sympathy* with you is likely to grow much livelier, rather than to fade—and not for the sake of regrets.—As for the other side, and Mother, and our all possibly meeting, I *can't* say anything. More than ever at this moment do I feel that if that *were* true, all would be solved and justified. And it comes strangely over me in bidding you good-bye how a life is but a day and expresses mainly but a single note. It is so much like the act of bidding an ordinary good-night. Good-night, my sacred old Father! If I don't see you again—Farewell! a blessed farewell! Your/ William"

Unfortunately, William James's father never received this farewell letter from his oldest son, who felt so close and grateful to him at the end. Henry James Sr. died on December 19, two days before Henry—no longer Jr.—arrived in New York. Actually, William knew of his father's death before his brother did, because he read the news on the 20th in the London *Standard*, the day before Henry's ship landed. Henry did not learn of his father's death until he disembarked in New York at noon on the 21st. His sister Alice and Aunt Kate had written to tell him that the funeral would be held that morning—in fact, it was over by the time Henry read the letters. William's wife did not cable him because she thought it would be kinder to break the news to him in a letter, but unknown to her or Aunt Kate, her sister-in-law had had her friend Katharine Loring send him a cable. William's reply to his sister's message was dated London, 3:30 p.m., December 20, 1882, and indicated that he had been almost on the point of starting when her cablegram arrived. He assured her that his greatest concern was now for her.

Henry was quite ill by the time his train arrived at the station in Boston, around eleven o'clock on the night of the 21st. Bob met him and took him to 131 Mount Vernon Street. Wilky had been too ill to come to the funeral, and Bob had to return to Milwaukee the next morning. Alice was in bed and was too exhausted to talk much, but she was calm. Before Henry went to bed Aunt Kate, who with the aid of a professional nurse had taken care of her brother-in-law during his last days, gave him a full account, which Henry summarized for William in a long letter written five days later after he had recovered from his fatigue and shock ". . . what they told me was deeply touching, and yet not at all literally painful. Father had been so tranquil and painless, had died so easily and, as it were, deliberately, and there had been none—not the least—of that anguish and confusion which we imagined in London.—The next morning Alice was ill, and went to Beverly—for a complete change, absence from the house etc—with Miss Loring."

Late on the 22nd, Henry, still confined to bed, had learned that William's wife and Aunt Kate had purposely refrained from cabling him (they still did not know of Alice's cable), and Saturday morning, "the earliest time possible," Henry had Aunt Kate go out and send a cablegram. Although he knew that William's Alice had been writing her husband almost daily, when Henry did feel well enough to write, on the 26th, he gave William all the details he had gathered from the three women, and on such occasions he was indefatigably —almost morbidly—exact.

"[The illness] appears to have been most strange, most characteristic above all, and as full of beauty as it was void of suffering. There was none of what we feared—no paralysis, no dementia, no violence. He simply, after the 'improvement' of which we were written before I sailed, had a sudden relapse—a series of swoons—after which he took to his bed not to rise again. He had no visible malady—strange as it may seem. The 'softening of the brain' was simply a gradual refusal of food, because he *wished* to die. There was no dementia except a sort of exaltation of belief that he had entered into 'the spiritual life.' Nothing could persuade him to eat, and yet he never suffered, or gave the least sign of suffering, from inanition. All this will seem strange and incredible to you—but told with all the details, as Aunt Kate has told it to me, it becomes real—taking Father as he was, almost natural. He prayed and longed to die. He ebbed and faded away—though in spite of his strength becoming continually less, he was able to see people and to talk. He wished to see as many people as he could, and he talked with them without effort. He saw F[rancis] Boott, and talked much two or three days before he died. Alice says he said the most picturesque and humorous things!

He knew I was coming and was glad, but not impatient. He was delighted when he was told that you would stay in my rooms in my absence, and seemed much interested in the idea. He had no belief apparently that he should live to see me, but was perfectly cheerful about it. He slept a great deal, and, as A.K. says there was 'so little of the sick-room' about him. He lay facing the windows, which he would never have darkened—never pained by the light. . . . He spoke of everything—the disposition of his things, made all his arrangements of every kind."

A week before he died Alice asked her father if he had thought about what arrangements he wanted made at his funeral. "He was immediately very much interested," she recorded in her diary, "not having apparently thought of it before; he reflected for some time, and then said with the greatest solemnity and looking so majestic: 'Tell him [the presiding minister] to say only this: "Here lies a man, who has thought all his life that the ceremonies attending birth, marriage, and death were all damned nonsense." Don't let him say a word more.' "

Only during the last ten or fifteen hours of the old father's life did he become inarticulate, because of the phlegm in his throat which he was too weak to cough up. The doctor gave him a little opium to clear his throat, and as a result he sank into peaceful unconsciousness, but he was heard to murmur clearly, "Oh, I have such good boys—*such* good boys!" He also repeated several times, "Mary—my Mary." He died at noon, in the broad daylight which he had loved from boyhood in Albany to old age in Boston.

On New Year's Day Henry wrote William that the day before he had gone out to the Cambridge cemetery, "and stood beside his grave a long time and read him your letter of farewell—which I am sure he heard somewhere out of the depths of the still, bright winter air. He lies extraordinarily close to Mother, and as I stood there and looked at this last expression of so many years of mortal union, it was difficult not to believe that they were not united again in some consciousness of my belief." At this moment Henry wanted to believe in immortality, but his more scientific brother could only say in his farewell letter to his father, ". . . if that *were* true, all would be solved and justified."

Henry sympathized with William alone with his grief "in those dark far-away rooms of mine. But it would have been sadder still if you also had arrived only to hear that after those miserable eight days at sea he was lost forever and ever to our eyes. Thank God we haven't another parent to lose. . . ." William was as lonely and miserable as Henry imagined him, but he found consolation in thinking of the heritage he had received from his father. To his wife he wrote: "For me, the humor, the good spirits, the humanity, the faith in the divine, and the sense of his right to have a say about the deepest reasons of the universe, are what will stay with me. I wish I could believe I should transmit some of them to our babes. We all of us have some of his virtues and some of his shortcomings. Unlike the cool, dry, thin-edged men who now abound, he was full of the fumes of the *ur-ursprünglich* human nature; things turbid, more than he could formulate, wrought within him and made his judgments of rejection of so much of what was brought [before him] seem like revelations as well as knock-down blows. . . . I hope that rich soil of human nature will not become more rare!"

Though Henry remained at 131 Mount Vernon Street, sleeping in his father's room, his sense of loss soon began to fade and to seem "a simple natural fact." But to William the loss of his father left a more painful void, not so much because he was on the other side of the Atlantic ocean as because of the different importance his father had for him. Two months after his father's death William confided to his mother-in-law: "It is singular how I'm learning every day now how the thought of his comment on my experiences has hitherto formed an integral part of my daily consciousness, without my having realized it at all. I interrupt myself incessantly now in the old habit of imagining what he will say when I tell him this or that thing I have seen or heard."

III

Having so deliberately and leisurely left the world of property and domestic responsibility, Henry James Sr. had of course made his will and distributed his possessions with what seemed to him justice to all his children. He had chosen Henry for executor of the estate, possibly because he regarded his second son as more reliable than the first, but certainly also because he knew his wife would have trusted Henry's judgment over William's. As it turned out, of course, Henry was in Boston when the will was probated and William in London, as if fate had confirmed the selection.

The estate, Henry reported to William, was roughly estimated at ninety-five thousand dollars and consisted of three business houses in Syracuse, the recently acquired house in Boston, and the rest in railroad stocks and bonds. The Mount Vernon Street house went to Alice, with the income from the stocks and bonds. Income from the Syracuse property valued at seventy-five thousand dollars was to be shared equally by William, Henry, and Robertson. The yield was fifty-two hundred and fifty dollars a year after taxes and agent's commission, which would give seventeen hundred and fifty dollars for each of the three sons. Wilkinson had been left out of the will because his father had recently given him five thousand dollars, in addition to all the other help in the past. Wilky, of course, was very unhappy at being excluded and complained bitterly. Henry's immediate response was that the brothers should all share alike, and he urged Bob and William not to abide by their father's terms—advice which curiously paralleled the breaking of the will of William of Albany by his sons and daughters. William argued at first that his father's wishes should not be ignored, though he offered to make up the difference to Wilky out of his own share. Bob made a similar offer—and actually he could afford such generosity better than William because his wife's father and grandfather were both quite "well off" and they had been generous to him and Mary (with whom he was for the time being reconciled).

On January 11 Henry begged William: "Don't judge that exclusion of Wilky harshly, as regards Father; *don't judge it at all*, in fact, for the present. Eventually when you have been home and we have talked about it, and you know the circumstances, you will see it all in a just light." Without further dissent William agreed to Henry's plan for equal distribution, and everyone was satisfied. Later Henry made over the entire income from his inheritance to his sister Alice because he felt confident that he could support himself by his writing.

Meanwhile, late in January, Henry visited his younger brothers in Milwaukee and was encouraged by Bob's "improvement" and dismayed by Wilky's condition, financial and physical—"broken down, dying, on the point of giving up his office and salary. . . ." And his wife, Carrie, seemed to have no judgment at all, so that Wilky's situation seemed hopeless. On the way back from Milwaukee Henry stopped in Syracuse to view his father's houses, which he found in excellent condition, rented to almost ideal tenants, and located in the best part of the city, on "James St., the 5th Avenue of Syracuse, one of the handsomest American streets I have ever seen—named after our poor Grandfather!"—doubtless "poor" only because dead; certainly not poor in worldly goods.

During the rapid exchange of letters about the settlement of their father's estate William and Henry also carried on a personal debate about William's abandoning his sabbatical plans and coming home. Henry could not believe that William was unhappy in London because he detested the city, and even found Henry's cherished flat uncomfortable. Henry thought at first that maybe William distrusted his administration of the will, and when this suspicion was dispelled, he became almost desperate in trying to keep his brother from giving up the amenities of London—or if he couldn't stand London, he could go to Paris—for barren Cambridge. The house at 18 Appian Way was rented until the end of the summer of 1883, and if William returned before September he would have to share his mother-in-law's crowded house on Garden Street with his wife, two children, and two in-laws, Mary and Margaret Gibbens. The idea finally occurred to Henry that William could occupy the third-floor bedroom of Alice's house on Mount Vernon Street: "I won't offer to give you up Father's room, because I lately made you a present of my rooms in London."

Here in skeleton outline is the running battle of words: William to Henry on January 9: "The complete absence of any aggregate and outward expression of pure and direct intelligence is what is so striking here. After Paris, London seems like a medieval village, with nothing but its blanket of golden dirt to take the place of style, beauty, and rationality. . . . England under a filthy, smeary, smoky fog, lusty and happy, hale and hearty, with the eternal sunlit ether outside, and she not suspecting, or not caring to think that with a puff of her breath she might rend the veil. . . . Then the theatres, and the hippopotamus-like satisfaction of their audiences! Bad as our theatres are, they are not so massively hopeless as that. It makes Paris seem like a sort of Athens. Then the determination on the part of all who write . . . to do it as amateurs, and never to use the airs and language of a professional; to be first of all a layman and a gentleman, and to pretend that your ideas came to you accidentally as it were, and are things you care nothing about."

Harry to William, January 11: "You speak of being 'determined to sail at latest in *Servia* of Feb. 11th.' This determination makes me really so sad. . . . I think that I must do what I can to keep you from breaking loose from Europe and giving up your stay there as a failure, prematurely. The *pity* of it almost brings tears to my eyes, and when I look upon the barren scene (bating your wife and babes) that awaits you here, I feel as if I were justified in doing almost anything to keep you on the other side. I left you so comfortably established in London with such promise of improvement and stability . . . that it seems a kind of 'irony of fate' that will bring you back in the midst of this harsh and rasping winter to narrow and, as it were, accidental accommodation in Mrs. Gibbens's small house. . . . All this came over me much as this morning I went out to poor *nudified* and staring Cambridge, and thought that *that* and your life there is what you are in such a hurry to get back to!" To this plea Henry added: what would people think of William's giving up his plans and coming back early?

William promptly replied on January 23: "Your solicitude is natural enough, but it certainly flows from a great misconception of all the premises that are operative in the case. . . . As far as the opinion of outsiders and their exclamations of 'failure' (which you seem so much to dread) go, I took great pains to say to everyone that I did not think I could stay the winter. . . . The horror you seem to feel at Cambridge is something with which I have no sympathy, preferring it as I do to any place in the known world. Quite as little do I feel the infinite blessing of simply being in London, or in Europe *überhaupt*. The truth is, we each of us speak from the point of view of his own work; the place where a man's work is best done seems and ought to seem the place of places to him. I feel tempted to go back now just to show you how happy a man can be in the wretched circumstances that so distress your imagination."

Then William confessed that, "The last two days I have written some psychology; and since yesterday noon a dry east wind and cold air has made me feel like a different man. . . . The fact is that although from a moral point of view your sympathy commands my warmest thanks, from the intellectual point of view, it seems, first, to suppose that I am a bachelor, and second, that I am one who suffers intensely from the skinniness and aridity of America." However, "If the psychology only keeps on as it has now started, and more than all, if the air either of Paris or of an improved London— they tell me that never in the memory of man has there been so uninterruptedly depressing a winter here—starts up my eyes and sleep again, I certainly shall not think of coming home for a good many weeks to come."

Long before Henry received William's January 23rd letter, he wrote on the 25th praising some of William's insights into the British character but insisting that, "There is more beside, and it is this *more beside* that I have been living on in London." On February 6 William admitted that he had indeed seen "the other side": "The great point about them [the British] seems their good-humor and *cheerfulness;* but their civilization is *stuffy.*" And he insisted that, "For some reason or other London does thoroughly disagree with me." Also, "Your allusions to my return continue by their solemn tone to amuse me extremely. Especially are the expressions 'confession of failure' and 'appearance of vacillation' comical. The only possible 'failure' would be to stay here longer than the refreshment, which was the only motive, either tacit or avowed, of my coming, lasted. And there can be no appearance of vacillation where there was no plan announced beyond that of staying on from week to week as long as I found it to pay. However, my reply to your first letter will have opened your eyes to all that; meanwhile the strength of your sympathy does equal credit to your head and heart."

While this dialogue with Henry was in progress, with Henry consulting William's wife between letters, William and Alice were carrying on a private correspondence about Henry. Yes, William wrote Alice in substance, Harry is a queer old boy, so good and yet so limited, as if he had taken an oath not to let himself out to more than half his humanhood in order to keep the other half from suffering, and he is unable to credit anyone else with the half which he has suppressed in himself. Of course he has not really taken an oath, or even made a conscious resolution: it is simply a matter of his own helplessness. William was curious about Henry's trip to Milwaukee; to Alice he wondered how his younger brothers and their uncultured households had affected the Anglicized Harry. William guessed there had not been much enjoyment on either side.

A little incident which took place about this time illustrates William's own humanity, bordering on gullibility, though it had no direct bearing on the controversy with Henry. One night on a London street William met an old Frenchman who wanted to sell him for a sovereign a pawnbroker's ticket to a 300-franc watch which he had pawned for four pounds; he said he needed the money to help him get back to Paris. William suspected the ticket was worthless, but he gave the sweet old man the sovereign anyway, and he wrote his wife that if he found that the pawnbroker didn't exist, he would still be glad he had rewarded the Frenchman for his enterprise and ingenuity in a foreign land. By a curious coincidence, that night William's own watch stopped, reminding him of the ticket. Next day he took it to the pawnbroker and found that the watch was a good one, made in Geneva, in a gold hunting case, almost new and worth from eight to ten pounds.

But to return to the argument with Henry, which continued in a letter he wrote to William on February 7: "I received this a.m. your letter of Jan 23d written on receipt of *my* letter (accompanying telegram) urging you to remain in Europe. I quite expected that you would be irritated by my long argument on the subject of your not coming home, and you may imagine how much I wished to put it before you that I should have written to you in the face of this conviction. . . ." Then a wordy defense of the "reasons" he had advanced, which he thought William's Alice shared. But if Henry's fervid pleas had irritated William, so had William's replies got under Henry's skin: "You speak of a 'Punchinello-life' in the evenings— but I don't know what you mean by this—and you must allude to something quite different from the state you were in a month ago. Different, and if you survive it, I venture to believe better! I stick to the doctrine of the 'skinniness' of Cambridge, even for you. . . . Let me add that so far from writing to you as a bachelor, my letter was a direct product of much talk with your wife about your return and much sympathy with the distress that the prospect caused her— distress I mean, on acct. of your homeless condition and the failure of your attempt. Now, I shall be equally satisfied, whatever you do. Don't use your eyes upon me, any more than simple business may require."

Four days later, however, Henry felt ashamed of the tone of this recent letter and apologized for what may have seemed to William "hasty or ill-tempered. . . . It *was* meddlesome in me to have so much to say about the question of your coming back. . . . I even persist in meddling, so far as to be glad that you have not yet come and that according to your last (of the 25th Jan.) to Alice [wife] you are probably now in Paris." This assumption was almost correct; William had not yet left London but did leave on February 13.

Part of this prolonged argument had evidently been relayed to William's mother-in-law, who had written him that she would be delighted to have him return and live with her at any time he chose. On February 14, from the Grand Hotel in Paris, he thanked her for her "beautiful and affectionate letter," which made him "feel altogether safe about going home as far as your welcome to 18 Garden St. was concerned. But Alice had already assured me of that; and in a letter written to her 2 days ago from London I have discussed the probabilities sufficiently to say no more to you about them now." The English Channel had been "rather boisterous" during his crossing, and nearly everyone else had got seasick. He had avoided it by vigorous massaging behind his ears, which confirmed a theory he had been pondering, though he did not say what it was. Mrs. Gibbens' daughter Margaret was in Italy, and William thought he might be able to see her there, for he was considering meeting an old friend (Thomas Davidson) in Florence to discuss "a certain point in Psychology." At any rate on Saint Valentine's Day William James was in good spirits again, was enjoying Paris, and considering further travel.

IV

Although William's personal worries—insomnia, trouble with his eyes, and finally the death of his father—had marred his sojourn in Europe during the autumn and winter of 1882–1883, another cause of his unhappiness was his inability to get started on his book on psychology. The actual difficulty was that he was not yet ready to write it, but he did not fully realize this and blamed his health and his undisciplined mind, and felt guilty over wasting time. The powerful German stimulation to his psychological thinking ebbed away in gloomy London, until the middle of December when a group of philosophers and psychologists who called themselves the "Scratch Eight" invited him to one of their meetings. It was held at the home of Edmund Gurney, author of a psychological study called *The Power of Sound*. In a letter to Alice, William called him "a magnificent Adonis, six feet four in height, with an extremely handsome face, voice, and general air of distinction about him, altogether the exact opposite of the classical idea of a philosopher." He was a fellow of Trinity College at Cambridge and had studied music, medicine, and law. With Henry Sidgwick, Professor of Moral Philosophy at Cambridge, Gurney had founded the Society for Psychical Research the previous February. Sidgwick, with the face of a saint and a long white beard which must have reminded William of his father, was the president of the recently founded S.P.R.

Other members of the informal Scratch Eight were G. Croom Robertson, professor of philosophy in University College, London, and editor of *Mind*, to which James had contributed several articles; Carveth Read, author of a recent book on logic; Frederick Pollock, then professor of law in University College, London, and later at Oxford; Leslie Stephen, editor of the *Cornhill Magazine* and soon to become editor of the monumental Oxford dictionary; James Sully, who had already published several books on psychology and was writing *Outlines of Psychology;* Frederic William Maitland, British jurist, later professor of English law at Cambridge; and, most important of all in James's development in the field of psychology, Shadworth H. Hodgson, an independent scholar who had already published voluminously, and with whom James would continue to exchange ideas for years to come. Hodgson was ten years older, a stern-looking man with bristling black whiskers, though William with his usual hyperbole, called him "an incarnate angel, the most exquisite human creature I ever knew, a *gentleman* to his finger tips and a professional philosopher as well. I love the rare combination." To his wife James wrote that he "felt quite at home" among these intellectuals, and that Stephen and Pollock had invited him to the next meeting. "The discussion, carried on by Sully, Hodgson, and Robertson principally, seemed to show me that there was a great opening for my psychology."

William was also invited to a meeting of the Aristotelian Society, where he met a brilliant young jurist, Richard B. Haldane, just starting on a distinguished career in which he would become Chancellor of the Exchequer and War Secretary. To Alice, William reported, "I went to the Aristotelian Society last night and had an instructive time. A . . . pupil of Caird [the Scottish Hegelian] was there, Haldane by name, and for all the world you would have thought it was dear old Palmer talking—same unrivaled fluency, same blamelessness of diction, same purity of thought." Instructive or not, this group was not half as congenial as the Scratch Eight.

The second meeting of the Scratch Eight to which James had been invited was on February 9 at the home of Carveth Read, at which time William presented a paper. Next day he wrote his wife:

"Yesterday I was parturient of psychological truth, being in one of my fevered states you wot of, when ideas are shooting together and I can think of no finite things. I wrote a lot at headlong speed, and in the evening, having been appointed, gave an account of it—the difference between feeling and thought—at the Scratch Eight. Unluckily neither Sully nor Robertson, the two men most capable of understanding and seeing the truth of it, were present. Hodgson is constitutionally incapable of understanding any thoughts but those that grow up in his own mind,—with all the desire in the world to do justice to them, he simply can't reproduce them in himself. But there was a fair amount of discussion afterwards, and the thing passed off well. I am sure the things I said were highly important scientifically."

This same subject William James treated more extensively a few months later in three lectures which he gave at the "rather absurd little" Concord School of Philosophy and published in *Mind* as "On Some Omissions of Introspective Psychology." He had already written and published an essay on "The Association of Ideas," which he later incorporated unchanged into his *Principles of Psychology*. In this he had used his famous metaphor of "stream-of-consciousness"; something is always in one's consciousness, but constantly changing, thus resembling the flow of a river. This awareness, he explained, is both of external objects experienced through the senses and of thoughts about objects remembered or imagined.

In his Scratch Eight paper James was trying to explain what links objects in consciousness, causing one to follow another—or in other words, what causes "association of ideas"—and he argued that it was their "halo" or the "fringe" surrounding them; "the difference between thought and feeling reduces itself . . . to the presence or absence of 'fringe.' " This was to become one of his most radical but characteristic doctrines: that there is no difference between *thought* and *feeling* except in the use the mind makes of them. "Through feelings we become acquainted with things, but only by our thoughts do we know about them. Feelings are the germ and starting point of cognition, thoughts the developed tree."

Ever since Plato most philosophers had been suspicious of *feelings* or *emotions*, and regarded them as hindrances to obtaining pure truth; thus a serious thinker must guard against the influence of his emotions or subjective states of mind. But now James not only restored feeling to respectability but argued that it was essential to cognition. In fact, it is only by feeling that one really *knows* an object; if the object is only present to the mind or consciousness and not experienced through the senses and emotions then one only *knows about it*. This distinction he would later carry into his mature philosophy, and especially in *The Varieties of Religious Experience*. Thus in working out his ideas on "the difference between thought and feeling" for the Scratch Eight, James made significant progress toward his book on psychology, enough to put him into a more cheerful state of mind and make him feel that he had not after all wasted his half year in Europe.

The "psychological problem" which James mentioned to Thomas Davidson that he wanted to talk over with him turned out to be "the question of objective cognition and the ego," or in simpler language, the relation of whatever one might be aware of in his consciousness to his own self or "I." This was not the epistemological problem (of Locke, Berkeley, and Hume) regarding the relation (if any) of a mental object to its physical existence outside the mind. James was concerned with how a person's sense of his own individual existence affected the contents of his consciousness—another "fringe" or "halo" effect. But why he thought Davidson could help him was a great puzzle to Professor Child, who wrote on March 11, mainly reporting the progress of spring in Cambridge and the boredom of Harvard faculty meetings: "The flitting to Florence for an opinion by Davidson causes (Alice says) much wonder to Harry, and I confess to myself. Perhaps you only want to be accurate about something which he can tell, but much as I value Davidson in his place, I should as soon go to a Baptist church in East Cambridge for inspiration. . . ."

Though fully aware of Davidson's eccentricities, James actually did have a high opinion both of his intelligence and of his historical knowledge of philosophy; in fact, after returning from Europe he did his best to persuade President Eliot to appoint Davidson to the Harvard Department of Philosophy. But the two men were intellectually and temperamentally very different. Both detested Hegel (though Davidson had been a Hegelian in Saint Louis before going to New England), but James did not share his reverence for Kant, and many years later in a memorial essay for his friend, he described the very antithesis of himself when he declared of Davidson, "Even if a philosophy were true, he could easily fail to relish it unless it showed a certain formal nobility and dogmatic pretension to finality." After leaving America in 1878 Davidson had become a follower of the Italian philosopher-priest, Antonio Rosmini-Serbati, whose works he was translating in 1882–1883—though he never became a convert to Catholicism. For several years William had joked about joining his cult in the Italian Alps. In all seriousness, the two men were eager to see each other again, and Davidson offered to meet William in Florence, but met his sister-in-law, Margaret Gibbens, instead. After returning to London, William thanked him on March 12 for this kindness, adding, "She writes me that the best things she has seen have been those to which you have helped her."

By this time, as William had written Davidson before leaving Paris, he was "sick of travel and vagrancy" and desired only "to get back to the bosom of my family. I've got all the good of being abroad in the way of mental refreshment, and a longer stay simply hinders my work. . . ." A few days later he left Europe and by the end of March was back in Cambridge and proving the groundlessness of Henry's fears that he would feel crowded and unhappy in his mother-in-law's house on Garden Street. To Davidson he wrote on May 2: "I need not say that I found America screeching with white luminosity and a little raw-looking to my London-blunted vision. I have not, however, an instant regretted returning when I did; the time had come that I should *ranger* myself. I have done more work in the past month since my return than in the previous six, and feel in a very different state of vigor than ever before at this time of year."

After his lectures at the Concord "Summer School of Philosophy," which had "an audience of from twenty to fifty persons, including the lecturers themselves," William James took his wife and the two babies to the "shack" at Keene Valley in the Adirondacks, from which he wrote Renouvier on August 5 that he was feeling stronger "than in many years at a corresponding period." But he had not done much writing and was still floundering around "in the morasses of the theory of cognition."

One interesting incident of the summer was James's reply to a solicitor of funds for a memorial to Schopenhauer: "I really *must* decline to stir a finger for the glory of one who studiously lived for no other purpose than to spit upon the lives of the like of me and all those I care for. . . . As for Schopenhauer himself, personally, his loud-mouthed pessimism was that of a dog who would rather see the world ten times worse than it is, than lose his chance of barking at it. . . . Then as for his metaphysics, they seem to me to unite every bad quality. He carried Kant's *Schnorkelwerk*, and machine-shop way of representing things, to an extreme where they became simply ludicrous; he ignored most of the really fruitful tendencies of his time; his only merits were his racy and pithy style, and his refusal to 'take stock' in a platitudinarian optimism."

Although the momentum attained in the Scratch Eight paper, which carried James through the writing of his important essay "On Some Omissions of Introspective Psychology" for G. Croom Robertson, editor of *Mind*, had slowed down by the end of the summer of 1883, the year of respite from teaching had been a fruitful one—though germinal rather than in its harvest. And not least of the benefits had been the friendships formed in Europe. From Brighton, Croom Robertson, now afflicted by a fatal illness though bravely carrying on, wrote him on August 13: "There has been no other meeting of the Scratch Eight since that night when you solved the whole mystery of the universe for the seven of them who were there, or for some of the seven. Next winter they will have to go on as seven—Wise Men of England—without the weak brother [himself] banned for the time from London."

CHAPTER XVI Fourteen Doors

Oh, it's the most delightful house you ever saw; has 14 doors, all

opening outside.   —W.J. *to his sister*

I

AFTER HIS RESTFUL SUMMER VACATION in the Adirondacks with Alice and his infant sons, William James began the new academic year in September 1883 in excellent physical condition and good spirits. Then early in October his sister-in-law Carrie summoned him to Milwaukee; Wilkinson was not expected to live more than a few days. William caught the first train possible, but the visit turned out to be harrowing and frustrating. The sight of his oldest brother so excited Wilky that the doctor asked William to leave. Feeling helpless and emotionally upset, William returned to Chicago. From the Palmer House he wrote his sister on October 12 about his painful experiences in Milwaukee.

Back in Cambridge two days later, exhausted and full of remorse, William tried to resume his duties as executor of his father's estate, which had been shifted to him so that Henry might return to London to his comfortable rooms in Bolton Street and the environment in which he could resume his writing. His sister Alice hated to see Henry depart because that left her alone in the Mount Vernon Street house except for a servant and Katharine Loring, on her visits. There were already indications that Alice's health might soon deteriorate again, and the strained relations between the two Alices made this prospect something that William preferred not to think about. To complicate matters, Bob had first decided to give away his inheritance, and then consented to a trusteeship for his children. As executor William had to juggle all these complications in settling the estate. Of course his sister Alice did not complain, and Henry tried to lighten William's burden by commanding him *not* to send him monthly reports, as William was trying to do. "Never, I again beg you," Henry wrote on November 24, now resettled in London, "take the trouble to tell *me* twice anything at all about my Syracuse dividend. I have made my income entirely over to Alice and take no further interest in it."

Wilky rallied again after William's painful visit and lingered on until November 23, when Carrie telegraphed William in Cambridge and Henry in London that he had died. Both brothers felt relieved that he had finally been delivered from his misery. As Henry expressed it, "It is a great weight off my spirit—not to see him lying there in that interminable suffering. Meanwhile your letter comes to me, forwarding Carrie's and Bob's notes and speaking of the days before his death—just as they came to you here, last winter, after you had heard that Father had gone." As usual, Henry was eager to receive exact information "about his last hours," and began worrying about having his body moved from Milwaukee to Cambridge to "lie beside Father and Mother, where we must all lie."

After Wilky's death William went through considerable vexation in reaching a legal settlement with Carrie about her husband's share of his father's estate. William was quite willing to abide by previous agreements, but thought some provision should be made for Wilky's two children, and a satisfactory solution was finally reached. Henry, meanwhile, contributed generously to the funeral expenses and for months afterward frequently sent sums of money to Carrie, not as part of the settlement but simply as gifts to her and Wilky's children, until William informed him that her father had amply provided for her. In his whole handling of legal and business details in administering the estate of his father, William exhibited a systematic thoroughness and reliability of judgment which would have surprised his mother. But he very wisely entrusted his own patrimony to Major Henry L. Higginson, a junior partner in the banking and investment house of Lee, Higginson, and Company in Boston. William also gained a valuable friend in Major Higginson, who would continue for three decades to give almost infallible financial advice.

But William was not so practical in other ways. His wife was expecting their third child in January, and William got the idea that he might lighten her responsibilities by importing a "nurse" from England. He outlined the plan to Henry, who replied January 25, 1884: "I shall be glad to do what I can for you in regard to the nurse; though your plan of importing one strikes me as rather bold. A modest, unaccomplished one (a 'nursery-maid' as they call it here,) would perhaps not be worth that cost and danger; and on the other hand, I fear, from what I am told, that a ripe, finished one (a Nurse, as distinguished from a n-m.,) might be rather a Tartar. She would be likely to have the exactingness of the English upper-servants, be discontented with a small establishment, expect a nursery-maid under her, as is always the custom here. Should you decide to risk it I shall be happy to help you, though I confess I shld. greatly feel the responsibility. Why don't you try for a good German?—or a German nursery-governess?" William apparently realized his ignorance of the British system of nurses, nursery-maids, and "nannies," and dropped this impractical idea, though he did, as Henry suggested, later employ a German governess.

The expected baby arrived January 31, another boy, which William announced to all his friends as his "little Israelite." Two hours after the birth William wrote Henry Bowditch: "Heute den 31ten Januar wurde mir vor 2 Stunden in rascher Aufeinander-folge *ein* (1) wunderschöner jüdisch-aussehender, kräftiger und munterer Knabe geboren. Alles geht nach Wunsch, und bittet um stiller Theilnahme der glückliche Vater." [Today the 31st of January, two hours since, there was born to me in rapid succession *one* (1) wonderfully beautiful, Jewish-looking, sturdy and lively boy. Everything is going as one would wish, and the happy father craves your hushed sympathy.]

Now that William and Alice had a Henry and a William, they had some difficulty in finding a name for their third son. William favored Tweedy, for his father's old friend Edmund Tweedy, foster-father to the Temple children. Henry, who had always exercised great care in naming his fictional characters, discussed this subject in several letters to William. He thought "the appellation of a child cannot be too much considered: it affects his life forever!" When William finally decided against Tweedy, Henry breathed "a sigh of relief," though he thought "Edmund James a very nice name." He was thankful their father had been content with simple "William," "Henry," and "Robertson" and "didn't make us (for the most part) William P's and Henry W., and Robertson F.," and urged William to follow his example. Finally William and Alice settled on Herman, for a German friend on the Harvard faculty, Hermann Hagen, a professor in the Scientific School. Henry liked

Herman but warned against using "Hagen" as a middle name: "it will eventually be pronounced Haygan and mistaken for the Irish Hagan"—not that Henry was prejudiced against the Irish. Anyway, the name remained Herman, without the German *nn*.

Although Alice was a little slow in recovering from the birth of her third son, little Herman flourished during the first months of his life in Cambridge and later with his parents on their vacation in the Adirondacks. In his favorite spot in the Keene Valley William reread his father's books, made a selection from them, and wrote a long introduction for the volume of "literary remains." But in September he barely got back to Cambridge before coming down with a severe fever of some kind which kept him in bed for eight days and affected his eyes for weeks afterward. Nevertheless, to his cousin Kitty Prince he wrote on October 20 from the small house on Appian Way: "We are embarking on what promises to be a much easier winter than the last—the house more furnished, two hours less of lecturing [his teaching load was now six hours a week], some pieces of work done which is a relief to my mind. . . ."

Bob had moved from Wisconsin to nearby Concord, where he was boarding—once again separated from his wife and children—but he often visited William and took dictation from him while William's eyes were bad. Bob claimed he had stopped drinking since settling in Concord, but William had little confidence in the permanence of the reform. Bob had confessed to his wife a little "innocent" love affair he had had in the country, and now Mary returned his letters unopened. To Henry, William expressed his growing conviction that Bob would never "work" again. Of course he painted for his own amusement and tried to write poetry.

But the most unexpected event of the autumn of 1884 was the sudden decision of sister Alice to go to England. In retrospect, the full pathos of the decision is apparent, though it surprised and somewhat alarmed her older brothers at the time. With Henry back in London, William occupied with his family, and sister-in-law Alice not only maternally occupied but also aloof, Alice James was so lonely in the Mount Vernon Street house that she sometimes felt like rushing out to the nearby firehouse to talk to the firemen. However, it was the prospect of losing Katharine Loring, for some months at least, that frightened Alice into action. Miss Loring's sister Louisa was suffering from "weak lungs," and it was thought that she might recuperate in Europe—still the land of magic health. Miss Loring was to accompany her. Alice James could not bear a separation from her friend, and announced that she would go with them.

Alice's excuse was that she would visit Henry for an indefinite time, and of course he encouraged her to do so, no matter how he really felt about it. No one expected her to stay longer than a few months. She closed her house on Mount Vernon Street and sailed with the Lorings in November, but the ship was scarcely under way before she collapsed with one of her mysterious spells, and Katharine was hard pressed to nurse two invalids. Henry met the ship at Liverpool and was astonished to find Alice so weak that she had to be carried ashore. He took her to a hotel, employed a nurse, and stayed with her until she could be taken to London a week later. Then he found rooms for her in Piccadilly, near his Bolton Street flat. To William he observed in a letter that it seemed to him that as soon as Katharine Loring arrived, "Alice takes to her bed. This was the case as soon as Katharine came to London to see her (she had been up before). . . ." Although the "Angel" did not complain, he had good reason to feel worried about the complications his sister was going to create for him.

II

The promise William James had made to his dying father that his "literary remains" would be "well taken care of," and that "your words shall not suffer for being concealed," he had kept with as little delay as possible, the second summer after his father's death. His father had not left a complete set of his books and William had had to have Henry search for some of them in England before he could complete his selection.

Since none of the books by Henry James Sr. had ever sold enough copies to pay for the printing, it was not likely that William's selection from them would sell, and consequently he had to pay for the printing himself. But late in 1884 (title page dated 1885) the *Literary Remains* was issued under the imprint of James R. Osgood of Boston, a firm of good reputation, which had also published Henry James Jr. The book of 471 pages, bound in red cloth, contained, in addition to William's long introduction (137 pages), an unfinished autobiography by Henry Sr.—a delightful and very readable account of his youth and early manhood, including his "vastation" near Windsor Castle when William was a baby, extracts from his books arranged to illustrate his theological ideas, and "Some Personal Recollections of Carlyle," an essay which Henry Sr. had published in the *Atlantic Monthly* the year before his death.

On January 2, 1885, Henry acknowledged receipt of his copies: "Three days ago . . . came the two copies of Father's (and your) book, which have given me great filial and fraternal joy. All I have had time to read as yet is the introduction—your part of which seems to me admirable, perfect. It must have been very difficult to do, and couldn't have been done better. And how beautiful and extraordinarily individual (some of them magnificent) are the extracts from Father's writings which you have selected so happily." Although he found himself unable to enter into his father's religious convictions and feelings, he admired their spirit and intensity, and felt that "poor Father, struggling so alone all his life, and so destitute of every worldly or literary ambition, was yet a great writer." The book had arrived at a bad time for Alice, who had suffered a temporary paralysis from an ineptly administered Galvanic treatment. But she held the book in her hands and burst into tears, exclaiming, "How beautiful it is that William should have done it!" Then they "talked of poor Father's fading away into silence and darkness, the waves of the world closing over this System which he tried to offer it, and of how we were touched by this act of yours which will (I am sure) do so much to rescue him from oblivion."

However, William's efforts did not rescue his father's "System" from oblivion; six months after publication William reported to Henry that only one copy had been sold! Most of the review copies mailed out were ignored, though the *Nation* published a savage critique which distressed both Henry and William. The latter wrote to the editor, E. L. Godkin, friend of Henry James Sr. for many years, asking, "Doesn't the impartiality which I suppose is striven for in the 'Nation,' sometimes overshoot the mark 'and fall on t' other side'? Poor Harry's books seem always given out to critics with antipathy to his literary temperament; and now for this only and last review of my father—a writer exclusively religious—a personage seems to have been selected for whom the religious life is complete *terra incognita*. A severe review by one interested in the subject is one thing; a contemptuous review by one with the subject out of his sight is another." Godkin responded promptly in great distress; someone else on the staff had assigned the review and he had not seen it before it was printed. William then replied to him: "Your cry of remorse or regret is so 'whole-souled' and complete that I should not be human were I not melted almost to tears by it, and sorry I 'ever spoke to you as I did.' . . . I am heartily sorry that the thing should have distressed you so much more than it did me."

Shadworth Hodgson thanked James so warmly for his copy that William replied on February 20, 1885: "Anything responsive about my poor old father's writing falls most gratefully upon my heart. . . . I thank you heartily for your interest. I wish that somebody could *take up* something from his system into a system more articulately scientific."

But however strongly William longed to "atone" for his own contribution to his father's loneliness, he knew he could never be the "somebody" he wished for. In preparing the book he had come to understand his father's ideas better, but the mental gulf which separated them in William's youth still remained. "With all the richness of style," William remarked in his Introduction, "the ideas are singularly unvaried and few. Probably few authors have so devoted their entire lives to the monotonous elaboration of one single bundle of truths. . . . His truths were his life; they were the companions of his death-bed; and when all else had ebbed away, his grasp of them was still vigorous and sure." This "bundle of truths" was not so much a rational theology as a combination of religious sentiments and personal convictions of the nature of God and of man's relations with him. And yet at bottom these rested on philosophical concepts, however difficult to articulate—and Henry James Sr. had never been satisfied that he had sufficiently articulated them.

In both Jewish and Christian theology God created the universe out of nothing (*cf.* the first chapter of *Genesis*), but William's father regarded a "magical" creation as childish. Such a creation would forever be tainted by its origin from nothingness. God, he believed, animated the void not with a supernatural fiat but by prolonged and continuous exercise of His creative energy. This process took place in two stages, which James called "formative" and "redemptive," the second not yet finished—or scarcely begun. "To speak very oracularly, *Nature* is for Mr. James the movement of formation, the first quickening of the void unto itself; and *Society* is the movement of redemption, or the finished spiritual work of

God. . . . for Mr. James a mere resistless 'bang' is no creative process at all, and that a *real* creation means nothing short of a real *bringing to life* of the essential nothingness, which is the eternal antithesis to God,—a *work*, therefore, upon that nothingness actually performed." In other words, *creation* is a long process of fecundation, growth, and maturation—not unlike the scientific theories of evolution if the motivating force is conceived of as spiritual and mystical. God creates continuously, and every creature is not only the result of His creation but is himself or itself a living, integral part; thus for man to *live creatively* is for him to live in harmony with God's energy working through him.

It was just here that the paradox which had always bothered William in his father's religion came into play, and now that he more fully understood it, he was no more able to accept it. His father believed that in order to animate the void into Nature, God had to permit self-consciousness or selfhood, which in man took the form of pride in his individuality, his personality, his own will power. In this stage man acquired conscience and religion. But, "after conscience and religion have played their part, and undermined the illusion of the self, so that men acknowledge their life to come from God, and love each other as God loves, having no exclusive private cares, will form the kingdom of heaven on earth, the regenerate social order which none of us yet know. In a word, God will be fully incarnated at last in a form that no longer contradicts his character, in what Mr. James calls, with Swedenborg, the Divine-Natural Humanity. God's real creature is this aggregate Humanity." This was the source of Henry James Sr.'s pervasive democracy. God could not be partial to "one fractional unit of us more than another." Even the redeemed and the unredeemed were one to Him, and He did not reward one and punish the other, though He was steadily working toward the redemption of all—to incarnate Himself in the whole of Humanity.

While rereading his father's books and planning his edition of the *Literary Remains,* William James had given a lecture (spring of 1884) to the Harvard Divinity students on "The Dilemma of Determinism." At the outset he admitted that "evidence of external kind to decide between determinism and indeterminism is . . . strictly impossible to find." But, anticipating his later Pragmatism, he urged the divinity students to consider the consequences of believing in one or the other. In a determined, "iron block" universe, their individual actions could have no effect. Everything was fixed, final, inevitable, with no open possibilities; nothing hanging in the balance waiting for human effort to sway the result one way or another. Here was the "dilemma": the determinist could never find a satisfactory explanation for evil in the world. "If God be good, how came he to create—or, if he did not create, how comes he to permit—the devil? The evil facts must be explained as seeming: the devil must be whitewashed, the universe must be disinfected, if neither God's goodness nor his unity and power are to remain unimpugned."

William James could see no basis for distinction between good and bad in a determined universe. "Calling a thing bad means, if it mean anything at all, that the thing ought not to be, that something else ought to be in its stead. Determinism, in denying that anything else can be in its stead, virtually defines the universe as a place in which what ought to be is impossible,—in other words, an organism whose constitution is afflicted with an incurable taint, an irremediable flaw." The only escape from pessimism was to abandon regret, become a cynic and a hedonist. Now of course his father had done nothing of the kind. He admitted the presence of evil in the world but regarded it as a transient stage in God's process, or "formation," of the world. It would disappear when God became incarnated in Humanity. To William this sounded like Hegel's fatuous doctrine of the merging of opposites, and it gave him no moral or intellectual satisfaction.

William did, like his father, prefer an unfinished universe, but it had to be one bristling with chance and possibilities; a universe in which both good and bad were real and eternally at war. But the outcome must not be foreordained, with man a mere pawn in the cosmological chess game.

Regarded as a stable finality, every outward good becomes a mere weariness to the flesh. It must be menaced, be occasionally lost, for its goodness to be fully felt as such. Nay, more than occasionally lost. No one knows the worth of innocence till he knows it is gone forever, and that money cannot buy it back. Not the saint, but the sinner that repenteth, is he to whom the full length and breadth, and height and depth, of life's meaning is revealed. Not the absence of vice, but vice there, and virtue holding her by the throat, seems the ideal human state. And there seems no reason to suppose it is not a permanent human state.

Thus the father and son shared many attitudes toward a universe still in process of being created, but the saintly father had a sublime faith in the outcome, not directed by human hands—and wills— while to his son the outcome was uncertain, and even God needed all the help He could get from faulty human beings.

III

While he was writing to his sister Alice on December 7, 1884, William's Alice called from the head of the stairs: " 'Don't you want to see the baby creeping on the floor?' I have rushed up and seen the phenomenon—a wonderful human turtle with nothing on but a diaper hitching himself all about the room." William never ceased to marvel at and be amused by his wife's complete absorption in the lives of her babies. She was soon to pay dearly for it. Three months later Alice caught scarlet fever and the whole family was quarantined. Without the help of her mother and sister from nearby Garden Street it would have been difficult for William to keep his household going. Then in June baby Herman caught whooping cough, and his mother contracted it from him. The other children escaped by being taken quickly to the country, but before little Herman had fully recovered he caught cold, which turned into pneumonia, and he died on July 9, 1885. To his favorite cousin, Kitty Prince, William wrote a full account three days later:

"Our little Humster, whom you never saw since his first boyhood, has gone over to the majority. We buried him yesterday, under the young pine tree, at my father's side. For 9 days he had been in a desperate condition, but his constitution proved so tenacious, that each visit of the doctor found him still alive. At last his valiant little soul left the body at nine o'clock on Thursday night. He was a broad, generous, patient little nature, with a noble head who would doubtless have done credit to his name had he lived. It *must* be now that he is reserved for some still better chance than that, and that we shall in some way come into his presence again. The great part of the experience to me has been the sight of Alice's devotion. I thought I knew her, but I didn't, nor did I fully know the meaning of that old human word *motherhood*. Six weeks with no regular sleep, 9 days with never more than 3 hours in the 24, and yet bright and fresh and ready for anything, as much on the last day as on the first. She is so essentially *mellow* a nature, that when the excitement is gone and the collapse sets in, it will be short and have nothing morbid about it. We are all pretty tired, and as I write this, I can hardly keep my eyes open.

"We leave for Jaffrey [in New Hampshire] in a day or two, little Billy staying here so as not to catch the whooping cough from his mother. He has been kept three weeks in the neighborhood of Jaffrey by Margaret Gibbens, and the climate doesn't seem to agree. What more permanent plan for the summer we shall make, I don't know, but will let you know when it is made. Dear Kitty, I have thought of you often, with the Angel of Death near by. It brings me closer to all mankind, this world-old experience."

William had arranged to board his family with a congenial couple on a quiet farm at Jaffrey in southern New Hampshire, near Monadnock Mountain, and a few miles from Peterborough. William went back to Cambridge in August to do some writing in his mother-in-law's house, while Mrs. Gibbens joined Alice and the children—Billy having already been restored to his mother. The barn, the farm animals, the hay wagon, and a berry pasture provided amusement for the little boys all day long, making them sleep like logs at night. Harry, now six, had the run of the farm, though of course Billy, only a little over three, had to be watched. But their father wrote their Aunt Alice that both were "in their element." Harry would hardly eat his supper for fear he wouldn't see the cows come home to be milked. To his cousin Kitty, William wrote on August 11 that he and Alice jogged about behind a slow horse in the afternoons and evenings. She was "enduring her loss beautifully, without a word or murmur or a bit of morbidness." They had received many letters of sympathy. From London Henry wrote how sad he felt never to be able to come "nearer to the little Herman than to see his small earthly mound nestling near father's." Sister Alice had had another collapse and was not told about her nephew's death for a few days, Henry said, but she would write as soon as she had recovered sufficiently.

After the Jameses returned to Cambridge in September life ran smoothly for them until December. Then William's mother-in-law suffered a "severe pulmonary illness" (presumably some variety of pneumonia) and decided to go to Italy for recuperation. Alice now detested the house in which little Herman had died, and she welcomed her mother's invitation to move into her house in her absence.

Meanwhile, also in December, Mary Gibbens, the second daughter, had married William Mackintyre Salter and gone to live in Chicago, where her husband was active in the Ethical Culture movement and was writing and lecturing on ethics. Thus William and Alice had the house at 18 Garden Street to themselves—and they continued to live there for several years after Mrs. Gibbens and Margaret returned—further disproving the grounds for Henry's worries about William's return in the spring of 1883.

On New Year's Day, 1886, William wrote his German friend Carl Stumpf from the new address on Garden Street, reporting the changes that had taken place. Mrs. Gibbens was "now on the Ocean, with her youngest and only unmarried daughter, the second one having only a month ago become the wife of that Salter whose essays on ethics have lately been translated by [Georg] von Gizycki in Berlin. So I have gained him as a brother-in-law, and regard it as a real gain. I have also gained a full Professorship with an increase in pay [five hundred dollars, bringing the salary up to four thousand dollars], and have moved into a larger and more commodious house. My eyes, too, are much better than they were a year ago, and I am able to do more work, so there is plenty of sweet as well as bitter in the cup."

IV

In the same letter to Stumpf James wrote also: "I don't know whether you have heard of the London 'Society for Psychical Research,' which is seriously and laboriously investigating all sorts of 'supernatural' matters, clairvoyance, apparitions, etc. I don't know what you think of such work; but I think that the present condition of opinion regarding it is scandalous, there being a mass of testimony, or apparent testimony, about such things, at which the only men capable of critical judgment—men of scientific education—will not even look. We have founded a similar society here within the year,—some of us thought that the publications of the London society deserved at least to be treated as if worthy of experimental disproof,—and although work advances very slowly owing to the small amount of disposable time on the part of the members, who are all very busy men, we have already stumbled on some rather inexplicable facts out of which something may come. It is a field in which the sources of deception are extremely numerous. But I believe there is no source of deception in the investigation of nature which can compare with a fixed belief that certain kinds of phenomenon are *impossible*."

James himself was obviously the chief instigator of the American group. Only he had had personal contact with the British researchers Edmund Gurney, Frederic W. H. Myers, and Henry Sidgwick, and he had been interested in such investigations at least since writing the review of a book on the use of the "planchette" in 1869. Also the other members of the little band that met in Boston in the autumn of 1884 were colleagues or personal friends of his, such as Stanley Hall, Dr. Henry Bowditch, Professor Asa Gray, the American Hegelian W. T. Harris, James's young protégé Josiah Royce, and a few others. None of these took a very active part in the investigations, and several, such as Hall and Royce, later made fun of the organization.

When Thomas Davidson, William's eccentric Scottish friend, still in Italy, heard of the founding of the American Society for Psychical Research he protested against what appeared to him to be its anti-spiritual bias, to which William replied that it had no bias whatever, either for or against anything. "For I take it the urgent thing, to rescue us from the present disgraceful condition, is to ascertain in a manner so thorough as to constitute *evidence* that will be accepted by outsiders, just what the *phenomenal conditions of certain* concrete phenomenal occurrences are. Not till that is done can spiritualistic or anti-spiritualistic theories be even mooted . . . what we want is not only truth, but evidence." Then William added, with true prophetic insight, "We shall be lucky if our scientific names don't grow discredited the instant they subscribe to any 'spiritual' manifestations."

Of course one field for the psychic researchers to investigate was the performance of mediums. Some time in 1885, after James had started the psycho-physics laboratory—in which he worked a couple of hours each day to counteract his tendency toward subjectivity—and had also begun to experiment on a large scale with hypnotism, using students as subjects, his mother-in-law heard of a medium in Boston who claimed to be able, while in a trance, to communicate with deceased persons. Mrs. Gibbens secretly visited the medium and was impressed by the intimate knowledge of the Gibbens and James families which the woman displayed in her trance. Then Mrs.

Gibbens's three daughters made visits, and were equally impressed, but especially William's wife. Of course they told William in great detail about their experiences and urged him to visit the medium and see for himself, which he promptly did with his wife. Thus began his observations, and later friendship, with Mrs. William J. Piper.

We hear of this medium through William's correspondence with his invalid sister. One of Mrs. Piper's methods of getting information from the spirit world about a person who was physically remote from her was to hold some possession of that person in her hands while she went into her trance. She asked for a lock of Alice's hair, which William duly requested of her, and his sister sent a lock of hair, but later wrote him: "I hope you won't be 'offended,' . . . when I tell you that I played you a base trick about the hair. It was a lock, not of my hair, but that of a friend of Mrs. [Humphrey] Ward who died four years ago. I thought it a much better test of whether the medium were simply a mind reader or not, if she is something more I should greatly dislike to have the secrets of my organization laid bare to a wondering public. I hope you will forgive my frivolous treatment of so serious a science." We hear nothing more of this particular experiment, but it is interesting that the invalid Alice was more skeptical than the other Alice, who continued to visit Mrs. Piper and receive visits from her for many years.

In 1886 James wrote an account of the séances with Mrs. Piper in which he, his wife, and his in-laws participated, and the account was published in the first volume of *Proceedings of the American Society for Psychical Research*. He began his report with another "trance-medium," Miss Helen Berry, who claimed to be able to "materialize" deceased friends of the sitters. But in twelve séances which he visited, and twenty-three by friends and relatives, "No spirit form came directly to any one of us. . . ."

To turn to the much simpler and more satisfactory case of Mrs. P. This lady can at will pass into a trance condition, in which she is 'controlled' by a power purporting to be the spirit of a French doctor, who serves as intermediary between the sitter and deceased friends. This is the ordinary type of trance-mediumship at the present day. I have myself witnessed a dozen of her trances, and have testimony at first hand from twenty-five sitters, all but one of whom were virtually introduced to Mrs. P. by myself.

Of five of the sittings we have *verbatim* stenographic reports.

Twelve of the sitters, who in most cases sat singly, got nothing from the medium but unknown names or trivial talk. Four of these were members of the society, and of their sittings *verbatim* reports were taken.

Fifteen of the sitters were surprised at the communications they received, names and facts being mentioned at the first interview which it seemed improbable should have been known to the medium in a normal way. The probability that she possessed no clew as to the sitter's identity was, I believe, in each and all of these fifteen cases, sufficient. But of only one of them is there a stenographic report; so that, unfortunately for the medium, the evidence in her favor is, although more abundant, less exact in quality than some of that which will be counted against her.

Of these fifteen sitters, five, all ladies [four were undoubtedly his wife, Mrs. Gibbens, Mrs. Salter, and Miss Margaret Gibbens], were blood relatives, and two (I myself being one) were men connected by marriage with the family to which they belonged [the other being his brother-in-law, W. M. Salter]. Two other connections of this family are included in the twelve who got nothing. The medium showed a most startling intimacy with this family's affairs, talking of many matters known to no one outside, and which *gossip* could not possibly have conveyed to her ears. The details would prove nothing to the reader, unless printed *in extenso*, with full notes by the sitters. It reverts, after all, to personal conviction. My own conviction is not evidence, but it seems fitting to record it. I am persuaded of the medium's honesty, and of the genuineness of her trance; and although at first disposed to think that the 'hits' she made were either lucky coincidences, or the result of knowledge on her part of who the sitter was and of his or her family affairs, I now believe her to be in possession of a power as yet unexplained.

James was curious to know whether Mrs. Piper's trance was hypnotic (self-induced), and he asked permission to hypnotize her. He found her at first a difficult subject, but on the fifth attempt succeeded "as far as muscular phenomena and automatic imitations of speech and gesture go; but I could not affect her consciousness, or otherwise get her beyond this point. Her condition in this semi-hypnosis is very different from her medium-trance. The latter is characterized by great muscular unrest, even her ears moving vigorously in a way impossible to her in her waking state. But in hypnosis her muscular relaxation and weakness are extreme." She had difficulty in making audible sounds, or even contracting her muscles, whereas in the medium-trance her pupils contracted and her muscles were restless, as stated above. James also tried to suggest to the "control" (the spirit of the French doctor) "that he should make her recollect after the trance what she had been saying" during the hypnosis, but this experiment failed. "In the hypnotic trance such a suggestion will often make the patient remember all that has happened."

To see, if possible, whether Mrs. Piper's peculiar power was "thought-transference," he had her try to name the suit of playing cards which he held invisible to her. Neither in her waking state nor in her medium-trance did she show any aptitude for this and similar experiments. "So far as the evidence goes, then, her medium-trance seems an isolated feature of her psychology." Four years later, after considerably more experience with Mrs. Piper, James was to offer a few more deductions about her trances, but he was still convinced that she did have some kind of "supernormal powers."

V

The report on the séances with Mrs. Piper was one of the few projects William James completed in the summer of 1886, though it was not on the whole an unhappy vacation from teaching. In June Alice felt so exhausted that she spent much of the day simply lying on the couch in the library while William read or wrote. His cousin Kitty had lost her husband, Dr. Prince, and she visited the Jameses during Alice's period of exhaustion. Fortunately the boys, Harry and Billy, liked her and she was able to help Alice keep a check on where they were and what they were doing. The first of July Alice took the boys to the farm at Jaffrey where they had stayed the previous summer, while William went for a week to the seashore at Portsmouth, New Hampshire, to be "alone with the waves and the pines and bayberries," he wrote his cousin Kitty on July 11, after he had rejoined Alice and the boys at the "peaceful and salubrious farm." His wife was pregnant again, but regained her buoyancy and cheerful temperament in the country air.

Around the first of August William returned to Cambridge to do some other writing on psychology—and perhaps finish the report on Mrs. Piper. But he also attended to some personal matters. Dr. Prince had been buried in nearby Newton, and on August 5 William paid the bill for an inscription on the doctor's tombstone, then went out to Newton to inspect it. "The inscription 'A new song before the throne' looked beautiful," he reported to Kitty, "and just fitted rightly into its place. I hope the blessed Doctor in some way takes cognizance of its being there."

Except for errands of this kind, William began writing at 8:30 in the morning and continued until mid- or late afternoon. But he soon had to give up this schedule and return to Jaffrey. There, on August 29, he wrote to Croom Robertson: "The moment I get interested in anything, bang goes my sleep, and I have to stop for ten days or a fortnight, till everything has grown cold again and the mood is off. One makes very slow progress at that rate." Alice no longer had morning nausea, and the boys were enjoying the farm as much as they had the previous summer, but William found it difficult to relax because he was not making any progress on the psychology book; consequently he was restless and impatient.

Finally, no longer able to stand his nervous tension, William decided, with Alice's encouragement, to take a week's jaunt by himself in the White Mountains. As usual, he carried a book which he had been intending to read, this time F. H. Bradley's *Logic*, which he praised extravagantly to his psychologist friends in England. The most important discovery during the trip was not an intellectual one, but one that was to shape the lives of the whole family for many years to come. The discovery was a farm for sale on the shore of Chocorua Lake, in New Hampshire, about ten miles from Conway. The farm consisted of ninety acres, most of it in forest—oaks, firs, maples and other trees typical of the region. Behind it was Chocorua Mountain, rising to a sharp, blue peak thirty-five hundred feet high. A rambling, shingle-covered, weather-beaten house in need of repairs stood in a narrow valley between the lake and a steep hill out of which a crystal-clear spring cascaded enough water for domestic use. Nearby was a brook which could be dammed up for bathing. William knew at once that he had found the right place for a summer home for his growing family, and it could be bought for seventy-five hundred dollars. When Alice saw it a few weeks later, she agreed that they should acquire it, as they promptly did, plus an additional piece of meadow land for five hundred dollars.

When William's sister Alice asked for more details about the house, he replied, "Oh, it's the most delightful house you ever saw; has 14 doors all opening outside." Then she added in her diary: "His brain isn't limited to 14, perhaps unfortunately." Whether fortunate or not, it was true that so many outward-opening doors exactly suited him—though he did reduce the number to eleven in the remodeling. It was not the orderly, logical house his wife would have preferred, but this did not restrain her enthusiasm for "Chocorua," as they would always call the place, though the nearest post office was named unromantically Tamworth Ironworks, which would be the postmark on their letters from their summer Eden.

Winters in the New Hampshire mountains are severe, and remodeling of the Chocorua house must wait until spring. But it was exciting for William and Alice to make plans, when they could find the time, for, with her mother away and the advent of their fourth child impending, it was a strenuous autumn and winter. When Mrs. Gibbens and Margaret arrived from Europe in November they had been through a harrowing experience. Their steamship had caught fire in mid-ocean, causing passengers to go overboard and float in the sea for an hour—Margaret did not have a life-jacket and someone had to hold her up. And when they unpacked their trunks, most of their clothes and the gifts they had brought back for members of the family had been ruined by water used in fighting the fire. In midwinter Mrs. Gibbens and Margaret visited the Salters in Chicago. While they were away Billy began to suffer from asthma, and his mother, now in advanced pregnancy, found it all she could do to keep the house running, even with a servant. Harry was going to school and gave little trouble, but Billy sulked and staged tantrums.

On February 5, 1887, William wrote his sister Alice that Mrs. Gibbens and Margaret had arrived home from Chicago and would take Billy in a few days to Aiken, South Carolina, to stay until May. Mrs. Gibbens, mindful of her own illness the previous winter, was "glad to go south for her own sake," and William thought the open air and Southern sunshine would be good for Billy. "He is the most utterly charming little piece of human nature you ever saw, so packed with life, impatience, and feeling, that I think Father must have been just like him at his age." And Billy's father too, one might guess.

For the present, William had given up the séances with Mrs. Piper—perhaps partly because his wife could not accompany him, though he said it was lack of time. But he confessed to his sister that he had paid "ten or eleven visits to a mind-cure doctress, a sterling creature, resembling the 'Venus of Medicine,' Mrs. Lydia E. Pinkham [a patent medicine called Mrs. Pinkham's Vegetable Compound used a picture of the buxom manufacturer to advertise the product], made solid and veracious looking. I sit down beside her and presently drop asleep, whilst she disentangles the snarls out of my mind. She says she never saw a mind with so many, so agitated, so restless, etc. She said my *eyes*, mentally speaking, kept revolving like wheels in front of each other and in front of my face, and it was four or five sittings ere she could get them *fixed*. I am now, *unconsciously to myself*, much better than when I first went, etc. I thought it might please you to hear an opinion of my mind so similar to your own. Meanwhile what boots it to be made unconsciously better, yet all the while consciously to lie awake o'nights, as I still do?"

Though the irony suggests skepticism, it is apparent that William was not visiting the "doctress" either for scientific observation or merely to satisfy his curiosity. He evidently felt desperate enough to try anything that promised relief from his insomnia. But the tone of this confession was also influenced by Alice's renewed attacks of her old invisible malady, about which she tried to be stoic and howled with derision whenever anyone tried to sympathize with her. "I will not moralize or sympathize," William wrote, "for fear of awakening more 'screams of laughter' similar to those which you wrote of as greeting my former attempts." He did, of course, frequently express sympathy in his letters, but usually in some humorous way. He also tried to divert her with amusing accounts of his activities, as in the following "adventure" in a horsecar—certainly exaggerated, maybe fictitious:

"The only *adventure* that has happened was two or three weeks ago in the horsecar. A little five-year old had been singing aloud from Harvard Square to Charles St. in such a hoarse nasal voice that I was on the point of getting out of the car twice. When by a mighty resolution, summoning all sorts of ethical, religious and sociological principles to the aid of my trembling courage, I managed to say in an ingratiating tone 'Sshh!' hoping the mother might take the hint. Instead of which she only said 'how can *I* stop the chayld?!' and appealed to the rest of the passengers, who forthwith rose as one man, and I thought I should be put out of the car. My next neighbor called me a jackass, I slapped his face twice & he collected the cards of the rest of the passengers, all eager to serve as witnesses in my trial for assault & battery. When I offered him my card, however, he tamed down immediately & the excitement subsided. I suppose he thought my card was a sort of romantic prelude to a duel—you know in novels & on the stage. Meanwhile the conductor had bulged in and we were at Bowdoin Square. I had spoken none but scrupulously polite words from first to last, & felt so gratified at having slapped his face with impunity, that I was friends with all mankind, and as we bundled off the platform together, I between the mother & her champion, I strove to engage them in reasonable talk. The mother however said 'I have nothing to say to you, Sir.' The man still more effectively replied to my advances: 'You may talk to the lamppost. I only talk with *gentlemen!*' Alice, on my return home, relates the adventure to Harry, who was in bed at his Grandmother's, but his only comment was 'Papa is more than a clown!' The moral is: 'never tackle an American infant unless you get him in a dessert [sic] spot.' There's no gain or glory in it. I suppose I seemed to the car population like an affected Anglomaniac. The American philoprogenitiveness is after all touching—the champion said to the mother as I walked away from them—'Don't mind it, madam, I've got a little one myself, & I know how it feels.' You may sell the incident to Harry for one of his novels if you like." James also told this improbable incident (or fiction) to his students around 1885–1886, according to Logan Pearsall Smith, who repeated it in *Unforgotten Years* with almost the same details.

In his letter of February 5 William said that during the examination period between the two semesters he had gone to Chocorua to "see just what was needed to make it habitable for the summer. It is a goodly little spot, but we may not, after all, fit up the buildings till we have spent a summer in the place and 'studied' the problem a little more closely. The snow was between two and three feet deep on a level, in spite of the recent thaws. The day after I arrived was one of the most crystalline purity, and the mountain simply exquisite in gradations of tint." An eccentric tenant, who called himself an "Attorney and Pension Agent," was occupying a room in the house, almost devoid of furniture, and keeping an eye on the place. William marveled at the old fellow's dream of self-importance, but felt sorry for anyone living for four months with "pure snow, always snow, and naught but snow." Later he learned that only two months in the summer were normally free of frost, and there were years in which Chocorua had some frost in every month. It was indeed a cool spot for a summer home, for wintry weather would come early and last well into the spring.

Alice's delivery seemed a long time in coming, but finally on

March 24 she gave birth to a daughter, and two days later William sent this message to Henry Bowditch: "My live-stock is increased by a *Töchterchen*, modest, tactful, unselfish, quite different from a boy, and in fact a really *epochmachendes Erzeugniss* [epochmaking manifestation]. I shall begin to save for her dowry and perhaps your Harold will marry her. Their ages are suitable. Grüsse an die gnädige Frau [greetings to your gracious wife]."

This was Alice James's first childbirth without the presence and assistance of her mother, who was still in South Carolina, with Billy, but there were no complications and she recovered with normal rapidity. To Henry, who was in Venice, recovering from "a sharp attack of jaundice (a most loathsome malady)," William wrote that the new baby looked like her mother. But they named her Margaret Mary, for her two maternal aunts. William's sister Alice, who was occupying Henry's flat in London in his absence, took great pride in her niece, who was in approximately the same chronological position in William's family as Alice in her generation.

VI

Living at Chocorua for a summer before deciding on what re-modeling the house needed might have been a sensible plan, but William could not be that practical. During the spring vacation in April 1887 he spent five days "at my sylvan home," he wrote to Henry on the 12th, "to see about getting the buildings in order for summer." When he arrived the snow was four feet deep on level ground, and at least eight where it had drifted. "The day before yesterday the heat became summer-like, and I took a long walk in my shirt-sleeves, going through the snow the whole length of my leg when the crust broke. It was a queer combination—not exactly agreeable. The snow-blanket keeps the ground from freezing deep; so that very few days after the snow is gone the soil is dry, and spring begins in good earnest. I tried snow-shoes but found them clumsy. They were making the maple-sugar in the woods; I had excellent comfort at the hotel hard by; with whose good landlord and still better landlady I am good friends; I rested off the fumes of my lore-crammed brain, and altogether I smile at the pride of Greece and Rome—from the height of my New Hampshire home."

He had a Boston architect draw a plan for repairing and re-modeling the house, and he now found that the expense would be nearer two thousand dollars than the eight hundred he had first estimated. "But," he assured Henry, "we shall have ten large rooms (two of them 24 x 24), and three small ones—not counting kitchen, pantries, etc., and if you want some real, roomy, rustic happiness, you had better come over and spend all your summers with us. I can see that the thought makes you sick, so I'll say no more about it, but my permanent vision of your future is that your pen will fail you as a means of support, and, having laid up no income, you will return like the prodigal son to my roof. You will then find that, with a wood-pile as large as an ordinary house, a hearth four feet wide, and the American sun flooding the floor, even a New Hampshire winter is not so bad a thing. With house pro-vided, two or three hundred dollars a year will support a man comfortably enough at Tamworth Iron Works, which is the name of our township. But, enough! My vulgarity makes you shudder." Perhaps even more than William could guess, for maintaining an independent life with his pen was no joking matter with Henry— aside from his feelings about America.

Early in the summer carpenters were at work on the house, and it was not ready for occupancy by the first of July, but William went up by himself to see how the carpenters were doing and to dig in his garden. He had done little writing for the past three or four months because of his eyes, but he now had "presbyopic spectacles" (lenses to correct the far-sightedness of middle age), and hoped for improvement after rest at Chocorua. To his sister Alice, who had had another "breakdown," he wrote on July 2: "I thought of the difference in our lots yesterday as I was driving home in the evening with a wagon in tow, which I had started at six-thirty to get at a place called Fryeburg, 19 miles away. All day in the open air, talking with country people, trying horses which they had to swap, but concluding to stick to my own—a most blessed feeling of free-dom, and change from Cambridge life. I never knew before how much freedom came with having a horse of one's own. I am be-coming quite an expert jockey, having examined and tried at least two dozen horses in the last six weeks; and I don't know a more fas-cinating occupation."

But later his oldest son thought his father had never been much of a horse trader:

The companion of one search for a horse reported James as accosting a man whom he met driving along the road and asking, "Do you know anyone who wants to sell a horse?" At Chocorua everyone was willing to sell a horse, and accordingly the man answered that he "didn't know as he did," but what might James be ready to pay? James replied that he was looking for a horse "for about $150, but *might* pay $175." There was a pause before the man spoke: "I've got a horse in my barn that would be just what you want—*for one hundred and seventy-five.*"

The third week in July William returned to Cambridge to pack some furniture and take his family back to Chocorua, though carpenters would continue working all summer. To a friend he wrote exuberantly: "The mother earth is in my finger-nails and my back is aching and my skin sweating with the ache and sweat of Father Adam and all his *normal* descendants." During his enthusiasm that first summer at Chocorua he cut down trees, cleared away brush and stones to enlarge the garden plot, dragged rocks from the bathing hole in the brook to enlarge it and make it safer for the children, and tried to garden. The thin glacial soil needed a great amount of fertilizer, especially natural humus such as rotted leaves or straw, to make it produce anything, and even then only the quick-growing plants were likely to escape an early frost; but much of the fun was in the doing and expectation. Except for berries, fruit trees, a potato patch, a vegetable garden and a meadow which yielded hay for the horse and cow (sometimes more than one of each), the Jameses did not attempt to operate their ninety-odd acres as a farm. They resolved early not to disturb their forest except to have enough trees cut for cooking and heating—the nights even in midsummer were often chilly enough to make a fire in the fireplace or in the cast-iron stoves in the bedrooms a welcome luxury.

For Mrs. James summers at Chocorua were a doubtful vacation, but she worked hard to make it a vacation for the other members of the family. Though she took with her a cook and a maid, and at least one local hired man was always employed, she had plenty to do in supervising the operation of the whole establishment. Her mother and sister Margaret were guests most of the time, and of course performed some chores, but it was Alice who provided the initiative, as she had done since her father's tragic death over twenty years earlier. Often there were other guests too, and when Alice became animated at the dinner table William would tease her about her "company smile."

Promptly at 7:30 every morning Alice went to the kitchen to see that breakfast was well under way. William would go to the bathing hole in the brook nearby and take a dip in the cold water. After breakfast he would walk or drive or chop wood for a couple of hours, and if it was a warm day, take another dip. In the afternoon, if Alice could leave the household responsibilities, he would take her, the children and perhaps two or three guests, for a drive through the country in the two-seated "democrat" wagon. Sometimes they would make a day of it, taking along a picnic lunch. In later summers the boys had ponies of their own, and they would either bring up the rear of the procession or dash ahead. They usually headed for some high hill which gave a commanding view of the Passipee Valley, the peaks of the Sandwich Range, and the White Mountains. Next to a brook William loved a hilltop, and he never ceased regretting that one could not have both in the same spot. It seemed to be one of nature's oversights.

But there were also periods when William could not sleep even at Chocorua, and then he would go off to his favorite retreat in the Adirondacks, to ramble by himself or lie under the trees and read. This happened even at the end of that first summer in Chocorua, as his wife's letters show—though he went not by himself but with a large party of mountain-climbers. On September 2, 1887, she wrote him in mid-morning: "The baby is much better, digesting so beautifully that I cannot think of moving her. I have been out of doors for nearly two hours superintending the strawberry bed and Ross's [the hired man's] work. All as far as I can see, very satisfactory. The strawberry plants came yesterday noon, before the bed was ready for them. I had Frank [another local helper] open the boxes, sprinkle them with water (they came packed in moss) and put them in the cellar for 24 hours. We had a great excitement about manure—Lord's man wouldn't sell—my book says good stable manure is an essential, but at the crisis of affairs Ross's son-in-law caved in and I have a cord of stuff from him. Before night the plants will all be in. It is a cloudy day fortunately."

"Mack" Salter, Alice's brother-in-law, was another guest, with his wife Mary, and he helped to look after the carpenters that first summer when William was away. A much-loved minister of the community, the Reverend John Runnells, had died, and some of the carpenters were not working in honor of him. "The work here is almost at a standstill, as the carpenters have not yet returned." Alice wrote William on September 6. "The painter works as satisfactorily as any man, and he gets through today. You must not be disappointed to find very little accomplished when you return. The 'help' are going up Chocorua (from the places on the lake) and so day after tomorrow we shall have to get our own dinner while Frank and the two women disport themselves on the mountain.

"Mother and Mack went to the old minister's funeral yesterday but could not get into the church it was so full. Mack said it was something to see, the crowd of decent country folks in their Sunday clothes, come from far and near. The old butcher this morning said 'that funeral had made him so late that he should not catch up all day,' then he added 'There ain't a man in Tamworth will be missed like him—*He always minded his own business.*' Was not that strange praise—yet it was adequate, in Woodbury's mind, worthy of a very good man."

"I really pity you to be receiving these dull lines from me," Alice continued, "but I can do nothing better. You will know from them that we prosper especially the baby and Billy [that is, William need not worry about the two most delicate members of the family]. We miss you tremendously but I am easy in my mind about you, and so thankful to have you away. We jog along very successfully." She was well aware of her meager literary abilities, and was always conscious of the contrast between her commonplace, domestic letters and William's pithy and witty epistles. But they told him what he needed to know, and reminded him of the dependable wife who so ably guarded their home and kept it operating while he sought relief for his jangled nerves in restless flight through one of his numerous doors.

CHAPTER XVII Epochal Year

With that work, your Tragic Muse, *and . . . my* Psychology, *all*

appearing in it, the year 1890 will be known as the great epochal year

in American literature.   —W.J. *to Henry James*

I

IN THE WINTER OF 1888 Billy's asthma returned, and his mother and grandmother decided to take the three children back to Aiken, South Carolina, until warm weather could be expected in Cambridge. Consequently, in February Mrs. James went south with Harry, Billy, and Margaret Mary, accompanied by Mrs. Gibbens, Margaret Gibbens, and a German governess who had recently been employed. William James found himself alone in the Garden Street house, except for a small pug dog named Jap, a great favorite with the children and regarded even by their father as a member of the family. In his loneliness William got out the love letters he had written Alice before their marriage (she had religiously preserved every letter), and in reading them he realized what a changed man he was. Of course he still had spells of insomnia, but his nerves were steadier and now he was seldom morbid. He wrote these thoughts to Alice and she received them in Aiken with great satisfaction, even with a sense of relief, for until now she had never been entirely easy in her mind that she had after all been the right wife for him.

The letters that William wrote to his children that spring also show how well he understood their psychology—proved, in fact, what a successful father he was. To eight-year-old Henry he wrote on March 1: "Beloved Heinrich,—You lazy old scoundrel, why don't you write a letter to your old Dad? Tell me how you enjoy your riding on horseback, what Billy does for a living, and which things you like best of all the new kinds of things you have to do with in Aiken." The house, he reported, was "so still that you can hear a pin drop, and so clean that everything makes a mark on it. All because there are no brats and kids around. Jap is my only companion, and he sneezes all over me whenever I pick him up." Then he said he would close with a fable.

"A donkey felt badly because he was not so great a favorite as a lap-dog. He said, I must act like the lap-dog, and then my mistress will like me. So he came into the house and began to lick his mistress, and put his paws on her, and tried to get into her lap. Instead of kissing him for this, she screamed for the servants, who beat him and put him out of the house. Moral: It's no use to try to be anything but a donkey if you are one. But neither you nor Billy are one.

"Good-night! you blessed boy. Stick to your three R's and your riding, so as to get on *fast*. The ancient Persians only taught their boys to ride, to shoot the bow and to tell the truth. Good-night!

"Kiss your dear old Mammy and that belly-ache of a Billy, and little Margaret Mary for her Dad. Good-night./ Your FATHER."

Henry did write his father, and on March 27 the latter replied: "Your long letter came yesterday P.M. Much the best you ever writ, and the address on the envelope so well written that I wondered whose hand it was, and never thought it might be yours. Your tooth also was a precious memorial—I hope you'll get a better one in its place. Send me the other as soon as it is tookin out. They ought to go into the Peabody Museum. If any of George Washington's baby-teeth had been kept till now, they would be put somewhere in a public museum for the world to wonder at. I will keep this tooth, so that, if you grow up to be a second Geo. Washington, I may sell it to a Museum. When Washington was only eight years old his mother didn't know he was going to be Washington. But he did be it, when the time came."

Dr. J. L. Hildreth was building a house next door. "The fence is taken down between our yard and his, by the stable, and teams are driving through with lumber. Our back yard is filled with lumber for the frame of the house. It is to be cut, squared, mortised, etc., in our yard and then carried through to his." Henry would always remember Dr. Hildreth's house, because a few months after his return home he hit a baseball through one of the doctor's windows, for which he was punished.

The letter ended with miscellaneous news and instructions. "Say to Fräulein that 'ich lasse Sie grüssen von Herzensgrund!' " [I send you heartiest greetings.] Jap's nose was dry and brown from holding it so constantly toward the fire. "We are having ice-cream and the Rev. George A. Gordon to lunch today." Evidently the cook had remained in Mrs. James's absence. "Now pray, old Harry, stick to your books and let me see you do sums and read *fast* when you get back. The best of all of us is your mother, though."

To five-year-old Billy, whom his father addressed as "Beloved Williamson," the style was a little more oblique because the letter would have to be read to him, and was written for his mother as well as him. "This is Sunday," a letter began on April 29, "the sabbath of the Lord, and it has been very hot for two days. I think of you and Harry with much longing, and of that infant whom I know so little, that I cannot help writing you some words. Your Mammy writes me that she can't get *you* to *work* much, though Harry works. You *must* work a little this summer in our own place. ["Work" probably meant "study."] How nice it will be! I have wished that both you and Harry were by my side in some amusements which I have had lately. First, the learned seals in a big tank of water in Boston. The loveliest beasts, with big black eyes, poking their heads up and down in the water, and then scrambling out on their bellies like boys tied up in bags." They had played on the guitar, banjo, and organ, and saved a child who tumbled into the water (part of the act). "When they have done well, their master gives them a lot of fish. They eat an awful lot, scales, and fins, and bones and all, without chewing." But speaking of dogs, Jap had been sick and vomited two days ago, and then "thought I was going to punish him, poor thing. He can't discriminate between sickness and sin. He leads a dull life, without you and Margaret Mary. I tell him if it lasts much longer, he'll grow into a common beast; he hates to be a beast, but unless he has human companionship, he will sink to the level of one. So you must hasten back and make much of him."

This may sound like William's indirect plea to his wife to come home, but the date had already been set. "On Monday morning the 14th or Sunday night the 13th of May, I will take you into my arms," he wrote Billy—"that is, I will meet you with a carriage on the wharf, when the boat comes in. And I tell you I shall be glad to see the whole lot of you come roaring home. Give my love to your Mammy, to Aunt Margaret, to Fräulein, to Harry, to Margaret Mary, and to yourself."

When summer came the whole family, including grandmother and aunt plus Fräulein and a tutor employed for Harry, returned happily to Chocorua. It was a bit more habitable than the previous summer, though on July 11 William wrote to his brother Henry that, "The place has yet a good deal to be done with it, but it can be taken slowly, and Alice is a most *vaillante* partner. We have a trump of a hired man." Henry had just written him of the death of Edmund Gurney, one of the chief psychical research men in England. He had apparently committed suicide by breathing chloroform.

In a postscript to his letter to Henry, William added some description of life at Chocorua in the summer of 1888. "I have just been downstairs to get an envelope, and there on the lawn saw a part of the family which I will describe, for you to insert in one of your novels as a picture of domestic happiness. On the newly made lawn in the angle of the house and kitchen ell, in the shadow of the hot afternoon sun, lies a mattress taken out of our spare-room for an airing against Richard Hodgson's arrival tomorrow." (This Hodgson, no relation to Shadworth H. in England, was an Australian, a hearty, jovial, athletic man, who would soon become the secretary of the American Society for Psychical Research.) On the mattress were "the madonna and child—the former sewing in a nice blue point dress, and smiling at the latter (named Peggy), immensely big and fat for her years, and who, with quite a vocabulary of adjectives, proper names, and a mouthful of teeth, shows as yet, although in her sixteenth month, no disposition to walk. She is rolling and prattling to herself, now on mattress and now on grass, and is an exceedingly good-natured, happy, and intelligent child." She liked to carry a hard cracker in her fist all day; she had even been known to take "it into her bath with her . . . holding it immersed till that ceremony is o'er."

Carpenters, painters, and paper-hangers were still busy, doing work not completed the previous summer. "Margaret [Gibbens] and Harry's tutor are off on the backs of the two horses to the village seven miles off, to have 'em shod. I, with naught on but gray flannel shirt, breeches, belt, stockings and shoes, shall now proceed across the Lake in the boat and up the hill, to get and carry the mail. Harry will probably ride along the shore on the pony which Aunt Kate has given him, and where Billy and Fräulein are, Heaven only knows. Returning, I shall have a bath either in lake or brook—doesn't it sound nice? On the whole it is nice, but very hot."

In other letters we learn that there were minor vexations, such as a new pump that had such strong suction it drew up mud from the bottom of the spring. And in August William was ill with "cholera morbus," which depressed him for a few days and made him wonder whether Chocorua might not bankrupt him, but to his sister Alice he wrote that it had already been worth the cost in the education it had given the two boys. On the whole the second summer at Chocorua was an even greater success than the first. William did not make any progress on his psychology book, but he returned to Cambridge with enthusiasm for the new academic year, and his family stayed on in New Hampshire until the end of October.

II

After getting his classes under way in September, William returned to Chocorua for the weekend of October 14–15. On the snowy Saturday morning of the 14th he wrote his brother and sister in England: "I am just up for the Sabbath to see the family, and go down again tomorrow. Another visit a fortnight hence, and we all go down together. We are moving the barn from the front of the house, so as to open the view a little more, down to the flat meadow below, with its margin of trees behind which the brook flows. Most people buy a site and then put a house on it. I have bought a house and am now creating a site around it, lowering the level of the landscape, in order to make the house appear on a little higher ground. I now know what people mean when they say you always spend more than you expect on a place. . . . Men and oxen, and the brown earth, and the new chopped wood, are goodly things to dwell among; and if one had plenty of money, I can imagine no more fascinating way of throwing it away than in owning a lot of land and playing the 'gentleman farmer'."

Of course he didn't have either the money or the leisure to make this dream a reality; he was still a professor at Harvard on a salary of four thousand dollars a year, not bad at the time for the academic profession, but inadequate for the needs of the James family. However, William was not dissatisfied with his profession, and this academic year was beginning well. As he expressed it to Henry and Alice, "The Cambridge year begins with much vehemence—I with a big class in ethics, and seven graduates from other colleges in advanced psychology, giving me a good deal of work. But I feel uncommonly hearty, and shall no doubt come out of it all in good shape. There will probably be no migration to the south necessary, and we shall have a dull and steady time at home." By "dull" he meant only much reading and preparation for his classes—Plato, Aristotle, Adam Smith, Butler, Paley, etc.—but he did not find them dull, and he found talking about them to his classes stimulating.

William James had now been teaching for fifteen years, and was nearing the peak of his effectiveness in the classroom. He really did not look or talk or think like a professor. In spite of the insomnia of which he so often complained and inner pressures which seldom permitted him to feel at ease with himself—except in his Chocorua woods—he walked with a brisk step, head erect, and never failed to recognize a student as he strode energetically across the Yard to his classroom. One of his students of this period, Dickinson S. Miller, who himself became a distinguished teacher of philosophy, recalled a class with James in one of the "tower rooms" of Sever Hall, with a dozen or more graduate students sitting around a table.

I can see him now, sitting at the head of that heavy table of light-colored oak near the bow-window that formed the end of the room. My brother, a visitor at Cambridge, dropped in for an hour and seeing him with his vigorous air, bronzed and sanguine complexion, and brown tweeds, said, 'He looks more like a sportsman than a professor.' I think that the sporting men in college always felt a certain affinity to themselves on one side in the freshness and manhood that distinguished him in mind, appearance, and diction.

James was almost a total contrast to Royce, the red-headed, freckle-faced Californian who had grown up as a country boy and was still sometimes taken by a freshman for a janitor. But in the classroom Royce was formal, composed, and eloquent, every word in the right place and given the right intonation. He had worked out his theory and had no misgivings about it. James was never satisfied with any theory, and was always exploring, examining, and experimenting. His students "felt his mind at work," as Miller expressed it.

Royce in lecturing sat immovable. James would rise with a peculiar suddenness and make bold and rapid strokes for a diagram on the blackboard—I can remember his abstracted air as he wrestled with some idea, standing by his chair with one foot upon it, elbow on knee, hand to chin. A friend has described a scene at a little class that, in a still earlier year, met in James's own study. In the effort to illustrate he brought out a black-board. He stood it on a chair and in various other positions, but could not at once write upon it, hold it steady, and keep it in the class's vision. Entirely bent on what he was doing, his efforts resulted at last in his standing it on the floor while he lay down at full length, holding it with one hand, drawing with the other, and continuing the flow of his commentary.

Another student, Rollo Walter Brown, who studied with James a few years later, is even more emphatic about the vitality which this professor communicated to his classes:

When he stood he was the nervous thoroughbred. If it had been possible to find and place beside him a man who was his perfect duplicate in size and clothing and beard, the duplicate still would not have suggested James, because there would have been lacking the vital mind and tingling nerves. Even in such details as the contour of the beard and the little fillip in the parting of his hair—in the middle—there was something expressive of intentness. To see him was never to forget what it means to be alive.

To another student at Harvard during William James's first decade of teaching, the restless energy had a negative as well as a positive side. This student was the brilliant, eccentric, mystical John Jay Chapman, who once in a strange mental state destroyed his left hand by deliberately holding it in the fire. His father had known Henry James Sr., and John, twenty years younger than William James, was well acquainted with the James family. Chapman appears not to have taken a course with William (he did take a course in philosophy under Palmer), but he knew James's ideas from conversation, reading, and public lectures, both while he was an undergraduate (1880–1884) and as a law student (1885–1887) at Harvard. He always believed that James's "mind was never quite in focus. . . . In private life and conversation there was the same radiation of thought about him. The center and focus of his thought fell within his nature, but not within his intellect. You were thus played upon by a logic which was not the logic of intellect, but a far deeper thing, limpid and clear in itself, confused and refractory only when you tried to deal with it intellectually." This was praise as well as negative criticism, for "James was always throwing off sparks. . . ."

And William James himself never took the tone in his classroom, as Royce did, that his was the voice of authority. He listened to questions, sometimes impertinent ones, and answered all with tolerance, and, perhaps surprising, with patience. He was one of the few professors of the period who did permit students to ask questions. More than that, they could stop him on the campus, or walk home with him discussing or arguing statements he had made in class. At the end of the term, he would even ask the students to write out criticisms of the course and make suggestions for improvements. Dickinson Miller thought he must have been the first college teacher in America to do that. In retrospect Chapman remembered how he himself had taken advantage of this humility.

> I should not have been abashed at being discovered in some mean action by William James; because I should have felt that he would understand and make allowances. The abstract and sublime quality of his nature was always enough for two; and I confess to having always trespassed upon him and treated him with impertinence, without gloves, without reserve, without ordinary, decent concern for the sentiments and weaknesses of human character. . . . I used occasionally to write and speak to him about his specialities in a tone of fierce contempt; and never failed to elicit from him in reply the most spontaneous and celestial gayety.

William James's humor was so natural and perennial that of course he displayed it frequently in the classroom, sometimes to the frustration of his more literal-minded students. James himself recalled the student who began his question with, "But doctor, to be serious a moment . . ." Chapman, too, declared that "he was a sportive, wayward, Gothic sort of spirit, who was apt, on meeting a friend, to burst into foolery, and whose wit was always three parts poetry. Indeed his humor was as penetrating as his seriousness." Chapman thought also that "There was, in spite of his playfulness, a deep sadness about James. You felt that he had just stepped out of this sadness in order to meet you, and was to go back into it the moment you left him." Possibly this impression belongs more to later years, but James's whole view of the world as containing evil which human beings must assist God in combating is basically a tragic view, which he held even before he began teaching.

In this connection, one other reminiscence of Miller is pertinent:

> Once when we were returning from two insane asylums which he had arranged for the class to visit, and at one of which we had seen a dan-

gerous, almost naked maniac, I remember his saying, "President Eliot might not like to admit that there is no sharp line between himself and the men we have just seen, but it is true." He would emphasize that people who had great nervous burdens to carry, hereditary perhaps, could order their lives fruitfully and perhaps derive some gain from their "degenerate" sensitiveness [an allusion to studies of "degeneracy" by Cesare Lombroso and Max Nordau], whatever it might be.

Probably none of the students guessed how much of James's own suffering had gone into this conviction, but both his tolerance and his understanding of human nature had come to him more from experience than from books.

Of course not all William James's students found his mind and personality congenial, though few actively disliked him. One who perhaps did was his most brilliant student, George Santayana, later a glittering ornament to the Harvard Department of Philosophy. He was half American and half Spanish, but his father's Spanish blood seemed to predominate in his Latin appearance and aesthetic tastes. He enrolled in Harvard in 1883, after spending the summer with his father in Ávila, where he had smallpox. President Eliot's "elective system" was in full swing, and Santayana went to see Professor James to enroll in a course in philosophy. "My face still had some marks on it," Santayana told his biographer, Daniel Cory, in recalling the experience, "and I must have appeared rather weedy and unpromising to James. At any rate, he frowned at me and said, 'You don't really want to go in for philosophy, do you?' " Quite probably James thought the immature freshman did not yet know what he wanted to study, but Santayana felt rebuffed, and never really forgave James for it. He suspected that the "intensely masculine" professor sensed some deficiency in him, and Santayana felt uneasy and unwanted. For James, as Cory has summarized, philosophy was "an invigorating and muscular kind of intellectual discipline. Beware of concepts and stick to raw facts of radical experience! Santayana, on the contrary, simply took philosophy to be an essential side of a fully civilized mind." Like William James and his brother Henry, Santayana and James could never really understand each other.

After a weak beginning, Santayana graduated *summa cum laude*, and was awarded a traveling fellowship (shared the first year with Charles Augustus Strong, who returned to America to accept an instructorship at Cornell), and spent two years studying in Europe, mainly in Berlin. But James thought his young student avoided the best German professors and lacked seriousness of purpose. On January 2, 1888, he wrote Santayana: ". . . our fellowships are for helping men to do some definite intellectual thing, and you must expect to have to show next May (if the fellowship is to be continued) that you are on a line of investigation of some sort which is likely to result in something more than a 'culture' which to the ordinary committeeman would look vague. I know your ability; and also your way of talking small about yourself. But your ability imposes arduous duties." And on April 22, after James had read the essay submitted by Santayana, he praised it for its originality, but protested, "This is a little too much like a poem . . . to count for much" in the eyes of the committee. "It must be backed by a good deal of prose and appearance of practicality."

In July Santayana left Berlin and announced that he was returning to Harvard so that he could prepare for the Ph.D. examination in his own way; he was oppressed by German "scholasticism" and "the absurd pretension to be scientific." In fact, he had gone through a series of disenchantments. "First I lost my faith in the kind of philosophy that Professors Palmer and Royce are interested in; and, then, when I came to Germany, I also lost my faith in psychophysics, and all the other attempts to discover something very momentous. A German professor like Wundt seems to me a survival of the alchemist." With some of these sentiments James should have been able to sympathize. To Stumpf he had written the previous year, in reply to Stumpf's grumbling about Wundt, "He isn't a genius, he is a *professor*—a being whose duty is to know everything, and have his own opinion about everything, connected with his *Fach*." But he grudgingly admired Wundt too: "Cut him up like a worm, and each fragment crawls; there is no *nœud vital* in his mental medulla oblongata, so that you can't kill him all at once." He wrote Santayana that the fellowship was intended for foreign study, and tried to discourage him from returning, though Santayana did and passed his Ph.D. examination in 1889.

Santayana's mature opinion of James as teacher and writer was that,

> On points of art or medicine he retained a professional touch and an unconscious ease which he hardly acquired in metaphysics. . . . He approached philosophy as mankind originally approached it, without having a philosophy . . . his doctrine, if he may be said to have had

one, was agnosticism. . . . In his own person he was ready enough to face the mystery of things, and whatever the womb of time might bring forth; but until the curtain was rung down on the last act of the drama (and it might have no last act!) he wished the intellectual cripples and the moral hunchbacks not be jeered at; perhaps they might turn out to be the heroes of the play. . . . The agnostic, as well as the physician and neurologist in him, was never quite eclipsed.

Some of these remarks apply more specifically to James's activities of the 1890s and early 1900s, but the last sentence quoted might be said to characterize his whole career as a teacher.

If James was unlucky in having Santayana as a student, and vice versa, he was fortunate in having Gertrude Stein, a few years later while she was attending Radcliffe as a special student. She thought him "truly a man among men; a scientist of force and originality embodying all that is strongest and worthiest in the scientific spirit; a metaphysician skilled in abstract thought, clear and vigorous and yet too great to worship logic as his God, and narrow himself to a belief merely in the reason of man." The story of her final examination is well known, but it is worth repeating because it illustrates so well James's unprofessorial conduct as a professor. After reading the questions, Miss Stein wrote on her examination book: "Dear Professor James, I am so sorry but really I do not feel like an examination paper in philosophy today." Then she left the classroom. Next day she received this reply: "Dear Miss Stein, I understand perfectly how you feel. I often feel like that myself." Then he assigned her the highest mark of the class.

James encouraged Miss Stein to make a career of philosophy, but Royce convinced her that to do so she would have to steep herself in logic. She shared James's repugnance for logic and mathematics, and when she sought further advice from him, he suggested that she go into psychology. Accordingly she next studied medicine, as a preparation for psychology, but ended by using the abnormal psychology she had learned in his laboratory and on field trips with him to hospitals and asylums to write *Three Lives* (1909), which established her reputation as a creative writer. Her later books probably owed little or nothing to her great teacher; but Gertrude Stein was one of the most sympathetic and grateful students he ever had, though he had many others who went on to distinguished careers in both philosophy and psychology.

III

In the spring of 1889 William James wrote his father's old friend E. L. Godkin, who was planning to go to England and wanted Henry James's address: "I settle the affairs of the Universe in my College courses, and have got so far ahead as to be building a big new house on that part of it known as the Norton estate." This house was to be the fulfillment of the dream William and his wife had talked about since they first considered building on Henry Sr.'s lot on Quincy Street. Their new house, on a street recently opened, was only a few blocks away from Quincy, in a little community forming in the region still called "Norton's Woods" by the older residents. Other faculty members were building there too, or soon would, and William would have several colleagues as neighbors, one of them Josiah Royce. Across the street would live a gentle minister and his wife, the Cummingses, whose son Edward Estlin would later become famous for his "lower case" poems.

But in the midst of drawing plans for the house, acting as his own architect except for technical specifications, and meeting his classes—even writing enough to interfere with his sleep—William James was distracted by the illness of Aunt Kate Walsh in New York and "Aunt" Mary Tweedy in Newport. In midwinter Aunt Kate fell and was never able to walk again. William visited her in the house on 44th Street in New York where she lived with her niece Lila Walsh and a wealthy relative Henry Wyckoff, himself an invalid. Several times during the spring William made hurried trips to New York, and went once to Newport to see Aunt Mary, who was becoming senile and helpless. Finally Aunt Kate died on March 6 and William and Alice made still another trip to New York to attend the funeral. This news was cabled to Henry and Alice in England, and amplified in letters. They were both shaken by the loss of the aunt who had been almost a mother to them in their youth. But they could not help being curious about her will, and indignant when they learned she had given the bulk of her estate, which turned out to be surprisingly large, to some obscure cousins in Stamford, Connecticut. When the estate was finally settled, however, Alice and William each received ten thousand dollars.

On May 12 William wrote his brother Henry: "I have been

feeling so dead-tired all this spring that I believe a long break from my usual scenes is necessary. It is like the fagged state that drove me abroad the last two times. I have been pretty steadily busy for six years and the result isn't wonderful, considering what a miserable nervous system I have anyhow. The upshot of it is that I have pretty much made up my mind to invest $1000 (if necessary) of Aunt Kate's legacy [though he had not yet obtained it] in my constitution, and spend the summer abroad. This will give me the long-wished opportunity of seeing you and Alice, and enable me to go to an international congress of 'physiological psychologists' which I have had the honor of an invitation to attend in the capacity of 'honorary committee'-man for the U.S. It will be instructive and inspiring, no doubt, and won't last long, and [will] give me an opportunity to meet a number of eminent men. But for these three reasons, I think I should start for the Pacific coast as being more novel. I confess I find myself caring more and more for landscapes than for men— strange to say, and doubtless shameful; so my stay in London will probably be short."

William admitted that it was a bad summer for him to be away, "with the house-building here, the Chocorua place unfinished, and the crowds set in motion by the Paris exhibition [another World's Fair]; and *perhaps*, if I find myself unexpectedly hearty when lectures end two weeks hence, I may not go after all." This was the way he had always felt and talked before a trip to Europe, but of course he went, sailing on the *Cephalonia* June 22. He disembarked at Queenstown and visited the Emerald Isle, stopping at Cork, Killarney, and Dublin, where he visited Trinity College. He had thought he would not go to Scotland, but on impulse proceeded to Glasgow and Oban, and by this time he had fallen so "dead in love wi' Scotland both land and people" that he went on to Edinburgh, and did not reach London until July 17.

Alice had not been told the exact date of William's arrival for fear she might become agitated in the anticipation. After spending the night with Henry at De Vere Gardens, William went out next day with his brother to Leamington, where Alice was now living, attended by a permanently employed nurse and part of the time by Katharine Loring. How Henry prepared his sister for William's visit was described later by her in her secret diary: "We had just finished luncheon and were talking of something or other when H. suddenly said, with a queer look on his face, 'I must tell you something!' 'You're not going to be married!' shrieked I. 'No, but William is here, he has been lunching upon Warwick Castle and is waiting now in the Holly Walk for the news to be broken to you and if you survive, I'm to tie my handkerch[ief] to the balcony.' Enter Wm. *not à la* Romeo via the balcony; the prose of our century to say nothing of that of our consanguinity making it super[er]ogatory. The *beforehand* having been so cleverly suppressed by the devoted H. 'it came out so much easier than could have been expected' as they say to infants in the dentist chair."

She continued: "Wm. had only got to London the day before, having been for three weeks in Ireland and Scotland. He doesn't look [much] older for the five years, and all that there is to be said of him, of course, is that he is simply himself, a creature who speaks in another language as Henry says from the rest of mankind and who would lend life and charm to a treadmill. What a strange experience it was, to have what had seemed so dead and gone all these years suddenly bloom before one, a flowering oasis in this alien desert, redolent with the exquisite *family* perfume of the days gone by, made of the allusions, the memories and the point of view in common, so that my floating-particle sense was lost for an hour or so in the illusion that what is forever shattered had sprung anew, and existed outside of our memories—where it is forever green!"

A few days later William wrote his wife his impressions of Henry, after their six-year separation: "Harry is as nice and simple and amiable as he can be. He has covered himself, like some marine crustacean, with all sorts of material growths, rich sea-weeds and rigid barnacles and things, and lives hidden in the midst of his strange heavy alien manners and customs; but these are all but 'protective resemblances,' under which the same dear old, good, innocent and at bottom very powerless-feeling Harry remains, caring for little but his writing, and full of dutifulness and affection for all gentle things. . . ."

William did not remain with Henry for all the two weeks he spent in England before going to the Paris conference. He went to Brighton and visited Mrs. Edmund Gurney, widow of his psychic-research friend, and F. W. H. Myers and Henry Sidgwick, the other most prominent psychic researchers in England. During his evening at the Sidgwicks' William tried "thought transference" with them, but without success. The most interesting thing he saw in Brighton, William wrote his wife, was "four cuttle-fish (octopus) in the Aquarium. I wish we had one of them for a child—such flexible intensity of life in a form so inaccessible to our sympathy." One is reminded of William's father, who at about the same stage of parenthood felt his love for his children to be so great that he almost regretted having them.

Next day William visited the Pearsall Smiths at Haslemere. Robert Pearsall Smith was a wealthy Quaker from Philadelphia, friend of Walt Whitman, who had gone to Europe as a Quaker evangelist, settled in England, and become an expatriate. His son, Logan Pearsall, then studying at Oxford, had, as we have mentioned, studied with James recently at Harvard, in the same philosophy class with his future brother-in-law, Bernard Berenson, the art critic and historian, who was also to remain a life-long friend of his teacher. In his autobiography, *Unforgotten Years*, Smith called James "the most charming man I ever met." At the Pearsall Smiths (whose friends did not use his first name) William spent "a really *gemüthlich* evening and morning. Pearsall himself as engaging as of yore." He was also interested in psychic research, and had joined the American Society on James's invitation.

Back in London in sunny and cool weather (at least compared to an American summer), William "mounted the top of a bus and went (with thousands of others similarly enthroned) to Hampton Court, through Kew, Richmond, Bushey Park, etc.; about 30 miles there and back, all 4s. 6d. . . . . a most delightful and interesting six hours," William wrote his wife, "with but the usual drawback, that *you* were not along. How you would have enjoyed every bit of it, especially the glimpses, between Richmond and Hampton, over the high brick walls and between the bars of the iron gates, of these extraordinary English gardens and larger grounds, all black with their tufted vegetation. More different things can grow in a square foot here, if they're taken care of, than I've ever seen elsewhere, and one of these high ivy-walled gardens is something the *like* of which is altogether unknown to us." The summer home at Chocorua had made William more perceptive of gardens, and Alice too, as she would discover later when she did see these sights with him.

On July 30 William left London for Boulogne-sur-mer, where at the age of fifteen he had performed his juvenile experiments in science to the annoyance of his brother Henry. He arrived in Paris in time for the opening on August 5 of the five-day session of the International Congress of Physiological Psychology. The delegates were mostly European, over a hundred of them, and they insisted that Professor William James preside at the opening session. Although he did not read a paper he was pleased to hear the several essays on psychology he had published referred to by the speakers. On August 15 he wrote Stumpf (who did not attend): "The sight of 120 men all actively interested in psychology has made me feel much less lonely in the world, and ready to finish my book this year with a great deal more *entrain*. A book hanging so long on one's hands at last gets outgrown, and even disgusting to one."

For Robertson's British magazine, *Mind*, James wrote an account of the conference, in which he said in part: "The most striking feature of the discussions was, perhaps, their tendency to slope off to some one or other of those shady horizons with which the name of 'psychic-research' is now associated. . . . The open results were, however (as always happens at such gatherings), secondary in real importance to the latent ones—the friendships made, the intimacies deepened, and the encouragement and inspiration which came to everyone from seeing before them in flesh and blood so large a portion of that little army of fellow students from whom and for whom all contemporary psychology exists. The individual worker feels much less isolated in the world after such an experience."

At the end of the conference William returned to London instead of extending his vacation in the Swiss mountains, as he had earlier planned. Then he and Henry revisited Alice on August 14 on William's way to Liverpool, to take ship for America. After his departure Alice wrote in her diary: ". . . William, instead of going to Switz[erland], came suddenly back from Paris and went home, having, as usual, exhausted Europe in a few weeks and finding it stale, flat and unprofitable. The only necessity being to get home, the first letter after his arrival was, of course, full of plans for his return plus wife and infants! he is just like a blob of mercury, you can't put a mental finger upon him. H. and I were laughing over him and recalling Father and William's resemblance in these ways to him. Tho' the results were the same, it seems to come from such a different nature in the two, in W^{m}, an entire inability or indifference 'to stick to a thing for the sake of sticking,' as some one said of him once, whilst Father, the delicious infant! couldn't submit even to the thralldom of his own whim, and then the dear being was such a prey to the demon homesickness." Although Alice undoubtedly held these opinions herself and with some justification, the influence of Henry is also quite apparent. One needs only to remember that protracted epistolary dialogue in the winter of 1882–1883.

But of course William was eager to get back home and see what progress had been made on his house in Cambridge. After the carpenters began working on it William had kept thinking of little improvements to add to his plans, and finally his contractor had told him that he could save several thousand dollars by going to Europe while the house was being built—not, of course, that this settled William's decision to go. But now he could scarcely wait to see what had been done in his absence, and in Chocorua as well as Cambridge.

IV

William James arrived back in Cambridge after dark on a late August evening. His whole family, including his mother- and sister-in-law, was at Chocorua, and the house at 18 Garden Street had been closed for weeks. But Grace Norton, who lived across the street from his new house on Irving Street, had invited him to spend the night in her house. In his first letter to Henry, written August 30 from Chocorua, William described his first glimpse next morning of the house under construction, and Henry replied: "I note gratefully the episode of your station in your night shirt at Grace Norton's window—gazing at your house in the August dawn—it must have seemed yours indeed. . . ."

Of course the interior of the house was far from completed, but in outward appearance it seemed almost ready for occupancy. It was a big, square, three-story house, with a gambrel roof, three chimneys, and a narrow porch with a balcony over the entrance. The sides were covered with cedar shingles, which would be oiled and would weather to a dark brown. The shutters and trimmings would be painted dark green. It looked like thousands of other nineteenth-century houses in New England and the Middle Atlantic states, but it was roomy, with a large, sunny library twenty-two and one-half by twenty-seven feet on the first floor, with a large fireplace, a triple window nearly half the length of the room, and built-in bookshelves from floor to ceiling. This would be William's study and living room, though he also would have a small room upstairs, with a stand-up writing desk, where he could write in complete privacy. This house at 95 Irving Street was to be the home of the James family for the remainder of William's life and of his wife for a decade longer.

After the Jameses moved to Irving Street, with carpenters and painters still administering the finishing touches to the house, William began working in earnest on his long overdue psychology book, though many interruptions plagued him. First of all, of course, there was Chocorua to close up for the winter. On returning there in September he heard that a farm adjoining his land was for sale for five hundred dollars, and he tried to interest Henry in buying it. Henry did consider the idea, but soon decided against it. In the autumn William also had to spend some time in New York during a legal battle over Henry Wyckoff's estate; one of the heirs was trying to break the will on the ground that Wyckoff had not been mentally competent when he signed it. But the will was sustained, and William received three thousand dollars in the settlement. Then during the winter one of the houses in Syracuse was badly damaged by fire. The insurance covered the expense of repairs, but a trip to Syracuse and ensuing correspondence took up valuable time. During the winter Billy also suffered an abscess in his head which made him scream with pain. As if this were not enough, in addition to keeping his Psychological Laboratory going, James treated in his home four "melancholics," as his wife called them in a despairing letter to Henry in England. On one he effected great improvement by the use of hypnotism. Yet through all these distractions William worked doggedly at his manuscripts, disproving his sister's opinion that he could not stick to a wearisome task.

Of course he did not write the big book in a few months. Three years earlier he had thought he had three-fourths of it written, though this estimate is hard to judge. He had also in ten years published sixteen articles that he could draw upon, and one very important one, "The Association of Ideas," that he could use without revision. The others required expansion, correction, or complete rewriting, such as "The Feeling of Effort," "What Is an Emotion?" (the theory that emotion is the result of specific body reactions and not the cause of them—enunciated independently by James and by Carl Lange of Denmark), and "The Perception of Space," which was published in four issues of *Mind* in 1887. But the book was in no sense a compilation of published essays; many gaps remained to be filled in, and even the published studies had to be assimilated into the context of the book.

In January 1890 James thought he saw the end of the writing in sight and sent Henry Holt 350 pages of manuscript with the request that he start type-setting and rest assured that he would have the remaining pages in his hands by May 1. Mr. Holt had had too much experience with authors' delusions to grant this request, and he replied that not one page would be set until he received the complete manuscript. It was not that he doubted James's belief that he could finish by May 1; but James had promised to do the book in two years, and it was now ten years overdue.

On March 21 James wrote Holt: "Publishers are demons, there's no doubt about it. How silly it is to fly in the face of the accumulated wisdom of mankind, and think just because one of them appears genial socially [Holt had invited Mr. and Mrs. James to dinner] that the great natural law is broken and that he is also a human being in his professional capacity. Fie upon such weakness! I shall ne'er be guilty of it again. . . .

"As for the manuscript, I confess I don't know why you need the whole of it *en bloc* in your own hands, before printing begins. After this week of recess I shall write a chapter which may take three weeks at the outside and complete the book. Some 1700 pages of manuscript will then be ready for the printer without another touch from me. There will remain five or six chapters, some of which need slight retouches and additions, which can be added by me perfectly well in the intervals of correcting proofs, thereby enabling the latter to begin about the first of May. . . . Write and tell me what is your decree. I want to get forward now with the least possible delay. . . . I find that I have lost the contract you sent me last spring. I did not even examine it then. Pray send another that I may see what to do."

Holt replied on April 2: "If 'publishers are not demons,' it is a striking instance of long-suffering. I have illustrations here made years ago for manuscript that has never appeared. Your letter makes plain what I took for granted,—that your manuscript will not be ready as early as May. *Of course* you 'don't know why I need the whole of the manuscript before printing begins.' It is not in your line to know. If you were gradually being converted into a demon, however, by the disappointments occasioned by authors, you would know all about it. I *never* began printing an instalment of a manuscript, so far as I can remember, without having to stop work before the book was finished, thus forcing the printer to put away the apparatus in place for it, and giving him excuses . . . for dilly-dallying with the rest of the work when it came. . . . One of the things that makes me a demon, is to have to go over this weary explanation again and again. . . .

"My demonical character has not been developed so much by authors failing to look at contracts and losing them, as by the other thing; so I'm angelic enough to send you duplicates, of which please sign both and return us one. I have just seen a contract signed by you to give us that manuscript June 12, 1880, and yet, you, you, you, Brute (two syllables) revile me for being a demon! I'm awfully sorry, all the same, that you're not coming here and to dine with us, but that all must be in due time."

On returning from a quick trip to Newport William found Holt's last reply waiting for him, and he immediately (April 5) retorted that it was "not fair to throw that former contract into my face," when ten years after signing it he had written to Holt that he should get someone else to write the book. And before returning the new contract James wanted to protest against pledging himself to prepare a revised edition whenever the publisher called for it; he would expect to do that, but did not like to bind himself legally. To this Holt wrote on April 7: "I don't want to 'throw anything into your face,' but upon my soul I don't see how after agreeing to do a thing, a suggestion that somebody else should do it is to be accounted a valid substitute for doing it; but your sins which are many are forgiven, as you know. Now, don't you be afraid of that provision about new editions . . . you are not going to be abused on the strength of it." Next day, on receiving the letter, James signed the contract, but still grumbled about the clause on a revised edition.

On May 9 James wrote that he still had two weeks of work on the manuscript. "What I wrote you, if you remember, was to send you the *heft* of the MS. by May 1st, the rest to be done in the intervals of proof-correcting." And then he added a paragraph which could hardly have been joyful news to the publishers:

"No one could be more disgusted than I at the sight of the book. *No* subject is worth being treated of in 1000 pages! Had I ten years more, I could rewrite it in 500; but as it stands it is this or nothing— a loathsome, distended, tumefied, bloated, dropsical mass, testifying to nothing but two facts: *1st*, that there is no such thing as a *science* of psychology, and *2nd*, that W.J. is an incapable. Yours provided you hurry up things, Wm. James."

Around the middle of May Alice took the children to Chocorua for the summer, leaving William at 95 Irving Street to finish his book and then see it through the press. On May 22, after sitting up the previous night until two o'clock working on it, William finally dispatched the manuscript—all of it—to Holt by express. Two days later he was still weary, but wrote his wife how relieved he felt to be "out from the shadow of that interminable black cloud," though he did find some comfort in having "something done to show for all the fuss. The joke of it is that I, who have always considered myself a thing of glimpses, of discontinuity, of *aperçus*, with no power of doing a big job, suddenly realize at the *end* of this task that it is the biggest book on psychology in any language except Wundt's, Rosmini's and Daniel Greenleaf Thompson's! Still, if it burns up at the printing-office, I shan't much care, for I shan't ever write it again!!"

Holt promptly began making arrangements for the printing, but in the interval before proofs would begin arriving William went up to Chocorua, where he wrote his brother Henry on June 4: "The great event for me is the completion at last of my tedious book. I have been at my desk with it every day since I got back from Europe [a slight exaggeration], and up at four in the morning with it for many a day of the last month. I have written every page four or five times over, and carried it 'on my mind' for nine years past, so you may imagine the relief. Besides, I am glad to appear at last as a man who has done something more than make phrases and projects. I will send you a copy, in the fall, I trust, though [the printer] is so inert about starting the proofs that we may not get through till midwinter or later." Actually, the publisher, not the printer, had received the manuscript only eleven or twelve days previously, so that the printer had scarcely had time yet to be "inert." But perhaps in his impatience he had forgotten that he had relinquished his "brain child" less than two weeks ago. Continuing to Henry, William now felt that, "As 'Psychologies' go, it is a good one, but psychology is in such an ante-scientific condition that the whole present generation of them is predestined to become unreadable old medieval lumber, as soon as the first genuine tracks of insight are made. The sooner the better, for me!"

Near the end of the first week in July William returned to Cambridge to receive the proofs and correct them. By July 23 he had corrected two batches, and wrote his sister Alice, "The printers are bent on overwhelming me and making me cry mercy now (I having complained of slowness at first), so that every mail, four times a day, is apt to bring a big bundle." After taking breakfast in their old house at 20 Quincy Street, which was now a kind of faculty club called the Colonial Club, William would return home and correct proofs all day. In the evening he would go over to Boston on the new electric street car and mail the package in the Boston Post Office, then get his dinner, sometimes as late as nine p.m., at the Parker House. During the last week of proofreading William had the help of his wife, who had come down from Chocorua to assist him in spite of the fact that she was expecting her fifth child in December.

On August 12 James wrote Holt: "Nothing remains now but the Index—hallelujah! The printing office did nobly, and so (though I say it as should not) did I, for I rarely got my dinner before 9 p.m. when I took the stuff into Boston to the late mail. My fears about not getting through before September were grounded on what you told me in the winter, that the printers could not be expected to do more than fifteen or sixteen pages a day." Now that the big job was over, William's weariness and disgust began to turn to elation. He still insisted to his friends that the book was "unreadable from any human point of view," but he felt that the whole "might be rather a vigorous and richly colored chunk." Actually, he was beginning to take pride in it, and this was the good feeling he had as he took the train for Chocorua, where he could still have a month's vacation before having to face his classes again. For him it was an "epochal year" after all.

CHAPTER XVIII Habit and Character

. . . the hell we make for ourselves in this world by habitually

fashioning our characters in the wrong way.   —W.J.

I

The Principles of Psychology was published in the autumn of 1890, with a dedication to François Pillon, "as a token of affection and acknowledgement of what I owe to the *Critique Philosophique*" —a reference to Pillon's having translated several of James's early essays, with the help of Renouvier, for the *Critique Philosophique*. *The Principles* filled two hefty volumes, each nearly seven hundred pages long. At the age of forty-eight (nearly forty-nine) William James had finally published his first book, and one that seemed to justify the twelve years of its gestation.

Why had it taken James twelve years to write the book? Of course his own character and erratic nerves had been factors in the delay, but everything in his career had been irregular. He had taken up scientific studies (chemistry first) at Harvard without the usual secondary-school preparation and had entered the Medical School without a college degree; then, finally, he had taught in the Graduate School without ever having been a graduate student himself. The irregularity of his own studies had not prepared him to march steadily toward any academic or scholarly goal, and perhaps the surprising thing is that he ever finished his first big, ambitious book.

But there were other reasons for James's delay in completing *The Principles*. One was the confusion of the subject matter itself, of which he had complained sardonically to his brother Henry in the letter quoted near the end of Chapter XVII. To a British psychologist, James Sully, a member of the Scratch Eight club and author of

Outlines of Psychology, James reiterated more soberly: "It seems to me that psychology is like physics before Galileo's time,—not a single *elementary* law yet caught a glimpse of." Scholars and investigators in Germany, France, and England were working hard to discover such laws, and James had given close attention to their efforts; yet he still felt, even after completing his book, that they had not been found, and that anything he published in the present state of inadequate knowledge would quickly become out of date.

Some of the confusion, however, may have been in his own mind. More specifically, he had not yet found a theory of cognition, which he had said in 1883 was the great impediment to his writing the book. How did man know? What could he know? On what basis could he trust his presumed knowledge? These questions had, of course, baffled all philosophers. Locke, Berkeley, Hume, and Kant, to name the major four in epistemology, had each thought he had found the answer, but later philosophers had shot their theories full of holes. For centuries thinkers had believed that man possessed a *soul* which was the seat of his intelligence and the force that held mind and body together, enabling one to operate on the other. But nineteenth-century science could find no way of discovering or dealing with this mysterious *soul*, and either ignored or eliminated it. James did not rule it out as an exploded superstition, but he did not see how a science of psychology could be built on such a hypothesis.

Still, without some theory to account for the relation of mind and body—or to reduce everything either to mind (spirit) or to body (matter)—how could he write a book on the processes of feeling, thinking, consciousness, etc.? He finally decided that he could treat this subject as a natural science and simply ignore metaphysical implications—not deny them, but postpone such unsolved problems as mind-body relationships. But if the most "elementary laws" of psychology had not yet been discovered, as he asserted, how could he treat it "scientifically"? Actually, he could not and did not, as his book reveals at many places. But he made an attempt, and succeeded in writing a book which eclipsed all rivals for a number of years.

As a medical student and teacher of physiology James had acquired about as much knowledge as possible at the time about the nervous system, and he hoped that he could describe, without having to go outside biology, how it functioned in receiving stimuli through the sense organs and transmitting the impulses (resembling electrical charges) to the brain, which then sent an activating impulse to some muscle, or stored up the stimulus for a future discharge. If there was one theory which all biologists of the late nineteenth century accepted, it was that of the "reflex arc," and James thought this theory would enable him to explain the phenomena of mental events, sequences, and concurrences. Two years before completing his book he had published in *Scribner's Magazine* an essay on "What the Will Effects," in which he stated:

> The only conception at the same time renovating and fundamental with which biology has enriched psychology, the only *essential* point in which 'the new psychology' is an advance upon the old, is, it seems to me, the very general, and by this time very familiar notion, that all our activity belongs at bottom to the type of reflex action, and that all our consciousness accompanies a chain of events of which the first was an incoming current in some sensory nerve, and of which the last will be a discharge into some muscle, blood-vessel, or gland.

This may sound like the automaton, deterministic psychology which James had always so vehemently opposed; but though he granted that much of the process of stimulation and response was automatic or reflex, he believed that indeterminism was still a reality. First, he found a purpose in all the neural activity: "the thinking and feeling portions of our life seem little more than half-way houses toward behavior; and recent Psychology accordingly tends to treat consciousness more and more as if it existed only for the sake of the conduct which it seems to introduce, and tries to explain its peculiarities (so far as they can be explained at all) by their practical utility."

In the second place, out of the welter of external (incoming) stimulations, consciousness selects some and ignores or suppresses others. There is a "fringe of consciousness" out of which the mind brings some object or objects into focus, as it were. Or, to use James's own words, "Every actually existing consciousness seems to itself at any rate to be a *fighter for ends*, of which many, but for its presence, would not be ends at all. Its powers of cognition are mainly subservient to these ends, discerning which facts further them and which do not." Here the influence of Darwin is also apparent: the mind has operated in such a way (through nerves and brain) as to enable an organism to adapt itself to its environment and to survive. Incidentally, if we extend this concept to all living organisms, then even the most primitive biological creatures have minds similar in kind though not in degree to those of higher organisms, and this raises the possibility that the processes of evolution have not been entirely fortuitous and blind—though this extension goes beyond James's purposes in his book. Yet it seems clearly implied by his words, and he would doubtless have approved of the statement of a twentieth-century biologist, John Langdon-Davies, in *Man and His Universe* that even plants have survived not because they were lucky but because they were clever.

In writing his *Principles* James drew upon the vast literature in the field, and when he mentioned a theory of interpretaton which he had borrowed or adopted, he not only gave the name of the originator but summarized the arguments of his opponents, so that these two volumes became almost an encyclopedia of nineteenth-century psychological theory. But he did have some doctrines of his own and a special point of view which reflected his own personality and character. One doctrine which became famous was that consciousness resembles a flowing stream. Although the concept was not entirely original with him, he gave it such a vivid and picturesque interpretation that he stamped his own character on it, and writers still attribute the "stream of consciousness" metaphor to him. First of all, he pointed out, the mind or consciousness is never empty, even in sleep; something is always in it, and the content is always changing, accumulating new images, points of attention, or "thoughts" in the process, so that, like a river, it seems to flow in one direction. Even when the mind attempts to retrace its course, it is never the same course because the contents have changed in many subtle ways. (An exception might be a recovered sequence of mental experience in a hypnotic trance.)

John Locke, the founder of the British school of empirical psychology, had divided "ideas" into simple and complex. After accumulating impressions of "simple" ideas through the senses, the mind could combine these into complex structures and test them by logical reasoning. James entirely rejected this classification, and also the doctrines of "association of ideas," because, he contended, it is not ideas but objects—pulsations in the nervous system causing images or mental units in the consciousness—which are associated. Furthermore, a person's *interest* influences the associations, so that the process is neither mechanical nor coldly logical and mathematical. So-called reasoning is often no more than "rationalizing," in the sense of self-justification, or satisfying emotional needs. All thought, James believed, is personal, colored by the thinker's individual peculiarities, needs, likes, and dislikes—all aspects of his unique self. Hence James's characterisic distrust of logic and his belief that every philosophical theory is personal—so that philosophers have seldom agreed with one another.

Another of James's contributions to psychological theory in his *Principles*—this too not entirely original—was that both space and time are directly felt by the senses, though the unit of temporal duration intuited is shorter than the amount of space directly experienced through the senses and nerves. David Hume had argued that the mind can perceive only disconnected dots or spots of time and space, and then hypothecate the connections. Thus the mind did not actually experience real duration or continuity in space. This argument cast extreme doubt on knowledge of time and space. Kant tried to find a way around the skepticism by arguing that the mind is capable of making its own constructs of time and space. But however useful such abstractions might be, James was not satisfied, because abstractions cannot be *felt*, and he believed that men could feel duration and have sensory knowledge of the three dimensions of space.

Henri Bergson had advanced a similar argument recently in *Les Données Immédiates de la Conscience* (1889; translated the same year as *Time and Free Will*), but this book came out too late to affect James in writing his *Principles*. Later the two authors became warm friends, and each found confirmation of his own doctrines in the other's works. Bergson argued that time is experienced as an unbroken unity, a continuous *durée*, and that the division into past, present, and future is an abstraction, not directly experienced. Later he expressed it this way in *Creative Evolution* (1907): "My mental state, as it advances on the road of time, is continually swelling with the duration which it accumulates: it goes on increasing—rolling upon itself, as a snowball on snow." This not only resembled James's theory of experienced time but also echoed his metaphor "stream of thought." But James did not work out a philosophy of intuition or, as some critics would say, of "mysticism," as Bergson did.

Another doctrine in James's *Principles* was the one Ralph Barton Perry calls "nativism." James had learned from Darwin to believe that the human mind has inborn traits, aptitudes, and predilections acquired by the nervous system in the process of surviving through "natural selection." These have been shaped by environment and heredity, as well as by each individual's experiences. In his chapter on "Habit," which was to become perhaps the most famous of all his chapters, James emphasized the importance of *first experience* in shaping future experiences. Once a neural path has been established, it will be traveled again and again unless some stronger force breaks a new path. The ethical implications of this "law of habit" are both negative and positive:

> The great thing, then, in all education, is *to make our nervous system our ally instead of our enemy*. It is to fund and capitalize our acquisitions, and live at ease upon the interest of the fund. . . . The more of the details of our daily life we can hand over to the effortless custody of automatism, the more our higher powers of mind will be set free for their own proper work. There is no more miserable human being than one in whom nothing is habitual but indecision. . . . Full half the time of such a man goes to the deciding, or regretting, of matters which ought to be so ingrained in him as practically not to exist for his consciousness at all.

William James spoke from experience. Ever since his early manhood, and perhaps earlier, he had wasted much time in indecision and regret; and even as a youth, shifted frequently by his father from one school or tutor to another, he had felt that he was not acquiring the right habits of mental discipline—though if he had done so, he might have lost some of the originality and spontaneity so pronounced in his adult mind and character; which is another way of saying that in failing to acquire the habits he admired in others, he unconsciously acquired others perhaps of more use to him.

Although attempting to write a "scientific" book, James did not refrain from "hortatory ethics," to use his own term: "The hell to be endured hereafter, of which theology tells us, is no worse than the hell we make for ourselves in this world by habitually fashioning our characters in the wrong way. . . . Let no youth have any anxiety about the upshot of his education. . . . If he keep faithfully busy each hour of the working-day, he may safely leave the final result to itself. He can with perfect certainty count on waking up some fine morning, to find himself one of the competent ones of his generation. . . ." This was the advice he had given, while still a dilatory medical student, to Tom Ward; it is doubtful that he yet realized the extent to which he had followed it in spite of all his anxieties and delays, but his competency was about to be recognized.

II

The Principles of Psychology was a smashing success. It quickly became the leading textbook in American colleges and universities (there had been several others by both American and British psychologists) and was translated into German, French, Italian, and even Russian. Most of the professional reviewers found some faults: nearly all thought it disorderly, though nearly all admitted the magnitude of the work. As Perry says: "It was read because it was readable, and it was read by people of all sorts because of the very qualities which condemned it in the eyes of some professional psychologists. Because it did not substitute the artifacts of analysis for the concrete, living mind, the reader constantly recognized *himself* in its descriptions and illustrations."

James's good companion and friendly enemy, Shadworth Hodgson, wrote him from England on August 19, 1891: "I am remorseful at owing you a letter for so long, which shall be something more than a mere reply, as my last was, to your kind present of your *Principles of Psychology*. I have long ago finished reading it, and have found it the most valuable and instructive book on the subject that I ever came across. This is chiefly because you make us see the reality of things, the real common-sense of the questions and problems at issue, while you go into full details on the moot points, and argue the whole out with the utmost fairness." Hodgson was especially impressed by "your speculation of the tissues covering the joints being the real seat or rather origin of the so-called muscular sensations of motor directions," and that an emotion is "a record of organic or systemic disturbances." But he thought that "your whole book contributes powerfully to the support of the so-called conscious automation theory. The more you explain, the less room do you leave for transcendental agency, since none of your explanations make any use of the latter." Of course James tried to reply to this charge, but it was difficult to answer.

The Cambridge University psychologist James Ward had criticized the book for the opposite reason in a letter written the preceding January 12. After admitting the "geniality, the incisiveness, the trenchant vigor" of the work, making the author "unique among psychologists," Ward said he was puzzled by the "treatment of the

causal relation of mind and body," and "your *penchant* for spiritualism in the new sense amazes me." This was a difference of opinion
which the two psychologists were to debate with each other for
years to come.

The reviewer for *Mind* was James Sully. Since William James had
published many of his important articles in *Mind* he was, of course,
particularly interested in the reception he might receive in this
British philosophical magazine. Sully found *The Principles* of great
importance, written with a facility, grace, boyish enthusiasm, and
irreverence for "authorities" which made it a joy to read, yet he
could not help wishing "here and there for just a *soupçon* of the old
spirit which has prompted mankind at all stages of culture to pay
reverence to ancestors." John Dewey, then teaching at the University of Michigan, wrote James: "One of my friends summed up
Sully's review in *Mind* for me as follows: 'A good book, but too
lively to make a good corpse and every scientific book ought to be a
corpse.' If we weren't indebted to you for any specific things, we
should be indebted to you for what you did to break down this
superstition."

But probably the most shocking critique James received was from
his prickly old friend Charles Peirce, who reviewed the two volumes
for the *Nation*. He, too, called the work "the most important contribution that has been made to the subject for many years," and
then went on to condemn it for the "idiosyncracies of diction and
tricks of language such as usually spring up in households of great
talent." Still more serious, he found the author

> materialistic to the core—that is to say, in a methodical sense, but not
> religiously, since he does not deny a separable soul nor a future life;
> for materialism is that form of philosophy which may safely be re-
> lied upon to leave the universe as incomprehensible as it finds it. . . .
> Brought up under the guidance of an eloquent apostle of a form of
> Swedenborgianism, which is materialism driven deep and clinched on
> the inside, and educated to the materialistic profession, it can only be
> by great natural breadth of mind that he can know what materialism
> is, by having experienced some thoughts that are not materialistic.

When William's brother Henry heard of this review, he was "unspeakably disgusted," and felt further alienated from his father's
old friend Godkin, still nominally editor of the *Nation*.

Stanley Hall reviewed *The Principles* for the *American Journal of Psychology.* Here was a man who spoke for the men of science. He characterized the author as on the whole

an *impressionist* in psychology. His portfolio contains sketches old and new, ethical, literary, scientific and metaphysical, some exquisite and charming in detail and even color, others rough charcoal outlines, but all together stimulating and suggestive, and showing great industry and great versatility. . . . Its very inconsistencies and incoherencies not only reflect but greatly magnify all the unrest, distraction and conflicts of the present hour. The author is a veritable storm-bird, fascinated by problems most impossible of solution, and surest where specialists and experts in his own field are most in doubt. . . . It is on the whole and after all the best work in any language. . . .

William Dean Howells stated, somewhat mischievously, in *Harper's Magazine:* "We suppose it would be rather damaging to Professor William James with other scientists to show that in his volumes on *The Principles of Psychology* he writes with a poetic sense of his facts, and with an artistic pleasure in their presentation." Howells thought his friend had "come dangerously near writing a 'popular' book." William thanked him handsomely too: "Surely never before did a work on mental science get so judged at the court of letters. I only wish you were not a friend of the family, so that my astonished eyes might read it as a tribute wrested by invincible evidence from an originally reluctant judge."

In view of George Santayana's personal feelings, or at least reservations, about his former teacher, it was perhaps a little surprising that he should write one of the most perceptive and subtly penetrating reviews for the *Atlantic Monthly:*

Individuality is here more than a charm, more than a human warmth and personal flavor pervading the discussions; it is a safeguard against pretension and hollowness. Those who deal with the abstract and general, who think impersonally and along the lines of a universal system, are almost sure to ignore their own ignorance. . . . But Professor James's simplicity and genuineness have saved him from this danger. He is eager for discovery, and conscious that too little is known for any final or comprehensive statements. The result is that in his book, more than in many books of philosophy, that which is known is set down, and the rest is omitted.

In later years Santayana would be caustic about James's "moral bias," but in 1891 he remarked tolerantly that James believed "with

Lotze, that our moral and emotional instincts are the best guides to ultimate truth." As for the loose structure, "it would be pedantry to regret the loss of logical unity in a book so rich and living, in which a generous nature breaks out at every point, and the perennial problems of the human mind are discussed so modestly, so solidly, with such a deep and pathetic sincerity."

But the finest and truest statement of all Santayana made thirty years later in *Character and Opinion in the United States* (1921), in which he said of *The Principles of Psychology:*

> This is a work of the imagination; and the subject as [James] conceived it, which is the flux of immediate experience in men in general, requires imagination to read it at all. It is a literary subject, like autobiography or psychological fiction, and can be treated only poetically; and in this sense Shakespeare is a better psychologist than Locke or Kant. Yet this gift of imagination is not merely literary; it is not useless in divining the truths of science, and it is invaluable in throwing off prejudice and scientific shams. The fresh imagination and vitality of William James led him to break through many false conventions. He saw that experience, as we endure it, is not a mosaic of distinct sensations, nor the expression of separate hostile faculties, such as reason and the passions, or sense and the categories; it is rather a flow of mental discourse, like a dream, in which all divisions and units are vague and shifting, and the whole is continually merging together and drifting apart.

III

Before becoming enslaved by his task of correcting printer's proofs, William James had completed for Frederic Myers, for publication in the British *Proceedings of the Society for Psychical Research*, a report on Mrs. Piper which he entitled "Certain Phenomena of Trance." On October 9, 1890, William was astonished to receive from his brother Henry this information: "Frdk Myers has written to ask *me* to read your letter on Mrs. Piper at a meeting of the S[ociety for] P[sychical] R[esearch] at the Westminster Town Hall on the 31st of this month: and I have said I would, though so alien to the whole business, in order not to seem to withhold from *you* any advantage—though what 'advantage' I shall confer remains to be seen. Therefore imagine me at 4 p.m. on that day, performing in your name."

On October 20 William replied: "I think your reading my Piper letter (of which this very morning proof came to me from Myers) is the most comical thing I ever heard of. It shows how first-rate a business man Myers is: he wants to bring variety and *éclat* into the meeting. I will *think of you* on the 31st at about 11 A.M. to make up for difference of longitude." And then in a postscript William added: "Alice says I have not *melted* enough over your reading of my paper. I *do* melt to perfect liquefaction. 'T is the most beautiful and devoted brotherly act I ever knew, and I hope it may be the beginning of a new career, on your part, of psychic apostolicism. Heaven bless you for it!" The final news of this bizarre event was written by Henry on November 7: "It was a week ago today that I read you at the S.P.R. with great *éclat*—enhanced by my being introduced by Pearsall Smith as 'a Bostonian of Bostonians!' You were very easy and interesting to read, and were altogether the 'feature' of the entertainment. It was a full house and Myers was *rayonnant*."

The report itself largely reiterated the observations of the earlier account written for the American S.P.R. *Proceedings*, but it did contain some additional personal details. For example, Mrs. Piper knew about the contents of a letter Aunt Kate had written to William's wife, warning her against all mediums: "Of course no one but my wife and I knew the existence of the letter in question." Mrs. Piper "was strong on the events in our nursery, and gave striking advice during our first visit to her about the way to deal with certain 'tantrums' of our second child, 'little Billy-boy,' as she called him, reproducing his nursery name. She told how the crib creaked at night, how a certain rocking chair creaked mysteriously, how my wife had heard footsteps on the stairs, etc., etc. Insignificant as these things sound when read, the accumulation of a large number of them has an irresistible effect." Of the two, Mrs. James was more profoundly impressed than her husband, but he was impressed, though unwilling to commit himself to definite conclusions: "The limitations of her trance information, its discontinuity and fitfulness, and its apparent inability to develop beyond a certain point, although they end by rousing one's moral and human impatience with the phenomenon, yet are, from a scientific point of view, amongst its most interesting peculiarities, since where there are limits there are conditions, and the discovery of these is always the beginning of explanation."

In the same letter in which he told of the success of William's Piper letter, Henry added: "Meanwhile, to compare great things with small, your Psychology has never turned up—though you told me you had ordered an early copy sent. Has there been some error or non-compliance? Will you kindly see? I yearn for the book—to lift me out of histrionics." The latter allusion was to Henry's play based on his novel *The American*. He had dramatized the book himself, and the production was soon to be tried out in provincial theatres before being taken to London. Although Henry had a very low opinion of the contemporary theatre, he had become convinced that he could make a great deal of money writing for the stage, and one of the successful producers had encouraged him in this idea. He could not help feeling contemptuous of and apologetic for the medium, yet it seemed to him that writers of inferior talent were making fortunes on their plays; so why should not he, with genuine literary talent, do as well or better? This ambition had become almost an obsession, and he wrote voluminous letters detailing his plans and imagined prospects, which also revealed an emotional tension unnatural for him.

On December 22 Alice James gave birth to her fifth child (fourth living), another boy. Of course William announced this event promptly to Henry and his sister Alice, assuring them that the delivery had been easy, and that both mother and son were flourishing—also that Margaret Mary had been so delighted with her new brother that she called him *her* baby. On January 3, 1891, Henry gratefully acknowledged the news, and then gave *his:* "It seems trivial at such a time to trouble you with *my* deliveries, but by the time this reaches you, you and Alice will have got a little used to yours. However, you are to receive news of the coming into the world of *my* dramatic 1st-born (which takes place here [at Southport, in Lancashire] tonight,) sometime tomorrow, through Alice from London, as I am to wire her early in the morning of the upshot of the dread episode (tomorrow unfortunately is Sunday, [when the cable office will be closed]) and she expressed to me before I left town day before yesterday the ardent wish that *she* might be allowed to cable you, as from herself, my report of the verdict that I am so oddly (till my complicated but valid material reasons are explained,) seeking of this Philistine provincial public. The omens and auspices are good—the theatre is bad but big and every seat in it has been taken for a week. . . . We are resting and quaking today—but we had yesterday a supreme, complete, exhaustive rehearsal, during which I sat in the stalls watching and listening as to the work of another. . . ."

Alice was able to cable that the play was a success—and so it was, in the provinces; months later, in London, the news was less encouraging. But meanwhile Henry still thought he was launched on a new and more profitable career. He was still excited on February 6 when he wrote William: ". . . I blush to say that I haven't had freedom of mind or cerebral freshness (I find the drama much more obsédant than the novel) to tackle—much more than dipping in just here and there—your mighty and magnificent book, which requires a stretch of leisure and an absence of 'crisis' in one's egotistical little existence. As this is essentially a year of crisis, or of epoch-making, for me, I shall probably save up the great volumes till I can recline upon roses, the fruits of my production fever, and imbibe them like sips of sherbet, giving meanwhile all my cerebration to the condensation of masterpieces."

But Henry was not too "possessed" with his dramatic ambitions to take the keenest and most personal interest in William's naming his latest son. William wrote him that he and Alice had finally settled upon "Francis Tweedy," and on February 12 Henry replied that he felt "strongly moved—even to tears—to supplicate you to *un*settle it. . . . *Francis* is very good, and I suppose it a friendship —certainly most just and grateful to F. J. Child. Besides I like the name itself. *Tweedy* I hate in itself—I think it woefully ugly—but accept willingly enough for its associations—though, as to this, they are essentially yours, not the child's, who will carry the name through life wondering, rather, why he was *affaibli* with it."

If *Tweedy* was bad, William's alternate was worse. He had written Henry that they had considered "Temple." "It is for Temple," Henry protested, "that I reserve all the horrors that an uncle and a brother may be judged by you to have a right to express; I don't understand it—I don't like it. . . . That it may be a sign, on your part of an attachment to Aunt Mary's maiden name [Mary Temple Tweedy], to the far-off dead Minny, or to the very near (me) living Elly's . . ." Henry had written that Elly (Ellen Temple, sister of the tragic Minny,) was living very extravagantly in London, cultivating aristocrats of dubious reputation, and, Henry suspected, intending to remarry. The American Temples had always prided themselves upon their aristocratic ancestry, being descended from

Sir John Temple. But they had "come by it through illegiti-
macy. . . . Aunt Mary's father was a bastard son of Sir John
Temple, the 'founder' of the family in America, and he housed himself, after burning the public office of which he was in charge, to
cover the tracks of his peculations." If William wanted to honor
Aunt Mary, wouldn't *Tweedy* be enough? Though Henry hated
"all surnames given to children when they are not [their] own
family-names."

If he were a father, Henry continued, he would give one of his
boys "the name or one of the names of mother's maternal grandfather, the worthy Alexander Robertson, who came from Scotland
to the U.S. in the middle of the last century and was a good and
solid burgess of New York. . . . Our Bob, as having Robertson,
needn't be a stumbling block, with a proper Christian name before
it. I, for my part, think Alexander Robertson James a very good
name. . . . At any rate think better of the 'Temple'—do, *do*, DO!
Alice [sister] feels as intensely on the subject as I do. . . ."

This impassioned protest of the novelist might not deserve such
extended quotation if it were only evidence of his offended sensibilities; but it had importance far beyond this one letter. In the
first place he did understand the effect of a name on a child better
than his psychologist brother, who was easily swayed by sentiment
or gratitude to friends. But—what is still more significant—William
and Alice later discovered that their son Francis (they dropped
"Tweedy" after using it a few years) detested his name. Consequently, they renamed him Alexander Robertson, as his uncle had
wisely urged—but by then his parents were so used to calling him
"Francis" that for many years they indiscriminately used both
"Francis" and "Aleck." He would grow up, like his uncle Robertson
("Bob") feeling neglected—not entirely as a result of the confusion
of names, but that was no doubt one factor.

IV

During Alice James's years of invalidism in England William
wrote her many letters, to which she replied when she had sufficient
strength or could dictate a reply to Katharine Loring—and of course
Henry shared his letters from William with her, so that she was always well informed about life in Cambridge. On May 31, 1889, she

had begun keeping the diary mentioned earlier, "as an outlet to that geyser of emotions, sensations, speculations and reflections which ferment perpetually within my poor carcass." Neither brother knew that she was writing the diary; had he known, Henry might have been more discreet in the gossip he relayed, with embellishments to amuse her, from his world of fashion, literature, and famous people. No brother could have been more devoted and thoughtful than he. On March 25, 1890, Alice recorded: "Five years ago in November, I crossed the water and suspended myself like an old woman of the sea round his neck where to all appearances I shall remain for all time. . . . He comes at my slightest sign and hangs on to whatever organ may be in eruption. . . ."

From time to time Henry found a new residence for her, first at Leamington, later in London in South Kensington or on Campden Hill, but in easy visiting distance from wherever he lived. She always had a maid, a nurse, and a great deal of the time the faithful Katharine Loring. Various physicians examined her and pronounced her trouble as "nervous hyperaesthesia," "spinal neurosis," "rheumatic gout" in the stomach, or something equally ambiguous. But her weaknesses, fainting spells, and neuralgia were unaffected by the high-sounding diagnoses. She read books, avidly followed national affairs through the newspapers, and vicariously participated in the Irish struggle for Home Rule. Henry thought that if she had possessed health and strength she would have been a real heroine in the Irish cause. Perhaps it was her Irish sympathies that made her so extremely satirical of British manners and intellects, which, to be sure, she knew only through reading, the conversation of her servants, and an occasional visitor.

Shut in as she was by necessity, Alice James took keen interest in the careers and experiences of her two older brothers—Bob seldom wrote her. William's *Principles of Psychology* she actually read, or most of it, skipping some of the more technical passages (Henry always intended to read the volumes but never found the time). On January 16, 1891, she wrote in her diary: "William says in his *Psychology:* 'Genius, in truth, is little more than the faculty of perceiving in an inhabitual way.' [This is slightly misquoted: he said "means little more. . . ."] This seems to the sisterly mind, or heart rather, more felicitous than the long-accustomed 'infinite capacity for taking pains,' but what length of tether does it allow to our greatly esteemed Cousin [British inhabitant] for browsing in unaccustomed fields and along the untrodden ways, for *he* only respects himself when he *is* habitual."

But of course William's *Psychology* did not provide the dramatic suspense for Alice that Henry's ventures in the theatre did. To her sister-in-law Alice (by this time the two women had become more sympathetic with each other) she had written on November 26, 1890, "I am going to ask of you a sisterly favour, that you should tell us of any *favourable* notices there may be of William's book, as we are quite out of the way of getting any here." Then Alice James continued: "Our absorbing interest just now is of course Harry's dramatic debut at the end of next month [the provincial, not London, debut]. . . . I have been on tenter-hooks about it for a year and a half now. If it succeeds at all, it will be a very brilliant success, and a very interesting illustration of the law that you can't hasten the moment, in any development. . . . How Harry, Katherine & I are to live through the first night I have no idea. There is little change in my state, the only variety in the day being the varying degrees of discomfort, & I find much entertainment therein. I am working away as hard as I can to get dead as soon as possible, so as to release Katherine, but this play of Harry's makes a sad complication, as I don't want to immerse him in a deathbed scene on his 'first night,' too much of an aesthetic incongruity! The trouble seems to be there isn't anything to die of, but there are a good many good jokes left still, and that's the main thing after all."

It was not a morbid obsession that made Alice James so often joke about her death but one of the ways in which she kept herself sane. Since her youth she had felt that her life was a "fight to death" between her body and her will. She had never conquered her ailing body, but she could assert her will by refusing to take the losing battle with tragic seriousness. In September 1890, while Dr. W. W. Baldwin, a famous American physician who practiced in Florence, was staying with Henry James in London, Henry asked him if Alice might die of her mysterious illness, and the doctor replied, "They sometimes do." On hearing this Alice wrote in her diary: "This is most cheering to all parties—the only drawback being that it will probably be in my sleep so that I shall not be one of the audience, dreadful fraud! a creature who has been denied all dramatic episodes might be allowed, I think, to assist at her extinction!"

But the joke took a grimmer tone in the spring of 1891. In March Alice moved into a small house on Campden Hill in Kensington, at 41 Argyll Road, where she employed a cook, a "house- and par-lour maid" whom she had brought with her from Leamington, and the nurse she had had for some months. This staff was supplemented by the ever faithful Katharine Loring. The comforts of this new home were soon negated, however, by an alarming increase in Alice's pain, and Dr. John Cooper Torry, a member of the Royal College of Physicians, was summoned. The diary entry for May 31, 1891, tells of the outcome: "Ever since I have been ill, I have longed and longed for some palpable disease, no matter how conventionally dreadful a label it might have, but I was always driven back to stag-ger alone under the monstrous mass of subjective sensations. . . . Dr. Torry was the only man who ever treated me like a rational be-ing, who did not assume, because I was victim to many pains, that I was of necessity, an arrested mental development too.

"Notwithstanding all the happiness and comfort here, I have been going downhill at a steady trot; so they sent for Sir Andrew Clark four days ago, and the blessed being has endowed me not only with cardiac complications, but says that a lump that I have had in one of my breasts for three months, which has given me a great deal of pain, is a tumour, that nothing can be done for me but to alleviate pain, that it is only a question of time, etc." Next day the diarist re-turned to this topic: "To any one who has not been there, it will be hard to understand the enormous relief of Sir A.C.'s uncom-promising verdict, lifting us out of the formless vague and setting us within the very heart of the sustained concrete. One would natur-ally not choose such an ugly and gruesome method of progression down the dark Valley of the Shadow of Death, and of course many of the moral sinews will snap by the way. . . . Having it to look forward to for a while seems to double the value of the event. . . . [Four days later] I cannot make out whether it is an entire absence or an excess of humor in Destiny to construct such an elaborate exit for my thistle-down personality, especially at this moment when so many of the great of the earth are gobbled up in a day or two by a microbe."

Though this new turn in her destiny naturally made Alice James even more introspective than ever, her tenderest sympathies were for her Henry and Katharine, "who will *see* it all, whilst I shall only *feel* it. . . . Poor dear William with his exaggerated sympathy for suffering isn't to know anything about it until it is all over." But of course Henry did write to William all about the situation, and on

July 6, 1891, William wrote Alice a long letter as frank and loving and thoughtful as his last letter to his father (unreceived) in 1882. He accepted the medical verdict as inevitably "a finite length of days; and then, good-bye to neurasthenia and neuralgia and headache, and weariness and palpitation and disgust all at one stroke—I should think you would be reconciled to the prospect with all its pluses and minuses! I know you've never cared for life, and to me, now at the age of nearly fifty, life and death seem singularly close together in all of us. . . . Your frustrations are only rather more flagrant than the rule. . . . Your fortitude, good spirits and unsentimentality have been simply unexampled in the midst of your physical woes; and when you're relieved from your post, just *that* bright note will remain behind, together with the inscrutable and mysterious character of the doom of nervous weakness which has chained you down for all these years."

Such experiences as hers, William continued to his sister, had made him feel that there was more in inhibitions, split-up selves, the enlargement of the self in trance, etc., than so-called science had been willing to admit, "bringing me to turn for light in the direction of all sorts of despised spiritualistic and unscientific ideas. Father would find in me today a much more receptive listener—all *that* philosophy has got to be brought in. And what a queer contradiction comes to the ordinary scientific argument against immortality (based on body being mind's condition and mind going *out* when body is gone), when one must believe (as now, in these neurotic cases) that some infernality in the body *prevents* really existing parts of the mind from coming to their effective rights at all, suppresses them, and blots them out from participation in this world's experiences, although they are *there* all the time. When that which is *you* passes out of the body, I am sure that there will be an explosion of liberated force and life till then eclipsed and kept down. I can hardly imagine *your* transition without a great oscillation of both 'worlds' as they regain their new equilibrium after the change! Everyone will feel the shock, but you yourself will be more surprised than anybody else."

Even with death now a near certainty, Alice James remained, as she had always been, more skeptical than her science-trained brother, and she took no consolation in anticipating immortality. But her stoicism enabled her to face the prospect of death without panic, and she did not resent William's writing her as he did. "It may seem odd," he continued, "for me to talk to you in this cool way about your end; but, my dear little sister, if one has things present to one's mind, and I know they are present enough to *your* mind, why not speak them out?" Then he spoke to her as a medical doctor: ". . . save yourself from bodily pain, if it can be done. You've had too much of that. Take all the morphia (or other forms of opium if that disagrees) you want, and don't be afraid of becoming an opium-drunkard. What was opium created for except for such times as this? Beg the good Katharine (to whom *our* debt can never be extinguished) to write me a line every week, just to keep the currents flowing, and so farewell until I write again."

On July 30 Alice replied to William's letter: "A thousand thanks for your beautiful & fraternal letter, which came, I know not when, owing to Katharine's iron despotism [withholding letters when Alice was suffering most]. Of course I could have wanted nothing else and should have felt, notwithstanding my 'unsentimentality', very much wounded & incomprise, had you walked round & not up to my demise." William's reading of Marcus Aurelius in his medical school days had never taught him the stoicism that his sister now exhibited without apparent effort: "It is the most supremely interesting moment in life, the only one in fact when living seems life, and I count it as the greatest good fortune to have these few months so full of interest & instruction in the knowledge of my approaching death. It is as simple in one's own person as any fact of nature, the fall of a leaf or the blooming of a rose, & I have a delicious consciousness, ever present, of wide spaces close at hand, and whisperings of release in the air."

She congratulated William on having attained "at nearly fifty" the philosophy "which I started at fifteen!" But she wanted him to know he greatly exaggerated "the tragic element in my commonplace little journey. . . . You must also remember that a woman, by nature, needs much less to feed upon than a man, a few emotions and she is satisfied; so when I am gone, pray don't think of me simply as a creature who might have been something else, had neurotic science [i.e., psychotherapy] been born." Although she had had a poverty of "outside experience," she felt that she had lived a rich inner life, and worshiped her own Deity in her own way. "This year has been one of the happiest I have ever known, surrounded by such affection and devotion, but I won't go into details, as I see a blush mantle the elderly cheek of my scribe [she was dictating to

Katharine Loring]. . . ." In a postscript she added: "I have many excellent & kind letters, but the universal tendency 'to be reconciled' to my passing to the summer-land might cause confusion in the mind of the uninitiated!" (F. W. H. Myers and other members of the British Society for Psychical Research referred to the land of spirits with which they hoped to communicate as the "Summer Land," and William had used the phrase in his letters to his sister.)

William received this letter from Alice in Chocorua, where he was spending the summer completing a condensed version of his *Principles of Psychology* for a one-volume "Briefer Course." On July 24 he had written Henry Holt that he would have the manuscript completed around the first of August. "By adding some twaddle about the senses, by leaving out all polemics and history, all bibliography and experimental details, all metaphysical subtleties and digressions, all quotations, all humor and pathos, all *interest* in short, and by blackening the tops of all the paragraphs, I think I have produced a tome of pedagogic classic which will enrich both you and me, if not the student's mind." Holt, of course, knew his author well enough to know how to take this grain of truth. "The larger book," James added to his publisher, "seems to be a decided success—especially from the literary point of view. I begin to look down upon Mark Twain!"

With the manuscript off his hands, William took a vacation in the mountains of western North Carolina. On August 23 he wrote his sister from Roan Mountain, sixty-three hundred feet high, which he had climbed the previous day, finding the air "round-edged and balmy," unlike the air of Mount Washington in New Hampshire. "I got your admirable, inspired and inspiring letter before I left home. It is good to hear you speak of this year as one of the best of your life. It is good to hear you speak of life and death from a standpoint so unshaken and serene, with what one of the Adirondack guides spoke of as such 'heaven-up-histedness' in the point of view. A letter from Harry, received only a few days later, confirmed me in this impression. He says he is less 'anxious' about you than at any former time, and I think we ought all to be so together now."

William refrained, probably deliberately, from telling Alice rapturously how enjoyable his vacation in the Carolina mountains had become. Two days later he wrote Miss Grace Ashburner, his elderly Cambridge neighbor, how he had "struck it rich" at Linville. He was staying in a new hotel in a tract of twenty-five square miles of wilderness. "The serpent has not yet made his appearance in this Eden, around which stand the hills covered with primeval forest of the most beautiful description, filled with rhododendrons, laurels, and azaleas which, through the month of July, must make it ablaze with glory." He had ridden that morning to the top of Grandfather Mountain with a North Carolina graduate of the Massachusetts Institute of Technology.

On September 12, 1891, William James sailed for England on the S.S. *Eider* for a ten-day visit to his sister, of course staying with Henry in London and spending several hours each day with her. It was perhaps not the best time to visit either Henry or Alice, for both were much preoccupied with the first night of *The American* in a London theatre on September 26, soon after William's arrival. The first night at the Strand Theatre was, indeed, a great social success, though Leon Edel calls it "a dubious artistic success." The American Minister occupied a box, William's Cambridge neighbor Grace Norton was there, rumor had it that several American millionaires were in attendance, and leading critics, artists, and writers were present. Although the critics did not really pounce on the play, most of them were far from enthusiastic about it. They saw that the author had turned a fine novel into a crude melodrama—Henry James had tried too hard to "write down to" his audience. The production could not be called a failure, for it ran for over two months, though attendance was often disappointing.

Probably William chose just the time he did for the visit in order that he might share Henry's "first night," knowing how excited both he and Alice were about it. And of course this excitement continued for the two weeks he was in London, during which the producer was using various devices—such as getting the Prince of Wales to attend—to stimulate the sale of tickets. During the last four days of his visit his sister seemed to be interested only in Henry's theatrical venture. Perhaps William even took advantage of this interest to avoid an emotional farewell. Although no account of his last days with her has survived—her diary is completely blank between September 20 and October 31—references to the visit in the correspondence of William with his sister and Henry indicate no faltering in her stoical planning for her demise or in the calm manner in which her brothers faced its inevitability.

On the last day of September William boarded the *City of Paris*, which he described next day in a letter to his sister as "like an enormous American hotel—very different from the gentlemanly *Eider* in which I came." Without actually saying so, he hinted that the excitement over Henry's "first night" and the necessity of limiting the duration of his visits to Alice to avoid overtiring her had left him with a feeling of unreality. "It seems absurd for me to have come and whisked about so soon after such short interviews and such contracted opportunities for conversation, but after all it is but part of the general queerness of all the deeper things of life. . . ." After he had left, Alice also began to feel that her "interest in the play" had prevented her getting the "full good" of her brother's visit, as Miss Loring expressed it in a letter she wrote to William at Alice's request. To this William replied, to reassure her: "It is a great mercy I went and got the impression of you which I did—seeing you so well-*minded* has colored all my imaginings of you with a cheerful tinge . . . [and] left so robustious an impression on my mind of the essence of you, that morbidness has no part of it."

William had urged his sister to try hypnotism both to kill the pain and to help her sleep and recommended a Dr. Charles Lloyd Tuckey, a pioneer in hypnosis therapy and author of a book William admired, *Psycho-Therapeutics: or Treatment by Hypnotism and Suggestion.* On December 2 Alice was able to dictate a letter to William reporting the success of the experiment:

"Supposing that your being is vibrating with more or less curiosity about the great hypnotic experiment on Campden Hill, I report progress. As far as pain goes the result is nil, save on four occasions the violent resuscitation of a dormant toothache, a wretched dying nerve which demands an agony of its own, impatient of waiting for, or too vain to lose itself in the grand mortuary moment so near at hand. What I *do* experience, is a calming of my nerves & a quiescent passive state, during which I fall asleep, without the sensations of terror which have accompanied that process for so many years, & I sleep for five or six hours uninterruptedly. But then, I slept like a dormouse all last year before taking morphia. Katherine has very much better results than 'Tuckums', that is so long as she remains silent & operates only by the gesture, but when she with solemn majesty addresses herself to the digestive Boreas & with persuasive accents suggests calmness & serenity of demeanour, cachinnation is the sole resource.

"We were fortunate in our ignorance, to have fallen upon an experienced doctor as well as hypnotist. He seems to be much penetrated with my abnormal susceptibility & says that to put me actually asleep would be a very risky experiment. He seems to look upon the reckless use of it as absolutely criminal. He is only coming once this week & then he will die, of course, a natural death. My pains are too much a part of my substance to have any modifications before the spirit & the flesh fall asunder. But I feel as if I had gained something in the way of a nerve pacifier & one of the most intense intellectual experiences of my life."

But Alice was distinctly not grateful to William for discussing her with Mrs. Piper, the Boston medium, and relaying instructions from her to Alice. On February 28, 1892, she wrote in her diary: "It is taken for granted apparently that I shall be spiritualized into a 'district messenger,' for here comes another message for Father and Mother; imagine my dragging them, of whom I can only think as a sublimation of their qualities, into gossip about the little more or the little less faith of Tom, Dick or Harry. I do pray to Heaven that the dreadful Mrs. Piper won't be let loose upon my defenceless soul. I suppose the thing 'medium' has done more to degrade the spiritual conception than the grossest forms of materialism or idolatry: was there ever anything transmitted but the pettiest, meanest, coarsest facts and details: anything rising above the squalid intestines of human affairs? And oh, the curious spongy minds that sop it up and lose all sense of taste and humour!"

Whether this last bitter comment was directed more toward her sister-in-law than her brother, we have no way of knowing. Mrs. James was credulous, but William was "curious," and probably they were both guilty in Alice's eyes. In fact, all talk about her "soul" left her completely unmoved. She had written earlier (February 2) in her diary: "If I could concern myself about the fate of my soul, it would give doubtless a savor of uncertainty to the fleeting moments, but I never felt so absolutely uninterested in the poor, shabby, old thing." But, like her father, she planned her funeral, made her will with agonizing care, and arranged to be cremated at Woking.

Finally on March 5, 1892, she cabled William: "Tenderest love to all. Farewell. Am going soon. Alice." Next day Henry cabled: "Alice just passed away. Painless. Wire Bob." On March 8 Henry wrote William a full account. She had died at exactly four o'clock on Sunday afternoon, the same hour and day as her mother. Up to Friday night she had suffered dreadfully, but Saturday morning it had suddenly stopped, permitting her to die peacefully. "We have made all the arrangements—they have been on the whole simple and easy—with the Cremation Society, for a service tomorrow afternoon (early) at Woking. Of course you know her absolute decision on this point—and she had gone into all the details. For myself I rejoice, as you doubtless will, and Katherine does, that we are not to lay her, far off from the others, in this damp, black alien English earth. Her ashes shall go home and be placed beside Father's and Mother's."

Alice James's estate was valued at something over eighty thousand dollars. Her largest bequests were to Henry, William, and Katharine Loring, to each of whom she left twenty thousand dollars, and to William the furniture and rugs she had loaned him from her Boston house. The remainder she distributed in smaller sums to nieces, nephews, cousins, and the servants and friends who had attended her.

From the Reform Club in London Henry wrote William on March 9: "It is all over—the painful business at the Crematorium achieved. I have just returned, and I stop here on my way from Waterloo home to scribble a word which will catch tonight's post. . . . There was a short simple service, read by an inoffensive, sweet-voiced young clergyman . . . after which the incineration. . . . It is the last, the last forever. I shall feel very lonely in England at first." But the final contribution to his sister's ceremony of dying was made by William, who selected a passage from Dante to be inscribed on her urn: "*Dopo lungo exilio e martiro/ Vienne a questa pace*" [After long exile and martyrdom comes to this peace], a line that took Henry "so at the throat by its penetrating *rightness*," he wrote later in his journal, "that it was as if one sank down on one's knees in a kind of anguish of gratitude before something for which one had waited with a long, deep *ache*."

CHAPTER XIX A Family Abroad

. . . coming abroad with a pack of children is not the same thing in

reality as it is on paper. —W.J. *to James J. Putnam*

I

LONG BEFORE HIS SISTER'S DEATH in March, William James had
planned to take his wife and possibly his children to Europe for
a year during his sabbatical leave from Harvard, which would begin
in June 1892. His sister's generous bequest would make the trip
easier, but it did not in any way alter his plans—if they could be
called "plans," for they had hardly gone beyond the date of sailing.
Henry, even in his letters describing Alice's last days, had begged
William for details of his intentions. Henry's flat in London was not
large enough for William's whole family, but on March 19 he wrote:
"I trust Alice and you, after planting your children [they had considered leaving them with their grandmother], are soon to come—
I mean *very* soon—to England: I mean during the rest of the
summer. I can put you *both* up *beautifully* [doubly underscored]
and will hear of your seeking no other asylum."

But there were several problems to be solved before vacation
plans could be completed, and what to do with the children was
the subject of endless discussion among their parents, grandmother,
and Aunt Margaret Gibbens. And meanwhile William was giving
a series of lectures which also marked a turning point in his life, the
beginning of a very successful career as a popular lecturer, which
was to cut into the time he could give to scholarship and directing
experiments in psychology. The publication of the one-volume edition of his work on psychology, which he called simply *Psychology:
The Briefer Course* to distinguish it from the two-volume *Principles*,
had greatly extended his reputation. The *Principles* had been too
long for some college courses in beginning psychology, but *The*

[341]

Briefer Course was just right. Both teachers and students liked it, and the latter quickly nicknamed the big work "James" and the shorter one "Jimmy." A whole generation of psychology students would read one or the other, or both.

In recognition of James's fast-growing fame the Harvard Corporation asked him to deliver a series of lectures to the teachers of Cambridge, and the preparation and delivery of these, later published as *Talks to Teachers*, occupied a great deal of his time during the late winter and early spring of 1892. But they, too, were loudly applauded. James's personality, his sense of humor, his sympathetic nature, and his ability to reduce abstractions to simple, concrete language and universal analogies enabled him to charm and interest almost any audience of ordinary people. And the moral implications in his theories on habit and will appealed to elementary and secondary school teachers.

James found lecturing to a popular audience much more fun than directing students in routine laboratory experiments. His lab course now averaged eighty students each term, and it was impossible to find enough original experiments for that many to undertake, even if they were capable of such investigations—and most of them were not, as he pointed out in letters to his friend G. H. Howison, who was trying to start a psychological laboratory at the University of California. In fact, the famous experimental laboratories of Germany had disappointed him in their trivial results. They had piled up great stacks of statistics, but their scales were always quantitative, not qualitative, and they had produced few new ideas. The German method, he had declared in his *Principles*, "taxes patience to the utmost, and could hardly have arisen in a country whose natives could be *bored*." It certainly bored William James.

And yet he believed that the psychological laboratory should be continued at Harvard, so that the students might learn to observe, touch, and handle nature while they studied the phenomena of the brain, nerves, and mind functioning in the animal body. Fortunately he and Palmer were now on excellent terms, and both Palmer and President Eliot told him to look for someone to take over the laboratory work for a trial period of three years, beginning with William's year of leave. The search did not take him long because he already had his eye on a young man at the University of Freiburg in Germany who had published impressive *Beiträge* (contributions) to experimental psychology. His name was Hugo Münsterberg; he was formerly a student of the great Wundt and only twenty-eight. His *Beiträge* had been fiercely criticized by a couple of German psychologists, but James attributed this to jealousy. On February 21, 1892, he wrote to sound Münsterberg out about coming to Harvard.

"The situation is this," James explained: "I, at the age of fifty, disliking laboratory work naturally, and accustomed to teach philosophy at large, although I *could, tant bien que mal*, make the laboratory run, yet am certainly not the kind of stuff to make a first-rate director thereof. We could get younger men here who would be *safe* enough, but we need something more than a safe man, we need a man of genius if possible." Although the appointment would be officially for only three years, and more money would have to be raised for equipping and operating the laboratory, it could become a permanent appointment and James was confident he could find the additional funds needed for the laboratory. Münsterberg was indeed interested, and President Eliot offered him the position on the terms James had indicated.

On May 3 William was able to write Münsterberg: "A telegram arrives from you 'joyfully accepting the call.' *Gottlob!* . . . It is an enormous relief to me to see the responsibility for experimental psychology in Harvard transferred from my feeble and unworthy shoulders to those of a man as competent as you. I shall proceed immediately to proclaim the news, as an early ventilation and publication of it will decide many wavering students to come to us next year." Münsterberg had been worried about his English, and James advised him to go to work on it immediately.

Not only was William now free of the irksome laboratory direction, but he was also free to take his vacation; his going on leave with half-salary (as customary for sabbaticals) had depended upon his securing someone to take charge of his psychology students in his absence. Meanwhile he and Alice had decided to take all the children with them. They would sail on the S.S. *Friesland* on May 25, and land at Antwerp. Their German governess would accompany them to her homeland.

II

Several years before her death Alice James had begged her brother William not to let his children "be torn up by the roots every little while as we were! Of all things don't make the mistake which brought about our rootless and accidental childhood. Leave Europe for them until they are old enough to have *the* Grand Emotion, undiluted by vague memories." Now William was about to forget that advice and repeat at least some of his father's mistakes. Of course he had not shifted his older sons Harry and Billy from one school or tutor to another every few months or weeks, and his wife was not going abroad for the first time with two babies under two, as William's mother had done in 1843. And yet what William and Alice were doing was perhaps even more complicated, for they were taking four children (Harry, thirteen; Billy, ten; Margaret Mary, five; and Francis Tweedy [later renamed Alexander], seventeen months). The German governess wanted to return to Germany, and Alice would have her help on the ship; but she had no faithful "Aunt Kate," as her mother-in-law had had on her three trips to Europe, besides always one or two servants.

Like his father, too, William had no very definite plans, beyond landing at Antwerp and taking his family immediately to Freiburg, where he would get acquainted with Münsterberg and his family could enjoy a brief vacation in the Black Forest while the next move was being decided upon. This part of the sketchy itinerary went smoothly enough: the ocean voyage was pleasant, though Billy proved not to be a good sailor; and the train took them down an enchanting strip of the Rhine Valley to the gabled, turreted old city of Freiburg, with its cobblestone streets, medieval university buildings, and boxes of bright flowers on nearly every window sill, while beyond the mossy banks of the Dreisam rose the mountain slopes of the Schwarzwald covered with dark-green spruce.

William was delighted with Herr Professor Hugo Münsterberg, a stout young man with typical German features: round head, bristling mustache, and stern eyes. He was friendly, in spite of his formidable appearance, and "gentlemanly through and through," James wrote Royce. He spoke German with a torrential eloquence, but was timid about even trying English, and William feared he would suffer a great *Hemmungsgefühl* (feeling of inhibition) when he tried to lecture to Harvard students. William predicted that Cambridge would "teem with anecdotes about him before he has been there a month."

The vacation at Freiburg was marred by almost incessant rain, which kept the children indoors, where they were restless, quarrelsome, and noisy. The older boys teased Margaret Mary until she became almost hysterical, and the noise and confusion caused the baby to cry a great deal. After ten days William left his family in Freiburg while he went on to Lake Lucerne to find, with Münsterberg's help, a *pension* for rent. By this time, William wrote Royce, the weather had "gloriously cleared up and nature's full orchestra [is] going it on this extraordinarily operatic lake." But delightful as Lucerne was, the older boys would not get there any instruction in the French language, and the parents wanted to find a place where this would be possible. William felt drawn to Geneva, as his father had been; consequently he took a week's trip through the Rhone Valley to Geneva to look for a *pension* and a pastor who would give instruction to the boys. By July 6 he had returned to Lucerne for his family, and he wrote Münsterberg, "We shall start tomorrow for Gryon," on Lake Geneva, "where I can probably get instruction for my boys in the pastor's family, as well as 'board' for ourselves in a big chalet near by." He had also engaged "a very promising Vaudoise girl for the children," meaning a nurse-maid for Margaret Mary and baby Tweedy (as he was being called at the time). She would join them when they passed through Aigle.

This, however, was only a temporary arrangement, and schooling for the boys during the coming autumn and winter was still the big unsolved problem. "Destiny," he confided to Münsterberg, "seems to be inevitably dragging us toward Paris:—I am sorry, for I rather hate the french language . . . , although I am much more at home in it than in German. But I see that I must resign myself to a year without the satisfaction of my *Gemut* [mind, desire]; and trust that by simply amusing myself with externals I shall be able to return to Cambridge fat and good natured, and full of metaphysical originality." He was still grateful to Münsterberg himself for giving up forty-eight hours to accompany him to Lucerne, when Münsterberg was making preparations for his trip to America. William had been able by cablegrams to his mother-in-law and Royce to find a place in Cambridge where Professor and Mrs. Münsterberg could get room and board for the coming academic year.

By the time the James family got settled at Gryon, William's exasperation with the children was almost beyond endurance. On July 13 he wrote Miss Grace Ashburner about the mistake they had made in bringing the children. "We have been in Europe five and a half weeks and are only just beginning to see a ray of light on our path. . . . It seems to me that the most solemn duty *I* can have in what remains to me of life will be to save my inexperienced fellow beings from ignorantly taking their little ones abroad when they go for their own refreshment. To combine novel anxieties of the most agonizing kind about your children's education, nocturnal and diurnal contact of the most intimate sort with their shrieks, their quarrels, their questions, their rollings-about and tears, in short with all their emotional, intellectual and bodily functions, in what practically in these close quarters amounts to one room—to combine these things (I say) with a *holiday* for *oneself* is an idea worthy to emanate from a lunatic asylum."

In his disgust with the situation he had got himself into, William declared that the wear and tear of teaching a whole year was not equal to one week with small children in a *pension* in a foreign country. Of course he was responsible for them, "and if a foreign education is required, they shall have it. Only why talk of 'sabbatical' years?—there is the hideous mockery! Alice, if she writes you, will (after her feminine fashion) gloze over this aspect of our existence, because she has been more or less accustomed to it all these years and *on the whole does not dislike it* (!!), but I for once will speak frankly and not disguise my sufferings." Miss Ashburner might have asked, when had he ever?

"Here in this precipitous Alpine village we occupy rooms in an empty house with a yellow-plastered front and an iron balcony above the street. Up and down that street the cows, the goats, the natives, and the tourists pass. The church-roof and the pastor's house are across the way, dropped as it were twenty feet down the slope. Close beside us are populous houses either way, and others beside *them.* Yet on that iron balcony all the innermost mysteries of the James family are blazoned and bruited to the entire village. *Things* are dried there, quarrels, screams and squeals rise incessantly to Heaven, dressing and undressing are performed, punishments take place—recriminations, arguments, execrations—with a publicity after which, if there *were* reporters, we should never be able to show our faces again." When the harassed father thought "of that cool, spacious and quiet mansion lying untenanted in Irving Street, with a place in it for everything, and everything in its place when *we* are there, I could almost weep for 'the pity of it.' "

Like his father before him in a similar situation, William worried about tutors for his children. If he could make arrangements with a pastor to board and instruct Harry and Billy, perhaps they could be left in Switzerland during the autumn and winter while William and Alice traveled with Margaret Mary and the baby—not that he disliked Switzerland, which he declared "an unmitigated blessing, from the mountains down to the bread and butter and the beds. The people, the arrangements, the earth, the air and the sky, are satisfactory to a degree hard to imagine beforehand. There is an extraordinary absence of feminine beauty, but great kindliness, absolute honesty, fixed tariffs and prices for everything, etc., etc., and of course absolutely clean hotels at prices which, though not the 'dirt cheap' ones of former times, are yet very cheap compared with the American standard."

A short time after William's writing Miss Ashburner, the James family was comfortably settled (temporarily) in a *pension* at Verschez-les-Blanc, near Lausanne. Billy was now boarding and studying with a nearby pastor, and Henry was living with another pastor at Vevey, a few miles east of Lausanne, near Montreux. It was at Verschez-les-Blanc that William's brother Henry paid them a visit during the first two weeks of August. He had not seen his sister-in-law for ten years or ever set eyes upon the two younger children, and of course in 1882 Billy had been only a few months old. Alice found the novelist so heavy that he was almost obese, and more formal and mannered than he had been when she first met him, but she liked him as much as ever, and he found her little changed by her decade of maternal cares. It was really much easier for each to understand the other than it was for either to understand the mercurial William. For several months Henry had been traveling and visiting in Paris and Italy. He had just come, in fact, from the Venetian palace rented for the summer by his good friend from Boston, Mrs. John L. Gardner, who had begun to form the fabulous art collection which would become the nucleus of the Boston Museum of Art in the Fenway.

Two days after Henry's arrival William left for a walking tour in the Engadine with two "psychical" friends, F. W. H. and A. T. Myers, and he did not return until August 23. Henry was overcome with sympathy for his sister-in-law, tied down with her two small children while her husband gaily tramped the mountains. On the evening of August 3, just after William's departure, Henry had visited a long standing friend of his, Henrietta Reubell, at nearby Ouchy, where she was spending the summer, and later recorded in his journal that "the conversation had run a little upon the way Americans drag their children about Europe."

To Mrs. Gardner, Henry had written the day after his arrival, "I have been since yesterday noon, intently occupied in realizing that I am an uncle." But the realization would not be complete until he could visit his two older nephews, and he was disappointed that they had been exiled to the homes of pastors, as he and Wilky had been in Germany in the summer of 1860. To his oldest nephew and namesake he wrote a formal request: "Will you please say to M. Ciresole [William spelled the name Cérésole in his letters], with all my compliments, that your uncle and brother, with your mother's consent, are coming to pay you this little visit—if he doesn't disapprove." After this polite gesture, Uncle Henry then took Billy by boat to Vevey to visit Harry. When it came time to say good-bye, he told his nephews he would turn his back if they felt embarrassed about embracing, Swiss-French fashion, before him; they should not think it unmanly, he told the little inhibited Americans, to show their emotions. This solemn advice from their Europeanized uncle deeply impressed them. On the fifteenth of August, a week before William was to return from his mountain tour, Henry James returned to London.

The day after he got back from his mountain trip, William wrote to Münsterberg, who would have reached Cambridge by the time the letter arrived: "When you get this, you will be housed in Sumner Street, and I can only hope that the shock of our bad streets and wooden houses will not be too great. Remember that the first weeks are always the lonely and unnatural ones, and that when work begins, your whole feelings toward America will change. I hope that Miss G[ibbens] will take you into my library and offer you the use of any books there which you may need. You will have a terribly hot week (we always do) the first week in September." William himself was homesick for his library in Irving Street.

Most of August and September William spent in traveling around in the mountains and lakes of this Alpine region. On September 8 he wrote Münsterberg again from Vers-chez-les-Blanc that he had just arrived back "from a flight of 8 days to the Engadin[e] and Italian lakes, solus." Münsterberg had been ill not long before sailing to America, and William was anxious to hear how he had stood the trip. As for himself, he was still worrying about his "infernal . . . educational problem." The boys were still in the families of the two pastors, and could be left there while he and Alice remained in the region. He had decided against Paris, but hankered "after Germany; and having just heard of the Realgymnasium at Stuttgart with Willman at its head, I am turning over the whole question again, and *may*, in a few days, run off to Stuttgart to see whether the place looks tempting for a winter abode. Had I foreseen this trouble, I should not have brought the children, nor taken my year of absence but simply given myself a long vacation of 4 months, bringing Mrs. James for perhaps two months, and gone back to work in Cambridge next year. At present I envy you your prospect."

Almost immediately after he had written Münsterberg this letter the weather in the region of Lake Geneva turned cold and wet, and William promptly decided that they would go to Florence for the winter. Harry and Billy were hastily summoned and the whole family crossed the Simplon Pass into Italy, pausing for ten sunny days at Pallanza on Lake Maggiore. On September 19, while still at Pallanza, William wrote Professor Théodore Flournoy, of the University of Geneva, whom he had met at Vers-chez-les-Blanc, to thank him for a philosophical critique written by a M. Sécretan criticizing Renouvier's doctrines. "I read it stretched on the grass of Monte Motterone . . . with all the kingdoms of the Earth stretched before me, and I realized how exactly a philosophic Weltansicht resembles that from the top of a mountain. You are driven, as you ascend, into a choice of fewer and fewer paths, and at last you end in two or three simple attitudes from each of which we see a great part of the Universe amazingly simplified and summarized, but nowhere the entire view at once. I entirely agree that Renouvier's system fails to satisfy, but it seems to me the classical and consistent expression of *one* of the great attitudes, that of insisting on logically intelligible formulas."

At Vers-chez-les-Blanc Flournoy had complained of the increasing burden of his psychological laboratory. James advised him to concoct "a programme of classical observations on the senses, etc., for the students to verify," as he had done at Harvard, and not get involved in laboratory research himself if he preferred to work with ideas. "You philosophize, according to your own account, more spontaneously than you work in the laboratory. So do I, and I always felt that the occupation of philosophizing was with me a valid excuse for neglecting laboratory work, since there is not time for both."

III

The Jameses might have remained longer at Pallanza if the food had been better—and they could have returned to Switzerland, where the weather was now reported to be delightful, but they went on to Florence and arrived there September 21. The autumn tourist season had not yet begun and they found a wide choice of furnished apartments for rent. The chief difficulty was that most were not large enough for all the Jameses, and again one is reminded of Henry Sr.'s troubles in Europe. But at 16 Piazza dell' Indipendenza an apartment was found, at a reasonable price and with a sufficient number of sunny rooms. It was clean and abundantly furnished with sofas and chairs, but had no housekeeping conveniences whatsoever: no oven for making macaroni *au gratin,* no place for keeping a week's supply of charcoal or a three- or four-days' supply of wood for the chilly days in winter, and no provisions for heat in the bedrooms. William rented it for six months, and the family moved in on October 4. Next day William wrote Münsterberg, from whom letters had now been received telling of his depressing first experiences in Cambridge: "Florence is pleasant, but the proper place for *children* is *home;* and my wife felt this morning very much as I think you must have felt when you first woke up in Cambridge. *No* conveniences in the house, and a man-cook with whom we communicate by naked Aryan roots without terminations. He seems nevertheless to catch our meaning even better than we do his!" William assured Münsterberg that "when work has once begun you will keep cheerful all the time." It was hardly possible for William to keep cheerful for any considerable time anywhere, but he did quickly adjust to Florence; or perhaps one should say that Mrs. James did, and she kept the family reasonably cheerful.

Both William and Alice soon became very fond of their Italian male cook, named Raffaello, who was quick to anticipate their wants, knew where to shop for the best vegetables, and devoted his life to making them happy. And other problems were more easily solved than expected. A good small English school was found for Harry and Billy, though their father was disappointed that it would teach them less French and German than they would have learned in their Cambridge school. Margaret Mary—now almost always called "Peg"

—was too young to send to a school, but three times a week "a poor little, humble, peering-eyed fiddler," an ex-ballet dancer, gave her gymnastic and dancing lessons at home in the big salon. They were all, of course, studying Italian, Alice proving the most adept because she had gained considerable facility in the language while living in Italy during her early womanhood.

On his previous visits to Florence William had always been depressed by the climate and cultural decay of the once-magnificent city, and he still had reservations about it, in spite of his declaring to Miss Grace Ashburner in a letter dated October 19 that, "For ourselves, Florence is delicious. I have a sort of organic protestation against certain things here, the toneless air in the streets, which feels like used-up indoor air, the 'general debility' which pervades all ways and institutions, the worn-out faces, etc., etc. But the charming sunny manners, the old-world picturesqueness wherever you cast your eye, and above all, the magnificent remains of art, redeem it all, and insidiously spin a charm round one which might well end by turning one into one of these mere northern loungers here for the rest of one's days, recreant to all one's native instincts. The stagnancy of the thermometer is the great thing. Day after day a changeless air, sometimes sun and sometimes shower, but no other difference except possibly from week to week the faintest possible progression in the direction of cold. It must be very good for one's nerves after our acrobatic climate."

The Jameses found all the social life they needed in Florence. Dr. W. W. Baldwin, Henry's friend, became their friend and counselor too. He had recommended the English school for Harry and Billy, and the dancing teacher for Peg. The husband of the late Lizzie Boott (she had died in 1888), Frank Duveneck, painted and sculptured in Florence, and the Jameses saw him occasionally, but more often were with Charles A. Loeser, one of William's former students at Harvard, who was now devoting his life to the scientific study of pictures. William found Duveneck, a native of Cincinnati, rather crude and difficult to talk to, but he called Loeser "a dear good fellow" and took up the study of pictures again under his instruction. He was delighted to find how much enjoyment he could still get from looking at great paintings, but was quite willing to leave the scientific study of them to Loeser and Baron Ostensacken, a nervous, intelligent, but rather egotistical old bachelor. And a former student who was to become a very famous art critic and historian, Bernard Berenson, was also in Florence. Fifty years later Berenson remembered a walk up Monte Vecchio to his favorite view: "I recall bringing William James here—I mean to the towered farm. He hated walking between high walls because they shut out the view. I protested that one enjoyed it all the more for not having it constantly before one. He would not listen. It was churlish to deprive one of the view. It made him mad."

With former students in Florence and the exchange of letters with Münsterberg and Royce in Cambridge, William did not feel entirely isolated from Harvard, which was frequently in his thoughts. He congratulated Royce on having been made a full professor, and thanked him for writing of Münsterberg's success in the psychological laboratory; he also sent messages to Palmer about the choice of graduate assistants and the planning of courses for the coming year. On December 18 he wrote Royce that he had gone to Padua the previous week to a celebration of the anniversary of Galileo. "It was splendidly carried out, and great fun; and they gave all of us foreigners honorary degrees. I rather like being a doctor of the University of Padua, and shall feel more at home than hitherto in the 'Merchant of Venice.'"

Back from Padua, William wrote that Mark Twain was spending the winter in a villa outside Florence, hard at work on something. "I have seen him a couple of times—a fine, soft-fibred little fellow with the perversest twang and drawl, but very human and good. I should think that one might grow very fond of him, and wish he'd come and live in Cambridge."

But for a restless man like William James, not even interesting acquaintances like Berenson and Mark Twain and a relaxing atmosphere could entirely save him from boredom. No one realized this better than his wife, who wrote her brother-in-law Henry on November 4: "I wish you could be as free from interruptions [which Henry had complained about in a recent letter] as we are, but you might find it monotonous or even a little depressing as William sometimes does. He misses, more than he is aware of, the excitement of his daily lecture and all the little hum of college life." She thought, however, that he would be stronger next year after the rest he was getting in Florence. For the boys, the benefit was quite obvious. "Last night Billy said 'I never got my eyes open till I came to Europe.' The[ir] school strikes me as better than anything we could have expected. The boys are doing French, German and drawing beside the regular school work. Peggy's needs are not yet provided for but I hope they will be soon. She is growing so very active that two hours of teaching at home does not seem just the thing. Mrs. Baldwin told me of a school now being started by an English lady which sounds cheerful and improving. These rainy days she has a wretched time with no play, and the boys hector her till she gets wild with excitement."

In-laws also passed through Florence. Alice James had expected to feel uncomfortable with Mary Holton (Bob's wife), but found her pleasant and genial. "Perhaps Bob's absence from the scene [they were still separated] helped. She is such a sound, energetic, major-key sort of a woman and so really good that I like to be friends with her." Carrie (Wilky's widow) had also been in Florence with her children. "If you could have seen William's . . . touching attempts to 'get acquainted' with Wilky's children you would have groaned in spirit. They were so cold [and] so absolutely indifferent." The girl, Alice, "evidently disapproved of him," though he made a great effort to be agreeable to her. Cary, the boy, was out when William called on him at the hotel, and he did not return the call until he came to say good-bye. "He could not dine with us because he was 'engaged to Detroit friends.' In short they were so evidently eager to escape us that I never again shall feel the slightest responsibility toward them. . . . Their coming saddened William as I am sure it did me, though for somewhat different reasons."

Mary Holton James was traveling with her mother, whom Mrs. William James thought a silly old woman, much as she liked Mary. "Poor old Mrs. Holton cried all the evening because her granddaughter is engaged to an Englishman, the disaster being aggravated by his title—Sir Philip Gray Egerton. I suppose few English mothers would take her view."

If a letter that William wrote to his sister-in-law Margaret Gibbens on January 3, 1893 can be believed (at least halfway), he and Alice did not often entertain in their own apartment: "My immediate purpose in writing is to celebrate Alice's social greatness, and to do humble penance for the obstacles I have persistently thrown in her path. By which I mean that the dinner which we gave on Sunday night, and which she with great equanimity got up, was a perfect success. She began, according to her wont, after we had been in the apartment a fortnight, to say that we must give a dinner to the Villaris, etc." (Professor Pasquale Villari, of the University of Florence, was at the time Minister of Education in Italy, and also a distinguished scholar and author.)

The almost total absence of housekeeping conveniences in the apartment has already been mentioned. "If you could have seen the manner of our ménage at that time, you would have excused the terrible severity of the tones in which I rebuked her, and the copious eloquence in which I described our past, present, and future life and circumstances and expressed my doubts as to whether she ought not to inhabit an asylum rather than an apartment. As time wore on we got a waitress, and added dessert spoons, fruit knives, etc., etc., to our dining-room resources; also got some silver polish, etc.; and Alice would keep returning to the idea in a way which made *me*, I confess, act like the madman with whose conversation at such times (dictated I must say by the highest social responsibility) you are acquainted."

At last Alice had invited the Lorings (Katharine's relatives), Baron Ostensacken, and Loeser for dinner on New Year's night: ". . . I groaning, she smiling; I hopeless and abusive, she confident and defensive, of our resources; I doing all I could to add to her burden and make things impossible, she explaining to Raffaello in her inimitable Italian, drilling the handmaids, screening the direful lamp most successfully with three Japanese umbrellas after I contended that it was impossible to do so, procuring the only two little red petticoats in the city to put on our two candles, making a bunch of flowers, so small in the centre of a star of fern leaves that I bitterly laughed at it, look exquisitely lovely—and then, with her beautiful countenance, which always becomes transfigured in the presence of company, keeping the conversation going till after eleven o'clock. I humbly prostrated myself before her after it was over,—for the table really looked sweet—no human being would have believed it beforehand,—threw the wood-ashes on my head, and swore that she should have the Villaris, and the King of Italy if she wished and whenever she wished, and that I would write to you in token of my shame. It will please your mother to hear what a successful creature she is."

From time to time Mrs. James experimented with diets for herself, though not for the rest of the family. William had to report that, "Her diet is still eccentric,—flying from one extreme of abstinence to another,—and her sleep fitful and accidental in its times and seasons. She sits up very late at night, and slumbers publicly when afternoon visitors come in, upright in her chair, with the lamp shining full on her beautiful countenance from which all traces of struggle have disappeared and [where] sleep reigns calmly victorious—at least she did this once lately." Then in a postscript: "On reading this to Alice she says she doesn't see what call I had to write it, and that as for my obstructing the dinner, I hadn't made it more impossible than I always make everything. This with a sweet ironical smile which I can't give on paper."

No doubt some of the credit for the success of the dinner—whatever the truth about it may have been—should have gone to Raffaello, whom Alice now admired and depended upon so much that she had declared her intention of taking him back to America with them. He seemed willing enough to go, too, but William feared the complications and asked Mr. Francis Boott, "Should you think it safe? He seems to have no friends or diversions here, and no love except for his saucepans. But I dread the responsibility of being foster-father to him in our cold and uncongenial land. It would be different if I spoke his lingo." And William now declared *"what a pretty lingo it is!* Italian and German seem to me *the* languages. The mongrels French and English might drop out!"

In January William also got involved in another episode which entailed a good deal of letter writing. He had mentioned to Henry that a Miss Vernon Lee (pseudonym of Violet Paget) had written him that she was living in Florence and would like to meet him, she being a friend of Henry. Immediately Henry wrote William not to have anything to do with her. But meanwhile on January 17 William had written Henry that he had met her and been much impressed by her brilliant mind and style of writing. On the 20th Henry wrote again from London: "Receive from me . . . a word of warning about Vernon Lee. I hope you won't throw yourselves [he did not mean a love-affair because the plural included William's wife] into her arms—and I am sorry you offered to go and see her (after she wrote to you) *first*." Henry had once befriended her, but he had been told that she had satirized him in a book called *Vanitas*. He had not read it and did not intend to, but he was greatly upset about it—he said because of her bad taste and ingratitude, but it was clear that his vanity was deeply wounded too; he begged William not to hint to Miss Lee that he, Henry, had even mentioned the subject. "But don't caress her—not only on this ground but because she is as dangerous and uncanny as she is intelligent—which is saying a

great deal. . . . At any rate draw it mild with her on the question
of friendship. She's a tiger-cat!" He felt sure that William, as his
brother, would agree on her "bad taste in her putting me *en scène*
(and the whole treachery of private relations of the procédé) a
thing to be judged as, on her part, *deterring*, or at any rate with a
hundred attenuations." The half-incoherent sentence evidenced his
emotional state of mind.

Of course William promptly read the book, and then wrote Henry
that he found it "clever" and not as malicious as Henry seemed to
think. Nevertheless he rebuked Miss Lee—to Henry's further embarrassment and vexation—telling her that her using a friend in such
an objective, detached way, void of all "sympathetic considerations
which usually govern human intercourse . . . has quite quenched
my desire to pay you another visit." This provoked such a tearful
response from the "tiger-cat" that William immediately forgave her:
"Your note wipes away the affront as far as I am concerned, only
you must never, *never*, NEVER, do such a thing again in any future
book! It is too serious a matter." When Henry heard of this exchange, he said he did not "find her note at all convincing—she is
doubtless sorry to be disapproved of in high quarters." He never
forgave her.

Actually, Miss Lee's appraisal of Henry James, disguised in
Vanitas as the novelist Jarvase Marion, contained observations like
those William himself had made in letters to his wife in 1883 and
1889. William was perhaps trying to pacify Henry by saying it was
not malicious; but whether maliciously intended or not, it was so
revealing, that it could not help deeply wounding Henry's *amour
propre*.

IV

Of course Vernon Lee's satire on Henry James was a caricature,
and caricatures always magnify partial truth in disregard of the
whole. His relations with William were often frustrating to both
brothers, though the blame did not always rest with Henry—as is
evidenced in William's going off on a walking tour during Henry's
visit to him in Switzerland the previous summer. Though he had
physically removed himself from his family, Henry James never
cut the strong emotional ties which bound him to his parents and

brothers and sister. He was now deeply attached to William's whole family, and he planned to visit them in Florence in the spring when the city, in his estimation, would be at its best. But both Peggy and Tweedy fell ill, in February, and their mother nearly exhausted her strength in nursing them. William meanwhile decided to place Harry in a small school near Munich for the coming summer months, and took him to Munich in time to enroll him on March 1.

When Henry heard of the illness of the children, and of William's debate over whether to take his family to Switzerland or Germany after leaving Italy, he felt like starting immediately to Florence to talk with his brother. William had been designing an urn for his sister's ashes, to be inscribed in Florence, and Henry approved William's designs and repeatedly thanked him for his efforts. On March 13 he wrote: "Weary and worn must Alice indeed be with the younger children's ills. She has my sympathy. . . . Is it out of the question or not worth thinking of, that you should come to *England* for the rest of the time (after leaving Italy,) till you sail?" He offered to help find a furnished house or lodgings, and assist in any other way he could to make the summer pleasant for all of them.

William had meanwhile arrived back in Florence on March 13 to find a letter from Münsterberg written while he was convalescing from diphtheria. William cabled the Münsterbergs to occupy his house while theirs was being fumigated. "I was surprised but also pleased," he wrote, "that you had Wesselhoeft [a doctor in Cambridge]. The prejudice against homeopathy is so strong amongst our doctors that I didn't conceive of an M.D. like yourself having even social relations with one. I however was brought up in a homeopathic family, and am as sure as I am of anything in the world that infinitesimal doses of their remedies are *effective*. The trouble is that they are men of one idea; and what with their narrowness, and the gross ignorance on the part of orthodox doctors of things that *they* know, there is no such thing as an all-round *physician* to be had—only sectarians. Wesselhoeft is a noble man, and I am right glad for his sake that you have had him." Dr. Wesselhoeft had not been able to save little Herman, but William said he would never forget his "devotion to the case."

Munich had given William great enjoyment: "after 6 months of this debilitated Florence, to breathe the strong smoky transalpine air, and to mingle with the strong German race and hear the deep bass voices again" had given him new life. In Munich he also "saw

Stumpf a good deal—an honest kindly man, and a clear headed one, for whom I have a real affection." But all the interruptions had prevented any serious reading, and James was already wondering how soon he could persuade his wife to return to America. "If I consulted my own personal interest I should go in August [alone] and have some quiet lonesome weeks of *recueillement* [musing] and meditation on my next year's work in my empty house. But conscience makes cowards of us all; and the 'sense of sin' that would come over me on leaving my wife behind to manage single-handed all our impedimenta, children, new servants [Alice would take three Swiss maids back with her], etc., will I think make me stay to the end."

Henry thought that William was leaving Florence too early, and William retorted on March 17: "I don't wonder that it seems strange to you that we should be leaving here just in the glory of the year. *Your* view of Italy is that of the tourist; and that is really the only way to *enjoy* any place. Ours is that of the resident in whom the sweet decay breathed in for six months has produced a sort of physiological craving for a change to robuster air. One ends by craving one's own more permanent attitude, and a country whose language I can speak and where I can settle into my own necessary work (which has been awfully prevented here of late), without a guilty sense that I am neglecting the claims of pictures and monuments. . . . In short, Italy has well served its purpose by us and we shall be eternally grateful. But we have no further use for it, and the spring is also beautiful in lands that will [be] fresher to our senses. There are moments when the Florentine debility becomes really hateful to one, and I don't see how the Lorings and others can come and make their home with it."

However, the Jameses did not immediately leave Florence when their lease on the apartment expired on March 31. They now had many friends in the city, who insisted on socializing at a furious rate as their time for departure drew nearer. And then, as William wrote Stumpf three weeks later from Switzerland (having finally escaped the Florentine hospitality), "a pair of young American friends came and *had a baby!!!* in our apartment, there being no other convenient place for the event to take place in. Fortunately my wife came away . . . and left them in possession—'mother and child well.'"

One of the last things that William did in Florence was to visit the cemetery in which Frank Duveneck had erected a statue of his own making for his wife, the Lizzie Boott to whom William had read Browning in the summer of 1869. When Henry saw it later he pronounced it a failure (Duveneck was really a painter, not a sculptor), but William wrote the artist-widower on April 13: "It will last after you are gone, as one of the monuments of Florence which people go to see. . . . Good bye, my dear fellow, I leave on Saturday night. I will write to F.B. [Francis Boott, Lizzie's father] my impression of the monument, and I shall hope within this year to see you at our home in Cambridge."

On April 15 Alice was not yet ready to leave, but William, impatient to have Billy resume his studies in the Cérésole home in Vevey, where he had stayed the previous summer, went on with his second son ahead of his wife and the two younger children. After getting Billy settled in Vevey and visiting some sick cousins in Geneva, William then returned to Meggen bei Luzern, where Alice and the children were waiting for him. William had learned that his oldest son, recently entered in the small private school in Munich, was not prepared for the Gymnasium; therefore, as he wrote Stumpf in the letter quoted above, "we concluded that the whole family had better return together in the summer to America. It is the *comfortable* decision, and we have been happy in it ever since. I believe that from the point of view of education, the best possible thing for American boys would be to pass the years from *six to ten* in German schools. At Harry's age, however, the advantages of only one single year are doubtful. . . . We are going to spend most of the summer in England, and have taken the road through Switzerland rather than through Tyrol for economical reasons. This means that my wife, and possibly I, will not have the chance of meeting you and Mrs. Stumpf this summer, which we both regret. . . . We are in this heavenly spot, with the trees all in bloom about us, and shall stay a fortnight at least . . . I am glad to have said good-bye to the sweet rottenness of Italy. . . ."

From Meggen William had also written his brother, then in Paris, of the present plans, and on the 26th Henry responded: "It's delightful to have something *settled* by your letter from Meggen, which gives wings to my impatience to join you. I shall leave this place for Lucerne—your distance from which is not sufficient to prevent our easy intercourse if I stay at one of the hotels there—preferable for me to one of the pensions of your suburb—on Monday

night next May 1st, in all *probability*. If I can't get off that day I
will the next—and shall promptly let you know. I suppose some of
the Lucerne hotels are open by May 1st. Your description of your
Lake is unspeakably alluring." Henry had also recently seen his two
other traveling sisters-in-law as they passed through London on their
way back to America. His encounter with Carrie had been as awkward and frustrating as William's, but he liked Mary Holton [Bob's
wife] "extremely—and relations with her are very possible and
comfortable."

On May 8 Alice decided to make a trip by herself, which William
described to her mother next day, addressing her as "Sweet Belle-
mère": "Alice, wonderful to relate, has started off all alone to
Munich to pay a visit to her first-born. Such is the power of maternal
love that she started up suddenly without misgiving or hesitation,
and resolved on it three or four days ago, and did it yesterday. She
insisted on going third class, in spite of the fact that it would only
save $2.50 on both journeys, that she would have a straight wooden
back to her seat and nothing to rest her elbows on for 12 hours, etc.
But, from this misguided Ideal, Providence rescued her (*I* could not)
by showing her at the station that she would have to spend the night
at a hotel in Zurich, there being no third class on through-trains. I
mention this only to show the spirit of which she is composed. We
always travel third class in Switzerland; but for a woman alone, on
an all-day journey it seems to me uncalled-for economy. The Swiss
trains are as clean and decent as one could desire and open throughout like ours, making an entirely different thing of the journey.
Well A's departure leaves a sort of emptiness which makes me turn
to you as the next best substitute, remote as you are."

One proof of the complete mutual trust of William and his
mother-in-law was the way he would turn to her for help in his
arguments with her daughter. They had been arguing now about
when to return home. "I *must* be back at least a fortnight before
the 26th Sept. (when College begins) to prepare for my work; and
I *ought* for the interests of my total character and standing, to return
as early as Aug. 5 and go to Chicago to the Psychical Congress, and
also to see the Exhibition [World's Fair] and meet the men of my
sort who are to be there. Alice on her part says that it is her and
the children's duty to drink to the last possible drop of Europe, and
not to sail earlier than Sept. 14, which would bring the boys home
on the eve of their school opening. Accordingly we have engaged

passage on the Pavonia for that date." He suspected that "what weighs most on Alice is a real dread (I am sorry to say) of Cambridge housekeeping, and no feeling of satisfaction in our house, and she hates to face what to her is an evil day. The house is to me such a luxury, and its calm wide spaces and outlook will be to me such a haven of peace after four months more of the fever and fret of our consolidated nursery-existence with Tweedy rousing us every morning between 5 and 6, and Peggy 'hanging' on all day, that I am quite unable to enter into Alice's state of mind. . . ."

If Mrs. Gibbens agreed with him, William hoped she would drop a hint (without giving away his having suggested it) that might budge the stubborn Alice—"hold out in your next letter some alluring picture of the sweetness of Cambridge in the latter ⅔ of September, which may soften her heart. If on the contrary you sympathize with her, as you very likely will, all I beg is that you will not actively write anything to encourage her in her resolution, for I should like it to be a fair fight between us two." Apparently it was not unfair to get his mother-in-law to fight on his side. But he was probably right in saying that the older boys "have but one desire and that is to get home; and they will (I fear) be impatient and listless and 'on her hands' all the time, when we get to England with nothing to do. . . ."

"Don't gather from this," William continued in his letter to Mrs. Gibbens, "that I am 'discouraged' about our trip. *Quite* the reverse! It has been very costly; but it has done us all lots of good and I wouldn't have it otherwise. It has had a *minus* side in the fact that we are primarily and essentially a *nursery*, with *adults* attached, and I don't think that my truest vocation is to be an appendage to a nursery. . . . Alice is rejuvenated mentally. The boys have a greatly enlarged horizon, Peggy gabbles french like an ash-shoot, and both she and Tweedy are *entirely* well just now. She has improved on the whole more than any of us, and now that Billy and the continuous opportunity of quarrel which he presented are removed, she has become really a charming little companion." Several pages later: "The day is cold and cloudy and a fire is lighted in the stove. Tweedy is now asleep in the adjoining room, Peggy comes in from a walk with a couple of the ladies of the house, and when asked for a message says 'I send 3 kisses and 100 loves.' "

Two days later William was still feeling lonesome for Alice, and began a letter to his sister-in-law Mary Gibbens Salter as a substitute for talking to his wife. He was oppressed by his nurse-maid duties and most of his letter was about the children and their mother. After a succession of digestive upsets, Tweedy was now thriving. Peg had "become a little trump, though in all her mental acts, of questioning, proposing, demanding and enunciating, she is . . . more remarkable for ponderosity and momentum than for the lightness and grace usually deemed characteristic of her sex." William had to interrupt the letter to give her a "reading" lesson and did not resume it until Sunday, the 14th of May. On this date Alice was still absent, but was to return on the morrow, and William planned to go as far as Zurich to meet her. With so many friends and acquaintances in the region, such as a Mrs. Evans, Miss Gardiner, and Harry at Lucerne, "that is the only way to get her an hour to myself."

Whether or not Mrs. Gibbens exerted influence on her daughter, William did win at least a compromise in his arguments. First of all, Alice agreed to leave the three children (Harry was still in Germany) in Switzerland with the Cérésole family at Vevey while she and William visited Henry in London. After stopping in Paris a few days, during which William was disappointed in his failure to find François Pillon, they arrived in London, unencumbered, on June 17. Writing Pillon to tell him how sorry he was to have missed him, William added: "Our three young children are all in Switzerland, the older boy in Munich, and my wife and I are like middle-aged omnibus-horses let loose in a pasture. The first time we have had a holiday together for 15 years. I feel like a barrel without hoops! We shall be here in England for a month at least. After that everything is uncertain."

William also just barely missed seeing his old friend Shadworth Hodgson. On June 23 he knocked on Hodgson's door and was informed that he had left England. What so disgusted him was that four evenings before, about 9:30 p.m., he and Alice had passed Hodgson's house and seen his library lighted up. Alice had said, "Let's ring and see him." But it was late and a warm night, and William feared that Hodgson might be "in tropical costume, safe for the night"; so they did not ring. But in spite of this one disappointment, they had a glorious second honeymoon in England.

After a month of their children-less vacation, during which Alice agreed to change their sailing to August 24 on the *Cephalonia*, the parents returned to Vers-chez-les-Blanc where they had stayed the previous summer. There William wrote to his colleagues and friends in philosophy and made plans for the coming academic year. Palmer had not arranged the courses for the Department of Philosophy the way William had recommended, and he thought Münsterberg had not sufficiently asserted his opinions. But he was more concerned with another subject—about which he had corresponded with Münsterberg at great length—the founding of a new journal to be sponsored by the American Psychological Association. The difficulty was that G. Stanley Hall had been editing a journal of his own, which he was reluctant to merge with the new publication. Also professors of psychology at Columbia, Yale, Cornell, and other places each wanted to edit or dictate the policy for the new magazine. On July 29 William wrote Münsterberg a long letter detailing how the project might be carried out with fairness to all parties, but the rivalry continued. On August 11, still in (or near) Lausanne, William wrote Münsterberg again: "I have already written to [James Mark] Baldwin and [James McKeen] Cattell about the Journal, asking Baldwin to send the letter to you, so, to avoid repetition, I will be very brief on that matter now. I am not altogether surprised that you have all come to grief in your negotiations with Hall, his personal psychology is a very queer and tortuous one. Containing, however, elements of sincere devotion to truth. He hates clearness—clear formulas, clear statements, clear understandings; and mystification of some kind seems never far distant from everything he does. Yet I think he does not mean to deceive, nor is he a liar in any vulgar meaning of the term. He shrinks with an instinctive terror from any explanation that is definitive and irrevocable, and hence comes to say & do things that leave an avenue open to retreat—at bottom it is connected with timidity in him—as a *dreamer* he is bold, when it comes to acting, he wills-and-wills-not. But what I least like in his journal and other writings of his as President [of the Psychological Society] is the religious cant he finds it necessary to throw in. Yet in a certain sense even that is not insincerely meant! He has too complicated a mind!"

Baldwin had asked James if he would accept the editorship—if offered to him—of the journal, if it were founded, and he had replied, James continued to Münsterberg, that he could not be any kind of editor, nor could he contribute money to the support of the journal—aside, of course, from a yearly subscription. "This year has been a perfectly ruinous one to me financially, making a far worse hole in my capital than I ever thought possible, or than I ever should have consented to in advance, and I must 'lie low' and live within my income for many years to come." Then, closing on a personal note, "both myself and wife are eager to see you again and hear all the gossip of your year from your own mouths. She starts tomorrow for London, I follow in 9 days, on the 24th we sail."

These plans went according to schedule, and early in September the James family, with the three Swiss maids, arrived without mishap in Boston. Alice had made purchases which she resented paying duty on (she always did, honest as she was in every other way), and she managed to smuggle a few things in. Not long after they were resettled at 95 Irving Street they entertained the great German physicist and physiologist Herman Ludwig Ferdinand von Helmholtz and his wife at a tea to which distinguished people of Cambridge and Boston were invited. William decided not to go to Chicago, and it was too late to open the Chocorua house for the whole family, but he and Billy went up to close it for the winter "and get a sniff of the place," William wrote Henry.

Coming back to America was no less an emotional wrench than it had always been. "The Salters have a noble hill with such an outlook! and a very decent little house and barn," William wrote Henry on September 22. "But oh! the difference from Switzerland, the thin grass and ragged waysides, the poverty-stricken land, and sad American sunlight over all—sad because so empty. There is a strange thinness and femininity hovering over all America, so different from the stoutness and masculinity of land and air and everything in Switzerland and England, that the coming back makes one feel strangely sad and hardens one in the resolution never to go away again unless one can go to end one's days. Such a divided soul is very bad!"

William, who had so many times twitted Henry on his preference for Europe, now wrote: "To you, who now have real practical relations and a place in the old world, I should think there was no necessity of ever coming back again. But Europe has been made what it is by men staying in their homes and fighting stubbornly generation after generation for all the beauty, comfort and order that they have got—one must abide and do the same. As England struck me newly and differently last time, so America now—force and directness in the people, but a terrible grimness, more ugliness than I ever realized in things, and a greater weakness in nature's beauty such as it is." Later (January 24, 1894) William James wrote to Carl Stumpf: "One should not be a cosmopolitan, one's soul becomes 'disintegrated,' as Janet would say. Parts of it remain in different places, and the whole of it is nowhere. One's native land seems foreign. It is not wholly a good thing, and I think I suffer from it." Such was the 'wisdom' the successful American psychologist had brought back from his sabbatical year in Europe.

CHAPTER XX Intimate Philosopher

A philosophy is the expression of a man's intimate character, and all

definitions of the universe are but the deliberately adopted reactions

of human characters upon it.   —W.J., A Pluralistic Universe

I

THE BIG, SQUARE, QUIET HOUSE on Irving Street was not as soothing and peaceful after the return of the James family in September 1893 as William in Europe had nostalgically dreamed it would be. It was a relief not to be cooped up with the children in two hotel rooms, and he did not mind their running up and down the stairs and calling to each other in their delight over being home, or the noise of the maids in their household chores. But the social whirl was giddier than it had been in that last week in Florence. Friends and neighbors dropped in at all times of the day, and there were invitations to dinners and teas to be accepted or tactfully declined.

The tea for the Helmholtzes required frantic preparations and a disrupted household for several days. And Alice and William had scarcely been home a week before F. W. H. Myers, the leading "psychic research" man in England, arrived on September 9 as a house guest, bringing with him Richard Hodgson, the secretary of the American S.P.R., and Mrs. Piper, whom Myers later called "that insipid Prophetess, that tiresome channel of communication between the human and the divine." But of course Mrs. James could not permit her to leave without holding a séance in the library, the seeress resting her head on a pillow on the table in front of the fireplace, with the saintly Henry James Sr. looking on benevolently from his portrait over the mantel. And Myers did not at that time find Mrs. Piper "insipid," for after returning to England he wrote William exuberantly: "Mrs. Piper is all right—and the universe is all right—and people will soon pay up more money to S.P.R.—and an eternity of happiness and glory awaits you . . . and the dear spirits are hovering around us in the Summer Land."

To his recent student Dickinson S. Miller, now studying in Germany, James described his state of mind in a letter dated November 19: "I have found the work of recommencing teaching unexpectedly formidable after our year of gentlemanly irresponsibility. I seem to have forgotten everything, especially psychology, and the subjects themselves have become so paltry and insignificant-seeming that each lecture has appeared a ghastly farce. Of late things are getting more real; but the experience brings startlingly near to one the wild desert of old-age which lies ahead. . . ." Although James was free of the psychological laboratory, and he reported to Miller that Münsterberg was "going *splendidly*" with it, he was still teaching a graduate seminar in psychology, which he had announced would be entirely devoted to mental pathology, "embracing a review of the principal forms of abnormal or exceptional mental life." He was also, for the first time, teaching a course on cosmology, described in the departmental announcement as "a study of the fundamental conceptions of natural science with special reference to the theories of evolution and materialism."

Soon after Myers returned to England, the British Society for Psychical Research invited William James to become its president—largely honorary, except for a Presidential address at the annual meeting. James declined on the excuse of his poor health, which provoked this response from Myers on November 16, 1893: "I am very sorry that you are feeling ill; but a touch of something is mixed with my sympathy that I may as well have out. It seems to me that your mental and physical disorganisation and decay is never by any chance perceptible to anyone but *yourself;* and, moreover, that when you are actually in the presence of friends you are able to make an effort (if such it be) which presents you to them as a source of wisdom and delight—'as light and light communicable'; which makes them rather wish that they were even as you, than grieve over any hidden malaise within you—and yet it seems to me that you lack one touch more of *doggedness* which would render you of even more helpfulness in the world than you are. Why on earth should you not in *public* matters act upon other people's view of you and not on your own? We all wanted you to place your name at our head—we should have been satisfied, however little you had actually *done;* why not have let us have our way? To *underrate* one's own importance in the eyes of others may be (though rarer) as great a nuisance to them as it is to *overrate* it. We must not push you further now; but I warn you that we shall ask you again another year, and that unless we have evidence to your decrepitude from someone besides yourself, we shall then take it somewhat unkind if you won't oblige us!"

A few weeks later James received a letter from Pearsall Smith informing him that the Council of the British S.P.R. still hoped that he would accept the presidency, whereupon he cabled December 17, "James accepts," and then wrote Myers: ". . . They are bent on having a King Log, so they shall be humored. I had no idea, when I got your first invitation, that it was a matter of the slightest real *importance.* . . . To tell the truth I supposed the true inwardness of the offer to lie in your friendly wish, yours and the Sidgwicks', to pay me a compliment; which friendly wish I thought almost as well acknowledged by 'declined with thanks' as by 'accepted.' "

Since William's wife took a lively interest in all psychical research, she was elated over this honor for her husband and promptly wrote Henry about it. On December 29 he replied flatteringly, as he always did about any distinction for his brother: "I greatly rejoice in Alice's announcement (which you, William, coyly don't mention) of the presidency of the S.P.R. I hope it's all honour and kudos and pleasantness, without a tax of botheration. . . ." Henry wished he could give "good tidings" of his own "ascensory movement," but he was having difficulty in getting his plays produced and he was discouraged, though determined to wage "this war ferociously for one year more." He did not say so at this time, but he was also alarmed over the decline in sales of his published novels. It almost looked as if William's humorous offer to support him at Chocorua might need to be made in earnest—not that Henry's discouragement had become so acute that he could even entertain such an idea.

William himself was in such low spirits during the autumn that he had resorted once more to an unidentified "mind-curer," probably a Christian Science practitioner in Boston. By the time he wrote Myers that he accepted the presidency of the S.P.R., he could report that his state of mind had been "revolutionized" since his first refusal. "I had a pretty bad spell, and know now a new kind of melancholy. It is barely possible that the recovery may be due to a mind-curer with whom I tried eighteen sittings. What makes me think so is that I am enjoying an altogether new kind of *sleep*, or rather an old kind which I have been bereft of for so many years that I had forgotten its existence, and considered myself sleeping as well as I ought to, and told her so, when I went to her, saying my only trouble was my mind." Two friends of his had also been treated with great success. "It is a good deal of a puzzle. I should like to get this woman into a lunatic asylum for two months, and have every case of chronic delusional insanity in the house tried by her. That would be a real test, and if successful would *have* to produce some effect. I may possibly bring it about yet!"

Whether or not the mind-curer was responsible for the improvement, James did not relapse into the depression of the early part of the first semester after his return. On January 24, 1894, during his intersemester recess, he wrote Stumpf: "I found it very hard to begin teaching again. I had been rather melancholy all summer, but it grew acute with my lectures. *I* shrank to nothing, *psychology* shrank to nothing,—etc. It passed away, however, and now not a trace of it is left. But it has taught me the lesson that fifteen months is too long a vacation for a man like me to take. Teaching is such an artificial discipline that one loses the habit of it immediately, and seems to forget all that one ever knew."

Stumpf had just accepted a professorship of philosophy and directorship of the psychological laboratory at the University of Berlin, on which James, of course, congratulated him, and noted with satisfaction that he would not have to take personal charge of the laboratory. "I may say that I myself enjoy inward peace and a good professorial conscience for the first time, now that Münsterberg has taken charge of the entire experimental field." He was still highly pleased with Münsterberg's performance at Harvard, but now feared that he would return to Germany to accept a professorship there.

Earlier James had written Stumpf to invite him to join the Editorial Committee of *The Psychological Review*. Negotiations with G. Stanley Hall had broken down completely, and the American Association of Psychologists had gone ahead with plans to start its own journal, to be edited jointly by Baldwin of Princeton and Cattell of Columbia. The editors had asked James to invite Stumpf to join the Editorial Committee and to contribute articles, or "give them timely advice about German books or news." It was a bad time, James admitted, to start a new magazine, because "the country is groaning under the worst financial depression it has ever known. . . . Our University has even had to dismiss instructors; but our *own* income is, so far, not reduced, although we are trying to spend as little as possible in order to repair the frightful ravages left by our European year." The only effect the financial depression actually had on William James was to make him more acutely sympathetic with reform movements in politics, and later a supporter of William Jennings Bryan and the "free silver" faction when Bryan ran for the Presidency.

James himself was elected to two presidencies in 1893. At the annual meeting of the American Association of Psychologists in December (like many learned societies it met during the academic Christmas recess) he was also chosen president of this society. The 1894 meeting was held at Princeton, where William wrote his brother Henry on December 29: "I have been here for three days at my co-psychologist Baldwin's house, presiding over a meeting of the American Association of Psychologists, which has proved a very solid and successful affair. Strange to say, we are getting to be veterans, and the brunt of the discussions was borne by former students of mine. It is a very healthy movement. Alice is with me, the weather is frosty clear and cold, touching zero this A.M., and the country robed in snow. Princeton is a beautiful place. . . ."

William James called his presidential address, "On the Knowing of Things Together" (later printed as "The Tigers in India"), which began: "There are two ways of knowing things, knowing them immediately or intuitively, and knowing them conceptually or representatively. Altho such things as the white paper before our eyes can be known intuitively, most of the things we know, the tigers now in India, for example, or the scholastic system of philosophy, are known only representatively or symbolically." This distinction in the different ways of *knowing*, which is too complicated for analysis here, was another indication of the direction in which James's philosophical thinking was taking him, toward the *naïve* or common-sense realism which would culminate in his Pragmatism, Pluralism, and Radical Empiricism, which might be reduced to the simplification: knowing by experience is better than knowing *about*.

II

Psychology as theory or "pure knowledge" interested William James less and less, but he was so eager to use his own knowledge to alleviate human suffering and unhappiness that he was willing to seize upon any means to apply it humanistically. Most contemporary psychologists were skeptical of "psychic research," but James saw in it a possible means of relieving people of delusions, disorders of personality, and such mysterious pains as he had suffered in his early manhood and his sister Alice all her life. It was not intellectual curiosity, therefore, nor even his desire to find proof of immortality (though he was not indifferent to this question) that made him willing to witness Mrs. Piper's trances, investigate for the American Society for Psychical Research such phenomena as clairvoyance, levitation, the "astral body," etc., and listen to Myers's credulous prattle of the "Summer Land" of spirits, but mainly his hope for eventual therapy for the neuroses of men and women.

In the spring of 1894 the medical profession in Massachusetts succeeded in getting a bill introduced in the Legislature to require all persons practicing mental therapy to pass a medical examination and be licensed—actually, it meant that only legally registered M.D.s could practice on either mind or body. The Christian Science movement, with headquarters in Boston, was growing rapidly, and the bill was specifically aimed at "Science" practitioners, but it would apply to all "faith" or "mental healers" of any kind. Though James had recently been helped by a "mind-curer," or thought he might have been, he was still skeptical of their claims; nevertheless, he thought they had a right to experiment, and they might after all be able to effect cures, or at least the amelioration of neurotic symptoms. How could society find out unless these practitioners were permitted to try? Consequently, he wrote a letter to the Boston *Evening Transcript* (published March 24, 1894) in which he argued in this way:

> I will confine myself to a class of diseases with which my occupation has made me somewhat conversant. I mean the diseases of the nervous system and the mind. . . . Of all the new agencies that our day has seen, there is but one that tends steadily to assume a more and more commanding importance, and that is the agency of the patient's mind itself. Whoever can produce effects there holds the key of the situation in a number of morbid conditions of which we do not yet know the extent; for systematic experiments in this direction are in their merest infancy. They began in Europe fifteen years ago, when the medical world so tardily admitted the facts of hypnotism to be true; and in this country they have been carried on in a much bolder and more radical fashion by all those 'mind-curers' and 'Christian

Scientists' with whose results the public, and even the profession, are growing gradually more familiar.

I assuredly hold no brief for any of these healers, and must confess that my intellect has been unable to assimilate their theories, so far as I have heard them given. But their *facts* are patent and startling; and anything that interferes with the multiplication of such facts, and with our freest opportunity of observing and studying them, will, I believe, be a public calamity. The law now proposed will so interfere, simply because the mind-curers will not take the examinations. . . . Nothing would please some of them better than such a taste of imprisonment as might, by the public outcry it would occasion, bring the law rattling down upon the ears of the mandarins who should have it enacted.

And whatever one may think of the narrowness of the mind-curers, their logical position is impregnable. They are proving by the most brilliant new results that the therapeutic relation may be what we can at present describe only as a relation of one person to another person; and they are consistent in resisting to the uttermost any legislation that would make 'examinable' information the root of medical virtue, and hamper the free play of personal force and affinity by mechanically imposed conditions.

Although holding an M.D. degree himself, James did not believe that the doctors were as "scientific" as they thought they were. Not only was medical science still very primitive, so that the licensed M.D. might himself do a great deal of harm in his ignorance or ineptitude, but the very spirit of science was to make a fair examination of all phenomena: "mental therapeutics should *not* be stamped out, but studied, and its laws ascertained." Whether it was the force of James's arguments or the political influence of the Christian Scientists themselves, the bill was tabled and not brought up again until four years later, when he was asked to testify before the Legislative committee considering the bill. He not only expanded his previous arguments but accused the medical profession of Massachusetts of having adopted "the fiercely partisan attitude of a powerful trade-union, demanding legislation against the competition of the 'scabs.' " Addressing the Committee he said: "You are not to ask yourselves whether these mind-curers do really achieve the successes that are claimed. It is enough for you as legislators to ascertain that a large number of our citizens . . . are persuaded that a valuable new department of medical experience is by them opening up. Here is a purely medical question, regarding which our General Court, not being a well-spring and source of medical virtue, not having any private test of therapeutic truth, must remain strictly neutral under penalty of making the confusion worse."

Some doctors, including his friend James Putnam, approved James's stand, though Putnam had to confess that he, and the "liberal" doctors whom he knew, did not have as much sympathy for the Christian Scientists as James and were more inclined to see "the harm that they sometimes do than you are." In a note to Putnam, dated March 3, 1898, James predicted that he would be "banded with the spiritists, faith-curers, magnetic healers," and other "strange affinities," and he was quite right. He would not only be hated for the remainder of his life by the medical profession in Massachusetts but would also be held in suspicion by a number of psychologists and other "natural scientists." In the scientific world he damaged his reputation by what he regarded as his support of science, i.e., men's freedom to pursue knowledge wherever it might be found. The "cures" claimed by the mental healers could not be judged by contemporary scientists because they were still raw experience which science had not yet found a way to test. But to examine *experiences* there must be experiences to examine, which there would not be if all Christian Scientists had to become licensed physicians.

James himself was, of course, trying to find a way to evaluate the claims of the "cures" scientifically. In the mid-1890s his chief activity in the field of psychology was with "psychical research." One of his projects was completing a census of hallucinations in the United States for the British S.P.R. This necessitated his corresponding with a large number of people who said they had seen ghosts, witnessed levitation, seen "doubles," dreamed of future events, etc. Sometimes he visited these persons and made a record of his interviews. And he required the students in his psychology seminar to make investigations or conduct experiments of their own.

In the academic year 1893–1894 Münsterberg was very enthusiastic about a most unusual student in his laboratory. It was Gertrude Stein, then enrolled at Radcliffe. James invited her to join his seminar in 1894–1895; she later wrote about her experiences there. She remembered that one student was investigating the psychology of religious conversion, another was studying the incubation of chickens, and Leon Solomons was working on problems of consciousness. Miss Stein and Solomons worked together on the experiments and published a joint report on "Normal Motor Automatism" in the *Psychological Review*, September 1896. They had investigated the effect of repetition on memory, the length of the "attention span," the effects of fatigue on attention and memory, and similar subjects.

These experiments had significance for psychical research because James was trying to find the relationship between the conscious and unconscious, and the point at which the separation took place, sometimes causing a "split personality." One of the means of studying this subject was experiments in automatic motor action, such as automatic writing, when the muscles (such as the hand and fingers in writing) perform actions unrelated to what the conscious mind is apparently paying full attention too. Solomons wrote the report of these experiments, combining his notes with Miss Stein's, and as her biographer John Malcolm Brinnin remarks, "In this way Gertrude made her first appearance in print. 'It was very interesting,' she wrote of the report, 'because the method of writing to be afterwards developed in *Three Lives* and *Making of Americans* already shows itself.' "

But at the time of her participation, Miss Stein found some of the experiments devised by William James distinctly unpleasant, as she indicated in one of her reports, referring to herself in the third person:

> . . . she finds herself with a complicated apparatus strapped across her breast to register her breathing, her finger imprisoned in a steel machine and her arm thrust immovably into a big glass tube. She is surrounded by a group of earnest youths who carefully watch the silent record of the automatic pen on the slowly revolving drum.
>
> Strange fancies begin to crowd upon her, she feels that the silent pen is writing on and on forever. Her record is there she cannot escape it and the group about her begin to assume the shape of mocking fiends gloating over her imprisoned misery. Suddenly she starts, they have suddenly loosed a metronome directly behind her, to observe the effect, so now the morning's work is over.

Miss Stein did not, however, believe that the experiments in which she participated actually proved that completely automatic writing took place in them, and she partly disagreed with Solomons' report. But she also conducted experiments of her own on college students, which she summarized in this way:

> . . . one of the things I did was testing reaction of the average college student in a state of normal activity and in the state of fatigue

induced by their examinations. I was supposed to be interested in their reactions but I soon found that I was not but instead that I was enormously interested in the types of their characters that is what I even then thought of as the bottom nature of them, and when in May 1896 I wrote my half of the report of these experiments I expressed these results as follows: In these descriptions it will be readily observed that habits of attention are reflexes of the complete character of the individual.

Although this made no contribution toward solving the problem that especially concerned William James in 1896, it is interesting that Miss Stein's conclusion exactly parallels his own philosophy, which he believed expresses "a man's intimate character." This is not to suggest that he influenced Gertrude Stein's conclusion, for it, too, was no doubt in harmony with *her* character. And just as it was William James's character to apply his psychological observations to finding methods of relieving human suffering, so it was Gertrude Stein's to apply her observations to the creation of a new type of fiction with a literary style that resembled the stream-of-consciousness of simple people (as in *Three Lives*) or automatic writing in some of her later books.

III

William James's "will to believe" has already been anticipated many times in this narrative of his life, because at least from the year (1868) when he first discovered Renouvier, and possibly earlier, he was always searching for faiths which would make his life easier, and then, as a teacher and psychologist, trying to make life easier for other people. The address by this title was first delivered at a "Summer School of Ethics" in Plymouth, Massachusetts in the summer of 1895 and repeated to the Philosophical Clubs of Yale and Brown Universities in the spring of 1896; it was published the following year in a collection of essays called *The Will to Believe and Other Essays in Popular Philosophy*. The term "popular philosophy" is significant, for most of his publications of this decade after *The Principles of Psychology* (and even parts of that great work) were intended to help people apply theories in psychology and philosophy to their common problems of human existence, or, to paraphrase his next major address, to make life worth living ("Is Life Worth Living?").

The major objective of "The Will to Believe" was to combat the agnosticism fostered by contemporary scientists and philosophical determinists. They argued that no one has a right to a belief that is not based on objective, scientifically verifiable evidence. If evidence is unobtainable, then belief should be held in suspense. An English philosopher, W. K. Clifford, had maintained that it is a man's *duty* not to believe until such evidence can be found. James admitted that this doctrine might be all right for the physical sciences, but he thought that in the field of religion and morality it is not desirable or often even possible to suspend action, and unless one has some faith in his choice of action, the psychological effects may be very harmful.

> The thesis I defend is, briefly stated, this: *Our passional nature not only lawfully may, but must, decide an option between propositions, whenever it is a genuine option* [i.e., one that has practical consequences if acted upon—or even if not acted upon] *that cannot by its nature be decided on intellectual grounds: for to say, under such circumstances, 'Do not decide, but leave the question open,' is itself a passional decision,—just like deciding yes or no,—and is attended with the same risk of losing the truth.*

This argument, and especially the emphasis on *willful* believing, was easily misunderstood. James did not use such extravagant language as Emerson, who declared in *Nature:* "Build therefore your own world. As fast as you conform your life to the pure idea in your mind, that will unfold its great proportions. A corresponding revolution in things will attend the influx of the spirit." Probably by this Emerson meant only that a person who holds fast to a great ideal and tries to make it a reality can change the world to what he thinks it should be. This James meant too, and it was one aspect of his doctrine. The "truth" of the proposition, in other words, need not be judged in terms of the world (either physical or social) as it exists at any given time; that may not be the most desirable world for human life, and the mind of man is capable of changing it. This should be self-evident when one looks at history.

James did not mean that one can believe anything he *wishes* without regard to the laws of nature, which also include psychology. Yet he thought that agnosticism stifled action, and that everyone had a *right* to adopt a helpful or useful hypothesis; and if experience confirmed its practical value, then one might have increasing confidence, or *faith* in it. To some of his critics James admitted that he should have called his essay not "The Will to Believe" but "The *Right* to Believe." This might have avoided some of the misunderstanding, but there was more than a tinge of Emersonianism and even Christian Science attitudes in James's thinking. He did not, with the Christian Scientists, actually believe there was proof that mind has control over the body and the physical world, and yet he was not sure that it did not have. This is obvious in all his patient assembling of documents and case histories for the two psychical research societies.

There was some irony in James's dedicating the book *The Will to Believe* "To My Old Friend, CHARLES SANDERS PEIRCE, to whose philosophic comradeship in old times and to whose writings in more recent years I owe more incitement and help than I can express or repay." For several years James had been trying to get Peirce appointed to the Department of Philosophy at Harvard, and did manage to get some brief lecture engagements for him. But Peirce's symbolic logic was so far over the heads of the best mathematical and philosophical students at Harvard (even James admitted that he could not follow it) that he was an almost total failure as a teacher, and President Eliot would not consider employing him. During the second half of this decade Peirce was busy planning and outlining a series of some fifteen books to explain his ideas (his "system"), and William James repeatedly encouraged him, pledged his subscription to the books, and secretly gave money to Peirce under the fiction that he had collected it from well-wishers and admirers. This secret support of a man who was often near starvation continued until the end of James's life, and there are no documents more poignantly revealing of James's tender human sympathies than his voluminous correspondence with Charles Peirce. Knowing his friend's impracticality, he made out checks to be cashed only by Peirce's wife, and doled out funds so that they would last for a year. And yet he was always considerate of Peirce's feelings, and tried to keep him from becoming despondent. William James did all this partly because of friendship, but mainly because he knew Peirce to be a genius, one of the most original thinkers of his time, who deserved to be supported.

Peirce was not unappreciative of James's attempts to help him, though often impatient, but sentiment did not soften his criticism of

James's publications. His review of *The Principles of Psychology* in the *Nation* has already been mentioned. He wrote William that his dedication of *The Will to Believe* to him "gave me more delight than you would be apt to believe." But, "As to 'belief' and 'making up one's mind,' if they mean anything more than this, that we have a plan of procedure, and that according to that plan we will try a given description of behavior, I am inclined to think they do more harm than good. 'Faith,' and the sense that one will adhere consistently to a given line of conduct, is highly necessary in affairs. But if it means you are not going to be alert for indications that the moment has come to change your tactics, I think it ruinous in practice."

In the main, Peirce found his own doctrine "that everything is to be tested by its practical results [which] was the great text of my early papers . . ." behind James's arguments, but his conception of the test was more literally practical (scientifically verifiable) than James's, which tended toward subjective and "psychological" verification, that is, judged in terms of its pacification or healthy stimulation of the emotions. Eventually this difference would cause Peirce to deplore James's borrowing of his term "pragmatism" to explain his ideas, but this would never affect James's loyalty to Peirce.

For the remainder of his life William James would continue to give more comfort to the "spiritualists" of all varieties (Christians, Christian Scientists, "psychic researchers" like Frederic Myers, etc.) than he himself found in his own ideas. And yet the contrast between them and him was not simply the result of his metaphorical or ambiguous language, they interpreting it more literally than he: it was the result of an unresolved dilemma in his own life. He longed for a religion, for faith in a spiritual world existing back of or parallel to the visible material world. Yet as a scientist he could do no more than accumulate data and hope for verifiable proof. The difference between him and the agnostic scientist was only that he wanted to give the "spiritualists" time and opportunity to prove their contentions. He, too, really suspended judgment, but his hopes were with them; in fact he would not only encourage but help them all he could, though he could never take a stand with them and say "I absolutely believe."

James's Presidential Address to the British Society for Psychical Research (read in his absence at the 1896 meeting) was unerringly characteristic of his stance in the field of "psychic" phenomena. The

Society, he reported, had investigated the performances of mediums, reports of experiences with ghosts, claims of thought-transference, etc., without finding any positive proof of supernatural forces at work. All the Society had done was to assemble a "collection of documents that may hereafter be resorted to for testing the conclusions and hypotheses of *anybody*," and he thought that they would be "permanently important." Science may say, " 'Such things are simply impossible': yet, so long as the stories multiply in different lands, and so few are positively explained away, it is bad method to ignore them. They should at least accrete for future use. . . . We must accustom ourselves more and more to playing the role of a meteorological bureau, be satisfied for many a year to go without definitive conclusions, confident that if we only keep alive and heap up data, the natural types of them (if there are any) will surely crystallize out. . . ." This, incidentally, is still the attitude and consolation of Dr. J. B. Rhine and his corps of "psychic researchers," who are carrying on the tradition in the spirit of William James. James's innate integrity protected him against the delusions of the more fanatical members of his Society for Psychical Research, but their tolerance and curiosity made him insist that no human experience is unimportant or too unnatural to be recorded and studied by science.

IV

During the academic year William James usually worked more or less all day, not because his academic duties were so heavy that he could not otherwise perform them, but because he was unsystematic and could not work to a schedule, so that he always had unfinished tasks or plans. Besides, he carried on an enormous correspondence with friends, in addition to the correspondence regarding "psychic research," and he had not yet acquired a typewriter or a secretary—except occasionally his wife, to whom he dictated letters, as we have noticed, when his eyes failed him. On a typical morning he would leave his home at about twenty minutes to nine to attend the fifteen-minute service in the College Chapel before classes began. He did not forget to wear his tie so that Alice had to run after him with it, as Royce's wife did, calling "Roycy! Roycy!" But he grabbed whatever coat was handy, often the old Norfolk jacket which he liked to wear in his study, or even his formal black coat.

After Chapel Professor James would meet his classes, go to the library for books, possibly "look in" on the psychological laboratory if some of his students were performing experiments, or visit a book store. If he returned home for lunch instead of eating with colleagues at the faculty club (Colonial Inn), he would likely be late and in a great hurry because students had asked so many questions after class. Royce remembered having once stood ankle-deep in snow at James's gate arguing about the "Absolute" while their lunches grew cold. In the afternoon James often but not always took a short nap, then read or wrote until he was tired and felt the need of fresh air. For recreation he would take a walk or, in good weather, ride his bicycle. On his return he would resume reading or writing, probably in the library; he seemed to be able to write a letter and carry on a conversation at the same time. To finish an important lecture he would go to his cubby-hole upstairs, but he kept his door open and from time to time would pop out to comment on some remark he had overheard in his children's conversation.

The College required each member of the faculty to announce an hour when students might consult him, and Professor James persisted in announcing 6 p.m. at his home. That was his dinner hour, and he would have to leave the table to see the caller, whom he was likely to invite to the table and hand a plate, much to the student's embarrassment—besides, he had usually eaten! Although this conduct somewhat annoyed Mrs. James, she liked to entertain her husband's students, and did so each year in spite of his protests. His oldest son later thought it fortunate that his student guests did not hear his father's lurid remarks before their arrival. But sometimes they did not altogether escape. Once, as the son Henry tells the story, "Mrs. James encountered a young man in the hall whose expression was so perturbed that she asked him what had happened to him. 'I've come in again,' he replied, 'to get my hat. I was trying to find my way to the dining-room when Mr. James swooped at me and said, "Here, Smith, you want to get out of this *Hell*, don't you? I'll show you how. There!" And before I could answer, he'd popped me out through a back-door. But, really, I do not want to go!' "

Somehow the terms got lived through, and as soon as he could, James would escape in June to the Adirondacks or to Chocorua. Summer schools were now flourishing in American colleges and universities, and William James as the author of two texts on psychology was in great demand as a lecturer to teachers, who were the chief enrollees in the short summer sessions. In the summer of 1895, after a too-brief vacation in the fragrant spruces and sweet ferns of the Adirondacks, James lectured to the summer-school students at Harvard in July, then went to Colorado Springs to repeat his "Talks to Teachers," leaving his family in Chocorua. The trip took three days and nights on the train, and made him for the first time "understand the vastness of my dear native land," he wrote on August 13 to his Swiss friend Théodore Flournoy. The scenery and topography reminded him of Switzerland.

The previous week, at El Paso in Colorado, James had written his eight-year-old daughter: "I went up a high mountain yesterday and saw all the kingdoms of the world spread out before me, on the illimitable prairie which looked like a map. The sky glowed and made the earth look like a stained-glass window. The mountains are bright red. All the flowers and plants are different from those at home. There is an immense mastiff in my house here. I think that even you would like him, he is so tender and gentle and mild, although fully as big as a calf. His ears and face are black, his eyes are yellow, his paws are magnificent, his tail keeps wagging *all* the time, and he makes on me the impression of an angel hid in a cloud. He longs to do good." Peggy had spelled "awfully" both "orphly" and "ofly", and her father said those were good ways too. He had once remarked to Professor Palmer that it was a shame everybody was "expected to spell the same way!"

This traveling around to deliver his "Talks to Teachers" increased James's bank account by a thousand dollars, and he now began to look upon his itinerant lecturing activities as another way to supplement his Harvard salary, which would have been adequate for most academic families, but was not sufficient to support his large family and maintain two homes, both of which required servants, a maid and a cook in Cambridge, and in addition to these a man in Chocorua to take care of the horses and keep the place in order.

V

Insufficiently rested from his traveling and lecturing during the summer of 1895, James began the new term in September with a responsibility he hoped to be rid of permanently. Münsterberg had decided at the end of his three-year appointment to return to Germany for a year while he considered whether to spend the remainder of his professional life in America—as it turned out, he did. James had never liked directing the work of the Psychological Laboratory, even though he would now have capable assistants to supervise the students in their experiments, and to have to resume this responsibility annoyed him greatly.

Nervous tension during the autumn intensified James's anger over the Anglophobia which swept the nation when President Cleveland startled the world on December 17 by defying Great Britain in a dispute over the boundary between Venezuela and British Guiana. This dispute had been going on for years, and there was no crisis in the negotiations until the President precipitated one by declaring "any permanent political union between a European and an American state [to be] unnatural and inexpedient," that the United States regarded herself as sovereign in both North and South America, "and its fiat is law upon the subjects to which it affirms its interposition."

On Christmas Eve James wrote E. L. Godkin, who was doing his best through the *Nation* to combat the growing jingoism, that he had not "slept right for a week." He greatly feared that the mob hysteria in Washington was undoing the peace habits of a hundred years, "and the only permanent safeguard against irrational explosions of the fighting instinct is absence of armament and opportunity." He predicted that the "labor of civilizing ourselves" would be more difficult for the next thirty years. To Frederic Myers he wrote on New Year's Day, 1896, that "our countries will soon be soaked in each other's gore. You will be disemboweling me, and Hodgson cleaving Lodge's skull." William exchanged similar sardonic comments with his brother Henry, who felt stupefied by "the absolute war-hunger."

Henry, like William, had personal worries to augment his political pessimism. In January at the "first night" of his play *Guy Domville* he was hissed off the stage when he tried to take a curtain call, and he wrote William long emotional letters about the brutality of the British theatre. The income from his published works had also declined, and he now needed his share of the rents from the Syracuse property (which he had resumed after his sister's death). Both he and William were also at this time often besieged by improvident cousins for financial aid, which they frequently gave. William himself needed additional income to meet the expenses of his uneconomical family, and for his oldest son's expenses in Harvard College, in which he had enrolled in September. Although Mrs. James did not complain of their poverty, she could not help some sarcasms at the expense of Wilky's widow, now flitting around Europe. Even Bob's daughter Mary was traveling. Her parents were still separated, and Robertson James lived in a studio in Boston, where he pretended to paint.

In the spring of 1896 William wrote Henry about seeing a neighbor run over in the street and killed, and he had had to tell the man's wife. On May 29 his brother commented: "Strange how practically *all* one's sense of news from the U.S. here is huge. Horrors and catastrophes. It's a terrible country *not* to live in." To this William replied June 11: "The horrors of *not* living in America, as you so well put it, are not shared by those who do live here. All that the telegraph imparts are the shocks." But he could not defend "the silly wave that has gone over the public mind—protection humbug [high tariff on imports], silver [currency], jingoism, etc."

In the same letter William said that he and Alice had decided to rent Chocorua for the summer, while he traveled and lectured again. He had already committed himself to fifteen hundred dollars' worth of lectures, more than the previous summer. Early in June he had gone up to Chocorua with Alice and Tweedy to get the house in order for a tenant, but two days had been "spoiled by a psychological experiment with *mescal*." Dr. Weir Mitchell had been experimenting with this drug, derived from the bud of a variety of cactus growing in New Mexico. Mitchell had seen glorious colors and felt himself in "fairyland," but James was violently ill for twenty-four hours— "no other symptom whatever except that and the *Katzenjammer* the following day."

The few days at Chocorua made William feel the "most curious mixture of sadness with delight. The sadness of *things*—things every one of which was done either by our hands or by our planning, old furniture renovated, there isn't an object in the house that isn't associated with past life, old summers, dead people, people who will never come again, etc., and the way it catches you round the heart when you first come and open the house from its long winter sleep is most extraordinary."

In July he began filling his lecture engagements. His repertoire

was still his "Talks to Teachers," and his first stop was Chautauqua,
New York, a combined summer resort and popular educational institution, where earnest people swam, boated, picnicked, and attended
lectures. At first he was quite delighted with his audience of about
five hundred in an open-air auditorium, but by the second day he
thought he had been "meeting minds so earnest and helpless that it
takes them half an hour to get from one idea to its immediately
adjacent next neighbor," and then "they lie down on it . . . like a
cow on a doormat, so that you can get neither in nor out with them."
But he tried to enter into the spirit of the place and attended demonstrations in bread-making, walking, telling stories to children, and
child pedagogy. To his wife he wrote: "There is hardly a pretty
woman's face in the lot, and they seem to have little or no humor
in their composition." One woman said she had his portrait in her
bedroom with the words written under it, " 'I want to bring a balm
to human lives'!!!!! Supposed to be a quotation from me!!!" He
baked a loaf of graham bread, which he considered sending Alice by
express, "only it seemed unnecessary, since I can keep the family in
bread easily after my return home." After six and a half days of
Chautauqua, he was glad to escape to Buffalo, having learned much
but "glad to get into something less blameless but more admiration-
worthy. The flash of a pistol, a dagger, or a devilish eye, anything
to break the unlovely level of 10,000 good people—a crime, murder,
rape, elopement, anything would do."

From Buffalo James went to Syracuse, Utica, Lake Placid, and on
to Burlington, Vermont, still sputtering about Chautauqua and the
dull school teachers in his audiences. "I have seen more women and
less beauty," he wrote one of his cousins from Burlington on August
2, "heard more voices and less sweetness, perceived more earnestness
and less triumph than I ever supposed possible." He felt like saying
to them, "*Smooth out your voices* if you want to be saved!!!"

James's lecturing was scheduled to end with six performances at
the University of Chicago during the first week of September. Late
in August he passed through Chicago and went on to Lake Geneva,
a summer resort in southern Wisconsin, for a few days' rest. On a
quiet Sunday, August 30, he wrote letters to his friends. The place
reminded him of Flournoy, though he had learned that the Wisconsin lake had actually been named for Lake Geneva in New York
rather than the one in Switzerland. "Still you see how dependent,
whether immediately or remotely, America is on Europe," he wrote.

As for himself, he had had a rather "busy and instructive, though possibly not very hygienic summer, making money (in moderate amounts) by lecturing on psychology to teachers at different 'summer schools' in this land. There is a great fermentation in 'pædagogy' at present in the U.S., and my wares come in for their share of patronage." But he was tired and bored, and planned to have his lectures "stenographed" after giving them in Chicago, then publish them, "and so remove from myself the temptation ever to give them again."

Another letter was to James's former student, Dickinson S. Miller, who had been attending a psychological convention in Munich: "I wish I could have been with you at Munich and heard the deep-lunged Germans roar at each other." He called his summer "unwholesome," too much talking and sitting up late with strangers. But in another week he could call it quits for this summer and head for Keene Valley. The lectures in Chicago went well, and James spent three and a half "life-and-health-giving weeks in the forest and the mountain air," he wrote Henry on September 28 from Burlington, Vermont, where he had stopped on his way back to Cambridge. The only sad note was that "dear old Professor Child" would not be there when he got home; he had died during William's absence. But otherwise he was eagerly looking forward to the new term. Münsterberg had decided to return to Harvard, and now James was again rid of that Psychological Laboratory. Tomorrow morning, he continued to Henry, he would take the train to Boston, "and read Kant's Life all day, so as to be able to lecture on it when I first meet my class."

VI

In the autumn of 1896 James delivered eight lectures in Boston at the Lowell Institute on "Abnormal Mental States." These were never published, but they covered the following subjects: "Dreams and Hypnotism," "Hysteria," "Automatisms," "Multiple Personality," "Demoniacal Possession," "Witchcraft," "Degeneration," and "Genius." James's approach was strictly psychiatric, mainly a description of "morbid" states of mind and the best known methods of treating them. For the next several years this field would occupy much of his attention, more than strictly "psychic research," though he did not regard these fields as entirely separate. Edinburgh University had invited him to deliver the Gifford Lectures on Natural Religion, supported by a liberal endowment, but no date had yet been agreed upon. Eventually in these he would deal with abnormal states in religious experience.

In February 1897, as if rehearsing for the Gifford Lectures, James gave a lecture to the Neurological Society at the New York Academy of Medicine on one of the Lowell Institute subjects, "Demoniacal Possession." A man much interested in this subject, Henry W. Rankin of East Northfield, Massachusetts, had been supplying him with references and a mass of material. Rankin apparently believed, like Cotton Mather in the seventeenth century, that human beings could be possessed by demon spirits. James, however, in a letter to Rankin dated February 1, 1897, insisted that he could only regard such cases as morbid-entities, "whose commonest homologue today is the 'spirit-control' observed in test-mediumship, and which tends to become the more benignant and less alarming, the less pessimistically it is regarded." And similarly with religious "conversion," he would not rule out a possible supernatural influence, but he thought that in many cases "it is less a new truth than a new power gained over life by a truth always known. It is a case of the conflict of two *self-systems* in a personality up to that time heterogeneously divided. . . ." And as to "true and false miracles . . . a miracle as a mere attestation of superior power is one that I cannot espouse. A miracle must in any case be an expression of personal purpose, but the demon-purpose of antagonizing God and winning away his adherents has never yet taken hold of my imagination. . . . You see that, although religion is the great interest of my life, I am rather hopelessly non-evangelical, and take the whole thing too impersonally." Nevertheless, at the end of the present school year he would begin gathering everything he could find bearing on religious biography and philosophy.

During the spring vacation in April while both her husband and oldest son were away, Mrs. James wrote her brother-in-law Henry a long letter about family matters. Billy had had "pink eye," and his father had caught it, so that he was unable to read for several days. This encouraged him to take a quick trip to the Adirondacks with his Scottish friend Thomas Davidson and Charles Bakewell, a professor at Yale, who had studied psychology at Harvard. Mrs. James's oldest son, Henry, in whom his uncle Henry took great interest, had gone to Chocorua with a classmate. He had been working hard to be chosen one of the editors of the Harvard *Crimson*, the student newspaper. Her brother-in-law Bob had recently returned from England, where he had visited Henry, whom he reported was looking tired, and that worried Alice very much.

In June they would all go to Chocorua, and they hoped to take with them a tutor who could supervise Billy, a reluctant student, and teach Peggy and Francis French. The youngest son had now been renamed, but instead of calling him "Aleck," as his father usually did, his mother merely shifted from "Tweedy" to "Francis." He had entirely forgotten French, she thought, and she wished she could send one of her children every summer to Mme. Cérésole on Lake Geneva. "Every spring I am most poignantly homesick for Europe. How our great grand-mothers must have longed for home when first transplanted to these bleak shores!"

But the most important, and to his wife the most painful, news was that William had refused the Gifford lectureship now set for three years hence. He hoped the invitation would be renewed for five years hence. What most annoyed his wife, however, was that in refusing he had recommended Royce. "Royce!! *He* will not refuse, but over he will go with his Infinite under his arm, and he will not even do honour to William's recommendation. William over-rates him. Knowing how I felt about the matter William wrote without telling me. I fear that he now sees his mistake so I say not one word to deepen his regret, and please do not allude to it in your letters. I shall tell William that I have told you. There is nothing now to be done but to accept cheerfully the irrevocable. But if ever a man was slow to take the just rewards of his labours, and quick to avoid recognition it is my dear William, bless him!"

The University of Edinburgh had offered to award James an honorary doctor's degree if he would attend the ceremonies in August, but he did not feel that he could afford to make the trip. He planned to rest at Chocorua during the summer of '97 so that he could go to California for more lectures the following summer. But first he had to deliver the "Oration" he had promised for May 31 at the unveiling of Augustus Saint-Gaudens' monument to Colonel Robert Gould Shaw, commander of the 54th Massachusetts Regiment, the first to be composed of Negro soldiers with white officers, in which William's brother Wilky had served in the assault on Fort Wagner. For the first time William memorized a speech, and even though he got through his performance to everyone's approval, he found it a nervous strain. The ceremony was in the Boston Music Hall, and, he wrote to Henry after it was over, "You have to shout and bellow, and you seem to yourself wholly unnatural. The day was an extraordinary occasion for sentiment. The streets were thronged with people, and I was toted around for two hours in a barouche at the tail end of the procession. There were seven such carriages in all, and I had the great pleasure of being with St. Gaudens, who is a most charming and modest man. The weather was cool and the skies were weeping, but not enough to cause any serious discomfort. They simply formed a harmonious background to the pathetic sentiment that reigned over the day. It was very peculiar, and people have been speaking about it ever since—the last wave of the war breaking over Boston, everything softened and made poetic and unreal by distance. . . ." He received many compliments on his oration, which his son Henry later published in *Memories and Studies* (1924).

VII

The year 1898 was one of great emotion and dire consequences for William James. His troubles began early in January with sleeplessness and consequent nervous exhaustion. Then on the 7th Bob arrived back from England, where he had again visited his brother Henry. Twelve hours before his arrival in Cambridge William and Alice received a cablegram from Henry warning them that Bob would be arriving and in an irresponsible condition. On the 13th Alice wrote Henry what had happened since Bob's return: "He came Friday evening very drunk. The cabby who brought him and lifted him onto the porch told me that he found him in Bowdoin Sq. [Boston] 'knocking about.' After some difficulty the man had got the name of our street and number and so brought him out. Billy luckily appeared just then & got him to bed. William had been very nervous all day and I had urged him to go to his Club dinner in town, so he did not see Bob till the morning. To judge by experience this meant days or even weeks of anxiety and care. Imagine our amazement therefore at finding Bob in the library next morning perfectly sober and strangely *sane*."

After breakfast Bob had a talk with William and then came up to ask Alice if she thought his mind was failing. "I was so wretched about him that I told him the whole truth; that it *was* failing, that he was much broken, and that another six months of such racking of himself could have but one end." The consequence was that he agreed to enter a sanitarium, chose a trustee to take charge of his money, and seemed genuinely determined to undergo a "cure." William chose a private sanitarium known as Danville near Buffalo, and departed that morning with Bob.

In the same letter Alice congratulated Henry on having bought Lamb House at Rye, in Sussex. She had purchased a set of blue china for him, which her son Henry would carry over in June. He planned to spend the summer in England, part of the time cycling with his father's former student and present colleague, Dickinson S. Miller. Young Harry was now on the staff of the Harvard *Crimson* and hoped to be chosen president of the paper next year. He had written an article on Kipling for the Harvard *Advocate*, which his proud mother was sending to his uncle. While in England he would stay part of the time with his parents' friends the Joseph Thatcher Clarkes at Harrow.

On February 15, 1898, the whole nation was excited by the blowing up of the United States battleship *Maine* in the Havana harbor, and of course the Jameses no less than most other Americans. Within a few months it would cause William James to join the Anti-Imperialist League, write letters to the newspapers, and make public speeches. On June 17 he wrote Flournoy that the declaration of war had been "the worst blow at the *prestige* of popular government that I have *erlebt* [experienced]. . . . Our Congress was *absolutely* sincere in disclaiming any desire of conquest or annexation. But see how in the twinkling of an eye a nation's ideals will change! With Dewey's sudden victory, an 'imperialist' party has arisen here, which, as it will command all the crude and barbaric patriotism of the country, will be a hard thing to resist." Much of James's precious energies for the next several years would go into resisting this "barbaric patriotism," for which he would be attacked and vilified by many people.

Professor George Howison had made arrangements for James to give a series of lectures at the University of California in August. Before starting on the long trip by train to California, he went by himself to the Adirondack camp to get himself in shape for the journey, but injured his health instead. Leaving his camp at seven o'clock on the morning of July 8, he spent five hours climbing to the top of Mount Marcy, carrying an eighteen-pound pack on his back. Next evening at Saint Hubert's Inn in the Keene Valley, William wrote his wife about the subsequent events: "At four, hearing an axe below, I went down (an hour's walk) to Panther Lodge Camp, and there found Charles and Pauline Goldmark [young friends whom he had met on previous camping trips], Waldo Adler [son of Felix Adler, the founder of the American Ethical Culture Society], and another schoolboy, and two Bryn Mawr girls—the girls all dressed in boys' breeches, and cutaneously desecrated in the extreme from seven of them having been camping without a male on Loon Lake to the north of this."

William's son Harry was on the ocean bound for Europe, and his father wondered how he was finding the trip. But his mind was mostly on the Edinburgh lectures, the invitation having been renewed and the date now set for 1899–1901 (two series). With these thoughts on his mind, in this high altitude after unaccustomed physical exertion, he spent one of the most memorable nights he had ever experienced. "I was in a wakeful mood before starting [up Marcy], having been awake since three, and I may have slept a little during the night; but I was not aware of sleeping at all. My companions, except Waldo Adler, were all motionless. The guide had got a magnificent provision of firewood, the sky swept itself clear of every trace of cloud or vapor, the wind entirely ceased, so that the fire-smoke rose straight up to heaven. The temperature was perfect either inside or outside the cabin, the moon rose and hung above the scene before midnight, leaving only a few of the larger stars visible, and I got into a state of spiritual alertness of the most vital description. The influences of Nature, the wholesomeness of the people round me, especially the good Pauline, the thought of you and the children, dear Harry on the wave, the problem of the Edinburgh lectures, all fermented within me till it became a regular Walpurgis Nacht. I spent a good deal of it in the woods, where the streaming moonlight lit up things in a magical checkered play, and it seemed as if the Gods of all the nature-mythologies were holding an indescribable meeting in my breast with the moral Gods of the inner life."

This experience made James feel that "the two kinds of Gods have nothing in common," and this realization gave his Edinburgh lectures "quite a hitch ahead." Some of his emotions resembled what he would describe in those lectures as the psychology of a "mystical experience," and indeed in some respects it certainly was mystical. "It was one of the happiest lonesome nights of my existence," he continued to his wife, "and I understand now what a poet is. He is a person who can feel the immense complexity of influences that I felt, and make some partial tracks in them for verbal statement." But to him it remained "a mere boulder of *impression*. Doubtless in more ways than one, though, things in the Edinburgh lectures will be traceable to it."

Next morning at six James shouldered his pack and went ahead of the party to the top of Marcy, where he was joined half an hour later by the others. Then they all plunged down Marcy, up Bason Mountain, "down again, away down, and up the Gothics, not counting a third down-and-up over an intermediate spur. It was the steepest sort of work. . . ." But the others had had a refreshing night of sleep "whereas I was 'on my nerves'." He lost his Norfolk jacket— "high time to say good-bye to that possession"—and staggered on to Putnams' shack in Keene Valley. "I got a bath at Bowditch's bath-house, slept in my old room, and slept soundly and well. . . ." Except for stiffness he thought he was no worse for the experience, but later he confessed in a letter to Howison, who himself had heart-trouble: "My heart has been kicking about terribly of late, stopping, and hurrying and aching and so forth, but I do not propose to give up to it too much." Later he discovered that his overexertion in the mountain-climbing had caused a valvular lesion and permanent damage to his heart. Of course his determination not to "give up to it" was another serious mistake.

Three days after his return to Cambridge, James wrote Howison on July 24 that he planned to arrive in San Francisco on the eve of August 26, though he actually got there two weeks earlier. His "month of practical idleness in the Adirondacks" had not got him into "proper working trim," but he thought after his lectures in California he would spend a fortnight in the Yosemite Valley resting up. He traveled to the West Coast by the Canadian Pacific Railroad, admiring the "ferocious scenery" but concluding that the British Empire's investment in Canada was so far only scenic. In Washington and Oregon he saw great tracts of conifer forests devastated by fire. In northern California he rode through a wheat field on a harvesting machine drawn by twenty-six mules and cutting a swath eighteen feet wide, leaving behind the ripe grain threshed and sacked, ready for hauling to the storage bin.

In San Francisco James stayed at the Occidental Hotel, "an old house cleaned into newness," redolent of the 1859–1860 period, hideous in architecture, vast, stuccoed with undulating balustrades and lace curtains. The food was good, but the Irish waiters walked as if their corns hurt and handled plates like men who had recently abandoned their picks and shovels. The town itself, "so full of the sea-port nakedness, yet so new and American," also seemed to be a survival of the mid-nineteenth century. On August 12 James started out for the Yosemite Valley with Charles Bakewell, his former student and Keene Valley companion but a native Californian.

For his lectures, the first one given August 27, James drew upon his familiar "Talks to Teachers," but at Berkeley he also gave a lecture to the Philosophy Union on "Philosophical Results," in which he first used the term "pragmatism" for a theory of "truth"; namely, that the test of any concept is an answer to the question, "What sensible difference to anybody will its truth make?" In other words, the *truth* of a concept lies in its practical consequences when applied to a real, as opposed to a theoretical, situation in human life. He had borrowed the term from his old friend Charles Peirce, who, however, had used it in the sense of a rational well-ordered life, whereas James made it a means of judging true from false by looking at results.

After completing his lectures at the two branches of the University of California, Berkeley and Los Angeles, James visited the newly constructed Stanford University campus at Palo Alto, where he was impressed by the youths and maidens lounging together "in cloisters whose architecture is purer and more lovely than aught that Italy can show." But he was not willing to start back East without a trip to the High Sierras, and that was not what a man with a heart making strange palpitations should have done.

William James arrived back in Cambridge to find all members of his family in good health, but Alice was much worried about Bob, who had suddenly left the sanitarium in Buffalo and returned to Boston, where he would be subject to all his old temptations. William himself was not feeling well, and tried to conceal his heart symptoms from Alice, though of course he did not succeed.

VIII

In spite of his poor health, James prepared that autumn to deliver his Ingersoll lecture on "Human Immortality." Miss Caroline Haskell Ingersoll had left an endowment to Harvard for an annual lecture on this subject, and in the spring of 1897 the Harvard Corporation had invited James to be the 1898 speaker. At first he had felt he ought to decline, because "my own personal feeling about immortality has never been of the keenest order, and that, among the problems that give my mind solicitude, this one does not take the very foremost place." But he had finally accepted the invitation, and for the past year and a half he had been trying to see what grounds a professional psychologist could find for entertaining a belief in immortality. His entire treatment must be speculative—showing what the physiological psychologists leave out of their answer, and what *might* be said for what they leave out.

In his lecture James said he would go so far as to say that the "supposed impossibility of [the soul's] continuity comes from too superficial a look at the admitted fact of functional dependence [of mind on brain]. . . . When the physiologist who thinks that his science cuts off all hope of immortality pronounces the phrase, 'Thought is a function of the brain,' he thinks of the matter just as he thinks when he says, 'Steam is a function of the tea-kettle, 'Light is a function of the electric circuit, 'Power is a function of the moving waterfall.' " This is *"productive function"*: there is also a *"transmissive function,"* such as the refraction of light passing through a prism, or the keys of an organ which "open successively the various pipes and let the wind in the air-chest escape in various ways." His thesis was that: "when we think of the law that thought is a function of the brain, we are not required to think of a productive function only: *we are also to consider permissive or transmissive function.* And this the ordinary psycho-physiologist leaves out of his account."

However, before he could make use of the hypothesis that the brain may be like "colored lenses in the wall of nature, admitting light from the super-solar source . . . ," or as Shelley expressed the same notion, staining "the white radiance of eternity," James had to resort to the idealistic philosophy of Berkeley which he had always rejected, namely, that the physical world we experience is perhaps only somehow an emanation of an unseen spiritual world. He had never been able to find a coherent explanation for the relationship of mind and body; now, he says, let us imagine that the brain is but a thin membrane separating the two worlds, and that sometimes spiritual energy flows through it. In cases of religious "conversion" the brain threshold has somehow been lowered, so that there is a great "influx," to use Swedenborg's term, of spiritual energy. The physiological psychologists have to say that "consciousness in the brain . . . is the absolute world-enigma,—something so paradoxical and abnormal as to be a stumbling block to Nature, and almost a self-contradiction." But, "we need only suppose the continuity of our consciousness with a mother sea, to allow for exceptional waves occasionally pouring over the dam. Of course the causes of these odd lowerings of the brain's threshold still remain a mystery on any terms."

This address was not remarkable either for originality or logic. The "threshold" theory James borrowed from the German "psychophysicist" Gustav Theodor Fechner, and the "mother sea" was but another name for Emerson's "Over Soul," which he, of course, had appropriated from Hindu religion and philosophy. And the reasoning ran perilously close to what Henry James had called William's "sky-larking" with ideas. Even the title was inaccurate, for James applies his speculation to all living things: he is "willing that every leaf that ever grew in this world's forests and rustled in the breeze should become immortal." But the metaphors, the humane spirit, the tolerance, and above all the lively imagination made this one of William James's more interesting lectures to hear or read.

IX

On the night of November 21, 1898, a terrible storm blew nearly all night in Cambridge, and William could not sleep. High winds always made him nervous, and this one gave him pains in the chest, so severe in fact, that he quit pretending that nothing was wrong and began consulting doctors, his friend Jim Putnam first. Alice went to Putnam herself, and he tried to reassure her by saying that the damage was slight and need not increase if taken care of properly. "But," she wailed in a letter to Henry, "was ever man born of woman harder to take care of than William!"

Mrs. James felt that the only hope for her husband was to get him away from the worries and distractions of Cambridge; and he, having learned nothing from earlier experiences, thought the mineral baths at Nauheim might help him. Fortunately he was due for another sabbatical leave at the end of the current academic year. They decided, therefore, to rent Chocorua and sail for Europe again, but this time take only the two younger children with them. (Francis, however, was finally left with his grandmother.) Henry, now managing editor of the *Crimson*, was working for the editorship and was very much absorbed in his college work. Billy had been admitted to Harvard and in the spring was assigned to highly desirable living quarters in the Harvard Yard. The two older boys had obtained employment for the summer with the United States Forestry Service for the Olympia Forest in Washington.

After learning of the seriousness of William's heart condition, his brother Henry had become extremely anxious about him and had urged him and Alice to take possession of his flat in London at 34 De Vere Gardens for the winter, or as long as they needed it— or he would be glad for them to stay with him in Lamb House. Near the end of May, while Alice and Francis were at Chocorua trying to get the place ready for a tenant—not yet found—she wrote Henry to thank him for his generosity and to explain their plans. "After the boys go [to Washington] and William has had a month of rest and reading we shall sail on the *Graf Waldersee*, July 15th, for Hamburg. I wrote two weeks ago to Mme Ceresole to ask her to take the two children and I can be at Nauheim with William, or anywhere else. We shall come to see you, if you promise not to turn out of your own room for me, as you did before. You cannot think what a comfort the boys have been. An irritable heart misbehaves on slight provocation so we all avoid discussions or anything disagreeable. I cannot be too grateful for the tact and gentleness the boys have shown." They had had to give up the merry Sunday night dinners to which their mother had encouraged them to invite any of their friends they wished.

Alice especially disliked to be away from home this summer because on June 1 her sister Margaret would marry a Scottish Canadian named Leigh Gregor, a professor in the University of Montreal. "Mother is a perfect saint, for she had ceased to expect Margie to marry, and she will miss her sadly. For mother's sake and for the boys I should rather stay at home this summer, but the other plan is the wise one."

At the beginning of June, after he was through with his classes, William wanted to return to the Adirondack Lodge. He insisted that if he went by himself, with no temptation to talk, and walked slowly at his own comfortable pace, the recreation would be good for him. His wife did not like the idea, but she let him have his way. The consequence was that one afternoon he took a wrong trail, got lost, and wandered until near midnight in the woods. He had not taken a coat, food, or matches. Twice he fainted, but at last found the Keene Valley road and reached a house, food, and transportation back to his lodge. After a few days' rest, he returned to Cambridge, made a joke of the whole experience, and prepared to sail on schedule.

CHAPTER XXI

The Dark Forest

We are like two strange way-worn birds perched in a strange dark

forest. —Mrs. William James *to William James Jr.*

I

AFTER RETURNING from Keene Valley in June 1899 William James was too busy making preparations for his forthcoming trip to Europe to heed the pains in his chest. Though he usually put off preparations for a trip until the last minute, and then loudly protested against his wife's packing his clothes for him, this time there were many things besides packing to attend to. The Irving Street house must be left in good order for its tenants, the Merrimans, Mr. Daniel Merriman having rented it for a year; Chocorua had been rented for the summer by Professor Eugene Wambaugh of the Harvard Law School.

William and Alice had decided at last to take only Peggy with them. One of the most delicate problems, psychologically, was leaving "Aleck" (his mother still called him "Francis," though he had now been renamed Alexander Robertson, as his Uncle Henry had suggested, and his father usually called him "Aleck"). His mother had wanted to take both children with her, but his father thought the boy would be a needless complication and better off with his grandmother, attending his Cambridge school in winter and staying at the Salters' Hill Top place in Chocorua during the summer. His mother had left him at Hill Top after getting their own house in Chocorua ready for the tenant who had finally been found, and both parents went up before sailing to spend two days with him. William took him a bull terrier puppy, which Aleck named Dinah, and his Aunt Mary let him have a hen to keep as his own. The nine-year-old boy seemed to be reconciled to being left behind, but unlike his father he so often kept his discontentment bottled up inside him that it was difficult to know how he really felt.

On July 15, at last safely aboard the big German steamship *Graf Waldersee*, William James dropped exhausted on his cabin bunk and lay there while Alice and Peggy went on deck to watch the ship pull away from the dock. It was a joy to Alice to hear the officers giving commands in their crisp, vigorous German. William was too tired to care, though he loved the language more than she did. The passengers seemed a dull lot, and it was a monotonous crossing. All that sustained William was the conviction that a few weeks at Bad-Nauheim would put him in condition to go to England and write the first course of the Gifford lectures he was to give, starting in January 1900. At Hamburg they would separate for a few days, he going straight to Nauheim while Alice took Peggy to Switzerland. With their daughter settled at Vevey, his wife would join him at Nauheim.

A couple of weeks after Alice arrived, William wrote his mother-in-law: "We inhabit one richly and heavily furnished bedroom, 21 x 14, with good beds and a balcony, and are rapidly making up for all our estrangement, locally speaking, in the past. It is a great 'nerve-rest,' though the listlessness that goes with all nerve-rest makes itself felt. Alice seems very well." For weeks he had been so irritable and short-tempered that any contradiction or frustration infuriated him, and Alice had had to exert her patience and tact with heroic effort to keep him from straining his heart by emotional tantrums. Perhaps the warm mineral baths did him some good by their enervating effects, but this was only a temporary benefit. For a short time he also found the place itself restful, with its "vast park with noble trees and avenues and incessant benches for rest; restaurants with out-of-door tables everywhere in sight; music morning, afternoon and night; and charming points to go to out of town." He especially liked a terrace-restaurant overlooking the park, from which he could see the little Gothic-spired town of Friedberg about a mile away. In the foreground was a broad fertile plain, checkerboarded with fields of wheat, rye, clover, timothy, and other crops, and on the horizon low wooded hills.

The weather was dry and cool, William wrote Mrs. Gibbens: "Today [August 22] is sunny but frigid—like late October. European weather is stagnant and immovable. It is as if it got stuck, and needed a kick to start it: and although it is doubtless better for the nerves than ours, I find my soul thinking most kindly from this distance of our glorious quick passionate American climate, with its transparency and its impulsive extremes. This weather is as if fed on solid pudding." But however monotonous Nauheim weather might be, it permitted William and Alice to spend much time outdoors. William did a great deal of reading or writing to friends while sitting in the shade of a tree with book or writing pad on his knee, or at one of the numerous restaurant tables.

To Pauline Goldmark, the young mountaineering companion of the Adirondacks who was spending the summer in Switzerland, William wrote on August 12: "I am afraid we are stuck here till the latter half of September." Then he told her of his mishap in June on their favorite mountain: "Once a donkey, always a donkey; at the Lodge in June, after some slow walks which seemed to do me no harm at all, I drifted one day up to the top of Marcy, and then (thanks to the Trail Improvement Society!) found myself in the Johns Brook Valley instead of on the Lodge trail back; and converted what would have been a three-hours' downward saunter into a seven-hours' scramble, emerging in Keene Valley at 10:15 P.M. This did me no good—quite the contrary; so I have come to Nauheim just in time." But whether "in time" or not, the benefits were doubtful. William especially disliked the morbidity of the place: "You have no idea of the moral repulsiveness of this *Curort* life. Everybody fairly revelling in disease, and abandoning themselves to it with a sort of gusto. 'Heart,' 'heart,' 'heart,' the sole topic of attention and conversation. As a 'phase,' however, one ought to be able to live through it, and the extraordinary nerve-rest, crawling round as we do, is beneficial. Man is never satisfied! Perhaps I shall be when the baths, etc., have had their effect. We go then straight to England."

Henry James was at Rye, where he had leased Lamb House for the third summer, and was eagerly waiting to hear from his brother and sister-in-law when they would visit him, either there or in London, where his offer of his flat at 34 De Vere Gardens still held. In mid-July he wrote William that their mutual friend the famous American physician in Rome, Dr. William Baldwin, was himself taking treatment at Bad-Nauheim, and was looking forward to William's companionship. Two weeks later Henry confided to William that he was considering buying Lamb House, although he was not sure just how he could raise the money. To Henry's great annoyance, William discussed his brother's plans with Dr. Baldwin, who agreed with William that the house was priced too high and would be a poor investment. William thoughtlessly trampled on Henry's sensibilities, as he had so often done in the past, not only by warning him that his dreams of becoming a householder might be foolish, but also by revealing confidences to someone outside the family. It was Henry's sister-in-law, not the professional psychologist, who understood the novelist and knew how to respond with the needed enthusiasm.

William's only excitement at Nauheim was news of the second trial of Dreyfus in France, which he followed in the full reports printed in *Figaro*. He still felt strongly about the American occupation of the Philippines, which the London *Chronicle* reported for him, but no new crisis had arisen over this issue. In a letter to his mother-in-law he exclaimed: "I hope that public opinion is gathering black against the Philippine policy—in spite of my absence! I hope that Salter will pitch in well in the fall." (William M. Salter was as strongly opposed as James to President McKinley's conduct in the occupation of the Philippines and had made some speeches on the subject.) On September 11 James wrote his brother-in-law: "The incredible has happened, and Dreyfus, without one may say a single particle of *positive* evidence that he was guilty, has been condemned again. The French Republic, which seemed about to turn the most dangerous corner in her career and enter on the line of political health, . . . has slipped Hell-ward and all the forces of Hell in the country will proceed to fresh excesses in insolence. But I don't believe the game is lost. 'Les intellectuels,' thanks to the Republic, are now aggressively militant as they never were before, and will grow stronger and stronger; so we may hope."

But the Dreyfus case had made William more patriotic: "We must thank God for America; and hold fast to every advantage of our position. Talk about corruption! It is a mere fly-speck of superficiality compared with the rooted and permanent forces of corruption that exist in the European states." In a postscript he repeated this conviction, almost in the words Lincoln Steffens—the "muckraker" who had studied Europe after having exposed the corruptions of the great American cities—was to use a decade later: "Damn it, America doesn't know the meaning of the word corruption compared with Europe! Corruption is so permanently organized here that it isn't thought of as such—it is so transient and shifting in America as to make an outcry whenever it appears." Of course, "*Every* great institution is perforce a means of corruption" and must be watched closely. William now distrusted institutions and "bigness" of all kinds almost as much as his father had, and like him too looked to the "free personal relation" to restore governments and society to health and sanity.

The Jameses had been visited for several days by an ardent Polish liberal and patriot, Wincenty Lutaslawski, whom they had met in September 1893 when he stopped off in Cambridge on his way to the Chicago psychological meeting which William had not attended. Lutaslawski was then a wandering student of philosophy in Europe, but he had recently received his Ph.D. degree from the University of Helsingfors and written a book called *Seelenmacht* (the power of souls) which William liked (with reservations) and for an English translation of which he had agreed to write an introduction (he did so, but the translation was not published until 1924). On September 17, 1899, to his long-standing Boston friend Miss Frances Morse, William described Lutaslawski: "36 years old, author of philosophical writings in seven different languages—'Plato's Logic,' in English (Longmans) being his chief work,—and knower of several more, handsome, and to the last degree genial. He has a singular philosophy—the philosophy of friendship. He takes in dead seriousness what most people admit, but only half-believe, viz., that we are *Souls* (Zoolss, he pronounces it), that souls are immortal, and agents of the world's destinies, and that the chief concern of a soul is to get ahead by the help of other souls with whom it can establish confidential relations." While at Bad-Nauheim Lutaslawski spent a number of hours making impromptu translations of Polish literary masterpieces for his hosts. William called him "a *wunderlicher Mensch* [strange man]."

Not long after the genial Pole departed, William and Alice began getting ready to go to England. On September 15 Alice wrote in her diary: "Two months ago we sailed. I have heart to begin again since William's heart is really better. This a.m. Dr. Schott said, 'I am pleased' and in answer to questions gave him [William] the precious word that his heart had resumed the normal size. The painful constriction of the chest remains but Schott says that will disappear after some weeks. It has been a good day. A letter from Harry [her son] of August 27 and from Peggy too—admirably well written. She says 'Please about England get a school where there are only girls and which is near Uncle Henry's.' "

II

William James was restless for more activity long before he and Alice left Nauheim toward the end of September. Their first thought was to rescue Peggy from Vevey; then they would visit Henry at Rye, where he waited in eagerness, and some trepidation, to give them the hospitality of Lamb House. On October 5, from Lamb House, William wrote another friend of his in Boston, Mrs. Henry Whitman, a concise account of their experiences since leaving Nauheim: "A glorious week in Switzerland, solid in its sometimes awful, sometimes beefy beauty; two days in Paris, where I could gladly have stayed the winter out, merely for the fun of the sight of the intelligent and interesting streets; then hither, where H.J. has a real little *bijou* of a house and garden, and seems absolutely adapted to his environment, and very well and contented in the leisure to write and to read which the place affords."

To Fanny (Frances) Morse, William gave a more detailed description a few weeks later: "Harry's place is a most exquisite collection of quaint little stage properties, three quarters of an acre of brick-walled English garden, little brick courts and out-houses, old-time kitchen and offices, paneled chambers and tiled fire-places, but all very simple and on a small scale. Its host, soon to become the proprietor [papers not yet signed], leads a very lonely life but seems in perfect equilibrium therewith, placing apparently his interest more and more in the operations of his fancy. His health is good, his face calm, his spirits equable, and he will doubtless remain here for many years to come, with an occasional visit to London."

To return to his impressions of October 5: "The land is bathed in greenish-yellow light and misty drizzle of rain. The little town, with its miniature brick walls and houses and nooks and coves and gardens, makes a curiously vivid and quaint picture, alternately suggesting English, Dutch, and Japanese effects that one has seen in pictures—all exceedingly tiny (so that one wonders how *families* ever could have been reared in most of the houses) and neat and *zierlich* [graceful] to the last degree. *Refinement* in architecture certainly consists in narrow trim and the absence of heavy mouldings."

Henry still had not sublet his London flat, and he had offered it to William and Alice, at least temporarily. On October 5, William wrote Mrs. Whitman that they expected to go to London in a few days, "where we shall in all probability stay till January . . . or till such later date as shall witness the completion of the awful Gifford job, at which I have not been able to write one line since last January. I long for a definitive settlement and ability to get to work. I am very glad indeed, too, to be in an English atmosphere again. Of course it will conspire better with my writing tasks, and after all it is more congruous with one's nature and one's inner ideals. Still, one loves America above all things, for her youth, her greenness, her plasticity, innocence, good intentions, friends, everything."

At De Vere Gardens William reached another low psychological ebb, and Alice and Peggy (now with them) were depressed too. On October 24 Alice was worried because she had not heard from Billy recently and wrote to ask him why. "Are you feeling hurt that you write us never a word? You always came in to see how I was getting on when I was having headaches and somehow your long silence in these dark days makes my heart a little heavier. Papa has been less well than at Nauheim and just now is housed for rest and care. We are like two strange way-worn birds perching in a strange dark forest. Uncle Harry has been kindness itself and this flat is comfortable in every way, but Sunday a great London fog shut us in, so heavy and dense that even with closed windows the rooms were full of a blue haze. It was awful, and nothing I have ever read had prepared me for the depressing experience. Peggy who is in bed with tonsilitis just observed mournfully, 'In our other troubles we have at least always had air to breathe.' By this you will perceive that she is not yet at school." Her mother had finally selected a school at Harrow, on the advice of the Joseph Thatcher Clarkes, American friends living at Harrow. Henry had thought a school at Wimbledon the ideal choice, and Mrs. James had been torn between the conflicting opinions of the Clarkes and her brother-in-law. Now Peggy's trunk was packed and as soon as she had recovered from the tonsilitis her mother would "take her to Northlands 'Englefield Green' and a more cheerful routine will begin for her." Her mother assured Billy, who had always been

Peggy's worst tormentor, "She has improved wonderfully, stands straight and talks very little."

But the news about Papa was not good. He was trying to write, but he had "no outside interests to amuse him or take his mind off his work and his illness." At Nauheim Dr. Baldwin had "staggered" Alice with his pessimistic diagnosis of William's heart condition, but now he had a new doctor, said to be the best heart specialist in London, Dr. Bezly Thorne, in whom she had much confidence. She herself had long adhered to a non-meat diet, but now Dr. Thorne had placed both of them on a low carbohydrate diet, especially avoiding starch and sugar, about which she intended to write her son Harry. He was living with Dickinson Miller, who was teaching in the Department of Philosophy during William's absence. But she wanted news about Billy's life in college, the courses he was taking and what boys he was seeing most often. Also whether he thought Harry was happy at Miller's. "And Grandma? Does Francis [Aleck] ever go to your room [in the Harvard dormitory]? Did the sight of Leland Stanford University make you wish that you had gone there?" Mrs. James's sons had taken a trip to California before returning from their summer employment in the forests of Washington.

William James's own version of these dark days in London was given to his mother-in-law on October 29, dictated to Alice. They had now received a "staving good" letter from Billy, evidently on the way even while his mother was writing him five days earlier. But the news about himself was not good. "Our short sunrise after Nauheim went down a fortnight ago in temporary clouds. . . ." In London he had seen little of the real sun, "I sticking to the house and my thoughts revolving about home affairs and Alice, though her body made daily sallies into the London streets, had her mind so bent on me that it was little better." Although Peggy had "turned into a refined, softly-moving, and wonderfully enunciating young lady in miniature," she had been listless and "seemed to have no desire to do anything but stay in the house and read Scott's novels." Then her mother came down with "a tremendous illness in her insides," followed by the worst head cold William ever remembered her having. At this point, "We had some pretty low spirits. . . ."

The depths of Alice's despondency seems to have been reached in her efforts to choose the school for her daughter. The school at

Harrow, where "Peggy was safely deposited yesterday [October 28]," William continued to Mrs. Gibbens, "and which seemed to me an unusually promising and charming place appeared to [Alice] a hopeless impossibility—and so did everything else. The attempt to satisfy our brother Henry and the Clarkes also made things no easier. I, trying to be cheerful for the crowd, reigned [*sic*] in all expression of my inward despair for several days till the afternoon when I went to [Alice's] bedroom where she was lying with a headache in the dark to console her. But nature was too much for me, and I soon found myself saying with a pathetic shiver in my voice 'Alice, if I could have heard one word escape your lips during all this time in recognition of the fact that we *have* a house beyond the sea, *one* syllable of tenderness for Cambridge, *one* pleasant allusion to our house, to all the life we left behind it would atone for everything,— in that ideal vision we might forget the present. But no! not a syllable, not a reference, not a relenting breath. . . .

" 'But no,' " William quoted himself as complaining, " 'I am left to suffer alone, alone, alone.' This involuntary cry of a suffering soul brought Alice to her feet again and with indignant tears she said that she was more homesick than I was really, but that the only reason I loved Cambridge and hated Europe was that in the one place I could keep away from her whilst in the other I was tied to her side. You see from this specimen of our conversation through what morbid depths we have drifted. Of course all sorts of clouds were cleared away and in five minutes we were laughing most heartily at the inner states which had taken such strange expression. I write them to you because they will remind you of old times and you are in no danger of viewing them seriously."

Now at least the psychological clouds had lifted. "Peggy sank into her school yesterday with more than equanimity. Alice has had a 2½ hour nap this P.M. and this forenoon I got out, we going together in a hansom to Kensington Gardens and loafing about there on benches for an hour. A moist south wind was blowing out of the full-bodied, multitudinous-clouded English sky with its shifting wells of strong light whilst the black elm trees shed their yellow leaves about us, and the misty atmosphere made rich softness of the distance wherever one cast one's eye. It was a great release and I shall go out every day now, taking more heed than hitherto of over-doing."

The social life of William and Alice was almost nil during these autumn days in London, but they did see Mr. and Mrs. Frederic Myers, who one evening brought a medium with them, "a lady who does it out of interest in the thing and not for money," Mrs. James wrote Billy on November 11. Her account of the performance made it sound quite ambiguous, though apparently she had not found it so. The medium talked for some time about a tall beautiful young man with a broad forehead until finally the name "Herman" came, and "an allusion to his going from us 13 years ago . . . later on she suddenly asked if *Billy* remembered playing dominoes with Herman. I must ask Grandma if there were dominoes for you two those last weeks of Herman's life." The answer— if any—seems to be lost.

For a couple of weeks the recovered cheerfulness continued in Harry's London flat. On November 14 William wrote (or dictated) another letter to his mother-in-law. His theme was Alice's spoiling him, which he elaborated almost to the point of burlesque. "She is making of me a perfect monster of self-indulgence." (Here the scribe interpolated in parentheses "not true! a.") ". . . she runs to anticipate every desire, agrees vociferously with every opinion, panders to every unreasonable whim with a face shining with that irresistible hypocrisy so characteristic of her sex in the connubial relation. . . . What I used to do for myself, tying shoes, putting on collar, moving chairs, picking up objects from the floor, writing letters, reading books and magazines, raising windows, putting change into my pocket and taking it out again, she must now do for me. She has almost come to feeding me. . . . After you, dear Mother, she is the blessedest phenomenon I have struck upon this earth and I have never shown you sufficient gratitude for consenting to let me have her." One of the family jokes was that William had forgotten to pay the minister after his wedding, and that his mother-in-law had given him $25, which William had never repaid. "Please note that in all this she is an unconscious medium, writing under 'control.'"

Even the weather had turned pleasant after that first depressing week in London. "Certainly fine weather in London," William could now declare, "has with its pink and opal and pearly effects a rare and precious and elaborated quality which makes the crude blue skies and hard bright light [of New England] seem very cheap and raw affairs from the aesthetic point of view. I don't say that from the *vital* point of view one doesn't hanker after them. How quickly one gets spoiled living here in the West End of London. Everything is better than the corresponding thing at home. . . . Every fish absolutely fresh, not a toss up for luck as in Boston or Cambridge." But good things have a way of coming to an end. "Harry has let his flat for a year to young Stopford Brooke and in some three weeks we shall be off not to return."

Of course Harry urged his brother and sister-in-law, with a warmth they knew to be sincere, to return to Lamb House and stay as long as they wished, but William knew how bored he would be in the atmosphere of that dainty place. Besides, Dr. Thorne thought the higher (though still moderate) elevation of West Malvern might do him good, and he could take thermal baths there. After their arrival, Alice wrote Billy on December 7 what the place was like: "The chief town or 'Great Malvern' [where Henry had tried to recuperate in the spring of 1870] lies in a wide river-valley but our little West Malvern is clinging to the hillside far above it. And it's a steep hill-side, into which the houses have to burrow like bank swallows, not to be washed into the valley below. We have seen a beautiful house called the 'Bungalow' the very ideal house for a hillside—just the kind of house we ought to have some day. It is low, wide-spreading, with lots of chimneys and a beautiful terrace just in front of the house. On the whole Papa and I agreed it was the house we should like to live in more than any house we have ever seen."

Two days later Mrs. James wrote from their hotel, the Westminster Arms, to their elderly friend Francis Boott, now languishing in Cambridge: "We made a bad 'after-cure,' and by the time we reached London William was worse than when we went to Nauheim. . . . Dr. Thorne has ordered him here to get up his strength in this tonic air. If we only had summer weather he could profit by it but the sun hardly appears these short December days and it is too cold to drive. It's a case for patience if ever there was one! William, however, was not created to practice this virtue. . . ." They were fortunate to find a clean comfortable inn, with excellent food, but since William found seeing visitors too exhausting, their life was as monotonous, he said, as in a convent, though Alice doubted that they would "be free to read about Buddha" in a convent. That was their present amusement, for William was still accumulating notes for the lectures he hoped to give in Edinburgh—now officially postponed for a year.

The bleakness of West Malvern in "drear-nighted December" was more than William could stand, and the baths weakened him; so he and Alice retreated to Lamb House for another short visit with Henry before they accepted the offer from William's friend at the Sorbonne, Professor Charles Robert Richet, of the use during the winter of his château near Hyères on the Mediterranean. Now that Peggy seemed satisfactorily settled in a good school—though she was not as happy as her mother thought she was—they could safely leave her in England. In her letter to Mr. Boott Alice confided, "I have not dared to let the boys know that she has already acquired an English accent!"

While they were still at Rye a great controversy arose in England over a national day of humiliation and prayer because of the disastrous defeats England had suffered in the war with the Boers in South Africa. A few weeks later William confessed to Francis Boott that the debate had moved him to write a letter to the London *Times*, suggesting, "in my character of traveling American, that both sides to the controversy might be satisfied by a service arranged on principles suggested by the anecdote of the Montana settler who met a grizzly so formidable that he fell on his knees, saying, 'O Lord, I hain't never yet asked ye for help, and ain't agoin' to ask ye for none now. But for pity's sake, O Lord, don't help the bear.' The solemn 'Times' never printed my letter. . . ." It is doubtful that Henry would have been amused if it had.

III

The Jameses made the trip to Hyères, in Provence, by way of Rome, where they made a stopover lasting from early January 1900 until about the middle of the month. On January 4, from the Hotel Primavera, Mrs. James wrote Billy a long letter, cautioning him to be careful not "to take cold before you have entirely recovered from mumps," and reporting that Papa "has bloomed up within the last two days after a very depressing fortnight. His nerves behave like the de'l but his dear heart keeps its moorings and his tension [blood-pressure] remains low so we know we are steering for port."

The Frederic Myers family had arrived, including three children, the oldest sixteen, and was staying in the same hotel. He was also suffering from heart disease and "poor Mrs. Myers is so frightened

about her husband that her best self appears." Ordinarily neither
Alice nor William had much patience with her, William especially
being annoyed by her chatter. Dr. Baldwin called twice a day to
see Myers, and of course William frequently saw him. Alice had
feared that "the Myers party would be a great strain on Papa but
though Mr. Myers quite clings to him, and Mrs. M. comes in and
talks the case over with him, it has not pulled him down." Another
couple in the hotel whom they saw frequently were the James
Frazers, he the author of the work on primitive religions, *The
Golden Bough*. Mrs. Frazer too was a strain on William's nerves,
though he enjoyed talking with her husband. But William was disappointed, his wife wrote her son, when the Frazers decided not to
move to another hotel, as they had announced they would, because
he liked the lamp in their room better than his and he thought that
if they left he could annex it.

Except for Billy's mumps, Alice and William had received good
news from their children, but she was anxious to hear about her
mother's trip to Montreal to visit her daughter and son-in-law.
Harry had delivered a speech on forestry conservation at a meeting
in Chicago which got reported in *Science*, and his parents were very
proud of him. Before leaving England Mrs. James had arranged to
transfer Peggy from the Northlands school to Hampstead High
School at Gayton Corner, near Harrow. Although at Northlands
Peggy was with excellent companions, had admirable lessons in
dancing and deportment, heard the best English spoken, and even
learned some German, her mother felt that the "spiritual effects" of
the school were not desirable. In a later letter to Billy she explained:
"She was growing terribly conscious of differences—felt herself
very much an outsider, was ashamed that she had never been christened (though she did not reveal her disgrace!) and in a dim way
was made aware that to be outside of the English church was tanta-
mount to being out of the world." When Mrs. James visited the
school at Gayton Corner she became conscious of a more vital
energy, more stress on the intellectual achievement of all the children, and thought that there Peggy would find herself with the
"daughters of everybody." Yet in spite of this, Mrs. James declared,
"She has no lack of refinement and is aristocratic in all her tastes.
She and Uncle Henry suit each other."

Later that spring Uncle Henry invited Peggy to meet him in London with some of her friends, and wrote William about the result:

"I met them at 4, at Baker St., lunched them, tea'd them, cabbed them and took them to a first-class variety entertainment (with Diograph war-pictures etc.) in a commodious private box. The affair was most successful. Peggy is a highly-developed Pro-Boer (and seemed surprised that *I* am not,) but she looked extraordinarily well—stouter and higher in colour than when at Rye—and pronounced herself, under my questions, perfectly happy and prosperous."

Mrs. James did not mail her January 4 letter to Billy for several days, hoping to hear from her mother, "and sure enough Grandma's letter gives me news of you." But it was written before her departure for Montreal. Anyway, Billy's mother could now say definitely that "things have brightened and opened up with the New Year and the way looks wonderfully less long. Papa is in working trim, full of ideas about his lectures. Yesterday he got in a big package of Catholic books out of which he will dig some wondrous quotations, and it doesn't look very long to April and Lamb House. Next Edinburgh and our Harry . . ."—their oldest son having been invited to join his parents in England. But Mrs. James was letting her enthusiasm run away with her usual sound judgment, for her husband had already written to the University of Edinburgh that he did not think his health would permit his giving the lectures in the spring of 1900, and offered to resign his appointment. And he had also written to President Eliot asking for an additional year's leave without salary.

Before William James had heard from either Edinburgh or Harvard, he and Alice stopped at the Hôtel d'Albion in Costelbelle-Hyères to recruit servants before taking possession of Professor Richet's big château. They would share the house with the Myers family, who had not yet arrived in Hyères. On the 19th of January Billy's mother wrote him: "I have been longing for and counting on, your first-rate letter which came an hour ago. After breakfast at 9 o'clock Papa goes into the garden and stays there till noon. Each morning he say[s], 'bring the letters right out if there are any,' and today five besides yours. I scrambled downstairs and Papa pulled his hat low over his eyes, while I read them in the order he directed —the least interesting first and 'Billy's for the best and last.' "

But the first, a typewritten one from President Eliot, proved good too. Eliot wrote: "I consulted the Corporation about your leave of absence for a second year. They regretted very much the illness which causes you to think of such a thing; but said they would give you leave of absence for a second year on the usual terms—that is, one-half pay. They distinctly declined your suggestion of a leave of absence without pay."

The University of Edinburgh had also written that Professor James's appointment for the Gifford lectures had been extended for two years. "So now he has nothing to do but to get well again. . . ." He still had to time himself in walking and not do more than five minutes before resting; also to be extremely careful about talking, which exhausted him easily. But his "old spirited look" was coming back, and his wife felt all sorts of plans and ambitions spinning through her mind. Harry could come over for a long summer in England, while Billy stayed at Hill Top and helped his Aunt Mary, Uncle Mack, and provided companionship for Francis and Grandma. Then the following summer Billy could come over.

In this happy state of mind Alice and William made arrangements to move into the Château de Carqueiranne the following Monday, January 22. She had engaged a cook and a housemaid, and with William's help "complicated" a letter to the gardener's wife announcing their arrival and asking her to order provisions. "What I wouldn't give," she continued to Billy in the long January 19 letter, "to have you children about me, to hear your voices in the hall, your steps on the stairs. There is a great billiard room and somewhere outside is a 'shed' about the size of our house in Irving St. only not so high, in which Richet used to keep his flying machine, his own invention. To my great relief he has taken it away—otherwise Papa would surely have tried it."

A Mrs. Roosevelt, whose daughter had attended Billy's dancing class, was spending the winter in a nearby villa, "But 'tis we who are to live in a château!" Billy's mother exulted. The fishermen were devoted to the Richet family "and ready to take Papa out if he wants to fish!" The Myers troop would not arrive until Friday, giving the Jameses four days of solitude. What William most dreaded was the fatigue of talking to the Myerses. But meanwhile he was enjoying the scenery and lush vegetation surrounding the Hôtel d'Albion: great beds of palms, oranges, roses, with winding walks and seats through a garden sloping down to gray-green olive groves, bordered by salt marshes. About three miles away was the Île de Hyères, and beyond that the Mediterranean. He felt that in this atmosphere he could begin writing the Gifford lectures—perhaps in a couple of weeks.

While still in the Hôtel d'Albion the Jameses were visited by Josiah Royce, who had come over to Europe for another round of lectures as a sequel to the Gifford lectures he had delivered early the previous year. The latter had just been published as the first volume of *The World and the Individual*, and the lectures Royce would shortly deliver would fill the second volume. He presented his published volume to James on his visit, and on January 21 William wrote him: "My wife can bear testimony to the cooings of rapture with which the reading of my daily stint of your pages was interrupted. I confine myself to this total impression, and don't at present venture on any criticisms of detail, not being well enough for polemics." This last statement hinted that he had some arguments against Royce's "absolute idealism," and he had actually already written (January 17) Mrs. Glendower Evans, an admirer of Royce's philosophy, that he found the book "a charming production," but "so trivial and so ponderous at once." And to Dickinson Miller next day: "We enjoyed Royce's visit very much, and yesterday I finished reading his book, which I find perfectly charming as a composition, though as far as cogent reasoning goes, it leaks at every joint. . . . In spite of the great technical freight he carries, and his extraordinary mental vigor, he belongs essentially among the lighter skirmishers of philosophy. A sketcher and popularizer, not a piledriver, foundation-layer, or wall-builder. . . . The subject is not really vital to him, it is just fancy-work. All the same I do hope that this book and its successor will prove a great ferment in our philosophic schools. Only with schools and living masters can philosophy *bloom* in a country, in a generation."

From this time on James's disapproval of Royce's philosophy continued and solidified into a "damn the Absolute" attitude. But this did not affect their friendship, and Mrs. James had doubtless been unfair in her suspicion of Royce's ingratitude. After leaving Hyères he gave lectures at Aberdeen, Edinburgh, Glasgow, and Oxford, then sailed home. Aboard the R.M.S. *Oceanic* he wrote William on February 7, 1900, reporting that "All went well enough," but "Everywhere they ask about you, and regard me only as the advance agent of the true American Theory. *That* they await from you. I received endless kindness; but they have still far more, I am sure, in store for you if only fate would permit them to get at you."

Two weeks later (January 31) William wrote Francis Boott that *he* had struck the right note about those Gifford lectures. Everyone else was writing, "We are glad to think that you are by this time in splendid condition, richly enjoying your rest, and having a great success at Edinburgh." But Boott wrote that "it is a great disappointment, more I should think than you can well bear. I wish you could give up the whole affair and turn your prow toward home." That is just what William wished he could do, but of course he couldn't. However, he did feel that his outlook had improved, and he was comfortable under his present circumstances. Their "broadbuilt sexagenarian Provençale" cook kept them well fed. "Especially is the fish good and the artichokes, and the stewed lettuce. Our *commensaux*, the Myerses, form a good combination. The house is vast and comfortable and the air just right for one in my condition, neither relaxing nor exciting, and floods of sunshine." He was mending, though slowly, and he found his "spirits now . . . first-rate."

One evidence of the improvement was the long letters he wrote to his most intimate friends and to his Harvard colleagues. Münsterberg had just informed him of the death of Solomons, the brilliant graduate student who had performed psychological experiments with Gertrude Stein. "Certainly the *keenest* intellect we ever had," William commented to Münsterberg. "But there was always a mysterious side to me about his mind; he appeared so critical and destructive. . . . He was the only student I have ever had of whose criticisms I felt afraid: and that was partly because I never quite understood the region from which they came. . . . Can you send me the address of his mother?—I think his father is dead. I should also like to write a word about him to Miss Stein, if you can give me her address."

To Palmer, his departmental chairman, James also wrote about employing new instructors and finding positions for their own graduate students. He was sorry to hear that Ralph Barton Perry was "out of place." He thought him "the soundest, most normal all-round man of our recent production," and he ought to be employed to give a course in Kant if he did not soon secure a good position elsewhere. Palmer did employ him, and Perry was regarded as James's successor at Harvard several years later.

The "great event" in James's life at Carqueiranne had been his reading of Santayana's book *Interpretations of Poetry and Religion*, just published. In 1896 Santayana had published an outline of aesthetic theory in *The Sense of Beauty*, and in this second book he was applying his own Platonic theory, which he defined in his Preface as the idea "that religion and poetry are identical in essence, and differ merely in the way in which they are attached to practical affairs. Poetry is called religion when it intervenes in life, and religion, when it merely supervenes upon life, is seen to be nothing but poetry."

"Although I absolutely reject the platonism of [Santayana's book]," James exclaimed to Palmer, "I have literally squealed with delight at the imperturbable perfection with which the position is laid down on page after page; and grunted with delight at such a thickening up of our Harvard atmosphere." If their students could now begin to understand "what Royce means with his voluntaristic-pluralistic monism, what Münsterberg means with his dualistic scientificism and platonism, what Santayana means by his pessimistic platonism . . . , what I mean by my crass pluralism, what you mean by your ethereal idealism, that these are so many religions, ways of fronting life, and worth fighting for, we should have a genuine philosophic universe at Harvard. The best condition of it would be an open conflict and rivalry of the diverse systems. (Alas! that I should be out of it, just as my chance begins!) The world might ring with the struggle, if we devoted ourselves exclusively to belaboring each other."

James now thought he understood Santayana the man for the first time. "But what a perfection of rottenness in a philosophy! I don't think I ever knew the anti-realistic view to be propounded with so impudently superior an air." Idealism seemed to James to ignore man's real experience, in which, for example, a bad egg at breakfast could not be explained away by some ideal harmony of goodness and badness. "Bah! Give me Walt Whitman and Browning ten times over, much as the perverse ugliness of the latter at times irritates me, and intensely as I have enjoyed Santayana's attack. The barbarians are in the line of mental growth. . . ." This was an allusion to the chapter called "The Poetry of Barbarism," in which Santayana attacked both Whitman and Browning.

William's letter-writing slackened when he finally got his long-postponed lectures started again. After breakfast he would lie

propped up in bed and scribble on them. But by April 13, he wrote
Fanny Morse, he had reached only page forty-eight of the third
lecture, and what he had written was "pretty slack" and would
need revision. "The problem I have set myself is a hard one: *first*,
to defend (against all the prejudices of my 'class') 'experience' against
'philosophy' as being the real backbone of the world's religious life
—I mean prayer, guidance, and all that sort of thing immediately
and privately felt, as against high and noble general views of our
destiny and the world's meaning; and *second*, to make the hearer or
reader believe, what I myself invincibly do believe, that, although
all the special manifestations of religion may have been absurd (I
mean its creeds and theories), yet the life of it as a whole is mankind's most important function. A task well-nigh impossible, I fear,
and in which I shall fail; but to attempt it is *my* religious act."

A Scots couple that called to see him at Hyères made James realize
that he would also fail to satisfy the semi-educated class who claimed
to have such experiences as he was collecting for use in his lectures.
They had heard that he would deliver the next Gifford lectures, and
came bringing a tract which the wife had written, but she impressed
James as a mass of "holy egotism and conceit based on professional
invalidism and self-worship." How his sister would have exposed
her with a scathing description! He wondered if this couple was
"a foretaste of what the Edinburgh atmosphere may be. Well, I
shall enjoy sticking a knife into their gizzard—if atmospheres have
gizzards? Blessed be Boston—probably the freest place on earth,
that isn't merely heathen and sensual."

The weather had been so cool, even in Hyères, that they had delayed their departure for Geneva, which would be much cooler,
until April 22. Then they would visit the Flournoys for a couple
of days and start once more for Nauheim by way of Heidelberg.
William rather dreaded the "nervous complications" of more baths,
yet felt that he must give them another try.

IV

From the time the Jameses left the Riviera at the end of April
1900 until April of the following year, they traveled the now all too
familiar zigzag route: from Geneva to Nauheim in May, back to
Switzerland for the summer, return to Nauheim in September,

thence to Rome again for the winter, and finally to Rye in April before the actual delivery of the lectures in Edinburgh, now scheduled for May 1901. Nearly all the stimulation of the unfamiliar was now gone, and the only variation in emotional experience was William's fluctuation of hope and despair and Alice's increasing homesickness for her children and mother. When her thoughts were not on William, they were on her loved ones in Cambridge, or at Chocorua in summer.

Three days after they reached Geneva (May 6), William wrote his mother-in-law, calling her "the only person who understands me on this globe." This compliment hints at some misunderstanding with his wife, and they evidently had had an argument about her buying clothes, not, as in the usual marital situation, because she had spent too much, but because she spent scarcely anything on herself. With fifty dollars her mother had sent her she had bought a ruby ring, but kept it in the bottom of her trunk instead of wearing it. She had also bought a sable muff and boa, for her mother, and then she "lay awake last night inconsolable over this last purchase, which, being paid for, is fortunately irretrievable." She already had a long Geneva fur cloak, but refused to wear it, or her boa, even though the weather was chilly and she had a severe cold. "Nothing can make her wear her good things. . . . She seems to think she is not good enough for anything good, and when we get home you must all join me in an effort to make her wear her best. In spite of this diseased humility she is an angel through and through."

It had now become a habit for Alice to try to shield her ailing husband from every exertion. "If I have a franc to pay, she gets between me and the payee, takes the money from my hand and passes it to him; tells me at table d'hôtes that I mustn't eat this and that, and gives the impression that I am a very henpecked man, not allowed to decide the minutest thing for myself—as indeed I am not able to, even if I were allowed. But her patience with my irritability and fits of despair, and invalid egotism is beyond all praise or description, so I bless her and thank you endlessly for giving her birth. Her hair is now more beautiful than it ever was . . . being quite silver white, in exquisite gradations, and hurled back from her forehead without a part. Her complexion is dazzling pink and white, her face as smooth as in infancy, and her expression without those lines of perplexity which sometimes, though rarely, cast a cloud over it when at home."

She had now gone out, he wrote, to perform errands, including mailing his translation of a French officer's diary at Manila Harbor, which he had dictated to her. William thought this would be good propaganda against President Cleveland's Philippine policy and was sending it to the Springfield *Republican* for publication. At 7:05 next morning they were to start for Nauheim, where they would arrive after eight in the evening and proceed next day to nearby Giessen to get the verdict of a physician who had been highly recommended by William's other doctors.

Meanwhile Peggy had been very unhappy at her new school. After alarming her parents with her "tragic outcries," she resorted first to silence, then to writing very ambiguously about her sorrows. On May 26 her father wrote her a long letter, analyzing her situation, her character, and patiently explaining what she must do—"a great lecture," he admitted, but "it is all true." As for himself, the baths were disagreeing with him again, and he would probably have to stop soon. But the good news was that the Merrimans had taken the Irving Street house for another year, and the Wambaughs Chocorua for another summer, though at a lower rent.

On May 30 Henry wrote William his disappointment over the failure of the Nauheim baths to help him, but he couldn't help pointing out that they had made his condition worse every time, and that surely he should look elsewhere for a "cure": "Better *here*, better at Carqueiranne, better at Geneva, etc.—you seem to have been *best* (in all your times abroad,) when you were furtherest away from them. . . ." It may seem strange that William James, M.D. could not recognize this fact himself—or rather that, knowing it to be true, for he did, he would go back to this treatment time and again. It was on the supposed best medical advice of the day that William James had acted contrary to his own experience. The irony is that he had little respect for the medical profession in general, and yet trusted the men whose theories were the most fashionable (not to say the most profitable) of the day.

But for the summer of 1900 it was back to Switzerland, mainly in the region of Lucerne, though Alice would go to England to spend August with Peggy during her vacation from school. At the end of June they were staying at the Hotel Saint Gotthard, near

Lucerne. There on July 1 Alice wrote Billy just how they had learned the exciting news about his boat race with Yale. They had known he was on the freshman crew, and as they were eating their evening meal outdoors on the 30th, she said to William, "How can we wait to hear how Billy has fared in the race?" Then they went into the reading room of the hotel and presently William thrust the London *Telegraph* at her and said, "Read that!" And there it was: The Yale varsity had beaten Harvard at New London, but the Harvard freshman crew had defeated the Yale freshman crew. William went immediately to the post office and cabled his congratulations. Now Billy's mother wanted to hear all about it, and especially whether Billy had fainted afterward. It seems that he had done that several times, and, much as she enjoyed hearing about the victory, she hoped he would give up rowing.

The day before they had seen Dickinson Miller off for Freiburg and Strasbourg en route to Nauheim. He also had a bad heart, and was going to take the baths. "He came way down here to see Papa," Mrs. James explained to Billy, "and then could not sleep. He has left a most pathetic impression on me and I only wish we could help give him a lift on his Nauheim expenses." The next day they were going up to Hotel Sonnenberg, half an hour from Lucerne on top of a mountain. "We want to settle down there and spend the month if Papa can sleep in so high an air." Fortunately he was able to, and here Alice heard that she was now an aunt: the Gregors had a daughter, and this news increased Alice's longing for home. She wrote her mother on July 8 that they planned to go to England early in August, and that she hoped to take passage to America the 5th or 6th, and then return early in November. ". . . William proposes that we shall take lodgings at Harrow and have Peggy with us till she completes her year at the High School." After Christmas they would take her to Geneva and arrange for French and riding lessons for her.

But it didn't work out quite that way. William's heart seemed to be worse at the end of the summer—so, it was back to Nauheim again in September. On the 16th he wrote Fanny Morse that his wife was still in England and had finally at his request given up "her long-cherished plan of a run home to see her mother, the children, you, and all the other *dulcissima mundi nomina* that make of life a thing worth living for. I *funked* the idea of being alone so long when

I came to the point. It is not that I am worse, but there will be cold weather in the next couple of months; and, unable to sit out of doors then, as here and now, I shall probably either have to over-walk or over-read, and both things will be bad for me. . . . The great Schott has positively forbidden me to go to England as I did last year; so, early in October, our faces will be turned toward Italy, and by Nov. 1 we shall, I hope, be ensconced in a *pension* close to the Pincian Garden in Rome, to see how long *that* resource will last."

It lasted very well for several months. On Christmas Day William declared to Fanny Morse that "Rome is simply the most satisfying lake of picturesqueness and guilty suggestiveness known to this child. Other places have single features better than anything in Rome, perhaps, but for an *ensemble* Rome seems to beat the world. Just a FEAST for the eye from the moment you leave your hotel door to the moment you return. Those who say that beauty is all made up of suggestion are well disproved here. For the things the eyes most gloat on, the inconceivably corrupted, besmeared and ulcerated surfaces, and black and cavernous glimpses of interiors, have no suggestions save of moral horror, and their 'tactile values,' as Berenson would say, are pure gooseflesh. Nevertheless the sight of them delights. And then there is such a geologic stratification of history! I dote on the fine equestrian statue of Garibaldi, on the Janiculum, quietly bending his head with a look half-meditative, half-strategical, but wholly victorious, upon Saint Peter's and the Vatican." William also enjoyed reading the inscriptions on the statues, such as Giordano Bruno's: *il secolo da lui divinato qui dove il rogo arse*—" 'here, where the faggots burned.' It makes the tears come, for the poetic justice; though I imagine B. to have been a pesky sort of crank, worthy of little sympathy had not the 'rogo' done its work on him. Of the awful corruptions and cruelties which this place suggests there is no end."

The Jameses were staying in the Hotel Hassler, not in a *pension* as William had anticipated. Their windows overlooked the Spanish Steps and Piazza di Spagna two hundred feet below, which William called in a letter to Billy, "a sort of Harvard Square . . . put through a wonderful sea change." Billy had been offered a job in Montana with the Forestry Service for the coming summer, but he also had an invitation to accompany friends to Hawaii, and was having difficulty choosing. Harry would work in Washington, D.C., for Gifford Pinchot, head of the Forestry Service, on a forestry magazine.

Mrs. James worried for weeks about Billy's having joined the "Dickey Club" at Harvard, which his father said was nothing but a drinking club. Harry had promised not to drink at all while he was an undergraduate, and she wished Billy would imitate him. But finally she got the idea that Billy could protest from within the club and at least partly reform it; at any rate this idea seemed to pacify her. William wondered if Billy would like to have an "English Express" rifle to shoot bears in Montana, but finally thought that maybe a good pair of Swiss binoculars would be more useful to him. On February 8 Mrs. James wrote Billy: "Are you aware that your sister, by order of her Uncle, is in complete mourning for her Majesty? . . . I am all black inside"—but not in grief over Queen Victoria's death. This is one of the few occasions on record when Alice James was sarcastic about her Anglicized brother-in-law, probably the result of the emotional strain she was under.

In the Hotel Hassler the Jameses once again had the J. G. Frazers as neighbors and "*commensaux* at meals." Although he was a world authority on "the religious ideas and superstitions of primitive peoples," William declared to Miss Morse, "he knows nothing of psychical research and thinks that the trances, etc., of savage soothsayers, oracles and the like, are all *feigned!* Verily science is amusing! But he is conscience incarnate, and I have been stirring him up so that I imagine he will now proceed to put in big loads of work in the morbid psychological direction."

William's "psychic research" friend Fred Myers was also in Rome, expecting to die soon. The story of his death, and its relation to William James, has been very dramatically told by Axel Munthe in his autobiography, *The Story of San Michele.* Dr. Munthe was not Myers' physician but was called in for consultation. Myers had completed his *Human Personality and Its Survival of Bodily Death,* but it had not yet been published; however, Dr. Munthe had attended a meeting of the Society for Psychical Research in London and had sat up all night with the author talking about survival after death. An examination showed that the poor man had only a few days, or even hours, to live, but Dr. Munthe called in a very famous heart specialist, a Professor Baccelli. His verdict was even more final: "*Il va mourir aujourd'hui.*"

James told Dr. Munthe that he had a solemn pact with his friend that whichever died first would do his utmost to send back a message as he passed over into the world of spirits: ". . . they both believed in the possibility of such a communication." James was so bowed by grief that he could not bear to enter the dying man's room, but sank down on a chair just outside the open door, his note-book open and pen ready to take down any message he might receive. In the afternoon the hard breathing of the patient signified that death was near. But he was still conscious and sent for Dr. Munthe. His eyes were "calm and serene" when he spoke:

"I know I am going to die," he said, "I know you are going to help me. Is it to-day, is it to-morrow?"

"To-day."

"I am glad, I am ready, I have no fear. I am going to know at last. Tell William James, tell him . . ."

His heaving chest stood still in a terrible minute of suspense of life.

"Do you hear me?" I asked bending over the dying man, "do you suffer?"

"No," he murmured, "I am very tired and very happy."

These were his last words.

When I went away William James was still sitting leaning back in his chair, his hands over his face, his open note-book still on his knees. The page was blank.

This painful experiment in "psychic research'" took place on January 17, 1901. On March 3, still in Rome, James wrote to the British psychologist James Sully that he felt the loss of Myers very deeply. "He died in this very hotel, where he had been not more than a fortnight. I don't know *how* tolerant (or intolerant) you are towards his pursuits and speculations. I regard them as fragmentary and conjectural—of course; but as most laborious and praiseworthy; and knowing how much psychologists as a rule have counted him out from their profession, I have thought it my duty to write a little tribute to his service to psychology to be read on March 8th, at a memorial meeting of the S.P.R. in his honor. It will appear, whether read or not, in the Proceedings, and I hope may not appear to you exaggerated. I seriously believe that the general problem of the subliminal, as Myers propounds it, promises to be one of the *great* problems, possibly even the greatest problem, of psychology."

James told Sully that he and his wife would leave Rome in three days, which would have been March 6. They visited other places in Italy before going north, among them Perugia and Assisi, where they spent a week, at the latter place visiting Saint Francis's retreat in the mountains, which caused William to declare that he could now see medieval Christianity face to face: "The lair of the individual wild animal, and that animal the saint!" Then they visited Florence, which brought back memories of their youth before either knew of the other's existence.

On March 24 Alice left William in Lucerne while she went to Geneva to see her dressmaker. She wrote Billy next day from the Hôtel de la Paix, congratulating him on his good grades in the mid-year examinations and bringing him up to date on his parents' wanderings. "The *Senatus* [of the University of Edinburgh] proposes May 15th as the date of Papa's first lecture. We should get through by June 20th. Let me say here that Papa can bear no contradiction. It's a nervous symptom, connected with his heart, and will wear off as he grows stronger. He has become very shy of people and I can see how the idea of Edinburgh preys on his spirits. He is in a tearing hurry to reach England and Lamb House. I must get some clothes for summer, and here is the only place I can do it in but Papa so fears the Flournoys [who would cause him to over-strain in talking] that he tents alone at Lucerne and Uncle H. cannot go to Rye till April 15 so *why* should he hurry so."

Promptly on April 15 William and Alice joined Henry at Lamb House, where they awaited the arrival of their son Harry, due two weeks later. In spite of his anxiety over the lectures, William found Lamb House more comfortable and enjoyable than he had on previous visits. The first course of ·lectures was now complete, and William was eager to deliver them before his health took another turn for the worse.

V

William, Alice, and their son Henry spent the night of May 13 in the Charing Cross Hotel in London and after an early breakfast boarded a train for Edinburgh, traveling, for once, first class. They were delighted to find that their Cambridge neighbor Mrs. Ole Bull, widow of the violinist, was taking the same train and they had a good chat with her. She was on her way to Norway to unveil a statue of her husband and was accompanied by a young English-woman named Noble, who had been converted to Vivekananda's philosophy and taken the name of Sister Vivedita, much to William James's interest; he regarded her philosophy as "more or less false," though "perhaps no more so than anyone else's."

In Edinburgh the Jameses were taken to the Roxburghe Hotel, which William thought "deadly respectable" because they had to ring the front-door bell to gain admission. He said he preferred "a cheerful blackguardly place like the Charing Cross." While Harry and his mother went out to see the town, William remained quietly behind, and to relieve his boredom he wrote his perennial confidante Miss Frances Morse. He dreaded the "social entanglements" that lay ahead, and felt like "a cake of ice in my epigastrium at the prospect, but *le vin est versé, il faut le boire* [the wine has been poured and one must drink it]. . . ." And since it was "real life beginning once more, it is perfectly glorious, and I feel as if yesterday in leaving London I had said good-bye to a rather dreadful and death-bound segment of life." Perhaps, the sociability might not be as bad as he feared because only the medical students and faculty were still in session, most of the others having gone on vacation. Even William's sense of humor returned; he had ordered summer clothes in London, before leaving Lamb House, but "the London tailor and shirtmaker, it being the height of the season, didn't fulfill their promises; and as I sloughed my ancient cocoon at Rye, trusting to pick up my iridescent wings the day before yesterday in passing through the metropolis, I am here with but two *chemises* at present (one of them now in the wash) and fear that tomorrow, in spite of tailors' promises to send, I may have to lecture in my pyjamas—that would give a cachet of American originality."

Apparently William James did not have to lecture in his pajamas, and two days later he could add to his unfinished letter to Miss Morse that he had made the plunge "and the foregoing chill has given place to the warm 'reaction.' The audience was more numerous than had been expected, some 250, and exceedingly sympathetic, laughing at everything, even when I used a polysyllabic word." Royce had warned him to expect a small audience, which might dwindle after a few days to fifteen—an estimate probably based on Royce's own experience. But James's audience soon grew to three hundred, in spite of rain, and no one could doubt that the lectures were a great success.

Of course this warm reception made James enthusiastic about the city and the people. The cool, bracing weather reminded him of the top of Mount Washington in early April, though the natives complained of the untimely heat, in spite of the fact that "one needs fires at night and an overcoat out of the sun. The full-bodied air, half misty and half smoky, holds the sunshine in that way which one sees only in these islands, making the shadowy side of everything quite black, so that all perspectives and vistas appear with objects cut blackly against each other according to their nearness, and plane rising behind plane of flat dark relieved against flat light in ever-receding gradation. It is magnificent." But he didn't want to become a Ruskin—though Miss Morse was probably glad he had not lost his ability to see with the eyes of a painter. He also wrote her that they had found "bully lodgings, spacious to one's heart's content, upon a cheerful square, and actually with a book-shelf two feet wide and two stories high, upon the wall, the first we have seen for two years!" Of course Lamb House had bookcases, but all so tightly packed that William found no space for his own books, of which he had accumulated a sizable collection on religion.

On May 30, to "dearest Fanny" again: "Beautiful as the spring is here, the words you so often let drop about American weather make me homesick for that article. It is blasphemous, however, to pine for anything when one is in Edinburgh in May, and takes an open drive every afternoon in the surrounding country by way of a constitutional. The green is of the vividest, splendid trees and acres, and the air itself an *object*, holding watery vapor, tenuous smoke and ancient sunshine in solution, so as to yield the most exquisite minglings and gradations of silvery brown and blue and pearly gray. As for the city, its vistas are magnificent." The Jameses were "*comblés* with civilities, which Harry and Alice are to a certain extent enjoying," but he had to spend much of his time in bed between lectures to rest his heart, which, however, "under the influence of that magical juice, tincture of digitalis,—only 6 drops daily,—is performing *beautifully* and gives no trouble at all." He had dined out once, where he was introduced to Lord Somebody, who said: "How often do you lecture?" —"Twice a week." What do you do between?—play golf?" Someone else invited him to "Come at 6—the dinner at 7.30—and we can walk or play bowls till dinner so as not to fatigue you." He politely declined, pleading his "delicacy of constitution."

On June 16, at the end of nine lectures with only one more to be delivered, James wrote his correspondent on psychic matters, Henry W. Rankin, about what he had been trying to hold up to his audience of "300-odd." He still found himself "permanently incapable of believing the Christian scheme of vicarious salvation," though he was sympathetic with those who did believe it. "In these lectures the ground I am taking is this: The mother sea and fountain-head of all religions lie in the mystical experiences of the individual, taking the word mystical in a very wide sense. All theologies and all ecclesiasticisms are secondary growths superimposed. . . . I attach the mystical or religious consciousness to the possession of an extended subliminal self, with a thin partition through which messages make irruption. We are thus made convincingly aware of the presence of a sphere of life larger and more powerful than our usual consciousness, with which the latter is nevertheless continuous. The impressions and impulsions and emotions and excitements which we thence receive help us to live, they found [lay the foundation for] invincible assurance of a world beyond the sense, they melt our hearts and communicate significance and value to everything and make us happy. They do this for the individual who has them, and other individuals follow him. Religion in this way is absolutely indestructible. . . . So I seem doubtless to my audience to be blowing hot and cold, explaining away Christianity, yet defending the more general basis from which I say it proceeds."

On Sunday, June 24, the Jameses traveled in a third-class compartment (which, however, they had all to themselves) back to London, spent the night at the Charing Cross Hotel, and returned Monday evening to Lamb House. There two letters written on the 26th, one by Alice to her mother and the other by William to Charles Norton, give us the two sides of their lives, the practical and the subjective at this point in time. Alice, of course, gave the practical view. She found Lamb House so restful and homelike that she had hoped they would spend at least a week there, but William was in "a fearful hurry to reach Nauheim and by hurrying we shall get off on Saturday." This necessitated a great amount of packing and preparation. He had received five hundred and fifty pounds for the completion of the first course of Gifford Lectures "and we can 'start afresh.' There will be no great outlay at Nauheim." In London Alice, Harry, and Peggy, who had joined them, had done some shopping Monday morning, then met William at the National Gallery. After lunch at the hotel, Alice accompanied her daughter back to Gayton Corner. Peggy now played tennis "with pleasure and spirit" and promised not to "drop into the resigned mood" again, and her mother thought she would not. Harry was to accompany his parents to Germany, then "swing off by himself" to see other parts of the country. She thought they would sail the last of August and arrive home about September 8.

To Norton, William wrote: "The lectures went off most successfully, and though I got tired enough, I feel that I am essentially tougher and stronger for the old familiar functional activity. My *tone* is changed immensely, and that is the main point." Edinburgh seemed to him much like Boston; but London, after Edinburgh, was "curiously profane and free-and-easy, not exactly *shabby*, but go-as-you-please, in aspect. . . ." He hoped to start for Nauheim the next day (Wednesday), after only one full day at Lamb House, leaving Alice and Harry to follow—probably on Saturday, as Alice had mentioned in her letter to her mother. "I confess that the Continent 'draws' me again. I don't know whether it be the essential identity of soul that expresses itself in English things, and makes them seem known by heart already and intellectually dead and un-exciting, or whether it is the singular lack of visible *sentiment* in England, and absence of 'charm,' or the oppressive ponderosity and superfluity and prominence of the unnecessary, or what it is, but I'm blest if I ever wish to be in England again. . . . England is ungracious, unamiable and heavy; whilst the Continent is everywhere light and amiably quaint, even where it is ugly, as in many elements it is in Germany. To tell the truth, I long to steep myself in America again and let the broken rootlets make new adhesions to the native soil. A man coquetting with too many countries is as bad as a bigamist, and loses his soul altogether."

The Nauheim baths did, as always in the past, prove debilitating again, though not disastrously so. On July 10 William was looking forward to ending this regimen, he wrote to Miss Morse, and taking a trip to the Vosges, "a week of touring up in higher air. . . . What I *crave* most is some wild American country. It is a curious organic-feeling need. One's social relations with European landscape are entirely different, everything being so fenced or planted that you can't lie down and sprawl." Both he and Alice were becoming homesick for their own country, and especially their own home. Peggy also wanted to go back with her parents instead of staying for another year in an English school, or studying French in Geneva, as her mother had once considered, and it was not difficult for her to persuade them to take her back with them.

Finally the summer passed, and Peggy and her parents were back at Lamb House, where William wrote E. L. Godkin, his father's old friend, who had suffered a crippling stroke, and was now living in England at Castle Malwood, near Stony Cross, that they would "leave for London tomorrow morning [August 30] and at four on Saturday [31st] we shall be ploughing the deep." Alice had sprained her ankle, yet insisted on hobbling about and doing all the packing. He would not be "aisy" till he got her in her berth on the steamship. But that was not the only reason that he could hardly wait to go aboard. "After all, in spite of you and Henry, and all Americophobes, I'm glad I'm going back to my own country again."

CHAPTER XXII Experience Is a River

Once admit that experience is a river which made the channel that

now, in part, but only in part, confines it, and it seems to me that all

sorts of realities and completenesses are possible in philosophy. . . .

—W.J. *to F. C. S. Schiller*

I

SOON AFTER REACHING CAMBRIDGE at the end of the first week in September in 1901, William James went up to Silver Lake in New Hampshire to get his fill of American scenery while Alice put the Irving Street house in order. Of course he longed for Keene Valley, though even he realized that to revisit it might be fatal for him; so as a substitute for returning to the Adirondacks he wrote his youthful mountaineering friend Pauline Goldmark. "I have reached home in pretty poor case," he confessed, "but I think it's mainly 'nerves' at present, and therefore remediable; so I live on the future, but keep my expectations modest." Remembering past experiences in returning to America, he had dreaded the "strangeness" after two years' absence—much too long to remain away. The country did look "pathetic and poverty stricken"—and as so many times in the past, he was comparing thin-soiled rural New England with humus-rich old England—but his consciousness of the difference would soon wear off.

From Europe James had written Palmer and President Eliot that he could not carry a full teaching load, and they had assigned him only a seminar meeting once a week for the first semester, leaving him entirely free the second semester, when he would return to Edinburgh to give the second course of his lectures. The topic announced for his seminar was "The Psychological Elements of Religious Life," the very subject of his Gifford lectures. Thus he could combine teaching and writing the remaining lectures, and get his manuscript ready for publication. Doubtless the one course

he taught from September to February was enriched by his satura-
tion in this subject, but his interest in academic affairs was minimal.

Even James's interest in philosophy—for he was more concerned
with the phenomena of religious experiences than philosophical explanations of them—was at a low ebb in the winter of 1901–1902.
To an invitation to join the newly founded American Philosophical
Association he replied to the secretary, Professor H. N. Gardner,
on November 14: "I am still pretty poorly and can't 'jine' anything
—but, apart from that, I don't foresee much good from a Philosophical Society. Philosophical discussion proper only succeeds between intimates who have learned how to converse by months of
weary trials and failure. The philosopher is a lone beast dwelling in
his individual burrow.—Count me *out!*—I hope all goes well with
you. I expect to get well, but it needs *patience*."

This winter was not, however, unproductive for James. On
April 1, 1902, he carried a copy of his completed manuscript to the
Boston harbor, where he and his wife boarded the familiar *Ivernia*
bound for England. The crossing was smooth, though cloudy, and
they landed nearly five weeks before William's first lecture in Edinburgh now scheduled for May 13. This gave them time for some
leisurely sightseeing, such as a visit to Stratford-on-Avon for the
first time. The bleak, shoddy appearance of the town made William,
he said, willing to believe almost any mythical story about the
authorship of the plays: ". . . a visit to Stratford now seems to me
the strongest appeal a Baconian can make." But he found the surrounding country "exquisite." This was true of Torquay, too, where
the Godkins were now living. Though the former editor of the
Nation was now an invalid, his mind was still clear, and bitter as
ever about the "Philippine conquest." The phrase was William's,
but he and Godkin were in complete agreement on this subject.

During the eight days the Jameses stayed at Torquay, William
answered a letter from Professor F. C. S. Schiller of Oxford, who
wanted to propose his name for an honorary degree from Oxford
University. Schiller was more than twenty years younger than
James, but he had found himself in close agreement with the American psychologist's ideas and would soon join him and John Dewey
in a brave defense of Pragmatism against all critics, who were to be
numerous. On April 20 William wrote: "I hope you are not serious
about an Oxford degree for your humble servant. If you are, pray
drop the thought! I am out of the race for all such vanities. Write

me a degree on parchment and send it yourself—in any case it would be but your award!—and it will be cheaper and more veracious. I *had* to take the Edinburgh one, and accepted the Durham one to please my wife. [The University of Edinburgh awarded James the LL.D. degree at the close of his Gifford lectures in 1902, but he did not present himself at Durham to receive the honorary doctorate that university had offered him until June 20, 1908.] Thank you, no coronation either! I am a poor New Hampshire rustic, in bad health, and long to get back, after four summers' absence, to my own cottage and children, and never come away again for lectures or degrees or anything else." He hoped by leading a cautious life to get his "small message to mankind on paper. That nowadays is my only aspiration. The Gifford lectures are all facts and no philosophy—I trust that you may receive the volume by the middle of June."

By May 4 William and Alice were once more at Lamb House, where they found Henry "tranquil and happy in his work," William wrote Charles Norton, "though he has been much pestered of late by gout." The weather was so cold that William claimed he had chilblains. But of course Edinburgh, a week later, was even colder, requiring, William wrote his mother-in-law on May 26, winter clothing and blankets at night, "and hardly a gleam of sun." He also confided that "the surprise of finding myself succeeding last year has this time been replaced by disappointment." But the failure must have been only in his mind, for the audience increased from the previous three hundred to four hundred. The Jameses did not receive as many social invitations as the previous year, but perhaps this was because he was presumed to be still a semi-invalid, though he was at least enough stronger to miss the invitations—partly for his wife's sake. Well aware of his eagerness to get back home and go to Chocorua, Alice suggested that he combine his last two lectures so that they could catch the *Ivernia* on June 10. He jumped at the idea," though he regretted her disappointment "at what promised to be so cheerful a trip socially, turning out so flat."

On the last day at sea before landing in Boston on June 19, William wrote a long letter to his Boston friend Mrs. Henry Whitman, who was now in London and considering where to go next. It had been a "cold and wet voyage, including two days of head-gale and heavy sea, and one of unbroken fog with the lugubrious moo-ing fog-horn," but now the sun had "risen upon American weather, a strong west wind like champagne, blowing out of a saturated blue sky right in our teeth, the sea all effervescing and sparkling with white caps and lace, the strong sun lording it in the sky, and hope presiding in the heart." But he understood Mrs. Whitman's "temptation to stay over." He had again found Scotland democratic and much like New England, though he did not advise her to go there. "Keep to the South and spend one winter in Rome, before you die, and a spring in the smaller Italian cities!" He had had "a bad conscience" about leaving his brother in Lamb House. "He and I are so utterly different in all our observances and springs of action, that we can't rightly judge each other. I even feel great shrinking from urging him to pay us a visit, fearing it might yield him little besides painful shocks. . . ."

II

The James family lost little time in closing the Cambridge house and opening their summer home in Chocorua. After four years they could all be together again. But William, happily, was not permitted to forget his Gifford lectures, for his *Varieties* was being more widely read and discussed than anything he had hitherto published, and throughout the summer he received many letters from readers, critics, and colleagues, praising, objecting, asking questions, and thereby indicating that the book had become a force in their lives. The Protestant clergy seized upon the book as confirmation of their beliefs in God and immortality; the Catholic press was friendly; and the Unitarians, Christian Scientists, Universalists, and others found something to bolster their individual "faiths." Perhaps a central teaching throughout the book, which James indicated on one of his manuscript pages, accounted for much of this enthusiasm; the note reads: "Remember that the whole point lies in really *believing* that through a certain point or part in you you coalesce and are identical with the Eternal. This seems to be the *saving* belief both in Christianity and in Vedantism. . . . It *comes home* to one only at particular times. . . . The more original religious life is always lyric—'the monk owns nothing but his lyre'—and its essence is to dip into another kingdom, to feel an invisible order."

The reception of the book astonished and amused James. The Harvard School of Theology asked him to give two lectures in the summer of 1902. On July 11 he wrote Münsterberg from Chocorua:

"I lecture in Cambr. on Monday and Tuesday. If I go on at this rate, they'll make me a bishop. As for my book, don't read it till you're on your deathbed, when it will save your soul." To Flournoy James wrote: "An enthusiastic clergyman wrote me yesterday that I am of the company of Isaiah and St. Paul. I have just replied: 'Why drag in St. Paul and Isaiah?' "

In writing Schiller back in April that the book was "all facts and no philosophy," James had been sincere. He had started out to write two books, or at least to cover his subject in two parts, the first descriptive (which he had completed), to be capped by a metaphysical treatment. The latter he had not written, though in Lecture XVIII he had discussed philosophy and religion, deciding that metaphysical attributes of religion have no pragmatic (or practical) value—this included dogmatic theology. Then in Lecture XIX he discussed how men intellectualize their religious experience, reducing it to abstractions. He found no fault with this procedure, but emphasized that the living, dynamic force in religion was the *experience* itself.

The whole book defended *variety*, and contained an abundance of examples. James admitted at the outset that there was no way to separate the religious from the neurotic, nor should the violently pathological be ruled out and called not genuinely religious. In fact, he did not attempt to define religion, but rather the *life of religion*, which "consists of the belief that there is an unseen order, and that our supreme good lies in harmoniously adjusting ourselves thereto." The examples cited ranged all the way from mild intuition to hearing voices and seeing visions supposedly emanating from the spirit world. And even if these depended entirely upon the condition of the person's nerves, the experience could still be useful or harmful by its effects on the person's life. Thus the *truth* of the religious experience is its pragmatic value. Does it work? What are the results? *How* it works may never be known and is a matter of scientific curiosity rather than essential knowledge. He was not indifferent to this aspect of the problem, as his own participation in "psychic research" showed, but men and women should not be denied the benefits of religion until science has such knowledge.

James found two main religious types, the "healthy-minded" and the "sick-souls." The former, like Walt Whitman and Emerson, believed that a divine goodness permeated nature and themselves as natural creatures. James admired the cheerful consequences of this "healthy-mindedness" (in fact, in the disguised story of his own experience, discussed in Chapter X above, he had included his own mother among the "healthy-minded"), but he thought they were not capable of fully appreciating tragedy in life or in art. He was also sympathetic with the "sick-souls," the sufferers of temporary or "chronic anxiety." Many of them he admitted, perhaps having himself partly in mind, were affected with a "sort of psychic neuralgia." But whether their malady came from the wrong theology, bad nerves, or abnormal sensitivity to pain, horror, and the evils of the physical world (which certainly included him), they needed such help as a religious faith could give. With him, as we have seen, this took the form of believing in his own power to *will*, and to believe in his will, rejecting pessimistic determinism.

The sick soul is also a "divided self." To some extent the difference between the "healthy-minded" and the "sick-soul" is physiological: "Some persons are born with an inner constitution which is harmonious and well balanced from the outset. Their impulses are consistent with one another, their will follows without trouble the guidance of their intellect, their passions are not excessive, and their lives are little haunted by regrets." But there are others "whose existence is little more than a series of zigzags, as now one tendency and now another gets the upper hand. Their spirit wars with their flesh, they wish for incompatibles, wayward impulses interrupt their most deliberate plans, and their lives are one long drama of repentance and of effort to repair misdemeanors and mistakes." This was his brother Bob, except as time went on his efforts of repair became rarer; and it was also William James himself to some extent, in his impatience, impulsiveness, and changeableness. A woman who had been converted to "mind cure" had written James that, "The first underlying cause of all sickness, weakness, or depression is the *human sense of separateness* from that Divine Energy which we call God." James was not sure that organic sickness could be so caused (though he did not think this impossible either), but he quite agreed that mental sickness and neurotic symptoms could be caused by such a feeling or conviction. Here we find all of James's observations and conclusions as a physiologist, neurologist, and psychologist of religion merging.

In Lecture XX James presented his "Conclusions," a summing up of the characteristic beliefs (which he also personally) held emerging from the religious life:

1. That the visible world is part of a more spiritual universe from which it draws its chief significance;

2. That union or harmonious relation with that higher universe is our true end;

3. That prayer or inner communion with the spirit thereof—be that spirit "God" or "law"—is a process wherein work is really done, and spiritual energy flows in and produces effects, psychological or material, within the phenomenal world.

Religion includes also the following psychological characteristics:—

4. A new zest which adds itself like a gift to life, and takes the form either of lyrical enchantment or of appeal to earnestness and heroism.

5. An assurance of safety and a temper of peace, and in relation to others, a preponderance of loving affections.

As a final observation, the book was dedicated to "E.P.G./ IN FILIAL GRATITUDE AND LOVE." Considering the sacrifices his wife had made for this book, or at least for the author while he was writing it, one almost feels that he was ungrateful not to dedicate it to Mrs. Gibbens's daughter, but of course the daugher was happy to have it dedicated to her mother. Furthermore, to both Alice and William Mrs. Gibbens was a living example of his fifth psychological characteristic, in her "temper of peace" and "preponderance of loving affections."

III

"*Dang* all schools and colleges, say I," William James exclaimed to Fanny Morse in a letter from Chocorua on September 18, 1902. He had spent a happy summer with his family in their New Hampshire home, though they had had guests, "too many of them, rather, at one time," and he had got little reading done. The weather had been cool, with much rain, which restricted his exertions out of doors and rested his heart, though not always his temper. But now the vacation was almost over and tomorrow Alice would be off to Cambridge "to start Billy for Europe—he will spend the winter at Geneva University—and get 'the house' ready for our general reception on the 26th."

James's plans for the one course he would teach during the first semester were already completed. The course was called Philosophy 3, devoted to "The Philosophy of Nature"—perhaps it should have been called "*A* Philosophy of Nature," for he still believed that all philosophical theories were personal, and he was now going to present *his*. Of course he had already published some articles on philosophical subjects, and had several times delivered his lecture on Pragmatism, but he had not yet published a book devoted entirely to philosophy. In his *Principles of Psychology* he had attempted to avoid metaphysics entirely, though actually he had not; but his discussions of the nature of the cosmos, how one knows and the limits of knowledge, and the dependence of the mind on the nervous system—even some speculation on immortality—had all been incidental to psychological exposition. He had attempted to make his *Varieties of Religious Experience* mainly descriptive, with a summary of some of his personal convictions and "over-beliefs" tacked on at the end. It did not add up to a "system," or even, he thought, an adequate development of the personal philosophy which was becoming his major concern in life.

Not only had he not written the book which would be *his* philosophy, James had not clearly thought it out, and he was already alarmed over the possibility that he might not live to do so. On December 14, 1902, he opened a correspondence with Henri Bergson, who four years before had sent him a copy of *Matière et Mémoire* [Matter and Memory]: "My health is so poor now that work goes on very slowly; but I am going, if I live, to write a general system of metaphysics which, in many of its fundamental ideas, agrees closely with what you have set forth, and the agreement inspires and encourages me more than you can well imagine." He had only recently been able to read Bergson with any satisfaction, but he now thought he was beginning to understand the Frenchman's ideas. Bergson had expressed a desire to meet him, and James was eager for a meeting—though it was to be delayed for two years.

Although James had corresponded with John Dewey since 1891, he had only recently begun to perceive the relationships between his own and Dewey's ideas. On April 8, 1903, James wrote to F. C. S. Schiller, his English pragmatist friend (though Schiller preferred the term "humanist" to "pragmatist"): ". . . it appears now that, under Dewey's inspiration, they have at [the University of] Chicago a flourishing school of radical empiricism of which I for one have been entirely ignorant, having been led to neglect its utterances by their lack of 'terseness,' 'crispness,' 'raciness' and other 'newspaporial' virtues, though I could discern that Dewey himself was laboring with a big freight, towards the light." Dewey never acquired the stylistic virtues which James admired and so brilliantly exhibited in his own writing. But the two men were to supplement each other in building a world-wide reputation for Pragmatism as the characteristic and genuine American philosophy, though Dewey would be more successful in influencing society and education.

In a further comment to Schiller, James indicated the nature of his own "radical empiricism": "Once admit that experience is a river which made the channel that now, in part, but only in part, confines it, and it seems to me that all sorts of realities and completenesses are possible in philosophy, hitherto stiffened and cramped by the silly littlenesses of the upper and lower dogmatisms, alternating their petty rationalistic and naturalistic idols of the shop." Later, in his book called *Pragmatism*, James stated his "thesis" that "the truth of an idea is not a stagnant property inherent in it. Truth *happens* to an idea. It *becomes* true, is *made* true by events." Thus, *truth*, like experience, like the cosmos perhaps, is always emerging and going through transmutations. At the end of the *Varieties* he had even intimated that God might be still evolving with His growing, expanding universe, and human beings could assist Him in building the right kind of world.

The letter to Schiller was written from Asheville, North Carolina, where James had gone for rest and recuperation from the colds and tonsilitis he had suffered that spring. He planned to go up to Chocorua the first of May to continue his recuperation, and, he hoped, "be as much better next year than this, as I have this year than last. But lord! how I do want to read as well as write, and with so much left undone, I am getting really anxious lest I be cut off in the bud. Another pathetic Keats case!" However, he would have to come back to Cambridge in May for the Ph.D. examinations. He not only found these a great nuisance; he had become critical of the whole Ph.D. system—"The Ph.D. Octopus," he had called it in the *Harvard Monthly*, March 1903. Already colleges wanted to employ only the holders of these magic letters, and James believed the degree was making graduate work mechanical and arbitrary, and discouraging originality. His observations convinced him that persons with a talent for passing examinations were often not good teachers or even productive scholars. To make the Ph.D. a criterion of employment was degrading and subverting American education.

James even found the awarding of honorary degrees a personal nuisance, though he was not opposed to the custom, as he was to the superstition about Ph.D.s. The Harvard Corporation, of which William's friend and banker Henry Higginson was a member, had wanted to award him an LL.D. degree at the June 1902 commencement, but he had announced that he felt too fatigued to attend, and the degree was deferred. To Higginson he wrote (July 3, 1902) that for the present he was "surfeited with the glory of academic degrees just escaped, like this last one which, in the friendliness of its heart, your Corporation designed sponging upon me at Commencement. Boil it and solder it up from the microbes, and it may do for another year, if I am not in prison! The friendliness of such recognition is a delightful thing to a man about to graduate from the season of his usefulness." Whether boiled or soldered, the degree was duly awarded the following June. Friends said that James worried for weeks before the event for fear that President Eliot would announce that it was being awarded to "William James, Psychologist," but this did not happen; he was recognized as a philosopher.

James's desire to be known as a philosopher, though his contributions in the field were as yet scant, bordered on the neurotic. In joking he would call philosophizing itself neurotic, but his laughter had a quiver of envy—or was it an intimation of pathos? On August 22, 1903, he wrote to his Boston society friend Mrs. Whitman: "I am convinced that the desire to formulate truths is a virulent disease. It has contracted an alliance lately in me with a feverish personal ambition, which I never had before, and which I recognize as an unholy thing in such a connexion. I actually dread to die until I have settled the Universe's hash in one more book, which shall be *epoch-machend* at last, and a title of honor to my children! Childish idiot—as if formulas about the Universe could ruffle its majesty, and as if the common-sense world and its duties were not eternally the really real!"

For the next two years, however, William James published very little, and this was not because his health became worse; on the contrary, it improved, except for an apparent lowered resistance to colds and influenza. His teaching continued to be light, and family affairs offered no greater distraction. Billy was happy in Geneva, took courses with Professor Flournoy, much to William James's delight, and seemed to be headed for a medical career, though after a couple of years he decided to become a painter instead. Harry, after finishing Harvard College and floundering around a bit trying to find a profession, entered the Harvard Law School and prepared for a legal career. Peggy continued to take dancing lessons, go horseback riding, and to acquire social rather than intellectual training, but her parents were pleased with her accomplishments. Aleck was to some extent a problem, though his health was excellent except for an appendicitis operation. He was a poor student, not because he lacked ability, but because he was not interested in academic work. Eventually he too became a painter.

On September 24, 1903, William was at Chocorua with Alice and his two older sons (the younger children were visiting friends), and they all planned to stay until the middle of October. William's only class met on Fridays (he would have to go down to Cambridge twice for that), which he called in a letter to Fanny Morse, "an arrangement which leaves me extraordinarily free, and of which I intend to take advantage by making excursions. . . . I am *vastly* better in nervous tone than I was a year ago, and my work is simplified down to the exact thing I want to do, and I ought to be happy in spite of the lopping off of so many faculties of activity." However, he had spent three days recently at the "Shanty" in Keene Valley without any ill effects. There he had been especially delighted by the "bare-headed and bare-legged" young people who had camped near him. "They lay around the camp-fire at night at the feet of their elders, in every attitude of soft recumbency, heads on stomachs and legs mixed up, happy and dreamy, just like the young of some prolific carnivorous species. The coming generation ought to reap the benefit of all this healthy animality. What wouldn't I give to have been educated in it!" Whatever else age had done to him, it had not made him pessimistic about the coming generation.

The winter of 1904 was not a crucial one for James's health, but the following June he wrote Pillon that it had been a bad one for work, "two attacks of influenza, one very long and bad, three of gout, one of erysipelas, etc., etc. I expected to have written at least 400 or 500 pages of my magnum opus,—a general treatise on philosophy which has been slowly maturing in my mind,—but I have written only 32 pages!" The philosophy which he felt "maturing" James called in his letter to Pillon "a radical empiricism, a pluralism, a 'tychism'. . . . It is theistic, but not essentially so. It rejects all doctrines of the Absolute. It is finitist; but it does not attribute to the question of the Infinite the great methodological importance which you and Renouvier attribute to it. I fear that you may find my system too *bottomless* and romantic. I am sure that, be it in the end judged true or false, it is essential to the evolution of clearness in philosophic thought that *someone* should define a pluralistic empiricism radically. And all that I fear is that, with the impairment of my working powers from which I suffer, the Angel of Death may overtake me before I can get my thoughts on to paper. Life here in the University consists altogether of *interruptions*."

Renouvier had recently died, and of course this news made James more apprehensive about failing to complete his own contribution to philosophy. The friends seemed to be dying off more rapidly now. Two weeks later (June 27, 1904) he had to come down from Chocorua to attend Mrs. Whitman's funeral in Boston. She had had "cardiac symptoms" for some time, but died suddenly of pneumonia. Although William's brother had never met her—rather surprising because Mrs. Whitman was intimate with Henry's good friend Mrs. Jack Gardner, William wrote him an account of the funeral. "She went to every dinner-party and evening party last winter, had an extension, a sort of ball-room, built to her Mount Vernon house, etc. The funeral was beautiful both in Trinity Church and at the grave in Mt. Auburn. I was one of the pall-bearers. . . ." Mrs. Gardner had arranged the floral display in "absolutely Whitmanian style." Mrs. Whitman left, James felt, a "dreadful vacuum in Boston." Perhaps William wrote Henry in such detail about the funeral of this woman whom he admitted to have been "a most peculiar person," because he wished his brother could have "known her whole life here more intimately, and understood its significance." Henry had never liked most Bostonians, but Mrs. Whitman might have been an exception. Now she could never be a link between Henry and the America of Alice and William.

IV

On April 10, 1903, Henry James had written William from Lamb House that the desire "to go 'home' for 6 months (not less,) daily grows on me. . . ." But he was in an economic dilemma: "It is more and more important I should go, to look after my material (literary) interests in person, and quicken and improve them, after so endless an absence—of that I am authentically assured, and *see* it, above all, for myself. But the process itself is so damnedly expensive—6 mos. of American hotels (for I can't *stay* with people—it's utterly impossible,) that I move, as it were, in a vicious circle. I say 6 months because I want and need the material and impressions that only that time would give me. I should wish to write a *book* of 'impressions' (for much money) and to that end get quite away from Boston and New York—really *see* the country at large."

It is clear even in Henry's twisting and turning syntax, that his primary motive for the trip (at least in his own mind) was to gather material for a book of "impressions." But William assumed that it was personal and sentimental, perhaps considering the book as a means of paying for the trip. That literary activities could dwarf personal one was difficult for him to understand. Consequently, when he replied on May 3 he said that the prospect of a visit from Henry "made Alice positively overflow with joyous anticipations. On my part they are less unmixed, for I feel more keenly a good many of the *désagréments* to which you will inevitably be subjected, and imagine the sort of physical loathing with which many features of our national life will inspire you."

Searching for an example of a crudity that would jar Henry's delicate sensibilities, William came up with soft-boiled eggs broken into cups and eaten with butter in dining cars and in hotel restaurants. "How irrational this dislike is, is proven by logic, and by the pleasure taken in the custom by the élite of mankind over here." Then there was American speech. "The *vocalization* of our countrymen is really, and not conventionally, so ignobly awful that the process of hardening oneself thereto is very slow, and would in your case be impossible. It is simply incredibly loathsome. I should hate to have you come and, as a result, feel that you had now *done* with America forever, even in an ideal and imaginative sense, which after a fashion you can still indulge in."

But the most obtuse misinterpretation was William's assuming that by "literary interests" Henry meant copyright—there was now an International Copyright law, but there were still some problems for an author such as Henry James, who lived on royalties from two countries. William said it would be much cheaper to employ an agent to look after these interests. And as for Henry's earning money by public lectures, they "have such an awful side (when not academic) that I myself have forsworn them—it is a sort of prostitution of one's person." William admitted that this was "rather a throwing of cold water; but it is well to realize both sides, and I think I can realize certain things for you better than the sanguine and hospitable Alice does." Still, if Henry really wanted to come, William suggested that he arrive in March or April of the next year and stay through October or into November. He could pass the entire hot summer at Chocorua, "where you could do as much writing as you liked, continuous, and undisturbed, and would (I am sure) grow fond of, as you grew more and more intimate with, the sweet rough country there." William at that time intended to resign his position at Harvard completely in June 1904—though he did not —and he would then be free to travel with his brother. "I could take you into certain places that perhaps you wouldn't see alone"— this in response to Henry's saying he was reluctant to prowl "alone in Western cities and hotels."

William could hardly have more misjudged the psychology of his brother, who replied promptly on May 24 in a two-thousand-word letter, striking down all William's imagined difficulties and clarifying his own actual intentions. He *was*, he insisted, making the trip for economic reasons, and far from dreading the crudities William mentioned, they would be so much grist for his literary mill. Furthermore, compared to William, he had traveled very little and felt that he had the right to do a little touring of his own. Even seeing America at its best in spring, avoiding the summer heat by staying at Chocorua, would not satisfy him either. He wanted to experience "the *whole* American autumn," and he thought he would leave England in mid-August 1904, and "arrive in time for the last three or four weeks of your stay in Chocorua. . . ."

None of Henry's reactions were what William had feared. He was delighted with Chocorua and with New England as a whole. This visit turned out to be one of the happiest periods he had ever spent with his brother. To Miss Pauline Goldmark, William reported on September 21, 1904, near the end of Henry's first stay at Chocorua, that he "seemed to enjoy nature here intensely—found so much *sentiment* and feminine delicacy in it all. It is a pleasure to be with anyone who takes in things through the eyes. Most people don't." One strong trait which the brothers shared was their ability to see a landscape with the eyes of a painter, a survival, in part, of their experiences together in William Hunt's studio in Newport during their youth.

In 1904 Saint Louis was holding an Exposition and many foreign scholars and scientists whom William knew were coming over to attend international conventions being held there because of its World's Fair attractions. Several visited the Jameses in Cambridge, especially in October while Henry was visiting some of his friends. Among the guests at 95 Irving Street were the French neurologist Dr. Pierre Janet and his wife; Professor C. Lloyd Morgan, a British psychologist; and Professor Harold Höffding, a Danish philosopher. To F. C. S. Schiller William James wrote on October 26: "Last night the Janets left us—a few days previous Lloyd Morgan. I am glad to possess my soul for a while alone. Make much of dear old Höffding [when he visits Oxford University], who is a good pluralist and irrationalist. I took to him immensely and so did everybody. Lecturing to my class, he told against the Absolutists an anecdote of an 'American' child who asked his mother if God made the world in six days. 'Yes.'—'The whole of it?'—'Yes.'—'Then it is finished, all done?' —'Yes.' —'Then in what business now is God?' If he tells it in Oxford you must reply: 'Sitting for his portrait to Royce, Bradley, and Taylor.'"

Whatever Henry James's conscious motives for returning to America may have been, perhaps William was not altogether wrong in assuming that the real "pull," possibly unconscious, was emotional. The November Henry spent with his brother's family in Cambridge proved to be the most unforgettable time of his whole trip. The "highest deepest note" was an evening hour he spent at Mount Auburn cemetery in Cambridge during which William's "inspired transcript, on the exquisite little Florentine urn of Alice's ashes" seemed such a "divine gift to us" that Henry felt an "anguish of gratitude."

On another day, in late afternoon or early evening, Henry went walking with William through the "umbrageous 'new' part of Cambridge," as far as Fresh Pond on the outskirts, where he had once walked on Sunday afternoons with William Dean Howells. "That return, with William, from the Country Club, hangs somehow in my mind, with the sense that one had, at the time, of the quality of this added grace to life—a note in the general concert of the larger *amenity* surrounding this generation." Of all the delightful walks and rides he took on this trip, what lingered most fondly in his memory was "the mild soft afterglow of that little excursion with William, at the end of which we walked home (after alighting

from the tram) through the still summerish twilight of the region.
. . . Whenever one is with William one receives such an immense
accession of suggestion and impression that the memory of the
episode remains bathed for one in the very liquidity of his extraordinary play of mind; and I seem to recollect, thus, how he gave
life and light, as it were, to the truth, the interest, of the change
wrought all about there. . . ."

If Henry had any unpleasant experiences with William during
the ten-mouth sojourn in America, he failed to record them, and
vice versa. In January Henry began traveling, and reached California in April 1905. But long before he had reached California,
William had once more sailed off in the opposite direction, con-
firming the fact that, comparatively, he was the traveler.

V

William James had announced that he would not attend a Philosophical Congress to be held in Rome the last of April in 1905, but
early in March, while Henry was still lecturing in the Midwest, he
suddenly decided that he would go, partly to escape the influenza-
inducing weather of Cambridge, partly to talk with European colleagues in psychology and philosophy, but also because he had long
wanted to see Greece. By starting early he could enjoy the Mediterranean sunshine, tour the Grecian isles, and take in the convention.
He sailed on March 11 on the *Romanic*, sharing a stateroom with
another American psychologist, Edwin Holt. Four days out the ship
was tossed by gale winds and heavy seas and it did not dock at
Naples until the 25th. After three days in Naples, William went
on to Capri the 28th and to Sorrento by steamer the 30th, then drove
through Amalfi to Ravello, and returned to Naples by train.

In Naples on the last day of March William walked alone through
the hilly streets of old Naples swarming with goats, donkeys, chickens, an occasional cow, and a multitude of shouting children, with
the cavelike shops and dark interiors forming a somber background.
"Such light and shade, and grease and grime, and swarm, and apparent amiability would be hard to match. . . . Tell Aleck," he
wrote Alice, "to drop his other studies, learn *Italian* (real Italian,
not the awful gibberish I try to speak), cultivate his beautiful smile,
learn a sentimental song or two, bring a tambourine or banjo, and

come down here and fraternize with the common people along the coast—he can go far, and make friends, and be a social success, even if he should go back to a clean hotel of some sort for sleep every night."

But it was Greece, the birthplace of Western philosophy, that William James had mainly come to see, and early in April he sailed for Athens. Santayana was staying at the Minerva Hotel, but after failing three times to find him in, William gave up the attempt and spent the next three weeks in visiting the Greek islands, a strenuous itinerary for a man with a serious heart condition. Finally on April 23 he returned to Rome, where he dined with his old Cambridge neighbor Charles Eliot Norton, actually rested two days, and then went to the meeting place of the Congress to register and get a program. What happened he described the same day in a letter to Alice: ". . . when I gave my name, the lady who was taking them almost fainted, saying that all Italy loved me, or words to that effect, and called in poor Professor [Francesco] de Sanctis, the Vice President or Secretary or whatever, who treated me in the same manner, and finally got me to consent to make an address at one of the general meetings, of which there are four, in place of Sully, Flournoy, Richet, Lipps, and Brentano, who were announced but are not to come. . . . So I'm in for it again, having no power to resist flattery. I shall try to express my 'Does Consciousness Exist?' in twenty minutes—and possibly in the French tongue! Strange after the deep sense of nothingness that has been besetting me the last two weeks (mere fatigue symptoms) to be told that *my* name was attracting many of the young professors to the Congress!"

During the next few days James worked on his speech, and was surprised to find that he wrote French more rapidly than English— partly, he decided later, because he did not have as wide a choice of words to draw upon. On April 30 he wrote his wife: "Yesterday till three, and the day before till five, I was writing my address, which this morning I gave—in French. I wrote it carefully and surprised myself by the ease with which I slung the Gallic accent and intonation, being excited by the occasion. Janet expressed himself as *stupéfait*, from the linguistic point of view. The thing lasted 40 minutes, and was followed by a discussion which showed that the critics with one exception had wholly failed to catch the point of view; but that was quite *en règle*, so I don't care. . . ." To Alice he declared: "The Congress was far too vast, but filled with strange and interesting creatures of all sorts, and socially *very* nutritious to anyone who can stand sociability without distress."

There was actually a small band of professed "pragmatists" in Italy, including Giovanni Papini, Mario Calderoni, Giovanni Vailati, Giovanni Amendola, and others, who published a monthly journal they called *Leonardo.* They "carry on a very serious philosophic movement," William wrote, "apparently *really* inspired by Schiller and myself (I never could believe it before, although [Dr. G. C.] Ferrari had assured me), and show an enthusiasm, and also literary swing and activity that I know nothing of in our own land, and that probably our damned academic technics and Ph.D.-machinery and university organization prevents from ever coming to birth. These men, of whom Ferrari is one, are none of them *Fach-philosophers* [specialists in philosophy], and few of them teachers at all. It has given me a certain new idea of the way in which truth ought to find its way into the world."

From Orvieto on May 2 James wrote to Santayana mainly to suggest that he send review copies of his *Life of Reason* to the editor of the *Revue de Philosophie* in Paris and the editor of *Leonardo* in Florence, but also reporting on the Rome meeting. "The most interesting, and in fact genuinely edifying, part of my trip has been meeting this little *cénacle,* who have taken my own writings, *entre autres, au grand sérieux,* but who are carrying on their philosophical mission in anything but a technically serious way, inasmuch as 'Leonardo' (of which I have hitherto only known a few odd numbers) is devoted to good and lively literary form. The sight of their belligerent young enthusiasm has given me a queer sense of the gray-plaster temperament of our bald-headed young Ph.D.'s, boring each other at seminaries, writing those direful reports of literature in the 'Philosophical Review' and elsewhere, fed on 'books of reference,' and never confounding 'Æsthetik' with 'Erkentnisstheorie' [theory of perception]. Faugh! I shall never deal with them again—on *those* terms!"

Throughout May James continued to travel on the Continent. On the 3rd he arrived in Siena and found his former student Bernard Berenson staying at the Grand Hotel. Siena was not *simpático,* but in the evening he heard *Trovatore* and did not get to bed until two in the morning. He was awake at five, and at eight started on a long drive with Berenson and Princess Marie von Thurn (spelled "Tarn" in his diary) of Austria. During the next several days he traveled on to Pisa, then to Genoa, to Cannes—where he had a long talk with Stumpf, who was on his vacation—to Antibes, Marseilles, and eventually to Geneva on May 16. After a good visit with the Flournoys, who praised Billy, and several days in the neighborhood of Lausanne, William went on to Paris May 25. Dr. Rupert Norton, son of Charles Eliot Norton, had invited him to stay in his apartment at 28 Rue d'Offémont, and it was there that he first met Henri Bergson. In his diary he merely recorded: "Visit from Beautiful Bergson." Twenty years later Bergson described the visit: "I believe that we did, indeed, say 'Bonjour,' but that was all; there were several instants of silence, and straightway he asked me how I envisaged the problem of religion." Bergson's friend Professor F. Abauzit was translating *The Varieties of Religious Experience*, for which Bergson was then considering writing a preface (he later declined), and the two philosophers had much to talk about.

On May 30 William James reached London, spent one night in his favorite "blackguard" hotel, the Charing Cross, then went on to Oxford. He returned to London June 1 to find all the hotels full. Finally the Cheltenham permitted him to sleep in a bathtub, and that was the way he spent his last night in England. Next day he caught the boat at Liverpool. He reached Boston on the afternoon of June 11, to be met by Alice. Five days later his brother Henry arrived from New York, but after only a few days of talk about their respective travels, Henry went to Lenox for a visit with the Whartons.

Henry did not return from Lenox until after William had departed on June 29 for Chicago, where he was to give another round of lectures in the summer school of the University of Chicago: "female teachers, such voices!" he recorded in his diary on July 3. On July 2, Henry wrote him from Cambridge: "Your good letter of farewell reached me at Lenox, from which I returned but last evening—to learn, however, from A., every circumstance of your departure and your condition, as known up to date. . . . Alice tells me that you are to go almost straight [from Chicago] . . . to the Adirondacks: where I hope for you as big a bath of impersonal Nature as possible, with the tub as little tainted, that is, by the soapsuds of *personal*: in other words, all the 'board' you need, but no boarders. I seem greatly to mislike, not to say mistrust, the Adirondack boarder. . . ."

But even William's visit to Keene Valley was not this time entirely for pleasure, because he had promised to give some lectures at a little summer school in Glenmore, which his friend Thomas Davidson (who had now been dead for five years) had started. According to William's diary he gave a lecture there on July 27 on "Witchcraft," and next day another on "Individualism." Although he had no disastrous experiences in the Adirondacks this summer, he probably depleted his reserve of strength more than he realized, for throughout August, back in Cambridge—Chocorua had been "let" for the summer—he suffered greatly from colds and grippe. It may have been an epidemic of some sort, for the whole family was afflicted, and Alice was confined to bed. On August 24 William's diary records: "I slightly better/ Harry no worse/ Alice better/ I make beds/ Alice undoes them." No matter how hard he tried he could never perform housekeeping chores to her satisfaction.

This illness must have somewhat tarnished the splendor of Henry's year-long visit. There is no evidence that the relations of the brothers became less harmonious, but William had become depressed before Henry left early in September. Even two weeks at Silver Lake, New Hampshire, did not restore him, and on October 1, when he met his first class, he could hardly speak. His low physical condition did not improve his appreciation of Henry's new novel, *The Golden Bowl*. On October 22 he wrote his brother that reading it had put him, "as most of your recenter long stories have put me, in a very puzzled state of mind . . . the method of narration by interminable elaboration of suggestive reference . . . goes agin the grain of all my own impulses in writing; and yet in spite of it all, there is a brilliancy and cleanness of effect, and in this book especially a high-toned social atmosphere that are unique and extraordinary." Nevertheless, "why won't you, just to please Brother, sit down and write a new book, with no twilight or mustiness in the plot, with great vigor and decisiveness in the action, no fencing in the dialogue, or psychological commentaries, and absolute straightness in style? Publish it in my name, I will acknowledge it, and give you half the proceeds. Seriously, I wish you *would*, for you *can*; and I should think it would tempt you, to embark on a 'fourth manner.' "

Henry responded on November 23: "I mean (in response to what you write me of having read the *Golden B.*) to try to produce some uncanny form of thing, in fiction, that will gratify you, as Brother—but let me say, dear William, that I shall greatly be humiliated if you *do* like it. . . . I *will* write you your book, on that two-and-two-make-four system on which all the awful truck that surrounds us is produced, and *then* descend to my dishonoured grave. . . . But it is, seriously, too late at night, and I am too tired." He said he was even sorry each time he heard that William had tried to read him: ". . . you seem to me so constitutionally unable to 'enjoy' it, and so condemned to look at it from a point of view remotely alien to mine in writing it. . . ." He also thought that William judged his subject matter too much by "an impossible analogy with the life in Cambridge. . . . And yet I can read *you* with rapture. . . ." Recently while visiting Manton Marble, a writer on politics and history living in Brighton, Henry had found "ever so many of your recent papers and discourses," which he had had time to read, "with the effect of asking you earnestly, to address me some of those that I so often, in Irving St., saw you address to others who were not your brother. I had no time to read them there. Philosophically, in short, I am 'with' you, almost completely. . . ."

When William first tried in the spring of 1907 to read *The American Scene,* the title Henry gave to his notes on his American tour, he found himself, as usual, not "with" Henry, who was still writing in his "third manner," with "innuendo and associative reference" on an enormous scale. Granting that "it does so *build out* the matter for the reader that the result is to solidify, by the mere bulk of the process, the like perception from which *he* has to start," William still found it "the rummest method for one to employ systematically, as you do nowadays. . . ."

By the following autumn, however, William had developed a genuine fondness for some parts of *The American Scene.* In October, while a house guest of the British Ambassador, Viscount James Bryce, and his wife at Intervale, New Hampshire (they had rented the Daniel Merriman summer home), William wrote Henry: "I have just been reading to Mrs. B., with great gusto on her part and renewed gusto on mine, the first few pages of your chapter on Florida in 'The American Scene.' *Köstlich* stuff! I had just been reading to myself almost 50 pages of the New England part of the book, and fairly melting with delight over the Chocorua portion." Back in June 1903, when he was inviting Henry to join him a year hence at Chocorua, William had urged: "Drop your English ideas and take America and Americans as they take themselves, and you will certainly experience a rejuvenation." Now William was delighted to read and reread in *The American Scene* that Henry had found at Chocorua

> a voice in the air, from week to week, a spiritual voice: 'Oh, the *land*'s all right!'—it took on fairly a fondness of emphasis, it rebounded from other aspects, at times, with such a tenderness. Thus it sounded, the blessed note, under many promptings, but always in the same form and to the effect that the poor dear land itself . . . would beautifully 'do.' It seemed to plead, the pathetic presence, to be liked, to be loved, to be stayed with, lived with, handled with some kindness, shown even some courtesy of admiration.

How much the affection of his brother's family had to do with this response, perhaps the novelist did not know himself, but the description of his emotions at Chocorua made William exclaim that "the book will last, and bear reading over and over again—a few pages at a time, which is the right way for 'literature' fitly so called. It all makes me wish that we had you here again, and you will doubtless soon come."

CHAPTER XXIII Philosophy without Humbug

I have grown more and more deeply into pragmatism. . . . It is abso-

lutely the only philosophy with no humbug in it. . . .

—W.J. *to Théodore Flournoy*

I

THOUGH THE HARVARD CORPORATION had refused to let William James resign in 1900 while he was recuperating in Europe, and President Eliot had persuaded him to withdraw a formal letter of resignation in 1903, James continued to debate the subject with himself. His diary for the last quarter of 1905 reads like a graph of his mental and emotional oscillation. From October 26 until December 8 he alternated between "Resign!" and "Don't resign!" President Eliot had also offered to appoint him the Harvard exchange professor at the Sorbonne for 1905–1906, and this posed another hard decision. Diary for November 16: "Don't resign." November 23: "Very tired. Resign—also from Paris." December 8: "Teach here next year." Apparently as his last class in philosophy (December 21) drew near, he felt less discouraged. He had already accepted an invitation to teach at Leland Stanford University from January until mid-May 1906, for five thousand dollars, and was eagerly anticipating this experience. Before leaving Cambridge he definitely declined the Sorbonne appointment.

On New Year's Day James started alone for California, with Alice to follow in February. Three days later he stopped at the Grand Canyon, which he pronounced "equal to the brag." However, it was three degrees above zero and he had brought only his spring overcoat. He had "meant to go down," though he disliked precipices, but he was saved from proving his courage by the refusal of the guides to take anyone down that day. After stopovers in Los

Angeles, Pasadena, Santa Barbara, and San José, he arrived in Palo Alto on January 8 and reported to President David Starr Jordan. His diary read: "All very beautiful & promising. Feel lonely & scared." But next day he felt better and lectured to two hundred students and as many visitors. Diary: "Funk is over! it went all right." January 15: "Lectured well—climate debilitates—air unspeakably soft and rainy. Thermometer about 60°." But he slept poorly and felt continually fatigued. He had not received any mail from Cambridge and wired on the 18th to ask if anything was wrong. Alice replied that she had been ill but was recovering. On February 1 he declined President Eliot's offer to appoint him exchange professor for the winter of 1906–1907 at the University of Berlin.

On February 14 Alice arrived in San Francisco, but William was suffering from gout and could not meet her. Her own account, written to her oldest son, was that she found William in "a truly deplorable condition." When her carriage arrived at the faculty residence assigned to them, he was hobbling around on crutches and could not carry the bags (there were no servants). In a few days, however, the swelling in his foot had subsided enough for him to wear a shoe and he was in fairly good shape for his address to the Assembly of the entire University on February 25.

The address was "The Moral Equivalent of War," perhaps the most famous and influential one he ever gave. James admitted that human history "is a bath of blood," and that the instinct to kill, pillage, and overcome the enemy has survived in men. "We inherit the warlike type; and for most of the capacities of heroism that the human race is full of we have to thank this cruel history." Although he himself looked forward to a time when war would be outlawed by civilized people, he did not want to lose the martial virtues of "intrepidity, contempt of softness, surrender of private interest, obedience to command. . . ." This could be accomplished only by finding "moral equivalents," such as mobilizing men in a conquest of nature, or for building a better society. Instead of conscripting young men for military service, they might be required to serve a few years in some kind of social-service army. (President Kennedy's Peace Corps was exactly the sort of organization James had in mind.) Of course Mrs. James thought the speech a great triumph, and she was right. She overheard a Scots professor of English say it was the most beautiful example of "form" in structure he had ever heard in a public address. The speaker was aware of his triumph too, for "today Papa seems like a new man," his wife declared next day.

William had written his impressions of Stanford to Flournoy on February 9. The architecture of the five-million-dollar buildings was truly beautiful; fifteen hundred students of both sexes paid no tuition; and a town of fifteen thousand had grown up a mile from the campus—Mrs. Leland Stanford, wife of the founder, would not permit shops nearer. "The landscape is exquisite and classical, San Francisco only an hour and quarter away by train; the climate is one of the most perfect in the world, life is absolutely simple, no one being rich, servants almost unattainable . . . and the professors' wives . . . do their own cooking. No social excesses or complications therefore. . . . There couldn't be imagined a better environment for an intellectual man to teach and work in, for eight or nine months in the year, if he were then free to spend three or four months in the crowded centres of civilization—for the social insipidity is great here, and the historic vacuum and silence appalling. . . . Unfortunately the authorities of the University seem not to be gifted with imagination enough to see its proper rôle." Instead of building up an excellent faculty, adequately paid, they employed young men at low salaries, who chafed at not being able to travel and their wives at their domestic drudgery, while a few famous men —himself among them, though he did not say so—were given large sums to teach for a few months.

The personal life of Alice and William James was most vividly described by him in a letter written April 6 to his daughter: "Sweet Peglein: *Won't* you enjoy your mother again! I wish that I could write an analytic biologico-psychological account of her *faits et gestes*, and various vital peculiarities. To begin with she is perfectly happy, has a tremendous appetite, and is beginning to grow *fat*, actually fat. Her face is smooth as a young girl's, and her voice, which lays down the law, communicating valuable information and advice to all, in a steady stream, is like clarified butter of a firm consistency. She has two speeds in going, a slower one which keeps her usually behind me, and a faster one which she throws into gear when we are approaching our destination, and which I can't keep up with at all, it being a kind of single-foot or running walk. It is easy to *offend* her, in entirely unexpected ways, but she gets over it always in about 3 hours, and is then the sweetest, most innocent child imaginable. Moving, or doing anything of my own accord offends her; but as I say, it doesn't last. She depends on me for almost everything, but when I am leading her about, explaining what we see, and fully cognizant of the way, she wants me to ask directions and consult everyone we meet, and she orders and directs me every foot of the way, as if I were incapable.—Since I wrote the above she has prepared our frugal meal, boiled eggs, sardines, triscuit, hot milk, and a roll (which she cabbaged from the brkfst table of the Del Monte Hotel) with apricot jam. . . ."

After an interruption from the assistant who was grading his papers and Miss J. L. Martin, of the Philosophy Department, who lived downstairs, William continued: "Suffice it that she is the most utterly delectable, devoted, wise, simple, fierce, dependent, sociable, kind-hearted, angry, forgiving, beautiful, helpful, radiant, affectionate treasure that ever a family were clustered round. Heaven bless and preserve her and keep us all under her wing. You ought to see her appreciative face when you are lecturing, as I do. She makes such friends wherever she goes, and how they do admire her! And she is getting a genuine vacation out of this, and I don't know when I have seen her more uncloudedly happy."

The last thing that James's former student from California, Charles Bakewell, said to him before his leaving Cambridge was, "I hope they'll treat you to a little bit of an earthquake while you're there. It's a pity you shouldn't have that local experience." On the morning of April 18, when he was lying in bed wide awake at about 5:30, the room began to sway, and James said to himself, "Here's Bakewell's earthquake, after all."

In describing the experience to Fanny Morse four days later, he said that "when it went crescendo and reached fortissimo in less than half a minute, and the room was shaken like a rat by a terrier, with the most vicious expression you can possibly imagine, it was to my mind absolutely an *entity* that had been waiting all this time holding back its activity, but at last saying, 'Now, *go* it!' and it was impossible not to conceive it as animated by a will, so vicious was the temper displayed—everything *down*, in the room, that could go down, bureaus, etc., etc., and the shaking so rapid and vehement. All the while no fear, only admiration for the way a wooden house could prove its elasticity, and glee over the vividness of the manner in which such an 'abstract idea' as 'earthquake' could verify itself into sensible reality. In a couple of minutes everybody was in the street, and then we saw, what I hadn't suspected in my room, the extent of the damage. Wooden houses almost all intact, but every chimney down but one or two, and the higher University buildings largely piles of ruins. Gabble and babble, till at last automobiles brought the dreadful news from San Francisco."

Miss Martin was so worried about her sister in San Francisco that William offered to go there with her, and they managed to get through by train. William returned on the last train that ran for several days, leaving Miss Martin with her sister. While they were away Mrs. James wrote to her mother—she had already sent a telegram by some students going to Oakland, where the telegraph office was still open. She said that when the house began to shake at 5:30 that morning, William had run into her bedroom saying: "This is an earthquake—are you frightened? I am not and I am not nauseated either." Miss Martin had shouted upstairs for them to get out of the house, which they did after grabbing some clothing. She and Miss Martin hurried to the Quadrangle, where they saw the beautiful buildings in ruins. The second floor of the girls' dormitory had dropped to the first with the girls in their beds. In the boys' dormitory a number were injured and several were trapped by falling beams, but, incredibly, only two people had been killed on the campus. When Alice and Miss Martin returned to their house William was picking up fallen bricks and trying to sweep out the broken plaster. All chimneys were down, but the Jameses had an oil stove, uninjured, and Alice made coffee and toast, which they ate on the porch.

San Francisco was a shambles. Explosions had been set off by the initial quake, followed by later damaging tremors, and most of the region of Market Street was in flames. The water mains were broken and firemen could do little except dynamite buildings in the path of the fire in a futile attempt to stop its spread. Federal troops were brought in to control the looting. In his letter to Miss Morse William said he was glad he had gone to the city with Miss Martin, "for the spectacle was memorable. . . . The fires most beautiful in the effulgent sunshine. Every vacant space was occupied by trunks and furniture and people, and thousands have been sitting by them now for four nights and will have to longer. The fire seems now [22nd] controlled, but the city is practically wiped out (thank Heaven, as to much of its architecture!). The order has been wonderful, even the criminals struck solemn by the disaster, and the military has done great service."

With no buildings to hold classes in, Stanford University had to be closed, but the trustees paid James for the full term. On Monday, April 23, he bought railroad tickets for the return home and they began packing. On Thursday morning friends drove them by motor to San Francisco. By this time Alice had located the ranch her father had bought and lost when she was a small girl, and she recorded in her diary for April 26: "A beautiful morning on this old country road we took with father 50 years ago." They spent Thursday night with friends in Oakland and boarded a Pullman car on Friday morning. After a brief stopover in Denver, they reached Cambridge on May 3. "Sunrise. New England, nearing home. Blessed country." This was the last entry in Alice James's diary for nearly two years.

Several cablegrams and a letter from Billy, who had returned to Europe and was staying with his Uncle Henry, made William realize that he had unintentionally kept them in suspense. He cabled their safe arrival home and wrote a letter to both of them on May 9, apologizing for his callousness: "For *all* the anguish was yours; and in general this experience only rubs in what I have always known, that in battles, sieges and other great calamities, the pathos and agony is in general solely felt by those at a distance; and although physical pain is suffered most by its immediate victims, those at the *scene of action* have no *sentimental* suffering whatever. Everyone at San Francisco seemed in a good hearty frame of mind; there was work for every moment of the day and a kind of uplift in the sense of a 'common lot' that took away the sense of loneliness. . . ." But it was a queer sight, even eight days after the disaster, to see groups of people cooking their meals at little brick camp-fires in the middle of the streets. "If such a disaster had to happen, somehow it couldn't have chosen a better place than San Francisco (where everyone knew about camping, and was familiar with the creation of civilizations out of the bare ground), and at five-thirty in the morning, when few fires were lighted and everyone, after a good sleep, was in bed. Later, there would have been great loss of life in the streets, and the more numerous foci of conflagration would have burned the city in one day instead of four, and made things vastly worse."

A week later, while the experiences were still fresh in his mind, William James wrote an article "On Some Mental Effects of the Earthquake" for the *Youth's Companion*. What he stressed was how the catastrophe had aroused the best instincts in people, suppressing their selfishness and binding them by mutual sympathy, and producing spontaneous leaders. It was also a "moral equivalent of war." By coincidence, the strange Pole Lutaslawski had been writing James about experiments with Yoga discipline, which had awakened deeper levels of will power in him. This year James was president of the American Philosophical Association, and for his presidential address at the meeting at Columbia University on December 28, 1906, he drew upon both his own observations after the earthquake in California and Lutaslawski's with Yoga. His theme was that most men have untapped energies which only a great disaster or disciplined will power can draw upon. He also discussed how "ideas" could help, and suggested again that the methods of the "mind curers" should not be dismissed without examination. Finally, he said, "We need a topography of the limits of human power, similar to the chart which oculists use of the field of human vision. We need also a study of the various types of human being with reference to the different ways in which their energy-reserves may be appealed to and set loose." Biographies could give us important clues.

II

Just before his sixty-fifth birthday on January 11, 1907, William James finally and definitely resigned his professorship at Harvard, and President Eliot accepted the resignation, granting him twenty-six hundred dollars a year as professor emeritus. As Professor James began his last lecture on January 22, he was surprised to see his wife and several colleagues slip into seats at the rear of the room, but he proceeded to teach his class in his usual informal manner. At the end of the period there was an enthusiastic ovation and then the class presented him with a silver loving cup. This was indeed the end of his formal teaching career, but he was not depressed about it. On the contrary, he felt relieved; now he could organize those lectures on Pragmatism into a book. Next day he wrote in his diary: "Delicious feeling of leisure." In the spring he wrote his brother Henry: "You can't tell how happy I am at having thrown off the nightmare of my 'professorship.' As a 'professor' I always felt myself a sham, with its chief duties of being a walking encyclopedia of erudition. I am now at liberty to be a *reality*, to be my own man, after 35 years of being owned by others. I can now live for truth pure and simple, instead of for truth accommodated to the most unheard-of requirements set by others."

But James certainly did not act like a man of leisure. He had agreed to repeat his Pragmatism lectures at Columbia University, and after several days of further work on them he left for New York on January 28. He put up at the Harvard Club on West 44th Street, attended a luncheon given by friends at the Century Club, and next day took the subway to West 116th Street. The lecture had been announced for Schermerhorn Hall, with two hundred and fifty seats, but over a thousand people were waiting to hear him; so the series of lectures was moved to the Chapel in Teachers College. As at Edinburgh, his audience increased with each performance. On February 2 he visited Peggy at Bryn Mawr, where she was doing well in her studies, then came back to New York on the 4th in a blizzard and on the 5th lectured to his biggest Columbia audience yet. Professor Edward Lee Thorndike, of Teachers College, entertained him in his home, and other members of the Columbia faculty drained his energy with their hospitality.

On February 14, back in Cambridge, William wrote his brother Henry and son Billy, the latter still visiting his uncle: "The first impression of New York, if you stay there not more than 36 hours, which has been my limit for twenty years past, is one of repulsion at the clangor, disorder, and permanent earthquake conditions. But this time, installed as I was at the Harvard Club (44th St.) in the centre of the cyclone, I caught the pulse of the machine, took up the rhythm, and vibrated *mit*, and found it simply magnificent. . . . It is an *entirely* new New York, in soul as well as in body, from the old one, which looks like a village in retrospect. The courage, the heaven-scaling audacity of it all, and the *lightness* withal, as if there was nothing that was not easy, and the great pulses and bounds of progress, so many in directions all simultaneous that the coördination is indefinitely future, give a kind of *drumming background* of life that I never felt before. I'm sure that once *in* that movement, and at home, all other places would seem insipid."

James had dined with Norman Hapgood, editor of *Collier's Weekly;* W. T. Jerome, District Attorney of New York County; Finley Peter Dunne, the humorist; and Mark Twain—"The latter, poor man, is only good for monologue, in his old age, or for dialogue at best, but he's a dear little genius all the same." Although Jerome was "in the very crux of the [Harry] Thaw trial," one of the most sensational murder-trials of the decade, he acted "as if he had nothing serious to do." James felt that his stay in New York was "certainly the high tide of my existence, so far as *energizing* and being 'recognized' were concerned, but I took it all very 'easy' and am hardly a bit tired. Total abstinence from every stimulant whatever is the one condition of living at a rapid pace. I am now going whack at the writing of the rest of the lectures, which will be more original and (I believe) important than my previous works."

In April Schiller wrote James that "humanism" would be a better title than "Pragmatism," but William replied that the book was already in type and it was too late to change. He disliked the word too, but it now seemed "to have the *international* right of way at present. Let's both go ahead—God will know his own!" Thus the book came out in the spring with the title: *Pragmatism: A New Name for Some Old Ways of Thinking.* In his preface, James tried to distinguish between *pragmatism* and *radical empiricism*, the latter holding that all knowledge is derived from experience and the testimony of the senses, while pragmatism was a method of thinking, using ideas as instruments of thought. While correcting proof William had written Henry: "I shouldn't be surprised if ten years hence it should be rated as 'epochmaking,' for the definitive triumph of that general way of thinking I can entertain no doubt whatever— I believe it is to be something quite like the protestant reformation."

This prediction was neither conceited nor delusive. Both the term and the concept of truth as an hypothesis always subject to change to make it work better impressed the world—though not always favorably—as *the* American philosophy. Heinrich Straumann in his recent *American Literature in the Twentieth Century* thinks it surprising that "the one aspect of American conduct generally accepted as outstanding found its philosophical interpretation at such a late date. The pragmatic view of life more commonly and also more honestly adopted in the United States than anywhere else in the Western world had its firm grip on the majority of Americans long before anyone attempted to describe it in terms of abstract thought." The significance of this in William James's biography is that his character, personality, and experience enabled him to *feel* the importance of the pragmatic view, and his familiarity with life and thought in Europe enabled him to *see* (intellectually) how it could be formulated into a theory, drawing on the work of John

Locke, John Stuart Mill, and other British and Continental fore-runners.

In June James thanked Bergson for sending him his *L'Évolution Créatrice*, which he predicted would bring about "an entirely new era in respect of matter. . . ." Its style left with him the same "after-taste" as reading *Madame Bovary*. Although he was not yet sure that he fully understood it, "To me at present the vital achievement of the book is that it inflicts an irrecoverable death-wound upon Intellectualism." He was sending Bergson a copy of his *Pragmatism*, but declared, "How jejune and inconsiderable it seems in comparison with your great system! But it is so congruent with parts of your system, fits so well into interstices thereof, that you will easily understand why I am so enthusiastic. I feel that at bottom we are fighting the same fight. . . . The position we are rescuing is 'Tychism' [chance] and a really growing world. But whereas I have hitherto found no better way of defending Tychism than by affirming the spontaneous addition of *discrete* elements of being (or their subtraction), thereby playing the game with intellectual weapons, you set things straight at a single stroke by your fundamental conception of the continuously creative nature of reality."

III

The excitement of his New York triumph had deceived James into thinking that his activities there had not tired him. Soon after returning home on February 10 he consulted a physician about his heart, and found that his angina was now in an advanced state. But he did not spare himself, continuing his work on the Pragmatism manuscript, and then the proof, except for an interruption of grippe in March. There were vexations, too, such as President Roosevelt's speech on February 23 at the Harvard Union, in which he had amused his student audience by making fun of scholarship. Recently his former teacher had come to admire him, and had even expressed the hope that "Teddy" Roosevelt might be considered for the next president of Harvard when Eliot retired. But this speech angered James; it seemed like a cheap trick, and he wrote in his diary "Déception!"

In April a bit of amusing excitement in the James household was caused by Mrs. James's decision to do something about their sorry lawn in Cambridge. She employed five men with two carts to scrape off the weeds and poor topsoil and then bring in a hundred and fifty loads of loam. On April 27 William wrote his daughter at Bryn Mawr an account of her mother, chubby, ruddy, bare-headed, and cloaked against the cold wind, supervising the operation, cheering the men on, giving them tea and doughnuts at four o'clock, and seeing that they did the work to her satisfaction—"Just like Chocorua!" But Alice, in her turn, was not amused, as she wrote Billy, by "the dreadful confusion of poor Daddy's days. Almost every morning come people who want his help in advice and *he sees them all*. One morning this is what I observed. Dr. Sidis, soon after 10 a.m. to have a long talk over his medical school difficulties, then Woodward Emery about Charles Peirce, next Kallen about his work [Horace M. Kallen, then a graduate student], and then Royce. It could all have been saved with a little planning. These morning hours ought to be kept for himself but I am powerless to help. . . ."

In May James was told by Aleck's teachers that there was no hope of his passing the entrance examinations for Harvard. Aleck was moody, emotionally unstable, and a great worry to his parents, who had quite unintentionally neglected him at a crucial stage of his adolescence. This and other worries were, of course, bad for William's angina, and in June the pains returned in full force. Unfortunately, too, he had rented Chocorua again to help with the expenses, and as a consequence was so restless and miserable during the summer that he made frequent trips away from Cambridge, mostly to the New England coast. In the autumn he became discouraged about keeping Chocorua because it needed repairs on the house and work on the grounds which he was not strong enough to do himself and he could not find anyone to employ. On October 14 his Polish friend Lutaslawski arrived for a visit, at William's invitation, and seemed to be in no hurry to leave. William did not mind this because he really did like the eccentric philosopher, who shocked the neighbors by his nude sun-bathing (in October!) on the balcony. Alice finally became so annoyed that she asked him to leave, much to her husband's chagrin.

In November Oxford University invited William James to give the Hibbert lectures in Manchester College in the spring of 1908. He cabled his acceptance on November 29, and in December began writing the lectures, which he later published as *A Pluralistic Universe*. By this time Billy had progressed enough in his painting to begin portrait work, and during December his mother posed several hours a day for him, doing meanwhile her darning and mending.

On Christmas Day William left for Cornell University to attend the annual meeting of the American Philosophical Association and read a paper on "The Meaning of the Word Truth." Many readers of *Pragmatism* had been unable to accept his concept of "truth" as a method of testing and verifying the workableness of any concept assumed to be "true." He now attempted to show that his account of truth was "realistic, and follows the epistemological dualism of common sense." In other words, he assumed an objective world independent of mind, the reality of which can be known only by exercising the senses and the mysterious process known as consciousness. The difficulty for James's hearers seemed to be his insistence that *truth* can not be known without some process (actual or imagined) of testing its reality, or the reliability of any statement assumed to be true. He came home from the meeting complaining that all he heard at Cornell was cursing of Pragmatism.

January was cold and blustery, with zero weather, and James suffered much from colds and a severe attack of grippe. There were times in February and March when he feared he could not possibly be ready to give the Oxford lectures in May, but on April 2 he wrote his daughter Peggy: "I think I see my way clear to go [to Oxford] now, if I don't get more fatigued than at present. Four and a quarter lectures are fully written, and the rest are down-hill work, much raw material being ready now."

On Tuesday, April 21, William and Alice James sailed from Boston on the *Ivernia*, which arrived at Liverpool on the 30th. Harry and Peggy were to come after their examinations were over (Harry's in law school, Peggy's at Bryn Mawr), and possibly Aleck. At the end of two restless days and sleepless nights for William at a hotel in Leamington, the family went to Oxford, where William gave his first lecture on May 4. The attendance was so great that many people could not get into the hall and were turned away. William could now relax and his sleep improved marvelously, though he still took heavy medication for his heart. On May 12 Oxford University awarded him an honorary D.Sc. degree, preceded by a ritualistic luncheon at St. John's College, and followed (quite unofficially) by a visit to Mrs. Ole Bull's house.

A letter written by Alice to her mother on May 26 indicates the busy social life she and her husband were leading: "Yesterday William gave his 7th lecture to an audience that was simply spellbound. On Thursday will come the last. I have been hoping that Harry [son] might get here and have written him at Queenstown [where the ship would pick up mail] to that effect. On Saturday the 30th Wm. is going to Birmingham to spend Sunday with Sir Oliver Lodge [an ardent supporter of psychical research]. I shall take that chance to go to Harrow. We shall both come back on Tuesday afternoon to spend 4 days with Mrs. Fiske Warren. I did not want to go there at first but I cordially like her now, so I can go. On June 5th Miss Sands sends over for us to spend Sunday at her country home 8 miles from Oxford. Monday we return for 24 hours with the [William] MacDougals (the professor of Psychology) and then we go, Harry too I hope, to the Cotswolds for a week of entire quiet. On the 20th we three are going to Durham to visit Professor [William Stanley] Jevons and let Wm. take the degree which was offered him 5 years ago. We shall have to be meeting Peggy by the 27th or 28th so you see our time is only too short. So much for our plans. Possibly we shall have Peggy come to London with the Cochrans and meet us in the Lake Country for it seems silly to travel to Southampton [to meet her ship] only to hurry north again. And I want to bring Peggy to Oxford in July to learn to love the beautiful old city. . . . Logan Pearsall Smith met us with his launch and took us together with Mr. Gilbert Murray and Val Worthington to a Tuesday lunch with the Bertrand Russells. The loveliness of the river of the old English village and the walk by footpaths to Bagley where the R[ussell]s live was beyond any words of mine. England is the most liveable, most homelike country in the world. It reminds me all the while of you. And what gardens! And this though we have nothing but cold, really cold weather."

On June 12 Alice wrote Billy: "We have struck up a most wonderful combination with Lady Ottoline Morrell—a lady of high degree whom all the artists want to paint. She looks like a Flemish saint of ages ago and she and Loving Dad are sworn friends. She and I do very well too. She is the only sister of the Duke of Portland and he is highly offended at her marriage to a commoner[,] just a liberal [sic] M.P. brother of Mrs. Edward Warren the architect with whom we lunched." Lady Ottoline recorded in her memoirs her opinion of James (no mention of his wife): "I walk again in memory with William James across meadows and down the Long Elm

Avenue [at Newington, her home near Oxford]. He was so appreciative and 'ravished by the greenness and luxuriance of the English country. The villages and lawns: the streams,' as he said, 'are endlessly perfect in their way and interesting. A country in equilibrium with itself and to Yankee eyes a fabulous antique and finished.' "

Lady Ottoline added that William had been distressed that in *The American Scene* Henry could have written as he did about his countrymen, especially about the commercial traveler's breakfast. "How could he have written that about a fellow human being—one for whom Christ died?" Although William had protested over the style of *The American Scene*, he had called the description of the "drummers" in the "best sense Rabelaisian," and one suspects that either the Lady misunderstood William or that he was being satirical for her amusement. She was also acquainted with Henry, and compared the brothers: William's nature was "intensely lovable, simple and human, with immense sensitive kindness and understanding of life and other human beings—he had above all people the intellect of the heart." Henry had the same temperament, "but added to it there was the inexorable artist who, when it takes command of a personality, is an autocrat over all the instincts, and a jealous taskmaster."

During June Alice and William were also the house guests of the Pearsall Smiths at their Sussex estate, and their son Logan Pearsall recalls (in his *Unforgotten Years*) another anecdote. William James declared he would like to spend the whole summer in England and enjoy the country life. "My father thereupon obtained a list of country houses to be let in our neighborhood, and orders to view them, and drove William James to see one after the other. This inspection he carried on with the utmost care, examining each house from attic to cellar, alloting the various rooms to be occupied by the various members of his family. When this process was over, and the gardens and even the stables had been examined, and he returned to our house to dinner, he genially remarked, 'I can't tell you how grateful I am for all the trouble you have taken; I have had my summer in England, and now we can go abroad!' "

However, the Jameses did not go to the Continent until the latter part of the summer. After the trip to the Lake Country, somewhat marred for William by a severe head cold, they visited Henry at Lamb House. Alice, Harry, and Peggy went down to Rye from

London on July 10, and William followed a week later. Some time after he arrived H. G. Wells witnessed an interesting "scene" between the brothers (told by Wells in his *Autobiography*):

> I once saw [Henry] James quarrelling with his brother William James, the psychologist. He had lost his calm; he was terribly unnerved. He appealed to me, to me of all people, to adjudicate on what was and what was not permissible behaviour in England. William was arguing about it in an indisputably American accent, with an indecent naked reasonableness. I had come to Rye with a car to fetch William James and his daughter to my home at Sandgate. William had none of Henry's passionate regard for the polish upon the surfaces of life and was immensely excited by the fact that in the little Rye inn, which had its garden just over the high brick wall of the garden of Lamb house, G. K. Chesterton was staying. William James had corresponded with our vast contemporary [William mistakenly thought Chesterton a convert to Pragmatism] and he sorely wanted to see him. So with a scandalous directness he had put the gardener's ladder against that ripe red wall and clambered up and peeped over!
>
> Henry had caught him at it.
>
> It was the sort of thing that isn't done. It was most emphatically the sort of thing that isn't done. . . . Henry had instructed the gardener to put away that ladder and William was looking thoroughly naughty about it.
>
> To Henry's manifest relief, I carried William off and in the road just outside the town we ran against the Chestertons who had been for a drive in Romney Marsh; Chesterton was heated and I think rather swollen by the sunshine; he seemed to overhang his one-horse fly; he descended slowly but firmly; he was moist and steamy but cordial; we chatted in the road for a time and William got his coveted impression.

Probably at this time Chesterton invited William to his house. At any rate, on August 2, two days after Alice and Peggy had left for Geneva, William wrote in his diary that he had motored with his brother to Mr. and Mrs. Ford Madox Hueffer's, then "at nine to Chesterton's where we sat till midnight drinking port with H. Belloc."

Meanwhile Aleck had come over and William took him to the National Gallery, where the paintings interested him as much as they had his father at the same age. Afterward his father found a private tutor for him at Oxford. Except for a business trip with Henry to London, William stayed at Rye until August 21, when he crossed the Channel to meet Alice and Peggy in Brussels, and they began a tour which took them to Antwerp, Rotterdam, The Hague, Haarlem, Amsterdam, Bruges, Paris, and back to London, where Aleck rejoined them. In September William revisited friends at Cambridge and Oxford, and on October 3 Henry came up from Rye to spend three days with them in London. They sailed on the 6th on the *Saxonia*, leaving Aleck in England, and arrived back in Boston on the 16th after a stormy passage.

IV

The kind of summer James had spent in Europe appears on the surface to indicate that he was stronger than he had been recently, but only excitement and will power had carried him through. By the time he got home, his heart was dangerously weak; yet instead of going to bed he went next day (October 17) to visit the Salters at Silver Lake. Three days later Charles Eliot Norton died, and James returned for the funeral on the 22nd. Though Norton's death was not unexpected, it was still a shock because he had been one of Henry Sr.'s closest friends, and the two families had been intimate for two generations. On the 27th William returned to Silver Lake, and after ten days he seemed sufficiently recovered to resume normal activities, repeating at Harvard some of his Oxford lectures (to be published early in 1909 as *A Pluralistic Universe*), continuing his support of the organizations for peace, mental health, and even attending more *séances*.

At the end of 1908 and continuing into 1909 he prepared a lengthy "Report on Mrs. Piper's Hodgson-Control," part of which was read in London at the January meeting of the Society for Psychical Research; the remainder (really a small book) was printed in the *Proceedings* for 1909. A short time after Richard Hodgson's death on December 20, 1905, Mrs. Piper claimed that he was communicating with her through a spirit, or "control." The S.P.R. asked James to evaluate the records of these *séances*, a total of seventy-five, and write a report for the Society. At the end of his report James repeated his earlier statement that the records of these sittings were "vastly more leaky and susceptible of naturalistic explanation than is any body of Piper material recorded before." Yet he was unwilling to say that they were fraudulent. In some parts of the *séances* he thought it was possible that some supernatural transaction had taken place, but it could not be proven. He was inclined to think it all came out of Mrs. Piper's subconscious dream life, but this did not rule out a seepage from other people's subconscious into hers.

James's last statement on this subject took the form of a popular article, "The Final Impressions of a Psychical Researcher," published in the October 1909 issue of the *American Magazine*. Here he frankly admitted that after twenty-five years of reading literature in the field, being acquainted with numerous "researchers," and himself "witnessing (or trying to witness) phenomena," meaning *séances*, telepathy, and supposed materialization of spirits, he was "theoretically no 'further' than I was at the beginning; and I confess that at times I have been tempted to believe that the Creator has eternally intended this departure of nature to remain *baffling*. . . ."

James did admit, however, to a conviction based on conjecture and intuition—which he had expressed many times before, but never quite so poetically as now—that "our lives are like islands in the sea, or like trees in the forest . . . [which] commingle their roots in the darkness underground, and the islands also hang together through the ocean's bottom. Just so there is a continuum of cosmic consciousness, against which our individuality builds but accidental fences, and into which our several minds plunge as into a mother-sea or reservoir."

None of this theorizing about an underground-consciousness had anything to do with Freud's theory, which had not interested James particularly and of which he had only skimpy knowledge. Freud had been in Boston in the autumn of 1908 and had conducted colloquia attended by William's friend Jim Putnam and by Münsterberg, but there is no record that he took any interest in the new doctrines. Of course James was just back from Europe then, and was tired and ill besides. He was also ill when Freud returned the following year, though he was able to go to Clark University early in September to hear his lecture. James's diary contains few entries for the summer and early autumn of 1909—another indication of physical weakness—and no mention of Freud, but Ernest Jones in *The Life and Work of Sigmund Freud* has a brief account of Freud's "moving encounter with William James, then fatally ill. . . . James, who knew German well, followed the lecture with great interest. He was very friendly to us [Jones had accompanied Freud from New York] and I shall never forget his parting words, said with his arm around my shoulder: 'The future of psychology belongs to your work.' "

Freud himself left a memory of James in *An Autobiographical Study:* "Another event of this time which made a lasting impression on me was a meeting with William James the philosopher. I shall never forget one little scene that occurred as we were on a walk together. He stopped suddenly, handed me a bag he was carrying and asked me to walk on, saying that he would catch me up as soon as he had got through an attack of angina pectoris which was just coming on. He died of that disease a year later; and I have always wished that I might be as fearless as he was in the face of approaching death."

On September 28, 1909, William wrote his Geneva friend Flournoy: "How much your interests and mine keep step with each other, dear Flournoy. 'Functional psychology,' and the twilight region that surrounds the clearly lighted centre of experience! Speaking of 'functional' psychology, Clark University, of which Stanley Hall is president, had a little international congress the other day in honor of the twentieth year of its existence. I went there for one day in order to see what Freud was like, and met also Yung [Carl Gustav Jung] of Zürich, who professed great esteem for you, and made a very pleasant impression. I hope that Freud and his pupils will push their ideas to their utmost limits, so that we may learn what they are. They can't fail to throw light on human nature; but I confess that he made on me personally the impression of a man obsessed with fixed ideas. I can make nothing in my own case with his dream theories, and obviously 'symbolism' is a most dangerous method. A newpaper report of the congress said that Freud had condemned American religious therapy (which has such extensive results) as very 'dangerous' because so 'unscientific.' Bah!"

James also told Flournoy in this same letter, "It hasn't gone well with my health this summer, and beyond a little reading, I have done no work at all." He did expect to be able to attend the inauguration ceremonies on October 5 for the new president of Harvard, Abbott Lawrence Lowell, though he would have no part in them except as a spectator. But it was not strictly true that James had done nothing in the field of philosophy during this summer of 1909, because he had put together a collection of essays, with a Preface and slight additions, which was published in October as *The Meaning of Truth*. Since his theory of truth was basic for his

Pragmatism, he thought these essays might clarify the theory and increase the understanding of *Pragmatism*. And the theory was also pivotal to his recent *Pluralistic Universe*, the first of his Oxford lectures having been on "The Types of Philosophic Thinking." In other lectures he tried to define and discuss monistic idealism, Hegelianism, the theories of Fechner (from whom James had largely derived his "mother-sea" metaphor for "cosmic consciousness"), and "Bergson and His Critique of Intellectualism." These philosophies were interpreted from the point of view of James's pragmatic-empiricist pluralism, but otherwise *A Pluralistic Universe* was not an original contribution; that is, it did not add up to the contribution to metaphysics which James had been desperately hoping to make before he died. In fact, the Oxford interlude had diverted him from that task, though the lectures had been a popular and literary success and one can hardly regret that he gave them.

James regarded his philosophy as embracing four doctrines: pluralism, radical empiricism, tychism, and theism. His *A Pluralistic Universe* was concerned with the first and second of these terms; his *Pragmatism* assumed a universe of constant flux and change; and the last chapter of his *Varieties of Religious Experience* had sketched out his theism. In 1909 and 1910 he was working on a book, tentatively entitled *Some Problems in Philosophy* (published posthumously with the subtitle *A Beginning of an Introduction to Philosophy*) which he hoped would tie all these theories together and explain them in a more logical and convincing manner. This was to complete the arch to his system.

CHAPTER XXIV

The Unfinished Arch

Call it 'A beginning of an introduction to philosophy.' Say that I hoped

by it to round out my system, which now is too much like an arch

built only on one side.   —W.J., *Memorandum dated July 26, 1910*

I

"DREADFUL ANGINA ON GOING TO BED," William James wrote in his diary for October 25, 1909. Several days earlier he had recorded, "Decided symptoms of nervous prostration all these days." Although he had never practiced medicine he had kept up with the advances in the field, and he was acutely aware of the seriousness of his condition. But he had never been able to relax and let nature help him recuperate. In fact, unless he was completely "prostrated," his pains and tension only drove him to more intemperate exertions. And the dyspnoea (hard breathing caused by angina) was worse in bed than out, thus making rest even more seemingly impossible for him. In desperation he again began taking Christian Science treatments, from a reputedly successful "practitioner," L. G. Strang, in Boston. On November 29, after his fourteenth visit, he recorded in his diary: "Good mental effect. [Physical] Symptoms bad." But next day he did not permit these "symptoms" to keep him from attending a luncheon given in Boston by the Anti-Imperialist League, at which he sat beside Mark Twain and listened to a stirring oration by Judge Moorfield Storey.

Fortunately, William no longer had any serious family problems. His son Henry was working in a law office in Boston and seemed to have a bright professional future. Peggy had finished her studies at Bryn Mawr and was living at home. (She was later to marry and would live in California.) Billy was busy painting portraits of the family, among them one of his father (*see frontispiece*). Even Aleck had solved his great problem in the choice of his life-work. Several months earlier his father had recalled him from England because he was making almost no progress with his Oxford tutors, and during the summer he had tried unsuccessfully to prepare for the Harvard entrance examinations by attending a "coaching school" in Cambridge. Finally in November he announced that he wanted to study painting in a small art school in Dublin, New Hampshire. This turned out to be a fortunate and happy choice—so happy that he would spend the remainder of his life in Dublin and win a respectable reputation as a painter.

In spite of a snow storm, the first of the season, William visited his brother Bob, again living with his wife, in Concord on November 24 and took lunch with them. Two weeks later Mary wrote him that she felt compelled to leave Bob once again and would soon go to Paris. Of course William was sorry to hear of this renewed discord in Concord, but there was nothing he could do to help. Bob was unable to change his character, and all William could hope for was that he would keep his unhappiness to himself.

Though on many nights William had difficulty in sleeping because of the dyspnoea, he still managed to accomplish a great deal. On December 13 he finished rewriting the speech he had given in 1906 at Stanford University on "The Moral Equivalent of War" and mailed it to *McClure's Magazine*. He promptly received two hundred dollars and assurance of publication in May 1910. Next day he began an article for the *Journal of Philosophy, Psychology, and Scientific Methods* on the phenomenon of the mystical experience, which he would attempt to explain in terms of the subliminal consciousness. Christmas Eve he was ill again, but was able to enjoy dinner next day with his family and his brother from Concord. On the last day of the year several colleagues in philosophy called to tell him about the recent meeting of the American Philosophical Society in New Haven, which he had not felt like attending, and that night he slept without medication. Thus, in spite of much pain and frequent exhaustion, James was able to keep in close touch with his professional world during the latter part of 1909; he even contributed to it substantially that year by publishing seven articles and two books, *A Pluralistic Universe* and *The Meaning of Truth*—three, if one counted the book-length "Piper Report."

At the beginning of 1910 William felt greatly encouraged by an apparent improvement in his health, discounting the usual colds and a touch of lumbago during zero weather. He had received a psychological lift from several fresh indications of his growing reputation in scholarly circles. One of these came in January when Bergson cabled him that he had been elected an *associé étranger* to the French Académie des Sciences Morales et Politiques. The Boston *Journal* received this information directly from Paris and publicized it, to the delight of James's many friends, but he pretended to think that Jack (John Jay) Chapman, one of the few persons to whom he divulged the message from Bergson, had "humiliated" him by giving the information to the newspapers, "so now I lie in the dust, spurning all the decorations and honors under which the powers and principalities are trying to bury me. . . ."

On January 11 William wrote in his diary: "68 years old today! Wrote. Good day. Called on Carrington and Eusapia P. at Adams House. Queer twisting of my chair." Eusapia Paladino was an Italian medium whom Professor Richet had told James about the spring the Jameses lived at Hyères. She had come to New York in the autumn of 1909 and been "exposed" by several investigators. James himself was not entirely taken in by her, and he had written in his "Final Impressions of a Psychical Researcher," published the previous October: "Eusapia Paladino, the Neapolitan medium, has been under observation for twenty years or more. . . . Everyone agrees that she cheats in the most barefaced manner whenever she gets an opportunity. . . . Yet her credit has steadily risen. . . ." But her "credit" had not risen with James's colleagues Royce and Münsterberg; in fact, their professional respect for him had declined because of his tolerance of her claims. Royce had even circulated a wicked little jingle:

> Eeny, meeny, miney mo,
> Catch Eusapia by the toe,
> If she hollers, then you know
> James's theory is not so.

Münsterberg was bluntly outspoken in condemning all psychical research, and in an article published in the *Metropolitan Magazine* for February 1910 he used Eusapia as a prime example of the bogus claims of the pseudo-scientists who called themselves "psychic researchers." James could forgive Royce's snickering jingle, but Münsterberg's attack angered him, and he wrote in his diary: "buffoon article!"

But these personal irritations did not diminish James's enjoyment of participating in a Eusapia performance on his birthday and talking to the Director of the American Psychical Institute, Hereward Carrington, afterward. Carrington had recently published *The Physical Phenomena of Spiritualism*, in which he had cautiously concluded that Eusapia's powers were not entirely "physical." This was James's own opinion, however suspicious he found the "queer twisting" of his chair while the lights were out. Yet he continued to investigate unusual "psychic" occurrences, and his wife's diary mentions several "sittings," her term for *séances*, with a "Mrs. Newman" in their home during February 1910.

Meanwhile William had been "sitting" in a different sense for his cousin "Bay" Emmet (Mrs. Ellen Emmet Rand), who was painting a portrait of him commissioned by his friends and former students. The official unveiling took place in his own home on Irving Street on January 18, 1910, and his guests turned it into an informal "testimonial dinner." On February 6 Mrs. James described the event in a letter to Henry: "The dinner on the 18th was a great success—an Erckmann-Chatrian feast William called it. [He had admired since his student days the works written in collaboration by Émile Erckmann and Louis Chatrian; the feast in his honor was a collaboration of his friends.] Mr. Peabody [Dr. Francis Greenwood Peabody, Professor of Social Ethics at Harvard] said there had never been anything like it in Cambridge. We all helped—behind the scenes. Billy broiled brant [wild ducks] he shot in New Brunswick, over the furnace fire, Aleck bore them up the cellar stairs and Harry carved. Meanwhile the cook was broiling chickens in the kitchen. Peggy had decorated the tables and the 22 men seated at three tables in the library[,] which we had handsomely lighted with candles[,] really enjoyed themselves. Bay's portrait was liked for the most part. The speeches were full of affection for William and of appreciation of his work for the College. He deserved every bit of it—but it is not often that the word of recognition gets spoken in time."

Mrs. James also mentioned in her letter to her brother-in-law that the day before (February 5) Mr. and Mrs. Boutroux had arrived from Paris to be their house guests for several weeks. Émile Boutroux, professor of philosophy at the Sorbonne and president of the French Academy of Moral and Political Sciences to which James had recently been elected to honorary membership, had come to lecture at Harvard for six weeks. He had written a eulogistic preface for the French translation of *The Varieties of Religious Experience* and shared his host's pragmatic theory of truth. The success of the hospitality at 95 Irving Street may be judged by Professor Boutroux's acknowledgment of it in an address he delivered—in the presence of former President Theodore Roosevelt—before the Academy of Moral and Political Sciences on April 23:

> . . . I had the good fortune to stay with Professor William James, whom we have recently elected an associated member of this group. How charming was the house of the illustrious philosopher! Standing by itself amidst lawns and trees, built of wood in the colonial style like most of the houses of the university part of Cambridge; large, filled with books from top to bottom, a dwelling-place marvelously suited to study and meditation. Reflection, furthermore, is here in no danger of degenerating into egotism. For there reigns a most amiable sociability, The 'library,' which serves as Professor James's place of work, contains not only a desk, tables and books, but couches, window-seats, morris-chairs, welcoming visitors at all hours of the day, so that it is in the midst of merry conversations, among ladies taking tea, that the profound philosopher mediates and writes.

Of course Professor Boutroux's picture of William James meditating and writing in his sociable library in the midst of the merry conversation and ladies taking tea was an exaggeration. In fact, the French professor probably did not realize that his presence had caused more people than usual to visit that library, making it at times more like a railroad station that a private study. Yet during his stay William had managed to do some writing on his intended introduction to metaphysics, the book in which, though intended for beginning students, he hoped to "round out" his own philosophical theories.

Mrs. James's letter to Henry of Sunday, February 6, had a special note of concern, for the previous Friday she and William had received a letter from Theodora Bosanquet, the novelist's secretary, telling them that Henry was seriously ill. "Within an hour," Alice wrote Henry, "William had written to you and cabled Dr. Skinner from whom we got an answer that afternoon, reassuring, thank Heaven!" Nevertheless, she felt a strong inclination to catch the boat next Tuesday and spend several weeks with him, "not to be 'on your hands' as William fears but just to keep you company a little when you are not strong enough to work." She had thought of surprising Henry with a visit, but "William's reasonable doubt of how you would 'take it' gave me pause. I can only say that if it would be just a little pleasant to you to have me you have only to cable a word and I come." William was planning, anyway, to go over in May, primarily to consult a heart specialist in Paris, a Dr. Moutier, who had devised a new electrical therapy. William also planned to return to Nauheim and Alice thought she ought to go too so that he would not be alone all summer. "He really seems and looks wonderfully well, more like his old self than he has for many months."

Henry did not immediately cable his sister-in-law to come to Lamb House, but he wrote several importunate letters urging both her and William to join him as soon as they could. The pathetic tone of his appeal must, of course, be attributed partly to the opening Alice had given him in her February 6 letter, but he was no doubt feeling very lonely, apprehensive, and utterly "lost" without his daily stint at his writing desk. His namesake nephew had come over to him while Mrs. James debated, and Harry was "an unspeakable relief and blessing," Henry wrote to his "dearest ones" on March 4. But the improvement which he had cabled at the time of Harry's sailing from Boston had not lasted. He had felt like saying to his nephew, "Take me back to them!—anyhow!" but with spring and summer coming, when he would be able to sit in his pleasant garden in the comfort of the English climate, this seemed like folly. Consequently, he urged his "dearest ones" to come to his comforts. "You and Peggy would have a long summer rest here, dearest Alice, and ease—alleviation—of burden and care—for I somehow feel that your mere being with me would work to see me through."

Although the physicians had thought at first that Henry James had had an angina attack, his major symptom was a recurring upset stomach, making it difficult to retain food. For six years he had been following a health fad started by a writer on dietetics named Horace Fletcher, personally known to the Jameses, who advocated thorough mastication as the way to health: a hundred chews for every mouthful of food. Now both Henry and his doctors were convinced that "Fletcherism" had ruined his stomach. Early in March he had sufficiently recovered to be able to go to London for examination by the famous Dr. William Osler, who agreed with Dr. Skinner that, in Henry's words, the "passionate and intimate Fletcherism" had done him serious harm, though his stomach itself was normal, and sensible habits would restore him to health.

While still in London, Henry wrote again to William and Alice on March 15, reiterating his appeal for their help: "I confess I am an arrant coward now over the solitude of Lamb House in anything of a prolongation of depressed sickness. This was the essence of the abject craven wail of my last letter." But all anginal symptoms had disappeared "since beginning to disFletcherize!" William had got the impression that his brother had suffered a nervous collapse, and Henry strongly protested that his "illness had no more to do with a 'nervous breakdown' than with Halley's Comet: I *had* no nervous breakdown whatever—and no reason to have one."

Meanwhile William had received Henry's March 4 letter on the 13th, and wrote in his diary: "Letter from H.J. very pathetic—decides me to go over immediately." Next day he received a cable from Henry in London saying that Osler was "intensely reassuring," but William had firmly resolved to go anyway. However, the gains he seemed to have made in his own health since New Year's also began at this time to ebb away, as the diary entry for March 22 shows: "Frightful night with angina pains and dyspnoea. Alice decides to accompany me abroad. Hurrah!" (To judge from her letters to Henry, she had never intended to let William go without her.) A few days before his own departure William wrote his old friend Fanny Morse, thanking her for sending roses to his house and apologizing for not having invited her to Cambridge recently. "I have about given up all visits to Boston this winter, and the racket has been so incessant in the house, owing to foreigners of late, that we haven't had the strength to send for you. I sail on the 29th in the Megantic, first to see Harry, who has been ill, not dangerously, but very miserably. Our Harry is with him now. I shall then go to Paris for a certain medical experiment, and after that report at Nauheim, where they probably will keep me for some weeks. I hope that I may get home next fall with my organism in better shape, and be able to see more of my friends."

But in spite of these plans and good intentions for "next fall," William closed this letter to Fanny with what he himself admitted was a "lugubrious" ending: "At present we are 'contemporaries,' that is all, and the one of us who becomes survivor will have regrets that we were no more!" Also a day or so before he sailed he took out his copy of the Harvard Catalogue and wrote at the top of the Faculty Lists: "A thousand regrets cover every beloved name." And then, as if in a pathetic gesture of farewell, "Forgive me!"

Obviously he was leaving his much loved Irving Street home with forebodings and strained emotions. Yet in some ways the leaving this time should have been easier, for Peggy was now mature enough to take care of the house, with the aid of two experienced servants. And of course Billy would help her until Harry returned only a few days after his parents' departure. Mrs. James was confident that she had never left her home in more competent hands. And if her children needed any advice, their grandmother was, as always, only a few doors away.

II

Before boarding the S. S. *Megantic* Mrs. James received a "wireless" telegram from her son Harry on the *Empress of Britain* asking if she were accompanying his father to England. Somewhere on the Atlantic, two or three days out of Boston, the parents passed their homeward-bound son, but they did not know exactly when. Until Monday, April 4, the weather was sunny, just cool enough to be stimulating, and the ocean was smooth. They spent many hours leisurely walking or reading in their deck chairs. William's nerves relaxed, and Alice wrote in her diary that he was "very dear." At Queenstown, where the ship paused briefly on Tuesday, April 5, they learned that Alexander Agassiz, son of William's teacher, had died while crossing the Atlantic two days before their own sailing.

The Jameses landed at Liverpool at five o'clock Wednesday afternoon, enjoyed a good dinner in the train dining car before they reached London at 10:30, and found comfortable beds waiting for them at William's favorite Charing Cross Hotel. Next day William was still tired, and consequently depressed, but they took a late morning train to Rye and received an emotional welcome not only from Henry but even from his servants. Henry was still in bed, and for several days Alice divided her time between sitting with him and taking walks with William or motoring with Henry's friends. Her presence seemed to do the invalid more good than the doctor's, and it was not many days before he was up and strolling or motoring with William and Alice.

Toward the end of April Henry suffered several temporary relapses during which he was mentally depressed, and at such time he was even more dependent upon his sister-in-law's cheerful presence, leaving William many hours of solitude for reading or writing letters. On April 30 William recorded in his diary: "During these last days, in addition to writing and mailing an article on [Benjamin Paul] Blood to [L. P.] Jacks [editor of the *Hibbert Journal*], I have read several french plays, H. Adams's *Mt. Michel & Chartres* [*sic*], Vol. IV of Joan of Arc by [Anatole] France, Butler on Shakespeare's Sonnets [Samuel Butler, *Shakespeare's Sonnets Reconsidered*, 1899], Masterman's Condition of England, etc." While trying to find some way to pass the hours in Lamb House, William had noticed these books in Henry's library.

Of all these books the privately printed *Mont-Saint-Michel and Chartres*, by William's old friend and former colleague at Harvard, now living in Paris, made the deepest impression on him, and he wrote to Henry Adams to let him know the delight he had experienced in reading it: ". . . [I] can't help sending you a paean of praise. From beginning to end it reads as from a man in the fresh morning of life, with a frolic quality of power unusual in historic literature so far as yet revealed to me, and I have found it powerful instructive. Where you stole all that St. Thomas, I shd. like to know! Of course I skipt much of the architectural detail, and found myself wishing that you would reprint the whole thing with innumerable fotografs or other designs—I'm sure it will last in literature—and in that case one will not feel inclined to skip."

Henry Adams had printed only a few copies of the book (it was not actually published until 1913) for friends to criticize. He had done the same thing with his *Education*, which he had sent to William, but he had apparently neglected to send *Chartres*. William now asked "why this shyness & anonymity in such a work? Are you afraid of german professors, noting the jokes and irony, calling it *oberflächliches Zeug* [superficial matter]?" Adams had remembered to send William a copy of his recent attempt to find a "law" in history, called *Letter to Teachers of History*, and William had brought the book with him, he said, but was saving it to read at Nauheim, where he would go in a few days, leaving Alice with the hypochondriac of Lamb House.

During the first days of May, Henry seemed much better. "What a relief!" William wrote in his diary on the 2nd. There was no longer any reason for him to delay his trip to Nauheim and the stopover in Paris to consult Dr. Moutier. Alice was torn by anxiety and remorse at the idea of letting William travel by himself, but Henry

LAMB HOUSE,
RYE.
SUSSEX.   *April 28. 1910*

Dear Henry Adams,

I got your "Letter to Teachers" before leaving home and have bro't it with me to read at Nauheim, whither I am ultimately bound. Meanwhile, seeing on Henry's table your M⁵. S⁵. M. et *Chartres*, I fell upon that as a preparation, & can't help sending you a pæan of praise. From beginning to end it reads as from a man in the fresh morning of life, with a frolic quality of power unusual in historic literature so far as yet revealed to me, and I have found it powerful instructive. When you stole all that St Thomas, I shd.

A letter from William James to Henry Adams, April 28, 1910.

like to know! Of course I skipt much
of the architectural detail, and found
myself wishing that you would reprint
the whole thing with innumerable
fotografs or other designs — I'm sure
it will last in literature — and in
that case one will not feel inclined
to skip.

Moreover why this shyness &
anonymity in such a work? Are you
afraid of german professors, noting
the jokes and irony, calling it Oberflächliches Zeug?

Henry here is poorly, and my
goodwife and I are relieving his solitude during these weeks. Believe me,
dear H. A., ever truly yours, Wm James

did not yet feel strong enough to leave Lamb House. Actually he had always hated Germany anyway and really did not want to go to Nauheim if he could avoid it. Alice was afraid that he would have a relapse if she deserted him, and William insisted that he could take care of himself. Thus, with great misgivings, she kissed him good-bye on the morning of May 5. On the Channel boat he met an old friend and former student, Charles A. Strong, who had retired from teaching psychology at Columbia University after coming into a substantial inheritance and was now living in Paris. Strong insisted that William stay with him in Paris, in his apartment at 21 Rue de Surène.

Strong had heard James's lecture on Pragmatism at Columbia in 1907, and had been trying since then to apply the Pragmatic theory in the field of religion. James had also criticized and annotated two manuscripts of Strong's called "Theory of Knowledge" and "Evolutionary Psychology." They had much to talk about, and it is not surprising that William was very tired by the time they reached Paris at eight o'clock that night. Although next day Dr. Moutier found his blood pressure only 150 mm., "which he wouldn't reduce if he could," William recorded in his diary, the anginal pains returned.

William had been urged by Henry to call on his friend Edith Wharton in Paris—in the past few years a great companionship had grown up between the two novelists—and on May 7 William visited her. That night he wrote in his diary: "Called on Mrs. Wharton. In very bad condition owing to perpetual talking with Strong, etc. To Moutier, who tried currents around chest—no effect." Next day: "Lunch with Baldwin [Dr. W. W. Baldwin, the American doctor in Rome]. Awful day!" May 9: "Moutier ditto."

On the 10th William and Strong called on Bergson, who invited them to lunch the following Sunday, the 15th. Before the 15th William moved from Strong's apartment to the Fondation Thiers, where he was the guest of Professor Boutroux, in charge of this institution. Boutroux also took William to a meeting of the Academy to which he had been elected *associé étranger*. In addition to seeing a cousin, granting an interview to a Madame Le Roux who was writing a thesis on Pragmatism, and having to listen to a quarrel between his French translators and publisher, William also dined several times with Henry Adams, which meant more hours of harmfully stimulating conversation. It was not until May 16 that William finally caught a morning train for Germany. Later he declared, "Paris killed me." And there can be no doubt that he arrived in Nauheim so exhausted from the many hours of "sitting and talking" that he never recovered from the fatigue. From this time on his health went steadily downhill.

After William had been at Nauheim for a week he wrote his friend François Pillon that he had said to himself every day in Paris, "I will get to the Pillons this afternoon," but each day the four flights of stairs to the Pillons' apartment were more than he could manage, and finally he had had "to run away from the Boutrouxs' to save my life from the fatigue and pectoral pain which resulted from my seeing so many people. I have a dilatation of the aorta, which causes anginoid pain of a bad kind whenever I make any exertion, muscular, intellectual, or social, and I should not have thought at all of going through Paris were it not that I wished to consult a certain Dr. Moutier there, who is strong on arteries, but who told me that he could do nothing for my case." Nauheim was now William's last hope.

III

A few days after William left Lamb House, Henry's illness took one of its numerous turns for the worse. Alice thought he missed William and wished she could recall him, which of course she could not, much as she wanted to do so. On May 29 she received a letter from William which, in the words of her diary, "made me half sick all day and at dinner I had to leave the table—wretched time."

In spite of his fatigue, William's first reaction to the country which he had loved since his youth was, "Grand, calm, handsome Germany!" At Nauheim Dr. Theodor Groedel examined him, and a "radiogram" (cardiograph) confirmed the diagnosis he gave to William—"Aorta enlarged and drawn down by heart's weight." But later Dr. Groedel said the valvular trouble was "insufficiency not *stendris*," probably meaning that the heart was not enlarged but was unable to pump sufficient blood—what is technically known today as "heart failure." Yet William continued to take those debilitating baths, to read, write letters, walk and visit friends, several of whom were taking baths or vacationing in the region. On May 29, the day so sickening to Alice, William was up early, and after taking his seventh bath noted sadly in his diary: "Letter from H. & A. saying they won't come—I absage [countermand] the rooms at Tielman's—Must tread wine press alone."

After breakfast William at least partly recovered from his disappointment and spent this quiet Sunday in reading, correcting proofs, and writing letters. One of the letters was to his daughter, who had been typing his manuscripts and keeping him posted on the activities of her brothers and herself. William needed a bibliographical reference for his "Blood" article and instructed Peggy where to look for it in his filing cabinet. He had just finished correcting the proof of his article for the *Hibbert Journal* and thought it would "make people sit up and rub their eyes at the apparition of a new great writer in English. [He had quoted extensively from Blood's writings.] I want Blood himself to get it as a surprise."

William's own surprise had been Peggy's "finely typed copy of the rest of my MS.," probably part of his intended introduction to metaphysics, on which he had worked during the spring and at which he had continued to peck away when his angina pains did not interfere too much. "You seem to be leading a very handsome and domestic life," he continued in his letter to Peggy, "avoiding social excitements, and hearing of them only from the brethren. It is good sometimes to face the naked ribs of reality as it reveals itself in homes. I face them *here*, with no one but the blackbirds and the trees for my companions, save some rather odd Americans at the *Mittagstisch* [midday table] and *Abendessen* [evening meal], and the good smiling *Dienstmädchen* [servant girl] who brings me my breakfast in the morning. . . . I went to my bath at 6 o'clock this morning, and had the Park all to the blackbirds and myself. This was because I am expecting a certain Prof. [Julius] Goldstein from Darmstadt to come to see me this morning, and I had to get the bath out of the way. He is a powerful young writer, and is translating my 'Pluralistic Universe.' But the weather has grown so threatening that I hope now that he won't come till next Sunday. It is a shame to converse here and not be in the open air."

Unlike his brother Henry, William had no foreboding that something was wrong with Germany. "The German civilization is *good!*" he declared in his letter to his daughter. "Only this place would give a very false impression of our wicked earth to a Mars-*Bewohner* [-dweller] who should descend and leave and see nothing else. Not a dark spot (save what the patients' hearts individually conceal), no poverty, no vice, nothing but prettiness and simplicity of life. I snip out a concert-program (the afternoon one unusually good) which I find lying on my table. The like is given free in the open air every day. The baths weaken one so that I have little brain for reading, and must write letters to all kinds of people every day." He probably meant that he was not doing professional reading, for he had been reading D. Halévy's life of Nietzsche and had bought two of Nietzsche's books, which he had not yet begun. He was "half through 'Waffen-nieder!' a *first-rate* anti-war novel by Baroness von Suttner. It has been translated [English title: *Ground Arms*], and I recommend it as in many ways instructive."

Writing to Henry Bowditch, who was now a complete invalid, William declared on June 4: "Germany is *great*, and no mistake! But what a contrast, in the well-set-up, well-groomed, smart-looking German man of today, and his rather clumsily drest, dingy, and unworldly-looking father of forty years ago! But something of the old *Gemüthlichkeit* remains, the friendly manners, and the disposition to talk with you and take you seriously and to respect the serious side of whatever comes along. . . . Alice is staying with Henry, but they will both be here in a fortnight or less. I find it pretty lonely all by myself, and the German language doesn't run as trippingly off the tongue as it did forty years ago. Passage back is taken for August 12th."

The first of June Alice had gone to London and made steamship reservations for their return. And she had also bought two first-class tickets to Nauheim for June 6–8, for Henry had now consented to go with her. He became despondent again before leaving Lamb House, but he stood the trip better than Alice, who was dreadfully seasick crossing the Channel and was weary when they at last reached Nauheim on June 8. But when they descended from the train, William was waiting behind the barrier, waving his hat. He looked much better than Alice had expected, but this may have been because he was flushed with excitement, for his angina pains had become more frequent and the dyspnoea bothered him at night.

Even the weather had become disagreeable, being unusually warm for northern Europe. After the excitement of the reunion had subsided, Alice wrote in her diary: "Sad night. Dreadful loneliness came down on me. But nothing matters if we can *do* something. The night and heat made me very weak." And next day, Thursday, was no better: "A slow sitting and walking in the noon heat. H. and W.

both silent. I very tired. Spent afternoon in waiting for the Proprietor to settle with me about rooms and then in moving into them. Very good ones on the 2nd floor."

Gradually Henry's condition improved, but the best that can be said of William's is that some days were less painful than others. Alice's diary testifies to the strain she was under. Sunday, June 12, was rainy and "A difficult day. Every word I spoke proved the wrong one. After dinner we three drove to the *Frauenwald*. Coffee, then H. and I walked a long way home [William evidently rode back]. W. & H. go out after supper. If I can only do my part!"

Two days later (June 14) William wrote his "Beloved Belle-Mère" that "Alice has work enough cut out for her in tending Henry, who is touchingly dependent on her presence, and on bad days of his, like yesterday, is really a heart-rending spectacle." He seemed to be definitely improving, "but the bad days return, and no doubt there will be many weeks more of it to face, both by him and by us. As for me, the baths are very debilitating, and if left to judge by my feelings alone, I should say that I was getting no good at all from them. With Henry in the condition he is in, and with the constant comings and goings of one or the other of us between his room and ours, & the attempts to walk or drive with him, the day is terribly chopped up, and the brain being inert, I shilly shally and neither read nor write letters these days." William hoped that his mother-in-law would be able to open the Chocorua house for part of the summer for herself and her grandchildren. He supposed that Billy had finished her portrait and hoped that he would now begin to get orders. The letter was interrupted by Alice's coming in "to summon me to go out (4 p.m.) with Henry for a drive. . . ."

On the 16th the Jameses were delighted with a call from Judge Moorfield Storey, who was vacationing with his family nearby. Afterward Alice noted in her diary that William was "very *kind as of old*" (her italics); it is not surprising that in his present condition he was often cross. Henry was frequently morose, but not cross, and for this reason Alice could peremptorily summon William to go riding to suit Henry's whim. As for herself, she was terribly homesick for her mother, as she confessed privately in her diary.

Meanwhile, William had read Henry Adams's *Letter to Teachers of History*. "I have been so 'slim' since seeing you," he wrote Adams on June 17, "and the baths here have so weakened my brain, that I have been unable to do any reading except trash, and have only just got round to finishing your 'letter,' which I had but half-read when I was with you in Paris. To tell the truth, it doesn't impress me at all, save by its wit and erudition; and I ask you whether an old man soon about to meet his Maker can hope to save himself from the consequences of his life by pointing to the wit and learning he has shown in treating a tragic subject, No, sir, you can't do it, can't impress God in that way."

What Adams had argued was that the time had come to make the study of social data scientific, to find, in short, a law of history: "Any science of history must be absolute, like other sciences, and must fix with mathematical certainty the path which human society has got to follow." He thought such a law could be found in the principle of entropy, i.e., as matter is consumed to produce energy, the energy is dissipated and can never be recovered. According to this second law of thermodynamics the universe is running down. James did not doubt that this was true, but he objected to applying the principle to human history. "So far as our scientific conceptions go," he conceded, "it may be admitted that your Creator (and mine) started the universe with a certain amount of 'energy' latent in it, and decreed that everything that should happen thereafter should be a result of parts of that energy falling to lower levels; raising other parts higher, to be sure, in so doing, but never in equivalent amount, owing to the constant radiation of unrecoverable warmth incidental to the process. . . . But I protest against your interpretation of some of the specifications of the great statistical drift downwards of the original high-level energy."

In the first place, James did not believe that "the *amount* of cosmic energy" was as important as the use made of it. "Certain arrangements of matter *on the same energy-level* are, from the point of view of man's appreciation, superior, while others are inferior. Physically a dinosaur's brain may show as much intensity of energy-exchange as a man's, but it can do infinitely fewer things, because as a force of detent it can only unlock the dinosaur's muscles, while the man's brain, by unlocking far feebler muscles, indirectly can by their means issue proclamations, write books, describe Chartres Cathedral, etc., and guide the energies of the shrinking sun into channels which never would have been entered otherwise—in short, *make* history. Therefore the man's brain and muscles are from the point of view of the historian, the more important place of energy-exchange, small as this may be when measured in absolute physical units." Thus the second law of thermodynamics "is wholly irrelevant to 'history'—save that it sets a terminus—for history is the course of things before that terminus, and all that the second law says is that, whatever the history, it must invest itself between that initial maximum and that terminal minimum of difference in energy-level."

To this argument Henry Adams replied in his characteristic self-deprecating, ironical manner: "Oh, Friend and Guide," he wrote from 23 Avenue du Bois de Boulogne on June 20, "indeed Nauheim has done wonders and miracles since it has left you the energy to think and write at such length and with such wisdom on the sandy wastes of time. I calculated, on my data, that out of five hundred readers, I should get five reactions. I have got one; and he is almost my oldest teacher! 'Tis something; nay, 'tis much! but I must reform my statistics.

"As for myself . . . Never have I held an opinion of my own, or ventured to trust a judgment. With humble heart I have chased the flying philosopher, trying to find out *his* opinions. . . . My philosopher runs like a rabbit when I seek his burrow. He denies frenziedly that he has ever expressed an opinion at all. He hides his tail.

"Therefore, just now, I am not asserting or rejecting anything. I am trying to find out what your friend Ostwald or Bergson . . . thinks or teaches or intends." Wilhelm Ostwald, a German chemist and philosopher, had lectured at Harvard in 1905–1906 and had recently (1909) won a Nobel Prize in chemistry. Probably Adams did not intend to insinuate that he was seeking more expert opinion, but it is obvious that William's protest did not shake in the least his commitment to finding a deterministic basis in the physical sciences for the course of social history.

On June 26 William replied by postal card: "Yours of the 20th, just arriving, pleases me by its docility of spirit and passive subjection to philosophic opinion. Never, never pretend to an opinion of your own! that way lies every arrogance and madness! You tempt me to offer you another illustration—that of the *hydraulic ram* (thrown back at me in an exam. as a 'hydraulic goat' by an insufficiently intelligent student). Three days later (June 29) Adams retorted: "Oh, best of Friends, I love that hydraulic goat! If ever I get hold of Ostwald, I will beg him on bended knees to let me have that goat. . . . It reminds me of the days when we were all hydraulic goats, and you were the light and joy of Beverly Farms [the site of Adams's estate in Massachusetts] and Harvard College." But Adams was weary of his *Letter to Teachers of History:* "I am a pretty well played out hydraulic goat now, and I don't much care how soon the brook dries up altogether."

The delay in William's receiving Henry Adam's letter of June 20 was caused by his having left Nauheim on the morning of the 23rd. The previous day Alice had pressed Dr. Groedel to tell her whether he thought William had benefited from the baths: "He excused himself by saying he must judge later," but she suspected that he did not see any improvement. She and her two patients stopped first in Konstanz, Germany (today spelled Constance, across the lake from Konstanz, Switzerland), where William wrote his latest note to Adams. By this time Henry was feeling very low again, and they hurried on to Zurich, and then to Lucerne, hoping that the Swiss air would be good for him. But the altitude was very bad for William's dyspnoea and Henry suffered again from nausea. On the Fourth of July they reached Geneva, and William and Alice called on Flournoy, who had recently lost his wife. But probably even this exertion was too much for William, for he became so ill that he had to send for a doctor. Henry, however, was better in Geneva and accompanied Alice on various errands, even helping her shop for clothes.

From Cambridge Harry cabled on July 7 that his uncle Robertson had died quietly in his sleep at his home in Concord. Alice received the cablegram and concealed it from William for two days, fearing that the news might upset him, but another cablegram was forwarded from Lamb House and William received it while she and Henry were out of the hotel. On her return she was surprised that the information had had no bad effects on William; on the contrary, he seemed relieved that Bob was now free of his miserable life.

William's former student Dickinson Miller, now teaching at Columbia University, was also in Geneva and came to see the Jameses several times. But William was too ill to see Flournoy again, and wrote him on July 9: "My dyspnoea gets worse at an accelerated rate, and all I care for now is to get home—doing *nothing* on the way. It is partly a spasmodic phenomenon I am sure, for the aeration of my tissues, judging by the color of my lips, seems to be sufficient.

I will leave Geneva now without seeing you again—better not come, unless just to shake hands with my wife! Through all these years I have wished I might live nearer to you and see more of you and exchange more ideas, for we seem two men particularly well *faits pour nous comprendre* [made to understand each other]. Particularly, now, as my own intellectual housekeeping has seemed on the point of working out some good results, would it have been good to work out the less unworthy parts of it in your company. But that is impossible!—I doubt if I ever do any more writing of a serious sort; and as I am able to look upon my life rather lightly, I can truly say that 'I don't care'—don't care in the least pathetically or tragically, at any rate. . . . I can write no more, my very dear old friend, but only ask you to think of me as ever lovingly yours, W.J."

On Sunday, July 10, William and Alice's wedding anniversary, William was too ill to get out of bed. But next day he summoned strength to board the train for Paris with his brother and wife. After spending the night in the Hôtel du Louvre, the three went on to London next day, William standing the trip surprisingly well but "Henry suffering again," Alice noted in her diary on the 13th. Dr. MacKenzie saw William several times in London, and Alice was greatly encouraged by a private talk with him. After they reached Rye on Saturday, July 23, Dr. Skinner began calling daily. On the 28th Alice recorded: "Another bad night. Dr. Skinner came. Wm. slept till nearly 1 o'clock. Since then he has been sitting in the sunshine in the garden. Such a good letter from Dr. MacKenzie! Wm. says he grows daily weaker. And he is so patient."

For weeks Alice had debated whether it would be easier on William to take a ship to Boston or the shorter ocean route to Quebec. She was inclined to think Boston would be easier, but William longed to see Chocorua again; so it was finally decided that they would land at Quebec. Harry would meet them there, where they would spend the night, and next day Billy would meet them at Intervale, some twenty miles from Chocorua, in a motor car. Brother Henry would accompany them and assist as much as he could during the ocean voyage. These plans were definite by August 5, when Alice wrote her son Harry from Lamb House: ". . . I want you to pass round the good tidings that Papa is really better. He is very weak and the breathing still troubles him, but he has had two good nights, and Skinner says his heart is *much* better. So we have a right to expect improvement now all along the line. Skinner says the voyage

will do him good and only think we shall have begun it by this time
a week from today." Although Henry still had days of depression
and discouragement, he seemed to be almost entirely recovered from
his illness of last spring.

"This will be my last letter," Alice wrote her mother on August
7, "and it can be a cheerful one, with a good report. Poor Mrs.
Oliphant [Margaret Oliphant, Scottish novelist and biographer]
says in one of her letters that there is no happiness in life to be
compared with the lifting of a great anxiety. And this joy has come
to me, and I am filled with gratitude. William is emerging from
what we can all now see to have been an acute attack. Why he
was so ill, why his breathing became so painful no one tries to
explain. But he is gaining strength, sleeping without narcotics, eating
better and beginning to take gentle exercise. Skinner has been an
invaluable help and had William put himself under his care last
April instead of knocking about to Paris and Nauheim much suffering would have been spared. It was a case, if there ever was, of 'let
down your bucket where you stand.' However I don't mean to look
back or refer to this again. I can only be thankful today. . . . William is looking forward with pleasure to the voyage—and so is
Henry. . . . It is a strangely haunted and haunting morning. The
sun comes and withdraws. The bees buzz about the great bush of
blossoming lavender beside the door. The wind sounds a menacing
note, as of rain to come, and I am thinking of all the anxious hours
I have lived through, of all the suffering Henry has endured, and
latterly William too, and as the end of our stay draws near I am
deeply conscious of the kindness that has never failed me. In our
perplexities, our journeyings, our decisions (and how faltering mine
have often been!) these two good men have been always full of
consideration for me—a good record for two nervous invalids among
all the emergencies of travel. Henry much exaggerates what I could
do for him, but I have helped some and that has made the summer
worth while. I really ought not to have left William to go alone to
Paris and Nauheim, but he was too eager to get off to wait for
Henry, and Henry didn't want to go to Paris. . . . To return to
the journey: our heavy baggage can be freighted straight to Irving
St. and we shall only take the state-room trunks to Chocorua. It
looks so pleasant,—Harry at Quebec, Billy at Intervale and you and
Peggy at the house. . . . It seems too good to be true."

IV

William James's last entry in his diary was made on August 11: "Skinner refuses fee. Must send it for 17 days. Left Rye today. Write this at Garland's." From his wife's diary, we learn that they had left Rye at twelve-thirty p.m. and at four on a rainy afternoon had reached London, where they found a comfortable room at Garland's Hotel. Next morning, Friday, they left for the Euston Station at eleven o'clock and at four William was carried aboard a ship of the Canadian Steamship Line. They had good staterooms and the voyage began encouragingly. Alice had bought a "basket chair" which she hoped would add to William's comfort. The second day out he was "disposed to walk about and explore," but thereafter he was too tired to do anything except sit during his waking hours. On Tuesday the 11th, the weather was very cold and he "sat most of the day in the music room by the fire."

On Wednesday the ship entered the Saint Lawrence River and began the final run of three hundred and four miles, "Wm. better but very suffering." On arrival next day at Quebec everything began to go wrong. Alice's diary tells the story laconically: "Arrive at 4, Harry, furious rain, horrid Hotel. Wm. walking too much. Very bad night, awake and dressing at 4 a.m. No breakfast Friday. Wm. sick at station. Customs. Long and terrible day in the cars. Intervale at 6 p.m. Billy motor home. Bad night." By the time the motor reached Chocorua, William's feet were badly swollen—the first evidence that his "heart failure" had become so acute that the fluids were now accumulating in his body. Both of Alice's sisters arrived on Saturday, and the Chocorua house was filled with the family and relatives, but Alice scarcely let anyone else attend her husband. At first William refused to have a doctor, but on Sunday Billy telephoned for Dr. George Shedd, who began, with his son, Dr. Harold Shedd, to make frequent calls. For Wednesday Alice recorded: "A terrible day of suffering. Dr. Harold Shedd was not to repeat the morphine till his father came—Feeding with milk every half hour to get the stomach going. He [William] said to me 'I can't stand this again—Cruel *cruel*.' And he added 'It has come so rapidly, rapidly.'" He knew he was dying and made a solemn request of

Alice to "go to Henry when his time comes." Of course she promised—and kept the promise six years later.

Near mid-day on August 26 Henry wrote Miss Grace Norton, who was eagerly waiting in Cambridge for news of the James family: "We arrived, William and Alice and I, in this strange, sad, rude spot, a week ago to-night—after a most trying journey from Quebec (though after a most beautiful, quick, in itself auspicious voyage too,) but with William critically, mortally ill and with our anxiety and tension now (he has rapidly got so much worse) a real anguish. . . . Alice is terribly exhausted and spent—but the rest she will be able to take must presently increase, and Harry, who, after leaving us at Quebec, started with a friend on a much-needed holiday in the New Brunswick woods (for shooting and fishing), was wired to yesterday to come back to us at once. So I give you, dear Grace, our dismal chronicle of suspense and pain. My own fears are the blackest, and at the prospect of losing my wonderful beloved brother out of the world in which, from as far back as in dimmest childhood, I have so yearningly always counted on him, I feel nothing but the abject weakness of grief and even terror; but I forgive myself 'weakness'—my emergence from the long and grim ordeal of my own peculiarly dismal and trying illness isn't yet absolutely complete enough to make me wholly firm on my feet. But *my* slowly recuperative process goes on despite all shakes and shocks, while dear William's, in the full climax of his intrinsic powers and intellectual ambitions, meets this tragic, cruel arrest."

In a postscript Henry added: "I open my letter of three hours since to add that William passed unconsciously away an hour ago— without apparent pain or struggle. Think of us, dear Grace, think of us!" That night (Friday, August 26) Alice recorded: "William died just before 2.30 in my arms. I was coming in with milk and saw the change. No pain at the last and no consciousness. He had [had] morphine. Since Wednesday at 6.30 without intermission. Two weeks ago we sailed for home. Poor Henry, poor children." She had lifted William's head from the pillow and was supporting him when the end came. Next day she was too sad and exhausted to make any entry in her diary, but on Sunday wrote: "Wonderful beauty of the dear face!" Billy photographed it, and then made a plaster mask. Dr. George Shedd performed an autopsy, and Alice summarized the results in her diary: "Acute enlargement of the heart. He had worn himself out. They have laid him in the coffin and I can see his face no more."

On Monday, Alice recorded: "Billy went to Boston yesterday. It is a strange quiet day, a day of memories and tears." Billy had gone to join his brother Harry in making the funeral arrangements. Before Billy left, his future father-in-law, Mr. John Summer Runnells, vice-president and general counsel for the Pullman Car Company, had offered to send his private Pullman car from Buffalo to Conway, New Hampshire, to convey the coffin and the family to Boston, and the offer had been gratefully accepted. The Runnells had a summer home in New Hampshire and Billy was informally engaged to Mr. Runnells' daughter Alice, who would become the third Alice James in the family.

On Tuesday morning the widow and her brother-in-law left Chocorua before six to accompany the hearse to Conway, while her mother and daughter followed in Mr. Runnells' automobile. Aleck was on a vacation in the West and could not get back in time for the funeral. But Harry and Billy met the train in Boston and accompanied the coffin to Irving Street, where the body was to remain until the funeral service that afternoon (August 30) at four o'clock, in the Appleton Chapel on the wooded grounds of the Harvard Yard, where William James had begun teaching twenty-seven years before.

One of James's former students, the Reverend George A. Gordon, pastor of the New Old South Church in Boston, returned from a vacation in Kennebunkport, Maine, to conduct the funeral service. The organist of the Appleton Chapel, Mr. Archibald T. Davidson, Jr., played Chauvet's "Funeral Prelude." The casket was covered with two palm branches and a spray of asparagus fern. The honorary pall bearers were: A. Lawrence Lowell, President of Harvard University; Major H. L. Higginson; Dr. James Putnam; Professor George Herbert Palmer; Professor James Crafts, former President of Massachusetts Institute of Technology; Charles Strong, the philosopher; George Doer; Henry S. Miller. Professor Ralph Barton Perry, the future editor and biographer of James, helped carry the casket.

In his tribute Dr. Gordon declared: "After all is said and done, it is the human aspect that lasts the longest. The scholar, thinker, teacher is merged at last in the human being. The man is the ultimate and everlasting value." These were William James's own strongest convictions, and what the words lacked in originality they made up in appropriateness. After the funeral service the body was taken to Mount Auburn Cemetery for cremation. The ashes were later taken back to Chocorua and scattered on the little mountain stream in which William had bathed on many a warm summer day.

It was to Chocorua that the widow and her brother-in-law returned the next day on the noon train: "Oh the unspeakable emptiness of the place! All the pathos of all the years!" Alice lamented in her diary. Henry tried to describe his feelings on September 2 to T. S. Perry: "I sit heavily stricken and in darkness—for from far back in dimmest childhood he had been my ideal Elder Brother. . . . His extinction changes the face of life for me—besides the mere missing of his inexhaustible company and personality, originality, the whole unspeakably vivid and beautiful presence of him. And his noble intellectual vitality was still but at its climax—he had two or three ardent purposes and plans. He had cast them away, however, at the end—I mean that, dreadfully suffering, he wanted only to die." One of those ardent plans had been his book for beginning students in metaphysics, which must now remain the "unfinished arch" in his philosophical structure.

The death of William James was important news throughout the United States and Europe. Of course the Boston newspapers gave generous space to the event, and the *Evening Transcript* published a series of evaluations of the man and his work. In one of these H. Addington Bruce declared: ". . . I am almost tempted to describe his death as the removal of the greatest of contemporary Americans. Certainly no other of his generation exercised such an international influence as did William James." This opinion was corroborated by the Paris correspondent of the London *Times*, who cabled his paper on August 29: "Commenting to-night on his death, the *Temps* characterizes William James as 'the most famous American philosopher since Emerson.' This judgment attests the great reputation of Mr. James in this country, but it fails somewhat uncritically to define the real character of his influence, since his scientific fame here was based on considerations which had little to do with his later reputation as the expounder of pragmatism. It is as an experimental psychologist of the school of Wundt and Ribot that William James secured a lasting reputation in this country."

Although his metaphysical views were never widely accepted in France, "his earliest admirers among French *savants*," the London

Times correspondent asserted, "have never allowed their views on Mr. William James's latter day philosophy to affect their opinion of the value of his work as a psychologist." But on the same day *Figaro* began a two-column obituary with "Le grand philosophe William James est mort . . ." and ended with, "C'est un des plus grand esprits philosophiques de ce temps, qui vient de mourir" [One of the greatest philosophical minds of the age has died].

Bertrand Russell, who had entertained James during his lecturing at Oxford, though he was not an admirer of Pragmatism, contributed a long article to *The Nation*, September 3, 1910, which began: "The great loss which philosophy has sustained by the death of William James will be felt also as a personal loss by all who knew him. He was one of the most eminent, and probably the most widely known, of contemporary philosophers. It was by his work on psychology that he first achieved fame, but his later years were devoted almost entirely to the advocacy of the philosophy known as pragmatism. The high value of his work on psychology is universally admitted, but his work on pragmatism is still the subject of controversy." This judicious statement gives an accurate estimate of James's reputation at the time of his death, though there were strong defenders of his Pragmatism, such as his former student Horace M. Kallen, in an article in the American *Nation* on September 8, 1910.

But it was still another former student and friendly critic for many years, John Jay Chapman, who made the most eloquent comment: "The world watched James as he pursued through life his search for religious truth; the world watched him, and often gently laughed at him, asking, 'When will James arise and fly? When will he "take the wings of the morning, and dwell in the uttermost parts of the sea"?' And in the meantime, James was there already. Those were the very places that he was living in."

Epilogue: "No Conclusion"

There is no conclusion. . . . There are no fortunes to be told, and

there is no advice to be given. Farewell.—W.J., *"A Pluralistic Mystic"*

I

SEVERAL WEEKS BEFORE HIS DEATH William James finished an essay
on a man he had long admired, an amateur philosopher and mystic
living at Amsterdam, New York, Benjamin Paul Blood. While re-
gaining consciousness after having been anesthetized, Blood had
experienced such a vivid awareness of "reality" and what he believed
to be the nature of the world that he spent the remainder of his life
trying to describe and interpret the experience. He began writing as
a transcendentalist, not unlike Emerson, but his mystical insight
gradually changed his impression (more impression than concept)
of the universe from "a oneness, a central wholeness" to "a number-
less many," and James therefore claimed him as "A Pluralistic
Mystic," the title of the essay published in the *Hibbert Journal* in
July 1910.

Like James, Blood had come to distrust reason and logic:

> Reason is neither the first nor the last word in this world. Reason is
> an equation; it gives but a pound for a pound. Nature is excess; she
> is evermore, without cost or explanation. . . . Go back into reason,
> and you come at last to fact, nothing more—a given-ness, a something
> to wonder at and yet admit, like your own will. And all these tricks
> of logicizing originality, self-relation, absolute process, subjective
> contradiction, will wither in the breath of the mystical fact; they
> will swirl down the corridors before the besom of the everlasting Yea.

The ending of this last essay of James's published during his
lifetime seems almost like a final commentary on his own contribu-

tion to philosophy: "Let *my* last word, then, speaking in the name of intellectual philosophy, be *his* [Blood's] word:—'There is no conclusion. What has concluded, that we might conclude in regard to it? There are no fortunes to be told, and there is no advice to be given.—Farewell!' "

In the memorandum directed to his son Henry regarding publication of his uncompleted introductory textbook for students in metaphysics, James regretted that he could not live to "round out" his system, "which now is too much like an arch built only on one side." It is not easy to imagine how he might have done so. He had published detailed expositions of his ideas, though mostly written in a popular style. He stated several times that he intended to make a final attempt to present his ideas in more technical language and a more formal style. But the ideas themselves were antimetaphysical and doctrinally unschematic. James had repeatedly asserted his conviction that no final philosophy—whether his own or someone else's—was possible because the universe itself was incomplete and ever-changing. As Blood had said: "Nature is excess; she is evermore. . . ."

In October 1910, James was to have given a series of lectures at Sainte-Croix in Switzerland to the *Association chrétienne suisse d'Étudiants*. When his death prevented this, the lectures were delivered with sadness by his good friend at the University of Geneva, Théodore Flournoy, who appropriately devoted them to "The Philosophy of William James." Published as a book in 1911, Flournoy's exposition is a clear, fair, and useful guide to James's philosophical thought. Of his friend's "unfinished arch," Flournoy said:

> No one was less likely than James to write a didactic treatise on philosophy. And when one attempts to put the very varied contents of his essays and lectures into precise and well-arranged formulae, one runs the risk of gravely misrepresenting him. It is very much like transforming a virgin forest by laying out roads and cutting vistas through it. James is one of those personalities who by their exuberance, their great originality, and their emancipation from everything conventional affect us like one of nature's primordial forces, which cannot be readily described or summarized.

Flournoy insisted that it is in William James's "works themselves— . . . in almost any one of them—" that one must look if one wished really to know him. "His genius is so abundant, so varied, and so little preoccupied with avoiding the appearance of contradiction that in gathering in his various utterances one does not easily frame them into a truly harmonious whole. Indeed, it is almost a question whether he himself would have been able to produce a perfectly linked and coherent system from the magnificent treasure of material which he has left to us.''

Although no summary can reduce this "treasure" to a neat "system," it is possible to describe James's basic attitudes and positions in his life and writings; and it would be difficult to find another man in the whole history of philosophy whose mental, physical, and emotional life was more completely unified. He at least had this unity and consistency. As we have seen many times in his biography, he believed that all philosophy is autobiographical, and certainly his own was.

Even as a child William James had a precocious curiosity about the relationships of his mind and body. The boy in Boulogne-sur-mer who took drugs to observe their effects on his own person was already an empiricist. The older boy who studied painting under William Hunt had spent years in observing the detailed structure of natural forms, from skeletons in the Geneva Museum to seascapes in Rhode Island. In his scientific studies at Harvard, he had the good fortune to come under the influence of Louis Agassiz, to whom he always remained grateful for having taught him "the difference between all possible abstractions and all livers in the light of the world's concrete fulness. . . ." But James's artistic talent and impatience with abstractions were also congenital; he was "made" that way, and his early training only developed his innate predisposition.

Rarely are artistic and scientific talents so happily combined and balanced as in William James, for as Flournoy remarked,

the artistic mind looks at everything in its concrete particularity and presents it as individual, while the scientific intellect analyzes, abstracts, and generalizes. All science is general, as Aristotle said, and when it deals with particular objects it at once dissolves their particularity. . . . But it is just this unique individuality, intact, immediate, and real, which is the exclusive interest of art. Now James's temperament led him to see that both of these points of view are indispensable to a complete knowledge of mental life, and that psychic facts must be observed in their integrity, as indivisible pulsations of the continuous 'stream of consciousness.' . . . One might reverse the familiar saying that "every landscape is a state of the soul," and say that for James every state of the soul was a landscape, in which he perceived with the eye of an artist the color, the atmosphere, and the indefinable charm of the whole; while at the same time his scientific eye distinguished the minutest detail and divined even the geologic structure of the earth beneath.

To Flournoy James wrote in 1903: "What I want to get at, and let no interruptions interfere, is (at last) my 'system' of tychistic and pluralistic 'philosophy of pure experience.'" At various times James used such neologisms as Tychism (from Greek τύχη, *chance*), Pluralism, Radical Empiricism, and Pragmatism to designate his philosophy of "pure experience," but what he was always trying to understand and translate into coherent language was how a human being experiences the world he lives in, and what sort of world it is he experiences. And he wanted to describe this not in retrospect and abstraction, but in the very act itself, with all its pulsating life and uniqueness.

II

The steps by which William James rejected belief in a monistic universe can be traced in the history of his mental crises. In 1870 he saved himself from despair and possible suicide by deliberately choosing to believe in free will. Realizing that he could sustain "a thought *because I choose to* when I might have other thoughts," he concluded that his freedom to act was not an illusion and resolved as his first act of free will to believe in free will. This resolution proved to be good psychiatric therapy for his morbid condition, and the discovery opened the way for his future career in psychology and philosophy.

To believe in free will one must reject the "iron block" universe of the determinists, which also means rejecting monism, or a universe in which all parts have already been formed and joined so irrevocably that they forecast all possible future conditions and combinations. In 1884 in "The Dilemma of Determinism" James defined and explained the consequences of believing in a determined or in an indeterminate universe. In the former, "The future has no ambiguous possibilities hidden in its womb; the part we call the

present is compatible with only one totality. Any other future com-
plement than the one fixed from eternity is impossible.''

In an indeterminate universe, however,

> the parts have a certain amount of loose play on one another, so that
> the laying down of one of them does not necessarily determine what
> the others shall be. It admits that possibilities may be in excess of
> actualities, and that things not yet revealed to our knowledge may
> really in themselves be ambiguous. Of two alternative futures which
> we conceive, both may now be really possible and one becomes im-
> possible only at the very moment when the other excludes it by
> becoming real itself. Indeterminism thus denies the world to be one
> unending unit of fact. It says there is a certain ultimate pluralism in
> it; and, so saying, it corroborates our ordinary unsophisticated view
> of things. To that view, actualities seem to float in a wider sea of
> possibilities from out of which they are chosen; and *somewhere*, in-
> determinism says, such possibilities exist, and form a part of truth.

These statements contain in embryo all of James's future doctrines:
Pluralism, Pragmatism, Tychism, and even Meliorism.

James did not argue, either here or later, that man has a wide
freedom of choice. His choice of action may, in fact, be quite
limited, but so long as events—some at least—hang in a delicate
balance of uncertainty, so that a human action may tip the scales
one way or another, there is *possibility*, hope, a chance to improve
one's life and possibly the world. The "dilemma" of determinism is
that it can give no satisfactory explanation of evil. "If God be
good, how came he to create—or, if he did not create, how comes
he to permit—the devil? The evil facts must be explained as seeming: the devil must be whitewashed, the universe must be disinfected, if neither God's goodness nor his unity and power are to remain unimpugned." If evil cannot be overcome, even in part, then
the only escape from utter pessimism is cynicism. On the other
hand if God has created evil only to banish it, the human will is a
fiction and life is nothing but boredom.

To James the universe seemed unfinished and therefore bristling
with chance and possibilities; a universe in which both good and
evil were real, and eternally at war.

> Regarded as a stable finality, every outward good becomes a mere
> weariness to the flesh. It must be menaced, be occasionally lost, for
> its goodness to be fully felt as such. Nay, more than occasionally lost.

No one knows the worth of innocence till he knows it is gone forever, and that money cannot buy it back. Not the saint, but the sinner that repenteth, is he to whom the full length and breadth, and height and depth, of life's meaning is revealed. Not the absence of vice, but vice there, and virtue holding her by the throat, seems the ideal human state. And there seems no reason to suppose it is not a permanent human state.

Throughout all James's essays and books we find this same attitude toward the never-ending dramatic conflict of forces in the universe of human experience. In *Pragmatism* he classified people in their attitudes toward this drama as the "tender-minded" and the "tough-minded." The "tender-minded" are rationalistic, "going by 'principles,'" intellectualistic (thinking in terms of abstractions), idealistic (in the philosophical sense), optimistic, religious, free-willist, monistic, and dogmatical. The "tough-minded," on the other hand, are empiricists, "going by 'facts'"; they tend to be sensationalistic (believing that knowledge comes only through the senses), materialistic, pessimistic, irreligious, fatalistic, pluralistic, and skeptical. Although James himself was basically a "tough-minded" empiricist and pluralist, strongly anti-intellectual, he shared optimism, free will, and at least sympathy for religion with the "tender-minded." Of course he was well aware of his ambiguous position, and he regarded his paradoxical tendencies as typifying the modern dilemma. The "tough-minded" are closely in touch with the actual world of finite human lives, but they find it hard to discover permanent values to give life meaning for the present and hope for the future. The "tender-minded" have their values but they live on such a high level of abstraction that they are out of touch with the contemporary world.

James hoped that Pragmatism would provide a needed bridge.

You want a system that will combine both things, the scientific loyalty to facts and willingness to take account of them, the spirit of adaptation and accommodation, in short, but also the old confidence in human values and the resultant spontaneity, whether of the religious or of the romantic type. And this is then your dilemma: you find the two parts of your *quaesitum* hopelessly separated. You find empiricism with inhumanism and irreligion; or else you find a rationalistic philosophy that indeed may call itself religious, but that keeps out of all definite touch with concrete facts and joys and sorrows.

Philosophy since the time of Plato has been mainly rationalistic, traditionally so to such an extent that the average man thinks that philosophy is not concerned with his everyday life and has no practical use for him. "The world of concrete personal experiences to which the street belongs is multitudinous beyond imagination, tangled, muddy, painful and perplexed. The world to which your philosophy-professor introduces you is simple, clean and noble. The contradictions of real life are absent from it. Its architecture is classic. Principles of reason trace its outlines, logical necessities cement its parts. Purity and dignity are what it most expresses. It is a kind of marble temple shining on a hill." James wanted to bring philosophy out of the marble temple into the street, the home, the private lives of men and women. His attempt to make philosophy useful shocked the professional philosophers as much as the ideas themselves.

Traditionally, the scholar and the philosopher were supposed to search for *truth* objectively, forgetting self, suppressing emotional desires, and becoming completely impersonal in the exercise of logical reasoning and impartial judgment. Plato even banned poetry from his ideal Republic because it stirred men's emotions, aroused their personal desires, and thereby endangered their benefit to the State. Throughout most of the history of philosophy we find suspicion of men's natural emotions, and this was as true of the modern positivists as of the ancient idealists. By James's early manhood the leading nineteenth-century materialists, such as Friedrich Büchner, Herbert Spencer, and Ernst Heinrich Haeckel, had reduced all emotional and mental processes to the blind operation of mechanical forces. These learned men reached their deterministic theories by what they believed to be infallible mathematical and logical reasoning. They gathered statistics, added and classified their examples, and abstracted their conclusions.

Early in his study of psychology James challenged the notion that any "thinking" is impersonal, no matter how eminent the thinker. Thought processes are influenced not only by the person's temperament, his constitution, the state of his health, but also by his personal desires, both conscious and unconscious—though it was not until later that James explored the potentiality of the "subliminal." In 1879 in an essay with the novel title "The Sentiment of Rationality" he contended that a "rational conception" is one which brings an emotional equilibrium to the thinker. "The transition from a state of puzzle and perplexity to rational comprehension is full of lively relief and pleasure." But what brings the relief to one person will not work for another.

Idealism will be chosen by a man of one emotional constitution, materialism by another. At this very day all sentimental natures, fond of conciliation and intimacy, tend to an idealistic faith. Why? Because idealism gives to the nature of things such kinship with our personal selves. Our own thoughts are what we are most at home with, what we are least afraid of. To say then that the universe essentially is thought, is to say that I myself, potentially at least, am all. There is no radically alien corner, but an all-pervading *intimacy*.

Although this conception of reality may have some admirable consequences, in some self-absorbed minds it

is sure to put on a narrow, close, sick-room air. Everything sentimental and priggish will be consecrated to it. That element in reality which every strong man of common-sense willingly feels there because it calls forth powers that he owns—the rough, harsh, sea-wave, north-wind element, the denier of persons, the democratizer—is banished because it jars too much on the desire for communion. Now, it is the very enjoyment of this element that throws many men upon the materialistic or agnostic hypothesis, as a polemic reaction against the contrary extreme. They sicken at a life wholly constituted of intimacy. There is an overwhelming desire at moments to escape personality, to revel in the action of forces that have no respect for our ego, to let the tides flow, even though they flow over us. The strife of these two kinds of mental temper will, I think, always be seen in philosophy. Some men will keep insisting on the reason, the atonement, that lies in the heart of things, and that we can act *with;* others, on the opacity of brute fact that we must react *against*.

If this description seems more favorable to the men who revel in the "rough, harsh, sea-wave, north-wind element," it does not accurately indicate James's intention. He was, it is true, bold, hardy, and adventurous in his thinking, but he was not wholly "tough-minded" either.

"Now, there is one element of our active nature," he wrote,

which the Christian religion has emphatically recognized, but which philosophers as a rule have with great insincerity tried to huddle out of sight in their pretension to found systems of absolute certainty. I mean the element of faith. Faith means belief in something concerning which doubt is still theoretically possible; and as the test of belief is willingness to act, one may say that faith is the readiness to act in a cause the prosperous issue of which is not certified to us in advance. It is in fact the same moral quality which we call courage in practical affairs; and there will be a very widespread tendency in men of vigorous nature to enjoy a certain amount of uncertainty in their philosophic creed, just as risk lends a zest to worldly activity. . . . In the average man, on the contrary, the power to trust, to risk a little beyond the literal evidence, is an essential function.

Some years later (1896) James returned to these arguments for faith beyond tangible evidence in *The Will to Believe*. This title led many critics to jump to the conclusion that he was saying that a person could *will* belief in whatever he chose, without respect to his external world. But James did not mean this at all, and later, as we have seen, regretted that he had not called his essay "The Right to Believe." What he was trying to combat was agnosticism, the position of such men as W. K. Clifford and Thomas Huxley, who in the name of science advocated that belief be withheld until all the evidence was in. James pointed out that the evidence is never all in so long as life and the world continue, and that refusing to take sides on questions of vital concern to men and society may permit the wrong side to win by default. He was as interested as any scientist in obtaining all the evidence possible and in continuing the search for it, for to him no conclusion was final.

This frame of mind, in fact, was to become the very foundation of his evolving Pragmatism, which was the doctrine that "truth" is only a temporary conclusion based on the evidence in hand: a conclusion on which to base action until new evidence indicates the need for change or modification. This became for him the only meaning of "truth." He admitted that his concept was "expedient," and spoke crassly of its "cash value," but he was only applying the scientific method of observation, hypothesis, and verification as a means of arriving at his tentative conclusion. The difficulty was that this experimental concept of "truth" violated the sanctity with which the metaphysicians and theologians had for centuries embalmed the word.

Another difficulty that James's audience experienced was in understanding that he applied the scientific method in arriving at subjective as well as objective "truths." His test was the practical, workable value of a truth-hypothesis in a person's private life. Observation of the effect of heat on protoplasm yields a more obvious and less variable kind of "truth" than the effect on the human psyche of believing that God exists. Yet James insisted that if for a given person a belief in God yielded practical benefits to health, personality, character, etc., that was pragmatic truth and the individual had the *right* to his belief—though he had no right to generalize his experience into a dogma for all men. Thus James comforted the religionists on one hand, but on the other rejected the Absolute Truths which most of them professed. Of course the scientists accused him of bowing to the superstitions of theology, while the theologians suspected him of undermining their institutions by making all truths relative.

That James could be fair and objective in his judgment was demonstrated by his conduct in extending his observations, over many years, in the field of psychic research. His own desire to find evidence of survival of the human psyche after the death of the physical body did not prevent his confessing near the end of his life that he had never in a single case found a shred of evidence of the mind's surviving the body. Yet he continued to believe that the search should go on, and criticized those scientists who rejected such theories outright without making any effort to examine reputed phenomenal occurrences. There was no inconsistency in James's application of his own pragmatic method, but his trying to apply it both subjectively and objectively led him into some paradoxical positions, such as defending "faith healers," attending *séances* of notorious mediums, and insisting in his *Varieties of Religious Experience* that no clear line of demarcation could be drawn between neurotic and religious experiences. This undiscriminating tolerance was the result of his basic psychological assumptions.

III

While writing his *Principles of Psychology*, James had attempted to avoid metaphysical questions by assuming a strategic "dualism," i.e., by holding that the mind is capable of reliable knowledge of objects existing outside itself but that it is not the task of psychology to show how this is possible. In his Preface James said: "This book, assuming that thoughts and feelings exist and are vehicles of knowledge, thereupon contends that psychology when she has ascertained the empirical correlation of the various sorts of thought or feeling with definite conditions of the brain, can go no farther—can go no farther, that is, as a natural science." However, he was not able to adhere consistently to this "positivistic" view, and, as Perry has pointed out,

> The pages of the book abound in such names as Locke, Berkeley, Hume, Kant, Mill, Lewes, Taine, Bradley, Hodgson, and Renouvier, to say nothing of Spencer. This is to be accounted for in part by the fact that James's philosophers were also, as a rule, psychologists; but mainly by the fact that he believed philosophy to be the only means of attaining that very emancipation of psychology from philosophy which he sought. Instead of attaining this emancipation in advance, James introduced it into the *Principles*, the result being that his psychology as it stands is inseparable from his philosophy. . . .

James thought that he could base his psychology on the physiology of the nervous system. Reduced to the barest fundamentals, this meant applying the current biological theory of the "reflex arc." In his essay "What the Will Effects" (1888) James stated:

> The only conception at the same time renovating and fundamental with which biology has enriched psychology, the only *essential* point in which "the new psychology" is an advance upon the old, is, it seems to me, the very general and by this time very familiar notion, that all our activity belongs at bottom to the type of reflex action, and that all our consciousness accompanies a chain of events of which the first was an incoming current in some sensory nerve, and of which the last will be a discharge into some muscle, blood-vessel, or gland.

It took James nearly a hundred pages in the *Principles* to describe these processes; a brief summary can say only that nerves carry the stimulus to some part of the brain, and the brain sends some sort of impulse (seemingly electrical) to muscle, blood-vessel, gland, etc. This process would be entirely automatic were it not that a "thought" or "idea" in the brain can start a discharge of energy. The brain also often seems to have a choice of which muscle to activate in response to a given stimulus-situation. In other words, the incoming and outgoing impulses do not follow a predetermined route. Here is James's much-valued *chance*, the possibility of *choice*, and the exercise of *will*. He also believed that *interest* influences what stimuli the brain pays attention to and suppresses or acknowledges by immediate or delayed response—and if delayed, will has again come into play.

The study of biological evolution had also convinced James that all of these processes have developed in the animal because they have "survival value." Except for this, they would never have existed at all in primitive animals, or developed into more complicated patterns in the higher animals, culminating in human consciousness. "Viewed in this light," he says, "the thinking and feeling portions of our life seem little more than half-way houses toward behavior; and recent Psychology accordingly tends to treat consciousness more and more as if it existed only for the sake of the conduct which it seems to introduce, and tries to explain its peculiarities (so far as they can be explained at all) by their practical utility."

Consciousness itself James simply accepted as an existing phenomenon. He could not explain it, though he was well aware of the epistemological debates on this mystery. The pantheists regarded it as a minute portion of God's consciousness; the panpsychists (such as Fechner) as the activity of a soul in a large community of souls inhabiting living things; the Idealists as existing, like the whole universe, in God's mind. To say, with the spiritualists, that it was the operation of a soul, individual or collective, in no way removed the mystery. A few years later in his address on "Human Immortality" James suggested that possibly the brain did not produce consciousness but only received and transmitted it from a transcendental world of spirit—"influx," Swedenborg called it. "We need only suppose," James told his audience, "the continuity of our own consciousness with a mother sea, to allow for exceptional waves occasionally pouring over the dam." This notion became more attractive as he became more deeply involved in psychic research, because the analogy offered the possibility of survival of consciousness after the death of the body, and also the "transference of thought" between living persons, or between a living and a deceased person. "Of course," James added, "the causes of these odd lowerings of the brain's threshold still remain a mystery, on any terms."

In his *Principles* and later writings James simply accepted the existence of consciousness as a fact verified by experience and turned to the study of its practical uses. As a psychologist he could study it by introspective analysis of his experiences. His most important discovery was that it was continuous in duration and constantly changing in content, like the flowing of a river. "Stream of thought" was the most appropriate metaphor for the phenomenon.

This description of consciousness contradicted the theory of "association" held by Locke, Hume, and their modern followers, who believed that some faculty of the mind constructed ideas by combining the separate characteristics of the object of thought, like placing a series of arcs together to form a circle. Complex ideas were formed by combining simple ideas. Ideas were stored in the memory, from which they could be brought forth to be compared and tested by logic. James completely rejected this mechanical and atomistic theory. Although he found that the objects in the consciousness varied in number, vividness, and complexity, their flow never ceased during a person's waking life, and apparently a similar flow continued during sleep, a glimpse of which could be observed at the moment of waking. The variation in flow might be compared to waves or pulsations, but the stream never ran dry, in health or in sickness, in reverie or in concentrated mental effort. To some extent a person could control the flow by will power, but he could not stop it entirely.

Although others had opposed the "atomism" of associationism, James seems to have been the first to discover and describe the flowing aspect of consciousness, as well as the intimately personal nature of the contents of the stream. In literary criticism the phrase "association of ideas" has been used to describe a certain literary method, especially in prose, but James pointed out that "*it is* THINGS, *not ideas, which are associated in the mind*. We ought to talk of the association of *objects*, not of the association of *ideas*. And so far as association stands for a *cause*, it is between *processes in the brain*— it is these which, by being associated in certain ways, determine what successive objects shall be thought. . . . Let us . . . assume . . . this law: *When two elementary brain-processes have been active together or in immediate succession, one of them, on recurring, tends to propagate its excitement into the other*." Thus the association might be free in the sense that it was not willfully directed, but the person's interest in one object would cause one "brain-process" to have more energy than another. This meant that the person's *interest* would determine which objects in the flow received attention and added energy. It also meant that *thinking* and *feeling* were all part of one dynamic process, and that feeling powerfully influenced the thinking.

The associationists had argued that the dimensions of space are not directly perceived through the senses, but that the mind infers the dimension from the sense data. James performed experiments which demonstrated to his satisfaction that the dimensions of space were directly experienced. In the same way he found that color "comes *to* the intellect, not from it." He also performed experiments on the feeling of effort and of muscular sensibility which led to his "ideo-motor action" theory. Simplified, this is that once the mind thinks of an action which the will desires, the action follows immediately, seemingly almost automatically. "All sorts of neuro-muscular processes come between, of course, but we know [i.e., are consciously aware of] absolutely nothing of them. We think the act, and it is done; and that is all that introspection tells us of the matter." This theory was of enormous importance for James's doctrine of habit: a person establishes a habit by repetition of ideo-motor action; the action is habitual when it has become a reflex. Like every other theory in William James's psychology, the ideo-motor action can be utilized to train a man's character and ultimately change the world nearer to his heart's desire. Its potentiality in the fields of education, sociology, and politics is enormous.

IV

Although James is best known for his doctrine of Pragmatism, he regarded as his major and most important contribution to philosophy Radical Empiricism, which he said had no logical connection with Pragmatism. And while it is true that one may accept Pragmatism without embracing the conclusions which James called Radical Empiricism, it was in the latter that he attempted to provide the missing links between his Pragmatism and Pluralism.

In 1904–1905 James published eleven essays in philosophical journals on problems of metaphysics and the theory of knowledge, with such titles as: "Does 'Consciousness' Exist?," "A World of Pure Experience," "The Thing and Its Relations," "How the Mind Can Know One Thing," etc. In 1907 he collected the essays for intended republication in a book, to which he added a twelfth printed in 1884 on "Absolutism and Empiricism." The book remained unpublished, however, until two years after James's death, when Ralph Barton Perry added a Preface and delivered the essays to James's publisher, Longmans, Green and Company. The book appeared in 1912 as *Essays in Radical Empiricism*.

James had defined the term *radical empiricism* in 1898 in the Preface to his *Will to Believe*, though he called it not a philosophy but a "philosophical attitude":

I say 'empiricism,' because it is contented to regard its most assured conclusions concerning matters of fact as hypotheses liable to modification in the course of future experience; and I say 'radical,' because it treats the doctrine of monism itself as an hypothesis, and, unlike so much of the half-way empiricism that is current under the name of positivism or agnosticism or scientific naturalism, it does not dogmatically affirm monism as something with which all experience has got to square.

Perry remarks that this describes "a temper of mind rather than a doctrine, and characterizes all of Professor James's writings." But in a Preface to *The Meaning of Truth* (1901) James had written: "I am interested in another doctrine [note the word] in philosophy to which I give the name of radical empiricism, and it seems to me that the establishment of the pragmatic theory of truth is a step of first-rate importance in making radical empiricism prevail." James then defined the term as containing a postulate, a statement of fact, and a generalized conclusion:

The postulate is that the only things that shall be debatable among philosophers shall be things definable in terms drawn from experience. (Things of an unexperienceable nature may exist ad libitum, but they form no part of the material for philosophic debate.)

The statement of fact is that the relations between things, conjunctive as well as disjunctive, are just as much matters of direct particular experience, neither more so nor less so, than the things themselves.

The generalized conclusion is that therefore the parts of experience hold together from next to next relations that are themselves parts of experience. The directly apprehended universe needs, in short, no extraneous trans-empirical connective support, but possesses in its own right a concatenated or continuous structure.

By insisting that "the parts of experience hold together," James was attempting to reply to the "un-radical" empiricists, beginning with Hume and John Stuart Mill, who had found it "inexplicable" and "incomprehensible," as Flournoy says in paraphrasing Mill, "that a succession of separate states of consciousness can take cognizance of itself, as succession, in a new state of consciousness." The rationalists had done so by introducing a mysterious "Ego" or "Soul" to organize the mosaic perceptions (sensations) into patterns of consciousness. Without something to act as a foundation or matrix for perceptual experience, Hume said, "I must plead the privilege of a skeptic, and confess that the difficulty is too hard for my understanding." James replied that there was no need for a "soul" because the stream of experience flowed continuously. Time, for example, is not experienced as past, present, and future, but only as a fluid moment of duration in which the past is uniting with the present, the present is becoming past, and the future is becoming present. Language, tied to words and logic, cannot accurately describe time-as-experienced.

James argued that the inner life is far richer than philosophers and psychologists had supposed. Even *relationship*, a great stumbling-block in epistemology, is directly experienced, because experiences overlap. All rationalists had contended that *causality* must be deduced from succession, but James found it to be experienced in personal activity. He pointed out that conjunctions and prepositions, such as *and, but, as, if, because, then, for, neither*, etc., were not empty of sensory content but aroused definite feelings of motion, anticipation, proximity, etc., and therefore served as "transitive states" between the "substantive states" (perceptions: images, sensations, memories). By such concrete examples and close—even subtle—reasoning James presented his arguments for direct or *radical* experience. Everything real could be experienced, and all experience was real. Thus *experience* and *reality* were the same thing, and could be summed up as: "a field of consciousness including its objects thought or felt, plus an attitude in regard to these objects, plus a sense of self to which this attitude belongs." Having to admit a "sense of self" was undoubtedly one of the problems in this theory.

Pure experience, James admitted, that is, experience devoid of all conceptual elaboration, exists only in the new-born babe, in the mind of a person coming out of sound sleep or narcosis, or in extreme phases of ecstasy. These might be called primordial states of consciousness, or "sciousness." Some mystics have testified to the phenomenon of "sciousness," when their sense of "me" was completely obliterated. This admission that *con*-sciousness, in which the "me" and the "not-me" are distinguished, is not *pure* experience—because to some extent a conceptual sorting and classifying of the primitive experiences has taken place—seems to make the mystic's "sciousness" more *real* than the "consciousness" of the normal person. But the author of *Varieties of Religious Experience* did not shrink from this implication.

V

The book called *A Pluralistic Universe* (1909), which James subtitled "Hibbert Lectures at Manchester College on the Present Situation in Philosophy," did not advance a new doctrine, but one which, as Perry remarks, was "almost coeval with James's philosophic maturity." A major purpose in these lectures was to counteract, in a playfully belligerent manner, the monistic philosophy entrenched at Oxford. The approach was essentially the same as in the *Radical Empiricism* essays. But if James did not have anything really new to say, he at least found fresh ways to say it.

James was acutely aware that he had not been entirely successful in salvaging a metaphysics of "radical empiricism" from his psychological "stream of consciousness." But recently a German philosopher, Gustav Theodor Fechner, whose earlier "psychophysicks" he had scornfully rejected, had helped him in formulating an ethical pluralism, which James called a "republic of semi-detached consciousness," presided over by a God whose finiteness absolves Him from responsibility for evil. James had long been familiar with Fechner's *Zend-Avesta*, and in 1905 he read *Über die Seelenfrage* (On the Question of the Soul) and *Die Tagesansicht gegenüber der Nachtansicht* (The Day View compared to the Night View *). James had always been fascinated by panpsychism, even while rejecting it, and he was now favorably impressed by Fechner's universe of pyramiding souls, intercepting each other like the epicycles on the circumference of larger cycles by which astronomers tried to "save" the Ptolemaic system. The largest of these souls was God, and beneath him an earth-soul which mediated between God and the human souls of the planet, while beneath these

---

* This title almost defies translation because in the context *Ansicht* means both the conscious awareness a person experiences during his waking hours and the different sort of psychic activity of his mind during sleep.

were infra-psychic states below the threshold of human consciousness. Of course James did not adopt this whole hierocratic scheme
—he was too republican to accept any hierarchy, human or divine
—but it suggested to him a modified analogy or hypothesis.

After reading *Seelenfrage* and *Tagesansicht*, James wrote his
British Humanist-Pragmatist friend F. C. S. Schiller: "I can't yet
get over the dialectic difficulty of seeing how a wide-span consciousness can be entitatively *constituted* of smaller consciousnesses,
but the dear old man's thoroughness and intimacy with his theory,
and the inimitable use he makes of the methods of induction and
analogy makes all these absolutists with their short-cuts to beatitude
shrivel, humanly speaking, to pellicles."

The epistemological problem of how two consciousnesses can
experience the same thing, without postulating an absolute mind
in which both consciousnesses exist, had bothered James for many
years, and as late as the writing of the *Radical Empiricism* essays. To
support his own doctrine of "pure experience" he had searched
frantically for some solution to this problem. In one of the Hibbert
Lectures he confessed,

> . . . I struggled with the problem for years, covering hundreds of
> sheets of paper with notes and memoranda and discussions with
> myself over the difficulty. . . . The struggle was vain; I found myself
> in an *impasse*. I saw that I must either forswear that 'psychology
> without a soul' to which my whole psychological and kantian edu-
> cation had committed me,—I must, in short, bring back distinct spirit-
> ual agents to know the mental states, now singly and now in combina-
> tion, in a word bring back scholasticism and common sense—or else I
> must squarely confess the solution of the problem impossible, and then
> either give up my intellectualistic logic, the logic of identity, and
> adopt some higher (or lower) form of rationality, or, finally, face the
> fact that life is logically irrational.

Reading Bergson encouraged James to give up logic, though what
he needed was instead to recognize the limits of logic. The special
stumbling block was the Aristotelian "law of identity": If A is B,
then A cannot be C. To James the universe seemed to have separate
identities, but they impinged, and were both identical (some at
least) and different from each other at the same time. In the "stream
of consciousness" there was an "endosmosis of adjacent parts of
living experience." Thus there was a pervading unity in the diver-
sity.

Perry notes that James's adherence to "realism" is vague in *A Pluralistic Universe* because his "position remains uncertain on a metaphysical point of first importance. Must reality be perceived, sensed, or felt in order to be? Rejecting a solipsistic or even humanistic limitation of existence, James represents it as stretching off beyond the horizon of human consciousness—accessible, but out of range." He might have distinguished *experience* from the *experienced*, but he did not. "Existence would then coincide with the content of experience, but would be independent of any *act* of experiencing on the part of mind. This alternative would be the most consistent with James's theory that mind is a peculiar type of relationship among terms which in themselves are neither physical nor mental." (Later realists called this "neutralism.") *A Pluralistic Universe*, Perry continues, "does not clearly affirm this alternative, and even compromises it through identifying the continuum of experience with consciousnesses great and small."

Nevertheless, James was determined to bring about a union between empiricism and some variety of theism which could restore religion to intellectual respectability. Fechner had written before Janet and Freud, but James thought that their discoveries of divided or split personality in hysterical patients made Fechner's speculation more plausible. "For my own part," James declared,

> I find in some of these abnormal or supernormal facts the strongest suggestions in favor of a superior consciousness being possible. I doubt whether we shall ever understand some of them without using the very letter of Fechner's conception of a great reservoir in which the memories of earth's inhabitants are pooled and preserved, and from which, when the threshold lowers or the valve opens, information ordinarily shut out leaks into the mind of exceptional individuals among us. . . . I think it may be asserted that there *are* religious experiences of a specific nature, not deducible by analogy or psychological reasoning from our other sorts of experience. I think that they point with reasonable probability to the continuity of our consciousness with a wider spiritual environment from which the ordinary prudential man (who is the only man that scientific psychology, so called, takes cognizance of) is shut off.

In his *Varieties of Religious Experience* James cited a multitude of examples of men and women who had been overwhelmingly convinced that they had genuinely experienced some sort of irrational flow of energy into their consciousness (or semi-consciousness in some of the "mystical" states). James believed that, whatever the explanation, the *experience* itself was real and must be reckoned with—merely to label it "morbid" or "abnormal" served no useful purpose. He was impressed also by the fact that since the time of Martin Luther these experiences seemed to flourish in times of human failure and despair—Kierkegaard's "fear and trembling," though the Danish mystic was still unknown to James.

"Religious experience of the lutheran type," James declared, "brings all our naturalistic standards to bankruptcy. You are strong only by being weak, it shows. . . ." He continued:

> The phenomenon is that of new ranges of life succeeding on our most despairing moments. There are resources in us that naturalism with its literal and legal virtues never recks of. . . . Here is a world in which all is well, in *spite* of certain forms of death, indeed *because* of certain forms of death—death of hope, death of strength . . . of everything that paganism, naturalism, and legalism pin their faith on and tie their trust to. . . . The sort of belief that religious experience of this type naturally engenders in those who have it is fully in accord with Fechner's theories. To quote words which I have used elsewhere, the believer finds that the tenderer parts of his personal life are continuous with a *more* of the same quality which is operative in the universe outside of him and which he can keep in working touch with, and in a fashion get on board of and save himself, when all his lower being has gone to pieces in the wreck. . . .

If this sounds like conventional Christian doctrine of the evangelical Protestant variety, that was not what James was trying to present. He felt that these experiences empirically verified Fechner's ideas rather than Luther's; and it was not pantheistic because the "higher mind in the cosmos" was "discontinuous with our own." Whether it was monotheistic or polytheistic, there was no way of knowing, but it seemed to James that the experiences indicated polytheism. At any rate, it was not an absolute mind, which would bring in foreknowledge, determinism, and responsibility for evil. The only escape from such an "iron block" universe seemed to James "to be frankly pluralistic and assume that the superhuman consciousness, however vast it may be, has itself an external environment, and consequently is finite." The finiteness of this supersoul or consciousness preserved free will and made it dependent upon other more finite souls for help in building and maintaining order out of chaos. Cooperation made the universe melioristic.

VI

Since *A Pluralistic Universe* was the last book that William James published in his lifetime, it might be regarded as his final word on philosophy. But of course the last book he actually wrote was the unfinished *Some Problems of Philosophy* (1911), a work specifically intended as an introduction to philosophy for beginning students. This book was written in the lucid style of his more popular works (e.g. *Pragmatism*, as compared to *Radical Empiricism*), but it also happens to be the most concise and best organized of any of his books.

The early chapters of *Some Problems* define the meanings of philosophy (the author prefers the older tradition of combining "mental and moral philosophy"), the problems with which metaphysics is concerned, the baffling problem of being (ontology), and the differences between "percept" and "concept," with James's confessed bias for the former as being nearer experience. Though he acknowledges the need for concepts, he teaches that their "significance consists always in their relation to perceptual particulars. . . . Had we no concepts we should live simply 'getting' each successive moment of experience, as the sessile sea-anemone on its rock receives whatever nourishment the wash of the waves may bring [what James called "pure empiricism" in *Radical Empiricism*]. With concepts we go in quest of the absent, meet the remote, actively turn this way or that, bend our experience, and make it tell us whither it is bound."

The philosopher, "unable as a finite being to compass more than a few passing moments" of perceptual experience,

> is yet to extend his knowledge beyond such moments by the ideal symbol of the other moments. He thus commands vicariously innumerable perceptions that are out of range. But the concepts by which he does this, being thin extracts from perception, are always insufficient representatives thereof; and, although they yield wider information, must never be treated after the rationalistic fashion, as if they gave a deeper quality of truth. The deeper features of reality are found only in perceptual experience. Here alone do we acquaint ourselves with continuity, or the immersion of one thing in another, here alone with self, with substance, with qualities, with activity in its various modes, with time, with cause, with change, with novelty, with tendency, and with freedom.

James's own character and temperament needed change, novelty, and freedom for healthy existence, and his own experience had convinced him that he lived in a world in which they could and should operate. He freely admitted that all his thinking about philosophical questions had this bias, but he also believed that every other thinker was influenced if not limited by his natural biases too. James did not see how by logic alone anyone could prove the universe monistic, dualistic, or pluralistic, but his study of the brain and the nervous system during his years of teaching psychology had shown him, he thought, that the world is perceptually experienced as continuous, related, and ever-changing; also that some part of the human mind has the power of making choices in response to sensory stimuli, and thus that free will is a reality. He believed, too, that his Empiricist and Pluralistic doctrines were confirmed both by science and the experience of individual human beings. Pragmatism provided a method for dealing with this sort of world.

Not only did science indicate to James that the world of experience was fluid and changing, but it seemed to him that only an unfinished universe held any incentive for human effort. Since effort and activity were so necessary for all living organisms—it would appear that they were innate in the existential world, and a proof of its built-in purpose (teleology). However, his reasoning to prove the existence of such a world was always circular. Beginning from a felt need, he proceeded to argue from effect to cause and from presumed cause to observed effect. Aware of this weakness in his metaphysics, he pleaded the inadequacy of logic.

James's professional contemporaries often arrogantly accused him of being a "popular philosopher," partly because he wrote in a highly successful literary instead of a technical, learned style, and partly because he was less concerned for ultimate truth than immediate, usable truths: doctrines or conclusions of personal use to his readers or hearers, such as calming their fears, giving them incentive for effort, enlisting their active support in building a better society, and, not least, in making life more enjoyable. If these are not proper goals for a dignified philosopher, then James was undignified and "popular," but it was his own deliberate intention to speak to mankind instead of to other philosophers. Some of the professional condemnation was motivated by snobbery and jealousy, though it was true that he never produced a closely reasoned metaphysical system. His Pragmatism, Radical Empiricism, and Pluralism were all aspects of his "universe unfinished, with doors and windows open to possibilities uncontrolled in advance. . . ."

Flournoy was right in his conclusion that "James's philosophy rests entirely upon his psychology." Although he founded no school in psychology—or philosophy either—his approach to every philosophical problem was psychological, and, as Flournoy says: "He transformed psychology by his analyses and theories of the perception of time, space, and reality; of the nature of emotion, the feeling of effort, of attention, volition, instinct, and reason; of the constitution of consciousness with its focus and fringe, and its incessant transformation; and of much else."

After a generation of neglect, psychologists are again turning back to James's contributions. His books are being brought back into print in inexpensive editions with introductions by distinguished psychologists. In an Introduction to a 1958 reprint of *Talks to Teachers*, Paul Woodring, of Harvard, points out that the "reversal of trends" in American education since World War II has given new importance to James's work:

> Today we hear from many quarters a demand for sweeping reforms that will place a greater emphasis on quality, values, clear thinking, and hard work. There is less stress on "growth" and more on learning, less on "needs" and more on accomplishment, less on permissiveness and more on that old-fashioned word, "discipline." The result of these new trends is that the views of William James seem a good deal more sound and realistic than do those of the leaders of what was called "the new education" a generation ago.

Another Harvard professor, Gordon W. Allport, remarks in his Introduction to a 1961 edition of the *Psychology:* ". . . now that we have recovered from the irreverent shocks administered by Freud, Pavlov, Watson, we begin to perceive that the psychological insights of James have the steadiness of a polar star." Allport also sees James's theory of "reasoning" as a useful corrective to the contemporary

> 'cognitive theory' . . . cast in terms of a machine model. Men no longer 'reason,' they behave like giant computers: they receive *inputs* and produce *outputs*, and in spite of *noise* and *redundancy*, they somehow manage to *code*—and so it goes. James, on the other hand, tells us that reasoning is the 'ability to deal with novel data' (which a

machine does poorly if at all). He shows us how we select and recombine attributes of experience, always following a course 'important for our interests.' Since machines lack interest it seems that James's simple scaffolding may outlast the currently fashionable computer model. James draws his designs from fresh daily experience, whereas today the tendency is to tailor human capacities to fit the alleged properties of the machine. Contemporary model builders will do well to return to James to see whether in fact their mechanical formulations do justice to the subtleties of process he depicts.

In the Introduction to a still more recent reprint of the "Briefer Course" *Psychology* Ashley Montagu says, in more general terms, that though much has happened in the seventy years since this book was first published, "nothing which has developed during that period or is likely to happen will ever render this book out-of-date." No one, Montagu asserts, "has ever written more illuminatingly and more helpfully on 'Habit,' the 'Stream of Consciousness,' the 'Self,' and 'Imagination.'"

The revival of interest in James's contributions to psychology has not yet extended to his philosophy, but the very foundation of both his psychology and philosophy, as this biography has emphasized again and again, was his belief in the ability of the human mind to choose between alternative theories and courses of action. Fully aware of the evils in the world which can be overcome only by the greatest exertion of human effort, self-sacrifice, and courage, James nevertheless believed that man is not a prisoner either of nature or of the race's accumulated mistakes of the past. Granting that the philosophical doctrine of "determinism" can never be definitively disproved—or proved either—he would, as Allport says, "invite us to take 'the livelier option,' for our choice of assumptions has effects on the human nature that we study. James warns psychologists that by their own theories of human nature they have the power of elevating or degrading this same nature. Debasing assumptions debase the mind; generous assumptions exalt the mind. His own assumptions were always the most generous possible."

If there is one indisputable characteristic of the twentieth century, it is the dynamic effort of people in almost every part of the world to achieve fuller social and political freedom and greater human dignity. William James was pre-eminently the philosopher of freedom and human dignity, and in his psychology he anticipated and prepared for the crises of humanity in this revolutionary century.

The James Family

Notes

Index

WILLIAM JAMES, OF ALBANY
b. Ireland, 1771; d. Albany, N.Y., 1832

m. (1st) Elizabeth Tillman   *Twin sons:* Robert, 1797–1821;
1796   1744–1797   William, 1797–1868

m. (2nd) Mary Ann Connolly   *Daughter:* Ellen, 1800–1823
1798   1779–1800

m. (3rd) Catharine Barber   *7 sons, 3 daughters* (2 d. in infancy):
1803   1782–1859   Augustus, 1807–1866
                                HENRY JAMES, SR., 1811–1882
                                Jeanette, 1814–1856
                                John Barber, 1816–1856
                                Edward, 1818–1856
                                Catharine Margaret (Temple),
                                    1820–1854
                                Ellen King (Van Buren), 1825–1849
                                Howard, 1828–1887

The James Family

A Genealogical Table

HENRY JAMES, SR.
b. Albany, 1811; d. Cambridge, Mass., 1882

    m. MARY ROBERTSON WALSH   *4 sons, 1 daughter:*
      1840   1810–1882   WILLIAM JAMES, 1842–1910
                                   Henry, 1843–1916
                                   Garth Wilkinson, 1845–1883
                                   Robertson, 1846–1910
                                   Alice, 1848–1892

WILLIAM JAMES (psychologist and philosopher)
b. New York City, 1842; d. Chocorua, N.H., 1910

    m. Alice Howe Gibbens   *4 sons, 1 daughter:*
      1878   1849–1922   Henry, 1879–1947 (lawyer,
                                       biographer, father's editor)
                                   William, 1882–1961 (artist)
                                   Herman, 1884–1885
                                     Margaret Mary (Porter), 1887–
                                       1947
                                   Alexander Robertson, 1890–1946
                                     (artist)

Notes

The primary sources of this biography are, as explained in the Preface, the hundreds of letters and manuscripts in the collection of the James Papers in the Houghton Library of Harvard University, and the unpublished letters and diaries of Mrs. William James and her family in the possession of Mr. John S. R. James. The two-volume edition of *The Letters of William James*, edited by Henry James Jr., and the letters and manuscripts published by Ralph Barton Perry in his *Thought and Character of William James* have also been used. For William James's contributions to psychology and philosophy, his published writings are of course the major source of information; Perry's monumental study is the most useful secondary source. Both primary and secondary sources are indicated in the notes that follow. These notes will enable the reader to identify quotations and references to authors and titles, but they do not reflect all the general sources of information for this biography, including hundreds of letters read but not quoted directly, or some of the family history conveyed informally by Mr. John James.

KEY TO ABBREVIATIONS

Manuscript sources:

HL Holographs in the James Papers, Houghton Library, Harvard University

JJ Private collection of Mr. John S. R. James, Cambridge, Mass.

Published sources:

AJ *Diary* *The Diary of Alice James*, edited by Leon Edel. New York: Dodd, Mead & Company, 1964.

CER *Collected Essays and Reviews*, by William James. London: Longmans, Green and Co., 1920.

LHJ *The Letters of Henry James*, selected and edited by Percy Lubbock. (2 vols.) New York: Charles Scribner's Sons, 1920.

LWJ *The Letters of William James*, edited by [his son] Henry James. (2 vols.) Boston: The Atlantic Monthly Press, 1920.

LRHJ *The Literary Remains of the Late Henry James*, edited with an Introduction by William James. Boston: James R. Osgood and Company, 1885.

P *The Thought and Character of William James*, by Ralph Barton Perry. (2 vols.) Boston: Little, Brown, and Company, 1935.

PP *The Principles of Psychology*, by William James. (2 vols.) New York: Henry Holt and Company, 1890.

NSB *Notes of a Son and Brother*, by Henry James. New York: Charles Scribner's Sons, 1914.

SBO *A Small Boy and Others*, by Henry James. New York: Charles Scribner's Sons, 1913.

VRE *The Varieties of Religious Experience: A Study in Human Nature*, by William James. New York and London: Longmans, Green & Co., 1902.

The James family:

AJ Alice James, sister of William
AHJ Alice Howe Gibbens, wife of William James
EPG Eliza Putnam Gibbens, mother of Alice Howe Gibbens
GWJ Garth Wilkinson (Wilky) James, younger brother of William
HJ¹ Henry James Sr., father of William
Mrs. HJ¹, Mary Robertson Walsh, mother of WJ
HJ² Henry (Harry) James, brother of William
HJ³ Henry (Harry) James, first son of William
MMJ Margaret Mary (Peggy) James, daughter of William
RJ Robertson (Robby, Rob, Bobby, Bob) James, youngest brother of William
WJ of Albany First American William James
WJ William James, psychologist, philosopher
WJ² William (Billy) James, second son of William

CHAPTER 1: *Rebellious Grandchildren*

Epigraph: SBO, 190.
New York City property: unpublished notes compiled by Dan Laurence from tax assessment records in the Municipal Archives and Record Center of New York City; Ward maps 1835–1850, Map

Room of the New York Hall of Records and Municipal Archives
and Record Center; Conveyance Records, Liber 422, pp. 279–81,
New York Hall of Records; Block Records #547 (15th Ward),
New York Hall of Records.

Katherine Hastings, "William James (1771–1832) of Albany," in *New
York Genealogical and Biographical Record*, LV (1925).

HJ¹, "Autobiography," LRHJ, 145–91.

Austin Warren, *The Elder James* (1934).

Harold Larrabee, "The Jameses: Financier, Heretic, Philosopher,"
The American Scholar, I (1932), 401–13.

Leon Edel, *Henry James: The Untried Years: 1843–1870* (1953).

"Of the eleven . . .": F. O. Matthiessen, *The James Family* (1948), 5.

Milly Theale's family: HJ², *The Wings of the Dove*, Book V, Chap.
III. P, I, 3–38.

CHAPTER II: *Transatlantic Infancy*

Epigraph: HJ¹ to mother, May 1, 1844.

Details of youth: Robert C. Le Clair, *Young Henry James* (1955);
  "Autobiography," LRHJ; SBO and NSB; P, I, 20–79; Edel, *op. cit.*

The Diary of Philip Hone, ed. Bayard Tuckerman (1889), II, 108.

John Sterling: "dying," HJ², *Substance and Shadow*, 322; "talk . . .
  depraved," 324.

Frogmore Cottage: HJ¹ to mother, May 1, 1844.

"spiritual creation," HJ¹, *Society the Redeemed Form of Man*, 43.

"one day . . . May," LRHJ, 58–60.

"curse of mankind," *Society the Redeemed Form of Man*, 46–48.

"Divine love," HJ¹, *Christianity the Logic of Creation*, 2.

Paris, 1845: SBO, 53–54.

Hudson steamboat: SBO, 178.

"Dame School": SBO, 9.

"I desire my child," HJ¹, *The Nature of Evil*, 99.

"curse and swear!" SBO, 259.

"Tell Henry and Mary," RJ to WJ, Feb. 24, 1898.

WJ drawing: SBO, 207.

Church: SBO, 233–34.

Profession of HJ¹: NSB, 69; profession for children: SBO, 219.

Robert James family: SBO, 181.

Art galleries in New York: SBO, 266–68.

"If this was Europe," SBO, 170.

Toeppfer: SBO, 293.

CHAPTER III: *Zigzag Voyages*

Epigraph: SBO, 293.

Switzerland, 1855: SBO, Chap. XX; P, I, 80–86; Le Clair, Chap. 6.

England: SBO, Chaps. XXII–XXIII; P, I, 80–86, 169–189; Le Clair, Chap. 7.

Paris: SBO, Chap. XXIV; Le Clair, Chap. 8, quotes letters of HJ[1] to mother. French painters: François Fosca, *Le Peinture Française au XIXᵉ Siècle, 1800–1870* (Paris, 1946); Lee Johnson, *Delacroix* (1963).

Boulogne-sur-mer: SBO, Chap. XXIX; Le Clair, Chap. 9.

CHAPTER IV: *Retraced Steps*

Epigraph: HJ[1] to Samuel Ward, Sept. 18, 1859.

Newport: NSB, Chap. IV; P, I, 190–201; Le Clair, Chap. 10; Edel, *op. cit.*, 136–44; Van Wyck Brooks, *New England Summer* (1940), Chap. IV; Anna F. Hunter, "Kay Street During My Life," *Bulletin of the Newport Historical Society*, No. 83, April 1932, 1–12; Bruce Howe, "Early Days of the Art Association," *Bulletin of the Newport Historical Society*, No. 11, April 1963, 5–29; Delphine Washburn, *Newport Historic Guide*, Preservation Society of Newport County, 1963; Cleveland Amory, *The Last Resorts* (1948), Chap. III; Percy Mackaye, *The Life of Steele Mackaye* (1927), 2 vols.; Virginia Harlow, *Thomas Sergeant Perry: A Biography* (1950)— letters from William, Henry, and G. W. (Wilky) James, 239–350.

William Hunt: Homer Saint-Gaudens, *The American Artist and His Times* (1941), W.H., 130–31, 154–55; Martha A. S. Shannon, *Boston Days of William Morris Hunt* (1923).

John La Farge: Royal Cortissoz, *John La Farge: A Memoir and a Study* (1911).

Julian Hawthorne, *Memoirs of . . .* , ed. by Edith Garrigues (1938).

Life and Letters of Edwin Lawrence Godkin, ed. by Rollo Ogden (1907), 2 vols.

Edward Waldo Emerson, *The Early Years of the Saturday Club, 1855–1870* (1918); chaps. on Henry James Sr., William Morris Hunt, Louis Agassiz, Jeffries Wyman.

HJ[2], "our poor father's," quoted Edel, *op. cit.*, 137–38.

"We can't get a house," HJ[1] to Mrs. Francis G. Shaw, quoted P, I, 186.

"I have grown," see epigraph.

Switzerland: NSB, Chap. I–III; Le Clair, Chap. 11; HJ², WJ, and RJ to T. S. Perry, Harlow, *op. cit.*, 239–59.

"Willy interrupts," RJ to HJ¹ [Dec. 1859].

"Willy . . . extraordinary," AJ to HJ¹, March 11, [1860].

Société de Zofingue: Theodore Flournoy, *The Philosophy of William James*, translated by Edwin B. Holt and William James, Jr. (1917), 1; HJ² to T. S. Perry, May 13, 1860 (Harlow, 247–48).

Saint Bernard: A letter to the Hospice du Grand Saint-Bernard in 1962 brought the information that the morgue described by HJ² to T.S.P. in 1860 is still in use. In the thin, cold air the skin dries like parchment, without odor, and the mummified forms last for centuries. But today the morgue is sealed with brick and mortar after each internment to prevent its becoming a curiosity for tourists.

Germany: P, I, 190–201; Le Clair, Chap. 11; WJ to HJ¹, Aug. 12, 19, 24, 1860; HJ¹ to Edmund Tweedy, July 18, 24, 1860; WJ to Charles Ritter, July 31, 1860.

CHAPTER V: *The Paternal Grip*

Epigraph: fragment of letter quoted by Edel, *op. cit.*, 137.

Newport, 1860: P, I, 88–95; Le Clair, Chap. 12; NSB, Chap. IV; see also titles on Hunt and La Farge for Chap. IV, above.

Sanborn's school: NSB, 221–23; P, I, 90–91.

Perry's diary, quoted Harlow, *op. cit.*, 13.

Edward Emerson's visit: *The Early Years of the Saturday Club*, 328; Godkin's visit: *Life and Letters*, II, 118.

"Never surely had so odd," NSB, 61.

"The broad sky," WJ to HJ², Aug. 24, 1872.

"the light is shrieking," AJ, *Diary*, Oct. 12, 1890.

WJ told WJ² (on becoming professional painter), orally by WJ² to author August 1959.

T. S. Perry's diary, quoted Edel, *op. cit.*, 167.

"I have had a firm grasp," quoted Edel, 171; "The way I excuse," *ibid*.

"To the Angels . . . Swedenborg," HJ¹ to R. W. Emerson [1861].

July 4th Oration: *The Social Significance of Our Institutions, an Oration.* Delivered by Request of the Citizens of Newport, R.I., July 4, 1861. By Henry James. Boston: Ticknor and Fields, 1861. "Mr. Lincoln and Mr. Seward," *ibid.*, 40.

Harvard: Samuel Eliot Morison, *Three Centuries of Harvard, 1636–1936* (1936); Hamilton Vaughan Bail, *Views of Harvard: A Pictorial Record 1860* (1949); Henry James [HJ³], *Charles W. Eliot, President of Harvard University 1869–1909* (1930), 2 vols.; Charles W. Eliot, *Harvard Memories* (1923).

Agassiz: Louise Hall Tharp, *Adventurous Alliance: The Story of the Agassiz Family of Boston* (1959); Edward Lurie, *Louis Agassiz: A Life of Science* (1960).

"We are . . . twelve," WJ to family, Sept. 16, 1861.

"I first came in contact," LWJ, I, 32–33.

"The first four days," WJ to family, Sept. 16, 1861.

"I haven't for one minute," WJ to family [autumn 1861].

Mrs. Upham's: NSB, 152–54.

"Do you know, Kitty," WJ to Kitty Temple [Sept. 1861].

"Wilky & I," WJ to family [early Nov. 1861].

Invitation to Perry: Harlow, 265.

"The *place*, to me," WJ to T. S. Perry, Dec. 25, 1861.

Sweetsers: NSB, 140.

"I am . . . chemistry," WJ to family, March 2, [1862].

Eliot's record: LWJ, I, 32 note.

Felton's death: WJ to family [March 1, 1862].

Bob Temple: NSB, 142.

"A few weeks' stay," *War Papers*, 10.

CHAPTER VI: *Medical Profession*

Epigraph: WJ to unidentified correspondent, P, I, 216; date Feb. 21, 1864, deduced by Perry.

Professor Child: NSB, 127, 152.

WJ's chemistry experiments: LWJ, I, 31–32.

Eliot on WJ's education: P, I, 207.

WJ's boil: WJ to AJ, Oct. 19, 1862; P, I, 213–14.

HJ² at Harvard: NSB, 326 ff.

"I have been with him," WJ to AJ, Oct. 19, 1862.

War news: NSB, 241 ff., 311; P, I, 185.

Wilky's wound: "The Assault on Fort Wagner," by Captain Garth W. James, *War Papers* (Loyal Legion, Milwaukee, 1891), 9–30; Peter Burchard, *One Gallant Rush: Robert Gould Shaw and His Brave Black Regiment* (1965).

Miss Appleton's: WJ to AJ, Sept. 13, 1863.

Wyman: WJ on, *Harvard Advocate*, Oct. 1, 1874, quoted LWJ, I, 48; *Early Years of the Saturday Club*, Chap. XIII.

"I am obliged," WJ to Katharine James Prince, Sept. 12, 1863.

"I feel . . . importance," WJ to mother, Nov. 11, 1863.

"I embraced," see epigraph, above.

Dr. Holmes: Eleanor M. Tilton, *Amiable Autocrat: A Biography of Dr. Oliver Wendell Holmes* (1947).

Harvard Medical School: *Charles W. Eliot*, I, 88 ff.; Tilton, Chap. 12.

CHAPTER VII: *With Agassiz in Brazil*

Epigraph: WJ to mother [March 30], 1865.

Agassiz expedition: WJ's Brazil notebooks (HL); WJ, "Louis Agassiz," *Memories and Studies* (1911), 3–16; P, I, Chap. XII; Tharp, 160–90; Lurie, 345–49; Mrs. Agassiz's diary (unpublished) on trip quoted by Tharp.

"We have been detained," WJ to mother [March 30], 1865.

"No one has a right," WJ to family, April 21, 1865; Rio Harbor, same.

WJ's smallpox: WJ to family, May 3–10, June 3, 1865.

"James, are you awake?" *Memories and Studies*, 11.

Pará: WJ to HJ², July 15, 23, 1865.

Solimões River: WJ to HJ¹, Sept. 12–15, 1865.

Tefé: WJ to family, Oct. 21, 1865.

Return plans: WJ to mother, Dec. 9, 1865.

Manáos: Mrs. A.'s diary, Tharp, 181.

"Well, James," quoted Tharp, 184.

CHAPTER VIII: *Unsettled Condition*

Epigraph: WJ to Tom Ward, June 8, 1866.

"I think Harry much improved," WJ to GWJ, Feb. 25, 1866.

John Allen: WJ to Tom Ward, March 27, 1866.

Wendell Holmes: above letter to T.W.; P, I, Chap. XXX; Catherine Drinker Bowen, *Yankee from Olympus: Justice Holmes and His Family* (1944).

Charles Peirce: P, I, XXXI.

Chauncey Wright: Edward L. Madden, *Chauncey Wright* (1964); *Chauncey Wright and the Foundations of Pragmatism* (1963)

AJ's breakdown: *Diary* (Edel ed.), 149.

"The Hidden Self," *Scribner's Magazine*, VII (1890), 7, 361–73.

RJ and GWJ in Florida: Anna Robeson Burr's Introduction to *Alice James: Her Brothers, Her Journal* (1934).

James: Her Brothers, Her Journal (1934).

"verge of suicide," WJ to Tom Ward, Jan. 1868.

"Where have I been," WJ to AJ, Nov. 14, 1866.

"materialism inconsistent," memorandum [winter 1866–67?], LWJ, I, 82.

AJ in New York: WJ to AJ [Feb. 18, 1867].

"present time . . . medical school," WJ to AJ, Dec. 12, [1866].

Medical School commencement: WJ to RJ & GWJ, March 13, 1866.

CHAPTER IX: *Baths in Bohemia*

Epigraph: WJ to HJ[1], Sept. 5, 1867.
WJ's unpublished diaries and notebooks (HL).
Aboard *Great Eastern*, WJ to AJ, April 27, 1867.
Paris: WJ to HJ[2], May 3, 1867.
Dresden: WJ to parents, May 27, 30, June 12, July 24, 1867.
Grimm and Saint-Victor on Venus de Milo: Edel, *op. cit.*, 258–59; WJ to parents, July 24, 1867.
Bad-Teplitz: WJ to AJ, Aug. 6–14, 1867.
Berlin: WJ to HJ[1], Sept. 5, 1867; WJ to Tom Ward, Sept. 2, 1867; WJ to O. W. Holmes, Sept. 17, 1867; WJ to HJ[2], Sept. 26, 1867; WJ to HJ[1], 1867; WJ to AJ, Oct. 17, 31, 1867.
Review for *Nation:* WJ to HJ[2], Sept. 26, 1867; HJ[2] to WJ, Nov. 22, 1867.
Philosophical debate: WJ to HJ[1], Sept. 5, 1867; HJ[1] to WJ, Sept. 27, 1867.
University of Berlin: WJ to Tom Ward, Nov. 7, 1867; WJ to AJ, Jan. 9, 1868.
Bad-Teplitz (2nd time): WJ to HJ[1], Jan. 22, 1868; WJ to RJ, Jan. 27, 1868; WJ to HJ[2], March 4, 1868.
"law-giving tone," WJ to HJ[2], April 5, 1868.
Criticism of "An Extraordinary Case," WJ to HJ[2], April 13, 1868.
Dresden (2nd time): WJ to AJ, March 16, May 14, June 4 (sentimentality of Germans), June 23 ("American petticoats"), 1868.
"scoundrel Agassiz," WJ to HJ[2], March 9, 1867.
Diary, "Greek things," April 14; "Harry . . . moping," April 27; Schiller, April 21; "queer state," May 1; "Miss H's playing," May 22; "Vorstellungen," May 27, 1868.
Heidelberg: WJ to HJ[1], July 3, 1868.
Geneva: WJ to HJ[2], Aug. 26, 1868.
Divonne: WJ to Henry Bowditch [Oct. 21, 1868]; WJ to Tom Ward, Oct. 29, 1868.

CHAPTER X: *The End of Youth*

Epigraph: NSB, 515.
Harvard in 1868–1869: Morison, Chap. V; *Charles W. Eliot,* I, Chap. III.
Lilla Cabot on James women: quoted by Van Wyck Brooks, *From the Shadows of the Mountain: My Post Meridian Years* (1961), 45.

Norton: Kermit Vanderbilt, *Charles Eliot Norton: Apostle of Culture in a Democracy* (1959).

Mrs. Fields: M. A. De Wolfe Howe, ed., *Memories of a Hostess: A Chronicle of Eminent Friendships Drawn Chiefly from the Diaries of Mrs. James T. Fields* (1922), 79–82.

WJ on HJ[1]'s "verbal combativeness," LRHJ, 76.

O. W. Holmes Jr.: "lead to Chief Justice," WJ to Henry Bowditch, May 22, 1869.

Peirce: WJ to Henry Bowditch, Jan. 24–25, 1869.

Thesis for M.D. degree: WJ to Charles Ritter, Jan. 21, 1869; WJ to Henry Bowditch, May 22, 1869.

La Farge: WJ to HJ[2], March 22, 1869.

Presidency of Harvard: HJ[3], *Charles W. Eliot*, I, Chaps. VI–VII; P, I, 106; WJ to Henry Bowditch, May 22, 1869.

M.D. examination: WJ to HJ[2], June 12, 1869; WJ to Henry Bowditch, Aug. 12, 1869; HJ[3], *Charles W. Eliot*, I, 276.

Pomfret: WJ to Henry Bowditch, Aug. 12, 1869; Mrs. HJ[1] to HJ[2], July 24, 1869.

HJ[2] in Europe: HJ[2] to WJ, Oct. 30, Dec. 27, 1869; Jan. 1, Feb. 13, March 8, 1869.

Minny Temple: NSB, Chap. XIII; WJ's diary, March 9, 22, April 30 ("a crisis"), 1870; HJ[2] to Mrs. HJ[1], March 26, 1870; "made a mark," NSB, 515; "Willy James tells me," NSB, 511; "one of the few people," NSB, 469.

Nervous collapse: WJ to HJ[2], Jan. 19, 1870; Diary, Dec. 21, 1869; Jan. 1, Feb. 1, "habits of order," n.d. (on or before April 30, 1870).

"case history," VRE, Lectures VI–VII, "The Sick Soul."

Reading list recorded in diary Jan. 1, 1870: Henry Maudsley's *The Physiology and Pathology of the Mind* (1867); Herbert Spencer's *Principles of Biology* (1863 and 1867, being Vols. II and III of his *System of Synthetic Philosophy*); Gustav Theodor Fechner's *Elementa der Psychophysik* (1860) and *Über die Seelenfrage* (1861). All these were concerned with the pathology of the brain, or mind-body relationships (*Seelenfrage*). WJ had heard Wilhelm Griesinger lecture in Berlin and had bought his *Pathologie und Therapie der psychischen Krankheiten* in 1868.

"swamped in an empirical philosophy," WJ to Tom Ward, March (?), 1869.

CHAPTER XI: *In a Permanent Path*

Epigraph: WJ to HJ[2], April 18, 1874.
"melancholy," WJ to HJ[2], May 7, 1870.

"William inspires me," HJ² to Jane Norton, May 20, 1870.

Reading, skimming: AJ *Diary*, June 18, 1890; Browning, Mrs. HJ¹ to HJ², July 10, 1870.

"brute power of resistance," WJ to HJ², May 7, 1870.

Franco-German war: WJ to Henry Bowditch, Dec. 30, 1870, Jan. 23, 1871.

Agassiz: voyage to San Francisco, WJ to Henry Bowditch, April 7–8, 1871 (A. going to Boston whorehouses deleted in LWJ, I, 161–62).

First teaching: P, I, Chap. XX; appointment, WJ to HJ², Aug. 24, Oct. [10], 1872; father's observations, HJ¹ to HJ², Jan. 14, 1873; WJ to HJ², Feb. 13–14, 1873; HJ¹ to HJ², March 18, 1873; "a solider job," WJ to HJ², April 6, 1873; "yesterday I told Eliot," diary, April 10; "discouraged by health," WJ to HJ², May 25, 1873; declines appointment, Mrs. HJ¹ to HJ², Sept. 12, 1873.

Mount Desert: WJ to HJ², Aug. 24, 1872.

Chauncey Wright in Paris: HJ² to WJ, Sept. 22, 1872.

Criticism of "Trans-Atlantic Sketches": WJ to HJ², Oct. [10], 1872; "Guest's Confession," WJ to HJ², Nov. 24, 1872.

RJ in Wisconsin: HJ¹ to HJ², July 14–16, 1872; HJ² to WJ, Nov. 31, 1872.

Summer 1873: "morbid sympathy," Mrs. HJ¹ to HJ², July 1, 1873; WJ considering Rome, WJ to HJ², July 14–16, 1873.

GWJ, visit with Carrie: Mrs. HJ¹ to HJ², Dec. 8, 1873; WJ to AJ, Dec. 11, 1873; WJ to AJ, Feb. 13, 1874; GWJ going into business, Mrs. HJ¹ to HJ², May 18, 1874.

Europe, WJ: (on way) WJ to family, Oct. 17–18, 1873; Paris, WJ to AJ, Oct. 29, 1873; with HJ² in Florence, WJ to GWJ, Nov. 16, 1873; WJ to AJ, Nov. 16, 1873; art treasures, Notebook, Nov. 20, 1873; "if one lived here," WJ to AJ, Nov. 23, 1873; Rome, WJ to AJ, Dec. 17, 1873.

HJ² and WJ on each other: WJ to AJ, Dec. 17, HJ² to HJ¹, Dec. 22, 1873.

Return from Europe: mother's premonitions, Mrs. HJ¹ to HJ², March 17, 1874; "morbid temperament," Mrs. HJ¹ to HJ², July 6, 1874; "happy here," WJ to HJ², April 18, 1874.

CHAPTER XII: *Muscles to Mind*

Epigraph: "Philosophy 1870–1929," by George Herbert Palmer, in Samuel Eliot Morison (ed.), *The Development of Harvard University Since the Inauguration of President Eliot 1869–1929* (1930).

WJ instructor at Harvard: P, I, Chaps XX, XXI.

Dr. Holmes's tribute to Wyman, *Early Years of the Saturday Club*, 427.

Charles Loring Jackson (amyl nitrite), P, I, 359.

Psychological Laboratory: P, I, 415, II, Chap. LVIII; G. Stanley Hall, *Life and Confessions of a Psychologist* (1923), 218.

Hall: Louise Pruette, *G. Stanley Hall: A Biography of a Mind* (1926).

"found bones and muscles," see epigraph, above.

"my business at the Museum," WJ to HJ², Nov. 14, 1875.

Spencer course: WJ to Tom Ward, Dec. 30, 1876.

Essay on G. H. Lewes, CER, 4 ff.; "We wish," 10. *"Pessimismus,"* CER, 13; "Schopenhauer's philosophy," 15; "These Germans," 16; "The world is," 19.

Wright's death: "the law," CER, 20; "cosmical weather," 23.

"Bain and Renouvier," CER, 26; WJ to C. Renouvier, July 29, 1876; *Some Problems of Philosophy* (1911), 165 note.

Hall's letter to *Nation*, LWJ, I, 188–89; WJ's amplification, LWJ, 189–90.

Roderick Hudson: WJ to HJ², Dec. 12, 1875.

Charles Peirce: HJ² to WJ, Dec. 3, 1875; WJ to HJ², Dec. 12, 1875.

Mrs. Sargent's tea: WJ to HJ², Jan. 22, 1876.

Renan review: CER, 36–39; "your letters breathe," HJ² to WJ, Feb. 8, 1876; WJ to HJ², July 5, 1876.

The American, Unitarian minister (Chap. V): WJ to HJ², July 5, 1876; HJ² to WJ, July 29, 1876.

London ("five rainy, foggy weeks"): HJ² to WJ, Jan. 12, 1877; Herbert Spencer, HJ² to WJ, Feb. 28, 1877.

CHAPTER XIII: *Psychology and Psyche*

Epigraph: WJ to F. J. Child, Aug. 16, 1878.

Hall, *Life and Confessions*, 218–24.

Chastity, PP, I, 22–23; instinct, PP, II, 437; "personal isolation," PP, II, 438.

Alice Howe Gibbens, biography and courtship, unpublished information supplied by JJ.

Lecture at Johns Hopkins: F. J. Child to J. R. Lowell, quoted P, II, 27.

WJ's engagement: WJ to Mary Holton James, May 12, 1878; HJ² to WJ, May 29, 1878.

"sad summer in Cambridge," HJ² to WJ, July 23, 1878.

Wedding: HJ² to WJ, July 15, 1878.

Henry Holt, contract for book on psychology; June 1878, LWJ, I, 194; Child to Lowell, 195.

Honeymoon: LWJ, I, 195; WJ to F. J. Child, Aug. 16, 1878.

"happily boarding," WJ to Frances R. Morse, Dec. 26, 1878.

Critique of Herbert Spencer, CER, 43–68.

"Brute and Human Instinct," CER, 69–82.

"The Sentiment of Rationality," CER, 83–136; *The Will to Believe* (1956 ed.), 63–110; *Selected Papers on Philosophy* (1917), 125–64.

"Quelques considérations sur la méthode subjective," *Critique Philosophique*, 6me année, 2 (1878), 407–13; CER, 69–82.

"Are We Automata?" *Mind*, IV (1879), 1–22—not reprinted in whole.

"Many persons nowadays," quoted P, II, 30.

"I have for many years," quoted P, II, 29.

"The truth is that science," P, II, 31.

"Reflex Action on Theism," *Will to Believe* (1956 ed.), 114.

CHAPTER XIV: *Fathers and Sons*

Epigraph: WJ to HJ[1], Dec. 14, 1882.

Birth of HJ[3]: HJ[2] to WJ, June 15, 1879.

Hall, WJ's course: "Philosophy in the United States," *Mind*, IV (1879), 97; quoted P, II, 13.

English Hegelism: WJ to G. S. Hall, Sept. 3, Oct. 10, 1879; WJ to G. S. Hall, Jan. 16, 1880.

WJ's isolation: WJ to HJ[2], Nov. 27, 1879; HJ[2] to WJ, Dec. 16, 1879.

Criticism of HJ[2]: *The Europeans*, HJ[2] to WJ, Nov 14, 1878; *Nathaniel Hawthorne*, "crude and simple society," 42.

Europe: HJ[2] to WJ, May 9, 1880; WJ to Henry Bowditch, May 30, 1880; HJ[2] to HJ[1], June 30, 1880; WJ to HJ[1], July 13, 1880; HJ[2] to WJ, Aug. 31, 1880; Germany, WJ to H. Bowditch, July 19, 1880.

Renouvier: P, I, Chap. XLI–XLIII; WJ to C. Renouvier, Aug. 21, 1880; WJ to C.R., Dec. 27, 1880.

Louisburg Square: HJ[2] to WJ, Nov. 13, 1880; HJ[2] to WJ, Nov. 27, 1880.

"Great Men and Their Environment," *Will to Believe* (1956 ed.), 216–54; *Selected Papers on Philosophy* (1917), 165–97.

RJ: HJ[2] to WJ & AHJ, March 22, 1881.

Burial of Mrs. HJ[1]: RJ to Mary Holton J., Feb. 4, 1882, quoted in Introduction to *Alice James: Her Brothers, Her Journal*, ed. by Anna Robeson Burr (1934), 55–56; *The Notebooks of Henry James*, ed. by F. O. Matthiessen and K. B. Murdock, (1955), 33 ff.

Royce: WJ to J. Royce, April 2, 1882.

HJ[1]'s partiality to HJ[2]: HJ[1] to HJ[2], May 9, 1882.

CHAPTER XV: *Ambassador of American Thought*

Epigraph: P, I, 383.
WJ's arrival in London: LWJ, I, 209–10.
Vienna: WJ to AHJ, Sept. 24, 1882; WJ to C. Renouvier, Sept. 28, 1882.
Venice: WJ to C. Renouvier, Oct. 23, 1882.
Prague: Hering, Mach, Stumpf, WJ to AHJ, Nov. 2, 1882.
Berlin: WJ to AHJ, Nov. 9, 1882.
Leipzig: WJ to AHJ, Nov. 13, Nov. 18, 1882.
Liége: WJ to AHJ, Nov. 20, Dec. 19, 1882.
Paris: WJ to C. Renouvier, Dec. 6, 1882.
Last letter to father: WJ to HJ[1], Dec. 14, 1882; WJ to AHJ, Dec. 19, 1882.
Death of father: HJ[2] to WJ, Dec. 26, 1882; AJ *Diary*, 217; HJ[2] to WJ, Jan. 1, 1883; W to EPG, Feb. 14, 1883; father's estate: HJ[2] to WJ, Jan. 11, 23, Feb. 5, 1883.
Debate over WJ's return: WJ to HJ[2], Jan. 9, 1883; HJ[2] to WJ, Jan. 11; WJ to HJ[2], Jan. 23; HJ[2] to WJ, Jan. 25; WJ to HJ[2], Feb. 6; HJ[2] to WJ, Feb. 7, 10, 1883; WJ to EPG, Feb. 14, 1883; WJ to AHJ, "Harry is a queer old boy," supplied by JJ from letter of this period.
"Scratch Eight": Edmund Gurney, WJ to AHJ, Dec. 16, 1882; Shadworth H. Hodgson, WJ to AHJ, Jan. 13, 1883; WJ to AHJ, Feb. 10, 1883; G. C. Robertson to WJ, Aug. 13, 1883.
"association of ideas," P, II, 798.
Thomas Davidson: WJ to T.D., Jan. 2, 1883; F. J. Child to WJ, March 3, 1883 (P, I, 596); WJ to T.D., March 12, May 2, 1883.
Keene Valley: WJ to C. Renouvier, Aug. 5, 1883; concerning memorial to Schopenhauer, P, I, 722.

CHAPTER XVI: *Fourteen Doors*

Epigraph: AJ *Diary*, 68 (Dec. 14, 1889).
Alice James: Edel's "Portrait" (Introduction), in *Diary;* private information from JJ.
Administration of HJ[1]'s estate: HJ[2] to WJ, Nov. 24, 1883; HJ[2] to WJ, Jan. 29, 1885.
WJ's second son: nurse, HJ[2] to WJ, Jan. 25, 1884; birth, WJ to H. Bowditch, Jan. 31, 1884; name, HJ[2] to WJ, March 26, 1884.
Appian Way: WJ to Kitty Prince, Oct. 20, 1884.
Re LRHJ: HJ[2] to WJ, Jan. 2, 1885; WJ to E. L. Godkin, Feb. 16,

19, 1885; WJ to S. Hodgson, Feb. 20, 1885; HJ¹'s "bundle of truths," WJ's Introduction, 10; HJ¹'s theology, 19 ff.

"The Dilemma of Determinism," *Unitarian Review*, XXII (1884), 193–224; in *Will to Believe* (1956 ed.), 145–83.

"If God be good," *Will to Believe*, 167; "calling a thing bad," 161; "stable finality," 169.

Herman James: "the baby creeping," AHJ to WJ, quoted to AJ, Dec. 7, 1884; death of H., WJ to Kitty Prince, July 12, 1885.

Jaffrey, N.H.: WJ to AJ, Aug. 11, 1885; AJ to WJ, July 24, 1885; WJ to Kitty Prince, Aug. 11, 1885.

Garden Street: WJ to C. Stumpf, Jan. 1, 1886.

Psychical Research: P, I, 161 ff.; *William James on Psychical Research*, compiled and edited by Gardner Murphy and Robert O. Ballou (1960); WJ to T. Davidson, *ibid.*, 64; Mrs. Piper, WJ to AJ, Dec. 24, 1885; AJ to WJ, Jan. 3–4, 1886; "Report of the Committee on Mediumistic Phenomena," reprinted by Murphy and Ballou, 95–111; "Mrs. P.," 96–97.

Jaffrey (summer of '86): WJ to K. Prince, July 11, 1886; WJ in Cambridge, WJ to K. Prince, Aug. 4, 1886; WJ to C. Robertson, Aug. 29, 1886.

Chocorua, information from JJ; AJ *Diary*, Dec. 14, 1889; see "sylvan home" below.

Aiken, S.C.: WJ to AJ, Feb. 5, 1887.

Horsecar "adventure": WJ's account in fragment of letter found by Leon Edel in MS of AJ's diary, presumably written to AJ in 1886; same story, Logan Pearsall Smith, *Unforgotten Years* (1939), 119–20.

Birth of daughter: WJ to H. Bowditch, March 26, 1887.

"sylvan home" (Chocorua): WJ to HJ², April 12, 1887; WJ to AJ, July 2, 1887; horsetrader, L, I, 271; "mother earth," WJ to Charles Waldstein, July 20, 1887; AHJ to WJ, Sept. 2, Sept. 6, 1887 (JJ).

CHAPTER XVII: *Epochal Year*

Epigraph: WJ to HJ², Aug. 22, 1890.

Love letters—restricted, some information from JJ.

WJ to sons: to HJ³, March 1, March 27, April 29, 1888.

Chocorua (summer–autumn '88): WJ to HJ², July 11, 1888; WJ to HJ² & AJ, Oct. 14, 1888.

Dickinson S. Miller, "I can see him," in "Beloved Psychologist," reprinted *Great Teachers*, ed. Houston Peterson (Vintage Books, n.d., reprint of 1946 ed.), 225; "Royce in lecturing," 227.

Rollo Walter Brown, *Harvard Yard in the Golden Age* (1948), 48.

John Jay Chapman, *Memories and Milestones* (1915); James's mind,

20; "I should not have," 19; "sportive," 25; "deep sadness," 26. "insane asylums," Miller, *op. cit.*, 226.

Santayana: "my face," quoted Cory, *op. cit.*, 42; WJ to G.S., Jan. 2, April 22, 1888; G.S. to WJ, July 3, 1888; see also P, I, 403, 405; P, II, 398; Santayana on J. as teacher, *Character and Opinion in the U.S.* (1921), 40; Bruno Lind, *Vagabond Scholar: A Venture into the Privacy of George Santayana* (1962), 70 ff.

Gertrude Stein: John Malcolm Brinnin, *The Third Rose: Gertrude Stein and Her World* (1959), 26–42; G.S.'s examination, 34.

England: WJ to E. L. Godkin, April 4, 1889; WJ to HJ², May 12, 1889; AJ *Diary*, Aug. 4, 1889; "Harry is a nice," WJ to AHJ, July 29, 1889; Smith, *op. cit.*, WJ's charm, 117; London bus, WJ to AHJ, July 29, 1889; "William instead of going to Switzerland," AJ *Diary*, Nov. 18, 1889.

Wundt: WJ to C. Stumpf, Feb. 6, 1887; P, II, 68.

Congress for Physiological Psychology: WJ to C. Stumpf, Aug. 15, 1889; account of, LWJ, I, 289.

Irving Street house: WJ to HJ², Aug. 30, 1889.

"The Perception of Space," *Mind*, XII (1887), 1–30, 183–211, 321–53, 516, 548.

Publication of *Principles of Psychology*: complete correspondence of WJ and Henry Holt in HL; WJ to H.H., March 21, 1890; H.H. to WJ, April 2, 1890; WJ to H.H., April 5, 7, May 9, 1890; WJ to AHJ, May 24, 1890 (about PP); WJ to HJ², June 4, 1890; WJ to AJ, July 23, 1890; WJ to H.H., July 24, Aug. 12, 1890; WJ to Mrs. H. Whitman, July 24, 1890.

CHAPTER XVIII: *Habit and Character*

Epigraph: PP, I, 127.
"psychology is like physics before Galileo," P, II, 113.
Re PP, WJ to James Sully, July 8, 1890.
"What the Will Effects," *Scribner's Magazine*, III (1888), 240–50—used in part in PP, II, 242–46.
"The only conception," *Scribner's*, III, 240; "Every actually existing consciousness," *ibid.*, 247, and PP, I, 141.
"The Stream of Thought," PP, I, Chap. IX.
Space, PP, I, Chap. XX; Time, Chap. XV.
"My mental state," Henri Bergson, *Creative Evolution*, translation by Arthur Mitchell (1911), 2.
"nativism," P, II, 80.
"The great thing," PP, I, 122.
"The hell to be endured," PP, I, 127.

Reception of PP: P, II, 90; S. Hodgson to WJ, Aug. 19, 1891; James Ward to WJ, Jan. 12, 1891; James Sully's comment quoted P, II, 104; John Dewey's, *ibid.;* reviews: Charles Peirce, *Nation*, LIII (1891), 15, quoted P, II, 105; G. S. Hall, *American Journal of Psychology*, III (1891), 585, 589–91, quoted P, II, 109; W. D. Howells, *Harper's Magazine*, LXXXIII (1891), 314–16, quoted P, II, 109; George Santayana, *Atlantic Monthly*, LXVII (1891), 553, 555–56, quoted P. II, 110; "work of the imagination," *Character and Opinion in the U.S.*, 41.

"Certain Phenomena of Trance," *Proceedings of the Society for Psychical Research*, Vol. II, pt. XVII (Dec. 1890), reprinted Murphy and Ballou, *op. cit.*, 102–11.

Report on Mrs. Piper: HJ² to WJ, Oct. 9, 1890; WJ to HJ², Oct. 20, 1890; HJ² to WJ, Nov. 7, 1890.

Birth of fourth son: HJ² to WJ, Jan. 3, 1891.

HJ²'s play: HJ² to WJ, Feb. 6, 1891.

Naming of WJ's son: HJ² to WJ, Feb. 12, 1891.

AJ in England: *Diary*, March 25, 1890; "William says," *Diary*, Jan. 16, 1891; AJ to AHJ, Nov. 26, 1890; Dr. Baldwin, will AJ die?, *Diary*, Sept. 12, 1890; "palpable disease," *Diary*, May 31, 1891; "Poor dear William," *Diary*, July 1, 1891; "a finite length of days," WJ to AJ, July 6, 1891; "A thousand thanks," AJ to WJ, July 30, 1891; Asheville, N.C., WJ to AJ, Aug. 23, 1891.

"Briefer Course": WJ to Henry Holt, July 24, 1891.

Vacation in N.C. mountains: WJ to EPG, Aug. 25, 1891.

London visit: HJ²'s "first night," Leon Edel, *Henry James: The Middle Years* (1962), 296–97; AJ's "interest in the play," WJ to AJ, Oct. 1, Nov. 22, 1891.

Hypnotism: AJ to WJ, Dec. 2, 1891.

End of AJ's life: AJ *Diary*, Feb. 28, 1892; HJ² to WJ, March 8, 9; motto for AJ's urn, *Notebooks of Henry James*, 321. WJ either misquoted or, more likely, used a popular version of *Paradiso X*, 128–29: *ed essa da matiro e da essilio venne a questa pace.*

CHAPTER XIX: *A Family Abroad*

Epigraph: WJ to James Putnam, Oct. 7, 1892.

"I trust Alice and you . . . are soon to come," HJ² to WJ, March 19, 1892.

"German method," PP, I, 192.

Hugo Münsterberg: WJ to H. Münsterberg, Feb. 21, May 3, 1892; "gentlemanly," WJ to J. Royce, June 22, 1892; see also Margaret Münsterberg, *Hugo Münsterberg: His Life and Work* (1922), for much WJ–Münsterberg correspondence (holographs in Boston Public Library).

"torn up by the roots," AJ to WJ, May 29, [1888?].

Europe 1892: Lucerne, WJ to H. Münsterberg, July 6, 1892; Gryon, WJ to Grace Ashburner, July 13, 1892; Vers-chez-les-Blanc, HJ² and WJ in Switzerland, Leon Edel, *Henry James: The Middle Years*, 328; "When you get this," WJ to H. Münsterberg, Aug. 24, Sept. 8, 1892; Pallanza, WJ to Th. Flournoy, Sept. 19, 1892.

Florence: "coming abroad with a pack of children," WJ to J. J. Putnam, Oct. 7, 1892; WJ to H. Münsterberg, Oct. 5, 1892; housekeeping in F., WJ to Grace Ashburner, Oct. 19, 1892; "Last night Billy said," AHJ to HJ², Nov. 4, 1892; Padua, honorary degree, WJ to J. Royce, Dec. 18, 1892; instruction for children, WJ to G. Ashburner, Dec. 28, 1892; AHJ's dinner party, WJ to Margaret Gibbens, Jan. 3, 1893; cook Raffaello, WJ to F. Boott, Jan. 30, 1893; "weary Alice," HJ² to WJ, March 13, 1893; homeopathy, WJ to H. Münsterberg, March 13, 1893; HJ²'s tourist view of Italy, WJ to HJ², March 17, 1893.

"I recall," Bernard Berenson, *Rumor and Reflection* (1952), 126.

Switzerland again: WJ to C. Stumpf, April 24, 1893; WJ to Frank Duveneck, April 13, 1893; HJ² to WJ, April 26, 1893; AHJ in Munich, WJ to EPG, May 9, 1893; WJ to Mary Gibbens, May 11, 1893.

London: WJ to F. Pillon, June 17, 1893; "Let's ring," WJ to S. H. Hodgson, June 23, 1893; founding a philosophy journal, WJ to H. Münsterberg, Aug. 11, 1893.

Return to Cambridge: AHJ habits, information from JJ; WJ to HJ², Sept. 22, 1893; "One should not be," WJ to C. Stumpf, Jan. 24, 1894.

CHAPTER XX: *Intimate Philosopher*

Epigraph: *A Pluralistic Universe*, 20.

Irving Street: LWJ, II, Chap. XI; F. W. H. Myers to WJ, Nov. 16, 1893; WJ to D. S. Miller, Nov. 19, 1893.

Psychical research: F. W. H. Myers to WJ, November 16, 1893; WJ to F. W. H. Myers, Dec. 17, 1893; HJ² to AHJ, Dec. 29, 1893.

Psychology: "I found it very hard," WJ to C. Stumpf, Jan. 24, 1894; at Princeton, WJ to HJ², Dec. 29, 1894.

"The Knowing of Things Together," *The Psychology Review*, II (1895), 105–24; reprinted as "The Tigers in India," *Meaning of Truth*, 371–400; "There are two ways," M. of T., 43.

Massachusetts Legislature: LWJ, II, 67–72; Boston *Evening Transcript* letter reprinted by Murphy and Ballou, *op. cit.*, 10–11.

Gertrude Stein: Brinnin, *op. cit.*, 26–42; G.S.'s report, 30–31.

"The thesis I defend," *Will to Believe*, 11; C. Peirce to WJ, March 13, 1897.

Presidential Address to British S.P.R., reprinted Murphy and Ballou, *op. cit.*, 58–63.

WJ's habits: P, II, 670–98; HJ³ on WJ, LWJ, II, 6–11.

Colorado: WJ to MMJ, Aug. 8, 1895; WJ to Th. Flournoy, Aug. 13, 1895.

Political views: WJ to E. L. Godkin, Dec. 24, 1895; WJ to F. W. H. Myers, Jan. 1, 1896; HJ² to WJ, May 29, 1896; WJ to HJ², June 11, 1896; WJ to Th. Flournoy, June 17, 1898.

Lecture tour: Chautauqua, WJ to AHJ, July 24, 26, 1896; WJ to Rosina Emmet, Aug. 2, 1896; WJ to Th. Flournoy, Aug. 30, 1896; WJ to D. S. Miller, Aug. 30, 1896; WJ to HJ², Sept. 28, 1896.

Neurology: Lowell Institute Lectures, not published, MSS in HL; WJ to Henry W. Rankin, Feb. 1, 1897.

Family affairs, spring 1897: AHJ to HJ², April 23, 1897.

Edinburgh invitation: AHJ to HJ², April 23, 1897.

Robert Gould Shaw Address: WJ to HJ², June 5, 1897; "Robert Gould Shaw," *Memories and Studies* (1911), 35–62.

Trials of autumn '97: AHJ to HJ², Jan. 13, 1898; lost in Adirondacks: WJ to AHJ, July 9, 1898.

Trip to California: WJ to G. H. Howison, July 24, 1898; San Francisco, WJ to HJ², Aug. 11, 1898; Palo Alto, WJ to Rosina Emmet, Sept. 9, 1898.

Ingersoll address published as *Human Immortality: Two Supposed Objections to the Doctrine*, Boston and New York: Houghton Mifflin, 1898. Reprinted as supplement to *The Will to Believe*, New York: Dover Publications, 1956 (photo-offset of 1898 ed.). "Steam is a function," *Will to Believe* (1956 ed.), 13; "influx," 27; "consciousness in the brain," 21; "mother sea," 27; "every leaf," 43–44.

Plans for trip to Europe: AHJ to HJ², May 21, 1899.

Overstrained heart: LWJ, II, 90–91.

CHAPTER XXI: *The Dark Forest*

Epigraph: AHJ to WJ², Oct. 24, 1899.

Unpublished diaries of WJ (HL) and AHJ (JJ)—also letters of AHJ to HJ³ and WJ² (JJ).

Nauheim: WJ to EPG, Aug. 22, 1899; WJ to Pauline Goldmark, Aug. 12, 1899; WJ to EPG, Aug. 22, 1899; WJ to W. M. Salter, Sept. 11, 1899.

Lamb House: HJ² to WJ, July 15, 1899; WJ to Mrs. H. Whitman, Oct.

5, 1899; WJ to Frances Morse, Dec. 23, 1899; WJ to F. Boott, Jan. 31, 1900.

Lutaslawski: WJ to Frances Morse, Sept. 17, 1899.

De Vere Gardens: AHJ to WJ², Oct. 24, 1899; WJ to EPG, Oct. 29, 1899; WJ to EPG, Nov. 14, 1899.

Great Malvern: AHJ to WJ², Dec. 7, 1899; AHJ to F. Boott, Dec. 9, 1899.

Rome: AHJ to WJ², Jan. 4, 1900; HJ² (meeting MMJ) to WJ, April [—?], 1900.

Costebelle-Hyères: AHJ to WJ, Jan. 19, 1900; WJ to Mrs. G. Evans, Jan. 17, 1900; WJ to D. S. Miller, Jan. 18, 1900; WJ to J. Royce, Jan. 21, 1900; J. Royce to WJ, Feb. 7, 1900.

Château de Carqueiranne: C. W. Eliot's letter to WJ quoted by AHJ to WJ², Jan. 19, 1900 (JJ)—same thought but different wording, C. W. Eliot to WJ, Jan. 1, 1900 (P, I, 430–31); WJ to F. Boott, Jan. 31, 1900; WJ to H. Münsterberg, March 13, 1900; WJ to G. H. Palmer (about Santayana), Apr. 2, 1900; "The problem I have set," WJ to Frances Morse, Apr. 13, 1900.

Switzerland: WJ to EPG, May 6, 1900.

Nauheim again: WJ to MMJ, May 26, 1900; HJ² to WJ, May 30, 1900. Switzerland again: AHJ to WJ², July 1, 1900; AHJ to EPG, July 8, 1900; WJ to Frances Morse, Sept. 16, Dec. 25, 1900. Rome again: WJ to WJ², Dec. 1, 1900; WJ to James Sully, Jan. 17, 1901; AHJ to WJ², Feb. 8, 1901.

Death of F. W. H. Myers: Axel Munthe, *The Story of San Michele* (1929), 371–72; WJ, "Frederick Myers' Services to Psychology," *Proceedings of Society for Psychical Research*, Part XLII (1901), 17 ff.; reprinted *Memories and Studies*, 145–70, and Murphy and Ballou, *op. cit.*, 213–24.

Geneva: AHJ to WJ², March 25, 1901.

Gifford Lectures (first): WJ to Frances Morse, May 15, 30, 1901; WJ to Henry Rankin, June 16, 1901; AHJ to EPG, June 26, 1901; WJ to C. E. Norton, June 26, 1901; WJ to Frances Morse, July 10, 1901; WJ to E. L. Godkin, July 25, 1901.

CHAPTER XXII: *Experience Is a River*

Epigraph: WJ to F. C. S. Schiller, April 8, 1903.

Diaries of WJ (HL) and AHJ (JJ).

Return to America: WJ to Pauline Goldmark, Sept. 14, 1901; WJ to H. N. Gardiner, Nov. 14, 1901.

England again: WJ to F. C. S. Schiller, April 20, 1902; WJ to C. E. Norton, May 4, 1902; WJ to EPG, May 26, 1902; WJ to Mrs. H.

Whitman, June 18, 1902.

"believing," MS, P, II, 331.

VRE: WJ to Hugo Münsterberg, July 11, 1902; WJ to Th. Flournoy, July 23, 1902; life of religion, VRE, 53; "such soul," 168; "separateness," 102; conclusions, 485–86.

"*Dang* all schools," WJ to Frances Morse, Sept. 18, 1902.

Philosophy: Syllabus for Philosophy 3, P, II, 745–49; WJ to H. Bergson, Dec. 14, 1902; WJ to F. C. S. Schiller, April 8, 1903; "thesis," *Pragmatism* (1907), 201; WJ to H. L. Higginson, July 3, 1902; WJ to Mrs. H. Whitman, Aug. 2, 1903.

Vacation 1903: WJ to F. Morse, Sept. 24, 1903.

Winter 1904: WJ to F. Pillon, June 12, 1904.

Mrs. Whitman's funeral: WJ to HJ², June 28, 1904.

HJ²'s trip to America: HJ² to WJ, April 10, 1903; WJ to HJ², May 3, 1903; WJ to Pauline Goldmark, Sept. 21, 1904; *Notebooks of Henry James, op. cit.* (AJ's urn), 321, walk with WJ, 323.

Guests, Irving Street: WJ to F. C. S. Schiller, Oct. 26, 1904.

Greece-Italy: itinerary, diary; WJ to AHJ ("Tell Aleck"), March 31, April 25, 30, 1905; WJ to G. Santayana, May 2, 1905.

Switzerland: WJ to H. Bergson, May 10, 1905.

London: slept in bathtub, diary, May 31, 1905.

Return to U.S.: HJ² to WJ, July 2, 1905.

The Golden Bowl: WJ to HJ², Oct. 22, 1905; HJ² to WJ, Nov. 23, 1905.

The American Scene: WJ to HJ², May 4, 1907; WJ to HJ², Oct. 6, 1907; "the *land's* all right," *American Scene,* 20.

CHAPTER XXIII: *Philosophy without Humbug*

Epigraph: WJ to Th. Flournoy, March 26, 1907.

Diaries of WJ (HL) and AHJ (JJ).

Stanford: AHJ to HJ³, Feb. 26, 1906; WJ to Th. Flournoy, Feb. 9, 1906; WJ to MMJ, April 8, 1906; WJ to F. Morse, April 22, 1906 (earthquake); WJ to HJ² & WJ², May 9, 1906.

"The Moral Equivalent of War," *McClure's Magazine,* Aug. 1910; *International Conciliation,* 1910, No. 27; *Popular Science Monthly,* LXX 77 (1910), 400–412; *Memories and Studies,* 267–96; "We inherit," 272; "contempt of softness," 287.

"On Some Mental Effects of the Earthquake," *Youth's Companion,* June 7, 1906; *Memories and Studies,* 209–226.

Retirement: P, I, 441–46; LWJ, II, 220–21.

Lecture at Columbia U.: diary and WJ to HJ², Feb. 14, 1907.

Pragmatism: A New Name for Some Old Ways of Thinking: Popular

Lectures on Philosophy (New York: Longmans, Green and Co.,
1907). On *Pragmatism*: WJ to HJ², May 4, 1907; WJ to H. Bergson, June 13, 1907.

Domestic life: WJ to MMJ, April 27, 1907 (JJ); AHJ to WJ², April
28, 1907; Lutaslawski sun-bathing, from JJ.

Oxford lectures: itinerary, both diaries; WJ to MMJ, May 2, 1909;
AHJ to EPG, May 26, 1908; AHJ to WJ², June 12, 1908; *Memoirs
of Lady Ottoline Morrell: A Study in Friendship 1873–1915*, ed. by
Robert Gathorn-Hardy (1964), 86; Logan Pearsall Smith, *op. cit.*,
120–21; H. G. Wells, *Experiment in Autobiography* (1934), 453–
54.

William James received the M.D. degree from Harvard University on
June 29, 1869, and the following honorary degrees: D. Phil. et Litt.,
Padua, 1892; LL.D., Princeton, 1896; LL.D., Edinburgh, 1902;
LL.D., Harvard, 1903; D. Litt., Durham, 1908; D.Sc., Oxford, 1908;
D.Sc., Geneva, 1909.

"Report on Mrs. Piper's Hodgson-Control," *Proceedings of the American Society for Psychical Research*, III (1909), 470–589; reprinted
by Murphy and Ballou, *op. cit.*, 115–210.

"The Confidences of a Psychical Researcher," *American Magazine*,
October 1909; reprinted as "Final Impressions of a Psychical Researcher," *Memories and Studies*, 171–206, and Murphy and Ballou,
op. cit., 309–25.

Freud: Ernest Jones, *The Life and Works of Sigmund Freud* (1961),
267–68, quotes Freud's *An Autobiographical Study*, 268 note; WJ to
Th. Flournoy, Sept. 28, 1909.

CHAPTER XXIV: *The Unfinished Arch*

Epigraph: Quoted by Henry James Jr. [HJ³] in his Prefatory Note
to *Some Problems of Philosophy: A Beginning of an Introduction
to Philosophy* (London: Longmans, Green and Co., 1911).

Diaries of WJ (HL) and AHJ (JJ).

"Subliminal consciousness," "A Suggestion about Mysticism," *Journal
of Philosophy, Psychology, and Scientific Methods*, VII (1910),
85–92; CER, 500–13.

Royce's jingle: P, II, 171 note.

Rand portrait: AHJ to HJ², Feb. 6, 1910.

Boutroux: P, II, 566–69; B.'s address, 568; Émile Boutroux, *William
James*, translated by Archibald and Barbara Henderson, New York:
Longmans, Green and Co., 1912.

HJ²'s illness: HJ² to WJ & AHJ, March 4, 15, 1910; WJ to F. Morse,
March 29, 1910.

England: trip, diaries; Henry Adams, WJ to Henry Adams, April 28, June 17, 1910; Henry Adams to WJ, June 20, 1910; WJ to Henry Adams, June 26, 1910; Henry Adams to WJ, June 29, 1910.
Charles Strong: P, II, 534–52.
Paris: WJ's diary; WJ to F. Pillon, May 25, 1910.
Nauheim: diaries of WJ and AHJ; WJ to MMJ, May 29, 1910; WJ to Henry Bowditch, June 4, 1910; WJ to EPG, June 14, 1910.
B. P. Blood: P, II, 553–62; "A Pluralistic Mystic," *Hibbert Journal*, VIII (1910), 8, 739–59; *Memories and Studies*, 369–411.
Geneva: WJ to Th. Flournoy, July 9, 1910.
Lamb House: AHJ to HJ³, Aug. 5, 1910; AHJ to EPG, Aug. 7, 1910.
Final days of WJ: trip to U.S., AHJ's diary; HJ² to Grace Norton, Aug. 26, 1910.
Funeral and tributes: Boston *Journal*, Aug. 31, 1910; London *Times*, Aug. 29, 1910; *Figaro*, Aug. 29, 1910; Bertrand Russell, *Nation* (British), Sept. 3, 1910; H. M. Kallen, *Nation* (American), Sept. 8, 1910; Boston *Evening Transcript*, Oct. 5, 1910; John J. Chapman, *Memories and Milestones* (1915), 28—"wings of morning," Psalms: cxxxix, 8.

EPILOGUE: *"No Conclusion"*

Epigraph: "A Pluralistic Mystic," *Memories and Studies*, 411.
"Reason is," *Memories and Studies*, 392–93.
Memo to son HJ³, *Some Problems* . . . , *op. cit.*, Prefatory Note.
Th. Flournoy, *The Philosophy of William James*, translated by Edwin B. Holt and William James Jr. (1917); "No one less likely," 40; "His genius," 41; "artistic mind," 4; WJ to Th. Flournoy, April 30, 1903.
"iron block" universe, *Will to Believe* (1956 ed.), 150; "the parts," 150; "If God," 167; "stable finality," 169.
Pragmatism (1907 ed.), "tender-" and "tough-minded," Lecture I; "You want a system," 20; "The world of concrete," 21.
"rational concepts," *Will to Believe* (1956 ed.), 63; "Idealism," 89; "sick-room air," 90; "Now, there is no element," 90.
"This book," Preface to PP, vi; "The pages of the book," P, II, 72.
"What the Will Effects," *Scribner's Magazine*, III (1888), 240.
"influx," Human Immortality (bound with *Will to Believe*, 1956 ed.—separate pagination), 27.
"things, not ideas . . . associated," PP, I, 554; "brain processes," 556; "All sorts of neuro-muscular processes," 522.
Philosophical attitudes: *Will to Believe* (1956 ed.), vii–viii; "another doctrine," xii; "field of consciousness," Flournoy, *op. cit.*, 94.

Pluralistic Universe: "almost coeval," P, II, 385; "wide-span conscious-ness," WJ to F. C. S. Schiller, 1905, quoted P, II, 588; "I struggled," *Pluralistic Universe,* 207; WJ's "position remains uncertain," P, II, 591; "Existence would then," 592; "For my own part," *P.U.,* 299–300; "The phenomenon," 305; "to be frankly pluralistic," *P.U.,* 310–11.

WJ "transformed psychology," Flournoy, *op. cit.,* 210.

Percept and concept, *Some Problems . . . , op. cit.,* 57, 64; philoso-pher "able to extend his knowledge," 96–97.

Paul Woodring, ed., Introduction to *Talks to Teachers* (1958), 16.

Gordon W. Allport, *William James: Psychology, The Briefer Course* (1961), xvi, xxi, xxiv. Another paperback edition: William James, *Psychology* [Briefer Course], Introduction by Ashley Montagu (1963).

Index